D1756451

A WORLD OF GIVING

A WORLD OF GIVING

CARNEGIE CORPORATION OF NEW YORK

A Century of International Philanthropy

PATRICIA L. ROSENFIELD

PublicAffairs

NEW YORK

ABOUT CARNEGIE CORPORATION OF NEW YORK

Carnegie Corporation of New York was created by Andrew Carnegie in 1911 to promote the advancement and diffusion of knowledge and understanding. In keeping with this mandate, the Corporation's work focuses on the issues that Andrew Carnegie considered of paramount importance: international peace, the advancement of education and knowledge, and the strengthening of democracy.

PublicAffairs books are available at special discounts for bulk purchases in the US by corporations, institutions, and other organizations. For more information, please contact the Special Markets Department at the Perseus Books Group, 2300 Chestnut Street, Suite 200, Philadelphia, PA 19103, call (800) 810-4145, ext. 5000, or e-mail special.markets@perseusbooks.com.

Book Design by Janet Tingey

LIBRARY OF CONGRESS CATALOGING-IN-PUBLICATION DATA
Rosenfield, Patricia L.
A world of giving : Carnegie Corporation of New York—A century of international philanthropy / Patricia L. Rosenfield.—First Edition.
pages cm
Includes bibliographical references and index.
ISBN 978-1-61039-498-7 (hardcover)
ISBN 978-1-61039-429-1 (paperback)
ISBN 978-1-61039-430-7 (ebook)
1. Carnegie Corporation of New York—History.
2. Charities—United States. I. Title.
HV97.C3R67 2014
361.7'650973—dc23
2013037928

First Edition
10 9 8 7 6 5 4 3 2 1

THIS VOLUME IS DEDICATED TO the generosity of one individual, his remarkable wife, and his family. Andrew Carnegie, his helpmate Louise, and their devoted daughter Margaret, all participated in the joyful but ceaseless work of giving away Mr. Carnegie's fortune. The bold spirit of the Carnegie family and their descendants has resulted, as this volume shows, in long-lasting societal transformations.

CONTENTS

INTRODUCTION:
IN TRUST FOR THE PUBLIC

WHEN ANDREW CARNEGIE LAUNCHED Carnegie Corporation of New York in 1911, his institutional vision inspired the field of modern philanthropy. Carnegie had already defined a new rationale and style for philanthropic giving. For more than twenty years he had been writing about and experimenting with a variety of approaches to philanthropy. Carnegie Corporation of New York was his final major American endowment.[1]

Carnegie's radical premise declared that money amassed by successful capitalists was not ultimately for their personal purposes, but rather that they held the funds in trust for the public and therefore should return those funds to the public.[2] In his seminal 1889 essay *Wealth*, he proclaimed that "the man who dies thus rich dies disgraced." This premise, arguably, launched modern philanthropy by eschewing the notion of giving for charity, that is, the short-term alleviation of human suffering. Instead, he embraced the notion of philanthropic giving to advance knowledge of the root causes of societal problems and to share that understanding widely, the mission he consequently bestowed on Carnegie Corporation of New York.

In today's world, a century later, when the concept of a philanthropic grant-making foundation is so widely accepted, it may be hard to understand what a conceptual breakthrough Andrew Carnegie's writings and subsequent actions constituted. Although philanthropic activities had been a constant of American life since the 1700s, the establishment of endowed philanthropic institutions was set in motion in part by Carnegie's energetic promotion of the idea.[3]

To set the context for Andrew Carnegie's bold creativity, imagine his challenge as the richest man in the world. He sold his company in 1901 for $492 million, the largest financial transaction of its day.[4] As his millions multiplied and his fortune accumulated, he was stymied in meeting his own standard. He could not give his money away fast enough. He established five major trusts, including one that provided pensions for teachers and another aimed at ending war; he built the world a Peace Palace in The Hague and another for Central America in Costa Rica. He funded libraries and church organs throughout the United States, Canada, and around the world. Each time he gave away his money he sought to put a dent in his fortune, and each time he discovered that his investments more than made up for the money donated.[5]

To ensure that he could give away all his money before he died, in 1911 Andrew Carnegie, the philanthropic industrialist, and Elihu Root, America's leading statesman and Carnegie's lawyer, designed a public trust corporation intended to give the money away in perpetuity and to support the most creative and talented people of future generations.[6] The founding of Carnegie Corporation of New York (the Corporation) began the age of the general-purpose foundation that gives grants to others. That is, in contrast to the operational foundations established earlier in the century, the institution would invest in the ideas and projects presented to it—to be carried out not by its staff but by people and institutions outside it. The Corporation's trustees would both decide and monitor implementation by others. The aim was to make a lasting difference by advancing the understanding of mankind's problems and by widely sharing that knowledge.

Carnegie Corporation of New York was incorporated through an act of the New York State Legislature, which approved its charter on June 9, 1911. The first meeting of the Board of Trustees was held on November 10, 1911; at that time Andrew Carnegie delivered the letter transmitting the deed of gift to the trustees and donated $25 million to the Corporation as his first gift. In that same letter, Carnegie also made it clear that he intended the philanthropic work he had set in motion to continue long after his own lifetime, writing, "My desire is that the work which I have been carrying on, or similar beneficial work, shall continue during this and future generations."[7]

The foundation's initial focus was on the United States, but that soon widened to include the British dominions and colonies in Australia, Canada, New Zealand, the Caribbean, Africa, and Asia. This study focuses specifically on the Corporation's role as an international foundation over the past one hundred years by examining its grants, investments, and activities around the world that have aimed to advance and diffuse knowledge and understanding. A century since its founding, this living institution today makes over three hundred grants totaling over $100 million annually, and nearly half of its grant-making resources are devoted to international activities.[8] It is not the money, however, but rather the history of how those resources have been applied that points the way toward a new century of international philanthropy.

SCOPE OF THE STUDY

ANDREW CARNEGIE WAS NOT CONCERNED about strategies or structures when he established Carnegie Corporation of New York. He knew the mission that he wanted to drive the institution, but he realized that conditions change, structures become inflexible, and strategies have limited lives. As a businessman, he had bet on good men and good ideas, seeking the most innovative approach, even if it reduced profit in the short run—he envisioned, for example, the advantage of iron over wood for bridges and established the Keystone Bridge Works Company. He adapted the Bessemer steel process for cleaner and more efficient steelmaking, thus providing the competitive advantage for Carnegie Steel Company. In establishing the Corporation and its twenty-some sister Carnegie philanthropies, Andrew Carnegie likewise sought to understand problems, not just throw money at them.[9]

Carnegie Corporation's international endeavors illustrate how a commitment to a wide worldview can be sustained and a variety of results obtained amid changing national and international governmental contexts and an increasingly complex cast of characters both within and outside the organization. The Corporation's body of work provides a time-tested set of experiences that illustrate the dynamics of grant-making, with a focus on understanding and contributing to international social change and enhancing the role that American citizens and American institutions can play internationally, as well as the role of immigrants and other transnational players, such as foreign scholars and international organizations, in the United States. The partnerships that have been forged with individuals and institutions in many countries and evolved over many decades of collaboration are another important component of this global philanthropy.

Andrew Carnegie, perhaps unintentionally, saddled the Corporation with creative tensions that are sometimes hard to balance. He not only endowed a foundation with a mission related to knowledge and understanding but also charged the trustees with shaping the foundation's mission to the changing context of their times.[10] The "pull" of mission and the "push" of changing context create the intellectual tension that drives decision-making—on the one hand, turning the focus toward central historical themes, and on the other, prompting an outward focus on an evolving world. A resolution of these oppositional forces has shaped Corporation responses to global challenges in times of both war and peace, of both economic prosperity and economic adversity, amid diverse nationalist and internationalist policies, and during ongoing variations in the demographic composition of the US population and that of other nations as well as dramatic advances in the civil rights of minorities and women. These significant contextual conditions and others provide the matrix for examining the pattern of the Corporation's international work.

Over the past one hundred years, the twelve individuals who have served as Corporation president have been the significant force defining the Corporation's interpretation of Andrew Carnegie's vision, principles, practices, and passions in response to the needs of a changing world. Their interpretations have incorporated guidance from trustees, staff members, consultants, the grant-seeking community, and other foundations, including, at times, the other Carnegie philanthropies. Over the decades the Corporation's fidelity to its mission as exemplified by the trustees and the presidents has resulted in a notable continuity of international commitment.

The Corporation has supported activities in two broad areas:

+ Extending access to knowledge and ideas through support of public libraries, technology-based information systems, and educational institutions in Africa, Asia, the Caribbean, Russia, and North America
+ Promoting peace, democratic institutions, socioeconomic develop-

ment, and international engagement through support of innovative partnerships and collaborations, travel grants, and exchanges, as well as institutions, organizations, and professional associations in the United States, Canada, Europe, Commonwealth Africa, and the Southern Pacific region

Historically, grants reinforced the development of libraries and educational research in Australia and New Zealand; increased American governmental and philanthropic attention to Africa in the midst of decolonization and independence movements; introduced new approaches to cultural understanding through development of the field of museum directorship; and promoted both music—originally through the support of church pipe organs and then by circulating music sets (collections of recordings of canonical music, as well as musical equipment)—and art, through the circulation of art education materials around the British Commonwealth and in the United States. Echoing grants made from the late 1930s to the mid-1960s, the Corporation, since the 1980s, has conducted research on, for example, ways to inform national security policies and reduce the likelihood of the use of weapons of mass destruction. This research is often conducted through approaches that connect scholars from the social sciences, policy studies, and occasionally the physical and natural sciences with key policymakers. A consistent theme has been the pivotal role of universities in building capable citizens who can effectively contribute to their societies.

With varying degrees of success, the Corporation has sought to educate Americans of all ages about the importance of understanding and engaging in world affairs. This effort began with support for the teaching of foreign languages in the United States and Canada and evolved into funding the early development of the field of international relations in the United States, South Africa, and Australia, along with country or regional area studies in US universities. These activities continued in the twenty-first century with a ten-year focus on public scholarship in the United States that specifically focused on Islam and Muslim communities in its last five years.

The Corporation was a prominent supporter of British Commonwealth–related activities from the days of the Empire, especially strengthening educational institutions, whether community-based or at colleges and universities. Corporation leadership did not shy away from controversy in its international grant-making, as illustrated by the range of Corporation activities in South Africa, such as supporting investigations into white poverty in the late 1920s and 1930s, promoting public interest law under apartheid in the 1970s and 1980s, and studying black poverty later in the 1980s, still under the regime of apartheid.

Soon after the founding of the Corporation, in 1913, the Rockefeller Foundation was established and also undertook grant-making overseas as well as in the United States. These two giants of the field prompted other philanthropists to expand their efforts around the world. A century later, American foundations continue to support international activities, not only work in other countries, including work on issues that traverse national boundaries, but also work in the United States to strengthen understanding of international issues.[11]

The history of the Corporation epitomizes the role of American foundations working internationally; straddling multiple worlds; and sharing priorities, grantees, and, especially, the same concern that has permeated society over the last one hundred years: how can individual generosity make a lasting contribution to social change? At the global level, foundations have played a significant role in building a new type of globalism—cultural, not political, economic, or legal—that seeks global understanding and a continuing emphasis on peace and social progress. As historian Akira Iriye has described it, such cultural internationalism "entails a variety of activities undertaken to link countries and peoples through the exchange of ideas and persons, through scholarly cooperation, or through efforts at facilitating cross-national understanding."[12] Cultural internationalism has defined the practice of international philanthropy as conducted by Carnegie Corporation and other American foundations over the past century.

The Early Years

Under Andrew Carnegie's presidency from 1911 to 1919, the Corporation continued his previous long-term practice of granting funds for libraries and church pipe organs, both in the United States and throughout the British Empire. These grants constituted the initial focus for the Corporation's international grant-making, following the receipt of Carnegie's second gift in January 1912: $75 million specifically earmarked for grants to the United Kingdom, Canada, and the British colonies.[13] In 1913, President Carnegie and his trustees decided to move beyond the international focus in support of church pipe organs and libraries with a grant for the endowment fund of Queen's University in Ontario; subsequently, universities in Canada became a major theme of the Corporation's international grant-making. Beginning in 1917, Carnegie's longtime support for libraries was expanded from the provision of books and bricks and mortar to the cultivation of librarians and library systems.

Responding to Carnegie's passionate promotion of peace by advocating for sound American policies and international arbitration arrangements, the Corporation considered how best to create an informed American citizenry by enhancing understanding of international conditions as well as supporting peace-related initiatives, including the Church Peace Union in 1914.[14] The Corporation also realized that great worldwide changes precipitated by World War I required enlarging the scope of its grant-making.

During the four years following the death of the founder, the presidency passed through the hands of three men.[15] The Corporation was helped through these transitions by a strong commitment among the trustees to pursue the mission and maintain the organization in perpetuity. Charter revisions in 1913 and again in 1917 helped to smooth out competing international and national priorities, and the focus shifted to major institution-building, with special emphasis on enhancing internationally related activities within the United States.

The Transformative Years: The 1920s to the 1940s

The Board of Trustees elected Frederick Keppel as the Corporation's fifth president in late 1922.[16] Under his presidency, which continued until 1941, the Corporation resolved tensions between international and national orientations in grant-making, and activities began to span the globe, fulfilling its international mandate with grant-making in Canada, Australia, New Zealand, and parts of Southeast Asia and throughout Africa and the Caribbean. During this period of energetic internationalism at the Corporation, the linkages between grant-making in the United States and

THE CARNEGIE FAMILY OF INSTITUTIONS
ESTABLISHED BY ANDREW CARNEGIE, 1891–1919[17]

CARNEGIE HALL (New York City) was established at the request of Walter Damrosch and Louise Carnegie. Work started in 1889 and was completed in 1891, with Carnegie's contribution of about $2 million toward the total cost of $2.2 million.

THE CARNEGIE INSTITUTE (Pittsburgh) was initiated in 1893 with a gift of $1.12 million, followed by a gift of $5 million and an endowment grant of $6 million. Eventually the Institute comprised the Carnegie Library of Pittsburgh, the Carnegie Museums of Pittsburgh (Art and Natural History), and the Carnegie Music Hall. It now also includes the Andy Warhol Museum.

CARNEGIE MELLON UNIVERSITY (Pittsburgh) was originally organized in 1900 as Carnegie Technical Schools; in 1905 it became part of the Carnegie Institute through an initial grant of $2 million with an additional $1.34 million for buildings, followed by $4 million more for endowment. Organized by 1912 into the Carnegie Institute of Technology, it became Carnegie Mellon University in 1967.

THE CARNEGIE TRUST FOR THE UNIVERSITIES OF SCOTLAND was established in 1901 and endowed with $10 million for use in Scotland. Located in Dunfermline, the Trust initially focused only on Scotland's four higher education institutions but now works with all Scottish universities.

THE CARNEGIE INSTITUTION FOR SCIENCE (Washington, DC), originally known as the Carnegie Institution of Washington, was established in 1901 for the promotion of science, especially the advancement of basic scientific knowledge. Carnegie endowed the Institution with a gift of $10 million; he added $2 million in 1907 and another $10 million in 1911.

THE CARNEGIE DUNFERMLINE TRUST, established in 1903, was intended to assist Carnegie's hometown—the site of his first library—with an endowment of £750,000 (then US$3.7 million).

THE CARNEGIE HERO FUND COMMISSION was established in Pittsburgh in 1904 with a $5 million fund covering the United States and Canada; the Carnegie Hero Fund Trust, established in 1908 with a fund of $1.25 million and based in Dunfermline, Scotland, extended the concept to the British Isles and Ireland, England, Scotland, Wales, Northern Ireland, the Republic of Ireland, and the Channel Islands; Fondation Carnegie (France) was founded in 1909; and the Carnegie-Stiftung für Lebensretter was established in Germany in 1910. In 1911, seven more Hero Funds were established: Carnegie Heltefund for Norge (Norway), Fondation Carnegie pour les Sauveteurs (Switzerland), Carnegie Belonningsfud for Heltemod (Denmark), Carnegie Heldenfonds (the Netherlands), Carnegiestiftelsen (Sweden), Fondation Carnegie

(Belgium), and Fondazione Carnegie (Italy). The eleven Hero Funds celebrate the heroic deeds of ordinary citizens in peacetime for their efforts to save the lives of their fellow citizens.

THE CARNEGIE FOUNDATION FOR THE ADVANCEMENT OF TEACHING, founded in 1905 in New York City, is now located in Stanford, California. With an initial endowment of $10 million, it was originally created to provide pensions for university professors but soon expanded its mission to working to increase respect for the profession of teaching and higher education in the United States, the Dominion of Canada, and Newfoundland. It received a congressional charter in 1906. The Foundation's work led to the establishment in 1918 of the Teachers Insurance and Annuity Association (TIAA), funded by $1 million from Carnegie Corporation, with resources added over the years; the Association became independent of both the Foundation and the Corporation in 1930.

THE CARNEGIE ENDOWMENT FOR INTERNATIONAL PEACE, now located in Washington, DC, was established in 1910 in New York City on Andrew Carnegie's seventy-fifth birthday with an initial endowment of $10 million to work toward achieving what by then had become his life's primary goal: to eliminate war. The first president of the endowment, Elihu Root, also served as acting president of the Corporation and chair of its board; the second president, Nicholas Murray Butler, succeeded Root as president of the Endowment and chair of the Corporation's board. The Endowment conducted major studies in international law, dispute settlement, the causes and impact of war, and international understanding; it also from the beginning established a branch in Europe, based in Paris with an advisory board.

CARNEGIE CORPORATION OF NEW YORK was established in 1911 with an initial endowment of $25 million, which increased in 1912 with another $75 million and, on the death of Andrew Carnegie, an additional $35 million.

THE CARNEGIE UNITED KINGDOM TRUST in Dunfermline was established in October 1913 with a gift of $10 million, with its own trustees, for the purpose of improving the well-being of the people of Great Britain and Ireland.

THE CARNEGIE COUNCIL FOR ETHICS IN INTERNATIONAL AFFAIRS (New York City) was founded in 1914 as the Church Peace Union, with a deed of gift from Carnegie and an endowment of $2 million from Carnegie Corporation; it has received several smaller grants over the years from the Corporation. Renamed in 1961 the Council on Religion and International Affairs, in 1986 it became the Carnegie Council on Ethics and International Affairs.[18]

overseas defined the themes pursued in several areas, including adult education, museum study, and support for higher education. A range of studies and associated grants revealed the sometimes ambiguous perspectives of the Corporation's approach to race issues, a major theme in the 1930s, as will be discussed in this volume in the context of the interplay of grants made in South Africa, the British colonies in East Africa, and the United States. In later years, however, the Corporation's work to advance racial and gender equality became a major commitment.

The travel grants program, initiated in 1928, represented the support that the Corporation provided for individuals in an effort to extend its reach across fields and regions. These efforts also led to building major fields of endeavor that carried forward into more recent decades, such as international security studies. In these fields and others associated with the international programs, the Corporation often began to work in partnership with other foundations, especially those that were already partners for the work in the United States, such as the Phelps Stokes Fund and the Rockefeller Foundation.   .

World War II and Its Aftermath

During the presidency from 1941 to 1944 of Walter Jessup, World War II brought a temporary halt to the Corporation's overseas grant-making, but it expanded after the war. The postwar period brought with it both an exuberant embrace of America's leadership role in the world and a burgeoning of American foundation efforts overseas, most notably those of the Ford Foundation, beginning in 1950. Under the two postwar presidents—first Devereux Josephs from 1944 to 1948, and then Charles Dollard from 1948 to 1955—the Corporation began to revive its international programming by reestablishing the travel grants program in order to reduce the isolation of both Americans and citizens of the British Commonwealth.

Starting in 1946, the Corporation moved beyond the experiential travel grants into a major program aimed at ensuring that the American public, academicians, and policymakers could participate in a knowledgeable way in international affairs. Along with the concern about atomic weapons, this era confronted the rise of communism and the Cold War. The fear of

Communist infiltration of American society led Senator Joseph McCarthy to organize congressional investigations that included philanthropic foundations among their targets. While these investigations did not lead to major legislative changes, Carnegie Corporation and other foundations suffered adverse consequences by having much of the time, energy, and work of their leadership diverted from grant-making.

The 1950s and Beyond

World War II galvanized movements for self-determination in the many colonies around the world. With decolonization and independence taking hold in the British colonies in Africa and the Caribbean, under the presidencies of John Gardner (1955–1967) and Alan Pifer (1967–1982), the Corporation worked closely with leaders in the new nations as well as with the British Colonial Office.[19] In addition, the Corporation succeeded in encouraging other donors and American foreign policymakers to focus their attention on these new African countries.

This period illustrates how the foundation was able to extend its influence beyond its grant-making. As other donors became increasingly active in Africa, the Corporation made every effort to work on themes that filled essential gaps without duplicating the work of other foundations. This was particularly evident in the mid-1960s, when the Corporation moved from a focus on African universities and their broader role in the new nations to a narrower concentration within those universities on the underaddressed area of developing human capital to ensure a high quality of teachers and promoting research on teaching and education.

The social, economic, and political disruptions around the world since the mid-1960s have significantly influenced the Corporation's work, perhaps even more so than in the immediate post–World War II period, and certainly as much as the equally disruptive events of World War I, the Great Depression, and World War II itself. A long list of societal fault lines—civil rights, women's rights, the Vietnam War, the Cold War, the end of the Cold War, apartheid, the end of apartheid, nuclear weapons, local wars, and the events of September 11, 2001 (all of which, in turn, have been significantly affected by technological, information, and communication transformations)—have led to wildly fluctuating US foreign and domestic policies. Though at times surprised by the rapid rise and fall of events, the Corporation has, on occasion, been far enough ahead of the curve—and lucky enough—to help shape the momentum of ongoing events as a result of astute judgment by the president, trustees, staff, and grantees. These large-scale social challenges have prompted the Corporation to maintain extensive continuing collaborations with American foundation partners such as the Rockefeller Foundation, the Rockefeller Brothers Fund, the Ford Foundation, and the John D. and Catherine T. MacArthur Foundation to enhance the effectiveness of their activities—especially efforts to confront apartheid or deter the spread of nuclear weapons.

Much like the turning point under Keppel that led the Corporation to become global in its reach through expansive grant-making around the world, during Pifer's presidency in the late 1960s the Corporation reshaped its board, staff, and programs to reflect a diverse American society. These two turning points—setting a global perspective and affirming respect for diversity—set in motion major changes that persist in the Corporation and are likely to remain major attributes of its grant-making in the twenty-first century.

In the 1960s and 1970s, the anti-poverty, anti-bias, and pro-inclusion zeitgeist at all levels of national and global society shaped the grant-making programs to promote equal opportunity, a major theme of Andrew Carnegie's, both in the United States and overseas. Under Alan Pifer, the program in the British Commonwealth focused on finding ways to reduce the impact of apartheid in South Africa and to increase opportunities for women's participation in society. These grant-making decisions represented a balance between two ethical "goods": supporting opposition to apartheid and advancing women's empowerment, on the one hand, and funding higher education and efforts to strengthen universities, on the other.

When Pifer retired in 1982, David Hamburg became the eleventh president of the foundation. Under his leadership, the Corporation reinvigorated its international grant-making, focusing particularly on tackling the intractable issues associated with reducing the availability of nuclear weapons and the potential for their use. Hamburg aimed to reduce international tensions by helping to change the nature of both official and unofficial US relationships with the Soviet Union. The foundation also continued Pifer's commitment to ameliorating the egregious impact of apartheid in South Africa. In addition to support for ending apartheid and enhancing women's opportunities, Hamburg broadened the focus in Commonwealth Africa and the Caribbean to include support for innovative policy research in science and technology for development, as well as in women's health, most notably drawing global attention to the persistence of maternal mortality in African countries and potential policy solutions.

Three major events directly related to its grants programs confronted the Corporation during the Hamburg era: the fall of the Berlin Wall, the dissolution of the Soviet Union, and the release of Nelson Mandela from imprisonment, which hastened the end of apartheid in South Africa. Hamburg responded by sustaining the continuity of the grant programs while at the same time introducing major changes in the specific grants made in response to the volatile conditions that followed these events. This period yet again serves to illustrate the need to balance the pull of mission and the push of dramatically changing context.

Entering a New Century

In 1997 Vartan Gregorian became the Corporation's twelfth president. As might be expected of a historian, Gregorian has drawn on each of the periods of the Corporation's past to shape both the patterns of the activities to be undertaken and the pattern of work within the foundation. The Corporation has extensively reshaped its efforts in Africa and Russia, for example, combining its earlier support for universities and libraries with a more recent focus, notably in African countries, on information technologies, women's advancement in higher education and the sciences, and the next generation of university faculty. Partnerships with other foundations have taken on a completely new dimension with the creation of a formal interfoundation partnership to support African universities.

The earlier strategy of making grants to individuals was revived in 2000 with the inauguration of the Carnegie Scholars Program, which provided significant support for American scholarly activity overseas. Concern about American public understanding of development, foreign policy, and Islam has been a modest but consistent focus of grant-making, with the recent addition of training journalists. The Corporation has also maintained and enlarged efforts in international peace and security, paying close grant-making attention to weapons of mass destruction, states at risk, Track II diplomacy, and the rise of a multipolar world of major international actors, both state and nonstate.

THE CHALLENGES OF PUBLIC ACCOUNTABILITY

SPECIAL CHALLENGES ARISE for grant-making institutions that are chartered in the United States and make grants overseas. The Sixteenth Amendment to the US Constitution, which went into effect in 1913, along with the 1917 law that allowed associated charitable deductions, transformed private foundations' societal accountability.[20] In accepting a donation on the public's behalf, through a charitable deduction, the government makes its decision based on governance by mission, not on governance by donor. Despite a donation's private origins, the legal standing of the money as a public trust leads to unalterable ethical obligations for present and future generations. When a donor endows a foundation, the money, in essence— and in accord with the inspiration for the foundation field, Carnegie's mandate in *Wealth*—is given to the public to serve the public.

This change in status from private funds to public trust complicates the process of grant-making for American philanthropic institutions as they embark on supporting specific programs in other countries. While the legal aspects are complex, the issue can be kept simple when viewed through the lens of Andrew Carnegie's vision: money made from the public is given back to the public. But when it comes to international work, two different publics are involved, in that the giving is controlled in the country of donation and the application is controlled in the country of expenditure.

The complex questions that arise from this set of issues are important to position at the front of a discussion of international philanthropy in the twenty-first century, when all aspects of international engagement are being sorted out. Which "public interest" should shape the purpose of an international grant: the public making it or the public receiving it? More specifically, is it necessary for the overseas work of foundations to be consistent with the American government's official positions in specific countries, under the assumption that those positions reflect the public's will?

If so, how can foundations respond to the public interest in the countries where they are working? While the US Internal Revenue Service (IRS) has enacted many regulations for work overseas, it has not explicitly acknowledged or addressed the dimension of public responsibility. Since one of the intended roles of philanthropy is to introduce new ideas and to press for change in problematic practices, given the context of the globalized framework within which foundations now operate, the "public trust" and "public will" issues need continued legal clarification and leadership by foundation governing boards. Donors cannot prescribe solutions here, but they can give to support sound process and practice.

Carnegie Corporation's century of grant-making shows that strength in international activities, much as in domestic efforts, comes from combining knowledge and skills in balancing mission with understanding of context and serious reflection before action. Consultation with partners, including other donors working in the same area, and importantly, with a sufficiently wide range of local experts and advisers provides multiple perspectives to inform staff members' understanding. With a few notable exceptions, the greater the involvement of local partners in shaping recommendations and actions, the greater the likelihood of grants having positive outcomes.

A CENTURY OF EXPERIENCES

FROM THE REVIEW of the Corporation's century of grant-making, institutional actions, and engagement with the ideas and issues dominating different eras, four interrelated attributes emerge as the significant properties informing its decision-making. These are discussed in more detail in the concluding chapter, which focuses on how lessons learned from a century of grant-making may help to point the way for developing philanthropic strategies crafted to meet the challenges of a new century. These four attributes are:

- *Significance of mission,* in shaping the grant-making decisions of the president and the trustees, confers an advantage for decision-making in complex, uncertain times.
- *Openness to risk-taking* is exemplified by the Corporation's social justice

grant-making starting in the 1960s, first in the United States and then in South Africa (foreshadowed by the support for the *American Dilemma* studies of Gunnar Myrdal in the late 1930s).

+ *Willingness to make long-term investments* underlies two broad areas: the Corporation's practice of funding institutional endowments or providing core support over many years, both more prominent in its early history, has now yielded enduring institutions, including the Brookings Institution and the Institute of International Education; the Corporation's support for "field" building has created ongoing programs that open new arenas of knowledge, and its grants have built individual and institutional capacity in major areas related to its mission, such as the work in the 1920s and 1930s on adult education in the United States and overseas and in the 1950s and 1960s on area studies.

+ *Openness to collaboration and partnership* began as early as 1920, when the Corporation provided matching support with the Rockefeller Foundation and the provincial government of Nova Scotia, Canada, for Dalhousie University, and continued throughout the century, as exemplified by the ten-year, multi-foundation Partnership for Higher Education in Africa starting in 2000.

Carnegie Corporation's centenary in 2011 provided the impetus for this publication, which aims to fill the gap in the analysis of the full range of the Corporation's international activities over the past century.[21] The study elucidates patterns of leadership, decision-making, and actions in each period as a contribution to public understanding of the ways in which an American foundation has worked in international settings and on international issues at home. Findings from the history of Carnegie Corporation and similar foundations that have acted on a global stage can inform philanthropic partnerships around the globe, all contributing to enabling, for the second century of modern philanthropy, a thriving "human community ... of various complementing organizations sharing the same concerns and seeking to solve them through cooperative endeavors."[22]

I

A GIFT BECOMES AN INSTITUTION,
1911–1920

AT 3:00 PM ON NOVEMBER 10, 1911, seven men gathered around a table at Andrew Carnegie's home on Ninety-First Street in New York City to agree to serve as its founding trustees and to officially accept his letter transmitting the deed of gift to establish Carnegie Corporation of New York. These men were at the forefront of the fields of peace, education, science, and philanthropy, the four areas of chief importance to Andrew Carnegie.[1] They were joined by Carnegie and his wife and daughter, Louise and Margaret, who embraced his commitment to give back to the public all the money he had earned in his highly successful business enterprises. At the time no one anticipated that this new foundation would grow and flourish to the extent that it has over the past one hundred years, contributing to the conduct of philanthropy not only in the United States but also, as this book details, abroad.

Andrew Carnegie, once the richest man in the world, had years earlier determined to shift his focus from making money to using it to enrich the lives of others, a commitment that helped shape a new age of philanthropy that continues today. The ripple effects of his vision are evident in the ongoing work of the Corporation and even in the promotion of philanthropy around the world by such twenty-first century philanthropists as Bill and Melinda Gates and Warren Buffett. The Corporation's initial grants to libraries and to fund church organs grew out of Andrew Carnegie's experiences as a youth in the United States. The roots of the broad, cosmo-politan understanding of the world he would later develop were in his early childhood upbringing in Scotland. Soon after the Corporation's founding, both he and his trustees began to expand funding beyond the borders of the United States, extending the Corporation's support overseas to Canada and the British dominions and colonies. This book tells the story of how the overseas grant-making of the Corporation blossomed over the century; today nearly half of its grant-making efforts are directed to international activities.

LAUNCHING THE CORPORATION

ANDREW CARNEGIE ESTABLISHED MANY PHILANTHROPIC institutions between 1893 and 1911, but still he was frustrated that he might die without returning all his money to the public.[2] When Elihu Root, a longtime trusted legal adviser and a senator from New York, suggested creating a foundation that instead of doing the work itself would support other institutions to do so, Carnegie happily adopted this idea as an improved way of administering philanthropy.[3] He founded Carnegie Corporation on that principle.

The Corporation is Andrew Carnegie's largest philanthropy. He endowed it with the broad mission to exist in perpetuity "for the purpose of receiv-ing and maintaining a fund or funds and applying the income thereof to promote the advancement and diffusion of knowledge and understanding among the people of the United States, by aiding technical schools, insti-tutions of higher lerning, libraries, scientific research, hero funds, useful publications, and by such other agencies and means as shall from time to time be found appropriate therefor."[4] A second deed of gift in January 1912 provided additional funds "for the continuance of the gifts for libraries and church organs, as heretofore made by me in Canada and in the United Kingdom and British colonies."[5] Unlike many foundation benefactors before and since, Carnegie did not tie the hands of his trustees. As he had stipulated when he founded the Carnegie Institution of Washington and the Carnegie Endowment for International Peace, his deed of gift to the trustees of Carnegie Corporation of New York—in which he employed the "simplified spelling" to which he was devoted—underscored what it meant to establish an institution in perpetuity:

My desire is that the work which I hav been carrying on, or similar beneficial work, shall continue during this and future generations. Conditions upon the erth inevitably change; hence, no wise man will bind Trustees for ever to certain paths, causes or institutions. I disclaim any intention of doing so. On the contrary, I giv my trustees full authority to change policy or causes hitherto aided, from time to time, when this, in their opinion, has become necessary or desirable. They shall best conform to my wishes by using their own judgment.[6]

The trustees of Carnegie Corporation not only were responsible for designing policies and programs to promote the advancement and diffusion of knowledge and understanding but also had to determine whether "conditions upon the erth" had evolved enough for them to change direction or whether they needed to stay the course. Subsequent trustees drew on those early efforts, learned what worked, discarded what did not, and built an enduring institution. Several of the trustees had the international experience needed to steward the Corporation's work outside the United States. Elihu Root, for example, in addition to being Andrew Carnegie's confidant and legal adviser as well as a US senator, was a (if not the) leading American public servant for international affairs in 1911—as a former secretary of war, former secretary of state, and Nobel Peace Prize winner. Henry Pritchett and Robert Woodward had been involved in international collaborations in science, particularly astronomy, and were known for their contributions in that field.[7] James Bertram, who had organized Andrew Carnegie's philanthropy before the Corporation was established, had spent several years in South Africa in the 1890s and reportedly spoke Zulu.[8]

Carnegie nested two major lines of action: mission within the charter and scope of action within the deed of gift. The dual documentation covered two tasks: one gave the legal standing, the other the guidance for how the new organization should conduct itself. The charter, the key to the structure, was a legal compact with the people of the United States and of the world. The second major component of the structure, the deed of gift to the managers of this trust, provided instructions for moving forward: "This is how I want you to proceed." Andrew Carnegie addressed and solved the challenge for a founder of seeking perpetuity—that is, ensuring that his intentions were followed.

Heritage and temperament shaped Andrew Carnegie and his philanthropic actions.[9] He was born to William and Margaret Carnegie in 1835 in Dunfermline, Scotland, and both sides of his family participated enthusiastically in the Chartist movement, abhorring privilege and charity as well as inherited wealth and titles and speaking out about the social justice issues of their day.

His proud father, a weaver of fine linens, was financially ruined when weaving machines replaced hand looms, and his mother, determined to provide for the family, opened a shop that sold basic household supplies. Andrew Carnegie grew up feeling the effects of poverty and with a disdain for privilege. In 1848, with the help of loans from friends, the family emigrated, steerage class, to the United States, where they settled near Pittsburgh, Pennsylvania. Young Andrew moved rapidly up the employment ladder, starting at age thirteen as a bobbin boy in a cotton mill. In 1853, at age eighteen, he was hired as clerk and trusted assistant to Thomas A. Scott, the superintendent of the Pittsburgh Division of the Pennsylvania Railroad. As Scott advanced in the railroad hierarchy, he brought Andrew along with him, and during the early part of the Civil War, Scott, then assistant secretary of war for transportation, placed Carnegie in charge of ensuring that the trains could transport Union troops into the city. Carnegie remained alert to business opportunities, and after watching a wooden bridge burn to the ground, he rapidly organized the Keystone Bridge Works Company in 1863 to build fireproof bridges of iron; in 1866 he established the Pittsburgh Locomotive Works and the Freedom Iron and Steel Company. By 1868, at age thirty-six, his multiple manufacturing businesses and investments earned him an annual income of $50,000, worth perhaps $11 million today. Carnegie decided to reinvest all his earnings above the $50,000 per annum in causes and institutions in which he believed. It was a natural progression of his Chartist abhorrence of unearned wealth and class-defined privilege and his devotion to self-improvement and open access to opportunity.

Andrew Carnegie's restless energies and curiosity led him to travel farther afield, and in 1878, at the age of forty-three, he took an eye-opening trip around the world that convinced him about the importance of "a cooperative spirit among nations, and his growing opposition to religious expansionism and wars of empire, were never firmer—he had 'suffered a sea change, into something rich and strange.'"[10]

His experiences in his new homeland enlarged his political views, melding the early family influence of the Chartist movement with the practice of American democracy. Carnegie's embrace of American democracy shaped his thinking about his country of origin, and he was an active promoter of Pan-Anglicanism, a movement of the last part of the nineteenth century that focused on "the community of ideals and institutions the United States shared with the United

Kingdom." His recognition of the connections and commonalities across geographic boundaries reflected the prevailing philosophy and practice of the cultural internationalism movement, which aimed to build the basis for peace around the globe through international understanding fostered by exchanges of ideas in literature, art, music, and science that linked scientists, scholars, and activists. These themes are reflected in Carnegie's varied philanthropies.

Carnegie was a member of a new generation of philanthropists who came to perceive the inefficiency of the general goal of charity, which was the alleviation of the immediate effects of "social dysfunction": poverty, sickness, and the various persistent forms of social disorder. A more scientific and business-like approach, these philanthropists thought, would be to attack the root causes of social dysfunction directly. The answers lay in the "scientific philanthropy" approach, promulgated as early as 1867 by George Peabody. Carnegie molded these influences and concerns into his formal statement on the societal obligations of private wealth, originally published in 1889 as *Wealth*, then subsequently expanded and republished several times; the last edition, retitled *The Gospel of Wealth and Other Timely Essays*, was published in 1900. His original essay with its provocative statement that private wealth should be returned to the public from whence it came also inspired John D. Rockefeller and others to establish their own foundations:

The millionaire will be but a trustee for the poor, intrusted for a season with a great part of the increased wealth of the community … the man who dies leaving behind many millions of available wealth, which was his to administer during life, will pass away "unwept, unhonored, and unsung," no matter to what uses he leaves the dross which he cannot take with him. Of such as these the public verdict will then be: "The man who dies thus rich dies disgraced."[11]

With his embrace of open access to learning, the focus of Carnegie's early grant-making was primarily on providing communities with the gift of a free public library; inaugurated by his mother, his library program started in his hometown of Dunfermline, Scotland, in 1881. His second major focus was the provision of church organs, starting with his father's Swedenborgian Church in Pittsburgh, where Carnegie had sung in the choir and developed a love of music. When he sold his company to US Steel and decided to devote himself full-time to philanthropy, one of his first major gifts was to the New York Public Library—$5.2 million for sixty-five branches. While devoted to these specific community- and church-based donations, Carnegie also sought to establish institutions that would contribute more broadly to enhancing community life and tackle the compelling global issues of peace, education, and science.

In his businesses, Carnegie had sought innovations that would enhance the bottom line, but he did not consider that kind of constraint on the actions of his grant-making foundation. He sought to benefit humanity in whatever way his trustees thought appropriate for their times. Carnegie Corporation was founded on trust: trust in the leaders, trust in knowledge, trust that its leaders would find worthy recipients and projects. The trustees responded to this challenge: "The Trustees realize that the execution of the trust will involve many difficulties of judgment and labors of administration, and they assume their obligation in the hope, and with the intent, to perform their duties faithfully, in a manner adequate to the great purpose of the trust, and in the disinterested public spirit which has moved the founder of the trust to this great benefaction."[12] A dialogue of implementation among the founder, the board, and the public was now under way: a charter with the public had been executed; guidance had been given to the managers that both freed and bound them; and the managers had responded by accepting responsibility for the trust, recognizing the judgments they would have to make.

At their first meeting, the trustees took care of the ground-building steps required to function: they approved a constitution and bylaws for the new institution, asked Andrew Carnegie to serve as president, and decided to move into the Fifth Avenue offices of the Carnegie Foundation for the Advancement of Teaching (CFAT). They determined many basic foundation details, and by establishing the Executive Committee, comprising the president and two elected members of the board, the trustees agreed that, in lieu of hiring staff, a board subgroup would be responsible for the management of the institution.

For the next ten years the Executive Committee conducted the work of running the organization, as stated in the newly approved constitution: "During the intervals between the meetings of the board the executive committee shall exercise the power of the board of trustees, in the management and direction of the business and the conduct of the affairs of the corporation. It shall hav supervision of the property of the corporation and shall determin the investment of its funds."[13] From 1911 through 1914, Andrew Carnegie was actively engaged in directing the Corporation's grant-making, both in the United States and overseas. Then, as was his practice in business and his other philanthropies, he devolved the management of the foundation to the trustees, while retaining the title of president.

These early actions of the trustees may seem remote from the issues of institution-building today. Yet philanthropists in the twenty-first century are likely to experience comparable challenges of birthing and weaning their foundations, particularly if they intend for them to support international activities and to thrive in perpetuity. The values that motivated Carnegie and his first trustees and shaped the activities of the first few years— private funds and public accountability, trust in the good ideas of others (as Carnegie had done for his business successes) and commitment to supporting people and institutions with those good ideas, building institutions that endure—were balanced by the trustees' own institutional obligations and the push and pull of national versus international opportunities and changing contexts.

American philanthropy began to take off rapidly in this period—the Rockefeller Foundation was founded in 1913, and as tax laws changed so were many other foundations. Competition, collaboration, partnership— these characteristics of philanthropy in the twenty-first century were shaping relations in the field right from the beginning. Predictably, opinions of members of Congress and of the public also became influential, if not always appreciated, factors in the politics of generosity. Many of these issues are well covered in other volumes; only those aspects most salient for the work of the Corporation are discussed in this book.[14]

During this first decade of the Corporation's history, the trustees set in motion the multiple interacting influences on decision-making that have influenced the work of this foundation and that of others, especially those working in other countries and on international issues in the United States. Pulled together, these many strands—including the mission of the foundation, the context in which it is situated (both local and more global), the special institutional standing of private foundations, and the foundation's human dimension: the trustees, president, staff members, advisers, and grantees, and the grant-seeking public—give shape to the efforts and effectiveness of all philanthropic institutions. Across these levels are the three closely related creative tensions that further inform decision-making: donor intent vis-à-vis the perspectives of the trustees, president, and staff members; external and public versus internal considerations; and for internationally oriented foundations, domestic priorities versus those in other countries that affect the balance between the national and international challenges facing the nation and the world.

THE FIRST YEARS OF INTERNATIONAL GRANT-MAKING

THE CORPORATION WAS LAUNCHED AGAINST the backdrop of impending world war. Despite Andrew Carnegie's passionate appeals for arbitration instead of violence and his efforts to organize meetings of Kaiser Wilhelm, the king of England, and US leaders, such as former president Teddy Roosevelt, more powerful pressures prevailed, culminating in World War I. As brutal and destructive as they were, the war years, 1914 to 1918, opened up new horizons for grant-making in the United States. World War I and its aftermath enabled the Corporation to make some of its most enduring grants.

In the first days and months after founding the Corporation, Andrew Carnegie took the initial steps that would lead to international grant-making. In January 1912, two months after he had given his gift of $25 million (worth approximately $571 million today) to establish the foundation, he gave a second gift of $75 million, of which $55 million was to be used in the United States for "general purposes" and $20 million in other countries, specifically to continue Carnegie's long-standing program of support for libraries and church organs.[15] He initially thought that half of the $20 million designated for the United Kingdom and Colonies could be used to establish a separate trust for the United Kingdom by taking funds from the principal. When he learned from his lawyers that the funds had to be drawn on the income—which would nearly deplete the grant-making resources of his new foundation—and that the Corporation would be liable for supporting the new foundation in the United Kingdom, Carnegie abandoned that plan.[16] Instead, in October 1913, he gave an additional $10 million from his own remaining accounts to establish the Carnegie United Kingdom Trust. The trustees now had the freedom to decide how to allocate those resources, which was Carnegie's original intention. The pressure to make grants in the United States probably weighed heavily on these trustees, many of whom, as presidents of other Carnegie institutions, often juggled the need to make up deficits in their own institutions with the need to maintain integrity in their role as trustees of Carnegie Corporation.

Despite these pressures, they decided to keep $10 million for work overseas, as originally intended, and to reallocate the remaining $10 million for grants in the United States. International activities soon began to enlarge the Corporation's focus, in keeping with Carnegie's vision of a foundation that would build stronger ties across the English-speaking world. In 1913 the trustees separated the overseas monies into a designated "Foreign Fund," or "Special Fund," with the monies for activities in the United States or occasionally Canada in the "Principal Fund," or "General Fund." This accounting decision has been maintained over the century: the funds for overseas activities are drawn out of a separately maintained fund.

One inspiration for this decision may have been the Rockefeller Foundation, which had a global presence from the moment it was founded in 1913. The two institutions focused on different areas (the Rockefeller Foundation mainly on health in its first years and Carnegie Corporation on education).[17] On occasion, they collaborated in support of an institution or program, especially in the American South and soon in Canada. From this time until World War II, even though many smaller foundations were established in the United States, the Rockefeller Foundation and Carnegie Corporation remained the two largest philanthropies active overseas, and for many years Carnegie Corporation had the larger asset base.[18]

After addressing the initial details of establishing and launching a new corporation, the trustees identified opportunities for national and international grant-making, in part in response to the demands created by the pre–World War I period, the war, and its aftermath, including the changing global role of the United States. Over the first year, however, the Executive Committee did not address international grant-making beyond maintaining Andrew Carnegie's commitment to support church organs and libraries in the United States and throughout the British Empire. On April 30, 1912, the Corporation made its first grant for library support (outside of Canada and the British Isles) in Potchefstroom, South Africa. Later that year, at the meeting on September 27, the committee recommended the first Corporation grant outside Canada and the British Isles, for church organ purchases in two parishes in Jamaica, British West Indies.[19] The Board of Trustees approved these grants at its annual meeting on November 21, 1912.

Over the second year the domestic program included support for endowments of small colleges and a wide range of modest grants to tackle various cases of human adversity. In 1913, in its first action related to an international issue at home, the Corporation provided $200,000 to the Chinese Educational Commission for Chinese students studying at American colleges, in response to their difficulties in receiving funds from the new Republic of China, which had been created in January 1912 following the overthrow of the Qing dynasty. The intention was that China would soon reimburse this grant, but the new Republic never achieved the stability needed to do so. Civil war in China began in 1913, and no evidence has surfaced that the Corporation ever pursued reimbursement.[20]

Following these early grants, the Corporation, less than two years old, quickly extended its international reach to supporting universities in Canada and providing organs and libraries elsewhere in Southern Africa and then in the southern Pacific. Support for students stranded in either the United States or Europe because of political and economic upheavals became a small but consistent area of grant-making over the next nine decades. Another natural interest of Carnegie's, maintained over the following century, related to pride in his background as an immigrant and concern about the treatment of immigrants; starting in 1913, Corporation trustees endorsed his support for immigrant-assisting institutions, such as the New Jersey Commission of Immigration, the North American Civic League for Immigrants, and the Society for Italian Immigrants.

In the first few years the trustees continued unchanged Carnegie's support for church organs and library buildings. They may have been asking themselves, however, how many more libraries and church organs were needed in the United States and overseas. Even Carnegie himself seemed to be rethinking his earlier program when, as chair of the Executive Committee, he agreed to recommend a grant in March 1913 to Queen's University in Ontario, Canada, for $100,000 to match the $400,000 already raised for a $500,000 endowment fund.[21]

This desire to broaden the mandate for international work led the board to undertake an early revision of the charter. In 1916 the Executive Committee—still chaired by Carnegie, though he no longer attended meetings—considered using the income from the Special Fund for purposes in Canada and in the United Kingdom and Colonies other than libraries and church organs. The board formally asked the legal counsel, Elihu Root Jr., to draft a bill requesting this change and to present it to the New York State Legislature.[22]

On April 23, 1917, the State Legislature voted to amend the charter as follows: "The corporation ... is hereby empowered to hold and administer any funds given to it for use in Canada or the British colonies for the same purpose in Canada or the British colonies as those to which it is by law authorized to apply its funds in the United States." This immediately legitimized and broadened both the range and scope of the Corporation's activities. The British Empire covered a large portion of the globe—23 percent of the Earth's landmass, with between one-fifth and one-quarter of the world's population.[23] With this repositioning in 1917, Carnegie Corporation and the Rockefeller Foundation became the dominant global foundations, a status they held for the next three decades.

The trustees, including the president/founder, were slowly building the institution and weaning it away from the structure of Carnegie's previous philanthropic activities. By April 1917, six years after the Corporation's founding, the trustees had revised the charter so that they could make grants overseas for the same purposes as they did in the United States; they had separated, instead of keeping combined, the funds for overseas activities and domestic activities; they had revised the Corporation to change the number of officers and the number of trustees; and soon they would consider modifying the original intentions of the donor for their grant-making priorities. These trustees took very seriously Carnegie's charge in the deed of gift: to build the institution for perpetuity by making it responsive to changing conditions as well as by assessing what was working and what was not. In 1918 the trustees reconsidered the support for libraries that had been established at the old Carnegie Steel Company. The following sentences reveal their thinking: "The plea is made by the Steel Company that Mr. Carnegie on various occasions emphatically stated that only his money should be given to or used by these libraries. Now what Mr. Carnegie might do as an individual is possibly very different from that which a Board of Trustees might consider within their province."[24]

With the establishment of the United Kingdom Trust and the charter changes, the Corporation had clarified its grant-making priorities to include the United States, Canada, and the British colonies, as well as the other British dominions, Australia, New Zealand, and South Africa. New places consequently appeared in the library lists, including Transvaal, Natal, Cape Colony, Trinidad, Mauritius, New Zealand, and more than twenty-six sites in Canada. In Canada, the trustees were moving beyond the focus on church organs and libraries to support universities. As with the grant to Queen's University, the requirement that grantees provide matching funds was maintained. Payment would not be made until "the conditions imposed by the rules of Carnegie Corporation of New York shall have been complied with."[25]

These stringent matching grant conditions incorporated an innovation previously pioneered by George Peabody, which is now a standard approach in philanthropy.[26] Especially in supporting the bricks-and-mortar of a library or the "hardware" of a church organ, these conditions were aimed at ensuring the sustainability of the investment for the benefit of the public.

ANDREW CARNEGIE'S PURSUIT OF PEACE

WHILE CONTINUING TO LEAD the Corporation, Andrew Carnegie was energetically pursuing his determination to prevent a world war, whose outbreak he, like many others, had feared for several years. Carnegie had spoken passionately against war, as when he proposed establishing a "League of Peace," which he later called a "League of Nations," in his 1905 Rectorial Address at the University of St Andrews. He closed that speech by urging the students to confront war: "So to us our time will come, and, as it does, let us hit accursed war hard until we drive it from the civilized world...."[27] Carnegie put his money, time, energy, goodwill, and contacts to use in trying to avert war that would entangle Europe—Great Britain included—Japan, and the United States, if not other nations.

Earlier in 1903 he had endowed the Peace Palace in The Hague. In addition to his writing about achieving world peace through arbitration treaties and the League of Peace, he invested considerable time and money in wooing President Theodore Roosevelt and Kaiser Wilhelm II of Germany to support the idea of the League.[28] In 1909, even when Roosevelt was no longer president, Carnegie worked hard to convince him to visit the kaiser and King Edward VII of Great Britain to discuss peace and the League. Roosevelt visited the kaiser, but King Edward died and all further meeting plans were canceled. Even with that failure, Carnegie did not give up. The successor to Roosevelt, President William Howard Taft, agreed with Carnegie on the importance of the arbitration treaty.[29]

To further assure the promotion of peace and the end of war, following consultations with advisers and statesmen, Carnegie established the Carnegie Endowment for Peace in 1910, one year before founding the Corporation. To serve as president, he selected Elihu Root, "that ablest of all our Secretaries of State, and in the opinion of President Roosevelt, 'the wisest man he ever knew' ... a great man."[30] He had hoped that the Endowment would serve as the platform for his advocacy, but by selecting Root he nearly guaranteed that it would not. Root was convinced of the importance of studies and research to underpin advocacy and saw that as the focus of the Endowment. Studies would shed light on the causes of war as the basis for sustaining peace; the Endowment would not actively conduct public outreach for peace in the United States or elsewhere.[31]

As part of the postwar peace efforts, and more in keeping with the Endowment's approach, in October 1918 the Corporation trustees provided the first substantive grant, of $90,000, for the publication and distribution of the controversial "Lichnowsky Memorandum"—a pamphlet written by Prince Lichnowsky of Germany that formed the crucial evidence for the German "war guilt thesis" that helped to shape the outcome of the Treaty of Versailles after World War I—as well as the distribution of the German Peace Treaties.[32]

Accepting the more academic orientation of the Endowment, Andrew Carnegie redirected some of his antiwar energies toward building the basis for peace through arbitration, promoting his ideas for establishing the League of Peace and engaging with groups explicitly oriented toward preventing a major international conflagration. He joined the board of a more activist organization, the American Peace Society, and soon became its chair. He wrote vigorously in newspapers and gave rousing talks about the importance of peace and the need for civilized nations to negotiate; he met with journalists, politicians, and kings to make his vision a reality.[33] Between 1910 and 1914, for example, he met with President Taft to lobby for the ratification of an international arbitration treaty; with Germany's

Kaiser Wilhelm II, whom he praised for refraining from military action in 1913; and with President Woodrow Wilson to persuade him to avert war with Mexico in 1914.[34]

Despite the impending war, or possibly to prevent it, the trustees in early 1914 considered the role of international exchanges to increase international understanding and the promotion of peace. This was consistent with the pre–World War I cultural internationalism movement, which stressed the importance of international connections as peace-building measures.[35] In March 1914, the trustees agreed to fund the Committee to Promote Friendly Relations Among Foreign Students to enable John Mott and Gilbert Beaver (leaders of the Young Men's Christian Association) to implement their idea of drawing closer together "those who labor for the arbitration of international disputes and the reign of peace under law" by promoting "friendly relations among students and professors in different countries." This furthered Andrew Carnegie's commitment to pursuing international arbitration for the peaceful resolution of disputes. The Executive Committee, with Carnegie signing the minutes as president, was also suggesting to the Board of Trustees the importance of fostering international activities in the United States.[36]

Also in 1914, the Rockefeller Foundation initiated its program of international fellowships for postdoctoral training. Both institutions were building on the concept of the Rhodes Scholarships, which were established in 1902 by Cecil Rhodes as a basis for building peace across the British colonies, the United Kingdom, Germany, and the United States. New grant-making was being broken open by the US philanthropies, all aimed at building peace through personal contact to share knowledge and understanding. These exchanges remained a hallmark of the Corporation's grant-making for the next fifty years.

Although reluctant to fund religious groups—beyond providing for spiritual uplift through church organ music—Carnegie gradually recognized that religious leaders and church groups might be enlisted as fellow antiwar advocates. With the encouragement of Mrs. Carnegie, he and the Corporation trustees appropriated $2 million (about $46.6 million today) from the Corporation as the endowment to establish the Church Peace Union, which brought together religious leaders from several Protestant denominations (Episcopal, Methodist, Baptist, Lutheran, Congregationalist,

Presbyterian, Church of the Disciples, Universalist, and Friends), a Roman Catholic, and a Jew. According to a website of the Carnegie Council for Ethics in International Affairs, the Church Peace Union's institutional descendant, "Carnegie hoped to mobilize the world's churches, religious organizations and other spiritual and moral resources to join in promoting moral leadership and finding alternatives to armed conflict."[37] On the eve of World War I, he sought to make war obsolete.

The Church Peace Union was the first grantee to support peace-related activities apart from the Carnegie Endowment. Indeed, until the 1980s the Church Peace Union was the main Corporation grantee completely dedicated to the promotion of peace other than the Carnegie Endowment. Even during the summer of 1914, Andrew Carnegie was convinced that war could be avoided. The inaugural international event of the Church Peace Union was a conference held on August 1, 1914, on the shores of Lake Constance in southern Germany. In the age before airplane travel, many conference participants had made long journeys and thus arrived just as war was being declared. The German, French, British, and American conferees met through August 2, released a declaration calling for the cessation of hostilities, and then fled quickly on the last trains to leave Germany.[38] Although Carnegie had warned how easily war could begin, when it was declared on August 3, he incredulously exclaimed, "It can't be true!"[39]

Andrew Carnegie never lost his vision of achieving lasting peace. In a *New York Times* interview on December 6, 1914, "he presciently predicted that if a League of Peace were not established at the end of this war, the vanquished would rise up again to renew the cycle of warfare."[40] Even as late as November 25, 1915, his eightieth birthday, he wrote to the *New York Times* that "the world grows better and we are soon to see blessed peace restored and a world court established."[41]

INTERNATIONAL PHILANTHROPY
DURING WORLD WAR I

A SMALL CLUSTER OF GRANTS related directly to the war effort. The trustees saw themselves as stepping forward to do their patriotic duty by purchasing $750,000 in Liberty Bonds as well as facilitating the purchase of the bonds by the staff of the Corporation and other Carnegie institutions.[42]

They also considered providing significant support for the American Red Cross with a grant of $500,000 for educational purposes. But the Red Cross did not fit Carnegie Corporation's mission: it was an organization devoted to service, not education. Again they needed to turn to counsel and explore the legality of making a donation.[43] Counsel authorized them to make that grant, and then another for $1 million at the May 20, 1918, board meeting. Support for the American Red Cross paved the way for additional war-related grants, including $320,000 for the War Service Committee of the American Library Association for library buildings at all US Army cantonments and $100,000 for the War Work Council of the National Board of the Young Women's Christian Association.[44] In 1918 the trustees granted $100,000 to the Khaki University of Canada, "for the purchase of books for its libraries among the soldiers."[45] That year they also granted $250,000 to the Knights of Columbus War Camp Fund.[46]

The trustees were torn between demands to be patriotic, on the one hand, and to honor charter obligations and donor intent, on the other—such as wrestling with the ethical decision about whether to support a service agency seen to be more appropriate for an individual donor and less so for institutional philanthropy, especially given Andrew Carnegie's philosophy. The trustees clearly respected the rationale underpinning institutional philanthropy in contrast to individual charity; in turning to counsel to ensure the institutional integrity of their decision, they set in motion a practice that has been gingerly used throughout the century, usually in the context of international grant-making.

The effects of the war also highlighted the question of how to balance old pledges with new understandings. With the "war to end all wars" under way, communities began to have difficulty meeting the commitments of their contracts for library buildings and church organs. Even as they were ending support for these programs, the trustees were flexible and sensitive toward communities experiencing this difficulty and understood that libraries in local communities could not always meet their promised collaborative support. Despite the firmness of their earlier decisions, they agreed that the promise for support from the communities could lapse, thus pioneering "no-cost" grant extensions, a technique now used widely by foundations.

During this period, the board also initiated several now-familiar grant-making procedures, including analyzing the proportion of grant applications received to grants made and requiring grantees to provide formal reports detailing the use of grants. As they began to recognize that it was necessary to build a sense of accountability and responsibility for the outcomes of the grants, both for the grantees and for themselves, the trustees instituted accounting practices to differentiate between the funds for grants in the United States and those for overseas grants, setting in motion a potential divide between domestic and international grant-making. In a way, they were creating a distinct subfoundation within the main foundation. Rather than limiting the growth of the overseas fund, this accounting method protected international activities against domestic demand. Thirty years later, with the monies sequestered in the overseas fund while the program was on hold during World War II, considerable resources accumulated, enabling the overseas program to restart very quickly after the war concluded. It is entirely possible that if the trustees had not enacted this policy in 1915, future trustees might have reread Carnegie's deed of gift and put all the money into the general-purpose fund for the United States.

NEW ISSUES ARISE

EVEN AS HE PURSUED his passion for peace, Carnegie retained his leadership role with the Corporation. The declaration of war changed that. He stopped attending Board of Trustees and Executive Committee meetings after presiding over the November 1914 board meeting. The founder's vision, as articulated in *The Gospel of Wealth*, had reshaped the image of philanthropy in the American psyche. His foundation was living up to his intentions, but the trustees, including Carnegie, were frustrated by his favorite grantees.[47] With the war effort now engaging Europe (and eventually the United States), the trustees had other ideas of how to spend the money, essentially honoring the charge in the deed of gift from Carnegie.

The trustees soon recognized, moreover, that requiring matching grants, formal proposals, and progress reports was not enough to build a sense of accountability and responsibility for the outcomes of the grants, for both the grantees and themselves. Unfulfilled promises from libraries and church organ recipients both overseas and in the United States led to changes in

the way the Corporation operated.[48] Unlike Rockefeller Foundation leaders, the trustees did not hire a grant-making staff. They were convinced of
the correctness of the founder's perspective that this institution should be
making grants for others to do the work, and administrative expenses were
kept to a low percentage, around 2.7 percent. But they still needed to be
on top of the work. The trustees recognized their fiduciary responsibility
to ensure sound fiscal management, but now they were also acting as program officers concerned about the impact of their grants. Yet given their
multiple responsibilities, they were not able to provide the regular oversight
that would be possible for a program officer assigned to make and monitor
grants.

Trustee concerns about how communities were meeting their pledges
for library buildings and church organs suggested a fundamental question about the Corporation's philosophy and practice: how far did the
grant-maker's stewardship extend from the time the grant was made? With
no staff members to conduct site visits and prepare detailed assessments,
the trustees agreed to hire external consultants to study the programs for
public libraries and church organs; these were the first "evaluators" hired
by Carnegie Corporation. Hiring consultants is routine in the foundation
world today, but this was the first time at the Corporation that professionals
were profiting from philanthropic assets.

Rather than turn to specialists to evaluate the library and church organ
programs, the trustees went to individuals who could look at a body of
work, give an objective assessment of it, and make recommendations that
the trustees could endorse because they trusted the person making them.
While there was clearly a role for special expertise, these trustees also saw
the value in the quality of mind and wisdom that a generalist would bring
to a task, the core trait of intellectual integrity being clearly transferable
from one field to another. Moreover, the trustees might have implicitly considered the fact that there would be no conflict of interest in these assessments; these gentlemen did not know others in the field, so there would be
no pressure or prejudice in their recommendations. The trustees would be
receiving analytical reports that were as objective and unbiased as possible.

This intention was evident as they began to move away from their original grant-making program, largely inherited from the founder. In May 1917,

the Executive Committee reviewed the report for the purchase of church organs and agreed not to give any new aid to this area. They recognized that changing global circumstances should influence their priorities:

> The great war now raging and the entry of the United States into that war has [sic] brought upon the Corporation new demands of great importance and of pressing urgency. It is therefore unlikely that the Corporation wil in the future be able to devote any part of its resources to the purchas of church organs ... the trustees of the Corporation feel sure that their action in this matter wil be completely understood by the patriotic men and women of the churches.[49]

The report on libraries prompted the trustees to reconfigure the library program; instead of building libraries, they would now support building the emerging field of library science. Their strategies for "the advancement and diffusion of knowledge" through grant-making were evolving. They broadened the focus to establish schools for the study of libraries and library services, to establish or strengthen librarian associations, and to provide support for the training of librarians. They maintained their commitments to the library buildings until they were completed, but only rarely did they vote to support new library buildings or to provide for book collections.

A highly sensitive issue surfaced in the midst of the review of the programs for church organs and libraries. At various points during the period 1912 to 1914, with Andrew Carnegie as chair, significant support (at the million-dollar level or more for endowment and other costs) had been granted to the Carnegie Institute of Technology and the Carnegie Institute (both in Pittsburgh), as well as to the Carnegie Foundation for the Advancement of Teaching. Paralleling concerns about the effectiveness of the main grants programs, at their December 1915 meeting the trustees decided to consider the appropriateness of funding for Carnegie institutions.

Although the men who represented the Carnegie institutions were each certain that Andrew Carnegie had promised Corporation support for the endowments of the institutions they headed, as trustees of Carnegie Corporation they also felt an obligation to fulfill its mission. From 1911 to 1916, five Carnegie institutions had been funded for a total of $13,116,099.[50]

An undercurrent of tension was growing around this funding and becoming a major issue as the endowments of these Carnegie institutions declined, deficits rose sharply, and pressures intensified. Despite varying views on Carnegie's intentions about the use of Corporation assets for this purpose, significant outlays of funds provided endowment and program support for these institutions, including the newest institution, the Church Peace Union, which the Corporation supported in 1914 with a $2 million grant, even though it was not represented on the Board of Trustees. This request reinforced the conviction that the Corporation's role was in part to replenish the Carnegie institutions' coffers. As Burton Hendrick clarified, Carnegie "also wished his already established foundations to be regarded as more or less under its wing; but he did not make these wishes definite stipulations, and, in subsequent clauses, gave the trustees and their successors full power to choose the objects of benevolence."[51]

A team of handpicked national leaders sat around the Corporation table, supporting the grand gift of one man. Yet each of these men, like grant-seekers everywhere, also sought some share for the institutions that they represented. They had come to the meetings and signed off in support as grants went to others. But was taking for one's own institution right or wrong? This question had entered the boardroom of Carnegie Corporation, without anyone acknowledging its delicacy. It is a question that haunts any philanthropist who places his name in perpetuity on the door of an institution: What is his continuing responsibility for supporting that institution? If he has more to give, does he have an obligation to support that institution, to leave more of the largess? These organizations tend to view such legacies as legitimately theirs, and the trustees' actions at this time suggest that they shared this tendency.[52]

Yet in December 1915, the trustees arrived at a Solomon-like solution, most likely inspired by the judicious acting chair of the board, Elihu Root, whom Andrew Carnegie considered the intellectual and moral equivalent of the entire Supreme Court.[53] The Executive Committee decided to request that each of the five institutions represented on the board[54] submit, in writing, the details of its current financial status, its policies, and the amount of funding needed to carry out the plans for the institution.[55] The reports were submitted and circulated to the trustees in November 1916. Over the next five years, drawing on these reports and submitted requests, significant grants were made to two of the institutions that had made compelling cases for their significant projects and dire financial situations, the Carnegie Institute of Technology (total support for this period: $18,145,377) and the Carnegie Foundation for the Advancement of Teaching, which included the teachers' pensions ($12,001,100, with $1 million additional to establish the Teachers Insurance and Annuity Association). Nearly $1.9 million was granted to the Carnegie Institute of Pittsburgh and $600,000 to the Carnegie Institution of Washington. The one institution particularly relevant to international grant-making, the Carnegie Endowment for International Peace, received relatively modest support, $396,000, which went to the publications mentioned earlier. The Church Peace Union was not one of the five represented on the board but was nonetheless an Andrew Carnegie–endorsed institution; despite its leaders' continued exhortations, it received only $25,000 during this period.[56]

THE INFLUENCE OF NATIONAL AND GLOBAL TENSIONS ON POSTWAR GRANT-MAKING

THE EXTERNAL POLITICAL TENSIONS prevailing at this time were both national and global. The threat of global war and then the reality of war and its aftermath caused large-scale tensions and disruptions throughout the world and led to major political and social changes. Times of disruption and uncertainty, such as this period, as destructive as they are, offer creative opportunities from the perspective of philanthropy. The trustees seized the opportunity and endowed institutions that could analyze these cycles and convey the results to policymakers and the public. They also began to explore the ramifications of the changing global context on American society.

In the midst of World War I, national tensions cropped up that were potentially destructive for the field of philanthropy and its institutions. Constructive external criticism is important for keeping a privately run, public-good endeavor like philanthropy accountable and responsible; gimlet-eyed watchdogs with clear standards and high expectations provoke healthy critical tensions. The congressional hearings of 1915 heralded a century punctuated by such investigations—for example, later on, in the early

1950s, and again at the end of the 1960s. While investigators' concerns have varied, the core issues that prompted the first hearings persist, as summarized by the historian James Allen Smith in his analyses of these investigations: Is endowing private foundations the best use for private wealth? Or should that wealth be taxed to benefit a broader public? And a corollary question: given the private nature of these institutions, what is the best way to ensure their accountability to the public?[57] Congressional oversight can be one of the most constructive tools for ensuring public accountability by foundations—whose resources, as Andrew Carnegie would be the first to agree, belong to the public. The resulting legislation (as discussed in later chapters) led to requirements for reporting to the public. Other lasting effects, particularly from the hearings and resulting legislation in the late 1960s, have constrained foundation support for individuals and certain types of international grant-making.

Following the establishment of both Carnegie Corporation of New York and the Rockefeller Foundation, these concerns about how private resources were being spent in the name of the public good prompted Congress's first interrogations of foundations in 1915. Frank Walsh, labor lawyer and reformer, was chair of the Industrial Relations Commission, which was established in 1912 by President Woodrow Wilson and enacted by the US Congress to explore industrial violence and labor unrest. Possibly as a result of its 1912 hearings with John D. Rockefeller Jr. about the Ludlow Massacre, the Commission expanded its reach to include the new large philanthropic entities, namely, Carnegie Corporation and the Rockefeller Foundation.[58] Walsh sought to attack foundations because of "their wealth, loosely defined powers, exemption from federal taxation, freedom from public control, subservience to donors, and benumbing effect on smaller philanthropic agencies."[59]

The first witness for the new hearings on the large philanthropies was Andrew Carnegie. He set the tone in the hearings, winning over members of Congress with his wit, sincerity about the correctness of the commissioners' questions, and genial efforts at building a bond of camaraderie and shared concerns about excess. The New York Times reported on February 5, 1915, that he was "the most remarkable witness that has yet appeared before the commission." He fully agreed with the Commission that "government should exercise some control over the foundations," and also agreed that foundations should exercise "all efforts to publicize their activities."[60]

The Commission's work did not result in any serious intrusion into the life of philanthropies, at least not those of Carnegie Corporation and the Rockefeller Foundation. The Corporation trustees, of course, were aware of these hearings; one internal outcome was their introduction of more systematic processes in the work of their institution. For the field, the passage of income tax legislation and subsequent deductions boosted interest in establishing philanthropic institutions. It is worth noting that the tax exemption for philanthropy had not been a factor in the founding of either of these two foundations, which were established before that privilege was enacted. Later congressional hearings, decades away, were more influential and led to serious and costly changes in the operations of philanthropic institutions.

In the wake of World War I, the worrisome convergence of increasingly polarized economic conditions with changes in population dynamics in the United States and around the world pinpointed the need to build a strong American society as a prerequisite for assuming a new global leadership role. Corporation trustees had a wide range of expertise and knowledge about the latest developments in science (Woodward), education (Pritchett), and foreign policy (Root) and were actively engaged in trying to shape American policy at the local, national, and international levels. Before the Corporation began extensive grant-making in the British dominions and colonies, it focused on ways to enhance American participation in the anticipated new postwar world order. With Woodrow Wilson as president, with Albert Einstein popularizing his theories of relativity, with John Dewey writing about democracy and education, the Progressive Era offered many opportunities for internationally oriented grant-making, beginning at home. At the same time, negative societal, demographic, political, and economic forces added urgency to this focus of the Corporation's grant-making.

To tackle these big issues—which have persisted over the decades—the trustees adopted a new approach for the Corporation, one that skated close to funding themselves to do the work, or hiring staff to undertake the groundwork, and thus becoming "operational," something they did not want to be. The trustees funded an idea suggested by two of their colleagues

and hired a consultant to design the approach. Instead of identifying a
grantee with a very smart idea and a grantee institution, they had the idea
and they made it happen. The two trustees—Henry Pritchett, president of
the Carnegie Foundation for the Advancement of Teaching, and Charles
Taylor, president of the Carnegie Hero Fund Commission, both founding
Corporation board members and longtime friends of Andrew Carnegie—
raised in May 1917 the issue of the immigrants then flowing into the country, and their assimilation.[61] The Executive Committee, on which Pritchett
also served, passed a resolution for discussion by the full board: "*Resolved,
that one of the most important matters which mite engage the attention of
the Corporation is the problem of the alien immigrant, and that individual
members of the Committee endeavor to get into touch with men who mite
be considered qualified to take charge of a survey of the problem of the alien
with a view to his more effectiv assimilation into American civilization.*"[62]

This resolution resulted in the Board of Trustees, in turn, asking
the Executive Committee to establish a three-person advisory council to develop the plans for what became "The Study of the Methods of
Americanization."[63] Although not named a commission, it was, de facto,
the first major Carnegie commission. The advisory council, one of whose
members was former president Theodore Roosevelt, not only designed and
planned the scope of the studies but worked with the trustees to hire consultants to conduct them and then had the studies independently reviewed.
Assisting with these efforts was a special editorial committee that consisted of three members, including Raymond A. Fosdick, then associated
with the Rockefeller philanthropies and later president of the Rockefeller
Foundation.

The overarching aim of the Americanization Study was "to set forth, not
theories of social betterment, but a description of the methods of the various agencies engaged in such work, [which] would be of distinct value to the
cause itself and to the public."[64] The report of Allen T. Burns, the consultant
hired to prepare the detailed plan of action for the Council, identified the ten
themes to be studied, detailed the specialists and staff needed, and set out
the time frame and budget.[65] The Corporation supported the Commission
at the level of $190,000 for eighteen months, beginning in mid-1918. In
January 1920, the Corporation appropriated another $3,000 to hire review-

ers of the study results. The study came at a crucial time when there was active debate about nativism and the anti-immigrant sentiment in Congress and in the country as a whole. The reports prepared under the aegis of the Americanization Study identified ways to work responsibly with immigrants and assist with their successful functioning in American society.[66] As the publisher's note to one of the volumes elaborated, "Americanization in these studies has been considered as the union of native and foreign born in all the fundamental relationships and activities of our national life. For Americanization is the uniting of new with native-born Americans in fuller common understanding and appreciation to secure by means of individual and collective self-direction the highest welfare of all."[67] Although the study reports did not stave off the anti-immigrant sentiment in the country in the 1920s, in at least one area—adult education—they led to major field-building investments by the Corporation and the government.[68]

At the same meeting in which the Corporation approved the Americanization Study, the trustees approved a $150,000 grant to promote the education of Americans in foreign policy issues through the work of the National Security League, headed by the politically active lawyer S. Stanwood Menken.[69] The minutes of that meeting characterized the grant as being

in aid of the intensive campaign which it [the National Security League] is now conducting to promote the education of the American people in the spirit and duty of citizenship…. The people simply did not know enough to appreciate the bearing of international problems on national existence and growth, or their related influences upon their own privileges and opportunities. We know that in the past a lack of popular understanding of great problems had been severely paid for, and that with new world conditions democracy could not prove successful without increased general knowledge by the people.[70]

This grant initiated the Corporation's century-long interest in increasing American public understanding of world conditions and issues in specific regions.

The Corporation, however, did not consistently address international issues with domestic impact. Although in 1913 the Chinese students stranded in the United States following the revolution in China received support, the trustees did not explicitly respond to the Russian Revolution of 1917. Even with the continued upheaval in Russia and the immigration of Russians to the United States, in 1919 the Corporation turned down requests from the League of Nations to assist the Russian Economic League and a request from the Russian People's University to establish an elementary school for Russian immigrants. The Corporation also rejected a proposal to support the education of Americans about the dangers of Bolshevism, although in 1920 it gave $10,000 to the Russian Collegiate Institute and $25,000 to the National Association of Constitutional Government for a project that aimed "to educate the people of the United States about the fundamentals of government as the most effective way to fight Bolshevism."[71]

As much as the trustees wanted to better integrate immigrants into American life, the Corporation was also committed to extending its reach overseas and educating Americans about the world beyond US borders. Modest support to increase the teaching of foreign languages in the United States began with a grant to the Foreign Language Governmental Information Service.[72] In 1917 it supported fellowships to the American Academy in Rome and grants to the American School of Classical Studies in Athens for a library, complementing grants from the Rockefeller Foundation to both institutions. The Corporation also funded scholarships for Americans to study in French universities.[73] These grants were precursors of a more comprehensive effort to build American understanding of the rest of the world through direct experience, which in the 1930s included individual fellowships for language training and institutional support for deepening public understanding of international affairs.

CREATING NEW INTERNATIONAL INSTITUTIONS IN THE UNITED STATES: LAYING CORNERSTONES FOR THE CENTURY

IN THE IMMEDIATE POSTWAR ERA, as the Corporation was taking modest steps to educate Americans about the world, it also made major financial contributions to establish enduring institutions at home that would advance knowledge and understanding about pressing global issues and help make the country a truly significant global player. This grant-making, which absorbed considerable resources from the Corporation, led to the establishment of institutions that today remain leaders in internationally related policy research programs and significant contributors to US policymaking.

After the war, Nicholas Murray Butler, president of Columbia University as well as director of the Intercourse and Education Division at the Carnegie Endowment for International Peace, urged the Corporation to support work on international education.[74] It was only after the Americanization Study had been funded that the Corporation seriously considered his request to establish an institution to promote overseas study by Americans as another effective way to promote peace.[75] This request had been deferred twice in the previous year, but in January 1919 the Corporation appropriated $30,000 to establish the Institute of International Education. The Corporation not only helped to establish the institute but also housed it, paid its rent, and nurtured its exchange programs, its work overseas, and its support of both American and international scholarship. The Institute remains a leading private agency in promoting and facilitating exchanges and fellowships and manages programs such as the Fulbright Awards.[76]

Such long-term support is not common in the foundation world, but the closely aligned missions of the Corporation and the Institute have made it a fruitful partnership that embodies the flexibility, even the mutuality, that can flourish in the most productive and promising relationships between a foundation and its grantee. Today Corporation support for the work of the Institute is minuscule compared to the resources of both institutions, but the ongoing grants explicitly recognize the ninety-year relationship between them.[77] Although Andrew Carnegie was the driving force in creating many new institutes, this was the second major institute—the Church Peace Union being the first—that was founded by his Corporation and did not bear his name. The Institute of International Education is the longest-standing non-Carnegie family institutional partner.

The trustees were setting the course, promoting the mission, not the man, and recognizing that a mission requires an institutional infrastructure. Although it is individuals who have ideas, conduct research, and disseminate their findings, a strong institutional base helps promote, encourage, and sustain the flourishing of individual initiative. The Corporation's trustees were convinced that building new institutions or nurturing existing ones in the United States for domestic and international activities was a wise way to contribute to meeting the mission of the foundation entrusted to them.

THE OVERSEAS GRANTS PROGRAM:
ITS ORIGINS IN THE UNITED STATES

IN 1906 JOHN D. ROCKEFELLER SR. had persuaded Andrew Carnegie to join the General Education Board, which focused on improving education in the American South for poor blacks and whites.[78] The Corporation continued this area of grant-making, and it ultimately became a model for the Corporation's education grant-making in Africa in the 1920s and 1930s. Dr. Thomas Jesse Jones, who was head of education for the Phelps Stokes Fund, dedicated his life to improving educational opportunities for poor, rural African Americans in the American South.[79] He was a controversial person in the field of what was then, at the turn of the century, called "Negro education." He advocated for vocational and community-based education and against the higher education urged by educated African Americans, including W. E. B. Du Bois and Carter Woodson, the first African Americans to graduate from Harvard University.[80] Jones instead embraced the self-help, basic-education approach that Booker T. Washington developed at the Tuskegee and Hampton Institutes.[81]

The General Education Board, the Phelps Stokes Fund, Carnegie Corporation, and eventually the Julius Rosenwald Fund backed the Tuskegee approach to public education for American blacks in the South. A key element in ensuring appropriate community-based education was the Jeanes teacher, usually a local woman, often trained by the Hampton or the Tuskegee Institute, who would go from community to community in her district to monitor implementation of community development–oriented education.[82]

Aware of the study of Southern education for poor blacks that Jones was conducting on behalf of Phelps Stokes, the Corporation trustees decided to defer consideration of support until they had seen its conclusions.[83] In the meantime, they entered into discussions with Jones about conducting a comparable survey of institutions devoted to industrial (that is, vocational) education for poor whites in the South.[84] The next month the trustees deferred consideration of the study of white industrial education; rather, they approved a grant to the Slater Fund of $20,000 over four years for the "establishment . . . of county training schools for the training of colored pupils in southern counties."[85] This was the beginning of Corporation funding for activities to improve community- and school-based agricultural, vocational, and technical education for blacks in the South, often supervised by Jeanes teachers. These efforts, including the promotion of the Jeanes supervisory teacher, became the basis for the Corporation grants in education in the British colonies in Africa, starting in the late 1920s.

CROSSING BOUNDARIES IN NORTH AMERICA

ALTHOUGH CROSSING THE ST. LAWRENCE RIVER does not quite constitute an overseas program, activities in Canada were the main international work of the Corporation until the late 1920s. Although it may seem surprising that Canada would feature in such a significant way in the grant-making of an American foundation in the early twentieth century, Canada, already in the mandate of the Carnegie Foundation for the Advancement of Teaching, was not merely America's neighbor to the north, but a self-governed dominion of the British Empire, with settlements by Scottish emigrants and a highly functioning democracy. These factors coincided with Andrew Carnegie's abiding interest in Anglo-Saxon democratic societies. Canada, moreover, provided a variety of easily accessible institutions and locales that enabled the Corporation—governed and run by trustees who had not yet started to make site visits—to test the waters of international grant-making without staff specialists.

In its support for US institutions of higher education, the Corporation targeted grants where the resources could be best put to use, primarily at underresourced institutions in less prosperous settings. Early grant-making in Canada, however, encompassed educational institutions that were already well funded as well as those less well funded. The initial grants, made as matching grants for endowment to Queen's University ($100,000)

and Dalhousie University ($40,000), were then followed by an uncondi-
tional $1 million endowment grant (worth $180 million today) to McGill
University. As the minutes of the Corporation show, this grant was made "in
recognition of the noble and devoted service and sacrifice of McGill toward
Canada's part in the Great War, upon which depends the rule of law among
nations, and the freedom, not only of Canada, but of the United States and
other democracies of the whole world."[86] Canada's Maritime Provinces in
particular represented for the trustees the region of that country in greatest
need of investment in higher education. With poverty reminiscent of that in
the bordering northeastern United States, the Maritime Provinces received
consistent and serious attention from the Corporation for nearly twenty
years.[87]

THE DEATH OF ANDREW CARNEGIE:
CONFORMING TO HIS WISHES

ALTHOUGH ANDREW CARNEGIE was no longer directly involved in the
work of the Corporation in 1919, John Poynton, his personal secretary, and
since 1916 a trustee, was at his side daily.[88] As he monitored postwar world
actions, Carnegie exchanged letters and telegrams with President Woodrow
Wilson. Enthusiastic about Wilson's commitment to the League of Nations,
another way of framing Carnegie's plea to establish a League of Peace,
Carnegie had, not surprisingly, shifted his support from the Republican
Party to the Democratic Party. He sought to ensure that Wilson would win
in 1916, since the League of Nations had been part of Wilson's agenda ever
since Carnegie had approached him about it in 1916. Ever optimistic even
as he became increasingly frail, Carnegie was counting on his League and
his associated arbitration efforts to lead the world into perpetual peace. He
had even urged Wilson to hold the peace conference at "his" Peace Palace in
The Hague.[89] When Carnegie died at age eighty-three on August 11, 1919,
following a bout of summer pneumonia, the establishment of the League of
Nations was almost certain; it began operations in January 1920.

Andrew Carnegie had sparked the imaginations of people everywhere
with his wealth, his writings, and his actions. At the first board meeting
held after his death, on November 28, 1919 (three days after what would

FOUNDING TRUSTEES OF
CARNEGIE CORPORATION OF NEW YORK, 1911

Besides Andrew Carnegie, the founding trustees of Carnegie Corporation were:

William Frew: President of the Carnegie Institute of Pittsburgh; on the board of the Carnegie Hero Fund Commission

Robert S. Woodward: President of the Carnegie Institution of Washington; on the board of the Carnegie Endowment for International Peace

Charles L. Taylor: President of the Carnegie Hero Fund Commission; on the board of the Carnegie Institute of Technology and the Carnegie Endowment for International Peace

Henry S. Pritchett: President of the Carnegie Foundation for the Advancement of Teaching; on the board of the Carnegie Institution of Washington and the Carnegie Endowment for International Peace

Elihu Root: President of the Carnegie Endowment for International Peace; on the board of the Carnegie Institution of Washington

James Bertram: Private secretary to Andrew Carnegie

Robert Franks: Business secretary to Andrew Carnegie; on the board of the Carnegie Foundation for the Advancement of Teaching and the Carnegie Endowment for International Peace have been his eighty-fourth birthday), the trustees recorded in their min-utes that Andrew Carnegie had "entrusted the largest endowment ever provided by one man for the increase and diffusion of knowledge among men."[90] They also elected Mrs. Carnegie to the board for an initial term of five years, an important symbol of their respect and love for her husband and a tribute to her own generous spirit. They then made Elihu Root chair-man of the board, Robert Franks vice president and treasurer, and James Bertram secretary.

Despite Andrew Carnegie's age and disengagement from the work of the foundation for the previous four years, the Board of Trustees had not given thought to identifying a successor, nor had it considered the appro-priate means to build the institution in the wake of the founder's passing. They took necessary but not sufficient steps to remedy this by amending the constitution and bylaws, expanding the board by another trustee, estab-lishing the position of chairman of the board, and enlarging the Executive Committee. The Executive Committee maintained its role in making deci-sions for the Corporation between board meetings, referring to the board all proposals for appropriations of money. They followed the structure of other foundations, establishing the role of president as executive officer under the direction of the board and the Executive Committee, creating the position of assistant to the president, and formalizing the position of trea-surer and secretary of the Corporation. The Corporation was inexorably moving away from the trustees-only model that the founder had originally envisioned. These institution-building activities indicate how some of the structures and positions needed to ensure a foundation's continuation in perpetuity are not always given the attention required while the founder is alive. For the Corporation, it was only on December 19, 1919, eight years and slightly more than a month after its founding, that the precursory structure of a professionally led foundation was established.

To honor the mission and the charge in Andrew Carnegie's deed of gift, the trustees appropriated $5 million to the National Academy of Sciences and its National Research Council to construct a building to house the insti-tutions and to establish a permanent endowment for the Research Council, recognizing the importance of the scientific community to maintaining a strong economy and society.[91] Andrew Carnegie had always been keenly interested in supporting science, as evidenced by the Carnegie Institution of Washington, the Carnegie Institute of Pittsburgh, and the charter of the Corporation.[92] This generous support, the equivalent of $62 million today, was approved following a presentation by Dr. James Angell, who was chairman of the National Research Council, and the person who would soon put the Corporation on a new footing to continue without the founder at the helm.[93]

2

THE CORPORATION AFTER CARNEGIE

"Carrying on the ... Beneficial Work," *1920–1923*

WHEN ANDREW CARNEGIE DIED ON August 11, 1919, nine months to the day after the armistice between the Allies and the Germans that ended the fighting in World War I, his Corporation was functioning, but still finding its way. It was not easy to follow in Andrew Carnegie's footsteps. Essential questions had to be addressed, such as:

+ What is the role of a philanthropy that makes grants to others to carry out the mission of the foundation?
+ How should decisions be made? On the merits of the ideas? On the quality of the people who suggest them? Or according to the priorities of the foundation's founder or its living leaders?
+ How much should the Corporation work with government and other philanthropic partners?
+ What is the best way to share grant findings with the public at large, scholars, policymakers, and others?
+ What is the best way to fulfill the international mandate of the founder?
+ How should practical administrative questions be dealt with?

Three different leaders in quick succession managed Carnegie Corporation in the four years after Andrew Carnegie's death.[1] The situation could have been catastrophic. With one new leader after another, opportunities might have been missed and the Corporation's reputation might have floundered; the aims of the donor might not have been respected and his resources could have been squandered. Indeed, Robert Kohler has suggested that, despite the preferences of Root, Angell, and Pritchett, from the limited perspective of support for science this is exactly what happened.[2] Not recognized by many later analysts, however, is that as the trustees assumed stewardship of the Corporation they were following the charge given to them by Carnegie, namely, to invest in what they deemed most promising to fulfill the mission of the institution.

This chapter illustrates more broadly the particularly crucial role of the board in moments of crisis. Under the leadership of Elihu Root and Henry Pritchett, the trustees made significant grant-making decisions during a precarious period of rapidly changing internal and external conditions and assumed more than routine fiduciary responsibility for the future of the institution. Andrew Carnegie had selected his trustees wisely. These men could simply have divided the money among their own institutions—after all, those institutions had been created by Carnegie—but instead they were committed to ensuring the continuity of his endeavors so that the Corporation could thrive in perpetuity, keeping close to its mission and to Carnegie's charge in his deed of gift. Not all of their investments have thrived, but several of the sizable domestic initiatives with major international reach continue to flourish today. Some now receive no support from the Corporation, and some only minimal support (particularly in proportion to the considerable amount of support they receive from other foundations).

The Board of Trustees as the leaders of the institution were willing to take the risks and spend the resources on ideas they thought met the needs of the moment and the anticipated needs of the future. They also knew how to structure the grants (sometimes over multi-year periods) so that they could assess the results. Increasingly, twenty-first-century philanthropists focus on achieving and measuring outcomes and impacts (often described under the rubrics of "metrics," "outcome-based decision-making," or "impact assessment"). These earlier philanthropists emphasized process and were acutely aware that they were building for perpetuity and that the future of the foundation hinged on their decisions and actions. In the early life of the Corporation, the board was the pivotal player moving the action from one scene to the next, albeit with some tensions, especially concerning the international work. Nonetheless, the trustees shared a commitment to supporting major national institutions with international reach and agreed on the importance of setting clear priorities for the Corporation's grant-making, even as they disagreed on other institutional matters.

This chapter is organized to illustrate the flow across the work of these men, not only the governance decisions they introduced or approved but also the grants they made. The continuity during these years set the stage for the new era that began in 1923 under the leadership of the Corporation's fifth president, Frederick Keppel.

THE GLOBAL AND NATIONAL CONTEXT: A SNAPSHOT

OF ALL THE CHANGES THAT OCCURRED in the tumultuous post–World War I period, most pertinent for the Corporation's soon-to-expand international grant-making was the handing over of German colonies in Africa to the other colonial powers, with Great Britain assuming responsibility for Tanganyika (which would become a site for Corporation grant-making over the next decade) and part of Cameroon. Changing the status of the self-governing British dominions (Australia, New Zealand, the Union of South Africa, Canada, Newfoundland, and the Irish Free State) was also under discussion; the Corporation would become increasingly active in these areas (except Ireland) in the late 1920s and 1930s. With the establishment of the League of Nations and other cross-boundary intergovernmental organizations, political internationalism began to take hold. Economic internationalism also revived, not only for capitalism (with trade agreements and the establishment in Paris of the International Chamber of Commerce) but also for communism (with the revolution in Russia that captured imaginations and support from nations around the world).[3]

Individuals and nongovernmental organizations (NGOs) revived the pre–World War I drive for cultural internationalism as a way to solidify the basis for peace. The internationally minded American foundations also found their conceptual home in the context of cultural internationalism. Akira Iriye highlights a prescient remark by Leon Trotsky, who stated in

1917 that "the war had established a connection between 'the fate of an individual and the fate of all mankind.'" As Iriye observes, "That connection was important because it imagined a worldwide community consisting of individual humans no longer separated by the artificial barriers of sovereign states ... those who struggled to reaffirm and strengthen internationalism in the wake of a calamitous war ... now vowed to dedicate themselves to resuscitating and expanding that movement [cultural internationalism] as the only hope for a sane world order."[4] As Iriye states, European intellectuals, particularly those in Paris, took the lead in this movement.[5] They established organizations that reinforced individual engagement with cultural internationalism in fields ranging from music, the arts, and mathematics to international relations.[6]

Andrew Carnegie had embraced the concept of cultural internationalism through his support of libraries and church organs as well as his untiring personal campaign to promote peace. Ever more extensively during the years between World Wars I and II, the two major American foundations active overseas, Carnegie Corporation and the Rockefeller Foundation, advocated and supported international exchanges, foreign language training programs, and scholarly and scientific networks. Together and in turn, these two philanthropies built enduring institutions in the United States that sought international connectivity in the postwar period and have flourished ever since.[7]

During the post–World War I period, international cooperation was shaped not only by treaties and efforts to promote peace but also by a series of man-made and natural calamities: famine in Europe and China, the 1918 influenza pandemic, and locally but massively destructive wars within and across neighboring countries in Europe and following the Allies-enforced dissolution of the Ottoman Empire. These dilemmas of modern complexity posed the challenges within which the internationally oriented American foundations sought to make their contributions. The global movements for peace, prosperity, and shared understanding and values were continually contending with and being countermanded by the violent forces of imperialism, brutal economic exploitation, and searing cultural prejudices. These countervailing conditions often impeded the progress of American philanthropy overseas, but also offered significant opportunities for promoting positive social change, especially through scholarly and activist exchanges across national boundaries, themes explored in depth by David Ekbladh in his study of American contributions to modernization and development over the twentieth century.[8]

President Woodrow Wilson had actively promoted volunteerism for military-oriented citizen service during World War I, including through the US Committee on Public Information (also known as the Creel Committee). After the war, nonmilitary volunteer organizations flourished and touched multiple aspects of American life, such as the Lions Clubs International, which were modeled on the tradition of Rotary International and other community clubs.[9] The aftermath of the war also launched the rapid growth of American philanthropy, encouraged not only by the spirit of volunteerism but in large part by congressional action, namely, the passage of the War Revenue Act of 1917 and the Revenue Act of 1918, which allowed individuals to take charitable tax deductions. Infused with altruism and pragmatism, the postwar climate proved propitious for the emergence of new foundations over the next decade.[10] Individuals who had contributed in significant ways to the war effort (such as the millions of dollars donated during the war to the American Red Cross) recognized the opportunity to use private wealth to study the root causes of social problems and find ways to use the results to improve policies. The US government moved from a position that criticized private donors to one that was supportive, as analyzed by Barry Karl and Stanley Katz: "Despite the periodic investigations through which the United States Congress expressed its uneasiness, governmental executive agencies at all levels looked to private donors, among them foundations, for the research on which they sought to base new social and economic policies."[11] By 1924 annual charitable contributions from private donors in the United States had reached $2 billion.[12]

The early 1920s was also a period of global economic and social fluctuations; in the United States, unemployment rose steeply from 4 percent to 12 percent in 1920.[13] It was also a time of contradictory tendencies within the United States—the interest of entrepreneurs and intellectuals in entering the world contrasted with the public's reluctance to do so and, later in the 1920s, the xenophobia of its representatives in the US Congress. Cultural internationalism was undermined in the United States, much as it was globally, by a fear of the influx of foreigners, a revived racism, and a preference for isolationist laissez-faire policies shared by the government and much of the public. This was a period notes Lynn Dumenil, "when massive immigration, swelled by refugees from war-devastated Europe, began again in the spring of 1920 at the rate of 5,000 people per day, restrictionists intensified their attacks, arguing that the literacy test should be replaced with more stringent restrictions.... The drive to restrict immigration reflected an unrelenting campaign of hostility toward immigrants that characterized the early 1920s.... Nativism was pervasive, respectable, and comprehensive."[14] Nativism reinforced racism. The Ku Klux Klan, for example, became increasingly brutal in attacking immigrants as well as African Americans and non-Protestants.[15]

The period from a few years after World War I and into the 1920s was one in which many Americans looked inward (as illustrated by the refusal of the United States to join the League of Nations), became mass consumers, and, as the decade progressed and Wall Street boomed, celebrated their revived prosperity, which was attained at the expense of others. While the framework of cultural internationalism helped shape the work of the Corporation and that of other foundations, these countervailing forces also played a role. Perhaps no one embodied those countervailing forces more than trustee and board chairman Elihu Root, who not only was a fervent internationalist but also supported both the Corporation's Americanization Study and passage of the Immigration Act of 1924 (also known as the Johnson-Reed Act), which codified after the war the anti-immigrant sentiment of the 1921 Emergency Quota Act.[16] The passage of this 1924 act highlighted as well the widespread high regard in America for the field of eugenics, which was supported by both the Rockefeller Foundation and Carnegie Corporation, the latter through support of the Carnegie Institution of Washington.[17]

GETTING IN SHAPE
TO TACKLE THE CHALLENGES

FOLLOWING THE DEATH OF ANDREW CARNEGIE, the trustees agreed on a new way of administering the foundation: they would hire a president to take over the handling of the many requests, analyze them, and then present the grant requests to the trustees for their decision. The trustees, like their Rockefeller Foundation counterparts, sought a distinguished, nonfamily president to lead the Corporation with ideas and time to fulfill the mandate bestowed on them by Andrew Carnegie.[18] They sought a fresh thinker to take over the leadership and advance the mission. Root agreed to serve as president for a short period—December 1919 to January 1920—during the search process. He became chair of the Board of Trustees and presided over the Corporation's work for those two months until they had identified four strong candidates: James Angell (chair, Department of Psychology, University of Chicago, and former president, American Psychology Association); A. A. Hammerschlag (president, Carnegie Institute of Technology, a colleague of Andrew Carnegie's since 1902); Livingston Farrand (president, University of Colorado, and Rockefeller Foundation medical consultant); and Henry Suzzallo (former dean, Columbia University, then president, University of Washington, later to become president, Carnegie Foundation for the Advancement of Teaching).

Following James Angell's December 1919 presentation to the board, Root and Pritchett must have found him an appealing candidate. (According to Ellen Lagemann, Angell thought that the combination of his presentation and his role as chairman of the National Research Council had enhanced his appeal.[19]) Pritchett confirmed this when he declared that Angell's "knowledge of science and education and his high personal qualities" made him "admirably fitted for their chief executive."[20] He was a renowned psychologist, educated partly in Europe, and the son and grandson of university presidents. He had built a superb reputation at the University of Chicago and was grounded in academic life. The trustees would not formally select Angell, however, until after he had met with Mrs. Carnegie and she had given her approval. Out of respect for her good judgment and for her late husband, the trustees gave her the deciding vote.[21]

James Angell was an academic through and through. His own writings made it clear that the university was the institution where he felt most at home. At heart, Angell wanted to lead a university, not a foundation (his father had been president of the University of Vermont, and his grandfather headed Brown University). This opportunity would present itself soon enough.

ANGELL AT THE HELM

JAMES ROWLAND ANGELL was named president of the Corporation at the tenth annual meeting of the Board of Trustees in April 1920.[22] Responding to board concerns, he began to build an institutional structure beyond the Board of Trustees and the Executive Committee. As president, he did not hesitate to shape these structures to reflect his own analyses of strategic ways to relate available resources to actions. Angell recommended putting in place program topics that could be funded over several years, noting that, "when I took up my duties as president of the Corporation, it was impressed upon me that the most important single problem confronting the Board of Trustees was the development of general policies determining the fields within which the Corporation should operate and the methods to be pursued."[23] Recognizing the need for flexibility, he concluded that "a highly exceptional case can always be accorded exceptional treatment."[24] Thus, he set the stage for a more systematic approach to grants and activity decision-making at the Corporation. First, as promised in his acceptance letter, he started "to familiarize [himself] with the past policies and traditions of the board."[25] He wanted to learn about projects that had been funded, both in the United States and elsewhere. He hoped to visit Corporation grantees in Canada, for instance.

Then, as part of his institution-building innovations, Angell introduced a new mode of professional management organized by priorities as well as budgetary allocations and percentages. In reporting to the board on his review of the previous five years, he grouped the Corporation's activities into five main categories and allocated percentages for the future.[26] The trustees agreed to the proposed structure and allocations for the next fiscal year. Given the change in charter in 1917 (see Chapter 1), these categorizations were equally applicable to grants made in Canada and in other areas overseas. For the first time at the Corporation, scientific and quantitative values were entering into the analysis of its philanthropy.

As Lagemann notes, the board was divided over the proposed way to run the foundation.[27] One of the main sources of tension in the Corporation was between the president and the board; another was among board members themselves. In this case, the two trustees with the deepest and longest association with the founder, James Bertram and Robert Franks, were uncomfortable with the proposed changes and soon found themselves isolated or marginalized. Quoting from the correspondence of Pritchett and Root, Kohler notes that they both had been trying to "dilute the power of Carnegie's 'former clerks'" since Carnegie's death.[28] Besides taking charge, Angell also recommended enlarging the board, not only to add to the diversity and quality of the members but to reduce the influence of the original trustees.

Further changes instituted by Angell made the Corporation more professional. Following the example of the Rockefeller Foundation, the Corporation began to publish an Annual Report that included a presidential essay. In his 1921 essay, Angell summarized the changes necessary to make the Corporation a durable institution: setting an overall budget with allocations by priority areas; establishing a definite reserve account for each fiscal year; committing resources for expenditures over several years; enlarging the Board of Trustees; and hiring a professional staff for a functioning executive office. Beardsley Ruml, the high-caliber staff assistant whom Angell brought from the University of Chicago, was the kind of mind he wanted to bring onto the board. (Following his time at the Corporation, Ruml went on to lead a Rockefeller philanthropy, the Laura Spelman Rockefeller Memorial.[29]) Angell sought to raise the Corporation's administrative functions to the same level of quality as its leadership role in grant-making: "To achieve these results, it is highly essential to establish a budgetary system, and in providing for this the Board has followed the well-established principle of other large financial agencies and particularly of those similar in character to the Corporation"—clear references to the Rockefeller and Russell Sage Foundations.[30]

Although Angell had sought to enlarge the board, only two changes were made in this period of leadership under Root, Angell, and Pritchett. In 1920 Robert Woodward had stepped down as president of the Carnegie Institution of Washington and John C. Merriam was elected in his place (after Angell had turned down the offer). Another new member appointed in 1922 was William J. Holland, likewise there in his capacity as head of a Carnegie organization, the Carnegie Institute of Pittsburgh. Both of these men had impressive credentials, but their appointments did not reflect the president's desire to bring on additional non-Carnegie members of the board.[31]

The broad vision presented in Angell's first and only Annual Report essay has informed the thinking of subsequent trustees and presidents. Recognizing that it takes time to build an institution or program, he formally introduced the idea of supporting grants for more than a year, even up to five years. Soon the Corporation was beginning to support significantly long-term grants, as long as ten years, something that requires a sufficient reserve, flexibility, and forward-looking vision. Angell also considered one of the persistent challenges of philanthropic decision-making: the question of "whether the Corporation should concentrate its energies upon a small number of very large undertakings, or should continue to countenance appropriations for a considerable number of smaller enterprises." He made explicit the constant tension between focus and scatteration, a complex dilemma for foundation presidents that continues to absorb considerable amounts of their time to this day. Angell firmly believed that, following a careful review of the "needs of our time" and exploration of the best use of resources, "in the long run the Corporation is likely increasingly to centralize its efforts and to disassociate itself from the great variety of minor interests such as those to which it has in recent years made contributions." He further emphasized that his conclusions resulted from widespread consultation "involving not only extended conferences with administrative officials of the other large foundations, but also intimate interviews with upwards of one thousand persons applying to the Corporation for assistance."[32] All later Corporation presidents have continued this type of consultation.

Angell paved the way for future international activities by introducing major institutional grants to strengthen scientific research capacity in the United States on pressing national and global problems. He introduced support for a major educational initiative in Canada and fundamental collaborative research by Canadian and American scientists. He also convinced the board to provide modest support for American cultural institutions located overseas. In addition, some of his other US-based grant-making provided major lessons for future overseas work.

Angell's tenure was the briefest of all the Corporation presidents, but he made lasting contributions to the foundation through his commitment to transparent, systematic, data-based decision-making. His first day as president was October 1, 1920; four and a half months later, on February 19, 1921, the Yale Corporation selected him to be the fourteenth president of the university.[33] He left Carnegie Corporation in June 1921, three months before the first Annual Report was to be issued, although his formal date of resignation was October 1, 1921.[34] His departure created a palpable sense of concern, so much so that even though the report was circulated to the trustees, copies were not printed or distributed to the public until 1931.[35]

ENSURING INSTITUTIONAL CONTINUITY

HENRY S. PRITCHETT, a founding member of the Corporation's Board of Trustees and longtime president of the Carnegie Foundation for the Advancement of Teaching, stepped in as acting president.[36] Pritchett embraced many of the changes that Angell had introduced, and his two years as president were vitally important for consolidating and solidifying these changes. Despite the internal upheaval with three leaders over four years, some of the Corporation's most enduring institutional grants were made during this period. International priorities were not yet in sharp focus, but under Pritchett's leadership, procedures were put in place that would affect general operations for grant-making both in the United States and internationally.

Pritchett's title was "acting president," but he was full president in practice.[37] He had decades of leadership experience and had also been a close and highly respected friend of Andrew Carnegie's. Pritchett clearly understood what the founder wanted and what kind of institution the Corporation was and should be—one guided by its mission but open to new ideas as "conditions upon the erth" changed.[38] The principles set forth by Pritchett, including those of Angell that he reinforced, have been followed continuously over the history of this institution, as have many of the practices. Following the example of Angell, Pritchett prepared an Annual Report, but he also printed copies for the public as well as the trustees; it contained his detailed president's report and equally detailed reports from the secretary and the treasurer, a model still followed.[39]

One thing that is striking about Pritchett's administration is that he seemed to ignore the fact that Andrew Carnegie empowered the Corporation to work in the British Empire, which was reinforced by the charter decision of 1917, even though Angell had suggested how best to move forward with this. As a consequence, while a few grants were made in Canada, and some libraries and church organ support continued to the end of their payments, grant-making elsewhere in the Empire did not begin for several more years. Nonetheless, under Pritchett's leadership, the Corporation supported institutions based in the United States that had international reach.

In setting the tone for the Corporation's work, Pritchett reviewed the rapid development of endowed foundations. He noted that some were limited to particular fields and approaches, and he differentiated the principles underlying the Corporation's approach to grant-making, emphasizing that it made grants so that others, not the Corporation's staff, could do the work. "According to this principle," he explained,

> the foundation has conceived its function to be not that of an operating agency in itself [like the Russell Sage and Rockefeller Foundations], but rather that of an agency charged with the duty of studying and estimating those forces and institutions that make for the advancement and diffusion of knowledge in English-speaking North America, and of aiding these institutions in such measure as may be possible within the income of the Corporation.[40]

Discussing "A Science of Giving" in the 1922 Annual Report, Pritchett reinforced Angell's notion of the desirability of long-term grants. He emphasized that the trustees believed "that their efforts will be more fruitful and more likely to be cumulative, if, taking up a particular cause, they assist it over a term of years long enough to try out the conception which lies back of its claims for usefulness and for support."[41] Pritchett went one step further, however. Perhaps recalling the early evaluations of the library and church organ programs, he hinted at an early approach to assessing ongoing grants, making it clear that the trustees had a responsibility to track what they were doing.

Even more insightfully foreseeing contemporary philanthropy's embrace of evaluation, Pritchett provided clear guidance for foundations created in perpetuity and, unknowingly, tossed down the gauntlet for twenty-first-century foundation officers, who often prefer to conduct short-term evaluations (that is, after three to five years) in the expectation of achieving and assessing immediate outcomes. Reiterating his understanding that the Corporation was "equipped to work with time," Pritchett's words resonate for those who seek to make contributions that will have a long-term impact: "The administration of such a trust will result in the greatest good when it confines its efforts, at least over a term of years, to designated lines of endeavor in which prolonged or repeated results can be compared and estimated."[42]

Pritchett then revealed the downside of grant-making: those making decisions need to have a certain toughness. "There will be needed in those who conduct such an enterprise a firmness to say 'No' to most of those who apply to them for aid. Not infrequently, it will turn out that, if there be the courage to utter a frank negative, the service of the trust may be greater in those requests which it refuses than in those which it grants."[43]

These and other reflections on the role and relations of grant-makers and grant-seekers still guide how the Corporation presidents and staff members conduct both their domestic and international work. It is very likely that when board members later referred to the "Carnegie tradition," they meant the tradition as interpreted by Henry Pritchett.

TYING UP LOOSE ENDS BEFORE THE NEXT STAGE

IN HIS FINAL REPORT as acting president, issued in 1923, Pritchett provided advice about organizing priorities and allocating resources. This advice built on Angell's 1921 analysis but added Pritchett's own perspective on how best to tie together the strands of Corporation activities to fulfill its mission. While acknowledging that at its core the mission was an educational one, he also observed that it "opens to the trustees an indefinitely large field of operation"—one that could include almost anything related not only to education but also to intellectual and scientific activities in the United States, Canada, and the British colonies. After studying the field of philanthropy, he concluded that it was best to limit the activities "to certain chosen fields in which they [the foundations] may hope not only to obtain cumulative results, but in which they may also hope to know with some degree of certainty the effects of their efforts."[44] He then analyzed how the Corporation had spent its resources and noted that in twelve years it had spent over $63 million (roughly $10.4 billion today). Casting his analysis in a slightly different way than Angell had, Pritchett related it to the charter of the Corporation and organized the grants by educational agencies and institutions, libraries, and scientific research: institutions founded by Andrew Carnegie (40 percent), public library buildings (20 percent), colleges and universities for educational purposes (15 percent), educational agencies engaged in war service (5 percent), and scientific research (3 percent).

While the Carnegie family of institutions received considerable support (and in contrast to Angell, Pritchett was very much in favor of that), he also emphasized the fields that were of interest to the Corporation: educational studies, economics, medical research and teaching, legal education reform, and scientific research, as well as providing some limited encouragement for special issues and opportunities. Both Angell and Pritchett were deeply dedicated to research, but Angell was equally committed to strengthening universities' ability to conduct research, while Pritchett had a more eclectic approach. It was in this period, however brief, that the Corporation trustees moved back and forth between support of universities and support of independent institutions and agencies that would contribute to the advancement and diffusion of knowledge and understanding.

For grants focused on international issues based in the United States or in other countries, this was the period of major institutional endowments. Pritchett preferred the big institutional grants that endowed enduring institutions as the most effective way to advance knowledge and understanding, suggesting "intelligent and discriminating assistance of such causes and forces in the social order as seem to promise effective service and the creation of new agencies which shall, however, be independent of the originating body."[45] Once the grant was made, the trustees needed to be confident in their choice and then let the individual or the institution do the work. The decisions of the trustees in the early 1920s established and strengthened intellectual institutions that contributed essential knowledge across the spectrum from science to foreign policy. Many of them—such as the Institute of Economics (which later in the 1920s became the Brookings Institution), the National Bureau of Economic Research, the Institute of

International Education, and the National Research Council—flourish to this day as vital institutions for promoting knowledge and understanding both in the United States and around the world.[46]

At the same time, the remarkably large contribution to Carnegie-related endowments and projects had repercussions for the assets of the Corporation, despite Pritchett's caution in keeping sufficient resources liquid for the next generation. Between 1911 and 1922, more than $23 million (40 percent of the Corporation's expenditures) was spent to support the Carnegie institutions.[47]

ENLARGING THE PATHS

PRITCHETT MAINTAINED the same general lines of approach to grant-making as Angell but gave greater priority to some new areas. Despite his scientific background as a renowned astronomer and president of the Massachusetts Institute of Technology, Pritchett had been selected as the first president of the Carnegie Foundation for the Advancement of Teaching in 1905 (and would serve until 1930 in that capacity). He was clearly committed to the overall field of higher education, not just scientific research in particular. Moreover, he "showed an unusual comprehension of the particular man at ease in social studies."[48] He maintained the commitment to the idea that education, broadly defined, was the main vehicle of the Corporation's mission. Grants related to science were still very attractive to the Board of Trustees, but with a few exceptions, they were made through the Carnegie Institution of Washington, just as peace-related grants tended to go through the Carnegie Endowment for International Peace.

Pritchett recognized the significance of the institutional research initiatives that Angell had recommended and fully endorsed them, recognizing that they offered the Corporation opportunities for work both in the United States and internationally and helped to bring American scientists together with scientists from other countries. As he noted when writing about the continuing support for the National Research Council efforts, the agency would, inter alia, "secure cooperation between American and foreign investigators in all branches of scientific research."[49]

In this crucially important period for the foundation, Root, Angell, and

Pritchett, together with the trustees, chose a mix of institutional investments that tackled the core of the crises related to food supply and economics and addressed basic science issues.[50] These major investments were
added to the portfolio related to understanding US connections to the world
through immigration, foreign languages, and international exchanges that
enabled Americans to engage the world. The grants in support of industrial
and community education for blacks in the rural American South in conjunction with the efforts of the General Education Board and the Phelps
Stokes Fund laid the groundwork for the major grants programs on this
theme in Africa in the late 1920s and 1930s. The grants in Canada in the
1920s opened up support for higher education in other dominions of the
British Empire. Modest funding for a series of grants enabled collaborative scientific research between Canadian and US colleagues that resulted
in a major medical breakthrough. The results increased the interest of
the trustees in supporting not just the institutions that brought scientists
together but also scientists themselves, which was reflected in the grants to
the Carnegie Institution of Washington. This institution and other members of the Carnegie institutional family remained on the agenda of the
Corporation's grant-making decisions but with different emphases under
Angell and Pritchett, continuing the board tensions on this issue from the
previous period.

One area the trustees did not tackle directly concerned sustaining the
peace after the Great War. With the US Senate turning down membership in the League of Nations, major efforts related to peace were left, at
least at this time, to the Carnegie Endowment for International Peace and
the Church Peace Union. The Corporation provided support to these institutions as well as limited support to the American Peace Society and the
Peace Palace in The Hague.

The trustees were keen to support institutions and activities related to
understanding the economic situation, both domestically and internationally. As Pritchett wrote in a 1922 confidential memorandum:

> The trustees, realizing how large a role economic questions today play
> in the government and prosperity of the country and of the world,
> appropriated last year a sum sufficient to maintain the Institute of

Economics, situated in Washington.... It may well be that certain other smaller grants can be made in the assistance of economic research which the Corporation may profitably consider. This matter is one to develop as the year progresses.[51]

The interest in establishing new institutions related to economics and food supply issues was complemented by support for the more traditional recipients of Corporation grants; universities and colleges in the United States and libraries in both the United States and the British colonies and dominions still featured in the grant-making, as did secondary schools, but these grants were relatively modest compared to other investments. In this period, the Corporation's annual expenditures fluctuated, from a high of $7.1 million in 1919 to $5.7 million in 1920, to $4.6 million in 1921, to $5.2 million in 1922.[52] With income from the investments averaging around $6.5 million, the trustees were cautious, taking into account the economic situation even as they were beginning to establish a modest reserve.

LAUNCHING TWO NEW RESEARCH INSTITUTES

THE BRUTAL FAMINE resulting from food shortages following World War I adversely affected countries in and around Europe, from Belgium to Armenia. The Rockefeller Foundation donated food supplies, at great cost to program activities. According to a time line on the Foundation's website, in 1918, as World War I came to a close,

> war relief efforts are substantial. The Foundation spends more than $22 million, sending food supplies to Belgium, Poland, Serbia, Armenia and other countries, even chartering its own ships. Laments President George E. Vincent, "I suppose we had to do it, and I suppose it was worthwhile, but think of the creative job we could have done with that money in a world of reason and sanity!"[53]

Providing emergency relief with goods and services was not how the Corporation trustees chose to invest. The charter legally prevented the trustees from investing directly in Europe, and the mission led them in the direction of supporting research to understand the nature of the problem and determine how best to prevent similar problems. Herbert Hoover asked the Corporation in late 1920 and early 1921 to invest in establishing an institution to conduct fundamental research on food production and distribution. Hoover was convinced that America's great capacity in food production could meet the global need for food security and thus merited the establishment of a significant new facility where basic scientific and economic policy research on food and nutrition could be conducted.[54] The expectation was that a new Food Research Institute at Stanford University would tackle issues related to problems both in the United States and around the world.[55] The trustees responded positively. In January 1921, the board appropriated $700,000 over ten years in support of the Food Research Institute to study the problems of the production, distribution, and consumption of foodstuffs.[56] At the end of 1930, the Corporation would determine if further support for the activities would be warranted. This grant exemplified the board's willingness to accept Angell's idea of making long-term commitments for institution-building, possibly because it also included an explicit exit strategy—the Institute's staff knew that the Corporation would decide at the end of ten years whether or not to continue support, depending on the work of the Institute and on Corporation priorities and resources at that point.

Angell declared that this first major internationally oriented investment of the Corporation was

> work of the first magnitude, the results of which will be watched with world-wide interest…. The problems to be attacked are … of the most far-reaching international character. So dependent are the nations of the modern world upon one another, particularly as regards their supplies of food, that no great contribution to our knowledge of the production, distribution, and consumption of foodstuffs can be lacking in interest to any nation, however circumstanced.[57]

The appropriation for the Stanford Food Research Institute as a multi-year initiative introduced a new approach to grant-making often endorsed by subsequent Corporation trustees and presidents in building new institutions or supporting new fields of research and practice.

This blending of financial and programmatic incentives resonated with the interdisciplinary mix of the Institute's directors, among whom were major scientists and economists. Over the ten years of the grant, they produced pathbreaking studies not only on the scientific and technical issues affecting the production and distribution of specific food commodities but also on "the economic aspects of world food production, consumption, and distribution."[58]

The Corporation renewed support in 1931 at the level of $750,000 for general endowment plus four more years of annual support totaling $70,000, based on the trustees' recognition of the impact of the Food Research Institute fellowships and graduate student dissertations as well as studies, articles, and books.[59] The latter included Holbrook Working's groundbreaking work in advancing understanding of the economics of futures trading through his research on wheat prices, which the Institute's historian Bruce Johnston assessed as "almost certainly the most significant body of work by a Food Research Institute staff member."[60] The Institute's track record reinforced the wisdom of both long-term support and a carefully constructed exit strategy.[61] These two issues, though handled in a matter-of-fact way in the 1920s and 1930s, nevertheless are thorny aspects of grant-making that continue to stymie foundations and grantees today.[62] In this instance and in others mentioned later, Angell and the trustees showed their commitment to supporting scientific and social scientific research related to national and global problems.

The support by Angell and then Pritchett for economic, scientific, and policy research through the Stanford Food Research Institute was part of their shared intention to create a new type of institution: the non-university-based social science research institute, comparable to those that had been supported for the sciences. The Rockefeller Foundation and the Corporation had already supported the Carnegie Institution of Washington and the National Research Council. Soon both foundations would help to establish two major social science institutions that have transformed American policies (both domestic and foreign) through the strength of their analyses and the prestige of their work among policymakers: the National Bureau of Economic Research (NBER) and the Brookings Institution.[63] The first transformed the field of economic research, the second defined economic policy research. The analytical scope of both the

NBER and Brookings has always been global: NBER's main focus has been the impact of world prices and conditions on the American economy, while Brookings has focused on the interaction of American and foreign policies in a global context. Both institutions also have interacted and worked with economists from other countries.

The National Bureau of Economic Research was conceived in 1920 to conduct rigorous, quantitative, scientifically sound research on the major problems of economic policy during the economic turmoil of the postwar period. The NBER was founded by a group of economists with differing analytical backgrounds, spearheaded by Edwin F. Gay of Harvard, Wesley C. Mitchell of Columbia, and John R. Commons of the University of Wisconsin.[64] Several leading economists had been approached by the Rockefeller Foundation in 1913 and 1914 to design an economics institute similar to the Rockefeller Institute for Medical Research (now Rockefeller University).[65] One prominent Rockefeller trustee, Frederick T. Gates, opposed the idea, however, saying, "The fundamental principles of economics are well known."[66] The founders of this institute were delayed but not detoured by this lack of support.

In early 1921, they submitted a modest request to Carnegie Corporation. The Corporation's Executive Committee approved their request in May for $15,000 a year for three years, with the condition that the institute secure $20,000 from other sources "for any year in which an appropriation is paid."[67] Possibly responding to a very well received National Bureau of Economic Research paper on national income accounts, the Executive Committee of the Corporation was soon willing to entertain a new proposal "in view of the excellent service rendered." The trustees reacted positively to the NBER's new proposal that stated in five years it would "finance its needs permanently through the development of an extensive subscription group and the securing of an endowment of One million dollars ($1,000,000)" by appropriating each year for three years, starting in October 1922, "an amount equal to one-half of the total amount collected by the Bureau for its current expenses during that year." In October 1925, the support would be reduced to one-third the annual expenses, and in October 1926, to one-fourth, up to $30,000 in any one year. This grant superseded the previous grant from 1921 of $15,000 per year for three years.[68]

When Corporation support ended, the NBER's leadership turned again to the Rockefeller Foundation, which then agreed to support it with comparably detailed conditions and instructions.[69] The National Bureau of Economic Research has more than fulfilled the multi-year confidence that the Corporation and others placed in it by conducting significant national and international independent economics research over the last ninety years, during which time its staff and associates have won sixteen Nobel Prizes in Economics.[70] Meeting the expectations of Angell, Pritchett, and the Corporation board, this significant research institution is not bound by government policy but critiques and informs it.

It took more persistent effort from Pritchett to convince the board to support the Institute of Land Economics under the leadership of one of the founders of the discipline, the University of Wisconsin's Richard T. Ely ("the Father of Land Economics"[71]), even at the much more modest level of $12,500 a year for five years, and despite its more traditional location within a respected university and the complementarity of its work with that of the Stanford Institute. When Ely first requested a grant for the Institute in May 1922, the board postponed a decision until November. When it then decided to provide support, it required a yearly matching grant from the Institute.[72] With support from the Corporation and others, Ely implemented a pioneering research program: "Beginning in the 1920s he and his fledgling institute played a leading role in creating the new sub-discipline of 'urban land economics.'"[73] In 1925 he started the journal *Land and Public Utility Economics* (now *Land Economics*) and that same year moved the Institute to Northwestern University. During the period at Wisconsin and Northwestern, the Corporation provided funds to the Institute of Land Economics of over $100,000.[74] In 1933 Ely moved to New York and took the Institute with him; it closed with his death in 1943.[75]

To reinforce the work of the National Bureau of Economic Research and the Institute of Land Economics, Pritchett also strongly recommended support for establishing an institute of economics as a partner institute to the Institute for Government Research. In 1914 the Rockefeller Foundation had encouraged developing the latter institute. The Foundation supported it for several years after Robert S. Brookings and several others in 1916 established the Institute for Government Research as the first federal government–oriented policy research institution, following the model of the Bureau of Municipal Research in New York City.[76]

The full Corporation board discussed Pritchett's detailed memo at its February 1922 meeting.[77] In contrast to merely covering the administrative costs, as the Corporation had done previously for the other two institutes, this Corporation initiative aimed to establish a full-blown institution, with Carnegie trustees reviewing, commenting on, and giving the terms for its purpose and the role of its trustees, even deciding how vacancies on the board would be filled and payment for trustees' expenses would be made. The Carnegie trustees specified, for example, that the trustees for the Institute of Economics could not receive compensation. As with the Stanford Food Research Institute, the Corporation provided very clear guidance about the amount of support it would provide over a specified time period.[78]

The Corporation was committed to the idea of establishing an institute "whose purpose shall be the ascertainment of economic facts and principles relating to the questions before the American people, and the dissemination in clear and simple form of the truth touching these fundamental facts and principles." So great was the trustees' commitment to this idea that they made it very clear in the minutes that the full administration of the funds would be out of their hands.[79] Pritchett, with board support, was adamant that the Corporation would relinquish any influence over the content of the work after making the grant, although they would, of course, look closely at the submitted reports and papers. The purpose of the Institute of Economics was to identify objective economic information and disseminate it to the American people—there would be no interference from the Corporation. The Carnegie trustees were acutely aware that a Washington-based policy research institute could be subject to donor influence.[80]

The Corporation's up-front commitment of $1,650,000 over ten years illustrates the kind of significant impact that can result from negotiating *ab initio* a long-term, multi-year grant. It enables the grantee to focus on the work, not core fund-raising. In 1927 the Institute of Economics merged with the Institute for Government Research and the Robert Brookings Graduate School to become the Brookings Institution. This launched a substantial institutional base for the new phenomenon: the freestanding Washington, DC, policy research institution that provides a home to policy researchers seeking to diffuse knowledge and influence policy by communicating clearly the implications of complex national and international economic conditions to policymakers and the public.[81] After World War II, these kinds of institutions would come to be called "think tanks."[82] The Corporation set the tone and approach for grantor-grantee relations, especially for major institutional grants. Paying considerable attention to the initial negotiations, and with confidence in the process and people involved, the Corporation intended to let the grantee institutions flourish or flail, free of Corporation interference.[83]

The Corporation's focus on food science and economics was complemented by a deep commitment to research in the physical and social sciences. The considerable efforts of some board members, particularly Pritchett and Root, led to the $5 million endowment grant made in December 1919 to the new study arm of the National Academy of Sciences, the National Research Council (then chaired by Angell), with the aim to strengthen the aggregation of American scientific expertise. This led the Corporation to another long-term engagement: its association with the National Academy of Sciences and the National Research Council has lasted for one hundred years and continues in the present day.[84] Support for the National Academy of Sciences and the National Research Council reinforced the other major institutional grants and provided funding for these institutions to bring together the scientific community to explore scientific research related to national and global problems. Recognition of the globalization of the world economy and social issues prompted support for these institutions, which would address the great global challenges of ensuring adequate food supply and nutrition, developing food policies to prevent famines such as those in Europe, assessing the impact of global commodities and other world prices and markets on the US economy and vice versa, clarifying for the government the global implications of its economic policies, and promoting scientific exchanges, particularly with scientists in Europe and throughout the British Empire.[85]

GRANTS REFLECT CHANGING AMERICAN SOCIETY IN A CHANGING WORLD

WITH ANDREW CARNEGIE'S VIGOROUS EMBRACE of the American system of government and education, reinforced by his belief in the importance of opportunity for advancement for all, it is not surprising that the Corporation in its early decades tackled (1) immigration and the challenge of how best to integrate new citizens into American life; (2) education for rural, usually poor, black and white populations so that they too could access opportunities for advancement; and (3) educational opportunities for Americans to engage with the world.

The Corporation-sponsored "Study of the Methods of Americanization" examined the question of how best to integrate immigrants into American life. The project started in 1918, and the first of what would eventually be ten volumes was published in 1921. Angell, always attentive to scientific research design, criticized the methodology of the studies. Nonetheless, he agreed that despite errors in design, data collection, and analysis, "such mistakes ... should not be allowed to obscure whatever is of permanent value in this mode of procedure."[86] Notwithstanding Angell's comments on the limitations of the Americanization Study, recent scholars consider the reports important early contributions to the field.[87] One parallel activity, the Foreign Language Information Service, which emerged from the wartime US Committee on Public Information (the Creel Committee), provided educational services for immigrant organizations beginning in 1921. A modest $5,000 Corporation grant stimulated other support for immigrant publications and a variety of civic initiatives.[88] The grant to the Russian Collegiate Institute supported education for Russian immigrants to help them adjust to life in the United States; the trustees looked more favorably on this request than on the earlier ones related to the Russian Revolution since it promoted neither capitalism nor Marxism but addressed integration into American life. These grants were taking place in the midst of anti-immigrant agitation, which led in 1924 to passage of the Johnson-Reed Act.[89]

The issue of poverty for whites and blacks in the US South was an early concern for the Corporation. As discussed in the previous chapter, it had explored appropriate educational opportunities for whites through industrial education, but this became a code term for a complex set of discussions surrounding the education of America's Southern blacks. Angell, possibly responding to heightened racist activity in the United States as well as pursuing his interest in improving the board's investigative methods, presented a request to the board to conduct a study of education in the South, especially in rural areas, to develop a program of grants "based upon trustworthy data regarding ways and means."[90] The program was intended to build on existing Corporation support for educational institutions in the South, including Fisk University, Berea College (the only white college to admit blacks at the time), Meharry Medical College, Tuskegee Institute, and Hampton Institute. The Corporation attempted to cover the field widely. In 1921 it also supported the Association for the Study of Negro Life and History, headed by the black historian Carter G. Woodson (the "Father of Black History"), at the level of $5,000 per year for five years, as well as Atlanta University, where the pioneering black scholar and activist W. E. B. Du Bois taught.[91]

At the same time, the Corporation continued to support Thomas Jesse Jones, the white educator-practitioner who had conducted, with Corporation support, the industrial school study in the South for whites as well as an earlier study for the Phelps Stokes Fund of the education of blacks in the South. Jones received support for a commission on interracial school operation, building on the approach taken by the Tuskegee and Hampton Institutes to promote technical, vocational, homemaker, and other skills-based education as best suited for the conditions of life in rural areas; this education was reinforced by the Jeanes teacher who traveled from community to community.[92] Jones represented the perspectives on education in rural, predominantly African American communities in the South promulgated by Booker T. Washington and his proponents. In contrast to the approach of Du Bois, Jones did not feel that it was necessary to add liberal studies such as mathematics, literature, and languages to the education of blacks.

Du Bois and Woodson argued that the advancement of blacks required the same opportunities for liberal higher education at the university level as whites had. Unlike Jones, who thought these courses of study would be appropriate only as rural populations progressed socially and economically, Du Bois and Woodson strongly believed that such progress could not happen without advanced classical higher education. These diametrically opposed perspectives were prominently debated during the interwar era.[93] Carnegie Corporation, through its grant-making, came down primarily on the side of Jones, a persuasive and insistent advocate. Despite the intense controversy attendant on Jones's views—particularly (but not only) among African American intellectuals—another one of his positive qualities for the trustees was his connection with Booker T. Washington, a person Andrew Carnegie had deeply respected.

Grant-making in support of education in the American South was not completely one-sided: universities and urban colleges were supported alongside the more rural-focused vocational efforts of Jones, the Phelps Stokes Fund, and the Rosenwald Fund. The Corporation's grant-making, albeit more modest in scope, reflected the program of the General Education Board, which since its founding in 1902 by John D. Rockefeller Sr. had promoted both community-based and higher education in the South and elsewhere in the United States.[94]

This work had implications far beyond the American South; in 1923 the International Education Board—founded in January of the same year by John D. Rockefeller Jr.—made a grant to the Phelps Stokes Fund to conduct a survey for the British Colonial Office of educational institutions in British West Africa.[95] Jones led that survey and then later a comparable one in East and Southern Africa. These studies provided the pathway for discussions in the late 1920s that determined the scope of the Corporation's investment in education in East and Southern Africa, even as the debate on these issues—that is, support for community-based vocational education versus classical university-based education—was taking place on the African continent in the 1920s and 1930s.[96] The results of these studies also led in 1922 to a Corporation grant of $250,000 to the Polytechnic Institute in Puerto Rico to offer general education and industrial training to young people in Puerto Rico.[97]

The progressive educators of this period, including those associated with Carnegie Corporation, such as John Dewey and Edward Thorndike, were working on educational reform issues. Thorndike led the field in the development of intelligence testing and other forms of aptitude-assessment within the context of comprehensive schools.[98] Issues of race, national origin, and poverty featured in these approaches, which were imbued with the contemporary progressive, not yet controversial, understanding of the role of eugenics in aptitude testing. The Corporation trustees tried to balance their portfolio by continuing to support higher education for African Americans along with Jeanes education; that is, they supported Du Bois as well as Jones. But the support was not at all at comparable levels; Jeanes and Jones received the far greater number and dollar amount of the grants. The trustees were men of their time and place who, like their counterparts in other foundations, sought to support a spectrum of educational institutions and approaches. Their underlying premises related not only to color (black versus white populations) but also to location and income (rural and poor versus urban and more middle-class).[99] The core issue for their grant-making was determining, from these premises, appropriate educational investments for African Americans, immigrants, and Native Americans.

As part of the Corporation's efforts to help US citizens understand the world by reaching out to it and meeting with people from other countries, the trustees approved a set of activities complementary to their immigrant education–related activities. In 1919 the Corporation, responding to a request from the Carnegie Endowment for International Peace, established the Institute of International Education. During the early years, there was limited programmatic support, but by covering its rent and general expenses, the Corporation enabled the Institute to conduct its work of awarding fellowships to Americans to travel overseas.

To broaden overseas educational opportunities for Americans, Angell, also keen to introduce the arts into the Corporation's agenda, persuaded the board to support two internationally based education programs. Linking the first to "the founder's well known interest in music," Angell submitted a request to fund music fellowships for Americans at the American Academy in Rome, in the hopes that this might lead to identifying a major American composer. The Corporation agreed to provide support for musical composition fellowships, at the level of $10,000 a year for ten years, if the Academy could raise at least $150,000 for the Division of Music and if a director in charge could be supported by additional funds.[100] Support for work at the Academy was continued for the ten years for an increased total of $190,000.

The second opportunity was support for the American School of Classical Studies in Athens: an endowment grant of $100,000 in 1921 followed an initial $25,000 grant in 1917. Pritchett recommended a grant of $200,000 for the construction of a library to house the 50,000-volume collection on Greek history and literature of the distinguished Greek diplomat Johannes Gennadius; the American School was also supported for nearly a decade for a total of $413,452.[101] The Rockefeller family and the Rockefeller Foundation supported both institutions as well.[102]

One area of both national and international significance that the Corporation left underaddressed was support for programs related to women and women's issues, including the increasingly widespread interest in family planning. The passage of the Nineteenth Amendment to the US Constitution on August 18, 1920, enabling women's suffrage seems not to have made a ripple at the Corporation. Support for women's colleges was maintained as it had been since the beginning of the foundation, but by ignoring larger educational concerns related to women, the Corporation missed an opportunity to address a critical area of social underdevelopment. The Corporation made no major grants aimed at enhancing women's role in society, whether in the United States or overseas, until the 1960s and 1970s under the leadership of John Gardner and Alan Pifer (as discussed later).[103]

THE CARNEGIE FAMILY OF INSTITUTIONS

MOST OF THE CORPORATION TRUSTEES also served as heads of other Carnegie institutions. And as grant-making to others rapidly increased under Angell, these trustees felt considerable anxiety about securing funds for their own institutions. Each of the Carnegie institutions seemed to be facing deficits despite their endowments. Different Corporation presidents struggled in different ways with the issue of support for the Carnegie institutions. Angell was not committed to these institutions; he saw more productive opportunities for the Corporation than spending the usual 40 percent of the resources on them. He thought the Carnegie institutions should have to compete with any other grant-seeker to make their case. Yet, given the membership on the board of the heads of the institutions, he realized that he had to address their concerns. Angell, a tough analyst, firmly clarified his sense of the Corporation's obligations to the Carnegie institutions following a major resolution providing support of $8 million over twenty-five years for the Carnegie Institute of Technology in Pittsburgh:

> The settlement involves a recognition of the principle that the Corporation has no binding obligation, based upon any alleged promises or instructions from Mr. Carnegie to come to the assistance of the Institute. On the other hand, it involves a specific recognition that the Institute has exactly the same claim upon the sympathetic interest of the Corporation as other meritorious institutions in this country or the British colonies, working in its peculiar field.[104]

Pritchett, who represented the family of institutions both under Angell and then as acting president, made clear his contrasting attitude, which indicated some softening about the other Carnegie philanthropies: Andrew Carnegie's "intention, as clearly expressed in his deed of gift, was that this foundation should, in reasonable measure, support and develop the existing institutions he had already created." At the same time, he emphasized and reiterated that the greater purpose Andrew Carnegie had envisioned for the Corporation "was to provide an endowment for all time, whose income should always be liquid, and should thus be available for generation after generation to be applied to the causes which each generation of trustees might find most significant."[105] Thus, while he was willing to support the institutions more generously than Angell was, he recognized that the use of the income from the Corporation's endowment extended beyond support for these institutions: to protect the assets of the Corporation in perpetuity, the endowment could not be invaded by those institutions.

The board spent the next few years reviewing requests from several of the Carnegie institutions. In addition to the major support for the Carnegie Institute of Technology in Pittsburgh, three in particular featured in the Corporation's grant-making during the 1920s and 1930s. From 1911 to 1941, the Corporation provided a total of $27,540,554 for: the Carnegie Endowment for International Peace, a total of $2,919,824; the Carnegie Institution of Washington, a total of $8,046,723; and the Carnegie Foundation for the Advancement of Teaching, $16,574,007 (excluding support for the pensions fund).[106]

Grants to these three Carnegie institutions, in particular, reflected the trustees' recognition of the importance of national and international social, political, and economic concerns as well as the charter restrictions constraining the Corporation's direct support. The continuing violence in Europe following the Versailles Peace Treaty led them to express their apprehension about world stability through a grant in 1920 to the Carnegie Endowment for International Peace, in support of efforts "to meet the need for a reconstitution of world conditions, with a view to laying the foundation for future peace and understanding among the nations."[107] Annual modest grants, following the earlier endowment support, also continued for the work of the Church Peace Union.

Such grants displayed concern for world peace, but surprisingly, Carnegie Corporation did not provide direct institutional support for the most important international body aimed at keeping the peace: the League of Nations (established in 1920). This lack of direct support may have been due to the multifaceted focus of the League's work; it may not have been clear to the trustees whether the League would attack the root causes of conflicts. Moreover, the League's more global work was considered outside the Corporation's restricted geographic scope of the United States and the British Empire. It was only later, in the 1920s and 1930s, that some small grants were made for activities indirectly related to the League, and it was not until the 1980s that the Corporation began to support organizations established as part of the international intergovernmental system, such as the United Nations, the World Health Organization, UNESCO, and UNICEF. The reluctance of the Corporation to provide direct support to the League of Nations is particularly ironic given Andrew Carnegie's passionate and persistent efforts to promote the establishment of a League of Peace.

The Carnegie Endowment for International Peace regularly requested support for its endowment and general program. Its president, Elihu Root, as the Corporation's chairman of the board, was well aware of the difficulty in making a persuasive case for the broad-based grants. Nonetheless, following the grant from the 1920 board meeting of $100,000 for the Endowment's work to understand ways to improve world conditions, in January 1921 Root presented a request for more significant support of $500,000. As he knew, the board had been reluctant to provide support at the level requested, but since other Carnegie family institutions had received significant funding, he persisted with his request. He noted that the Endowment was facing increasing demands "as a result of the Great War" and that "the cost of publication has more than doubled during the past five years. This increasing cost alone severely taxes the work of the endowment in going forward with its work as organized before the war." In conclusion, Root noted that "the Trustees of the Carnegie Endowment for International Peace respectfully request a special allotment of $500,000 from Carnegie Corporation, of which $250,000 is needed at once for defraying the extraordinary and unexpected expenses made necessary by the work described above, namely, the study of the economic and historical aspects of the war, the development of new agencies in the field of international education, the promotion of additional agencies of the cultivation of American goodwill in Europe, and to defray the enormously increased cost of printing and publication."[108]

In their extended discussion following Root's presentation, the trustees focused on his request for sufficient funds to bring to completion *The Economic and Social History of the World War.* The members of the Executive Committee thought the work was of great value, but some trustees expressed the opinion that financial assistance given for this purpose should be coupled with the requirement that the Endowment undertake certain structural changes, including improved coordination of its activities, to develop a program that would lead to results like the publications rather than statements of aspirations. The board awarded a grant of $250,000 solely to publish the history; later, in 1922, the Corporation trustees, recognizing the value of this specific work, provided the remaining $250,000 for its publication. As it turned out, the full series of about 150 volumes is the most extensive and important set of publications on World War I. A review of an early volume, *War Government of the British Dominions,* highlighted the importance of this monograph's focus on the political facts of the role of the dominions following World War I.[109] This insight was of particular relevance to the Corporation: the authors of the volume had clarified the basis for a different relationship between the Corporation and the dominions than it had with the colonies.

This focus on supporting concrete results rather than abstract aspirations set a pattern for the future: in response to constant requests for support from the Carnegie Endowment—which over the next twenty years was the main institutional vehicle through which the Corporation supported work on peace and international security—the Corporation routinely provided much less funding than requested or shaped the request toward a tangible product. Root's actions and reactions reflected the sense of responsibility to the legacy of Andrew Carnegie that all the trustees of that era, many of whom had known him well, brought to the work of the Corporation. They argued the case for their own institution, but then accepted the decision if it could not be supported exactly as presented. These were principled board members, role models for their successors.

The Church Peace Union leaders also considered themselves part of the family of Andrew Carnegie philanthropies. They were correct in that Louise and Andrew Carnegie's committed advocacy for peace had led Andrew Carnegie to consider something that was not quite in his comfort range: working with religious leaders whatever their denomination (as discussed in Chapter 1). But the Church Peace Union leaders were mistaken in thinking that their organization was at the same level as the others. While not explicitly stated, it is clear from reviewing the minutes of the trustees' meetings that there was no deep commitment to the Church Peace Union's work.

The Corporation had made its original endowment grant in 1912 and 1913 and had supported the institution at modest levels for several years. Then, in 1922, the Church Peace Union sought another endowment grant of $2 million. Its request noted that it had established contact in twenty-seven countries through the World Alliance for Promoting International Friendship Through the Churches. Its leaders informed the trustees that they had used half the income of the endowment to fund annual conferences to promote international goodwill. They emphasized that they had made a concerted effort during the war to keep the possibility of peace alive. The Union had petitioned Congress and supported outreach efforts through publications and speakers. In the request, the Union sought support to continue these activities and extend them into other countries, to promote similar efforts among Catholics and Jews, and to fund local work in the United States. After much deliberation and a presentation by the president and secretary of the Union, the trustees decided that it was impossible to make a grant

of that size, especially from the endowment or from income for the organization. Mrs. Carnegie, of course, was sitting on the board at the time of
the discussions, but maintained a discreet silence.[110] The trustees agreed to
provide support at the level of $25,000 per year for three years; they even-
tually continued making annual grants at this level for nearly twenty years.[111]

It was relatively easy for Root, Angell, Pritchett, and the board to maintain
their commitment to science and concrete results by funding the requests
from the Carnegie Institution of Washington. Although some of the support to the Institution was quite far afield from the Corporation's mission, it
was justified as being undertaken by a Carnegie family institution. Pritchett,
in response to a contemporary natural disaster, "called attention to the interesting scientific questions involved in the great earthquake that had just
occurred off the coast of Chile, the results of the action of certain forces of
nature which science may be capable of interpreting."[112] This earthquake was
of particular interest to the United States, he reasoned, because it seemed
to be related in origin to similar seismic phenomena that had been observed
in North America. The support of nearly $5,000 contributed to conducting
a survey on the earthquake's origins and impact to shed light on preventing
future ones. Possibly because of the clear relationship of the Institution's
activities to the advancement of knowledge, it seemed that all the Carnegie
Institution of Washington had to do was make a request—albeit generally
modest—and, without debate, it would receive support.[113]

The educational mission of the Carnegie Foundation for the Advancement
of Teaching, however, was squarely related to the work of the Corporation,
and it acted as a partner in the education grant-making. The Foundation's
close association with the Corporation ensured that it received considerable
support, both for its teachers' pension program and for collaborative activities, including overseas grant-making. Andrew Carnegie had chartered the
Foundation to work in both the United States and Canada, and Foundation
staff participated actively in the Corporation's early efforts in Canada.

A BOLD EXPERIMENT IN CANADA

THE CORPORATION'S GRANT-MAKING IN CANADA, beyond libraries and
church organs, began in 1918 with a $1 million grant to McGill University
in Montreal, along with support for two universities in Nova Scotia and

one in Ontario.[114] Beginning in 1920, possibly because of the volume of requests received from Canada, the trustees became particularly interested in the Maritime Provinces, a small area on Canada's eastern seaboard comprising New Brunswick, Nova Scotia, and Prince Edward Island and adjacent to the British dominion of Newfoundland.[115] Under Root, Angell, and Pritchett, the Corporation intensified its work in these provinces, which were home to about 1.25 million people.[116] In April 1920, the trustees agreed to support a matching grant to Acadia University in Wolfville, Nova Scotia, of $75,000. Seeking productive matches for its grants, in May of the same year the Corporation provided $500,000 to endow several chairs in medicine at Dalhousie University in Halifax, on the condition that the school obtain the matching support it sought from the Rockefeller Foundation and the government of Nova Scotia. The Rockefeller Foundation provided another $500,000 for buildings, equipment, and endowment, and Nova Scotia's government contributed $675,000 for buildings and additional costs. Medical care also featured in a subsequent 1922 Corporation grant to Dalhousie University of $50,000 for teaching facilities in the hospital, with the proviso that the university raise $150,000 for the same purpose.[117]

These grants to Dalhousie University, Acadia University, and St. Francis Xavier University prompted a wave of requests from other educational institutions in the Maritime Provinces and Newfoundland. Angell, committed to the concept of evidence-based decision-making, acknowledged that the Corporation's lack of firsthand knowledge of educational conditions stood in the way of informed grant-making in Canada, other dominions, and the British colonies. As he firmly stated, without such information, "we are in no position to pass intelligently" on the requests coming from those locations.[118] He proposed that a small commission be appointed to collect information in Canada that would serve as the basis for any allocations made there by the Corporation.

Conducting surveys prior to considering grants in the United States was a standard procedure used by the Corporation and other philanthropies; this was the first time the Corporation had embarked on one in another country. Over the next seven years, the work in eastern Canada yielded a variety of lessons about "investing" in other countries in support of others' projects, which was the premise for the Corporation's grant-making. Angell's commission proposal was reinforced when "the Government of

Nova Scotia joined with the colleges and universities in officially inviting the Corporation to make a study of the situation."[119] The government's invitation convinced the board—which was equally desirous of "reliable data"—to authorize Angell to provide funds for a small commission to examine the educational system in the provinces and in Newfoundland in collaboration with the Carnegie Foundation.

The commissioners' schedules did not permit the study to begin until the fall of 1921, after Angell's departure for Yale. The team members, William S. Learned, vice president of the Carnegie Foundation, and Kenneth C. M. Sills, president of Bowdoin College and originally from Nova Scotia, spent two months in the region. With an expense account of $5,000, they met with many of the region's key officials and education leaders. Their final fifty-page report, published as a Carnegie Foundation bulletin entitled *Education in the Maritime Provinces of Canada*, set in motion a major commitment pursued by the Corporation for the next nine years.[120]

In their report on the needs of the different institutions, Learned and Sills noted the limited resources available for institutions scattered around the provinces and, especially, the deep poverty in rural areas. Modeling their proposal on the University of Toronto, an educational hub with affiliated Roman Catholic, Anglican, and Methodist colleges, they recommended that the various universities pool their resources as a federation, with Dalhousie as the central institution and the others as satellite residential colleges. As Robert M. Lester described it, they proposed a University of the Maritime Provinces comprising the different denominational institutions as satellites around the base of Dalhousie University, all located in Halifax, Nova Scotia.[121] This plan for the federation of the institutions, which would draw together the colleges, students, and faculty, was expected to result in a better-integrated curriculum, cost savings through resource-sharing, and more effective education.

The boards of trustees would remain separate, and each would have its own residential structures and some classrooms, as well as a chapel. The university facilities would be open to all students. As Lester described it, the federation would become a "cooperative system of college and university instruction."[122] The plan would also serve to build close ties between the regional governments. The Learned and Sills report endorsed the

University of Toronto model, even though they recognized the major economic resource differences between Ontario and the Maritimes.[123]

The report generated extraordinary levels of discussion and debate. Pritchett in the Corporation's 1923 Annual Report described the conversations taking place in the region with the governments and institutions and efforts to work out "a plan for the establishment of such a provincial university with which the various denominational colleges might be related."[124] Dalhousie University, the prospective hub, was well disposed to the plan, as was the University of King's College, which was in dire need of financial support. Regardless of the considerable religious differences involved, Father James J. "Jimmy" Tompkins of St. Francis Xavier University became a "tireless advocate" for the plan, seeing it as the region's path to prosperity. "Success," he wrote, "will bring a new and glorious era to these provinces and give our poor people a chance for life in these strenuous days."[125]

Maritime Provinces historian John Reid has commented that although the Learned and Sills report generated debate, discussion, and dissension in the region, it "was based upon an intelligent appraisal not only of the situation of education in the Maritime provinces but also the political and societal characteristics of the region."[126] Learned and Sills were also well aware of the local sense of relative poverty, due to the small size of the Maritime Provinces in comparison with the enormous resources of other Canadian territories. Their report also noted the decentralized social organization of the region: small towns predominated, and fragmented religious affiliation played an important role in daily life. In Reid's assessment, however, "the commissioners did not allow these characteristics to influence significantly their findings or recommendations. For them, the principal justification for the reforms they advocated was that the cause of educational efficiency would be advanced." Reid noted that Learned and Sills thought their ideas constituted "an illuminating experiment almost certain to succeed," and they envisioned the experiment becoming a model for American institutions.[127]

Reid concluded that the Learned and Sills report did not link what the commissioners observed and understood about local economic justice concerns with the opportunities for educational development represented by the plan for federation, although the two factors were "directly and inseparably linked."[128] These were primarily rural provinces with populations that

were "struggling" economically. Although Father Tompkins felt that the economic issues provided the main reason for supporting the federation idea,
the other institutions did not want to incur the costs and dislocations that
would result from associating with Dalhousie University and moving from
their small-town settings to Halifax and at the same time would lead to the
loss of opportunities and resources for their localities. Religious concerns
about exposing students to urban Halifax were also a factor. Nonetheless,
for the time being support for the federation was not formally refused.

Pritchett, having determined that $1.33 million was available from the
interest accrued in the foreign fund, proposed that the entire fund and the
income for the next three to four years (and, as it happened, for the next six
years) be used in support of the regional federation for higher learning. A
former university president and head of the Carnegie Foundation, Pritchett
clearly embraced the advantages of such consolidation and coordination.

Although the board did not want to commit itself without having firm
assurances from all the institutions involved that they would participate,
in January 1923 the Corporation's Executive Committee recommended $3
million in support, "as soon as the essential features of the whole undertaking shall have been effectively and informally agreed upon by the institutions and provincial governments concerned."[129] Mrs. Carnegie and seven
of her colleagues on the board voted in favor of this recommendation; one
unnamed trustee abstained. James Bertram, the sole trustee to object, raised
a potent concern: six years of income from the special fund would only benefit, as Lester quoted, "less than six per cent of the population of the British
Dominions and Colonies, and for that matter ... less than thirteen per cent
of the people of Canada."[130] Notwithstanding his objection, the recommendation was approved.

Even as they were discussing the federation plan, the trustees were
offered an opportunity to provide a grant to one of the potential partner
institutions and thus initiate the federation. The oldest English-speaking
colonial university in the British Empire (outside the United Kingdom), the
University of King's College, chartered in 1789, was in very bad condition.[131]
There had been a disastrous fire in 1920; when the Corporation team visited in 1922, they saw half-built buildings and learned about the equally sad
state of the school's finances. Even before the commission had submitted its

final report, the leadership of King's College had asked the Corporation for a grant of $20,000 per year for three years to help rebuild the institution's structure as well as its morale. In May 1922, the Corporation agreed. By the fall of 1923, King's College was the first institution to reach agreement with Dalhousie University. Pritchett had presented this agreement to the Board of Trustees of the Corporation as an opportunity to carry out the plan and, failing that, to strengthen both institutions. The trustees agreed and authorized the acting president to provide a $600,000 endowment to King's College, with the conditions that it create a permanent endowment with monies it already had and that it also raise $400,000 to match. It took the college until 1928 to raise the $400,000 in matching funds, even with generous help from Dalhousie in the fund-raising; the Corporation then made good on its pledge.[132]

Along with others on the board, Pritchett recognized that the plan for federation constituted a major commitment for the Maritime Provinces institutions. He summed up his perspective in 1923, based on the experience of promoting the $3 million plan and the ongoing debate: "Whether it comes to full fruition or not, the Carnegie Corporation feels a genuine satisfaction in lending itself to a movement which seems so reasonable and so credible to those who conduct higher education in the maritime provinces."[133] Despite the considerable efforts of the Corporation and the plan's local proponents, the institutions of higher education in the Maritime Provinces would remain decentralized. The next chapter narrates the dénouement.

AN INTERNATIONAL MEDICAL COLLABORATION

DURING THIS PERIOD, not only did the Corporation fund American medical schools and various aspects of medical education when opportunities arose, but Root, Angel, and Pritchett were also interested in supporting scientific discovery and practicing scientists. Their interest led to Corporation support of a remarkable international research collaboration between scientists in the United States and Canada. The work of these scientists produced a medical discovery of lasting importance for people around the world.

As early as 1916, the Corporation had begun to support the work in nutrition-related diseases of Dr. Nathaniel Bowditch Potter, who "founded, with money from the Carnegie Corporation and others, the Memorial Laboratory and Clinic for the Study and Treatment of Nephritis, Gout, and Diabetes."[134] His renowned clinic in New York received from the Corporation $7,500 a year for over three years, with a matching condition of $20,000. Dr. Potter was diabetic and for health reasons relocated his clinic, renamed the Potter Metabolic Laboratory Clinic, to Santa Barbara, California.

During the course of Potter's grant, the research of Dr. John James Rickard Macleod and Dr. Frederick G. Banting of the Physiological Department at the University of Toronto came to the attention of the trustees. Banting had isolated a secretion from the pancreatic tissue of a dog—which a colleague had named "insulin"—and had been in contact with the Potter clinic in Santa Barbara to obtain some of this substance from the pancreas of a human being. Using the human insulin, the Toronto researchers successfully treated patients who were severely ill with diabetes. In 1923 they were awarded the Nobel Prize in Physiology or Medicine for this work. A total of $74,000 in Corporation grants to laboratories in the United States and Canada had supported an international collaboration that produced a life-transforming medical application for millions of people.[135]

The aspect of this work that most appealed to Pritchett was "the admirable attitude in which the two sets of investigators, each of which has received modest help from the Carnegie Corporation, have cooperated toward a common end. It was a graceful and generous act on the part of Dr. Macleod and his colleagues to put at the service of the Potter Metabolic Clinic the full results of their important researches. This action is in entire consonance with the spirit and the purpose of true scientific research." Pritchett also noted that "the brilliant success of this study formed the source of the greatest encouragement to the Trustees of the Corporation that their gifts may, if given with discretion, advance the cause of medical knowledge and thereby increase human happiness and usefulness. Mr. Carnegie had always in mind the desire to 'find the efficient man and enable him to do his work.'"[136] This approach has continued to shape grant-making intentions throughout the history of the Corporation.

SETTING THE STAGE FOR A NEW ERA

IN THE FIRST FEW YEARS following Carnegie's death, in areas other than Canada, the Corporation's programs for libraries and church organs had dwindled to fulfilling the last of the earlier commitments. Pritchett's 1922 Annual Report noted that these programs had ended because they had largely accomplished their goals in the English-speaking world. Yet, even though the thrust of the program for libraries had changed to librarian development and the church organ program had ended altogether, the Corporation trustees maintained the earlier commitments; they had a sense of responsibility to grantees and were concerned that all grants would meet their goals.[137]

Root, Angell, and Pritchett and their fellow trustees, however, committed the foundation to projects that moved well beyond the building of libraries and the installation of church organs. They believed that the United States needed to play a more significant role in the world. In remembering the public trust, all three men were firmly dedicated to increasing the capacity for research as the basis for developing national and international policies—hence their early commitment to freestanding research institutions, which were rare then but now, as today's think tanks, are ubiquitous.[138] They encouraged long-term grants, up to ten years, especially when investing in those institutions. Such investments directly contributed to fulfilling that part of the Corporation's mission that had to do with the advancement of knowledge and understanding. Pritchett was also concerned about the second part of the mission, dissemination; research results needed to reach the public as well as policymakers in order to help inform public opinion and understanding. The concern about dissemination would shape the Corporation's continuing interest in experimenting with different types of media for communication purposes, such as radio and, much later, television and newspapers, as well as its support for different types of education programs for the public at large.

When James Angell resigned, the Trustee Presidential Search Committee of Robert Franks, John Merriam, and Henry Pritchett interviewed candidates ranging from a Princeton University professor of biology to the secretary of the Rockefeller Foundation. They recommended Frederick P.

Keppel, whom the trustees invited to become president in November 1922.

The future of Andrew Carnegie's largest philanthropic endeavor had hinged on the extraordinary dedication of three men, none of whom had actively sought the job of president: Elihu Root, James Angell, and Henry Pritchett. Despite differing temperaments and wide-ranging outside commitments, they not only shared a deep-seated commitment to the Corporation's mission but also demonstrated keen insights about the steps needed to build a strong and responsible public trust institution. Furthermore, they shared a willingness to take intellectual risks by supporting enduring institutions and making creative, if contentious, international grants. They paved the way for Frederick Keppel to deepen the work of Carnegie Corporation in the United States, Canada, and throughout the British Empire.

3

ENTERING THE WORLD, 1923–1941

FREDERICK M. KEPPEL TRANSFORMED the intellectual scope and geographic reach of Carnegie Corporation. Under his leadership as president from 1923 to 1941, the Corporation spanned across the Pacific to Australia and New Zealand and across the Atlantic to Europe, the United Kingdom, and Africa; it extended the programs in the Western Hemisphere, entering the Caribbean and widening the range of its earlier grant-making in Canada. The Corporation programs, while maintaining the traditional focus on educational institutions and libraries, reflected national and international social themes emerging in the 1920s and 1930s that brought the Corporation into new areas in the United States and overseas, including: expanding opportunities for lifelong learning through adult education, vocational education in rural schools, music and art appreciation, and museum studies; promoting American understanding of foreign affairs by providing training in foreign languages, nurturing the interdisciplinary study of international security, and reinforcing international connections through travel grants and international conferences; and supporting groundbreaking, even occasionally controversial, work in social survey research, technology for education, psychological testing, and the natural and physical sciences.

Keppel's procedural innovations made the work overseas more relevant to local conditions by establishing committees of local experts to recommend promising grant opportunities; in South Africa for a limited period, these committees even dispersed the funds. He also fostered formal collaboration with key decision-makers in the United Kingdom to support closer cooperation in the British dominions and colonies. Keppel, like Root, Angell, and Pritchett before him, focused on the long view rather than on short-term results; he sought to advance and disseminate understanding of the big ideas, even the controversial ones, of the new age related to international cooperation and security, trans-Atlantic versus pan-Pacific relations, education across demographic divides of age and race, and the role of the humanities in nurturing human well-being.

Keppel introduced new ways for the Corporation to fulfill its public trust responsibility. Following a casual comment from a trustee that "in industry much better use is made of past experience as a guide to future action than in philanthropy," he instituted a system of documentation and evaluation of grant-making that went beyond the information in the Annual Reports.[1] Starting in 1935, Robert M. Lester, the corporate secretary, began methodically taking stock of all the grant-making programs since 1911. These audits of experience, which continued until 1941, became the basis for refining and advancing both the national and international activities.[2]

Questions raised about foundations by the public and "doubts as to the basic social utility of these organizations" led Keppel to reinforce the publications program in order to fulfill the commitment to public dissemination of the Corporation's work.[3] Each Annual Report included a listing of all the publications from that year. For the centenary celebration of Andrew Carnegie's birth, James Gourley and Robert Lester produced a volume of 314 pages covering the period 1911 to 1935 and containing 5,000 entries.[4]

In this period, to reduce the mystique of foundations and allay continuing concerns about their use of accumulated wealth, Keppel played a new role for foundation presidents by speaking and writing about philanthropy and foundations. He placed high value on obtaining external advice at all stages of grant-making. A wide range of colleagues from many different institutions and countries helped inform the actions of the Corporation during this era. As a consequence, Corporation programs would explicitly take into account what other foundations and agencies were doing. This chapter analyzes the context and approach of President Keppel and the trustees as backdrop for a discussion of the Corporation's international program activities throughout the British Empire and in the United States.

KEPPEL: A MAN FOR THE LONG RUN

DURING THE TUMULTUOUS INTERWAR PERIOD—the Roaring Twenties, the Great Depression, and the buildup to World War II—Frederick Keppel grew as a leader of American philanthropy. When he died unexpectedly in September 1943, the *New York Times* eulogized: "The attributes of Mr. Keppel, which won him a high place in the educational, governmental and philanthropic fields, were based upon living things. He had a genius, it seems, for persuading people to work together in harmony."[5]

His insights into social forces, his capacity to stay the course (even when navigating in choppy waters), and his commitment to Andrew Carnegie's mission for the Corporation, combined with his good humor and organizational skills, made him the right person to lead the foundation in this era. Russell Leffingwell, a Corporation trustee, board chairman in the 1940s and 1950s, and one of Keppel's oldest and dearest friends, said, "He was a wise and prudent administrator of a great and beneficent trust.... There was no end to his curiosity or to his capacity to absorb knowledge and understanding and to disseminate them among the people. There was a Spartan and relentless purpose in his life: to be good and to do good, and he pursued that purpose and achieved it."[6]

Keppel's presidency was informed by his early life in academics, his professional commitment to public service, his international perspective, and his view that philanthropy should be proactive as well as responsive. He had acquired experience with complicated decision-making in previous leadership positions, first at Columbia University as the youngest dean of the college and adviser to two of its presidents, Seth Low and Nicholas Murray Butler, and then as third assistant secretary of war in the War Department during World War I. Based in Paris after World War I, he gained international experience as head of the Foreign Relations Department of the American Red Cross and then as the first commissioner for the United States at the International Chamber of Commerce. Keppel, influenced by the cosmopolitan European atmosphere and open to new ideas, returned to New York in 1921 to lead the New York Regional Plan Initiative of the Russell Sage Foundation. In November 1922, he was appointed a trustee and the fifth president of Carnegie Corporation, to take office in October 1923.[7]

Keppel followed and enlarged upon the earlier comments of Angell about the need, before embarking on grant-making overseas, to conduct fact-finding surveys and site visits, to meet with many different people, and to listen carefully to what they said; Corporation staff members still adhere to this approach. Keppel grasped the planning and implementation strategy for effective grant-making even before it was articulated in foundation literature. He consolidated his philanthropic ideas in *The Foundation*, his 1930 book drawn from a series of lectures he delivered at the University of Virginia on foundation best practices.[8]

A CHANGING WORLD CONTEXT

THREE MAJOR TRENDS in these years are most pertinent to the Carnegie Corporation story, especially its entry onto the global stage. First, increased leisure time was making education across the human life cycle desirable and feasible. Second, intellectual and scientific ferment was combining with increasing ease of communications and travel to enhance a high level of cooperation and collaboration. Third, boom-and-bust economic conditions were fostering political and social uncertainties in the United States and around the world.

During the interwar period, American philanthropy flowered, even during the Great Depression, in part because the US Tax Act of 1936 allowed corporations to deduct as much as 5 percent of pretax income for charitable giving.[9] American philanthropy in the late 1920s and 1930s mirrored the era's broader globalism, which sought to counter the inward-looking nativist views of the 1920s, the effects of the Depression, and the rise of totalitarianism in the 1930s. Frederick Keppel defined the philanthropic decision-making challenge for this period: "There has perhaps never been a time when it was harder to think clearly in terms of the long run, as contrasted with the calls of the moment, never a time when it was more necessary that the attempt should be made."[10]

Edward Shuman, a well-known journalist of the day, commented on American philanthropy's "ever widening reach." He noted that Stephen Edward Harkness's recent $10 million grant that founded the Pilgrim Trust to help Great Britain was a prime example of the role that Americans were playing overseas to emphasize "the common brotherhood of man irrespective of national boundaries.... It also illustrates once more the injustice of the charge, so often made in the press of foreign countries, that Americans are selfish isolationists, interested only in accumulating wealth for themselves."[11] He gave as further evidence the "increasing trend toward the international philanthropic programs, as pointed out by Frederick Keppel, president of the Carnegie Corporation of New York." The data Shuman used showed that of the more than 150 endowed philanthropic foundations—capitalized at about $1 billion and giving away about $60 million a year—about one-half made grants on a national level, one-quarter made international grants, and the rest concentrated on local areas within the United States.[12]

The Rockefeller Foundation had been active through its health and scientific grant-making and operations in every region of the world since 1913.[13] During this period, the Corporation entered the wider world as well, though its outreach was focused by charter on the British dominions and colonies. Both these institutions maintained strong ties to cross-Atlantic partners, and they were also intrigued by the countries around the Pacific Rim, recognized even then as a central feature in American foreign policy.[14]

At the same time as foundations were reaching out internationally, national legislation reflected a different set of American public and policy priorities. Ongoing immigration to the United States had generated a populist backlash, leading to the 1924 Immigration Act, which severely restricted entrance from southern Europe and Asia. Approval by the US Senate of the 1928 Kellogg–Briand Pact, an anti-aggression treaty signed by countries around the world, reflected both pacifist and isolationist perspectives in the United States. While the treaty had no direct repercussions for the Corporation and did not affect its international activities, some of its grant-making in the United States for teaching foreign languages reflected the Corporation's continuing interest in both promoting the Americanization of immigrants and enhancing American understanding of the rest of the world. Indeed, the roiling political and economic conditions around the world, as well as the American academic community's limited capacity to address these interrelated conditions, led the Corporation to back the development of a new field of international security studies in the United States, in much the same way as the Rockefeller Foundation was deepening the work in international relations.[15]

The British Empire was changing in ways that reflected the increasing pressure for self-determination, following Woodrow Wilson's "Fourteen Points" presented in January 1918 and the Versailles Peace Conference in 1919. In 1926 the Corporation's potential bailiwick of the British dominions—Canada, Newfoundland, Australia, New Zealand, and South Africa—all achieved autonomous status.[16] With the passage in Great Britain of the Government of India Act of 1935, which established India as a federation, that country became ineligible for Corporation funding: the British Dominions and Colonies Fund (BDC), by charter, was limited to the British dominions and colonies.[17]

As cultural internationalists, the American foundations were keen to promote values that emphasized democracy and the free exchange of ideas and opinions with the aim of building a peaceful world based on knowledge and understanding. Toward that end, foundations funded "the interchange of graduate students among the nations, with the consequent interweaving of the lines of advanced thought all over the world."[18] The Corporation reinforced the transmission of knowledge by funding a set of interlocking activities connecting scholars, practitioners, policymakers, and advocates across the dominions and colonies and also connecting them to the United States. Early forays into building international networks of scholars and practitioners within and across fields included, for example, the travel grants program, initiated in 1928, which facilitated a flow of people from one country to another, and support for international conferences to promote the sharing of information across geographic boundaries. Fellowships and travel grants funded by the Rockefeller Foundation, the Rhodes Trust, and the Commonwealth Fund had been connecting people and ideas even earlier; these three institutions, along with the Corporation, tended to focus on the English-speaking world. As Keppel noted, the Rockefeller Foundation and the General Education Board (founded by John D. Rockefeller Sr.) together had "given appointments to no fewer than 5,827 individuals at the cost of almost exactly nine and a half million dollars. The program of a single year, 1929, includes 1,451 such appointments."[19] Over the period 1921 to 1934, Lester reported, 439 individuals received support from the Corporation totaling $1,815,000 for travel awards from the British dominions and colonies to travel to the United States, Canada, Europe, the United Kingdom, and occasionally other parts of the British Empire to be exposed to new ideas and to expose others to their ideas, or awards to Americans to travel to the dominions or colonies; grants-in-aid for specific research projects; or fellowships for study, primarily in the arts, music, and librarianship.[20]

The international connectivity promulgated by American foundations in the 1930s has led some later scholars to characterize the Rockefeller Foundation and Carnegie Corporation in particular as the "foreign policy hegemons of the 1930s"—that is, as private players serving as public good institutions to shape and enhance the impact of US foreign policy.[21] Keppel described quite a different perspective, noting that a foundation "must ever be on its guard against indulging in propaganda."[22] For the Corporation international grants program (as described later in the chapter), local actors influenced and recommended the directions for work in their settings. These scholars are right in one respect, however: Like their counterparts at Rockefeller and elsewhere, Keppel and the trustees anticipated that exposing Americans to thoughtful ideas about the role of the United States in the world, through the grants in the United States focused on international issues, would promote greater international understanding by the public and policymakers, thereby enabling the United States to be a responsible and dynamic global player.

The Board of Trustees and the Executive Committee for the most part supported Keppel's efforts in fulfilling Andrew Carnegie's Commonwealth mandate (see the introduction to the book) and organizing grant-making according to the mission and program priorities.[23] In meeting the 1922 board mandate to enlarge the number of trustees from eight to fifteen, Keppel and his colleagues selected new trustees who were open to new thinking about social change and geographic reach.[24] The trustees covered a wide range of international activities and maintained support for the Corporation's overseas program over the period of the 1920s, the Depression, and the pre–World War II years.[25]

As David Ekbladh and others have observed, these progressive views might well be called elitist because they were embraced by educated and well-traveled people.[26] Yet these men were deeply concerned about enhancing American international understanding and knowledge of how the United States could play a constructive role in the world. Most of them had served in government during World War I and wanted to prevent future wars. For the most part, they were proponents of the League of Nations, and like those progressives who pursued activities and experiences that frequently took them to Europe and elsewhere, they often hosted visitors from overseas.[27] Bucking the tide of isolationism, chauvinism, and parochialism, they and their counterparts at the Rockefeller Foundation represented the modern progressive global persona that is taken for granted today in the leading international American-based foundations.

In selecting board members, nonetheless, Keppel was aware of the "murmurings which are heard from time to time as to the dominant influence of what is called the 'New York point of view' in the affairs of American foundations."[28] He addressed these "murmurings" in part by mentioning where trustees came from and where they lived.[29] In almost every Annual Report, Keppel would include lists of the advisers who participated in Corporation studies and programs and emphasize that they were drawn from all areas of the United States as well as from overseas; in the 1925 Annual Report, for example, he provided the names and areas of contribution of all the external advisers.[30]

NEW GRANT-MAKING APPROACHES: KEY MEN AND LOCAL ADVISERS

IN KEEPING WITH HIS DESIRE to seek the opinions and expertise of others, Keppel introduced the Corporation to the concept of relying on "key men"—or in the Rockefeller Foundation terminology, "circuit riders"—rather than hiring a cadre of permanent professional staff.[31] These key men served as trusted advisers to the Corporation and explored the world to identify the most appropriate grantees and promising opportunities. Keppel often relied on these men (and even a couple of women) to serve as the eyes and ears of the foundation in the areas of the world where it could be active. Keppel also welcomed international visitors to the Corporation and maintained an extensive correspondence with many of the key players in the United Kingdom and elsewhere overseas.

When opening new areas of grant-making in Australia, New Zealand, and South Africa, the Corporation would usually send an American or British adviser, paired with a local consultant, to survey the field and advise on program strategy. Following his early trip to Canada, Keppel had determined that the most effective way of working in the dominions was to establish local committees that would follow up on the team's report and recommend, without interference from the Corporation, the local grants.[32] As international travel grants became more prominent in the Corporation's grant-making, these committees identified people who merited such grants. Advisory committees were organized, first in the southern dominions of South Africa, Australia, and New Zealand, and later in Canada.

The backgrounds of the local advisers differed depending on the status in the British Empire of the region or country to be explored. In the dominions—Canada, South Africa, Australia, and New Zealand— the advisers were primarily local residents and citizens. In South Africa, there were both British and Afrikaner South African advisers, with fewer than a handful of colored, Asian, and African South Africans.[33] In contrast to advisers in the dominions, in the colonies there was little or no advice from Africans or white settlers; the voices listened to in New York usually reflected the British colonial perspective, although occasionally, especially as the 1930s continued, the mix was slightly more balanced, notably in the Caribbean colonies. A London-based committee organized under the auspices of the Royal Institute of International Affairs provided advice for all the British colonies and Commonwealth-wide opportunities.[34]

FINANCIAL CHALLENGES

KEPPEL BECAME PRESIDENT of Carnegie Corporation at an inauspicious financial time for the institution. Not immune to the economic exuberance of the 1920s, the trustees had committed such a high level of resources to future obligations that there was very little money left for new grants. That is, the major endowment grants from the late 1910s and early 1920s—for instance, to the Institute of Economics—had obligated the Corporation to yearly payments. In 1923 and 1924, these obligations required payouts that put significant pressure on the budget, dramatically reducing the scope for new grant-making. Unable to make many new commitments, the Corporation had only limited capacity to institute new programs, including international ones.[35]

A perennial quandary for philanthropy is whether to make the world better today and reduce available resources for new grant-making or hold back resources to create capacity to address future challenges. Keppel took advantage of these budgetary concerns to make the case for reducing support for endowments (in 1921 about 67 percent of the grants made and 71 percent of the money appropriated) that supported new institutions such as the policy research institutes, bringing to a close the general-purpose grants that had supported educational institutions and further reinforcing the shift in grant-making for libraries from paying for bricks-and-mortar construction to development of the profession and practice of librarianship.

Furthermore, the amount of money the Corporation had to give away, even if there had been no outstanding commitments, was very small compared to the increasing resources available for philanthropic endeavors in the United States. The Corporation's annual grant-making budget of around $6 million to $7 million seemed paltry compared to the nearly $1 billion that was being spent in the United States at that time by philanthropies, the government, and other entities on issues of concern to the Corporation. Despite the Depression, by the 1930s university and college endowments along with the federal government's resources far outstripped those of the foundations, even with the new ones established in the 1920s and 1930s. In his observation that the power of the philanthropic dollar had to go beyond its nominal dollar amount to make a difference, Keppel became an early spokesperson for what would later be called "strategic philanthropy." Given his assessment of how to make a difference, Keppel defined the grant-making challenge for the Corporation: "The Corporation must of necessity restrict its angle of vision and, at the best, it can support only a very small percentage of the projects which are brought to its attention, even from among those regarding whose usefulness to humanity there can be little question."[36] He suggested several criteria for deciding in favor of a proposal: limited availability of funds from other sources, such as a local community or alumni association; activities at an early stage, such as unproven approaches or ideas, that cannot "call upon any particular clientele"; clarity about the program of work and the source of additional resources following the Corporation's support; and a reasonable time frame for the completion of the project, with no need for continuing support over the long term.[37]

With the mission as the overarching frame, Keppel highlighted new areas of focus for the foundation, including opportunities for grant-making within and beyond the borders of the United States. He recommended the following framework for organizing the Corporation's grant-making:

1. Promoting research and studies that will advance newly discovered knowledge to the world (e.g., continuing the insulin research studies, educational testing studies, social surveys, and support for science through the Carnegie Institution in Washington)
2. Promoting acquaintance with the highest educational aims and policies in order to make possible the ready diffusion of knowledge (e.g., building the field of adult education, improving library services, and foreign language training; and outreach on world affairs and peace, including grants-in-aid and traveling fellowships)
3. Furthering the understanding of that deeper stratum of knowledge and feeling that involves philosophy, art, and the comprehension of human relations (e.g., support for museums and museum studies, music and art appreciation material, and a major program on the fine arts)[38]

The Corporation initiated major support for international grant-making in 1927, and that support continued during the 1930s. Surprisingly, the Crash of 1929 and the ensuing Great Depression had a limited effect on the Corporation's grants programs. Nonetheless, while the stock market crash itself did not dramatically affect the Corporation's grants budget, over the next four years, as the Depression began to permeate American society and the economy, the trustees and the president moved forward with fiscal caution.

In 1932, for example, at the December Executive Committee meeting, the president recommended a formal plan for reducing the expenditures of the Africa program; the committee agreed to it, in principle.[39] In February and March 1933, the Executive Committee again reviewed the financial situation and found that it was not as unfavorable as anticipated. The trustees agreed to increase the funds available for overall grant-making by $325,000, to $2,325,000. They also recommended "that the President should be conservative in making his plans for the next fiscal year," taking into account, "the considerably reduced amount of money being at his disposal."[40]

International activities continued, notwithstanding Keppel's recommendation, with minimal loss of momentum, including, for example, grants
for libraries and books at Canadian institutions, grants for the expenses
of the British Commonwealth conference of the Canadian Institute of
International Affairs, and grants for the South African Institute of Race
Relations, as well as for the international education initiatives in the United
States and overseas. Despite the troubled financial situation of the late
1920s and early 1930s, the Corporation's leadership displayed a firm commitment to initiating and extending programs in Africa, the Caribbean,
Australia, and New Zealand and maintaining the ones in Canada, starting
from an annual level of $375,250 in 1929–1930 (out of a total of $7,729,750)
and reaching a maximum of $1,532,500 in 1933–1934 (out of $5,028,420).[41]

ENGAGING THE WORLD THROUGH GRANT-MAKING: PROMISING OPPORTUNITIES AMID ENDURING THEMES

THE THEMES AND APPROACHES promulgated by the Corporation throughout the United States often served as templates for the grants made in the
British dominions and colonies and for the Commonwealth in general.

In the late 1920s and 1930s, social and cultural conceptual breakthroughs
became as relevant for Corporation grant-making as economic institutional
innovations had been under Root, Angell, and Pritchett. Keppel and his
assistants, first Morse Cartwright, followed by Robert M. Lester in 1926,
John Russell in 1932, and Charles Dollard in 1938, targeted several developments as high-priority grant-making opportunities: the increase in leisure
time that made it possible for more adults to engage in intellectual pursuits;
the importance of the humanities and social sciences to understanding the
human condition; and the relevance of on-the-ground research to local
decision-making as well as Corporation grant-making.[42]

New developments in human biology and mental testing were showing
no diminishment in adults' capacity for learning. This finding led to increasing education opportunities for adults, a social and cultural change that
was "one of the most vital which faces the world today."[43] In Keppel's view,
this not only was an American phenomenon but was happening throughout the Commonwealth world. He and Cartwright categorized the field of

information for adults into library service; education and appreciation in the arts, modern languages, and literature; and adult education. These were areas in which the Corporation, through preliminary investigations, could work with existing organizations or develop new ones.

Despite the overarching thematic connections between adult education and access to knowledge and culture, the extent and variety of the opportunities pursued by Keppel and supported by the Board of Trustees led to later criticism that grant-making was scattered during this period of the Corporation's history. Keppel surely heard such remarks when he was president. In his 1942 report on the grants to the British colonies and southern dominions prepared for the new president, Walter Jessup, Keppel commented on the Corporation's work as a whole: "The list of individual grants would give the impression that we had done a good deal of spattering. We have done some, as was, I think, inevitable, while we were feeling our way, but most of the small items were really part of a larger program, as, for example, the wide distribution of art and music sets, or the development of the educational services of museums throughout the Empire."[44]

From 1923 to 1941, Keppel noted the Corporation expended the following resources in the different regions of the British Empire, except Canada:

Africa, including the Union of South Africa and African colonies: $1,955,925
Australia: $1,026,795
New Zealand: $669,030
Other colonies in the Southern Hemisphere: $42,975
Centrally administered from London: $473,000
Travel grants: $599,658

This total of more than $4.7 million for the work in the Southern Hemisphere did not include the support in the United States for internationally oriented activities or for some Commonwealth-wide grants, such as for the Imperial College of Tropical Agriculture in Trinidad.[45]

In its overseas grant-making, as described in the following sections, the Corporation pursued activities that often shared common themes but displayed distinct characteristics arising from the local responsibility to design and implement the grants. As program leaders, through travel grants, visited other sites, shared ideas, and brought back new approaches, new connections were built across dispersed individuals, institutions, and regions.[46]

MAINTAINING THE MISSION IN CANADA— SUCCESSES AND FAILURES

BY FAR THE MOST PROMINENT LOCUS of the Corporation's international grant-making from 1912 through the 1930s was Canada, where grants covered an extensive range of activities. The Corporation's initial vision for its work there centered on strengthening Canadian universities in multiple dimensions, building the capacity of public and university libraries and library systems, strengthening basic scientific and social scientific research, and developing the same initiatives in adult education it was supporting in the United States and elsewhere.[47] During this era, the Corporation spent nearly $6 million in Canada and Newfoundland, half of which supported enterprises in the Maritime Provinces.[48]

The commitment to establish a federated university system in the Maritime Provinces illustrates one approach in philanthropy: social change driven by grant-making-led educational reform. A foundation, even one hundred years ago, could choose to use its money to change the institutions to which it was giving or to improve the communities within which the institutions operated. In this instance, the Corporation hoped to achieve social change by promoting the consolidation of higher education in Canada's Maritime Provinces to improve institutional arrangements, rather than by making direct investments in the communities. Each year for more than nine years the trustees asked if the federation idea had been accepted by the local decision-makers so that they could release the $3 million put aside for this initiative.

One prominent public concern was that each institution represented a different denomination and such a federation might dilute this trait. A second major public concern was the economic loss in the rural areas where these institutions were based that would result from the move to Halifax.[49] The Corporation trustees, while endorsing the plan, also debated about providing support that would affect only 6 percent of the population of the

British dominions and colonies and fewer than 13 percent of the people of Canada.

When Keppel visited Canada in July 1923 as president-elect, he heard the local criticism and realized that it was important to form a local organization to provide advice to the Corporation. Outside experts could be helpful in raising ideas, but the important lesson from this experience was that local expertise and advisers played a vital role. This idea had ramifications for how the Corporation would work in other settings throughout the world.

From this effort with its record of mixed success, a few initiatives had lasting positive effects. Dalhousie University, University of King's College, and Mount Allison University developed a federated arrangement. The Corporation facilitated the establishment of the University Matriculating Board representing thirteen colleges in the region. After that initiative, the Corporation contributed to the establishment in 1924 of the Central Advisory Committee for Higher Education in the Atlantic Provinces to advise the Corporation and the region.[50] Discussions on the committee led to the establishment, with Corporation contributions, of a university in Newfoundland (then a dominion) called Newfoundland Memorial University. Following his visit in 1934, Lester observed, "The work of the Central Advisory Committee has accustomed executives and teachers to think regionally rather than locally upon educational matters."[51]

A second enduring institution resulted from the work of Father J. J. Tompkins, vice president of St. Francis Xavier University, after he had been banished to Canso, Nova Scotia, by the university administration for supporting the federation.[52] Through the extension program of St. Francis Xavier, he and Reverend Moses Coady initiated a self-help program for poor fishermen called "The Antigonish Experiment," which blended study, self-reliance, and economic development. Trustee James Bertram, in giving his full approval to the request (after having earlier raised objections to the federation idea), commented, "If we can help people to help themselves instead of putting out a life line to the Red Cross or their fellow taxpayers' pocket every time they get into a jam, we shall be carrying out the ideas of the Founder."[53] The initial support of $3,000 in 1932 was renewed regularly until 1943, for a total of $79,500.[54] The Antigonish Experiment, which became the Coady Institute in 1959, today trains practitioners from all over the world in the Tompkins/Coady approach to community education.[55]

Grants to a variety of universities and colleges in other provinces made from 1923 to 1940 encouraged extension work in other settings, adult education, library development, and music and art teaching; professorships ranging from arts to foreign languages to physics; and innovative institutes. Following the Corporation-funded American Library Association (ALA)'s 1930 commission of inquiry on library conditions in Canada, the Corporation seized the opportunity to act on the ALA's recommendations in support of its regional demonstration of a public library service on Prince Edward Island and other public library programs in Nova Scotia, New Brunswick, Newfoundland, and British Columbia.[56] Support for scientific research institutes continued, including grants for the work on insulin at the University of Toronto and the University of Alberta from 1922 to 1926. New institutes and schools receiving grants included the Institute of Child Study at the University of Toronto and the Library School at McGill University; grants to Canadian institutions and programs continued until 1960.[57]

One of the earliest area studies programs took place, with backing from the Corporation, under the aegis of the Carnegie Endowment for International Peace; the Endowment's Canadian-American studies program drew together scholars in the United States and Canada to address shared and distinctive issues. From 1933 to 1941, the Corporation provided funds for this part of the Endowment's work at the level of over $200,000 to organize educational programs and research projects and to conduct special studies on Canadian-American relations. About twenty years later, the Corporation supported the first Canadian-American studies program based in an American university, the University of Rochester.

PROMOTING THE MISSION IN SOUTH AFRICA AND THE AFRICAN COLONIES

THE TRUSTEES IN 1926 authorized Frederick Keppel and James Bertram (a trustee as well as corporation secretary) to visit Africa during the summer of 1927 "to study on-the-ground educational opportunities for effective use of the Special Fund within the limits of the charter."[58] This two-month visit initiated an enduring relationship. For more than eighty years, Corporation grant-making in support of African initiatives with African institutions and individuals has centered on education and access to information; corollary investments have been made to support exchanges and fellowships and to study issues related to culture, health, gender, and social and economic development at the policy and research levels. Commonwealth countries in Africa have been the Corporation's predominant overseas grant-making focus since the 1960s.

On the 1927 trip, Keppel and Bertram had to navigate more than an ocean voyage. To reassure the British Colonial Office that the Corporation sought to be collaborative, not competitive, the team's first stop was London; only after discussions with the Colonial Office staff and other officials in London did they continue the journey and disembark in Mombasa, Kenya Colony. The Corporation's commitment to education, including adult education, placed the team in the center of controversy between the British Colonial Office, the colonial settlers, and the native population. In the African colonies, white settlers and the native populations alike advocated for their own local higher education institutions to eliminate the necessity of traveling to the United Kingdom or the United States.[59] The Phelps Stokes Fund study conducted by Thomas Jesse Jones had recommended instead a focus on vocational education and local community-based training for the native populations. Supportive of the Jones study but seeking to appease the settler and native populations, the British government had taken tentative steps to upgrade the local colonial colleges.[60] South Africa, as a dominion with its Union government status, was responsible for its own education system and had already established full-scale universities. The issue in South Africa concerned who could attend which institutions. Non-Europeans could only attend the English-language universities or the South African Native College at Fort Hare, not the Afrikaans-language universities. This distinction was indicative of the complexity of the situation in South Africa concerning race and ethnicity that became increasingly evident as the team traveled through the dominion.

In July 1927, the Corporation team visited schools, libraries, and missionary programs in Kenya, Tanganyika, Southern Rhodesia, and one town in Northern Rhodesia; they spent August in the Union of South Africa and visited Transvaal, Orange Free State, Natal, and the Eastern and Western

Cape Provinces.[61] The Keppel and Bertram team identified many opportunities for Corporation activities in the trip report; at the same time, they explicitly recognized that they had to be wary of the political controversies and mindful about entering areas where other agencies, including non-African ones, were active.[62]

Given the prevailing social, economic, and political conditions in South Africa, it is not surprising that the team shared with the other trustees their observations on the race issue; they identified "a present lack of sympathy and understanding of certain important matters as between East Africa and South Africa, and between the English and Dutch elements in the latter; the conflict of races, not only as between black and white but with the Indian and coloured elements further complicating the situation."[63] Their program recommendations attempted to balance these concerns. The report set the groundwork for what became criteria for action in the ensuing decades, focusing "upon fundamentals ... to take the long view ... so that instead of scattered results, there may be a cumulative effect, even if within relatively narrow limits.... It is also important, even more so than in the United States, to group the enterprises with which the Corporation concerns itself."[64]

From this trip, they recommended a five-year, $500,000 program of cooperation with the Union government in South Africa and the British government in the colonies.[65] In making their recommendations to the board, Keppel and Bertram commented that conditions in Africa more greatly resembled those in the United States and Canada than in the United Kingdom, leading them to recommend a program of travel grants for individuals from Africa to American and Canadian institutions.

The trustees approved the overall program on November 17, 1927, with the Executive Committee authorized to recommend grants for specific proposals within the program. The program continued substantially beyond the initial five-year limit, until Keppel retired in 1941; about $520,000 worth of grants supported initiatives in the African colonies and about $1.3 million supported activities in South Africa.[66]

For the grants in the colonies, the Corporation consulted with the British Colonial Office, advisers in the United Kingdom, advisers in the United States, and colonial officers and missionaries on the ground. In South Africa, following on the Maritime Provinces experience, the Corporation encouraged the establishment of a local committee. Launched in 1928 as the South African Advisory Committee, the members called themselves the South African Trustees of Carnegie Corporation of New York, almost a precursor of a country office. For nearly seven years they not only recommended the grants but also had the resources from the Corporation to pay for them.

The original committee, chaired by Sir Patrick Duncan (a respected lawyer, member of Parliament, and later governor-general of the Union of South Africa), had difficulty distributing the funds to the recipients in a timely fashion. Thus, starting in 1935, at Duncan's request, the Corporation gave the money directly to the institutions. Although local committees were established in other dominions, a similar arrangement—that is, establishing a group of trustees and giving them a pool of money to disperse when the grant was approved in New York—was not repeated elsewhere or in later eras.

A second committee was established to recommend recipients for the travel grants, the Carnegie Corporation Visitor Grants Committee.[67] Both committees were composed of more liberal South Africans of British origin and more conservative Afrikaners; the members acted as "gatekeepers," that is, the key decision-makers regarding who would receive support in the increasingly fraught situation in South Africa. The process became problematic. Indeed, the Corporation's chief liaison in the country, Charles T. Loram, moved to the United States in 1931, partially as a result of the situation. This left only Ernest Malherbe, who played an important role in the Corporation's educational initiatives in South Africa, including the work on intelligence testing and educational measurement there.[68]

As the 1927 trip report and subsequent discussions made clear, the Corporation's intent was to pursue its educational mission for whites, "natives," and "Coloureds" in South Africa as well as in the colonies. To achieve this goal, the Corporation worked with some of the most liberal and progressive elements of white South African society to design its grant-making for the benefit of nonwhites as well as whites. The dilemma this posed was that most liberals agreed with Afrikaner nationalists on the benefits of segregation for the different population groups. Keppel and Bertram chose a strategy of legitimizing the Corporation with the conservative white

South Africans by underwriting projects that both Afrikaner nationalists and pro-British liberals would approve. Premier among these legitimizing projects was the Poor White Commission (known formally as the Carnegie Commission of Investigation on the Poor White Question in South Africa).[69] Marita Golden, in a review of the work, noted that "the Carnegie Commission of Investigation on the Poor White Question in South Africa … was at that time the largest and most complex social science study ever conducted in Africa. More than a sociological inquiry, this investigation was to become a watershed event in South African social and political history."[70]

The Poor White Commission was not the largest financial investment made in South Africa by the Corporation, but it has generated the most enduring scholarly attention and controversy.[71] While it applied the results of the lesson learned from the Canadian Maritime Provinces experience in South Africa, the Corporation was soon to learn another lesson: supporting politically charged research, even if undertaken in a well-designed social scientific manner, can have unintended adverse consequences.[72] When making grants under cultural and political conditions only seemingly reminiscent of the foundation's home base, a major lesson—and one the Corporation would apply much later in South Africa—was to think through the possible implications of such work before approving it. The Corporation, in this instance, raised many questions with the local committee and local advisers about the approach and the people involved; the concern was to achieve a scientifically unbiased set of results. That goal was reached, but as discussed later, those results contributed eventually to destructive political abuse.

Scholarly assessments of the Poor White Commission and its subsequent Poor White Study have focused in part on the Corporation's motivation for funding the study and considerably more on later uses of the study results. Although a comparative discussion of race and racism in the 1930s in South Africa and the United States is outside the scope of this book, the period when the Poor White Study was conducted can usefully be interrogated against the following point made by Robert Miles and Malcolm Brown, British scholars of racism: "The effective expression [of racism] always interacts with the extant economic and political relations and other ideologies…. It should always be remembered that those who will articulate it and those who are its object are located in a wider, complex web of social relations."[73]

The Poor White Study took place at a moment in time when its results could be used to reinforce the political trajectory that later consolidated the imposition of apartheid policies in South Africa with the election of the National Party in 1948. The Corporation's support of the Poor White Commission was intended to increase understanding of the conditions of poor Afrikaners and arrive at recommendations for improving those conditions. Undertaken over the period 1928 to 1932, the study involved detailed field research at the household and community levels and was conducted by scholars, clergymen, and activists and advised by two American consultants.[74] The project, at a total cost of $30,500, resulted in five volumes that pulled together reams of statistics and analyses to undergird a deeper understanding of what constituted poverty in South Africa for Afrikaners; the volumes also included policy recommendations for building self-reliance among poor Afrikaners and reduce their dependence on the state.[75] These analytical results were the intended direct outcomes of the commission and the study, namely, to delineate the extent and nature of white Afrikaner poverty and recommend ways to alleviate it. Such studies, especially ones of such scope and in politically complex settings, as noted have significant unintended consequences—sometimes positive, but in this case destructively negative in both the short and long term.

The results have generated decades of scholarship across a wide spectrum about this "watershed event." Some scholars have claimed that the study provided the blueprint for apartheid. Golden noted the widespread publicity it received when it was published in 1932: "With unprecedented swiftness the Poor White Study spawned a movement uniting the destinies of privileged and downtrodden whites."[76] Just a few years later, the study results contributed to more dire effects: "At national conferences in 1934 and 1936, Afrikaner political and social activists used the Poor White Study as a guide for creating the blueprints to solidify Afrikaner economic and political dominance.... The Poor White Study and the response to it was widely recognized as leading to the rise of the National Party [in 1948]."[77]

Other scholars in South Africa and elsewhere, however, have situated the work of the Poor White Commission as an integral contribution to the long-standing political debates around race and poverty in South Africa since the late 1890s, when the issue of "poor whites" became a concern.[78] Current scholarship, drawing on detailed research conducted by Deborah

Posel and others, has concluded, in the words of Steffen Jensen, that "there is a consensus among many scholars in the field: there was no blueprint for apartheid."[79] As South African scholar Saul Dubow notes, perhaps the most important factor was the fifty years of segregation policy that preceded it: "It is inconceivable that apartheid could have been imagined, let alone implemented, had it not been able to build on segregation."[80] Nonetheless, it is clear that the study aided the Afrikaner nationalist cause, as well as white supremacy in general, by adding scientific legitimacy to the inherently racist concept of "white poverty."[81]

Several study participants, for example, were later active in the Afrikaner nationalist movement, but at that stage such involvement was not always the same as promoting the eventual post–World War II harsh apartheid laws. A couple of the study participants, however, combined both nationalist and racist ideologies. Geoffrey Cronjé, who co-authored the study's volume *The Poor White and Society* with a social worker from the Dutch Reformed Church, Reverend J. R. Albertyn, was the first South African PhD in sociology; even before his participation in the study, he had been active in right-wing nationalist circles. According to Dubow, Cronjé is "commonly regarded as being one of the key exponents of apartheid theory."[82] But not all were as virulent as Cronjé. Mrs. M. E. Rothmann, author of the report on women and the one female member of the team, was a nationalist, but expressed concern for nonwhite populations: "Are we not going astray if we think of the welfare of the Afrikaner or of the white populace as our only task?"[83]

One unambiguous result of the study was its part in launching the study of sociology in South Africa with the creation of several sociology departments across the country: "the commission recommended 'that a department of social studies' be created in a South African university to train social workers and conduct scientific studies on how to reduce white poverty," Paul Sager notes. "Stellenbosch University created such a department in 1932, even before the report was published, with Hendrik Verwoerd [a student of psychologist R. W. Wilcocks, a member of the Poor White Commission].... He would play a central role in the follow-up conferences of 1934 and 1936, [in] the Continuation Committee dedicated to promoting reforms to eradicate white poverty, and ultimately, in the 1950s and 60s, as Prime Minister, would become known as the 'architect of apartheid.'"[84] Verwoerd wrote extensively in the press about the study results, emphasizing the importance of the study in combating white poverty.[85]

The Corporation also funded some activities that directly benefited the African and Colored populations. It did so at the urging of Charles T. Loram, one of the Corporation's most trusted advisers in South Africa, as well as of Ernest Malherbe, both of whom had earlier recommended support for the Poor White Commission.[86] They both recognized the importance of undertaking equally detailed studies of black poverty. Loram wrote to Keppel in 1929 that the South African Research Grants Board should "undertake a survey of social and economic conditions of the Natives of the Union."[87] He suggested that it be headed by Thomas Jesse Jones and funded by Carnegie Corporation.

Malherbe commented on the implications of the Poor White Study for the black population: "What we have on our hands today is the *poor black problem*, a problem of greater magnitude and complexity than ever the Poor White Problem was."[88] Malherbe also acutely predicted in 1929 that "in less than 50 years' time the Carnegie Corporation will perhaps feel it incumbent upon them again to appoint a research committee, but this time to investigate the cause of the poor black problem—a problem which may prove to be very black indeed, because I have not the least doubt that if things are allowed merely to drift, the natives will, if they are not already, be victims of the same ruthless process."[89]

Fifty years later, the study had one more unintended consequence. Fulfilling the recommendations of Malherbe and Loram, the Corporation embarked on the Second Carnegie Inquiry into Poverty and Development in Southern Africa. As Francis Wilson, co-principal investigator of that study, has commented:

Politically, the Carnegie Commission [the first one] was incredibly important, because if we could have a second Carnegie commission or inquiry, that immediately gave it political coverage, because nobody in Afrikaan-speaking South Africa could be anti–Carnegie Inquiry into Poverty. It had been too important in the Afrikaner drive against poverty, in both good and bad aspects, but it had a resonance that Carnegie meant battle against poverty. And so it had very good political vibes for the white establishment.[90]

The Second Carnegie Investigation on Poverty in Southern Africa is discussed more fully in chapters 6 and 7.[91]

Both Loram and Malherbe pressed the Corporation to back the new South African Institute of Race Relations, where Loram served on the board. The Institute was created in 1929 to address the nonpolitical aspects of race relations, and the Corporation supported its research into the "native problem."[92] The Phelps Stokes Fund provided support as well.[93] The support kept the Institute solvent when few other resources were forthcoming; from 1929 to 1940, the Corporation provided a total of nearly $40,000, exceeding the $30,500 for the Poor White Study.[94] Additional grants included research into native problems and related nonpolitical activities. Support for the Lovedale Press at the Lovedale Institute strengthened this missionary undertaking dedicated to providing access to books for Africans, including the printing of books in local languages. The modest amount of $10,000 enabled the African population for the first time to have access to the works of a wide variety of African authors.[95]

The library program in South Africa as shaped by specific reports from two expert librarians, S. A. Pitt from Scotland and Milton Ferguson from the United States, also reinforced the practice of segregated programmatic activities. The library consultants recommended establishing "a free public library system serving all communities in South Africa ... school library service" including "population groups other than whites on a segregated basis."[96] The Library Service Committee agreed to hire an African to be in charge, Herbert Isaac Dhlomo, a poet, playwright, and author. Dhlomo was outspoken against the discriminatory policies, and he dedicated extensive time, effort, and imagination to public outreach to ensure the success of the service.[97]

In several colonies, the Corporation supported the technical and vocational Jeanes education initiatives promoted by the Phelps Stokes Fund and approved by the colonial authorities. Through modest grants, the Corporation supported public libraries and initiated relationships with some of the colleges, including Achimota College in Ghana, which in the 1950s became the core of the University of Ghana, a later partner of the Corporation. A major survey of conditions throughout Central and Southern Africa complemented the Poor White Study and the pan-Africa survey (discussed later).

Although the total funds for the Africa program represented only 0.84 percent of that spent for the main endowment fund for the United States and only a modest 7.5 percent of the total spent in the British dominions and colonies, these grants resulted in the development of a close working relationship with the colonial offices. That relationship put the Corporation in good standing for the postwar era as colonies were becoming independent and Africa was moving onstage in the Cold War era. At the same time, South Africa was becoming increasingly rigid in enforcing apartheid against the nonwhite population and making it more inappropriate and uncomfortable for the Corporation to be working directly in support of institutions in the country. Corporation grant-making to institutions in South Africa ended in the mid-1950s; travel grants continued until 1968. It was only in 1975 and 1976 that the Corporation began to consider reinstituting activities in South Africa.[98]

RACE RELATIONS FROM THE DOMINIONS AND COLONIES TO HOME

CHARLES T. LORAM, one of the Corporation's key men in South Africa, took an appointment at Yale University in 1931. There he introduced the question of race explicitly into the academic curriculum. Loram, who advocated for the Poor White Commission and then for a comparable study of the black population, had immersed himself in the study of native education and the conditions surrounding black poverty under colonial rule. He persuaded the Corporation to fund a new program at Yale on the study of racism and race relations, called the Education of Primitive Peoples Program, through its grants-in-aid program; this decade-long initiative has not yet attracted as much scholarly attention as the Poor White Commission. Based in Yale's Department of Race Relations—where Loram was chair, director of graduate studies, and the Sterling Professor of Education—the program had several objectives: "The work offered in the field of race relations has been set up for students interested in the effects of the contact of Western civilization on other civilizations and cultures and the race problems resulting therefrom. In particular, it is designed to provide opportunities for study and research for those who are engaged in work as officials, educators, and missionaries among non-Western peoples."[99] The department attracted students from all over Africa and beyond, including India and Hawaii. Students were black, Asian, white, Hindu, Muslim, Christian, and Jewish.

Faculty from a wide range of departments participated. In an early example of an interdisciplinary academic program, students could take courses in all the participating departments, which included anthropology, sociology, law, and education; the Divinity School was involved as well. Loram organized meetings in the field, such as a lengthy summer conference on education and race relations held at the University of North Carolina in 1936. He organized field trips during the school year and over the summer with the help of the US Department of Education and the US Bureau of Indian Affairs.[100] Loram kept track and reported to the Corporation on what happened to the graduates once they left. In a 1938 report to the Corporation, he noted that two graduates became college presidents; thirteen, professors; three, high school principals or assistants; eleven, government servants; one, a businessman; and five, missionaries who transferred to other departments. No one was unemployed. Up to 1938, the Department of Race Relations had awarded thirteen master's degrees and six PhDs. In reviewing the program in 1937, Keppel noted for the Executive Committee that $40,500 had been expended between April 1932 and January 1937, covering thirty-five allocations. "This is probably the largest sum of money spent by the Corporation for grants-in-aid in one field at a single university."[101]

The program was carried on even after Loram's death in 1940. Yale sent the Corporation the report from the final field trip Loram had organized, to the Negro schools in the South and the Indian reservations of the Southwest.[102] Prepared by Esther Strong, one of the students (and also a Brookings fellow), the report underlines the distinctive nature of the program:

To be a member of the Seminar on Race Relations at Yale University, where individuals of a variety of types of cultural training and experience come together to study and discuss the problem of dominant interest to all of us, the problem of culture contact and culture change, is a great privilege.… We went, *as a group*, to visit those areas of the country where day by day the American people are hammering out their policies of racial adjustment.[103]

Loram made sure they experienced a wide variety of race issues: throughout the South and Southwest, from Hampton to Tuskegee, from Howard University in Washington, DC, to Atlanta University in Atlanta and Xavier University and Dillard University in New Orleans, from El Paso to an Apache reservation in Tucson and a Navajo reservation in Los Angeles. The trip ended in Washington with a visit to the Bureau of Indian Affairs; Strong concluded that the trip enabled the travelers "to gain perspective in the consideration of a problem integral to the corporate life of the American people, the race problem, which will probably not be solved for another two hundred and fifty years."[104]

The program further sensitized Keppel and the Corporation to the conditions confronting American blacks in the South: the correspondence with Loram, the students he met, the papers and dissertations he read, and the conferences Loram organized reinforced the vital importance of understanding this societal fault line in the United States. Loram's activities contributed to Keppel's abiding commitment to Gunnar Myrdal's study of race relations in the United States and his insistence that Myrdal leave the library and go to the field to observe firsthand the conditions confronting American blacks in the United States.[105]

THE OTHER SIDE OF THE GLOBE

THE ENGLISH-SPEAKING DEMOCRACIES bordering the other side of the Pacific Ocean had attracted the attention of the American foundations in the 1920s. In 1925 the Rockefeller Foundation sent a team to explore opportunities for grant-making in Australia and New Zealand, as well as Hawaii.[106] Two of the team members, Edwin Embree, the former corporate secretary of the Rockefeller Foundation, and Dr. Clark Wissler of the American Museum of Natural History agreed to share the report and recommendations with the Corporation on their return. The Rockefeller Commission suggested opportunities in the fields of education, arts, and libraries, all familiar areas from Corporation grant-making in the United States and Canada.

As Keppel told the trustees, "Through the courtesy of the members of the Rockefeller Foundation Commission to Australia and New Zealand, the Corporation has been well informed as to opportunities for useful action in that part of the world."[107] The Rockefeller Foundation staff also introduced Keppel to Australians and New Zealanders visiting the United States with foundation support. Although the Rockefeller Foundation and Carnegie Corporation often collaborated in grant-making throughout the 1920s and 1930s, this interchange illustrates a rare time when their shared interests led one of the institutions to directly inform the grant-making of the other.

With the information gleaned from the Rockefeller scouts, the trustees agreed that the Antipodes merited exploratory visits. In 1928, James Russell, former dean of Teachers College at Columbia University, visited Australia, New Zealand, and, briefly, South Africa on behalf of the Corporation. His report led to activities that shaped not only the Corporation's grant-making but ultimately the educational systems in Australia and New Zealand. Throughout the 1930s, other visitors sent by the Corporation addressed issues related to adult education, library service, museums, and the arts—the arts being particularly pertinent to the range of themes suggested in the Rockefeller report.[108] In a complementary fashion, the Rockefeller Foundation continued its grant-making around issues of anthropology to enlarge that field, in both Australia and New Zealand.

All Corporation visitors to Australia and New Zealand provided comparable analyses of the differences across these two dominions. In his 1935 trip report, Keppel commented on the following commonalities: pioneer conditions, homogeneous populations, isolation from the rest of the English-speaking world and from each other, and dependence on commodity products for their prosperity. He noted that both countries shared characteristics highly relevant to what the Corporation was trying to promote in the region: "They are proud of being outdoor folk and often offer their opportunities for sport and their love of out-of-door recreation as an explanation of the limited circulation of books."[109] Moreover, he and other visitors pointed to the centralized public education systems in the two countries: "In New Zealand the system is dominion-wide, in Australia it is under the control of the separate states. With a lack of local tax revenue, there is a corresponding lack of local responsibility, not only for formal education but for other cultural agencies, as libraries and museums."[110] These attributes, along with the more limited effects of higher education, determined the nature of the Corporation's programs in both Australia and New Zealand.

In his extensive travels around Australia and New Zealand, Russell met the key educational and political leaders as well as local individuals outside of education. He homed in on the conditions of the schools and universities, the role of the state ministries, and the high quality of the individuals he met. The combination of talented individuals and opportunities to strengthen educational institutions had already been established as a basis for Corporation grant-making in Canada and the United States, so it is not surprising that such findings would inform Corporation initiatives in Australia and New Zealand. In his unpublished trip report, Russell suggested that the US relationship with these countries bordering the Pacific was as important as its relationship with the countries bordering the Atlantic.[111]

James Russell recommended a variety of actions compatible with the Corporation's programs and goals to improve local conditions. The following discussion illustrates a few of the differences and commonalties of the programs in Australia and New Zealand that he and other Corporation key men recommended in education research, adult education, libraries, and museums, with a few forays into international affairs and social science research. A small note follows, describing Corporation outreach across the Pacific in areas not covered by the charter.

Australia

In Australia, Russell spent considerable time with three local key men: H. T. Lovell, a professor of psychology at the University of Sydney; A. Mackie, a professor of education at the University of Sydney and the principal of Sydney Teachers College; and most importantly, Frank Tate, director of education in the state of Victoria.[112] Russell encouraged Tate and his colleagues to prepare proposals for the Corporation as soon as possible, and they listened. As Australian historian of education W. F. Connell commented in his analysis of the Russell trip, Russell emphasized to his Australian hosts that the Corporation had learned from their work elsewhere, "that models introduced from other countries were seldom a success. It was better to use them as suggestions and stimuli to planning that would be undertaken by local interested people who with appropriate support might develop, for their own felt needs, vital institutions and practices of their own creation."[113] Following a local model in Australia, the Council for Scientific and Industrial Research, which had a strong but small executive committee, the local organizing group began to develop the request to the Corporation to fund a major center devoted to educational research. Tate championed such a research institute. It would give Australian educators the wherewithal to examine in more detail "the fundamental conditions determining the best lines of educational advance."[114] Frank Tate had greatly impressed Keppel and Russell, "with his quick grasp of ideas, his ability to formulate policy and ... make decisions, and the confidence which his fellow directors of education placed in him."[115]

With buy-in from all the state educators, the proposal to establish the Australian Council for Educational Research was approved at the October 15, 1929, meeting of the Corporation's Board of Trustees at the level of $250,000 over ten years. In 1930 a second request was received and approved to cover the support of the executive director. After selecting Kenneth Cunningham, who held a doctorate from Teachers College, for this position, Tate and his colleagues organized a conference of educators, held in Melbourne, Australia, on February 10 and 11, 1930, to launch the Council.[116] As Russell had urged, "In all its negotiations the executive kept firmly in mind that the new institution was an Australian body, planned by Australian educators in the interest of education ... of the whole Australian community."[117]

Together, Cunningham, Tate, Lovell, and Mackie embarked on the scientific study of education, providing research findings to Australian educators for their use in supporting progressive education. Serving at the helm of the Australian Council for Educational Research from 1930 to 1954, Cunningham remained committed to scientific accuracy in the course of developing sound educational research and testing programs, improving the teaching position, and instituting progressive actions in the schools.[118]

The travel grants suggested by Russell were also managed by the Council. These grants exposed Australian researchers not only to research in the United States but also, just as importantly, to other work going on in the Pacific Rim region, based on recommendations from Russell. The Council's initiatives marked the beginning of international studies in Australia that included enabling Australians to learn more about their own region, as discussed later.[119]

A pivotal event for Australian and New Zealand education was a Corporation-sponsored, two-month-long meeting that brought together people from all over the Commonwealth to examine educational developments across Australia and then New Zealand. The conference, from August 4 to September 18, 1937, was modeled after a meeting of the New Educational Fellowship, which was founded in 1921 by educator and theosophist Beatrice Ensor and focused on highly progressive educational experiences.[120] Nearly eight thousand educators from Europe, Japan, the United States, and Canada attended; one lecture drew over ten thousand people. The idea for holding the conference in Australia and New Zealand came from Cunningham's attendance at the New Educational Fellowship conference in 1934 in South Africa, the first time it had been held outside Europe. Cunningham had met Ernst Malherbe, one of the Corporation's key men in South Africa, and seen firsthand the positive effect of such a conference. The discussions at the 1937 conference focused on overhauling the educational systems in Australia and New Zealand to better relate curriculum "to the needs and conditions of modern life," promoting "education for citizenship that would produce persons with a highly developed sense of democratic, social, and political responsibility."[121]

It was an unqualified success. The conference put the Australian Council for Educational Research on the global map and inspired new thinking in education. Although the war came too soon after the conference for immediate changes to be made, the greatest effect of the conference was initiating a change in the climate of Australian education. After the war, the conference discussions were revisited and would seriously influence educational thinking.

Critical goals in the Corporation's effort to professionalize the field of librarianship and enhance university libraries and public libraries in Australia included educating librarians and building the capacity of libraries to serve as full, functioning arms of universities. The first visitor, Lotus Coffman, the president of the University of Minnesota, after reviewing the weaknesses in Australian libraries in 1931, recommended taking a cautious approach until a more detailed survey could be done. In the summer of 1934, Ralph Munn, chief librarian of the Carnegie Library of Pittsburgh, and Ernest Pitt, a leader among Australian librarians who was based at the Melbourne Public Library, surveyed library conditions across the country.[122] The result of the trip was "the first thorough appraisal of Australian libraries by an outside expert, and the consequences were remarkable. Librarian experts in Australia commonly divide the history of Australian libraries into the eras 'BM and PM—Before Munn and Post Munn,' so great was the influence."[123] Key people in Australia had fully vetted the highly critical 1935 Munn-Pitt Report ("Australian Libraries: A Survey of Conditions and Suggestions for Their Improvement") before its publication; because of a carefully planned dissemination campaign, the response to the penetrating criticisms was overwhelmingly enthusiastic.[124] In the first phase, the library system was reorganized, new buildings were planned, and a free borrowing service was introduced (implemented following World War II).

The Munn-Pitt Report became legendary in Australia, and authors of even recent articles remember it as a key document in Australian history: "Sir Grenfell Price, at the opening of the building of the National Library of Australia in 1968, said the Munn-Pitt survey led to a 'revolution in Australian libraries.'... Indeed, it is undoubtedly true that no library report before or after in the history of Australia has made such an impression."[125]

Following a $25,000 grant in 1937 through the Australian Council for Educational Research to respond to the report, the Corporation provided modest support for university libraries. As Michael Birkner points out, there was much less success in professionalizing Australian university libraries:

Although the Corporation's philanthropic enterprise at the university level yielded mixed results at best, it was not inconsequential. It provided a blueprint for future university library development in Australia. In one instance, at the University of Melbourne, it inspired a vice chancellor to articulate a vision of a library future that comported with the best practices in Great Britain and the United States. In another, at the University of Adelaide, it showed how, with philanthropic intervention, university library modernization could be expedited with salutary results.[126]

Promoting higher education research and strengthening university and public library systems were not the only educational institutional initiatives of the Corporation in Australia, even if they were the most extensive ones. Lotus Coffman, who had also examined the adult education system in the early 1930s, recommended that in Australia and New Zealand the extension programs go through the universities. Efforts at promoting adult education through a university-based system were modeled on the Workers Extension Association, which was started in the United Kingdom in 1903 and provided lectures and other extension activities designed for the urban "proletariat" or working man. From July to December 1932, one of the leading adult educators in the United Kingdom, C. O. G. Douie, surveyed potential situations in Australia and New Zealand for building on the Workers Education Association approach. In Australia, these efforts had mixed success.[127] The efforts in New Zealand yielded more positive results, as described later.

Museum and art activities, resulting from the 1932 visit of Sir Henry Miers and S. F. Markham, were also extensively pursued.[128] Perhaps the most significant grant led to the major four-year exhibition, starting in 1941, of Australian art in the United States and Canada. It was the first time that aboriginal art was shown in North America, and it generated widespread interest.[129]

A small but significant set of grants to the Australian Institute of International Affairs (for library development, a major Commonwealth conference, and travel grants) and to the Australian Institute of Political Science (primarily for attendance at conferences and for bringing people to the Institute's summer school as well as for travel grants) is considered by two analysts, James Cotton and Michael White, to be of extraordinary importance in introducing Australian scholars to the broader field of Pacific affairs and the development of Asian-Pacific studies.[130] The travel grants enabled Australian scholars to connect with other Pacific-region scholars, most importantly through participation in the Hangchow Conference of the Institute of Pacific Relations. White concluded that one value of the travel grants was that they built the basis for furthering American-Australian relations.

W. F. Connell in 1980 and Michael White in 1996 and 1997 paved the way for a thoroughgoing examination of the Corporation's grant-making in Australia that took place in February 2010, organized by the Academy of the Social Sciences in Australia.[131] White pointed to tough issues, such as the value placed on educational testing by the Corporation and its Australian key men.[132] But he also mentioned that the surveys by local and overseas experts—and particularly the New Educational Fellowship conference in 1937—brought much more radically progressive perspectives to Australia. These, too, helped to shape the research and the educational culture.[133] White commented that while the grants may have been modest, "their impact on Australian education was impressive. A whole generation of educational, library, and adult education leaders was given rare insights into overseas developments at a time when the nation was reeling from the depression. Institutions involved, which are the backbone of cultural formation, received a much needed injection of new ideas that eventually percolated to the surface of the nation's cultural life." White concluded: "The Carnegie Corporation activities, whatever else they might represent, stand out as perhaps the most remarkable phenomenon in Australian education between the two world wars."[134]

At the 2010 meeting, scholars questioned the positive tone of White's conclusions and the role of the Corporation and, in certain fields, the Rockefeller Foundation in shaping Australian culture. As discussed in the meeting papers, their impact was not confined to the introduction of American educational practices, including testing, but also was felt in the promotion of different academic fields, such as anthropology, international affairs, and public health, as well as the provision of travel grants. These impacts resonate, as noted by the conference conveners, in the current expansion of philanthropy in public culture and the increasingly important role of transnational academic networks.[135]

A total of approximately $1,026,795, according to Keppel, went to support the universities, libraries, and the arts, as well as a smattering of other institutions and activities in Australia. Most of the $340,000 in university grants in Australia went to six universities for library development, adult education activities, various faculty appointments, and music and art teaching. A total of $704,000 supported libraries, museums, and research-related institutions. The bulk of this support, $482,000, went to the national institution that was the major outcome of the Russell visit: the Australian Council for Educational Research. Three other programs and efforts received fairly modest support: $20,000 went to the Australian Institute of International Affairs, $35,000 to the Australian National Research Council, and $25,000 to Australian library development.[136]

New Zealand

Russell's trip to New Zealand covered comparable ground, but it took longer to establish comparable activities in education research. The adult education and public library initiatives took off more rapidly.

Kenneth Cunningham, the director of the Australian Council for Educational Research, and Frank Tate, the chairman, thought it might be a good idea to have a sister institution in New Zealand and suggested that idea to Corporation visitor Lotus Coffman when he was on a tour similar to Russell's. Keppel considered it an essential prerequisite for establishing a new institution in New Zealand that the idea come from New Zealanders themselves. Nonetheless, when Coffman was in New Zealand, he explored the idea with the governor-general and the minister of education. They turned the proposal down. Some people in New Zealand, however, were interested in the idea, namely, James Hight, rector of Canterbury University College, Thomas Hunter, principal of Victoria University College, and D. M. Rae, principal of Auckland Training College. The three of them went to the United States to discuss educational developments in New Zealand, including this idea, with Keppel, Coffman, and James Russell. In a meeting with Coffman and Russell, the latter reinforced the concern of the Corporation that the New Zealand Council for Educational Research should be independent of the Australian Council and not under the sway of the New Zealand government. Based on the evidence of "a real and serious demand for the Institute in New Zealand," Keppel recommended approval of the request received on October 19, 1933.[137] The trustees agreed to provide an annual sum of $14,000 over five years for the research part of the Council and $3,500 for general expenses per year.[138] The grant was renewed for another five years at the same level. At the young age of thirty-two, C. E. Beeby, considered an outstanding scholar and educator, was appointed the executive director.[139]

As Beeby described it, the New Zealand Council started off differently from the Australian Council and then did different work. Possibly because it was smaller and the situation in the country required something different, the Council did not get involved in detailed research. Essentially it conducted surveys of the educational system and made recommendations as an adviser to the government.[140] The Council's recommendations changed the government's policy and agenda concerning secondary schools, and it conducted the first sociological studies on education and the history of education in New Zealand. The New Zealand Council also organized the 1937 New Educational Fellowship conference, which affected New Zealand as dramatically as it did Australia.

As Beeby recalled, "This gang of people arrived, some of them conservatives, some of them radicals, an astonishing mixture! And New Zealand simply hadn't had anything like this before. Apart from the few the Corporation had sent, it hadn't seen many educators of any kind from overseas for a very long time."[141] As a consequence, the government realized the importance of education and educational research and started to pay attention to the work of the New Zealand Council. In his assessment, Beeby concluded, "there can be little doubt that the Corporation had a very considerable effect on New Zealand's educational policy."[142]

As he had done in Australia, librarian Ralph Munn visited New Zealand to examine library conditions. He was joined by John Barr, a librarian from the University of Auckland. Their recommendations led to the establishment of "an informal advisory group to report on library problems and development."[143] Their recommendations then resulted in Corporation support for the New Zealand Library Association and the libraries of the different colleges of the University of New Zealand, including its adult education libraries. Most of the art and teaching material went to the universities and training colleges, although there were also travel grants for New Zealand artists.

Grants of $15,000 each went to college libraries in Auckland, Christchurch, and Wellington to develop book purchasing programs, and another grant of more than $100,000 went to support a traveling library and home-science project to provide practical education and access to knowledge in rural populations in the South Island of New Zealand.[144] The focus on bookmobiles with book boxes—efforts linked with adult education—was seen to be the only way to reach rural peoples and have a significant impact in those settings. Separately, Ann G. Strong, an American educator based in New Zealand, developed a program of traveling home economics programs that provided books and materials as well as tutors to teach the courses.[145] This program later became the Association for Country Education, a modification of the Workers Education Association.

In New Zealand between 1928 and 1942, in contrast with Australia, a much smaller proportion of the total grant of $669,020 as noted by Keppel—$184,000—went to universities, colleges, and schools, with most of it going to the University of New Zealand at Auckland, Canterbury, Otago, and Victoria. Much of this work involved extension and outreach in local communities as well as library development. Other institutions and programs that received support included the New Zealand Library Association ($29,700), the Traveling Librarian and Home Science Project ($102,500), the New Zealand Council for Educational Research ($177,000), and the New Zealand Museum program ($50,000).[146]

The Pacific Region

Keppel visited not only the southern British dominions of Australia and New Zealand but, through the Institute of Pacific Relations meetings, Japan and China as well. As a result of participating in these meetings, he developed respect and admiration for Asia. The Laura Spelman Rockefeller Memorial had provided support for the Institute after its founding in 1925 "as a private nonpartisan forum for the promotion of mutual understanding amongst nations of the Pacific rim through discussion, research, and education."[147] There were national councils in all the countries around the region, and the secretariat was based in Hawaii and New York. The Corporation helped fund its American council.[148]

After participating in an Institute meeting in Kyoto, Keppel underlined the importance of such meetings, especially when the threat of war in the future was an underlying concern at the meetings:

> For all of us the Kyoto conference had much to teach about the new world in which we are living today. It is a peace loving world, but a world which doesn't believe that peace can be maintained by preaching about the evils of war. It is a world which is beginning to realize that wars don't happen from spontaneous combustion—wars start from little hot points, and if we really understood what our neighbors were thinking about and particularly what they were feeling, these hot points could be recognized and attended to before they develop high temperatures and tension, and finally cause a state of national hysteria when it's too late to do anything but fight. And I honestly think the conference did contribute to an all round understanding of what our neighbors are thinking and feeling.[149]

The Corporation continued to provide modest support for the Institute of Pacific Relations and participate in its meetings until it was closed in the Second Red Scare of the late 1940s and early 1950s, also known as the McCarthy era.

SMOOTHING THE WAY FORWARD IN THE COMMONWEALTH: THE LONDON CONFERENCES

AS CARNEGIE CORPORATION began to extend its grant-making outward from North America to the far reaches of the British Empire, trustee Russell Leffingwell suggested that the Corporation consider consulting not only the British Colonial Office but also experts in London who worked on or in the British colonies and dominions.[150] For many years the Rockefeller Foundation had been working closely with the Royal Institute of International Affairs (Chatham House), the meeting place for politicians, scholars, practitioners, and policymakers that was the sister organization to the US-based Council on Foreign Relations (CFR).[151] Since the trustees who traveled across the Atlantic were familiar with Chatham House meetings, it was the logical choice of venue for Corporation discussions.

Historian Richard Glotzer emphasized Keppel's ability to make astute connections across distinctive ideas and individuals, along with his "unique insight into the complex relationship between the growing international stature of the United States and the preeminence of Great Britain as a world power. He understood the Anglo-American relationship was cultural, economic and strategic."[152] Keppel realized that working with key advisers in London would not only facilitate the Corporation's entrée throughout the British Empire but would also bolster the program's credibility with Corporation trustees. J. H. Oldham, the head of the International Missionary Council and the International Institute of African Languages and Culture, and Dr. Iverson Macadam, secretary of the Royal Institute of International Affairs, worked closely with Keppel to establish the London conferences, which would convene a committee of advisers every other year from 1931 to 1939. They not only asked colonial authorities to serve as advisers but also sought out intellectuals, scientists, and scholars with experience in the different parts of the Empire.

The Colonial Office was represented by Hanns Visscher, secretary of the Advisory Committee on Native Education, and Sir William G. A. Ormsby-Gore, undersecretary of state for the colonies; political leaders among the advisers included Lord Lothian (Philip Henry Kerr) and former prime minister Stanley Baldwin. The nongovernmental luminaries covered a very broad swath, ranging from scholars such as the historian Arnold Toynbee, the economist William Beveridge, and the anthropologist Bronislaw Malinowski to labor union leaders such as Ernst Bevans.

These conferences not only contributed to regular external critical reviews of the Corporation's efforts but also led to suggestions about enlarging the scope to include Commonwealth-wide initiatives, work in the Caribbean, and some additional studies, including the pivotal Africa Survey by Lord Malcolm Hailey (discussed later). One factor contributing to the success of these meetings and the advisory committee process was the role of the Carnegie United Kingdom Trust in establishing the credibility of Carnegie Corporation. Some of the success of the conferences may have been attributable to their timing during the Depression: the Corporation on occasion picked up the costs of some programs that could not be maintained or new initiatives that could not be funded out of the colonial resources, especially those related to agricultural research and Empire-wide activities.[153] Mainly, however, Keppel and the Corporation trustee who accompanied him to each conference always made it clear that they listened carefully and acted on the comments and suggestions arising out of the meeting, reinforcing the confidence of the British participants, who under other circumstances might have been highly skeptical of American initiatives. On the other side of the Atlantic, the Corporation's Board of Trustees frequently expressed their satisfaction with the results of the meetings.

One enduring grantee resulted from these meetings, the Association of Universities of the British Commonwealth, then called the University Bureaus of the British Empire. Corporation support of $40,000 enabled vice chancellors from the dominions to meet with each other and with their counterparts in Britain to discuss shared problems and ideas. The University of London also received, among other grants, $139,000 for the work of the Institute of Education in providing training and grants-in-aid for overseas students. Sir Fred Clarke, the Institute's head, served as a major adviser for the work in Africa for the Corporation.[154]

The most important outcome may have been the suggestion made at the 1933 conference to provide support for the work of Lord Malcolm Hailey. He had been a diplomat in the British Colonial Service in India and on his return to London was asked to conduct the first full survey of conditions in Africa. Funded by the Corporation at the level of $115,000, the "Study of Equatorial and Southern Africa" took over four years to complete.[155] The final report, Keppel emphasized, would be of great value to students and diplomats going to Africa. He noted in the 1939 Annual Report its publication as follows: "Special mention must be made of the appearance of An African Survey, the outcome of an epoch-making study by Lord Hailey with which the Corporation is most proud to be connected."[156] As important as the report was for that era, it also had staying power.

Historian Andrew Roberts in 1990 reinforced Keppel's perspective: "Hailey's African Survey presented an enlightened and cautiously reformist view of the continent. It was the first British work to give serious attention to the African empires of other European powers, which Hailey himself visited during a tour of Africa in 1935. He confronted many of the implications of economic change and implicitly at least offered a critique of indirect rule."[157] Recently historian Rohland Schuknecht has noted that the survey crystallized the value of economic development assistance for Africa: "One of the most influential works of the decade was Lord Hailey's African survey (1938) which had been initiated by the International African Institute and whose author would become a major voice for political and economic reform in the colonial office in the 1940s."[158] Most recently, Helen Tilley has provided extensive detail on the planning and impact of the survey, agreeing with Lord Lothian that the survey was "an unparalleled undertaking: the entire continent became the object of transdisciplinary study."[159]

In his 1942 exit memo to the new Corporation president Walter A. Jessup, Keppel reinforced the positive attributes of the London conferences and their important role in the entire British dominions and colonies program: "The contacts with the Colonial Office put the Corporation into direct touch with the permanent offices of the Department and through them with opportunities in isolated colonies of the Empire." However, Keppel also acknowledged the occasional downside, saying, "I admit that enthusiastic Colonial Office functionaries have occasionally pulled our leg, particularly as to archaeological enterprises, but in general the results have been satisfactory."[160] As he said to the conferees at their final meeting in 1939, when World War II seemed inevitable, "There was no place where the Trustees could get better help than here in London."[161]

These meetings proved to be of considerable value in establishing the Corporation as the main interlocutor between the British and Americans in Africa following decolonization and independence. No other American entity had established such close working relationships with the British on the situation in the African colonies, and this relationship would facilitate the Corporation's continued engagement with the region after World War II.

Moving Closer to Home: The Caribbean Colonies

Despite the proximity of the Caribbean, it was the last of the major British Empire regions to be considered for Corporation grant-making during Keppel's administration. Earlier support there had gone to libraries and church organs; a grant in 1927 of $5,000 provided for some library equipment at the Imperial College of Tropical Agriculture in Trinidad. The London conference advisers' interest in the region led them to suggest investing in programs related to agriculture, especially given some of the economic constraints resulting from the Depression. Despite the adverse economic situation in the United States and the caution being expressed by the trustees about opening up new areas of grant-making, Keppel convinced the board that there were special opportunities in the Caribbean. They agreed to his proposal that he visit all the islands, including the Virgin Islands and Puerto Rico.

Essentially, he found that there was "a real opportunity to develop closer relations between the different scientific agencies in the Caribbean area," especially those engaged in agricultural research, and he identified Puerto Rico as a good center. Keppel saw the potential for collaboration around the overlapping activities in the region, even as he recognized that there would be difficulties. He was optimistic, however, commenting that even with "the difficulties of establishing a spirit of cooperation, in view of the problems of race, language, and jurisdiction.... I feel that the situation may offer a real opportunity to the Corporation."[162]

In 1933, after discussions with the trustees and the London group, the Corporation asked Ernst Savage of the Edinburgh Public Library to investigate conditions in the British West Indies, Bermuda, Bahamas, British Guiana, British Honduras, the Virgin Islands, and Puerto Rico. His report led to a book purchase program for almost all the libraries in the region; it was the basis upon which the Corporation made a series of small grants totaling some $30,000 for the development of public libraries in the colonies there. In 1940 a $70,000 grant helped to establish the Eastern Caribbean Regional Library in Trinidad, which represented regional cooperative institution-building of the kind Keppel had envisioned in 1932. The Trinidad library system had developed an innovative way of training and reaching inaccessible areas that would become the model for the regional library's training programs; even years later, in 1964, an analysis by scholar Alma Jordan concluded that the Trinidad library system was a leader in regional collaboration.[163]

Following the suggestion of George Vincent, former president of the Rockefeller Foundation, the Corporation continued to back the Imperial College of Tropical Agriculture in Trinidad from 1932 to 1936, for more than $140,000 in total. Elsewhere in the Caribbean, Keppel was impressed with the potential for wealth in British Guiana yet recognized the oppressive poverty, describing it as "one of the poorest" colonies in the Empire.[164] Over the period 1932 to 1935, the Corporation subsequently approved a total of about $74,000 for educational and scientific development, museum development, and a women's trade center—which was one of the few overseas grants in this era to focus on the condition of women.[165]

One small example shows the continuing validity of Henry Pritchett's perspective on the benefits of perpetuity. That perspective enables the assessment, as appropriate, of the impact of a foundation's grant-making across generations, rather than in the short term. This example also shows the results from very modest grants and from Corporation efforts to make connections across the Empire, in this case connecting an able researcher from one region with a problem in need of analysis in another.

In 1935, through the grants-in-aid for the Department of Race Relations at Yale University, the Corporation provided support of $865 for William M. Macmillan, a former professor (and founder of the history department) at the University of the Witwatersrand, South Africa, now based in Britain, to study the conditions of the black and disadvantaged members of the Jamaican population.[166] Macmillan was appalled by the education provided to the population and recommended a fellowship program to enhance the education of the most promising high school students. Following riots in subsequent years, the British colonial government in Jamaica instituted the fellowship program that had been recommended by Macmillan. A bright but impoverished young woman won a fellowship, was able to go to a better school in Jamaica, and eventually earned another fellowship to study in England, where she met her husband. After they were married, they moved to Canada and gave birth to Malcolm Gladwell, the best-selling social trends author of the early twenty-first century.[167]

BUILDING PEACE AND INTERNATIONAL
UNDERSTANDING THROUGH NEW APPROACHES TO
EDUCATING AMERICANS AND
CONDUCTING POLICY RESEARCH

DURING THE 1920S AND 1930S, the Corporation dedicated significant resources to educating Americans about international affairs through a combination of institutional grants, specific research projects, travel grants, and publications. As part of the effort to enhance Americans' understanding of the world and the policy options facing the United States in its foreign activities, the Corporation emphasized the importance of education, particularly in foreign languages, and the participation of Americans in international institutions and international conferences. Rather than invest in university-based international education to achieve the aim of educating and involving Americans in international activities, the Corporation worked, under the rubric of adult education, through leading nongovernmental and freestanding scholarly institutions.[168] Travel grants and grants-in-aid covered the cost of sending Americans abroad, primarily to the colonies and dominions but occasionally to international conferences and meetings in Asia and Europe (including the United Kingdom).[169]

Two sets of grants best reflected the thrust of these activities. One set of grants to the Council on Foreign Relations aimed to build up not only its research and publications program but also its effort to educate Americans throughout the country.[170] The other set was to the Institute for Advanced Study to support the innovative work of Edward Mead Earle and his colleagues as they developed new interdisciplinary approaches for the field of international and national security studies.[171] (A third set of activities, loosely grouped together as the National Emergency Program, helped sustain a number of the grantees immediately before, during, and, briefly, after the war years.)

The Council on Foreign Relations was established in 1921 to organize meetings and study groups that brought together leading scholars, politicians, policymakers, and businessmen to participate in intense discussion and examination of the major foreign policy issues of the day.[172] The meetings took place primarily in New York and Washington, DC. With the aim of providing opportunities for Americans from different perspectives to be exposed to new thinking and global thinking on foreign affairs, the Corporation worked with Walter Mallory, then executive director of the Council, to establish regional committees around the United States. Corporation trustees saw the Council as the main institution for "development of interest and knowledge in the field of foreign relations" and agreed to increase support for research, meetings, and publications by the Council in order to include the regional committees. On January 20, 1938, the trustees approved a separate grant for the committees as a "continuation of the research, study group, and publication program of the Council; extension of its work to include experiments in cities other than New York." Consequently, between 1921 and 1941, the Corporation provided $284,430 in support of the wide range of Council activities, of which $105,430 went primarily to support the work of the regional committees.[173] An independent study of the Council conducted by British social scientist Inderjeet Parmar confirmed the expected effect of the committees in educating a wide range of Americans at a certain level about the complex issues in foreign affairs. He also revealed a somewhat surprising outcome: a national perspective began to permeate the work of the Council as a consequence of the national committees.[174]

In addition to educating adults about foreign affairs, the Corporation recognized during the immediate prewar years that with Europe in a state of war, its work might need to change. Instead of changing the Corporation's basic thrust, particularly in the program for the British dominions and colonies, Keppel suggested to the trustees that the Corporation focus more explicitly on "questions of peace and war." When Lord Lothian, the British ambassador to the United States, suggested that there was a need for studies on these questions and on the changing balance of power, Keppel responded by asking trustee Russell Leffingwell to organize a private meeting for the trustees at his house in October 1939.[175]

The wide-ranging discussion at this meeting set in motion a concern about how best to respond to what the trustees called the national emergency.[176] At the October 4, 1940, board meeting, trustee Elihu Root Jr. submitted a memorandum that organized such a response. Using the memorandum as a guide, the Corporation's main efforts in response to the national emergency were activities that would reinforce or extend the impact of its grant-making, including a special effort to ensure a more fully informed American worldview about the situation.[177] As war preparations began in earnest, there was increasing concern about the foreign students stranded in the United States and the Americans stranded abroad, as well as about the morale of soldiers in their training programs. From 1940 to 1944, through its National Emergency Program, the Corporation provided about $1,700,000 in support of thirty-three organizations for ninety-seven projects.[178] All grants were aimed at reinforcing the war effort at home and enabling Carnegie grantee institutions to remain viable.

In addition to its efforts through the Council on Foreign Relations and the National Emergency Program as World War II commenced, the Corporation provided support for Edward Mead Earle in his efforts to define a new theoretical and analytical framework for the study of international security. This grant, though neither explicitly stated as such nor mentioned at the private trustee gathering, seemed to come closest to meeting Lord Lothian's 1939 suggestion that studies of peace and war and the balance of power be initiated.[179] Earle was convinced that the proper study of international security required bringing a wide range of disciplines— economics, psychology, sociology, anthropology—together with the more traditional ones of history, law, and political science. New research by historian David Ekbladh reveals that this was the beginning of the field of international security studies in the United States, which grew out of Earle's insistent efforts and the Corporation's increasingly acute awareness of the important need for a new field of analysis to help understand the fraught times.[180]

Earle had left his academic position at Columbia University to join the newly created Institute for Advanced Study, where he thought he could best promote his interdisciplinary approach to the study of international security. He had originally approached the Corporation in 1937 for support to create this new field of research; when he again broached the subject in November 1939, the response was positive. The initial grant of $6,500 was approved on February 1, 1940. The board anticipated that Earle's theoretical and analytical studies of foreign policy would yield "a realistic governmental program in this field ... devised and effected only by conceiving diplomacy and armaments as being complementary to each other." The trustees endorsed his "special emphasis on the interrelation of diplomacy and arms as an alternative and interdependent means of achieving national security."[181] When the grant for $10,000 was renewed at the Executive Committee meeting on November 7, 1940, staff remarked that "the importance of this study has been emphasized by international developments since the original grant was made."[182]

NOT FORGOTTEN:
THE FAMILY OF CARNEGIE INSTITUTIONS

IN THIS PERIOD, as earlier, the Carnegie family of institutions made a major call on the resources of the Corporation.[183] Some of the work directly related to the international agenda, especially the work of the Carnegie Institution of Washington and the Carnegie Endowment for International Peace. Although not represented on the Corporation's founding board of trustees, the Church Peace Union, endowed by the Corporation at the request of Mr. and Mrs. Carnegie, also received continuing but modest levels of support.[184]

Keppel, following the lead of James Angell and Henry Pritchett, continued to recommend support for a range of international scientific investigations under the auspices of the Carnegie Institution in Washington, including archaeological digs in the Mayan highlands and Cyprus, earthquakes in Chile, and land use and geological patterns in the Himalayan region of Asia.

The Carnegie Endowment for International Peace was for many years the main vehicle for the Corporation's policy-related research and outreach in the field of peace.[185] For the period 1922 to 1941, the Corporation provided grants totaling $2,523,824 for Endowment-related activities that educated Americans about the financial and economic problems that threatened peace and that showed ways to solve those problems through a charter-related "educational program for the promotion of the advancement and diffusion of knowledge and understanding among the people of the United States."[186] The amount included Corporation funding of the program on Canadian-American studies discussed earlier.

WHAT CAME OF ALL THESE EFFORTS?

WORLD WAR II ENDED the vibrancy of international grant-making in the Keppel era. Nonetheless, after the war, when the Corporation began to reestablish its international role in the United States and the British dominions and colonies, it could easily move forward because of the groundwork laid during this era. What were the broad achievements of this groundwork? What choices were made? What was not pursued or funded? What was done to support advancement of new knowledge, especially with respect to building fields, institutions, and careers? Were new institutions in the dominions and colonies built to endure and old ones strengthened? Did education in these regions achieve a broader reach? Did Americans adopt a broader worldview? Did the new research make a difference? What efforts did the Corporation bring to a close, and why?

Two contemporary assessments made partial attempts to answer these questions. Both were conducted at the request of the newly elected Corporation president, Walter A. Jessup: one by Keppel in 1942, and the other by Harvie Branscomb, a distinguished educator and university president who in 1943 prepared an external desk review. In a short report to President Jessup dated January 26, 1942, Keppel provided his own assessment of the strengths and weaknesses of the Corporation's work under his own leadership. With nearly $5 million spent during this period (not including the work in Canada or the internationally focused work in the United States), Keppel raised the key question that continues to haunt all philanthropists: "What has the Corporation got for all this money?"[187]

Keppel shared his list of "indisputable strikes": the educational research councils in Australia and New Zealand; the application of Jeanes education work from the United States to African native education; the Poor White Commission;[188] Lord Hailey's Africa Survey; the travel grants (for the colonial officers and more broadly); and building up undergraduate college libraries throughout the dominions ("This was, of course, an extension of our current activities in the United States," he noted).[189] While positive about the public library programs throughout the dominions, Keppel related the challenges that remained to the underlying conditions—"a subscription basis ... a pioneering character ... the unfavorable economic situation and ... the war."[190]

Keppel was less positive about the results from the grants for scientific research in South Africa, the museum grants, the Association for Country Education activities in New Zealand, the East Africa Agricultural Research Station in Amani, Tanganyika, and the National Research Council of Australia. He thought the Workers Education Association grants "proved disappointing." He recognized that it was "a fundamental mistake to transplant a type of organization which had proven very satisfactory in England to the very different conditions which obtain in other parts of the English-speaking world."[191]

Keppel acknowledged that the grants "in the interest of the African natives, while frankly spotty as to the results in individual cases, were probably justified as supplementary to larger enterprises." He highlighted as positive in this regard the work of the Corporation in supporting the South African Institute of Race Relations, the International Institute of African Languages and Culture, and the Yale Department of Race Relations established by Charles T. Loram. A concluding sentence of this section sheds light on many of his actions: "It must be remembered that the whole subject of the treatment of the natives is red hot politically—this is particularly so in the Union of South Africa—and what might be regarded as outside interference would accomplish more harm than good."[192]

Although he thought that the university organization grants were "reasonably successful," he felt that he should have done more to support the general purposes of the institutions of higher education in the southern dominions. Keppel concluded his assessment of the programmatic work with a reminder of the challenges of measuring impact in philanthropy:

Perhaps the most important result of the Corporation activities taken as a whole is rather an intangible one. These activities have, I believe, resulted in a better understanding of the best things in American life and in confidence of the disinterested and intelligent goodwill of the Corporation in particular.... Our doings in these Dominions have uniformly received attention in the press far beyond anything we have achieved either in the United States or Canada. I think it may fairly be said that our spadework for the past fourteen years in Australia and New Zealand as well, is now bearing fruit in these critical days for all the democracies touching the Pacific Ocean.[193]

Branscomb's assessment, coming nearly two years after Keppel's, and one month after Keppel died, was part of a larger effort by Jessup to assess the work of the Corporation and lay the groundwork for the postwar era. Branscomb, who had talked several times with Keppel before he died, submitted a somewhat longer assessment and noted that by this time the total expenditure for the program amounted to $5,500,000. Even from the distance provided by his external perspective, his observations were similar to Keppel's, of both the good and the problematic.

Approving the practical approach taken to education in the colonies, Branscomb underscored the fact that "in Africa the problem which overshadows all others is the race question."[194] The programs in South Africa in support of higher education for natives, literature for native use, educational institutions for interracial understanding, and research into the conditions surrounding native life, mainly the cultural conditions, made him think, from his desk perspective, that "the attitude in South Africa toward the native, at least toward native education, seems to have become more generous." Like Keppel, he agreed that the Poor White study was important because of its findings about the nature of the problem, "but also in that it impressed South Africans with the possibilities of further self-examination by the same techniques."[195] Branscomb concluded that "in Africa, the problem which overshadows all others is the race question," but that "the ultimate value of the experience and studies [in the African colonies and South Africa] which it has made possible remains, however, to be seen, now that the race problem has become a global one."[196]

In the dominions of Australia and New Zealand, Branscomb noted the tentative nature of the work. He pointed out that the Corporation had to modify programs that were adapted from the United States. He saw value in the two educational research councils and felt that their work was timely. He thought it especially noteworthy that "in the spring of 1939 when the period of the Corporation support of the Council was coming to its end, five of the six Australian state governments promptly agreed to contribute their share of the funds needed for its continuation."[197]

Branscomb was enthusiastic about the grants-in-aid, the fellowships, the travel grants, and the visitors' grants. He concluded, "These may well have been the most useful part of the program. One finds repeated instances in the correspondence of individuals who have received these grants being responsible for fresh beginnings in their communities or being appointed to key positions after their return from abroad."

Even with his positive assessment of the work in the southern dominions, he doubted that the Corporation could sustain those efforts because of the distance, which precluded frequent external visits and led to heavy reliance on a limited number of local advisers. He was more confident about the sustainability of the work in Africa because it involved many agencies, multiple local and external advisers with differing viewpoints, and a resulting diversity of activities. His assessment was "that the Australian and New Zealand programs did not have the inner forces of expansion of the African one." Although he concluded that "the Corporation may well be proud of its work during these years in these regions," his findings directly and indirectly informed the Corporation's geographic and programmatic scope following World War II.[198]

The reviews of Keppel and Branscomb addressed both overall and specific institutional and travel grants, and their comments were both positive and negative. Among the policies, procedures, and approaches introduced in this era, some have remained valid and continue to be practiced, while others merit renewed consideration in this new century of international philanthropy. These enduring contributions include:

- The role of key advisers in conducting preliminary analyses and visits as a way to identify major new opportunities
- The importance of regular visits and informal communication by program staff once grants have been made
- The reliance on local initiative, or as Keppel stated, "We have done well to support the interest of people on the spot ... regardless of whether their recommendations fit conveniently into the pattern of our activities in the United States and Canada."[199]
- A corollary, the willingness to take intellectual risks and support new ideas even if they are out of program (as long as they are within the charter restrictions)
- The intellectual courage and creativity not to shy away from field-building, but to do it thoughtfully and over a sufficient number of years

+ The support for research as the basis for decision-making and new
  policies
+ The confidence to work in partnership with key institutions, even if
  they are larger in scope and resources, and to establish others that
  could become potential partners

From its early tentative steps overseas via Canada, Carnegie Corporation
matured into an active player on the world stage. Frederick Keppel and the
trustees pursued a balanced strategy that would set the course for the foundation in areas that would have long-term implications rather than short-
term impact.

4

ENGAGING THE EMERGENCY AND RE-ENGAGING WITH THE WORLD, 1942–1954

W ORLD WAR II GALVANIZED AMERICAN energies, and a positive can-do attitude permeated the United States.[1] During the war, the deep engagement of physical and social scientists with military policymakers elevated the value of science-based decision-making, echoing the Corporation's mission to advance knowledge and understanding. Developments in the interdisciplinary studies that informed the conduct of the war and the planning of postwar peace offered new opportunities for grant-making. Allied victories reinforced the firm conviction that America had the resources and the reach to help Europe and the world rebuild.[2]

The exuberance and national pride following World War II were comparable to the heady atmosphere of the years following World War I; fortunately, no major economic downturn occurred in the immediate post–World War II years, and the United States benefited from a sound economy into the 1950s.[3] The optimism that followed the end of the war in Europe and Asia and the signing of the United Nations charter in 1945 was tempered by the dropping of the atomic bomb and by the rise of aggressive communism. The American response, a fervent policy of anticommunism for the next forty years, first came into distressing focus with the Second Red Scare at the end of the 1940s. The Korean War, fought from 1950 to 1953, and the increased political strength of the American military establishment further dissipated the optimism that peace could be sustained.[4]

These complex political conditions, reinforced by the lack of deep knowledge about communism and the Soviet Union and the global existential threat of atomic bombs, motivated Corporation leaders to reshape the international programs in the United States for a new era.

In the 1930s, the Corporation had promoted international activities primarily by investing time and money in overseas endeavors. In contrast, during World War II and in the years immediately following, the Corporation emphasized activities that would enhance the American capacity to play a leadership role in a new global order. The grants programs opened up new territory, not in the British Empire, as before the war, but at home. The Corporation launched into addressing the compelling issues of the era: deepening the work in international security studies, tackling the challenges of atomic energy, backing university-based area studies programs and international exchanges, and encouraging investigations into the effectiveness of technical assistance in the underdeveloped regions of the world. The dual aim of these efforts was to create an educated, globally knowledgeable American populace and to inform and better educate American foreign policy makers.

The changes unfolding in the British Empire yielded a different set of opportunities, almost uniformly positive, that the Corporation welcomed and embraced. Throughout World War II, the British prepared for the transition to independence in the colonies. The movement for self-determination that arose in the post–World War I period had firmly taken hold in the British colonies, accelerating the movement to independence much faster than the British planners had anticipated.[5] This evolutionary, not revolutionary, process gradually transformed the British Commonwealth from a group of dominions and colonies into independent nation-states.

In the postwar years, the Corporation revived the overseas program, which had been on hold during World War II. Continuing the thrust from the past era to relate these grants to programmatic priorities in the United States, staff sought, for example, to enhance the capacity of the independent educational research institutions established with Corporation support in the 1930s. The Corporation, working closely with its counterparts in London and in the British colonies, ventured into strengthening the relatively new higher education institutions in Africa and the Caribbean. A cluster of grants in the dominions provided support for freestanding institutes of international affairs and social science research councils. The goal of a renewed emphasis on travel grants was to reduce the isolation created by the war for academics, scientists, and educational policy practitioners in the dominions and colonies by supporting their visits to the United States, Canada, and the United Kingdom. Program staff also continued the practice of supporting Commonwealth-wide initiatives, following consultations with local decision-makers.

Reminiscent of the period after World War I, the Corporation faced potentially destabilizing situations among its personnel. Abrupt leadership changes due to death, resignation, and illness led to abbreviated presidential terms, but this time the trustees could depend on core staff members until a new leader was at the helm. The trustees also confronted changes in their group: they lost the last of the board members who had been personal associates of Andrew Carnegie. Although many trustees and staff members remained who had served under Frederick Keppel, during this period the carriers of institutional memory gradually declined in number.

Throughout this time the leadership of Carnegie Corporation—Walter A. Jessup from 1941 to 1944 and Devereux C. Josephs from 1945 to 1948—embraced the national spirit of optimism but tempered it with a seriousness of purpose in reshaping the foundation to participate in this new world, while staying true to the Corporation's values and mission. Grim national and international political circumstances shaped the more sober period from 1948 to 1954, when Charles Dollard was president. Nonetheless, he too sustained the commitment to internationalism. Although each president naturally brought a distinct perspective, all three displayed such a continuity of commitment that this era was recognizably shaped by their cascading efforts. Indeed, this era illustrates that when presidents of foundations share the passions of their predecessors, collectively they can transform and then sustain grant-making, cohesive programs, and relationships with constituents.

Corporation efforts to reorient American higher education toward much deeper international understanding paralleled and often intersected with those of the Rockefeller Foundation and soon attracted the interest and resources of the newly configured Ford Foundation and the US government.

The Corporation and the Rockefeller Foundation maintained, and even enhanced, their close collaboration established in the prior decades on many aspects of the international program in the United States and overseas. This period ushered in proactive shared funding initiatives, including some highly sensitive ones, around the themes of national defense, social adjustments to the atomic bomb, and technical assistance.

STABILITY AMID TRANSITION: CHANGES OF PRESIDENTS, STAFF MEMBERS, AND TRUSTEES

WALTER JESSUP HAD GREATLY EXPANDED the University of Iowa during his tenure as its president from 1916 to 1934. After Henry Pritchett's retirement in 1934, Jessup assumed the presidency of the Carnegie Foundation for the Advancement of Teaching. When Frederick Keppel retired in 1941, the board selected Jessup to serve as president of the Corporation as well. Circumstances limited Jessup from playing an expansionary role at the Corporation.[6] Because his presidency from 1941 to 1944 coincided with the war years, he was compelled to be an institutional consolidator for the Corporation and to pull back from the extensive activities, especially overseas, of the previous era.

In contrast to its continuing, although limited, wartime grant-making in the United States, the Corporation halted its activities in the British Empire.[7] With the limited communications and the "uncertainty prevailing in world conditions," the board temporarily halted new overseas programs and projects, except for ones in Canada.[8] With many staff serving in the war effort, the trustees had assumed more responsibility for the detailed work of the Corporation. With his leadership experience from other institutions and his service on the Corporation board, Jessup recognized the importance of balancing the board's involvement in strategic and policy discussions with active review of every request submitted to the Corporation. Jessup began the process—which would not be completed until the early 1970s—of gradually redesigning the board's role away from deciding on program design and reviewing details of grant-making proposals to working with the president on developing and approving policy and strategy.

Jessup sought board approval to establish a limited discretionary fund to respond to grant requests under the National Emergency Program. The board approved in January 1942, for the first time, a separate fund of $20,000 for such requests, giving a measure of flexibility to the president; these grants would not need board approval.[9] To make sure that Jessup focused the Corporation on the priority activities, the board endorsed his intensive review of all the grant-making, including the overseas grants. Anticipating the future emphasis on promoting the international education of Americans, he brought forward a proposal in March 1942 to plan more extensive work on this theme following World War II. A request for support to develop a national program of general education in foreign relations, in conjunction with a national agency in the field, came from Brooks Emeny, who was president of the Foreign Policy Association, a former Carnegie fellow in international law, a leader of the World Affairs Council in Cleveland, and a close associate of a former board member, the late Newton Baker. The board did not feel that it could consider such work positively at that time, but the request sowed the seeds of interest in international education. The trustees would reconsider work in this area just a few years later.[10]

Fortunately, because of the charter protection for the British Dominions and Colonies (BDC) program, that program could not be easily canceled.[11] Given the special interests of the founder and the international bent of the board members (Nicholas Murray Butler was chair at the time), Jessup would have found tough opposition had he suggested closing the fund. Thus, monies accrued to the fund. At the beginning of US involvement in the war in September 1942, the fund was valued at $12,932,759; in the year after the end of the war in September 1946, the assets reached $14,305,061. (For the Main Endowment Fund, the respective numbers were $153,055,508 and $152,937,620, reflecting fairly modest grant-making expenditures.) The surplus income for the BDC program equaled $1,418,636 (approximately $17,460,000 in 2011 dollars), a sizable amount of money with which to start a program once the war ended.[12]

In September 1943, Keppel, who had been providing guidance to Jessup, even as he advised the State Department on the relief situation, died of a heart attack.[13] His passing was a serious blow to the already restrained mood of the foundation, but Jessup's unexpected death in July 1944 was even more devastating since he had been personally reviewing the work of the Corporation to determine future grant-making as well as running the Carnegie Foundation—all with greatly limited staff. It took several months of contentious discussion to select trustee Devereux Josephs as the seventh president of the Corporation; he took office on June 1, 1945.[14]

With Josephs, the board had selected as president a relatively new member of its group and a dedicated internationalist. Josephs, an insurance executive and investment banker, originally joined the Corporation's board in his position as the head of the Teachers' Insurance and Annuity Association (TIAA).[15] In that capacity, he worked in the Corporation's offices.

Most members of the board in the 1940s, much like Andrew Carnegie, were born disadvantaged and had become self-made men as academic and business leaders. Many originally came from the Midwest and held intellectual, academic, public service, or business leadership positions. In contrast, Devereux Colt Josephs was born in Newport, Rhode Island, a descendant of the inventor of the Colt revolver. He went to Groton School, then Harvard, and later was chairman of the Harvard Board of Overseers. He served on innumerable boards, was an active member of New York society, connected by birth and marriage to many of the social powerhouses, and had founded a literary magazine called *Contemporary Verse*.

These details say little, however, about Josephs's abilities and the quality of his mind. In their reminiscences, his Corporation colleagues gave a more well-rounded assessment of the kind of person Josephs was and why he was the right person at the right time to lead the Corporation into the post–World War II world. Charles Dollard, for example, held Josephs in high regard, calling him "superbly competent," with "courage," even if he disagreed with Josephs's view that authors of research studies—such as Myrdal's *An American Dilemma*—were "interchangeable."[16] Pendleton Herring, who joined the staff in 1946, characterized him as a man of "vigor and imagination and verve and style and élan" who was well suited to getting off to "a new start," and also "a very effective person, a very persuasive person … full of energy."[17] John Gardner, who also joined the staff in 1946, emphasized the value of Josephs's leadership through a difficult transitional era: "I really think he saw it [the Corporation] through a transition period with great shrewdness and great good judgment." Josephs's philosophy of philanthropy—treating staff and grantees as partners—would have a "permanent" impact on Dollard and Gardner.[18]

Drawing on Jessup's analyses, Josephs immediately began to make changes in the way the Corporation functioned. Like Jessup, he wanted to establish more businesslike procedures and to make modest grants more efficiently. He persuaded the board to expand Jessup's concept of the discretionary grant, moving beyond its use for the emergency grants to more general ones and increasing the discretionary fund level to $50,000. Slowly, like Jessup, Josephs began to expand the president's scope for grant-making vis-à-vis the prior responsibilities of the board.[19]

Because the Corporation, out of a sense of patriotic duty, had bought war bonds instead of stocks, it had lost income during the war years. Fortunately, because of the curtailed grant-making, the overall asset base increased slightly between September 1941 ($166,504,969) and September 1946 ($167,242,681).[20] At the same time, funding increased from private and other sources for the areas of traditional Corporation interest.[21] Financial prudence and the availability of new monies for older areas of interest further motivated the board to set new programmatic priorities for the new postwar world.

Josephs had been with the Office of Strategic Services (OSS) during the war, and that experience had also influenced his global perspective.[22] He knew that information mattered and that information had to be accurate and culturally appropriate. He envisioned an America with citizens who were knowledgeable about the world, and he was determined to make that happen. In his first presidential essay, he set forth the underlying purpose: "Most important of all, fundamental in the concept of the work of this foundation, is its purpose—to raise the spiritual and ethical level of American society. Culture will enrich the spirit; education is a means of building character; but this foundation should never be so engrossed in the means as to forget that the intent is to help make a nation wiser."[23] He ended his essay by elaborating on the appropriate grantees for a postwar world: "What we do seek and hope to be able to consider, are proposals from practical visionaries.... It is the ambition of this foundation to share in creative enterprises. It can supply money and a measure of accumulated experience ... the Carnegie Corporation offers partnership to active and able men or institutions with imagination."[24]

When Josephs walked down the hall to become president, he counted on inheriting a core group of staff with whom he could build internal capacity for program expansion, rather than rely mainly on consultants. (Until the late 1930s, Keppel, with less than a handful of staff members, had engaged consultants to assist with the identification and monitoring of grants.[25]) Josephs encouraged those staff members—Charles Dollard, Stephen Stackpole, and Florence Anderson—following their service in the military or the War Department, to return to their positions to join him and Robert Lester at the Corporation. In particular, he twisted the arm of a reluctant Dollard to return by offering him a partnership, the modus operandi he had been comfortable with in his insurance and banking business.[26] In the interest of building a professional institution with strong capacity in international as well as national foundation priorities, Josephs hired four more people during his first year: Oliver Carmichael, Pendleton Herring, John Gardner, and Whitney Shepardson.[27]

Having decided to give special attention to the overseas work, Josephs broke with former practice by making the British Dominions and Colonies (BDC) program its own department within the Corporation, calling it the BDC Fund. He hired a high-profile director, Whitney Shepardson, a distinguished, senior international figure. Shepardson, along with several trustees—including the former board chair and a member of the original board, Elihu Root Sr., and current trustee Russell Leffingwell—had been responsible for the 1921 founding of the Council on Foreign Relations. Shepardson had been an aide to Colonel Edward House for the Paris Peace Conference, a director on John D. Rockefeller Sr.'s General Education Board, and a leader prior to American entry into World War II of the Council on Foreign Relations' Rockefeller Foundation–funded "War and Peace Studies" project. During the war, he served as head of the Secret Intelligence Board in the Office of Strategic Services (OSS), the precursor to the CIA. His focus was primarily European; however, from 1934 to 1940, he edited and wrote much of the annual volume *The United States in World Affairs.*[28]

With this team, Josephs thoroughly internationalized the Corporation during his short tenure by promulgating a worldview for the foundation centered on the vital importance of American international understanding. Like his counterparts at the Rockefeller Foundation, he recognized that in the postwar era it was essential for citizens to have in-depth global knowledge.[29] Toward that end, he and his "partners'" recommended new area studies institutes and programs, promoted continued work on international relations and international affairs at universities, and maintained funding for significant foreign-policy outreach and advisory institutions.[30]

When offered the presidency of New York Life Insurance Company, the third-largest insurance company in the United States,[31] Josephs could not resist the call to return to his preferred career, even though he had been president of the Corporation for less than four years. Josephs remained committed to the Corporation and agreed to stay on the Board of Trustees. An active trustee until 1967, he would be one of the board's longest-serving members.

By 1948, when Josephs stepped down, the Corporation had a sophisticated team of seasoned grant-makers whose wartime experiences had opened their eyes to the opportunities and the constraints of working overseas and to the need for developing programs to educate Americans about their country's role in the world. The international thrust continued to thrive with the election of Charles Dollard as president. Dollard, a dedicated social scientist, had been hired in 1938, originally to handle the grants-in-aid, but he also assisted with the international activities.

The trustees and Josephs shared a high regard for Dollard.[32] In the few years of his sadly abbreviated presidency, Dollard initiated innovative work in the social sciences and maintained strong support for the area studies and international relations programs, along with the overseas grant-making. Dollard also followed the Josephs standard—namely, their promise as partners—in hiring new staff members.[33]

In his first presidential essay, Dollard wrote about the opportunity to promote research in a different way now that there was such extensive funding from the federal government, especially since foundation support no longer accounted for half the resources available for research support but closer to 1 percent. As he noted, "they must husband … limited funds for the germinal work … increasingly responsive to the opportunities which balance great risk of failure against great promise of social and scientific gain."[34] Committed to promoting research in both hard and social sciences, particularly in the field of human behavior and mental health, he introduced a fundamental program in cognitive research with ramifications that continue to today. He also aspired to strengthen the social sciences throughout the British dominions and colonies.

Returning to Keppel's tradition of welcoming new foundations in his presidential essays, Dollard formally welcomed two significant ones in 1951: the National Science Foundation (NSF), on whose board he was to serve, and the Ford Foundation, whose enormous endowment in 1950 resembled the impact on other foundations that the Bill and Melinda Gates Foundation would have nearly fifty years later.[35] As Dollard noted to the board, the Ford Foundation presented an "'embarrassment of riches' ... the Foundation's income this year might approximate $100,000,000.... It [is] clear they intend to operate in the same fields which we are plowing, but also because the new tax legislation will create a compulsion for them to get rid of their money fast, let the chips fall where they may. We have, of course, discussed this problem with the Ford people and are doing what we can to encourage wise polices."[36] Dollard ended his reporting on the two foundations by commenting on the Corporation's commitment to individual talent: "Money *is* barren until and unless it is put in the hands of people with hearts and heads, with energy, confidence, intelligence and goodwill."[37]

The postwar enthusiasm palpably began to wane during the Dollard presidency as the currents of suspicion about foundations (and other institutions and individuals) emerged from policymakers in Washington, DC. A series of congressional investigations of foundations, the Cox Commission and the Reece Commission, aimed to reveal the foundations as "un-American." The commissions called on foundation presidents, trustees, grantees, and others to give testimony about whether or not foundations were subversive institutions intent on damaging America. Dollard and his staff dedicated months of his presidency, in 1952, 1953, and 1954, to preparing detailed testimony. The Cox Commission hearings of the House Select Committee to Investigate Tax-Exempt Foundations and Comparable Organizations were relatively benign.

One member of the Cox Committee, however, Representative B. Carroll Reece of Tennessee, would not let the matter die. He organized a second round, the Special Committee to Conduct a Full and Complete Investigation and Study of Educational and Philanthropic Foundations and Other Comparable Organizations Which Are Exempt from Federal

Income Taxation, "'to determine if any foundations and organizations are using their resources for purposes other than the purposes for which they were established, and especially to determine which such foundations and organizations are using their resources for un-American and subversive activities; for political purposes; propaganda, or attempts to influence legislation.'"[38] Dollard and Russell Leffingwell, then chairman of the Board of Trustees, prepared written testimony at the invitation of the committee in the spring of 1954; a sixty-eight-page document reviewed the history of the foundation.[39] The material was sent to the committee on June 22, and the Corporation was soon informed that there would be no public hearings; Dollard and the trustees were never called to testify. When the Reece Commission issued its report, it mainly included testimony from witnesses who were negative about foundations and only one foundation representative. To ensure that the public was aware of the material, the Corporation then published its testimony in an effort to answer those negative witnesses.[40] The commission never formally published its report, the recommendations were not adopted, and there was no follow-up legislation.[41]

The Cox Commission's pressing for more openness and accountability by foundations led the Corporation to move away from the "audits of experience" Review Series that had been prepared by Corporation secretary Robert Lester to a more accessible form for communicating grant results. Although the earlier reviews remained invaluable for understanding the rationale that led to grants and the crucial data concerning whom, what, when, how much, and for how long, they were often more limited, as Lester himself often acknowledged, when it came to describing and assessing the results. Suggesting the experiment of conducting in-depth reviews of the major programs over $100,000, Dollard raised concern about communication as a problem that "plagues every foundation ... we know of no fund which has achieved a completely satisfactory answer to it."[42]

In January 1953, the Corporation launched a new type of publication, the *Carnegie Quarterly Report*, to provide more frequent and more in-depth reporting as the grants came to completion. An editor was hired specifically to write it. For almost fifty years, the quarterly would serve as the main vehicle for broad public dissemination of the Corporation's activities.[43]

The Corporation sacrificed more at this time than the hours and energy spent in preparing documents for the congressional investigations. In 1952 the Corporation announced that Dollard had taken ill in the midst of the extensive preparations for the Cox Commission. The board appointed John Gardner, in his capacity as vice president, to manage the institution during Dollard's first medical leave, and then to serve officially as acting president during the president's next leave. Dollard resigned in November 1954.[44] In light of the revolutionary changes he had hoped to make through grants to promote social science and interdisciplinary research, his departure left a gap in both continuity and substance. Moreover, he was the active connection between Keppel, the war years, and the postwar opportunities. Again, a cluster of seasoned staff members who had been working together as a team, many throughout the 1940s, sustained institutional stability during this near-crisis transition; these staff members included, most notably, Stephen Stackpole, Florence Anderson, John Gardner, James Perkins, and, starting in 1953, Alan Pifer. Gardner's formal presidency, begun a few months after Dollard's resignation, is the subject of Chapter 6.

Much as had happened after Andrew Carnegie's death, even with experienced staff members, the board's stable and firm leadership made these successive presidential transitions manageable. Keppel had recommended all but one of the thirteen trustees who served during the war years; several stayed on the board well into the 1950s and some into the 1960s. Jessup, Josephs, and Dollard recommended ten more, many with extensive international connections. These trustees maintained a strong sense of the Corporation's history, a deep respect for the mission, and a clear understanding of the charge from Andrew Carnegie that the Corporation should evolve with changing times. This combination of talent, knowledge of the Corporation, and openness to change reinforced the board's sense of shared purpose in moving forward with the newly enlarged international agenda and addressing the critical issues of the era. Without term limits, it was possible for a cluster of committed board members to serve for many years and thus gain the confidence to support risky undertakings with uncertain results.[45]

Reinforcing their commitment to internationalism, in May 1946 the trustees elected General of the Army George C. Marshall to join the board.[46] The later addition of Charles Allen Thomas and others further reflected the changing world conditions.[47] With experienced and knowledgeable leadership, the internationalists on the board reinforced the internationalist tendencies of the presidents and staff during this entire period. Over the years, this alignment—rare in any institution—enabled the Corporation to undertake extensive grant-making, both at home and overseas, that responded to rapidly changing international conditions.

AN AGENDA FOR AMERICA: ENGAGING THE WORLD THROUGH EDUCATION AND EXPERIENCE

THE GLOBAL WORLDVIEW that Josephs and his colleagues represented in their discussions with the board reflected Andrew Carnegie's political passions. Like the Corporation's founder, they vehemently opposed war—not as isolationists, but as internationalists convinced of the need for a durable peace. They wanted to make sure that the world would never again face a global war, and that the atomic bomb would never again wreak devastation. Echoing his words to the board on several occasions, Josephs wrote in his second Annual Report essay, "Without peace and the prospect of peace, all other plans are worthless.... World peace is made up of many elements ... the Corporation has selected for its attention one that is double-starred on every list, and one that is fundamental enough to have lasting influence. The goal chosen is adult appreciation of international responsibilities."[48]

The world had changed, and to help maintain peace America needed to play a different role. Josephs and his team were concerned about the capacity of Americans—the public and policymakers—to play that role with wisdom and knowledge. Slightly more than a year after Josephs took office, and after the end of World War II, the Corporation launched a new vision that maintained the focus on education but—following Andrew Carnegie's charge to the original trustees—revised it to take the changing context into account. A committee comprising both trustees and staff was appointed by the board to propose the most effective way forward; it concluded that the Corporation could build on its comparative advantage in the education field by making grants to improve civic education in the United States as a corollary to those that promoted education in international relations and bolstered the social sciences. The programmatic justification addressed the challenges and rationale.[49] Josephs suggested the measure of success: "the extent to which we of the United States are conscious of the existence of the other peoples of the world and of the view that these other people have of us."[50]

Before presenting the revised program for final approval to the Board of Trustees, the trustee/staff committee reviewed and refined the plans, one of the few examples of active intra-institutional "teamwork" in any period of the Corporation's history.[51] The final plans approved by the trustees in September 1946 called for "A Long Term Program, dealing with the relation of the Corporation to such matters as education in international relations, development of recognition of responsibilities of citizenship, promotion of the social sciences, aid to educational institutions, uses of surveys, and other topics."[52]

The team proposed three areas for work: the official area of work on international relations and international security, along with outreach to policymakers and the public; international exchanges; and education for international understanding. In the official area, grants for the Foreign Policy Association, the Council on Foreign Relations, the Institute of Pacific Relations, the Brookings Institution, the Social Science Research Council, and the Carnegie Endowment for International Peace would be continued. These institutions had already compiled a solid track record of policy-oriented research regarding international peace and security—that is, they provided "constructive and nonpartisan criticism of government policy"—and routinely presented their research findings to the government and private citizens as well as to the public. Moreover, the Corporation was familiar with their research. Nonetheless, staff members and trustees also recognized the limitations of these institutions, especially "the limited extent of their influence and the limited nature of their objectives."[53]

In the second area, promoting international exchanges, the team suggested working primarily through the Carnegie Endowment for International Peace and the Institute of International Education. Since these institutions were independent of government, they could "help to maintain communication between private citizens of various nations in crucial periods when official communication is broken or badly strained."[54] They also saw a role for the British Dominions and Colonies Fund, as well as backing for unofficial international meetings.

The third area, the field of education, was the main area for the new program thrust. As part of the Corporation's determined effort to build a citizenry educated in world affairs, the goal of this area was to achieve "greater knowledge and understanding, and more mature attitudes on the part of the people." The theory of change, although not so named, was that an educated population would be more likely to approve government policies focused on securing peace. The team was not interested in what they called "education in breadth," that is, propaganda through mass education. They proposed "to educate in depth." The program would focus on the colleges and universities, to "educate the teachers who instruct the youth ... their alumni [who] constitute a great body of influential citizens ... [and who] in recent years ... have furnished the government many of the practical men in administration and policymaking."[55] To implement the program the team suggested a variety of approaches using different methods and funding different activities, to "encourage development of departments of international studies ... stimulate institutions to provide international education programs for their alumni ... encourage institutions to emphasize international relations in their adult education programs ... encourage the development of foreign area and language studies for training of area specialists ... [and] promote efforts looking to improvement of curriculum and instruction in history and associated courses."[56] The Corporation pursued all these goals in varying ways over the next ten years.

In presenting the plan and clarifying Josephs's earlier comment about preservation of the peace, the team emphatically stated that "the Corporation does not propose to promote peace through advocating any particular foreign policy; it is concerned only with facilitating the formation and exposition of that policy."[57]

International affairs and education grant-making continued under Josephs and Dollard until 1953, when, under Gardner's acting leadership, staff prepared a board memo assessing the international work in the United States. Staff reported first that from 1946 to 1953 the Corporation spent over $10 million (approximately $82 million in 2011 dollars) under the broad category of international affairs.[58] The memo was written with an intent and tone that reflected a shift to a Cold War perspective. The rationale had changed over the seven years from 1946 to 1953, but the goal of educating Americans about the world remained the same. According to reviews conducted in 1953, the results achieved in foreign area studies, teaching, and research in international relations, international cultural and scientific exchanges, and civic education on international affairs had yielded lessons about ways to move forward and where to focus in selecting the themes of the next era.

The increasing interest in international affairs shared by the Corporation and the Rockefeller Foundation informed both institutions' agendas for grant-making in the years immediately following World War II. The two foundations collaborated in support of research, study groups, consultancies, and exchanges. Sometimes, such as with the area institutes, the collaboration was more parallel than joint; in contrast, the work on what the Corporation had designated as its own three areas of focus—international relations, international exchanges, and civic education on international affairs—exemplified foundation collaboration. By the early 1950s, the Ford Foundation began to make grants on international affairs issues in the United States and engage in a wide range of international activities overseas. It soon dominated many of the fields where Rockefeller and the Corporation had been active. Occasionally collaborating with the Ford Foundation in internationally oriented activities, the Corporation developed closer ties with the Ford Foundation by the mid-1950s.[59]

IN-DEPTH EDUCATION ABOUT THE WORLD:
THE AREA INSTITUTES

CORPORATION TRUSTEES AND STAFF MEMBERS believed in the vital importance of reinforcing the core values of the mission to advance and disseminate knowledge and understanding, particularly about the places in the world that were increasingly in the headlines and the focus of American foreign policy. As Josephs made very clear, their intention was not to influence or endorse policy, but to make Americans more internationally oriented so that academics, policymakers, businesspersons, diplomats, and citizens would have a deeper understanding of the issues confronting the world and the country and be more effective in meeting global challenges. This may seem obvious today, but in the mid-1940s it was a new way of thinking for American education.

During this period, the Corporation, along with the Rockefeller Foundation, dedicated a significant amount of time and money to deepening Americans' understanding of different geographic areas of the world. Before World War II, both the Rockefeller Foundation and Carnegie Corporation, working in parallel ways, contributed to strengthening American academic capacity in international relations. Together the two foundations started to focus early in World War II on what eventually would be called "area studies."[60]

As part of the war effort, four major scholarly institutions—the American Council of Learned Societies, the Social Science Research Council, the National Research Council, and the Smithsonian Institution—joined forces to establish the Ethnogeographic Board, housed at the Smithsonian in Washington, DC. As stated in the proposal to the Carnegie Corporation and the Rockefeller Foundation, the Board's purpose was "to furnish to governmental war agencies, military and civilian, needed information of all sorts relating to any areas outside the United States where military, economic, or other action is carried on or planned." The proposal emphasized the nature of the work of the board as "interdisciplinary in character; the information it secures derives from research in the fields of the sciences, humanities, and the social sciences. In short, it seeks all useful information respecting a given area and its inhabitants."[61] The request for $20,000 from each foundation was matched by $15,000 contributed by the four partner institutions. Rather than conduct original area-based research (clearly not possible given the war), the board oversaw the collection of available information from experts, publications, atlases, and on-the-ground institutions; contacts were made throughout the United Kingdom, in Europe, and in any region where troops might disembark. The intent was to organize conferences, collect and review the materials, and then put the information together in accessible ways for all the agencies associated with prosecuting the war.[62]

The Ethnogeographic Board, although not explicitly acknowledged by the foundations, contributed to the postwar grant-making of both foundations related to area studies. Their recognition of the value of crossing discipline boundaries to prepare reports for military and civilian war agencies directly influenced the design of the area studies institutes and programs supported by the Corporation and the Rockefeller Foundation.[63]

Beginning in 1945 and continuing for nearly two decades, the Corporation sponsored a range of area studies that brought the world to American (and Canadian) higher education institutions. These area institutes combined the Corporation's strong commitment to the field of international studies with its efforts to make the results more accessible to the public, while at the same time expanding the interdisciplinary nature of these studies. The focus of nearly every program on a core geographic region provided the common frame of reference to meld the disciplinary differences.[64]

From 1946 to 1953, the Corporation funded over thirty area studies programs in twenty-five universities, ranging from Arctic studies in Canadian institutions to Venezuelan studies at the University of North Carolina. Despite that breadth, a disproportionate interest in certain regions and countries reflected staff members' recognition of the world areas that were imperative for Americans to understand better. The Soviet Union and Latin America clearly received the most attention. From a foreign policy and national security perspective, it was crucial to increase knowledge about the former, and a focus on Latin America made sense because of its proximity in a shared hemisphere. The Corporation did not feel the urgency to seek the same breadth and depth on Canadian studies, although it did fund a pioneering program about Canada at the University of Rochester; it also provided fairly significant aid for a variety of institutes that focused on Inner Asia, East Asia, Japan, Southeast Asia, the Near East, Africa, Europe, and the Commonwealth itself.

It was perhaps impossible to live in the United States in 1946 and not see the importance of having a deeper understanding of the Soviet Union. This major ally during World War II was rapidly becoming America's major adversary. In 1945 the Rockefeller Foundation had funded a significant program at Columbia University to provide Russian language training and a focus on history and politics, especially for students who were planning to enter the US Foreign Service.[65] Corporation board member Frederick Osborn encouraged staff members in 1947 to survey the current state of research on the Soviet Union. He was then a US delegate to the United Nations Atomic Energy Commission. As Paul Buck, provost of Harvard University in the late 1940s and 1950s, explained, Osborn's frustrating experiences with Andrei Gromyko, the Russian ambassador to the United States, prompted him to encourage the Corporation to develop a program that would help in understanding Russian behavior.[66] All the officials surveyed saw a need for long-term studies but believed that neither the government nor the academic world had the capacity to produce them. Explorations around the country undertaken by staff member Oliver Carmichael were followed by the decision that Harvard University would be the best location for funding a new broadly interdisciplinary approach to a Russian studies program that would teach not only the language, economics, and history of Russia, as was being taught at Columbia University, but also the culture, the humanities, and the sociology of Russia, as well as the psychology of the Russian mind to better understand Russian behavior. The basic premise was, "whatever the goals of the USSR may be, Russian policy will be set within certain definable limits. These limits are imposed by national traditions, ideology, and economics, modified by Soviet assumptions as to the intentions of other great powers."[67]

Although Harvard had Russia experts, the Corporation sought different academic expertise for the Russian Research Center. To lead this interdisciplinary effort they wanted a social scientist; the decision was influenced in large measure by the Corporation's support for Harvard's Department of Social Relations, which drew together the disciplines that were considered the intellectual underpinnings for innovative studies of Russia— sociology, anthropology, and psychology. The Corporation persuaded the Harvard leadership that anthropologist Clyde Kluckhohn, with his proven capacity to understand complex cultures, should take the helm and build the Russian Research Center.[68]

The early experience with the Russian Research Center at Harvard was highly positive in that it produced deep, well-informed studies, but it has been tainted by two areas of controversy: the Center's ties to government, and the Corporation's interference in the selection of the deputy director.[69] Both controversies point to the fraught nature of grant-making around sensitive policy issues, even in an ivory tower setting such as a university.

The controversy concerning the Center's ties to government arose from the Corporation's post–World War II shift to grant-making that would address the need to enhance the understanding that policymakers brought to foreign policy in the new world order. Staff wanted to enable policy-makers to develop a sophisticated understanding of the world's cultures, economies, and politics that would then inform national decision-making. The fact that the dynamics of the Cold War era were impeding open access to on-the-ground knowledge reinforced the Corporation's support for an array of international affairs studies, including projects related to the increasing concern about secrecy in government. The Russian Research Center's contact with the US State Department, for instance, was related to efforts to ensure that US diplomats were well informed about the cultures of the countries where they served. But as Buck explicitly states, at Harvard, secrecy or governmental pressure would not have been allowed to play a part in the shaping of the research at the Center, especially research on the important question, in Buck's words, of "what makes the Russians tick?"[70]

At the same time, because of the policy-sensitive nature of the research, a more delicate question came to the forefront almost right away: what freedom did academics have to engage as citizens in democratic life? Buck, in discussing this aspect of the Center's work, provided a rationale for limiting staff involvement in political activity, including political campaigns, by stating that it was "a privilege—to have the freedom to study the fundamentals of this question [Russian behavior and culture]. ... The staff of the Russian Research Center voluntarily took this self-denying agreement not to meddle in politics."[71] In other words, because staff members working in this sensitive area, especially at the leadership level, needed to be unbiased, their involvement in political campaigns for either party might compromise the credibility of the Center.

The Corporation's concern about this relationship between the freedom to explore fundamental questions and involvement in politics partially explains—though it does not excuse or deny—its inappropriate role in an initial personnel decision at the Center. Both Dollard (then vice president) and Gardner (the program staff member responsible for the grant) called on Buck to discuss the appointment of H. Stuart Hughes, an assistant professor of history, not yet tenured, as assistant director. Hughes was becoming active in the highly controversial 1948 political campaign of the Progressive Party presidential candidate Henry A. Wallace, who had been vice president under President Franklin D. Roosevelt; the issue of concern was the alleged Communist role in the Progressive Party.[72] As Buck related the story, a "very embarrassed" team of Dollard and Gardner made the request to remove Hughes, since it was thought by some at the Corporation that his political participation would compromise the objectivity of the work of the Center. It would appear, however, that the Corporation did not question Hughes's qualifications or capabilities. While Buck was uncomfortable with the Corporation's foray into academic decision-making, he considered the positive intellectual impact that Hughes could have later on the field and the country and advised him to step down from the Center and stick with history. Buck made sure, however, that the Corporation supported Hughes for the next four years of his assistant professorship.[73]

From the first grant in 1947 through the review made in 1953, the results from the $1,575,300 provided for the Russian Research Center received high marks from the Corporation.[74] As the review memo concluded, even after only seven years, the Center already had "had a decided impact upon the study of Russia in this country.... There is no serious student of Russian in this country today who has not read one or more of the books produced by the Center over the past five years." The Center staff also helped stimulate Russian studies around the country.[75]

The Corporation promoted work on Russia and the Soviet Union in other institutions as well: it provided training fellowships at Columbia University, reinforcing the Rockefeller Foundation investments, and developed Russian studies for undergraduates, notably at Dartmouth College, Yale University, and the tri-college program at Bryn Mawr, Haverford, and Swarthmore Colleges. Another grant related to Russia that turned out to be a precursor for Corporation-funded work in the 1990s enabled the Massachusetts Institute of Technology to complete a government-funded study of Soviet scientific and engineering education.[76] Despite all the controversies from the 1950s and 1960s, which were reinvigorated in the 1980s, the field of Russian studies continues in the twenty-first century at Harvard's Davis Center for Russian and Eurasian Studies (the current name for the Center), Bryn Mawr, Dartmouth, Yale, and Columbia—as well as at many other universities and colleges around the country.[77]

Following Carmichael's survey, Gardner was given responsibility for the area studies program. As he reveals in his oral history, he avidly encouraged institute programs for other areas besides Russia. Because of Latin

America's proximity to the American South, the Corporation made Latin American studies a second major area of focus. Building on the earlier efforts in this field by the Rockefeller Foundation, the Corporation expanded the prior investments in Latin American studies, with support to Vanderbilt University, the University of North Carolina, Tulane University, and the University of Texas at Austin. The rationale given for investing in these centers, however, was not that the Rockefeller Foundation had already built the infrastructure for the field, but rather that a collaborative program linking these institutions in the South could be established.[78] The staff initially presented the area studies program as an array of institutions throughout the country; the Corporation would fund those where resources could be strategically used, either to start pilot programs whose costs would then be absorbed by the university or to reduce "duplication and rivalry"—hence the Latin American area studies collaborative grouping.[79]

Area study institutes developed to conduct research on countries and regions primarily according to their prominence in foreign policy and Americans' lack of familiarity with them. Sometimes area studies extended work that was already under way in another institution. For example, the assumption was made that Inner Asia and Asiatic Russian (or Eurasia) studies at the University of Washington would be well placed because of the university's prior commitment to Russian and Far Eastern studies (the latter areas funded initially by the Rockefeller Foundation).[80] Modest grants had already been made, however, to Johns Hopkins University for work in the same area. But the geographic proximity assumption was often not the determining criterion. Carnegie Corporation helped underwrite what staff members considered to be the country's foremost research center on Japan at the University of Michigan.[81]

The Corporation also funded the only significant research programs in the United States on the Philippines (at the University of Chicago) and on the Pacific Islands (connecting Yale University and the University of Hawaii's Bishop Museum).[82] Grants for Arctic studies went to the Arctic Institute of North America at McGill University in Montreal (now at the University of Calgary in Calgary), along with support for study centers on Greenland and Scandinavia. (Scandinavian studies were also supported at the Universities of Minnesota and Wisconsin.[83]) At the University of

Toronto, the Corporation backed work on East Asia.[84] The Corporation even trained missionaries in the United States and Canada to have a broader worldview through grants to the Hartford Seminary in Connecticut.[85] A grant enabled Yale University to develop one of the first programs in the country on Southeast Asia studies, and both the Rockefeller Foundation and Carnegie Corporation bolstered Princeton University's efforts to revive its Near Eastern Studies Program and expand its program of instruction in Arabic. Other grants helped Columbia University develop a program in European studies and one in Asiatic studies under general education; the latter was the first such program in the country.[86]

The Corporation had considerable interest in supporting work on African studies, perhaps the most relevant area for the Corporation since it had been making grants on that continent starting in 1925. However, this was a most difficult area to get off the ground. In late 1950, John Gardner discussed the matter with the Rockefeller Foundation's Robert Calkins, who indicated later that Carnegie Corporation had concluded "that there was no adequate basis for such a program in any American institution."[87] Rather than invest in an institute, the Corporation decided to send a team of individuals to East Africa with the aim of trying "to increase the number of first-rate social scientists with an interest in Africa."[88] The team was led by Cornelis de Kiewiet, a longtime Corporation associate who was originally from South Africa and now was at Cornell, and it included Leonard Doob, a psychologist from Yale, along with an agricultural economist and a political scientist. One outcome of this trip was that Doob became so interested in Africa that he went on to receive considerable Corporation support for his work on cross-cultural psychology and testing in nonliterate societies.[89] He also became the chair of the Yale Council on African Studies.

In 1948, in lieu of a full-fledged African studies program, the Corporation provided support for Professor Melville Herskovits's research programs at Northwestern University because the university was not willing to endorse an institute like the ones the Corporation supported elsewhere. The Corporation, though reluctant to act in support of Herskovits because it had been hoping to support a broader program, determined that "African studies are almost at a standstill in this country.... The officers of the Corporation believe that support of the research activities of Professor

Herskovits offers the best available opportunity for the encouragement of African studies in this country."[90] The Corporation followed up with two grants to Northwestern in 1951 in support of Herskovits and his work— one to establish the Institute on Contemporary Africa, at the modest total outlay of $10,000, and then a five-year $100,000 grant for the work in African studies.[91]

In May 1953, the Corporation critically reviewed all its initial investments in international affairs in the United States. The review of the area studies institutes also drew on the prior analysis conducted by Caryl Haskins, a highly respected scientist and science adviser in the fields of foreign policy and national security.[92] In the assessment, staff noted the importance of "expert knowledge of foreign lands and peoples" to maintaining a position of credible American leadership.[93] They concluded that Corporation efforts to fill that gap had not only enhanced the quality of the research conducted and the knowledge accumulated but also increased the number of trained scholars and practitioners who could contribute as better-informed policy-makers and citizens.

But they also noted that the area of popular education remained a challenge. It was not a question of promoting interest or providing information. As they wrote, "It is, rather, the more complex problem of discovering ways in which the American people can be given a clearer comprehension of the realities which condition their survival." They concluded this section of the basic report with a theme that became a focus for future activities: it "is a problem which the offices regard as yet unsolved."[94]

But by this time the funding situation had significantly changed. The Corporation and the Rockefeller Foundation were no longer the two lone proponents of area studies. In 1950, as noted earlier, the Ford Foundation came on the scene. The US government became even more involved in area studies through the National Defense Education Act (NDEA), with its Title VI program—which, when initiated in 1959 and 1960, provided significant resources to centers of research and language studies—and then through the Fulbright-Hays Act, which, after being passed in 1961, amplified support for international travel, research, and teaching.[95] Within only a few years, a field of study that the two foundations had created with generous, although not vast, funds was inundated with resources. As Frank Sutton wrote in his analyses of the Ford Foundation's history: "By 1951

... ideas on the importance of educating Americans on foreign areas and how it might be done through university area centers were shaping into a kind of enthusiastic orthodoxy. Rockefeller and Carnegie Corporation led the way with grants totaling $8.5 million by that year but ... much more needed to be done."[96] Sutton estimated that, over the next nearly thirty-four years, the Ford Foundation invested nearly five times as much as Carnegie Corporation.[97]

Corporation staff members also realized that, in addition to conducting interdisciplinary research and creating new knowledge on these areas of the world, it was vital for students to see firsthand the countries they were studying. Thus, at the same time that they were supporting the area studies institutes, they also decided to consolidate in one place support for fellowships, since they had also been receiving a considerable number of requests to support fieldwork. Rather than respond on an institution-by-institution basis, the staff recommended to the board that "a fellowship program on a national scale" be established. They eliminated fellowship funds from the area program budgets and began in 1947 to allocate annually $130,000 for research fellowships and travel grants under the auspices of the Social Science Research Council.[98] Over the main years of this program, 1949 to 1953, the Corporation provided about $780,000 for fellowships. The Rockefeller Foundation, as noted earlier, had funded area-specific fellowships and exchanges as well since the 1930s. At the end of World War II, the US government also became involved, with Congress enacting the Fulbright Program in August 1946. An interesting footnote is that Carnegie Corporation and the Rockefeller Foundation helped launch the program by covering the first six months of operation.[99] Two additional programs greatly enhanced the availability of fellowships for Americans who wished to study overseas and opportunities for exchanges across countries. In 1948 the US Information and Educational Exchange Act was passed with the aim "to promote the better understanding of the United States among the peoples of the world and to strengthen cooperative international relations."[100] After it established the Foreign Area Fellowship Program in 1952 with an initial amount of $500,000, the Ford Foundation soon became the major nongovernmental supporter of overseas fellowships and exchanges, spending $35.1 million by 1977.[101]

TRAINING, RESEARCH, AND OUTREACH IN
INTERNATIONAL RELATIONS

IN PARALLEL TO THE EXTENSIVE EFFORTS to enhance American understanding of specific geographic areas of the world, the Corporation
embarked on a series of grants to improve training in international relations, conduct specific research on fundamental issues integral to the conduct of foreign policy, enhance think tanks' capacity for public and policy
outreach on international affairs, and strengthen institutional capacity to
provide international exchanges. In the grant-making devoted to building
the field of area studies, the Corporation and the Rockefeller Foundation
provided the major support but did not work as partners. For the panoply
of work in international relations, the two foundations collaborated much
more closely and developed grants jointly. Both saw the work in this area as
essential for deepening understanding—especially that of policymakers—
of the nuances in the conduct of American foreign relations, particularly
in light of the challenges posed by policies related to anticommunism and
military engagement. The Ford Foundation soon began to make a significant contribution, often enlarging support in areas where the Rockefeller
Foundation and Carnegie Corporation had already been working together.

Before World War II, these two foundations had addressed different
dimensions of the field of international relations in the United States, even
though they often supported the same institutions. Beginning in the early
1930s, Rockefeller Foundation focused on foreign policy and international
relations, while Carnegie Corporation's greater priority was international
security and public outreach.[102] The Rockefeller Foundation was deeply
concerned about the ability of American policymakers and policy advisers to understand the complex foreign policy issues of the day. Rockefeller
Foundation staff had provided early backing to create deeper capacity for
discussion and action through institutions such as the Council on Foreign
Relations. In the 1930s, the Corporation also supported the Council on
Foreign Relations' plan to reach interested opinion-shapers outside of
Washington, DC, and New York by establishing local or regional commit-
tees in cities across the United States.[103]

Edward Earle, an innovative foreign policy researcher and Corporation grantee, had been funded since 1939 to define a new interdisciplinary approach for the study of international security studies at the Institute for Advanced Study at Princeton. With Earle bringing together virtually the entire next generation of prominent leaders in the field, the Corporation support continued through World War II as part of the National Emergency Program. This work, and the planning of the new program from 1945 to 1946, led Josephs and his team to observe the increased interest at the undergraduate level in a wide range of courses in international relations. This piqued the interest of Corporation staff members, who realized "that college graduates … exposed to such training would form the core of an informed American public." That realization led to a commitment to ensuring that the courses would be "of the highest quality." Staff members sought to give such courses "a drastic overhauling" by having them move away from the "excessively legalistic approach, and a strong strain of idealism," which limited the introduction of real-world questions such as those of "power conflict." To update these courses so that they would expose students to current realities, "such as the Truman Doctrine, the Marshall Plan, the ECA [Economic Cooperation Administration], NATO, and Point IV," Corporation staff believed that faculty had not only to grasp but to understand and be able to present coherently "the revolutionary unrest throughout the world, intensified class and racial conflicts, and the complexities of the Cold War." They recognized that both junior and senior faculty would need further training to be effective teachers and advisers.[104]

For six years the Corporation invested more than $400,000 in grants to the Brookings Institution for summer seminars, organized by Leo Pasvolsky and co-funded by the Rockefeller Foundation, to improve the teaching of foreign affairs and international relations, as well as involve relevant representatives from the State Department and armed services.[105] Brookings rotated the seminars around the country, to Dartmouth, Lake Forest, Stanford, and elsewhere; shorter seminars also achieved positive results. Convinced that the seminars had become a major factor in shaping the teaching of international affairs at colleges in the postwar period, Corporation staff, feeling that still more needed to be done, sought additional opportunities.[106]

One approach to strengthening teaching in this area built on the Earle

seminars and emphasized research in departments of international relations. Starting in 1947, the Corporation supported departments of international relations at Yale, Columbia, Johns Hopkins, Stanford, and Princeton,
covering research, conferences, and publications. As noted in the 1951 review
for the Board of Trustees, "Much remains to be done, and there are probably many ways in which a foundation might assist in the further development of this field."[107]

At the same time that Corporation staff were concerned about the relationship between technical assistance and the spread of communism in
underdeveloped countries, they also raised the issue of the changing atmosphere in Washington, with special concern about the secrecy surrounding
American national security programs, the increased size and role of the military establishment, and the increase in international enmity since the end
of World War II, engendered in part by the Korean War. Staff members
believed that scholars and the public sphere at large were not paying enough
attention to these three post–World War II developments that could fundamentally affect American society.

To address these concerns, Corporation staff member James Perkins
and his colleague Don Price of the Public Administration Clearing House
(Price would soon join the Ford Foundation) prepared a background memo
on the wide range of issues associated with civilian and military relationships in the emerging Cold War. At the request of the secretary of the army,
Frank Pace, and the secretary of the air force, Thomas Finletter, the memo
was discussed over a "small dinner" in Washington, DC, organized by the
Corporation. Board member Elihu Root Jr. participated, as did Dollard. The
memo posited the two framing issues for the discussion of civilian-military
relations: "Our security program has greatly increased the weight of military considerations in the formulation and execution of national policies …
military officers participate in government and public counsels to a greatly
increased extent."[108] With support from the participants at this meeting, and
following extensive discussions with academics, government officials, and
others, the Corporation organized a subsequent meeting that discussed all
of these issues in greater depth. The opportunities for research and action
became clear as a result of these discussions. The initial major partner for
the Corporation in this endeavor was the Twentieth Century Fund; the

Rockefeller Foundation soon joined. As highlighted in the agenda item for the board, a main outcome of this second meeting was "a general feeling on the part of this group that the time is more than ripe for serious academic and public attention to the problem."[109]

The next steps included asking the Social Science Research Council to establish a committee on civilian-military relations, drawing together key scholars from a few campuses. The Council served both as a "clearing-house" on existing material for researchers in the field and as a promoter of new research. In addition, the Public Administration Clearing House was encouraged to hold dinner discussions with key officials in Washington to raise awareness among those officials and enhance "the availability of material" for scholars. The group encouraged cross-fertilization across the two efforts.[110]

Central to these discussions was the academic international relations specialist William T. R. Fox, renowned for his theoretical work.[111] The Corporation knew Fox from his work at the Yale Institute of International Studies in the late 1940s. He had moved to Columbia University in 1950 to focus more on his writing. As a highly distinguished scholar in international relations, Fox was asked to chair the Social Science Research Council Committee on Civilian-Military Relations.[112] Through the grants program, funded for nearly twelve years by the Corporation, the committee began its work by preparing a major bibliography for the field to enable scholars to better examine questions such as: What is the appropriate role of the military in foreign policy? In diplomatic missions? In on-the-ground assignments? Then, in 1952, it focused on taking a different approach to American military history, through the lens of military policy and the political and economic aspects of war. Corporation staff members believed that this committee helped shape a new field of research and continued to provide support throughout its lifetime. The initial grant was in September 1952 for $12,225 and was then enlarged in March 18, 1954, to the level of $75,000 over three years for the work on American military policy.[113]

Columbia University president Dwight D. Eisenhower persuaded Fox to head the newly formed Institute of War and Peace Studies.[114] The Corporation also provided two grants—starting in 1953, and under Fox's aegis—at the Institute to examine the civil-military issues involved in establishing national security policy. Fox described the policy orientation of this effort as based on

> the notion that the historic way of looking at civil-military relations, in American history ... could be phrased as the problem of how to keep the high brass from taking over. We found ourselves living in a period in which it seemed to be the problem not of how to maintain civilian control but of how to maintain competence in civilian control. It wasn't simply a matter of improving the system of checks and balances to make sure the general didn't get up on his horse and ride away with our Constitutional liberties.... The new problem was how to orchestrate the expertises, civilian and military, of our society so that, while maintaining our American way of life we are also reasonably efficient in being able to meet the external threats.[115]

In addition, the trustees approved $45,000 for a program at Dartmouth College to educate military leaders so that current career military officers would have an adequate liberal education.[116]

A different set of grants, also funded jointly with the Rockefeller Foundation, helped establish another field of research around "social adjustments to atomic energy." Staff members at both foundations recognized the importance of "public understanding of energy and its effect on attitudes toward foreign policy, universal military training, etc."[117] Toward that end, the two foundations shared support at the level of $23,875 each, bringing together a new Social Science Research Council Committee on the Social Aspects of Atomic Energy, comprising social and natural scientists, technical and administrative support staff from Cornell University, and representatives of the polling agencies and the Program Survey Bureau of the US Department of Agriculture.[118] The intent was to measure public attitudes in response to Operation Crossroads, the post–World War II program for atomic bomb testing starting in the Bikini Atoll.[119] The foundation saw this as a model for assessing public attitudes toward other sensitive governmental activities, as well as one that would shed light specifically on these experiments with the bomb. In addition to studying the impact on American public attitudes about the bomb test, the committee examined attitudes about foreign relations with the Soviet Union and Great Britain, about the United Nations, and about America's role in the world.

The joint program on public understanding at Cornell University and the Social Science Research Council Committee on Social Aspects of the Atomic Bomb and the probing analyses of civilian-military relations undertaken by Columbia University's Institute of War and Peace Studies and the Social Science Research Council Committee on Civilian-Military Relations produced innovative and timely results; nonetheless, the policy impacts were limited.

The poll on the atomic bomb testing did lead to useful results on the role of public opinion testing; the public was convinced of the importance of the testing but also was in favor of international controls.[120]

According to Fox, the activities probing civilian-military relations were successful in helping to establish the interdisciplinary field of national security studies, following on the work of Earle on international security studies. Although the Columbia Institute on War and Peace Studies and the Social Science Research Council efforts generated serious studies and major publications for a number of years, the effects of this work on public understanding and decision-makers were not as deep as the Corporation staff had hoped they would be.

All these efforts reflected the Corporation's concern about giving "systematic attention to problems involving the relations of military and civilian authorities in the conduct of national defense."[121] These prescient discussions continued well into the 1960s at the Social Science Research Council. Yet, the impact on clarifying and harmonizing civilian and military relations in the context of the Defense Department and the conduct of foreign policy has never been fully assessed. The conduct of the Vietnam War, for example, which intensified soon after the ending of these activities, illustrates how difficult it is for the scholarly community to make a difference, even when earnestly committed to improving policy.

OUTREACH ON INTERNATIONAL AFFAIRS
TO THE PUBLIC AND POLICYMAKERS

IN HIS 1950 PRESIDENT'S REPORT, Dollard noted that the Corporation had spent more than $5.5 million on increasing knowledge in the United States about the rest of the world, through activities ranging from formal university education to more limited programs aimed at elementary school students. He calculated that nearly half that amount, 42 percent, had supported a mix of education and outreach activities.[122] Dollard argued that greater public understanding of a wide range of international activities was needed, along with humility, especially when labeling "those peoples who do not share our social, economic and religious institutions as 'backward' nations." He noted that such arrogance "has cost us the friendship and confidence of millions."[123] These concerns underlined the aim of the outreach programs to enhance public understanding of "'the rest of the world.'"[124]

In closing his essay, Dollard commented on the difficult decision concerning South Korea and the need in December 1948 for military operations to sustain the "uneasy peace that began in 1945," albeit this time under the UN flag. Highlighting security concerns, he said that the results of the 1948 and 1950 elections, with their divisive divisions of political power, further reinforced the Corporation's commitment to public and policymaker global understanding.[125] The Corporation maintained support for its long-term grantees in this area, namely, the Institute of Pacific Relations, the Foreign Policy Association, the Council on Foreign Relations, the Carnegie Endowment for International Peace, and the Church Peace Union.

The Corporation's grants to the Institute of Pacific Relations exemplified its commitment to international public education. In early 1946, staff reported to the board that the Institute had accumulated important information about the Pacific area and was focusing on popular and secondary education. It also prepared materials for the US military drawn from its educational activities. The teaching materials reached 1,300 public school systems, and the Corporation had contributed to the development of this extensive work on public education. The board agreed to continue to fund the program at the level of $55,000.[126] By early 1947, the staff of the Institute had identified new sources of income so that the 50 percent of its income provided by the Rockefeller Foundation and Carnegie Corporation could be replaced. As a result, the Corporation made a final grant for annual support of $120,000 over three years, but encouraged the Institute to identify projects for specific support in the future.[127]

But it was the Council on Foreign Relations that the Corporation officers considered the preeminent institution for providing information to the educated public and policymakers on complex foreign policy issues. Nearly every year from 1938 to 1954, the Corporation renewed its support for the Council at various levels through separate grants for research and publications, fellowships, and the nationwide locally organized Committees on Foreign Relations. In 1954 the trustees agreed to make one large grant covering the traditional three activities—research and study programs, local committees, and fellowships (for scholars and journalists)—at the level of $500,000 over a five-year period. The board also backed complementary programs of the Foreign Policy Association, enabling it to build on its successful outreach in the Midwest and to develop new programs on the United Nations charter, economic problems (such as cartels), the Anglo-American oil agreement, postwar trade in the United States as well as newly liberated areas, colonial issues, and other issues affecting the foreign policy of the United States. In these activities the Rockefeller Foundation was also a major supporter of both these institutions.[128]

The Carnegie Endowment for International Peace did not receive much assistance in this period, at least not as much as desired by Nicholas Murray Butler, chair of the Endowment's board as well as the Corporation's. When Butler was stepping down from the latter board in 1945, he made one last, equally unsuccessful, effort to obtain a significant grant for the Endowment. The Corporation deferred the Endowment's postwar request of $150,000 for educational programs until "such time as the direction and the programs of the Endowment are clarified and the purposes to which Corporation funds are to be applied can be clearly defined."[129] When the Endowment appointed Alger Hiss as the new president in 1947, the Corporation had more confidence in the direction and leadership of the institution; they approved his tightly focused request to support work on public education around the UN.[130] The Endowment then became a regular grantee for nearly two decades, at the annual level of about $75,000.

The Corporation also continued to support the work of the Church Peace Union, a longtime grantee, in education on peace both for the public and throughout the church community. The modest level of $10,000 per year was maintained throughout World War II and in the years immediately following. The Corporation in 1946 also made a discretionary grant of $7,500 to the Federal Council of Churches of Christ in America for a conference of churchmen on the problem of world order and the establishment of the Commission on International Relations.[131]

In the 1953 review, the officers commented to the board that there was now abundant information on international affairs, which had not been the case earlier. They highlighted for the trustees the set of grants to the Council on Foreign Relations for the local Committees on Foreign Relations as one of the Corporation's most successful and distinctive contributions.[132] They were also positive about the results of the World Affairs Councils that they had fostered, including help with launching the one for Northern California.[133] These efforts, however successfully they were reviewed in 1953, did not saturate the public arena. That concern was explicitly addressed in the next era, when John Gardner, as Corporation president, promoted a major thrust on public affairs for international understanding with the intent of achieving such saturation.

INTELLECTUAL AND SCIENTIFIC EXCHANGES

THE CORPORATION SINCE THE 1920S had sponsored international exchanges as a critical component of building American awareness of the world; this theme informed the last part of the 1946 core plan to advance and disseminate international knowledge and understanding. In the interwar era, primarily through the Institute of International Education, the funds, either as grants-in-aid or travel grants (the latter mainly for residents of the British dominions and colonies), covered individual overseas travel, participation in international conferences, and exchanges of publications.

In association with the Phelps Stokes Fund and the Institute of International Education, the Corporation tackled specific areas of concern, such as the conditions faced by students from overseas studying in American colleges and universities. Following support of an extensive survey of the situation facing the hundreds of African students in the United States, the Corporation and the Phelps Stokes Fund co-funded a proposal—developed with the backing of the US State Department, the British Colonial Office, and the Committee on African Students in North America—that would have the Institute take responsibility for providing improved services for these students, from selection to return home, including "counseling, placement, and supervision."[134]

In 1946, because of the greater number of governmental and intergovernmental agencies providing support for international contacts, the Corporation chose to focus on ways to increase "the vitality" of private providers such as the Institute of International Education. The aim was to ensure that "their operating machinery is in order and their objectives more clearly defined."[135] As noted in the initial 1946 agenda item, the Corporation had provided nearly $1.3 million worth of support since the founding of the Institute in 1919 by the Corporation and the Carnegie Endowment.[136] Over the period 1946 to 1953, the Institute experienced leadership changes and a lack of direction that caused enough concern that Corporation staff had strongly considered recommending a final grant in the early part of this era. When a new leader was appointed in 1950, however, nearly one and a half years after the death of the previous president, Dollard organized a luncheon at Carnegie Corporation with other foundation supporters of the Institute. The group agreed on the importance of having a "strong private agency to handle international exchange of students, and a disposition on the part of most of the foundations to do their part in maintaining such an agency."[137] Nonetheless, the discussion raised many "friendly questions" about the functioning of the Institute and its role in the international exchanges of students and scholars.[138]

Following the completion of two studies supported by the foundations, it had become clear by 1953 that the Institute had "major responsibility for the coordination and direction of virtually all programs involving exchange of students between the United States and foreign countries."[139] With other supporters, including the Ford Foundation and government contracts, covering about 40 percent of the administrative costs, the Corporation's annual contributions were no longer as significant, covering only about 13 percent of the budget. In the same report to the board, staff members highlighted the fact that foreign student enrollment had risen from 7,000 in 1933 to 30,000 in 1951 and that the Institute had played a major role in handling the scholarships for the increasing number of foreign students. The Corporation felt that the studies of the Institute's operations showed great improvement and that, rather than contribute annually, they and other foundation supporters should begin to make longer-term grants to contribute to the operating costs of the Institute. Consequently, in 1953 the trustees approved a grant of $450,000 over three years to the Institute.[140]

At the same time, Dollard and his colleagues persisted in questioning the overall effect of these fellowships and exchanges. The Rockefeller Foundation had for years, along with the Corporation, funded exchanges; now, with the Ford Foundation active in this area, together the three foundations asked the Social Science Research Council and the Institute of International Education to study the benefits of such exchanges. Questions they explored included: How do these fellowships contribute to international understanding as well as understanding of the United States? Are these fellowships more effective for people who are younger or for those who are more mature? They also were concerned about the educational benefits of such exchanges.[141] The questions they raised, never fully resolved and resonating across the decades, remain the salient questions about how to support exchanges, including junior year abroad programs (as discussed in Chapter 5), in deepening and sustaining American public understanding of the world.

ANOTHER NEW FIELD: ASSESSING THE EFFECTIVENESS OF TECHNICAL ASSISTANCE TO UNDERDEVELOPED COUNTRIES

THE QUESTIONS CONCERNING INTERNATIONAL EXCHANGES were reminiscent of an earlier set of questions that Corporation staff members began to ask in the mid-1940s about another area of American foreign policy endeavor, namely, the provision of technical assistance, whether by voluntary agencies or by the government. Two distinctive trends, starting immediately prior to World War II and continuing through the war and beyond, fueled American public and policymaker engagement with what became known as "foreign assistance." The movement toward self-determination and independence in the colonized regions of the world that emerged during and following World War II prompted policymaker and academic involvement, especially around issues of governance, education, and leadership in what would become the new nation-states.[142] The extraordinary relief needs starting in 1939 with the early war in Europe prompted a great outpouring of American citizen resources that continued through the war and afterward, including support for the government's Marshall Plan in Europe and for extensive private efforts in the Near and Middle East.[143] Concern about relief efforts in countries that were emerging from the British Empire also became a focal point of the voluntary and US government technical assistance, especially after President Truman's inaugural speech on January 20, 1949, which led to the Point Four Program, the first systematic US governmental effort to provide technical assistance in developing countries.[144]

These trends directly influenced the grant-making of the two major international American foundations in the 1940s, Carnegie Corporation and the Rockefeller Foundation. Much like the grant-making for area studies, international relations, and the social adjustment to atomic energy, the foundations collaborated in the field of technical assistance, but even more closely. Both foundations not only shared concerns about how such assistance would be delivered and received but also understood analytically its potential for damage, which could undermine the intended benefits. The Corporation's most significant early work in this area comprised three activities that included two major grants, and one long-term consultancy.[145]

The grants to Cornell University and Michigan State College (now University) to examine the social, cultural, and political problems involved in technological assistance in developing countries, initiated over the period 1947 to 1949 and continuing for more than ten years, were pioneering grants that helped to define a field. Many of the people involved became the leading scholars and policymakers on these subjects (much as happened with the area studies, international relations, and international security). Cornell University received the first grant in 1947 for a program of study and training that directly tackled the question of how "technological advances can be presented to a society so as to minimize conflict with old traditions and folkways."[146] Initially the program focused on incorporating cultural anthropology into training programs for engineers and agriculturalists (from both the United States and overseas); it also included research on the psychological aspects of introducing new technologies in the "so-called backward areas of the world."[147] The four field sites were a Peruvian hacienda, a village in central Thailand, a village in India, and a Navajo reservation in New Mexico. When Cornell requested additional funding for the remaining two years, Corporation staff members were sympathetic because they understood the difficulty of predicting the outcomes and continuing expenses of this experimental work.

By this time, the Point Four Program had come into existence and become a focus of the program as well: "The research program has been concerned with specially-induced technological changes of the sort associated with the Point Four Program, and also with the slower processes of change resulting from the normal diffusion of Western ideas into underdeveloped areas."[148] Agreeing with the suggestion that the program be expanded to include work in nutrition and public health, and recognizing the importance of analyzing and writing up the findings of the nearly ten years of research, the staff recommended the additional support of $40,000. The agenda item also noted that this amount was small compared to the $500,000 that had already been invested. Several aspects of this program were bolstered by support from the Rockefeller Foundation, especially for the anthropological work in Southeast Asia.[149]

The grant to Michigan State College, starting in 1949 and continuing over ten years at the level of $30,000 per year, began by supporting a study based at a field site in Turrialba, Costa Rica. As a staff member described the effort in the agenda item, "Everyone who has had firsthand contact with attempts to provide assistance to nonindustrialized peoples recognizes that such ventures encounter serious obstacles which lie well outside the economic and technological problems involved."[150] The ties of Michigan State College president John Hannah (later administrator of the US Agency for International Development) and other faculty to officials in the US Agriculture and State Departments led this work to focus directly on the human dimensions of introducing new technologies for improvements in agricultural production. In renewing the support in 1954 at the level of $150,000 over another five-year period, the Corporation recognized the value of the Michigan State work conducted through the Inter-American Institute of Agricultural Sciences in Costa Rica, particularly in the ways it had expanded understanding of how to handle the complex societal problems of introducing technological innovations.

These results led the Corporation to endorse the extension of the work to a new place: the United States–Mexico border. Here the aim was to examine the different approaches to accepting new technologies by farmers on either side of the border where the land conditions were the same. The circumstances that differed were the farmers' levels of economic development and their adoption of innovative approaches; the American farmers, according to the proposal, were more willing than the Mexicans to accept new approaches. Corporation staff members posited this difference as "one of the many puzzles which must be solved if we are to understand fully the roots of economic and cultural backwardness."[151]

The expansion of technical assistance programs by the US government prompted Charles Dollard, by this time president of the Corporation, and the two vice presidents, James Perkins and John Gardner, to raise with a colleague at the Rockefeller Foundation, Vice President Lindsley F. Kimball, their concern about the increasing overlap in foundation and government activities. In 1950 Dollard and Perkins met with Kimball, Flora Rhind, secretary of the Rockefeller Foundation, and Andrew Warren, director of the Foundation's Division of Medical and Public Health, to talk about hiring an outside person to conduct a review for them. Gardner identified a current consultant and former editor at W. W. Norton, Elling Aannestad, as someone with the appropriate skills who might be available.[152] From that initial meeting in October 1950 emerged a partnership between the two foundations to hire Aannestad, with the Rockefeller Foundation covering his salary and Carnegie Corporation providing the office space, secretarial support, and traveling expenses. Aannestad suggested that an area of shared interest might be the increasing role of governmental activities in the developing world, with special attention to technical assistance. This led to a remarkable consultancy over nearly three years that examined and reported to the foundations on developments, inter alia, in the implementation of the Point Four Program, including the role of social science research and development of the field of technical aid through the Technical Cooperation

Administration and the Economic Cooperation Administration, as well as UNESCO (United Nations Economic, Social, and Cultural Organization) in Paris.[153]

By December 1951, after attending congressional hearings, talking with State Department officials, researchers, and scholars, examining the different executive branch agencies involved in technical systems, exploring the role of voluntary agencies in providing assistance, and spending time talking with UNESCO staff about their work, Aannestad summarized his findings and asked nine prescient questions that still haunt programs of development assistance in the twenty-first century, such as, "How can programs of aid be developed which build independence instead of dependence in the recipient countries, and which rely principally on the resources, capacities, and desires of the peoples assisted?"[154]

Unfortunately, this particular consultancy, which never led to publications, appears not to have directly influenced the programs of either foundation related to the work on development assistance or the original question of foundation-government relations around research. The one possible contribution, although not acknowledged, can be seen in the essay by Rockefeller president Dean Rusk in the Rockefeller Foundation's 1954 annual report; Rusk raised questions about technical assistance that reflected the list prepared by Aannestad.[155] The Corporation began in the 1960s to fund a series of in-depth studies on development and modernization that implicitly reflected questions raised by Aannestad and the Cornell and Michigan field studies. The Corporation tackled closely related issues in the 1990s, but without access to the knowledge of the precedent it had set in the 1940s and 1950s.[156]

RECONNOITERING, THEN RECONSTRUCTING, THE BRITISH DOMINIONS AND COLONIES PROGRAM

THE MAJOR STRENGTHS AND WEAKNESSES of the British Dominions and Colonies Fund in the interwar era had been assessed in the reviews that Jessup sponsored in 1942 and 1943 (see Chapter 3). Because the program had been put on hold during World War II and the funds had not been mingled with the Corporation's main fund, the BDC Fund had accumulated $1.5 million that was available for grant-making (the equivalent of $17.9 million today).[157] Combined with the growing movement for change throughout the British Empire, the potential for significant grant-making was clear. Josephs was as eager to revive the foundation's work in the British Empire as to enhance American understanding of the world. To move forward, he needed to obtain trustee approval, put staff in place, and then design and present a compelling program to the board. In October 1945, the trustees agreed to reopen the program and appoint a new staff member, but they also requested a fresh review of the history to identify the best possible uses of the protected resources.[158]

Possibly recognizing that with the changes under way in the dominions and colonies, the British government would be even more sensitive to the involvement of American foundations in the dynamics of decolonization, Josephs hired a true Anglophile, Whitney Shepardson, who had worked in London and had British friends at many levels of government and throughout the policy research community. Shepardson brought deep experience along with recognition of the different approaches that Carnegie Corporation might take to play a constructive role and work effectively at the local level in this turbulent postwar period.[159] Josephs also asked Stephen Stackpole (hired by Keppel in 1940) to remain at the Corporation with the title of staff member, to continue in his assignment to the British Dominions and Colonies Fund, and to focus on the work in Canada.

The rapid evolution from decolonization to independence in the African and Caribbean colonies posed a series of questions for the Corporation to consider. What could an outside institution contribute to these momentous changes? Was education still the appropriate point of continued contact? Where could considerable but still limited resources make the greatest difference? Was there a way to build on the carefully nurtured collaboration with the British Commonwealth, which was always sensitive about American interference in the Empire? Would the status changes taking place as a result of British Commonwealth ministerial conferences make a difference for the program?[160] As a consequence, the Corporation amended the charter in 1948, abolishing the BDC Fund as an entity and combining its assets with the Corporation's general endowment. The amendment authorized the trustees "to use the income from $12 million of its general funds … in Canada, the British colonies or the British dominions, whether such colonies or dominions attained such status prior to or after the passage of the act."[161] With the definitions clarified, the Corporation proceeded to act as it always had.

It was clear to the seasoned Shepardson that an effective program would require more than building on what had been done before World War II. He needed to take the measure of those who were responsible for policy in the British Empire: the British Colonial Office, the British colonial government, the government leaders in the dominions, and local leaders in the colonies. He also needed to see the situation on the ground for himself. Starting in London, Shepardson visited the dominions and some colonies and consulted "all friends and counselors of the Corporation." But he also looked for "new friends … to suggest how the Carnegie Corporation can make the income of the Fund go far, by marrying small sums of money to enterprises of real promise and to individuals of great faith."[162]

Shepardson traveled extensively throughout the Commonwealth, in sub-Saharan and South Africa, in Australia and New Zealand, touching base in London as needed. Describing his findings about the success of the investments in educational research made "under Mr. Keppel's inspired direction" in Australia, New Zealand, and South Africa, Shepardson wrote that "it was always the intention and the hope that these efforts, if they prove their worth, would pass under the aegis of government and would continue to expand with solid government support. It is one of the satisfactions of foundation work to report that as of today, after the war and in spite of that, these results have been achieved. The credit belongs to those in the three dominions who put their hands to the plow and did not turn back."[163] With these findings, he recommended continued backing for the adult education initiatives of the past as well as for the institutes of international affairs (all associated with the UK-based Royal Institute of International Affairs) in several Commonwealth countries. He also pointed to the isolation of professionals in the dominions resulting from severed contact during the war, highlighting the need to revive the travel grants program in order to freshen and sustain Commonwealth connections.

The travel grants became the cornerstone of the new BDC program. Yet even as he made the case to continue them, Shepardson raised some concerns. He had pointed out that others were also undertaking programs for foreign study and travel: the Fulbright Program, the US Information and Educational Exchange Act, UNESCO, the Nuffield and Imperial Relations Trust in Britain, the British Council, and other Commonwealth institutions. The Rockefeller Foundation and the Commonwealth Fund also offered travel and study grants. But Shepardson could not bring himself to shut down that part of the program. He emphasized instead that for the Corporation "this multiplication of sources of support means that it must keep its own program under constant review to make sure that it does not compete with, or seriously overlap, other programs." He further identified the rationale for maintaining the travel grants: "For the time being, however, the Corporation's travel grants to individuals seem to occupy an otherwise unoccupied place amongst the various programs particularly when dollars *qua* dollars are required to carry out a plan." And it remained the case that the Corporation also filled an almost empty niche by making it possible to send individuals from the colonies and dominions to visit elsewhere in the Commonwealth, not just the United Kingdom, the United States, or Canada. As Shepardson commented, "Not many such opportunities are offered by other grant-making bodies."[164] Moreover, it was clear from the number of people receiving travel grants that senior leaders on both sides were supportive.

Shepardson soon refined the focus from a wide range of senior and junior recipients covering a wide range of Corporation grant interests to awarding travel grants to more senior educators and researchers in science and the field of education; education policymakers were also included. Many grant recipients, such as Professor Sydney Brenner from South Africa, a future Nobel Prize winner in medicine, were already fairly distinguished. Shepardson also created a special category of travel grant: bringing journalists from foreign countries to Harvard University as Nieman Fellows. The intent was to give them exposure that might enable them to write with more understanding about the United States and its values and developments. Over time the travel grants program increasingly focused on centrally placed individuals or those from institutions whose work was of the highest quality and addressed problems of broad national or international concerns, and away from the junior faculty members and local arts teachers who had been supported alongside the more senior recipients in the 1930s.

Shepardson visited the British colonies as local leaders were demanding power-sharing and, especially in African colonies, serious investments in higher education.[165] Those leaders knew that eventually they would be taking over the running of their countries. Rather than continue the focus on technical and vocational training, they knew that independence and economic development would require a cadre of national administrators, managers, technical experts, and teachers capable of developing an informed and educated citizenry.

Moving away from the Jeanes education vocational grants of the interwar years, Shepardson and Stackpole saw the need to build up Africa's educational infrastructure before independence. The Corporation was an eager partner in British efforts to establish or strengthen universities in nearly all of its African and Caribbean colonies.[166] Together they also addressed a number of related questions: What constituted effective leadership in the African context? Effective teaching? Appropriate curriculum? Did nutrition affect learning? How was it possible to put together African history in a way that would reach African populations? The Corporation made a few exploratory grants in each of these areas before the major investments in universities and the field of higher education.

For example, a grant to Makerere University in 1953—three years of support at a level of $125,000—established the East African Institute of Social Research for the study of African leadership.[167] One grant in rural Nigeria established an agricultural training and demonstration center in Asaba (the site of a similar grant thirty years later). This grant, at the level of $60,000 over five years, was a fairly considerable activity: it complemented the resources provided by the Colonial Welfare and Development Fund, the Nigerian government, and missionary societies by providing support for hiring a public health worker and a director for development of the village centers.[168] Another grant addressed the issue of food security in Africa, one of the first to delve into this ongoing issue; in 1953 the Stanford Food Research Institute, which had not been funded by the Corporation for nearly two decades, received support to conduct in-depth studies on this issue with the aim of developing better policies.[169]

During a three-month, summer-long visit to South Africa in 1948, Shepardson was fully aware of the fraught situation in that country, but also recommended a series of continuing grants for travel, library support, international relations at the universities, and publications, as well as some limited field research. This was a time when South Africa's National (soon to be called Nationalist) Party, having won the general election of 1948, was actively implementing its policy of apartheid. In response, Shepardson did make some changes—for instance, he put decisions on the selection process for travel grants back in New York with the staff members and shifted the South African role to an advisory one. But he retained the funding role of the South African trustees at least until the resources that they had maintained during the war ran out. He expressed naive optimism about the capacity of South Africa to deal with a "number of difficult problems, political, economic, social and racial." He ended his report to the trustees by emphasizing that "in no other of the old dominions of the Commonwealth is it necessary for the Corporation to take such careful thought before acting. On the other hand, there is probably no other Dominion where funds of the Corporation, voted after careful thought, can be so effective."[170]

By 1953 Corporation officers had made clear their anxiety about working in the country. The minutes from the May 1953 Board of Trustees meeting reported: "In discussing … present conditions in [South] Africa, the members … were in agreement that the officers … should exercise particular caution in making grants in that area and should even consider the possibility of suspending any plans for new activities in the Union during the present crisis."[171] The country was pursuing, some thought, "a naked, legalized racism that drew its ideals from the Nazis."[172] Of all the areas in which apartheid changed South African society, perhaps the most destructive was education. As Francis Wilson, a major Corporation grantee in the 1980s, remarked in a recently published history of South Africa, "The Bantu Education Act of 1953 embodied a philosophy that specified that it would not educate black South Africans for positions in the economy beyond those they were expected to occupy…. The consequence was to poison the well of education in a way that would cripple the society for decades to come."[173] Limited grant-making by the Corporation continued for a few years, including to institutions trying to counter the destructive policies and their devastating impacts through education, research, and access to knowledge.

Library support dominated much of the work in South Africa, but the program also funded other activities, including research on the conditions of natives, even at this difficult time. The Institute for Social Research at the Natal University College, where longtime Corporation grantee Ernst Malherbe was then vice chancellor, received grants starting in 1948.[174] Appointed principal of Natal University College in 1945 by Premier Jan Smuts and inaugurated with Smuts by his side in March 1949, Malherbe was in a particularly sensitive position at Natal.[175] Nonetheless, he succeeded in fighting "the Nationalist government to keep the university multiracial, including the only black medical school in Africa, an even more important institution to the formation of a black elite than Fort Hare."[176] An anthropological research project at the University of Cape Town[177] and book purchases for Rhodes University also received support.[178]

After World War II, earlier grantee institutions, the South African Institute of Race Relations and the South African Institute of International Affairs, received funds, the former a travel grant in 1949 and the latter for its library over the period 1950 to 1954, but not for specific field projects, as in the past.[179] The Corporation underwrote basic scientific research in partnership with the Carnegie Institution of Washington and the University of the Witwatersrand for continuing the prewar collaboration on research in embryology (over the period 1942 to 1946) and geophysics (in 1952).[180]

Grant-making continued in the other two southern dominions, Australia and New Zealand, although not at the same level as before World War II. Some of the grants reflected the Corporation's interest in promoting the social sciences in the United States, such as those for a travel grant in anthropology at the Australian National University (in 1951), for developing the Australian Social Science Research Council (1953), and for teaching and research in social anthropology and psychology at the University of Western Australia (1954).[181] Public and university libraries also received funding. Similar to the support in South Africa, the Corporation pursued the theme of scientific collaboration by underwriting a partnership between the University of Western Australia and the Carnegie Institution of Washington for geophysical research.[182] Australians continued to get the bulk of the travel grants.

Similarly, in New Zealand, support helped to strengthen the social sciences at the University of New Zealand.[183] Continuing a major prewar focus, the Corporation backed the New Zealand Council for Educational

Research in developing programs in sociology and examining the question of forming a social science research council.[184] A linkage grant went to the New Zealand Council for Educational Research and to the Australian Council for Educational Research to encourage the two groups to develop closer ties and coordinate their research and programmatic efforts.[185] Modest support over several years also continued for the New Zealand Library Association, and New Zealanders were also high on the list of travel grant recipients.[186]

A Special Cross–Southern Dominion Initiative

Having created the Educational Testing Service in 1947—in a merger of the main American testing organizations—the Corporation similarly began a fellowship program for several years for psychologists and educators from the dominions and colonies that involved training in psychometric testing; that is, the attempt to measure mental capacity objectively with the intent to channel societal resources accordingly. The Educational Research Council leaders in the three countries had already identified the work on testing as high-priority areas for investment. Grants to the Australian Council for Educational Research and in South Africa developed their educational testing services.[187]

In Australia and New Zealand, the Corporation supported psychometric fellowships to reinforce the program of testing that had originally been introduced by Kenneth Cunningham, the first director of the Australian Council for Educational Research. It was then shared with colleagues at the New Zealand Council for Educational Research.[188] This approach to testing has been criticized by modern scholars for its impact on Australian society, as it reshaped the objectives of Australian education.[189]

The most alarming of these fellowships for psychometric work went to the South African Council for Scientific and Industrial Research. The grants also included mobile laboratories for research on the mentality and aptitudes of Africans and studies of the development of African children.[190] As Johann Louw and others have shown, this focus on testing contributed to solidifying the argument for apartheid.[191] The quantitative normalized testing approach could bolster the bogus claim that native populations were "mentally deficient." The program in psychometric fellowships to overseas recipients, like standardized testing in the United States, was idealistically aimed at increasing scholarly capacity and contributing to improved education policy decision-making and practice by creating a level playing field for applicants to higher education institutions. In a situation like South Africa, such testing provided not immediately lethal but still highly dangerous ammunition for the Nationalist Party.

Ironically, despite the controversial past of educational testing in the three southern former dominions of the British Commonwealth, in the twenty-first century it provides global comparisons and a standard best-practice tool for educational assessment. As noted in Chapter 3, the institution the Corporation helped establish in Australia, the Australian Council for Educational Research, is now the preeminent global institution responsible for global comparison testing.

Canada

The Corporation's historic relationship with Canada, along with the nation's proximity, led it to continue activities there throughout World War II and during the immediate postwar period. On a reconnaissance visit to Canada in March 1942 to identify grants appropriate for support under the Corporation's National Emergency Program, Charles Dollard talked extensively with local residents in eastern Canada and observed the Canadian government's determination "not to permit serious impairment of its system of higher education either through lack of financial support or lowering of standards of educational performance." Dollard noted the increasing conflict between regionalism and nationalism in Canada, as well as Canadians' warm feelings toward the United States. These findings led Dollard to suggest that the Corporation identify grants that might address and minimize the conflicts within Canada. Much as the Corporation twenty-five years earlier had sought to bring order into Canadian higher education in the Maritime Provinces, now it considered how to build harmony across the country.[192]

Dollard's report led to continued support throughout World War II, especially for the educational extension work started in the 1930s and for examinations of economic and social conditions in various areas. For example, aid to the Canadian Association for Adult Education enabled it to continue its program in rural education and community life, as well as to provide extension services for French-Canadians, and in Newfoundland the Workers' Educational Association was also funded for its outreach efforts.[193] Universities such as St. Francis Xavier, McGill, and the University of Manitoba also continued to receive grants for their extension services.[194] The Royal Institute of International Affairs in the United Kingdom received a small contribution of about $8,000 for its study of the internal economic conditions in Newfoundland, still officially a dominion but inevitably associated with Canada. The Canadian Institute of International Affairs, the Canadian Library Association, and the Central Advisory Committee on Education in the Maritime Provinces (the institutional successor to the Corporation's failed federation effort in the 1920s) all received continued funding during the war years and for many beyond. Grants for museums and libraries continued, along with continuing grants to Mount Allison University and Queen's University.[195]

Following World War II, the Corporation picked up on Dollard's observations about the tensions between the country's French- and English-speaking provinces. By the early 1950s, the Corporation was making grants to examine in greater depth French-Canadian relations from historical and present-day perspectives. Such grants went for research projects on French-Canadian relations at universities as far removed from the situation as the University of British Columbia[196] and as closely enmeshed in it as Memorial University, Newfoundland (an institution the Corporation had helped to support in its earliest days in the 1920s). They also supported studies of Canadian biculturalism at the Canadian Social Science Research Council and the outreach activities of the Quebec Association for Adult Education, Société Canadienne d'Enseignment Postscolaire, the Canada–United States Committee on Education, and the Committee on Cultural Relations in Canada.[197] The Corporation's interest in promoting Canadian integration underpinned the aid it gave to a wide range of Canadian institutions.[198]

The commitment to support work on Canada led to Corporation support for Canadian-American studies at the University of Rochester, now a thriving field on both sides of the border.[199] Grants to the Canadian Mental Health Association, McGill University, and McMaster University were complemented by a cross-border collaborative project jointly funded over several years by the Corporation, and the Milbank Memorial Fund grants to study social factors were channeled through Cornell.[200]

The Caribbean

For the colonies in the Caribbean, also rapidly progressing to independence, Corporation staff members maintained higher education as the entry point for grant-making. The Corporation awarded $10,000 over three years to the University College of the West Indies, founded in 1948, to strengthen primary and secondary education and teacher training to ensure a higher standard of education in the Caribbean region. Several more grants to the University College followed, including funding for an educational research center, travel and study grants, and educational radio broadcasting.[201] These grants were precursors to the Corporation's more active engagement with institutions and issues in the Caribbean in the next era.

Commonwealth-Wide Activities

In this early postwar period, the United Kingdom was actively investing in the colonies, "expending millions of pounds a year under the Colonial Development and Welfare Acts."[202] The agenda of support for "education, public libraries, museums, scientific research, and social services" paralleled the Corporation's from the 1930s.[203] Support for Commonwealth-wide investments was especially prominent in the emphasis maintained since before the war on bringing together educators and scholars, now as members of the Commonwealth, to share ideas and experiences, such as at the meetings of the University Bureau of the British Empire, which became the Association of Universities of the British Commonwealth. The grants enabled vice chancellors and other university leaders throughout the dominions to participate in these meetings.[204] Grants also allowed the Association of American Universities to send delegates to such conferences. In accordance with the British government's increased interest in higher education, the Corporation underwrote meetings and fellowships through the Inter-University Council for Higher Education Overseas.[205] It backed the Royal Institute of International Affairs for the first demographic survey of the British colonial empire, conducted by Robert Kuczynski and published in several volumes beginning in 1948, and for a significant survey of British Commonwealth affairs conducted by Nicholas Mansergh from 1947 to 1951.[206] Carnegie Corporation also funded an update in 1952 of Lord Malcolm Hailey's African Survey, along with a bibliography of social science studies related to British territories in tropical Africa.[207] Support for one longtime grantee, the International African Institute, was revived after World War II for its special studies and publications programs, with a focus on the impact of colonization on African family life, with the intent "to find a way to adjust existing inconsistencies between missionary practices, government laws, and tribal customs."[208]

An early Commonwealth-wide grant in 1948 co-sponsored by the General Education Board built on the long-standing collaboration between Teachers College, Columbia University, and the Institute of Education, University of London. In the 1930s, the two institutions with the same donors brought together for two separate conferences state agents for Negro education in the United States and educators working in Africa from the British Commonwealth. In 1948 they held a third conference, lasting three weeks, that covered an in-depth review of issues in African education. As E. Jefferson Murphy points out, this was a transition grant that had significance for the later work of the Corporation. New educators with more modern views were involved, particularly Karl W. Bigelow, who would help define the new Africa program for the Corporation later in the 1950s and 1960s.[209]

PRELUDE TO A NEW ERA
FOR THE COMMONWEALTH PROGRAM:
NEW STAFF, NEW STRUCTURE, NEW APPROACH

IN 1953 A NUMBER OF CHANGES led to a refocusing of the work in the British dominions and colonies. Whitney Shepardson resigned from the Corporation in February 1953 to become president of the National Committee for a Free Europe. Rather than appoint Stephen Stackpole as the director of a special fund apart from the regular grant-making of the corporation, Charles Dollard promoted him to the more customary title of executive assistant and shifted the separate fund back into a program that was incorporated into the Corporation's regular grant-making portfolio. The change in title, according to Dollard, "symbolized the intention of the senior officers of the Corporation to participate more directly in the guidance of the program."[210] Nearly $1.5 million was still available for grant-making, and the intention of the leadership was to enlarge activities to make use of this accumulation. Later on in 1953, Dollard hired Alan Pifer to help Stackpole.[211]

Dollard also commented on the "mixed bag" of proposals and projects in this area, a recurrent concern in the developing-countries work of the Corporation. As Keppel had recognized and future presidents would as well, Dollard noted that "this may always be the case to some degree since each area of the Commonwealth has its peculiar needs and problems." To reassure the board he added, "The officers are convinced, however, that as the present program develops, certain consistent emphases will emerge."[212] As more colonies became independent nations and contacts shifted more decisively from London to new capitals, and as more donors entered the field, the Corporation started in the next era to focus the grant-making to respond even more specifically to opportunities identified jointly between local leaders and Corporation staff.

With the concerns raised by Dollard, the staff again conducted a major review of the British Dominions and Colonies Program in November 1954, similar to the review that had been undertaken the previous year on the international affairs activities. In Stackpole and Pifer's assessment of program progress and new opportunities, they highlighted the expansion of the travel grants program. Between 1947 and 1954, the Corporation had spent $1 million for such grants to scholars and administrators from the dominions and colonies. Stackpole and Pifer also reported that institutional grant activities included "significant new developments in teaching, professional training, research, or the dissemination of scholarship," for a total of $3,700,000.[213]

In summing up the 1954 review, they concluded that

these grants over the past nine years have made a positive contribution to the strength and vitality of the Commonwealth and, hence, of the free world … with a carefully designed and accelerated program in the three to five years immediately ahead, the Corporation's funds for the Dominions and Colonies can have a significance and impact out of all proportion to their size, for they can provide not only the leverage for educational ventures of broad consequence but also the basis for strong and fruitful relations with the United States.[214]

The two officers made the case that because of their success, postwar grants to colonial universities offered a sound way to focus future grant-making. In the review they also explained that they would continue support for the dominions, but that the emphasis would be on grants to the colonies, particularly to support them in responding to "the urgent need for support of certain lines of development in Colonial universities, particularly the new university colleges and research institutes of Africa and the West Indies."[215] They suggested that the board consider "an extraordinary expenditure," that is, the $748,000 that remained from the amount accumulated during the war years to support the new institutions—the university colleges of the Gold Coast, Nigeria, East Africa, the West Indies, and, most recently, Rhodesia—and strengthen the older universities of Malta and Hong Kong. They also noted that the British government had established institutes of social and economic research as part of the colleges in Nigeria, East Africa, Central Africa, and the West Indies, as well as new colleges of art, science, and technology in both West and East Africa.

Stackpole and Pifer pointed out that "the United Kingdom Government has provided capital grants totaling 8,000,000 [pounds] for these institutions from funds available under the Colonial Development and Welfare Acts. Operating expenses are provided in each case almost wholly by local Colonial governments. In 1953 about four thousand students were enrolled … this remarkable development in the Colonies affords opportunities now for a program of grants which might be particularly productive and timely."[216]

To implement the program, Stackpole and Pifer explained that they would continue the practice of consulting with British officials and intellectuals, including the Inter-University Council for Higher Education Overseas in the colonies and the British Social Science Research Council. Much like Keppel and Bertram before them, Stackpole and Pifer identified the need to ground local universities in their local societies as a critical issue. They also recognized that the Corporation's key opportunity would be to fill the gap in the financing of local projects, since such support was not available from either the British or the colonial governments: "There is a large and unexploited area of enterprise here to which the officers believe the Corporation should turn its attention. They are assured this would be welcome."[217]

They then proposed grants that would increase the number and capabilities of local staff, develop programs to study local cultures, support social science research on regional problems, and support conferences to strengthen professional training in selected fields. They highlighted their enthusiasm by emphasizing that "the development of higher education in the colonies is both impressive and exciting."[218] As they observed, "distinctive contributions to scholarship are likely to come from local studies ... the colleges should branch out in ways which give them a greater identification with their constituencies."[219]

As noted throughout the earlier sections in this chapter on the British Dominions and Colonies Program, the Corporation was able to develop a new and more targeted set of grants in the colonies and increasingly began to focus its work on the dominions as well. These geopolitical changes in the areas of the world where the Corporation could be active clearly helped shape new directions in new areas of opportunity within the broad field of education, while continuing the Corporation's commitment to research, institution strengthening, and international connectivity over the next several years.

CONCLUSION

THE GRANT-MAKING AND THE WRITINGS of the immediate postwar era were noteworthy for the excitement of Corporation trustees, presidents, and staff members about the opportunities for building greater global understanding in the United States. The collaboration in this endeavor between Carnegie Corporation and the Rockefeller Foundation soon had a multitude of partners sharing their commitment. With the participation of the Ford Foundation and the impact of a variety of government programs from the late 1940s to the late 1950s—the Point Four Program, the Technical Cooperation Administration, the Economic Cooperation Administration, the Fulbright Awards, the National Defense Education Act, and the Fulbright-Hays Act—considerable resources became available for training and education at the college, graduate, and postgraduate levels.

Much as had happened at the end of World War I, toward the end of World War II and in the decade following the Corporation experienced disruptive, unexpected leadership changes. The three men who had taken the helm, Jessup, Josephs, and Dollard, departed early through death, a new position, and debilitating illness. Not one of these three presidents completed his expected full term, which, though not predetermined, was certainly expected by the trustees to be longer than these gentlemen served: less than two years for Jessup; less than four years for Josephs; and less than five years for Dollard. These unanticipated institutional disruptions in leadership could have had disastrous effects for the Corporation, but, instead, there was clear continuity during the period reviewed in this chapter. With the departures of Jessup and Josephs, firm board leadership helped keep the work on an even keel; when Dollard became debilitated, dedicated staff commitment reinforced and bolstered board leadership.

The Corporation also maintained its institutional contributions to building the field of international education in the United States during this period. Following World War II, the Corporation revived its commitment to the institutions it had helped to establish in the dominions; it also built the basis for sound reflection and action in support of the transitions under way in the British colonies in Africa and the Caribbean.

The critical reviews that the Corporation undertook in 1953 and 1954 to assess the effectiveness of the area studies, international affairs, and overseas grant-making significantly influenced the work of the next era. The assessments shaped the focus of the new president, John Gardner. With new players on the scene, the Corporation's resources could be more sharply honed to make a difference; other organizations could, and did, take over some of the Corporation's grantees. The sense that comes through the documents of the era is not a sense of competition but one of opportunity to move into new areas with confidence that what the Corporation had been working on would be continued by other organizations.

What does seem to have been missing in this era, however successful the grants were, was a sense of building on the knowledge gained in both the area studies and the international affairs activities and sharing that knowledge more widely with the public, a continuing concern of the Corporation. Nor did the results of these grants inform the British Dominions and Colonies Program, an issue, however, not explicitly addressed except by Dollard when he changed the structure from a separate fund to a program. Because these activities were often establishing and extending a field of learning, the emphasis was on the number and geographic coverage of the grants; indeed, area studies grants covered a wide geographic range of countries and regions. Moreover, so many US university programs received these grants that practically the entire nation was covered, as were parts of Canada through area studies grants to several universities there. Field-building went beyond the university programs; also funded were fellowships through the Social Science Research Council and the American Council of Learned Societies and activities that prepared publications, encouraged linkages with policy-makers, and reached out to the interested, albeit not general, public through the Council on Foreign Relations, the Foreign Policy Association, and the Carnegie Endowment for International Peace.

Interdisciplinary approaches informed not only area studies but also the projects on defense policy, civilian-military relations, and international affairs. While much of this work has become internalized in university-based foreign policy and international relations programs, its impact on public understanding, depth of scholarship, and better-informed foreign policies has yet to be fully assessed.[220]

During this period, the Corporation maintained a consistent focus in the British Dominions and Colonies Program on access to higher education and the availability of information through libraries, as well as the importance of engaging with British decision-makers and intellectual leaders. It also continued to support the surveys and research conducted in the 1930s throughout the colonies and dominions and to provide travel grants.

Finally, another significant aspect of this period relates to leadership. It was in the postwar decade that most of the trustees who had deep historical connections to the Corporation rotated off the board; a handful remained, however, up to the late 1960s. Their deep knowledge of the Corporation and its early leaders continued to help them find ways to engage in shaping, not only approving, the Corporation's programs. That level of engagement would change in the Gardner era as the attention that board members gave to the Corporation in relation to their other activities began to wane and the president became more dominant. As staff from one era remained connected to staff from the next, however, historical continuity was maintained.

This period differs in one crucially important respect from all others, except for the years of trustee leadership following the death of Andrew Carnegie: the three presidents from 1948 through 1982 had all been staff members for some years before their selection as president. In the wartime and postwar periods, Jessup and Josephs had been on the board, and Dollard had been a staff member for ten years prior to becoming president. Context influenced how innovative Jessup and Josephs could be: the former operated under many constraints, while the latter had few. Context also undermined Dollard's strong leadership capacity, in the form of the McCarthy era, the Cox Commission, and the Reece Commission. Still, he was able not only to maintain continuity in the international field but also to deepen it by enhancing its social science dimensions. Josephs and Dollard made it possible for Gardner to build on both the international and domestic programs when he assumed the presidency after his nine years as an energetic and creative staff member. Gardner saw the need to maintain a commitment to continuity but also recognized that the continually changing context affected the role of foundations. These twin insights shaped his tenure. As the next chapter shows, Gardner devoted considerable attention during his presidency not only to the international arena but also to making a more concerted impact on the public aspects of international education.

5

STABILITY IN MOTION, 1955–1967

T HE TUMULTUOUS TWELVE YEARS from 1955 to 1967 encompassed neither an economic depression nor a war, yet the tumult proved to be as
insidious and pervasive as the Great Depression of the 1930s and the two
world wars.[1] The political and social climate for Americans, and throughout much of the world, posed stark challenges, not only for policymakers
and the public but also, not surprisingly, for foundation leaders and staff
engaged in international philanthropy.

The intensifying Cold War reinforced fears about the potential for communism to entrench itself in both newly independent and more established
countries as well as at home, prompting ever more intense anticommunist
rhetoric and responses in domestic and foreign policies.[2] The fear of atomic
weapons defined the psychic landscape of the 1950s and early 1960s for
American citizens: the government tested weapons below- and aboveground,
and bomb shelters were built. Then the Soviets launched *Sputnik* in 1957,
amplifying the fear about nuclear weapons with the reminder of the weak
American competitive capacity in science and technology. CIA operations
were in full force, as were military spy flights—a U-2 plane shot down by
the Soviet Union at the end of the Eisenhower era helped shape the results
of the 1960 election. In his speech at the end of his presidency, Dwight
D. Eisenhower could very well have been talking about the Corporation's
US-based international program, its rationale, and its areas of emphasis:

America is today the strongest, the most influential and most productive nation in the world. Understandably proud of this pre-eminence, we yet realize that America's leadership and prestige depend, not merely upon our unmatched material progress, riches and military strength, but on how we use our power in the interest of world peace and human betterment.... In the councils of government, we must guard against the acquisition of unwarranted influence, whether sought or unsought, by the military industrial complex.... Only an alert and knowledgeable citizenry can compel the proper meshing of the huge industrial and military machinery of defense with our peaceful methods and goals, so that security and liberty may prosper together.[3]

This theme undergirded the Corporation's continuing focus on civilian-military relations. The Cuban Missile Crisis of October 1962 drew even greater American public attention to foreign policy.[4] That event, along with increasing guerrilla warfare in Indochina, further reinforced the Corporation's emphasis on national security, internal warfare, and the economics of disarmament. On the more positive side, independence movements throughout Africa, Asia, and the Caribbean gave birth to new nations from old empires, and these changes invigorated the Corporation's British Dominions and Colonies Program.

As President Kennedy launched the Alliance for Progress in Latin America and the Peace Corps around the world in 1961, the Corporation's work in the United States continued to emphasize Latin American studies and the other area institute programs, as well as grants to better understand successful development assistance and modernization. With Kennedy's assassination and President Lyndon Johnson's focus on poverty and equality issues, the Corporation maintained its active international program but began to shift its emphases toward the domestic social concerns that featured even more prominently in its grant-making in the late 1960s and 1970s.[5]

The volume of philanthropic resources increased alongside the federal government's role in areas where foundations had traditionally been active. In 1960, for example, philanthropic giving was estimated at $10.92 billion; the Corporation's assets equaled approximately $214 million.[6] In addition to Carnegie Corporation, the Rockefeller Foundation, and the Ford Foundation, during this period a number of smaller foundations also became active internationally, along with development assistance agencies in the United States and elsewhere and major players such as the World Bank and the United Nations.

When Carnegie Corporation and the Rockefeller Foundation were established in 1911 and 1913, respectively, and through the 1920s, their assets were comparable to the endowments of the major research universities and even to earlier federal government expenditures. These relative positions started to change in the 1930s; after World War II, the foundations had to rely more on their comparative advantage in the flexibility of their spending than on the levels of their spending. As noted in the Corporation's 1964 Annual Report:

> Today the income of foundations is in the neighborhood of *one half of one per cent* of federal revenues. Foundations hold between $15 and $17 billion in total assets at market value, a sum which is about three-fourths of one per cent of the financial assets of all banks, savings and loan organizations, insurance companies, major corporations, and other wealth holders in this country … foundation grants today account for only about 8 per cent of the total philanthropic giving from private sources. More than 85 per cent of the dollars given annually to philanthropic causes are … individual gifts and bequests.[7]

Government expenditures had dramatically changed in relation to foundation expenditures:

> In 1913 the federal government spent about $5 million on education, and in that year Carnegie Corporation spent $5.6 million on various philanthropic projects. In the fiscal year 1963–64 the federal government spent about $2 *billion* on education (a 400-fold increase) while Carnegie Corporation spent a little over $12 million. Endowed institutions of all sorts—universities, museums, churches, and hospitals, as well as foundations—are losing ground steadily to government-supported institutions.[8]

These analyses were originally prepared in response to questions gener-ated by Representative Wright Patman of Texas, yet another congressio-nal investigator reconsidering tax exemption privileges in light of a wide range of questions related to possible abuses of that privilege by founda-tions. Patman's 1961 hearings continued for ten years and led to the 1969 Tax Reform Act, which would have enduring repercussions for foundations.[9]

INTERNAL TRANSITIONS

WHEN CHARLES DOLLARD RESIGNED in November 1954, the easy thing for the board to do was to make John Gardner president, since he had already served as acting president during Dollard's most recent illness. Instead, the trustees spent a few weeks considering a nationwide search to identify an external candidate. Some trustees were concerned that since Gardner would be the second internal promotion (after Dollard), the Corporation was becoming "self-infatuated." According to Devereux Josephs, former president and current trustee, they were looking for someone "more glam-orous." Everyone respected Gardner's intellect and competence, but he was not yet a figure of national prominence. Josephs opposed their view as "hero worship." When no competition emerged, he pushed for Gardner; he did not see how they could consider anyone else.[10]

The other trustees soon agreed with Josephs and selected John Gardner to be the ninth president of Carnegie Corporation on January 20, 1955.[11] At the same time, like Jessup before him, he was asked to serve as president of the Carnegie Foundation for the Advancement of Teaching. Not only did that appointment continue to make sense, given the two institutions' shared commitment to higher education and academic testing, but it also mitigated the financial woes of CFAT to have the Corporation cover the salary of its leadership.

As a staff member, Gardner developed a reputation for displaying the strategic planning skills flagged earlier: he would select an idea that needed to be worked on, home in on it, and then develop innovative, gap-filling grants programs to address it.[12] For example, although Gardner did not originate the area studies program, he made it a full-scale, nationwide effort. With the perspective on national security and the anticommunism of the congressional investigations pervading the public sphere, he was also increasingly exposed to policy challenges in the making of US foreign policy.

Gardner's conceptual framework for approaching institutional management was shaped by life experiences rather than by management training.[13] He quickly dissipated any trustee doubts about his institutional leadership capacity by coherently reorganizing the Corporation's programs. He had soon arranged the programs into a framework of three areas for considering grants: higher education, public affairs and international affairs, and the British Dominions and Colonies Program (soon to be the Commonwealth Program). This restructuring gave a sense of order to the review of proposals, grant recommendations, and presentations to the board; it also gave shape to the writing of the Annual Report.

While other presidents of Carnegie Corporation, starting with Andrew Carnegie, were prolific writers, Gardner's writings received considerable national recognition; he also used them to inform his leadership at the Corporation.[14] His 1963 book *Self-Renewal: The Individual and the Innovative Society*, while primarily addressing social systems and individuals, also applied to the dynamic and creative tensions resulting from the Corporation's mission and Carnegie's charge to the trustees. His analyses emphasized that "purposes and values ... evolve in the long run; but by being relatively durable, they enable a society to absorb change without losing its distinctive character and style. They do much to determine the direction of change.... As Peter Drucker has pointed out, in a world buffeted by change, faced daily with new threats to its safety, the only way to conserve is by innovating. The only stability possible is stability in motion."[15]

Gardner's phrase "stability in motion" epitomized his presidency. He maintained stability by closely following the Corporation's mission, through grants in education aimed at advancing knowledge, and he developed the first organized dissemination fund for promoting the work of the grantees and the Corporation, explicitly responding to the second element of the mission.[16] Hewing to Andrew Carnegie's charge to the trustees, he also identified new areas such as curriculum overhaul in mathematics, gap-filling research on national security policy, and a considerably sharpened British Dominions and Colonies Program. As part of his commitment to internal institutional self-renewal, Gardner brought a focus on adult education into the Carnegie Corporation itself: in 1959 he recommended to the board that the Corporation support foundation officers in learning foreign languages if this would be useful for their work.[17]

In contrast to previous presidents of the Corporation, Gardner personally advised American political leaders, particularly at the presidential level.[18] From the work he did to strengthen governance in the United States, and with his focus on excellence as a way of improving conditions for all Americans at the appropriate levels (a perspective comparable to the Andrew Carnegie philosophy), it was inevitable that he would be appointed to a national leadership position.[19] In 1965 President Johnson asked Gardner to become secretary of health, education, and welfare. With permission from the Board of Trustees to take a leave of absence, Gardner accepted and then renewed his leave of absence in 1966. Alan Pifer served as acting president during that period, and in 1967 Gardner formally resigned from the foundation.

Board membership in this period reflected stability more than motion. Throughout much of Gardner's tenure, the internationally minded board membership was much the same as under Josephs and Dollard; even new trustees for the most part maintained the international outlook.[20] While board support remained significant for approving initiatives—both the continuing and new ones in the United States and overseas—Gardner engaged the trustees more at the overall strategy and policy levels and not, as in earlier eras, at the detailed programmatic level, which had become increasingly unnecessary with the number and expertise of staff.

With a staff that was as internationally oriented as the trustees, the Corporation could maintain considerable continuity in its international and overseas grant-making. James Perkins, Corporation vice president until he left in 1963 to become president of Cornell University, had responsibility for promoting the international affairs grants, especially the work on national security policy. He also worked in part with Gardner on the area studies programs. When Perkins left, Stephen Viederman was hired from the Corporation-funded Russian studies programs at Columbia and Indiana Universities to take responsibility for many of these efforts. In the British dominions and colonies, Stephen Stackpole and Alan Pifer's sophisticated, ear-to-the-ground efforts thrived under Gardner's leadership and were reinforced by the able contributions of Frederic Mosher (hired from the Corporation-funded Social Relations Department at Harvard University) and Katherine Ford, who had been program assistant since 1954. Corporation secretary Florence Anderson—at this time the staff member with the longest tenure—also remained involved in documenting the progress on both international and national grants.

To guide grant-making in this period characterized by complex challenges and the increasing resources of others in the areas of the Corporation's interests, Gardner introduced the idea of "strategic philanthropy"—that is, identifying where it would be possible with limited resources to make a difference, and then developing an organized plan with a stated goal, lines of activity for meeting that goal, and a plan for communicating results to the public and policymakers.[21] In the following discussion of international grant-making in this period, the Corporation's strategic philanthropy, reflecting both dynamic stability and deliberate motion, is clustered into two areas. The first section covers the domestic grant-making related to efforts to strengthen Americans' international knowledge and to support basic and policy research on national security policy and on broad-based international affairs, in a wide range of countries, with results intended to inform American foreign policy. The next section describes how the overseas grant-making responded to the fundamental transformations in the British dominions and colonies and highlights the Corporation's leadership in attracting more attention and funding from foundations and the US government for the British colonies in Africa. The resulting increase in external resources for African development enabled the Corporation to reset its program on themes that were not as attractive to the broader donor community but that related closely to the Corporation's comparative advantages in the field of education.

REINFORCING INTERNATIONAL PROGRAMS
IN THE UNITED STATES

TAKING THE STRATEGIC PHILANTHROPIC APPROACH, Gardner and his colleagues extended the reviews of the international programs that had taken place in 1953 and 1954 in the context of an overall assessment of Corporation prior grants and plans for the future. Their recommendations led to changes, not in overarching goals but in specific priority areas for the Corporation. As Gardner reported, "The trustees agreed that the Corporation should concentrate its resources [in the United States] in the two fields to which it has given primary attention in recent years, eliminating or drastically reducing the various other interests which it had developed over the years. The first of these two fields is higher education; the second is public and international affairs."[22] Although he noted that higher education would get most of the attention and resources, he expected that the latter area would also grow over time, and indeed it did expand to cover a wide range of issues.[23] The international themes laid out at the beginning included area studies, international exchanges, American representation abroad (including American missionaries), undergraduate courses in international relations, and research in underaddressed aspects of international affairs. For programs in the Commonwealth, strategic grant-making required building on the deep knowledge of staff to identify key points of opportunity where other donors were not active, still remaining within the broad area of education.

A NEW FOCUS FOR AREA AND INTERNATIONAL STUDIES

ONE BASIC PREMISE INFUSED THE Corporation's area and international studies programs at both the undergraduate and graduate levels: for American citizens to become knowledgeable supporters and, when necessary, effective critics of American foreign policy. The intention was that all students should have some exposure to world affairs, even those who did not intend to specialize. Recognizing that since the end of World War II American universities (some with significant resources from the Corporation) had greatly enlarged their graduate-level international programs, the Corporation embarked on finding new ways to reach a larger number of students at the undergraduate level: by developing new undergraduate curricula related to different geographic areas; by strengthening undergraduate exchange programs, including some associated with learning foreign languages; and by initiating programs reaching out to high school students and teachers, with an emphasis on teaching international affairs and learning major critical languages.[24]

The Corporation's support for Latin American studies exemplified the

kind of effort it found promising to deepen American student understanding of particular regions and countries. The rationale for a special focus
on Latin America reflected the recognition by scholars and policymakers
of the increasing importance of this neighboring region, first expressed
in the mid-1930s by the Rockefeller Foundation and then sustained by
both the Foundation and Carnegie Corporation in the 1950s. In this era,
the Corporation promoted language learning, scholarly conferences, and
higher-level policymaker exchanges; additional support enabled professors
and students from American universities and universities in the region to
collaborate in field-based research on a wide range of topics.

Building on the earlier Latin American studies grants to Tulane
University, Vanderbilt University, the University of North Carolina, and the
University of Texas at Austin, the Corporation identified other universities
for Latin American–focused fieldwork and exchanges of both students and
faculty, in many instances creating cross-institutional collaboration:[25]

- Through the University of Kentucky, students from several American
  universities conducted work over the summer with specialists in
  the fields of geography, geology, Spanish history, Spanish language,
  and Mexican history and literature at the Technological Institute in
  Monterrey, Mexico.[26]
- Two "sister universities," the University of Kansas and the University of
  Costa Rica, fostered undergraduate and graduate student and faculty
  exchanges.[27]
- Cornell University focused on training and research in the Andean
  part of South America, covering such fields as political behavior, economic development, social psychology, comparative administration,
  and demography in Peru, Chile, Bolivia, Colombia, and Ecuador.[28]
- Columbia University created opportunities for anthropology students
  from Columbia, Cornell, and Harvard to work in Mexico, Ecuador,
  and Peru with senior anthropologists from these countries.[29]
- Massachusetts Institute of Technology (MIT) seminars brought
  together engineering and engineering education students and faculty
  to work on common problems with their counterparts from Latin
  American universities.[30]

+ University of Wisconsin engineering students took their junior year abroad in Monterrey, Mexico.[31]
+ The University of Arizona developed an honors program in Spanish in Guadalajara, Mexico, which included home stays as well as exposure to Mexican and Spanish culture.[32]
+ Vanderbilt University students and faculty conducted research and training in modernization in Latin America.[33]

As a complement to this work, and to advance and disseminate more widely research on and in Latin America by both US and regional scholars, the Corporation in 1959 provided support for the Social Science Research Council and the American Council of Learned Societies to develop a joint committee on Latin America studies with funds for research grants as well as special conferences.[34]

Recognizing the value of exchanges for higher-level education policymakers, in 1960 the Corporation supported the Institute of International Education to create and house the Council on Higher Education in the American Republics.[35] The Council's scope included organizing meetings so that leading educators in North America and Latin America could get to know one another, visit other campuses, exchange views, and carry out joint research. Staff members continued to endorse this activity because they saw the accomplishments as building a base for continued communication in the Western Hemisphere, reinforcing the area studies work on Latin America and the other research programs on technical assistance and modernization.

One unanticipated negative impact of the fellowships and exchanges that involved students from Latin American countries and other newly independent nations was "brain drain" (a term not widely used in 1966): students from developing countries would come to study in the United States and not return home. In that era, staying in the United States was not considered an immigration issue, as it is in the early twenty-first century. Rather, the concern was about the negative implications for strengthening human capacity in those countries so that they could be effectively led at all levels. Although the Corporation itself was not providing the fellowships that some students were using in this way—except in one instance in 1960 for students from Nigeria—staff sought to encourage studies to understand the factors involved and identify remedies, particularly among Latin American students. Robert Myers of the University of Chicago's Center for Comparative Education, together with colleagues from Pennsylvania State University, examined the information available on foreign students to see if there was a relationship between student characteristics, country of origin, and the likelihood of returning.[36] These studies helped to establish "brain drain" as a serious topic of scholarship for researchers and policymakers.[37]

A second area of regionwide attention was Asia. Staff members recognized that, unlike scholarly collaboration with Latin American countries and scholarly counterparts there, the field of Asian studies posed distinctive educational and collaborative challenges because of the distance, the language barriers, and the different educational systems. The Corporation's broad scope on Asia encompassed specific study programs for Asian countries, including fieldwork with counterparts in the region; study groups; language teaching at the high school level as well as at higher levels of education; and when possible, visits to China and exchanges between Chinese and American scholars.[38]

Grants to the University of Wisconsin led to a program of study in India for undergraduates from Midwestern colleges. A similar kind of hub grant renewed support for the University of Chicago to bring "young professors" from other institutions to Chicago and help them develop courses for their institutions on non-Western civilizations. The University of Chicago also received support to continue the program on Philippine studies. Another Asian studies program continued to receive Corporation support at the University of Michigan. Grinnell College became a hub for research on and in Hong Kong, Malaya, British Borneo, Burma, and the Tibet borderlands. Cornell University filled the same role for research in Taiwan, the Philippines, Thailand, and Indonesia.[39]

Two institutions outside of the Midwest and Northeast received support for programs on Asian studies. In 1957, the University of Washington received support for its program on Inner Asian studies, first funded in 1950; the focus was on the little-studied areas of Tibet, Turkistan, Inner and Outer Mongolia, and Sinkiang, China, all in relation to Soviet, Chinese, Indian, Japanese, and US policies in the area. Corporation staff remarked on the unusual nature of the grant, proposed also in 1957, on Asian studies to the University of Arizona: "The Corporation does not often have an opportunity to support a genuinely promising project in the southwestern part of the United States. The present project is excellently planned and formulated, and is recommended with enthusiasm." [40]

Massachusetts Institute of Technology received support for a study on Burma. In a comment that resonates with developments later in the century and early into the next, staff defined Burma as "one of the most complex, possibly *the* most complex of the southeast Asian countries." They also highlighted "the shortcomings" of American foreign policy makers' understanding of "the forces at work" in Burma and in all "these new nations." [41]

Again, the Social Science Research Council became the institutional base for seminars and research grants in a particular field of interest to the Corporation, in this case a study of modern Chinese society. The Council was supported over several years to fund research grants and hold seminars and conferences in order to "define the existing state of knowledge about Chinese society, evaluate research methods and strategy, and determine what further steps are necessary to strengthen work in this field." [42]

In partnership with the Edward W. Hazen Foundation, the Corporation aimed to improve communications with scientists and scholars in China through an exchange that started with modest resources but great expectations. In 1966 the National Academy of Sciences, the Social Science Research Council, and the American Council of Learned Societies formed the Committee on Scholarly Exchanges with Mainland China to improve communications with scientists and scholars from China. [43] At the same time, through the University Service Center in Hong Kong, the Corporation supported the program to help scholars of contemporary Mainland China "from America and a few other countries who come to the Crown Colony because it is now the most important base in the world for research on Mainland China." [44]

In this era, the Corporation made its last grant to the Russian Research Center at Harvard University, and only as part of a major grant to build international studies at the university. As the agenda item reads, the intent was to enable Harvard to build a focus "on other strategic areas of the world" but still maintain support for the center. A grant of $750,000 over eight years provided $350,000 toward the Russian Research Center and $400,000 toward the university administration to develop the broader international studies program.[45] As soon as it was possible for Americans to visit the Soviet Union, in 1956, Columbia University received a Corporation grant to enable American scholars to do so. Although Columbia managed the grant, it was intended to attract specialists from all over the country; to this end, Columbia established the Inter-University Committee on Travel Grants to review requests for travel to the Soviet Union and related research grants.[46]

The Corporation maintained an active grants program to increase American scholarly engagement with the continent of Africa, building on the earlier support for African studies at Northwestern and Yale Universities. In 1956, with a grant of $100,000, the Corporation supported a five-year program at Tulane University in democratic governance in West Africa.[47] Following the inter-university collaborative approach, the research program brought together younger scholars who were to become the major American Africanists of the next decades: David Apter from Northwestern University; James Coleman from the University of California at Los Angeles; L. Gray Cowan from Columbia University; George Horner from Boston University; and Robert Lystaad from Tulane University.

To connect the disparate, and still few, scholars in the field of African studies, a series of meetings took place in Alan Pifer's office, starting in 1955, to discuss the possibility of building "a scholarly association concerned with Africa that would be free of government influences." In March 1957, about thirty-six scholars met and agreed to form the African Studies Association (ASA).[48] The Corporation supported the conference at the level of $6,500, but organizing it was left to the scholars themselves. Ford Foundation staff members Melvin Fox and Wayne Fredericks also participated. More than fifty years later, the association thrives and has a global membership.[49]

In this meeting the Corporation decided to fund, also in 1957, an American Assembly on Africa. In recommending support, Corporation staff, not so modestly but still realistically, made the case in the agenda item that, "as the Trustees know, the Corporation has done more than perhaps any other single group to stimulate serious interest in the problems of Africa on the part of scholars and other informed Americans." The conference aimed to have the policymakers, scholars, and practitioners who participated in the assembly meetings develop "long-range guiding principles" for American policy toward Africa.[50]

Among the other grants made in support of African studies, the African-American Institute stands out as one that brought together the Corporation, the Rockefeller Brothers Fund (RBF), and the Ford Foundation to assist in weaning the institute from reliance on government support. In 1962 the Corporation provided a grant of $290,000, which included support for the ongoing African Scholarship Program of American Universities.[51]

Having long been interested in enhancing American understanding of the Commonwealth as a whole, the Corporation responded positively to requests from Duke University for assistance in establishing a center for Commonwealth studies, which it funded for several years, starting with an initial grant of $350,000.[52] The Corporation continued to support the program on Canadian-American studies at the University of Rochester. In this era, Rochester remained the only major university in the United States that devoted "more than passing attention to the study of Canada and the problems of Canadian-American relations."[53]

Another way of exposing American undergraduates to international affairs was the junior year or summer spent abroad. The Corporation did not introduce the concept of junior year abroad, but it did seek ways to make it a more valuable learning experience for students; it was especially concerned about ensuring that institutions without the requisite level of expertise or international connections could also provide overseas experiences for their students.[54] The Corporation selected institutions that were strong in a particular academic area as the hub of a network for other academic institutions that lacked that strength but were interested in providing opportunities for their students in the field. For example, Princeton University, in collaboration with Colgate, Columbia, Rutgers, and Swarthmore, was the hub institution to provide a joint undergraduate study program in international relations. This program enabled juniors from all of these institutions to study at the Institute for Social Studies in The Hague and then conduct individual research projects in Europe.[55]

COMPARATIVE AND SPECIAL STUDIES

THE CORPORATION MATCHED the interdisciplinarity of the area institutes in other aspects of its US-based international activities. A modest but innovative focus on comparative studies—primarily but not entirely undertaken in relation to Cold War concerns—contributed to new approaches in survey research, quantitative methods in the social sciences, and comparative case study work.[56]

In 1965 Alan Pifer, then acting president, noted that although mainland China was considered Communist,

> the more we learn about contemporary China the more we see that she is quite different from these other nations in many respects—and they are quite different from each other. What, then, does communism consist of? To deepen understanding of this major political phenomenon, scholars are turning more and more to comparative studies—studies comparing communist nations with noncommunist nations and with each other. As yet, however, this is a new and not much explored approach, and one that presents complicated organizational and training problems.[57]

With grants from the Corporation, the American Council of Learned Societies convened a working group in 1966, and then again in 1967, to plan and sponsor research and training for comparative studies on communism. Also in 1967, the University of Pittsburgh and Columbia University received grants to enable them to develop inter-university comparative research programs, the former on communist political and economic systems and comparative Marxist ideology and the latter on elites and interest groups in Communist nations.[58]

Linked to the study of elites and political power, but with a focus on capitalist systems, a grant to Stanford University examined citizen participation in political life between elections, both in the United States and in non-European countries; the Corporation continued the collaborative, comparative model here as well, noting in the agenda item for the board that "the entire effort is under the overall, cooperative management of a group of

American scholars and foreign scholars of non-European countries."[59] One of the aims was to encourage scholars from abroad to study the American system of governance to balance the increasing number of American scholars going overseas to study foreign systems; by collaborating, the scholars would be able to introduce different perspectives into each other's work.[60]

The Corporation provided support, for example, for an undergraduate suite of courses on foreign affairs at the University of Chicago that included Chinese civilization, Indian civilization, and the Islamic world.[61] This grant was later complemented by one to the University of Wisconsin that expanded its program on the history of tropical areas of the world by building "a comparative approach to history rather than the usual division by countries and centuries."[62] Corporation support enabled Wisconsin to include a full-time history teacher on every major culture of the world in its history curriculum and then to develop a course on Afro-Asian history, further illustrating the comparative approach to teaching history. For several years, Northwestern University received support to strengthen its work in international affairs and to train teachers, as well as to reinforce the Wisconsin hub. One of the grants enabled Northwestern to expand the teaching of international issues into the larger introductory courses, particularly history, government, and economics courses.[63]

Other curriculum experiments in international studies took place at the University of Rochester, Lawrence College, and Brooklyn College.[64] Moving away from the Eastern states, a major grant went to the University of Oregon for training and research in international studies and overseas administration, at the level of $150,000; grants also bolstered experimental programs in international affairs at Southwestern University in Memphis, Tennessee; Western College for Women in Miami, Ohio (now the Western College Program); and San Francisco State College.[65] The University of Denver, striving to become a center of scholarship in this field, received support as a hub program in its prime location between the Midwest and the West Coast. The cooperative international relations program at Denver, under the leadership of Joseph Korbel, brought together other institutions in the region to enhance their teaching and research.[66]

BRINGING IN THE HIGH SCHOOLS:
LANGUAGE TRAINING FOR STUDENTS AND TEACHER
TRAINING IN INTERNATIONAL AFFAIRS

DETERMINED TO DEEPEN THE KNOWLEDGE of American citizens on international affairs, the Corporation began to focus on high school students
and teachers. Reminiscent of the grants to the Brookings Institution from
the late 1930s to the early 1950s, the Corporation made modest grants to
the University of Michigan and the University of Arizona, not to focus on
college- and university-level faculty but rather to reach out to high school
teachers for teacher training in international affairs. In Arizona, teachers
from public schools spent a year at the university working on this program.
At Western Michigan University (a state university with major responsibility for teacher training), faculty members were given support for study and
travel, reinforced by a program of faculty seminars.[67]

Despite the intensive and well-organized support given to language training programs at the undergraduate level through programs of the National
Defense Education Act (NDEA) of 1958 and the work of the Corporation,
the Rockefeller Foundation, and the Ford Foundation, Corporation leadership expressed dismay over "Americans failure to learn any language other
than their own."[68] Recognizing that some of the languages related to areas
of greatest concern—namely, Chinese, Japanese, Russian, and Arabic—and
required an early start to learn them well, the Corporation began in 1962
to assist, along with a handful of other language programs, "a number of
budding Chinese and Japanese programs in high schools throughout the
country."[69]

In some cases the Corporation complemented the support that the
NDEA was providing to Chinese language institutes for public high school
teachers. For example, at Thayer Academy in Boston, Seton Hall University
in New York, and San Francisco State University in San Francisco, the
Corporation's grants enabled the hub schools to bring in private high school
teachers. The most promising students from the Thayer program were able
to spend the summer in intensive study at Yale University's Institute of Far
Eastern Languages. A similar approach, including Japanese instruction, was
supported at the University of Southern California. In the Midwest, the

Mark Twain Summer Institute, based at Washington University in St. Louis, developed a program for high school students in Chinese and Japanese that became year-round. Several years of support backed a similar program at Evanston Township High School and New Trier Township High School, both outside of Chicago, for Chinese and Japanese instruction.[70]

In 1963 John Gardner highlighted the immediate success of the Corporation's program: "Six years ago only about five secondary schools in the continental United States taught Chinese, and even fewer offered Japanese. Now more than 75 secondary schools teach Chinese and about 10 are teaching Japanese. Similar strides were made in Russian a few years earlier, and at least two high schools now offer Arabic."[71] Yet the Corporation never fully analyzed the results of these programs and did not sustain funding past the mid-1960s.[72] Very soon (by the early 1960s), the Rockefeller Foundation, the Ford Foundation, and the new Title VI program of the US government deepened and greatly expanded funding for area studies, so much so that the Corporation's efforts have often been overlooked by scholars of these efforts.[73] In addition to posing the question of the Corporation's impact on building international awareness and connectivity for Americans, the increasing activity of other institutions in this area raises another question: What was the impact of this work on American foreign policy making, since the expressed aim of the Corporation and others was to improve such capacity through better-informed citizens and carefully formulated research? How did the results shape work in those areas? From the scope of these activities, it seems that the Corporation, on balance, focused primarily on advancing research and education, leaving more extensive diffusion of the knowledge and understanding gained to the grantees and others.[74]

A MULTIFACETED APPROACH TO NATIONAL SECURITY RESEARCH AND POLICY

MUCH LIKE THE WORK in international education, the Corporation's programmatic activities related to national security spanned a broad spectrum, widening the scope of the previous era. The Corporation maintained its support for the field of national security studies through the work on civilian-military relations and the ramifications of the atomic bomb and atomic energy. Staff also recommended support for studies that explored newer themes, such as the economics of disarmament and understanding internal conflicts and their causes, along with continuing examination of approaches to sustaining peace, strengthening international law, and achieving world order. In 1962 Gardner noted that "as recently as 15 years ago the universities were giving almost no attention to national security policies, despite the great relevance of the subject to anyone concerned with the future of the nation or the world."[75] By the time he became president, Carnegie Corporation, the Rockefeller Foundation, the Rockefeller Brothers Fund, and the Ford Foundation had put in place programs on national security policy at the university level, and the results were well recognized, seemingly in contrast to the international affairs and area studies efforts.

In the recommendation for continued support of Columbia University's Institute of War and Peace Studies, for example, Corporation staff members quoted the comment of *New York Times* columnist James Reston that "the most interesting new ideas regarding national security and military strategy seemed to be coming out of the universities these days rather than out of government." Staff also wrote that some of the credit could go to the efforts of the Corporation (and other foundations) to stimulate "serious attention to these new areas."[76] The Corporation continued supporting William T. R. Fox's work at Columbia University and that of his colleagues at the Institute of War and Peace Studies and the Social Science Research Council Committee on National Security Policy Research, and of John Masland and his team at Dartmouth College. Bernard Cohen and his colleagues at the University of Wisconsin conducted research and training programs "on the international factors that create security problems for the United States, the relationship of U.S. military policy to national security, and the formulation and execution of national security policy."[77]

In its continuing concern about atomic weapons and the rapid changes to the patterns in relations among nations being wrought by scientific and technological developments, in 1955 the Corporation supported Columbia University in establishing the Council for Atomic Age Studies as a clearinghouse for research on the interrelationship of science and society, co-chaired by Philip Jessup, professor of international law, and I. I. Rabi, professor of physics. The Corporation and Columbia also hoped to stimulate research on the issues associated with the space age, such as "the political and legal problems of outer space."[78]

And then came *Sputnik*. Reaction to the Soviet launch in October 1957 reinforced the national security, science, and technology thrust of the Corporation, while maintaining the policy dimensions.[79] For example, the concern about atomic weapons led to grants that enabled Henry Kissinger, then at Harvard University, to hold his Defense Policy Seminars, starting in 1960, following support through the Council on Foreign Relations for his seminal 1958 book, *Nuclear Weapons and Foreign Policy*. That publication had already "added to his reputation as a leading expert on international relations and national defense policy."[80]

The Corporation identified one of the underaddressed issues related to national security and atomic weapons, namely, the economics of national security policies and, in particular, disarmament as a theme deserving special attention. As Gardner noted, "It is only recently that the field of national security policies has attracted much attention from the academic world. And so far, those academic people who have done research in the field have usually been either historians or political scientists. Although the subject matter of economics is tightly bound up with our defense effort and the planning of our future strategy, economists have been conspicuous by their absence from this field of investigation."[81] Once again, the Corporation sought to encourage new work through the Social Science Research Council; this particular submission to the board explained why the Corporation and other foundations in the development of new fields of research, such as national security policies, continued to turn to the Social Science Research Council. With the recognition that scholarship on foreign policy issues had to be "healthy" and "up to date," the staff praised the Council: "Of the efforts that the Corporation has made in this direction, perhaps the most widely effective and influential has been the work of the Committee on National Security Policy Research of the SSRC [Social Science Research Council]." Staff emphasized that through its conferences and individual research grants, "the Committee has probably done more than any other single group to bring able social scientists face to face with the realities of national security policies today."[82] In 1958 the committee received a grant to explore the economic issues in this area.[83]

Gardner and his colleagues noted that despite the extensive attention given to arms control and disarmament, since World War II "few systematic studies have been made of an extremely important aspect of the problem: what the economic consequences of disarmament, if it were achieved, would be."[84] Toward that end, the Corporation supported soon-to-be-renowned economists Emile Benoit and Kenneth Boulding to conduct a joint study on the economic consequences of disarmament, bringing together researchers from academic institutions, the private sector, and government.[85] Boulding, whose area of interest was the economics of peace, headed the recently established Center for Research on Conflict Resolution at the University of Michigan; Benoit was an associate professor of international business at Columbia University. Their joint research focused on issues of stabilization, reconversion, growth, equity, and international economic development. Boulding (who would become one of the most distinguished and unorthodox of American economists) and Benoit published the first book in the field in 1963, and Benoit then published a more popular, less technical edition. Not only was this work the earliest in the field, but it was also the first research effort in Boulding's new center.[86] The Corporation was impressed by the results and made a major research grant to support Boulding and his "excellent research team." Staff members were impressed by the plans for a "promising long-range program." They also underlined the basic premises of the group "that a stable peace can never be a happy vacuum. The only hope is to develop the kinds of mechanisms and instrumentalities which will diminish tension as it arises, and resolve conflicts in an early stage."[87]

Closely related to the economic analyses—in what has now become a more traditional field of study in national security policy and conflict resolution but then was new—was the field of game theory, which the Corporation jumped into by funding two grants at Princeton University. One grant went to Princeton's Center of International Studies for research on internal warfare, and the other supported the research on game theory and economic behavior of Oskar Morgenstern, co-founder with John von Neumann of the field of game theory.[88]

By the end of the 1950s, the increase in the number of internal conflicts related to the Cold War and other internal violence, whether "rebellion, revolution, mob violence, guerilla warfare, and all types of civil uprising," had not yet become a topic of scholarly attention, although as Corporation staff noted, the military had been expressing the need for greater understanding in this area.[89] The Corporation supported a small cluster of grants related to the political dimensions of internal conflicts (Princeton's Center of International Studies), the anthropological aspects (Northwestern University), and international legal approaches (American Society of International Law).

Grants to Northwestern University supported Donald Campbell, a professor of psychology there, and Robert LeVine, assistant professor of anthropology at the University of Chicago, in co-directing a project to bring together as many as twenty psychologists and anthropologists from a variety of universities to "examine the attitudes that approximately 100 different primitive societies, shielded from the complexity of civilization, hold toward their neighbors and themselves."[90] With their findings, the project team aimed to understand the factors that caused intergroup tensions, determine how they might be mitigated, and contribute an anthropological perspective to developing the emerging field of conflict resolution.

Recognizing that international law did not address the concerns generated by internal conflicts, the Corporation asked the American Society of International Law (ASIL) to clarify "what contemporary role, if any, international law could play in regulating international strife."[91] In studies presciently relevant for the 1980s, 1990s, and 2000s, the Society was supported to organize a panel of legal experts and to commission "a series of studies of actual civil wars (for example, the American civil war and the Congolese) each of which will analyze how laws of war were applied; how much and in what way outside powers intervened; whether and how international organizations were involved; and what role law played in terminating the war and establishing a viable domestic order."[92]

Despite the extensive focus on national security policies, economics and disarmament, international law, and internal conflicts, it is striking that only a couple of grants focused on peace. Two grants each of $75,000 a year over three years supported scholars coming to study and write about peace and international affairs under the auspices of the Carnegie Endowment for International Peace.[93]

Another approach to achieving peace caught the imagination of acting president Alan Pifer and his colleagues. In 1967 the World Law Fund received a grant from the Corporation to further discussions on how to promote world order and eliminate war. The Corporation was interested in the four volumes of research that had been published by the World Law Fund, including a book by Richard Falk at Princeton University and Saul Mendlovitz at Rutgers University, *The Strategy of World Order*.[94] Corporation support enabled them to write two more volumes, one on regionalism and the world order and the other on the individual and the world order.[95]

Complementing this work was a research and writing grant to Richard Gardner, a professor at Columbia University and former deputy assistant secretary of state for international organizations; Gardner was one of the scholars concerned about delineating pathways to redefining the world order. During his sabbatical year, Gardner examined "the kinds of international institutions required to resolve conflicts that could lead to war, promote economic development in the less-developed nations, and handle other major problems of long-term and worldwide importance."[96]

PUBLIC UNDERSTANDING OF WORLD AFFAIRS IN THE UNITED STATES

AS THE CORPORATION BEGAN to expand public affairs grant-making in the John Gardner era, a new focus on public scholarship developed as part of the work to promote international understanding. The Corporation encouraged individual scholars as well as universities to intentionally reach out and better inform their communities. Gardner reflected on this approach to extending the reach of international education in his 1959 presidential essay: "Some people … criticize the universities for giving their chief attention to long-term goals…. Such people often urge that the universities should give more attention to educating the public. Of what use are fine research and brilliant experts, they ask, if the public is so ignorant of international affairs that it stands as an immovable obstacle to a sound foreign policy?" Gardner goes on to explain that the "universities have not ignored this problem."[97] The Corporation on occasion provided funds for such efforts; for example, the University of Wyoming's Institute of International Affairs received a grant that enabled Gale W. McGee, professor of history and director of the Institute, to speak at the 1956 Laramie, Wyoming, Summer Seminar for the public organized by the university. Soon after this grant, in 1958, McGee was elected to the US Senate.[98]

For the public outreach, the Corporation more commonly supported its operating partners in this area, namely, the Council on Foreign Relations and the Foreign Policy Association. An omnibus grant of $500,000 to the Council on Foreign Relations in 1960 brought together the different lines of support that the Corporation had funded separately over the past thirty-three years to cover research, fellowships, and assistance for the national committees, which by then were in twenty-seven cities throughout the country.[99] More modest grants than those awarded to the Council on Foreign Relations enabled the Foreign Policy Association to hold meetings around UN issues, often through its World Affairs Councils in different cities.[100]

Even without formal assessment, it is evident that the research on the multiple dimensions of national security helped shape the field and build national reputations. The outreach efforts had at least an indirect impact on policymakers; again, the direct impact on policies and public understanding for this era is much less clear. Another prominent issue for this particular cluster of grants is the lack of internal memory at the Corporation regarding the work they supported—the direct cause of the lack of internal awareness of the work later. Many of the national security themes tackled in this era and the previous one were reprised by the Corporation in the 1980s with limited awareness of the scope and results from the earlier work.

"MODERNIZATION" AND NEW NATIONS: FROM TECHNICAL ASSISTANCE TO ECONOMIC THEORY TO POLITICS AND CULTURE

THE RAPID MOVEMENT of British colonies in Africa, Latin America, and Southeast Asia toward independence in the 1950s and 1960s was unprecedented. Carnegie Corporation, through grants in the late 1940s through the 1960s, contributed to the theory, practice, and critique of economic development and modernization; its overseas efforts, discussed in a later section, related more to education and development.[101] The Rockefeller Foundation and the Ford Foundation were early partners, both in the United States and overseas, supporting activities on these issues both separately and together. As Gardner noted in his 1960 Annual Report essay:

> The economic, political, and social emergence of these [underdeveloped] countries into the modern world is one of the most momentous developments of modern times....What all these areas share in common—for some of them are "new nations" in the political sense, others will soon become so, and some are in fact old nations—is that the process of modernization lies ahead for them. In highly telescoped fashion, these emerging nations are striving to create modern economic and political structures in the merest fraction of the time it took the West to do so. Their success will represent the best hope for a peaceful world for all of us; if they fail at that, it will represent failure—and tragedy—for all of us.[102]

The Corporation's initial efforts related to the study of economic development were influenced by the focus in the late 1940s and 1950s, on the part of the US government and private organizations, on the role of technical assistance in contributing to the growth and development of newly independent countries, often by introducing new technologies and techniques for applying them. The rationale that increasingly attracted researchers and policymakers, as well as foundation staff, throughout the 1950s and 1960s was the idea of modernization—bringing development along with liberal capitalism—as a counter to the attraction of communism.[103] The Corporation in each of these periods was an early supporter of research efforts that first supportively and then critically examined these issues. In both the United States and overseas in the decades between World War I and World War II, as well as earlier, the Rockefeller Foundation and Carnegie Corporation had been involved in what was called "community development" to support educational, social, cultural, and economic developments at the local level.[104] Starting in the mid-1950s, the shift in focus beyond the community to the nation was understandable in an era of nation-building following the success of decolonization and independence movements, although complicated by the competition between political and economic systems.

When the Ford Foundation in the 1950s joined the Rockefeller Foundation and Carnegie Corporation in addressing these issues, bringing considerably increased resources, each foundation also brought a distinct perspective: Ford in its early work focused on international organizations and peace, along with nation-building in the developing world; Rockefeller focused on agriculture, population, and health, along with strengthening work on economics and history in many universities in the developing world; and the Corporation, in its US-based work, focused on the development of models of economic growth and development and interdisciplinary research on non-economic perspectives on modernization.[105] In the late 1950s and 1960s, the three foundations converged in their support for higher education in newly independent countries.[106]

ENLARGING THE FOCUS ON TECHNICAL ASSISTANCE

THE CORPORATION ALREADY WAS INVOLVED, through early grants to Cornell University and Michigan State University, in supporting projects that questioned how foreign technical assistance was conducted, who conducted it, and what impact it had on the intended beneficiaries. John Gardner, James Perkins, and William Marvel built on these grants to address the larger field of economic development. The Cornell project, for example, in its work with small landholders to improve their productivity with new techniques and technologies, informed what would be called in the 1970s "farming systems" research.[107]

The Cornell program, nearly ten years after it had started, was helping farmers raise crop yield, improve the health and literacy of their families, and engage in self-government.[108] Allan Holmberg and the team in Los Vicos, Peru, worked closely with the local community but generated a backlash from the local landowners.[109] The "Vicos Project" was one of the first to combine approaches to local governance and community engagement with new technologies and techniques—in this case with regard to potato production, the major staple crop in Peru. This project also garnered funding from the Rockefeller Foundation and the Wenner-Gren Foundation. The more than twenty years of support for the Vicos Project has engendered considerable debate in academic circles as to foundation motives, the role of American anthropologists versus local anthropologists, choice of approaches, and impact. The debate still flares in the twenty-first century, with probing questions about external interventions into local communities and the social responsibility of scholars and funding agencies.[110]

At the Center for Comparative Education at the University of Chicago, under the direction of Robert Havighurst, researchers studied the relationship between education and occupational choice in Brazil and West Africa. Another grant enabled a team of Brookings and Dartmouth college researchers, led by Kalman Silvert (previously the head of the Tulane University program on Latin American studies funded by the Corporation), to apply modern survey interview techniques to study the role of education in economic and social development in modern Latin America.[111] Prior to the establishment of the Latin American Studies Association in 1966, these university programs were connected in the United States through the Committee on Latin American Studies of the Social Science Research Council and the American Council of Learned Societies; individual programs were separately in positions to influence the design of technical assistance programs.[112]

Concern about the impact of development assistance projects led the Corporation to help build the field of ex-post analyses of these projects. Recognizing that the World Bank was the dominant provider of development assistance, through loans since its start in 1945 of about $8 billion for projects in Africa, Asia, Europe, and Latin America, Corporation staff decided that enough time had elapsed so that lessons could be learned.[113] One of the leading development economists, Albert Hirschman, who was then at Harvard University, received backing from the Corporation in 1964 to direct a study under the auspices of the Brookings Institution to assess the impact of those projects. The goal was to analyze the projects to "yield information useful in the selection and evaluation of development projects, shed light on both the potentialities and limitations of foreign aid, and contribute to knowledge about the processes of development."[114] The 1967 publication that resulted from that study, *Development Projects Observed*, raised controversial questions about the nature of development and development project analysis; indeed, Hirschman's analyses prompted debate on development project evaluation and the state of development economics.[115] Moreover, as Hirschman later wrote, this publication served as a bridge to the equally influential and "broader social science themes" of his later writing.[116]

The Corporation complemented the range of international work in the United States with studies of how best to prepare Americans for representation and work overseas. The American Assembly on Representation of the United States Abroad offered the Corporation "an excellent opportunity … to encourage informed public discussion of this problem."[117] This meeting foreshadowed the publication of the 1958 novel *The Ugly American*, which reinforced the widespread concern about how Americans were representing their country overseas, whether in business, diplomacy, or research.[118] The negative repercussions of the actions abroad of arrogant and uninformed Americans would surely counter any of the positive work undertaken by those who were more culturally aware. Another way the Corporation responded was to fund Harlan Cleveland, dean of the Maxwell School of Public Administration, and his colleagues at Syracuse University to conduct interviews of overseas Americans who were diplomats, technical experts, military officers, and representatives of private interests. In the resulting book, *The Overseas Americans*, Cleveland and his team made the case for new forms of international education, at both the undergraduate and graduate levels in colleges and universities.[119] Concerns about "contractors"—those individuals implementing the development projects of the new agencies established to provide technical assistance, such as the United States Agency for International Development (USAID) and the World Bank—led to support for improved training programs for overseas work, such as the one at Montana State College.[120]

Another approach to improving the caliber of Americans working abroad and at the same time meeting the needs expressed by the newly independent countries resulted from a 1959 meeting sponsored by the Ford Foundation at the request of the State Department to explore more specifically how universities could contribute to international activities.[121] For several years the staff of the Corporation—especially Perkins, Marvel, Pifer, and Stackpole—had been working with the Rockefeller Foundation and the Ford Foundation to encourage American universities to participate in international development activities, particularly those focused on education. Following the meeting, the three foundation presidents at the time (the Rockefeller Foundation's Dean Rusk, the Ford Foundation's Henry Heald, and Carnegie Corporation's John Gardner) and their staff members held consultations with a wide range of academics, other education leaders, and government officials. That resulted in the establishment in 1962 of a new coordinating entity, Education and World Affairs (EWA). Gardner's staff assistant, William Marvel, became the EWA president and chief executive, and Herman Wells, the president of Indiana University, was chairman of the board.[122]

Both the Corporation and the Ford Foundation agreed to support the first five years at the level of $500,000 each. The initial purpose of Education and World Affairs was in part to meet the increasing demand for education specialists from the United States to participate in educational activities in the countries of Asia and Africa.[123] It was also to serve as a clearinghouse on American higher education activities overseas, to bring together higher education leaders to examine the policy issues arising from such activities, and to provide a channel of communication on these topics between the government and the universities. In addition, foreign educational organizations and governments could work with EWA to develop relationships with the appropriate elements of American higher education. Eventually Education and World Affairs merged with a new organization led by James Perkins, former vice president of Carnegie Corporation and former president of Cornell University: the International Council for Educational Development.[124] This, too, had come to a close by 1995, and other institutions, like the Institute of International Education, filled the gap.

The Corporation also examined the other side of the manpower challenge by exploring ways to fill local manpower requirements. Much as it had done with the work in international studies and international relations, the Corporation sought to build collaboration across American institutions to address this issue. This grant, first made in 1959 to Princeton University, brought together a team of economic powerhouses: John Dunlop of Harvard University, Frederick Harbison of Princeton University, Clark Kerr of the University of California, and Charles Myers of the Massachusetts Institute of Technology.[125] They conducted the basic studies on high-level manpower requirements in developing countries, elucidating through their research how to make modernization work with the right human capacity. As noted in the grant recommendation to the board, they were pulling together the data to make "long range projections of manpower requirements in modernizing countries, and to set up some guideposts for determining patterns of investment in education appropriate to different levels of development."[126] This work led directly to the manpower studies conducted in Nigeria, described later in this chapter, and shaped the field of manpower planning in developing countries. As Gardner explained, "So far our gains in understanding the process of modernization have been chiefly on the economic side, although everyone concerned acknowledges the powerful role which the development of human resources plays in modernization. The inter-university study should supply some missing pieces in the jigsaw puzzle of modernization."[127]

One unusual grant, the only one like it in this particular era, brought some of the issues about technical assistance in developing countries back to the United States. Sol Tax, a professor of anthropology at the University of Chicago, prepared self-teaching materials for Native Americans so that they could learn on their own about the culture of the United States and how to read and write English. Tax developed the fields of action anthropology and intercultural communication; he helped shape international anthropology with support from the Corporation and the Rockefeller Foundation.[128]

FACTORS INFLUENCING MODERNIZATION: ECONOMICS, POLITICS, AND CULTURE

ALONG WITH THE GRANTS to study ways to improve the provision of technical assistance, the Corporation was one of the backers of studies on economic theories of development and interdisciplinary approaches to modernization, both then considered intellectually compelling new themes for academic attention. For a variety of reasons, this work has been severely criticized. First, many analysts now consider the promotion of modernization as a major ideological, not analytical, economic vehicle aimed at confronting the spread of communism. Second, many critics have pointed to the pressures brought to bear on governments to move in somewhat financially destructive ways. But in the late 1950s and throughout much of the 1960s, this field of study and action attracted scholars and practitioners in both the newly independent countries and the United States. The Corporation, despite its grants examining in depth the potential success or failure of technical assistance activities, and despite the work, albeit contradictory, on economic development, chose not to focus solely on economic and financial dimensions. Instead, it harked back to its interdisciplinary thrusts in the late 1940s and posed questions about the social, psychological or attitudinal, and political dimensions of modernization—the dimensions that lay at the core of human development, in the Corporation's estimation—and their impact on developing countries. As Gardner assessed the field in 1960,

> The vast problems of rapid modernization, taken together, pose the greatest challenge ever to confront the advanced Western countries. They also represent a singularly fruitful field for foundation activity. Whatever advances can be made in knowledge about the multi-faceted process of modernization can contribute to the formation of sound policy on the part of the United States with respect to the emerging nations. At the same time, the state of the social sciences in the United States will be advanced. As we accumulate data and observations on political, economic, and social phenomena in Africa, the Near East, Asia, and Latin America, something so basic as our knowledge of man himself will be expanded and strengthened.[129]

Just six years later, recognizing the potential social backlash from modernization (perhaps as a consequence of the actions of landowners in Vicos), Pifer, as acting president, advanced a fundamental issue involved in political and social change in developing countries: "how to bring about much-needed social change without causing political chaos." This key point emphasized the vital importance of political institutions for social change, institutions "that can withstand or even introduce necessary reforms without themselves being destroyed, and to promote patterns of social change compatible with necessary institutions."[130]

Amid the cluster of grants made on the political and social dimensions of modernization in transitional societies, two major institutional grants supported such interdisciplinary work at Harvard University and the Massachusetts Institute of Technology. Following the practice of building collaboration within and across academic institutions, the Corporation backed a $250,000, four-year program of studies led by Samuel Huntington, professor of government, at Harvard's Center for International Affairs. Huntington and colleagues drawn from other departments and other institutions examined the role of government and social change: "The emphasis is on ... to what extent reform can substitute for (or provoke) revolution, and what impact social diversification has on a one-party system."[131] Of the several major books resulting from these studies, the first one, *Political Order in Changing Societies*, published in 1968, has been called "perhaps Huntington's most important book."[132] At MIT, where the Corporation supported the efforts of the Center for International Studies, directed by Max Millikan, to contribute to long-term understanding in the field of modernization, staff assessed the situation as follows: "There is no disguising the fact that ... we have been for the most part groping blindly. Our understanding ... is extremely limited ... and in the absence ... we have assumed that a sufficiently heavy application of dollars would somehow accomplish a useful result."[133]

As a contribution to theory-building in the field of economic development and modernization, the Corporation funded two radically different economists, one based at MIT, the other at times at Harvard, and both were associated with the Council on Foreign Relations. These two further exemplified the commitment to public scholarship: their work sparked many more analyses of and controversies over the conditions for sustainable growth and successful development in developing countries. Perhaps the contribution to understanding the modernization process in relation to economic development that was most discussed at the time was Walt W. Rostow's *The Stages of Growth: A Non-Communist Manifesto*, which would become a classic.[134] Rostow, an economic historian, had served in the Office of Strategic Services (OSS) in World War II. He had been at MIT since 1951, and in the 1960s he was a presidential adviser, first to John F. Kennedy and then to Lyndon B. Johnson. His advocacy for the Vietnam War soon overshadowed his personal and professional reputation. Nonetheless, when his book was published in 1960, prior to that period, it was a major success.[135] Rostow described a linear path for development that he claimed all countries followed, drawing on the experience of the US and European societies: "It is possible to identify all societies, in their economic dimensions, as lying within one of five categories: the traditional society, the preconditions for take-off, the take-off, the drive to maturity, and the age of high mass-consumption."[136] Foreign assistance agendas for the next twenty years drew on Rostow's conceptual framework of stages of growth leading to "take-off." In the 1970s, new perspectives and analyses brought to bear on economic development showed the fallacy of this approach, but for decades it provided the core concept and terminology used in development assistance programs and came close to dominating the work in development studies.

It was indicative of the Corporation's effort to advance knowledge by funding the finest minds of the day, even when they presented rival analyses. Barbara Ward, a British-trained economist and journalist, received support for her analyses of economic development based on her experiences in developing countries. Ward had lived in Ghana and India with her husband, Sir Robert Jackson, and had seen firsthand the problems with development assistance and Western approaches to modernization.[137] In 1958, the Corporation started funding her research and writing at the Harvard-based Radcliffe Institute and at the Council on Foreign Relations.[138] One of her early books, published in 1962, *The Rich Nations and the Poor Nations*, was a best-seller. In this volume, drawn from the Massey Lectures, which she delivered over Canadian radio, Ward addressed economic development not as a matter of linear stages but as a series of interrelated factors that lead to "success" in the rich nations but that, for newly emerging societies, pose challenges that arise from issues of equality, the power of ideas, population growth, and the application of science to achieve economic progress. She emphasized that "here we are concerned primarily with equality as a force making for social, economic and political change."[139] *The Rich Nations and the Poor Nations* is still on reading lists in economic development courses and provides a critical analytical counterpoint to the work of Rostow.

Another senior scholar who would have considerable influence on the field of economic development and modernization was Myron Wiener, professor of political science at MIT.[140] With grants from the Corporation, Wiener examined the "patterns of political participation and organization in Europe—especially in Eastern Europe ... [to] understand what is going on in today's developing nations ... how social theorists analyzed those patterns in the nineteenth and early twentieth centuries as well as what students of developing nations have to say on the subject today."[141] He then compared those observations with the actual development of political systems in Europe. One of the resulting books was the prize-winning *Party Building in a New Nation*.[142]

The view of modernization as a key element in achieving economic, social, and political development led to new funding for the Church Peace Union. In 1960 and 1961, many years after the last grant had been made to the Union, the Corporation provided a modest three-year grant to examine the issue of religion and the state in Asia in the context of the interplay between religious issues and modernization in developing nations.[143]

Following on the Corporation's support for studies on the economic and political elements of modernization, staff members brought to the forefront an issue that was hotly debated in the field: would political independence combined with advances in economic well-being, prompted in part with external donor assistance, lead to an automatic rise in democratic institutions? The relationship of economic development and growth to democratic institutions is still an issue. By 1965, even after all these studies and meetings, there was palpable concern at the Corporation over what was actually meant by "development" or "modernization." As Acting President Alan Pifer wrote, "Actually, very little is known about what it consists of and how it is stimulated."[144] Rather than end grant-making in frustration, this question led to funding a sociologist at Columbia University, Theodore Caplow, to analyze the nature of development by pulling together economic, demographic, and welfare statistics and constructing what was perhaps the first "index of modernization." Caplow's initial findings led him to conclude that modernization was much the same anywhere; the only difference he found between societies was the rate of change, which was "tied in with the world system of communication and commerce." Clearly this early data-based statement of the relationship of local conditions to the global system required greater testing; the Corporation continued to support Caplow in his research and writing about practical applications of these insights in foreign aid. About fifteen years later, the Overseas Development Council, soon followed by the World Bank, the UN Development Program, and UNICEF, began to create development indexes.[145]

SCHOLARLY COMMUNICATIONS:
MEETINGS AND EXCHANGES

GARDNER AND HIS COLLEAGUES MAINTAINED the Corporation commitment to travel grants and, increasingly, scholarly exchanges in order to build bridges across cultures—whether different cultures of ideas, geography, or background. These grants bolstered education research in the critical areas affecting all "modern and would-be modern" states; Gardner and his colleagues were convinced that "the sharing of knowledge and in many cases the pooling of energies toward solving common problems assumes mounting importance in our shrinking world."[146] Although funds for exchanges and travel grants were provided to individual universities, especially to bolster area studies or technical assistance studies, four organizations served as the Corporation's operating agencies (as they did for the Rockefeller and Ford Foundations) for fellowships, exchanges, and meetings both within the United States and between the United States and other countries and regions: the Institute of International Education, the Social Science Research Council, the American Council of Learned Societies, and the National Research Council (National Academy of Sciences).

In nearly every decade since the launching of the Institute of International Education in 1919, the Corporation had either housed or funded special initiatives under its auspices.[147] In 1956 the Corporation made what staff considered to be a final grant of $1.5 million, having provided, over thirty-seven years, a total of $2.7 million (the equivalent of $23.2 million today). This grant was to be spent over the next ten years for any "legitimate purposes within the scope of the Institute."[148] Since its founding in 1923 by the Laura Spelman Rockefeller Memorial, the Social Science Research Council had been the backbone of the Corporation's support for fellowships and special research initiatives, including the area studies committees, which were carried out jointly with the American Council of Learned Societies. The Social Science Research Council was also given support, somewhat similar to that provided for the Institute of International Education, to assist American scholars who sought to attend international meetings or congresses in their areas of expertise.[149]

The American Council of Learned Societies, founded in 1919 by thirteen learned societies in the humanities, had been another longtime grantee, usually supported to provide fellowships on key themes of interest to the Corporation.[150] In 1960, the Corporation funded ACLS to organize one of the first US-USSR scholarly exchanges under the newly negotiated official exchange agreement between the two countries.[151] The National Research Council (NRC), founded in 1916 and supported with a $5 million grant from the Corporation in 1919, formed in 1965–1966 the Committee on Scholarly Exchanges with Mainland China to explore exchanges of publications, scientists, and scholars. The committee was co-funded by the Corporation and the Edward W. Hazen Foundation and run in partnership with the Social Science Research Council and the American Council of Learned Societies.[152]

Through these activities, the Corporation and the Rockefeller and Ford Foundations could extend their reach far beyond the institutional grants; the grants to IIE, SSRC, ACLS, and NRC enabled individuals from a wide range of disciplines and institutions across the United States to participate in working groups (often including colleagues from other countries) and receive research grants. Essentially, in the 1950s and 1960s, these three foundations sustained the connecting tissue for the scholarly communities in the social sciences, in the humanities, and, somewhat less often given the significant government support through federal agencies, in the sciences.

THE CORPORATION OVERSEAS:
RESHAPING AND RECONFIGURING
THE BRITISH DOMINIONS AND COLONIES PROGRAM

THIS TWELVE-YEAR ERA WITNESSED THE sea change in the British Empire and global alliances. Most of the members of the British Commonwealth that were originally colonies or dominions had become fully independent by 1967. In the mid-1950s, the Corporation's grant-making overseas, along with that of the Rockefeller and Ford Foundations, reflected and reinforced the continuing process of decolonization, independence, and nation-building.[153] By the mid-1960s, the opportunities had become more topic-specific, driven by local concerns, and there were many more partners.[154] Similar to the approach of Whitney Shepardson in the late 1940s and early 1950s and

Frederick Keppel in the late 1920s and throughout the 1930s, Corporation staff during this period took their program cues from local perspectives in the British dominions and colonies—the main difference being that in the colonies these perspectives were now voiced by African, Caribbean, and Asian interlocutors, not by British colonial residents and governors, as in the past.

In those early years of independence in the British colonies, the Corporation's decades-deep experience throughout the British Commonwealth conferred an advantage in its work both with the colonial governments and with the new leaders in the new nations.[155] The relationships were strengthened by mutual trust, familiarity, and recognized commitment to partnership. Stephen Stackpole, for example, had some exposure to the overseas grants when he was hired in 1940. When he returned to the Corporation after World War II in 1945, he joined Whitney Shepardson, the newly hired director of the program, who had worked closely with his British counterparts since the 1920s. Together, from 1946 to 1953, Shepardson and Stackpole revived the Corporation's activities in the British dominions and colonies. When Shepardson resigned in 1953, Alan Pifer was hired to work directly with Stackpole on the Commonwealth issues; he had been with the US Fulbright Commission in London, so was also familiar with the British Commonwealth and its national African counterparts. And of course, John Gardner, who had been at the Corporation since 1946, was increasingly aware of the work in the Commonwealth countries, having served as vice president and then acting president on and off since 1953. One of the first actions Gardner took when he became president in 1955, for example, was to change the name of the program from the British Dominions and Colonies Program to the British Commonwealth Program and then, in 1962, upon Stackpole's urging, to the Commonwealth Program, the name used for almost twenty years.[156]

Like the team making grants in the United States, Stackpole and Pifer were seasoned practitioners who understood the changing context for the overseas grant-making. Stackpole and Pifer therefore continued working with the colonial—now Commonwealth—institutions, mainly the Inter-University Council for Higher Education Overseas, the Association of Universities of the British Commonwealth, the Royal Institute of International Affairs, the Colonial Office in London and in the colonies, and leading national educational institutions. In addition, they maintained a good rapport with British officials, such as Sir Andrew Cohen, undersecretary for Africa in the British Colonial Office, and Sir Christopher Cox, chief educational adviser to the British government from 1940 to 1970; both men had responsibility for the transformation of education, particularly higher education, in the colonies.[157] Cox, an indefatigable extrovert, was well known and highly respected throughout the colonies for his dedication to education; according to Clive Whitehead, he had significant "influence on the course of educational development in Britain's former Colonies."[158] From his time at the Fulbright Commission, Pifer knew both men well enough to raise sensitive subjects with them and come to agreement, even if Cox was initially reluctant (as happened with the collaboration between Michigan State University and the University of Nigeria at Nsukka to establish an American-style land-grant university, not one more traditionally British).

Much like other presidents, Gardner at first endorsed an opportunistic approach for grant-making in the British Commonwealth Program: "The Corporation's program for the British Commonwealth must always enjoy a somewhat greater freedom from rigorous definition than does the main program. With a modest income to be spread over large areas of the world, this program must be shaped to accord with the opportunities and realities under which it functions. At any given time it will reflect clearly the major emphases of the main program, but it can never be bound by them."[159] Soon, however, Stackpole and Pifer determined that as an external American-based institution, the Corporation could make the most productive contribution, not opportunistically, but rather by concentrating its contributions on a major theme. Keeping in mind the historical and contemporary comparative advantage of the Corporation, and considering the Rockefeller Foundation's focus on the specific problems of health, agriculture, population, and nutrition and the Ford Foundation's focus on a wide range of development issues, the team homed in on higher education as a core component of successful nation-building. Thus, the initial programmatic priorities were maintaining the travel grants, with an increased emphasis on Africa; continuing support for universities in a variety of areas in Canada and the other former dominions; and staying actively involved

with the "emerging countries of the Commonwealth, primarily African but
including [the] West Indies and Southeast Asia."[160] Also, staff continued
to be interested in finding interconnections between the domestic focus on
higher education and overseas grant-making, particularly around supporting universities and enhancing the capacity of local staff. (As noted in the
prior chapter and here, this seemed not to extend to the more theoretical
and comparative work on modernization and development or the fieldwork
on technological change.)

Gardner endorsed this approach, even as he acknowledged the more
opportunistic nature of the program. He made the connection between the
educational activities in the United States and those being considered for the
soon-to-be-independent countries in Africa: "Americans have long regarded
education as indispensable to progress. We are now, however, seeing more
clearly than before that our continued national development and indeed our
survival depend on the effective utilization of our best minds. If this is true
in the United States, it applies with particular force to new countries and
those at the threshold of independence."[161]

RESHAPING THE COMMONWEALTH PROGRAM
WITH NEW PARTNERS IN AFRICA

FROM 1955 TO 1967, THE Corporation's programs in Africa reflected the
growing capacity of African educators and the rising number of partners in
support of African education. Initially, in the mid-1950s, the focus was on
strengthening higher education planning. When, in the late 1950s, the gap
in teacher training to support the entire education system became apparent,
the program then targeted relevant activities in that domain. These activities led in the 1960s to concerns about students and learning, including child
development, with the aim of improving the educational curriculum and
teaching approaches. This latter orientation dominated the grant-making
toward the end of the Gardner era and carried over to the next. Stackpole
and Pifer demonstrated during these programmatic transitions their
effective application of strategic philanthropy and their capacity to target
grant-making in light of the ever-increasing local capacities in African countries and the number of donors—private, national governmental, and international—all working in support of education in African countries.

Ghana's independence in 1957 and the selection of the dynamic pan-African leader Kwame Nkrumah as prime minister spurred the different approach for working in sub-Saharan Africa. The Corporation-supported book *Decolonization and African Independence* by Prosser Gifford and William Louis analyzed the conditions under which the Corporation developed its active program support for universities in Africa:

> At the time of the transfer of power, in the late 1950s through 1970s, the British and the French, at least, handed over an administrative apparatus, a judiciary, and an educational system. These were imperfect and fragile creations, designed for European as well as African purposes. Nevertheless, they are vital parts of any modern state, in Africa as elsewhere.... What has become clear is that the time of the transfer of power marked a significant juncture in the Africans' management of their own affairs.[162]

By sustaining the friendships and relationships with colleagues in the United Kingdom and the newly independent—or about to be so—nations, Pifer and Stackpole were able to take on a significant leadership position with regard to US assistance and the work of the other foundations to increase support for the transition efforts and development assistance investments in African countries. Indeed, as E. Jefferson Murphy noted in his unpublished 1975 memo on the program for the Board of Trustees, the Corporation played a key role in introducing other foundations to the leadership in both Africa and the British Commonwealth organizations during the period of decolonization and independence.[163]

Murphy elaborated on how the Corporation used its special connections with the British Colonial Office and the countries themselves to enlarge the number of actors providing support for development in these new countries:

> Carnegie Corporation was especially committed to the idea of mobilization of resources: the small size of its own available funds, especially for such a vast area of need as African development, made it eager to use these funds to stimulate interest in effective aid on the part of institutions with greater resources.... Some of the earliest Commonwealth Program initiatives in this area were taken to mobilize American

resources cooperatively with those of the United Kingdom. A small, select, carefully planned conference at the Greenbrier Hotel in White Sulfur Springs, West Virginia, held in 1958, brought together key representatives of American foundations, universities, and government agencies with Britons responsible for British aid to Africa.... Greenbrier served as a stimulus both to greater American interest in West African development and Anglo-American cooperation and coordination. A somewhat similar meeting at Gould House, on the Hudson River outside New York City, brought together university heads from Africa, America, and Britain, to help lay the foundation for later work in higher educational development.[164]

Other meetings were held to stimulate similar interests, such as a meeting at Princeton to promote interest in East Africa and another at Lake Mohonk in New York State on education and teaching. Each of these events gathered American foundation and government representatives with partners in the United Kingdom—and on occasion educators from throughout the Commonwealth—to enhance support for African development, in particular for higher education development.[165]

Following the Greenbrier conference, in late 1959, Pifer embarked on a three-month trip throughout Africa to determine how best to reshape the program.[166] He visited the United Kingdom, Ethiopia, Kenya, Uganda, Tanganyika, Southern Rhodesia, Northern Rhodesia, Bechuanaland, and Basutoland, traveling over 12,000 miles in Africa and meeting with nearly 1,500 people—such as Sir Roy Welensky, the prime minister of the Central African Federation, and Kenyan political leader Tom Mboya, as well as educators, missionaries, students, and ordinary citizens. Pifer analyzed conditions throughout the continent, emphasizing the importance even with all the changes under way of working with the British, not around them, especially given "the friendly new attitudes of British administrators toward American participation." He also compared political and educational differences between West, East, and Central Africa, highlighting the opportunities for supporting university colleges and continuing Anglo-American-African cooperation in West Africa and introducing it into East Africa. From this trip ultimately emerged the plans to support university research and development, education planning, and a continuation of the travel grants and fellowships.

As an outcome of the Greenbrier conference, the Corporation made a small grant in 1959, along with the Ford Foundation, to the American Council on Education to establish the Africa Liaison Committee under the leadership of J. Lewis Morrill, president of the University of Minnesota, with the active involvement of Harvie Branscomb (who had reviewed the British Dominions and Colonies Program for President Jessup in 1943) and Cornelis de Kiewiet (a longtime Corporation grantee and adviser). The Committee called together a group of educational leaders to meet with leaders in the United Kingdom and Africa for consultations on the role of the United States in the educational development of the countries moving toward independence.[167] The Committee's work ultimately received Corporation funding for sixteen years for a total of $1.1 million.[168]

To address educational concerns in East Africa, the Africa Liaison Committee, with support from the Corporation, the Ford Foundation, the Rockefeller Foundation, and the Edward Hazen Foundation, planned a conference at Princeton (as mentioned earlier).[169] In December 1960, the forty-five conference participants from Britain, East Africa, and the United States endorsed the University of East Africa and called for considerably more foreign aid.[170] One tangible conference outcome was the Teachers for East Africa Program, funded by the International Cooperation Administration (the forerunner to USAID), which provided for American teachers to assist in training local teachers in East Africa. In existence for nearly ten years, the program "supplied 631 teachers for secondary schools and teacher training colleges in Kenya, Tanzania, and Uganda."[171]

The Africa Liaison Committee's work encompassed many dimensions: studies of the educational problems of developing countries; the impact of American aid on African institutions; advisory services on national education systems; and coordination of American, British, and Canadian assistance efforts. In 1965, when the Committee had been in operation for less than six years, it organized another meeting, supported in part by the Corporation, at Lake Mohonk. The Conference on the American University and National Educational Development brought together twenty-five universities from developing countries, including seven from outside Africa, as well as university, private, and government agency officials from the United Kingdom, Canada, New Zealand, and the United States. At this meeting, it was agreed that the Committee's success with its work in Africa made it seem "logical … to extend this approach to other developing areas."[172] Its name was changed from the African Liaison Committee to the Overseas Liaison Committee; in this new capacity, it helped the Corporation and others elsewhere in the Commonwealth.

THE ASHBY COMMISSION:
LAUNCHING A NEW INITIATIVE IN AFRICA

RARELY IS IT POSSIBLE to identify one major activity as the launching pad for a whole new program. For Carnegie Corporation's work in Africa in the 1960s and early 1970s, there was one such pivotal grant that would define the program activities. The Commission on Post–School Certificate and Higher Education in Nigeria, better known as the Ashby Commission, had a goal that was originally broached at the Greenbrier conference: to provide a new way of planning and supporting higher education in Nigeria to strengthen national development in the soon-to-be newly independent nation. It was the right idea at the right time and with the right partners expressing strong support and enthusiasm for it. The Ashby Commission joins a handful of other examples in the Corporation's history that clearly stand out as having made a difference in both the short run and the long run, with scale-level—in this case, continent-wide—multiplier effects for many years. The impact was so prolonged and so pervasive that in Anglophone African educational circles today, more than fifty years later, even beyond Nigeria, the Ashby Commission strikes a chord of recognition and debate.

In his oral history, Pifer fully described how the Ashby Commission evolved, and much of his account is reflected in Murphy's book *Creative Philanthropy*.[173] The ongoing conversations about new approaches to higher education between Sir Andrew Cohen, undersecretary for Africa in the British Colonial Office, and Pifer crystallized at the Greenbrier Conference around the idea of a Nigerian commission. Pifer followed up with several leading educators in Britain, East Africa, and West Africa, including the influential Sir Christopher Cox, the UK overseas education adviser.

In high-level shuttle diplomacy, Pifer consulted with colleagues in these countries over several months, and in 1959 he held intensive discussions with Nigerian ministry officials and educators, including Chief Minister Sir Abubakar Tafawa Balewa (who was also the first prime minister when Nigeria became independent); as a former teacher, Balewa warmly supported the idea.[174] To engage all partners, the tripartite (African-Anglo-American) idea was endorsed. The plan was to start before the declaration of independence, set for October 1960, and to be ready with a blueprint that could be acted on immediately afterward.

The Ashby Commission was to project the needs of higher education over the next twenty years in Nigeria, hold meetings, conduct field studies, organize critiques of the findings, and prepare a major report with recommendations for action. Maintaining the tripartite approach, nine commissioners were appointed—three from Nigeria, three from the United Kingdom, and three from the United States. The Corporation provided support of $100,000.[175]

The Ashby Commission was launched on May 4, 1959, in Lagos, Nigeria. It was the only meeting John Gardner attended in Africa, a clear indication of the importance he gave to this effort. Writing about the grant, Gardner noted that "the Corporation has high hopes for this study. Its findings are likely to prove of immediate practical value to Nigerian leaders. It may also be of wider significance if, with the tripartite approach, it can cut through the jungle of conflicting views on the relative merit of British and American educational philosophy for emerging countries and show the way to constructive joint efforts."[176] The commissioners and their consultants conducted studies, held meetings, and prepared the report in record time, by September 1960. The total costs of the Ashby Commission came to $87,168; in 1961 the Nigerian government returned the unspent balance of $12,832.[177]

The 139-page negotiated report, *Investment in Education,* generated both controversy and support. The commissioners themselves disagreed over what kind of education was most important for development: should the focus be on producing practitioners and vocational experts, the US land-grant model of education, or on producing an educational elite, the University of Ibadan–UK liberal arts model? They ultimately compromised by agreeing to build on the past and to introduce more diversity in the future. The report served as the basis for the university expansion plan in Nigeria after independence and gave impetus to the idea that external funding would be acceptable for higher education.[178] The Ashby Commission recommended creating a Bureau for External Aid as part of the Ministry of Education, and the Corporation helped fund it in 1961 with a grant of $225,000. A second grant in 1964 of $102,000 helped support the Committee of Nigerian Vice Chancellors, the precursor of the Nigerian Universities Commission, a Corporation grantee in the twenty-first century.[179]

In addition to the controversy over the model for higher education, the report had another equally controversial effect: it inspired the creation of universities all over the country, thus reducing opportunities for the economies of scale that would have come with regional universities, which had been recommended by at least one of the Nigerian commissioners. A third area of controversy resulted from the manpower studies conducted and organized by Frederick Harbison, the American labor economist. He worked with already collected data to minimize time and costs and arrived at estimates that the government considered unacceptable because they were too low, especially with regard to technical and teaching needs. Despite the controversies, the report made a major statement about the value of education and support for it: "It began by announcing that its recommendations deliberately disregarded budgetary prudence; vast sums of money would be required to expand Nigerian higher education to the level appropriate for the country's size and importance."[180] The report highlighted the most critical ingredient in ensuring high-quality primary, secondary, and higher education throughout the country: having a sufficient number of well-trained, effective teachers.

The results from the external funding recommendation stimulated considerable foreign aid for Nigerian education and prompted interest in such aid from other parts of the continent as well. G. Mennen Williams, the American assistant secretary of state for Africa in 1961, pledged $30 million over ten years for Nigerian higher education "soon after reading the Ashby Commission report," according to Murphy.[181] Stephen Stackpole calculated in 1964 that about $83 million for higher education had been loaned, granted, or pledged as a result of the Ashby Commission. Murphy's assessment concludes:

In its cost-benefit effectiveness, the Ashby Commission project is very likely the best expenditure the Corporation made in Africa.... The Commission helped to stimulate major American, as well as British and European, aid to most of Africa during the 1960s and helped clear the way for the founding of new institutions of large size and great concern for national relevance, ... The Commission's Report ... served as a pivotal force in the rate and nature of African educational development throughout the 1960s.[182]

For the Corporation, the Ashby Commission marked a major advance in sharpening the focus of the British Commonwealth Program. The Corporation felt that the Commission had "boldly" taken up the challenge of determining how best to meet the demand for education resulting from the rapid rate of change on the continent. From the report, the Corporation embraced the recommendation about the need for teacher training as the highest priority. A new strategy for the Commonwealth Program emerged:

The Commission found that the gap between demand and supply in this field constituted a national emergency for Nigeria ... the problem is one of major proportions in most of the Commonwealth countries of tropical Africa.... The upgrading of inadequately prepared teachers at both secondary and primary school levels ... is an urgent matter for all ... there is the increasing need for teachers of advanced qualifications to staff training institutions themselves. Government departments of education are grappling with the shortages.... A special responsibility falls on university institutes and departments of education to give preparation to teachers, ... to conduct research on educational problems and, above all, to provide guidance and set standards for teacher training colleges.[183]

Drawing on the recommendations of the Ashby Commission about teaching and teacher education, the Corporation became interested in the new institutes of education that had been established in the university colleges in different African countries, institutions that they had funded earlier. The institutes of education, the Corporation envisioned, could play an effective connecting role between government, universities, and local communities, aligning teacher education curricula with local needs and local languages as well as conducting research to assess the effectiveness of new teaching curricula.

To strengthen the capacity of the new institutes to meet the human capital needs in African education, Stackpole and Pifer responded positively to discussions with Karl Bigelow, a leading American researcher in the economics of education on the staff at Teachers College, Columbia University since 1936.[184] Bigelow had participated in several of the Corporation's earlier initiatives and become passionate about African education. With support from the Corporation and the Ford Foundation, he eventually became one of the leading spokespersons in the United States for promoting education, especially higher education, in Africa.

Bigelow proposed linking the Institute of Education of the University of Ghana, the Institute of Education at the University of London (a Corporation grantee in the 1930s), and Teachers College at Columbia University to organize a professional association that would enable educators to maintain regular contact on issues related to teacher education and curriculum reform. Corporation staff members welcomed the idea of maintaining the tripartite approach across African, American, and British institutions, but suggested that additional institutions be included, both in the United States and in Africa. At the same time, staff members were loath to impose their own perspectives on this initiative. After all, Bigelow and his colleagues were the experts, and their ideas fit perfectly with Corporation thinking about ways to help the universities become much more closely tied to local needs and their societies and meet the increasing demand for education, starting with primary and secondary schools. The program began with the three partner institutes; Bigelow and his colleagues ultimately extended the reach to include other Anglophone university colleges in East and West Africa.[185]

The Afro-Anglo-American Program for Teacher Education (the AAA program) led to the establishment at Teachers College of the Center for African Education "to award fellowships and organize exchanges of teachers, researchers and practitioners from the partner institutions; assist African educators to have access to publications from the UK and the United States; promote and disseminate research on education, particularly teacher education, throughout Africa; and ... organize annual conferences to build relationships and exchange ideas and experiences with educators from across African countries, the UK and the United States."[186] As the Ashby Commission studies were becoming available but before the Commission presented its report, the Corporation in May 1960 provided a three-year grant of $450,000 to launch the program.[187] Although this was not the only field-building initiative that the Corporation undertook to support the African teaching profession in Africa, it was the most extensively supported for the longest period of time and led to an African organization that is still active.[188]

Over the next three years, more institutes of education were founded on the continent, and the organization's membership grew to include five other African institutions in addition to the original partner in Ghana.[189] Faculty exchanges became a regular activity across the departments in the different universities, and three well-attended annual conferences were held. The request in 1963 for a second round of support at $450,000 over three years was warmly approved by the trustees. All agreed that the AAA program was meeting a real need in the newly independent countries. The Corporation provided additional support for an Institute for Africa at Teachers College, and other teaching programs, such as Teachers for East Africa, were also based at Teachers College.

A FOCUS WITHIN A FOCUS

BY THE MID-1960S, Stackpole again began to take stock of the role of the Corporation in promoting higher education in Africa. He realized that he had succeeded beyond board and staff expectations; the Ford Foundation, the Rockefeller Foundation, the US Agency for International Development, and other agencies were providing considerably more support for African higher education than the Corporation. The other donors were supporting high-priority institutional concerns and creating new departments in areas related to economic development and growth, such as veterinary science, agriculture, science, commerce, and medicine.[190] This welcome increase in resources going to a wide range of initiatives in education in Africa led Gardner, Stackpole, and the board of trustees to make another significant decision.

By 1963 Alan Pifer was vice president of the Corporation and Stackpole had a new associate, Frederic Mosher, who had joined from the Social Relations Department at Harvard. In analyzing the situation, Stackpole noted that over the past four years the Corporation had spent in the Commonwealth Program about $646,000 a year, or a total of $2,564,750. Over the four years, slightly more than 65 percent of the resources were devoted to Africa, around 30 percent had gone to the travel grants, and the remainder, about 4 percent, had been for expenditures in the rest of the Commonwealth, mainly in Canada. The nearly $1.7 million expended in Africa encompassed planning for higher education, university programs, and teacher training; educational research; library training and development; university programs in adult education; and the undergraduate scholarship program.[191] And Stackpole made explicit the Corporation's influence on other donors:

[US]AID's support of the Teachers for East Africa scheme ... grew directly out of the Princeton Conference of 1960 ... and the present interest of [USAID, the Rockefeller Foundation (RF), and the Ford Ford Foundation (FF)] in the development of the University of East Africa was undoubtedly stimulated by that meeting. I'm inclined to think that the Carnegie program, with its focus on higher education in Africa, had a fairly direct influence on the exploratory FF Africa team which ultimately recommended for Africa ... [a program] which in many respects has paralleled our own. I would not claim a similar effect on the new RF program, but it is interesting to speculate that in their decision to go for institution building in the interest of national or regional development ... the example of CC's [Carnegie Corporation's] approach may have played some part.[192]

Stackpole went on in his memo to analyze the two partner foundations' expenditures, which had increased since five years earlier ($10 million over that period for the Rockefeller Foundation and $6 million for the Ford Foundation): each was planning to expend about $3 million a year, considerably more than the Corporation could spend. He also noted the field-based staff appointments that both foundations had made: namely, the Ford Foundation's regional offices and the Rockefeller Foundation's faculty appointments and consultants in a variety of countries and institutions.

Even with the considerable resources of the sister foundations and the continuing, although limited, opportunities elsewhere in the Commonwealth, Stackpole concluded by saying that he was "convinced Africa should remain the center of our interest.... Yes, we *should* continue for a further period, say two or three years, to devote a substantial portion of Commonwealth income to Africa—but on a new and more sharply-focused basis."[193] Cognizant of the success of the AAA Program for Teacher Education, as well as the changing level and pattern of donor support, he recommended that the opportunity to break new ground and develop innovative programs revolved around strengthening "a university's capacity to do something substantial about the shortage of qualified teachers for secondary schools and training colleges, to become the hot beds of curricular reform, to give leadership to the ministries and to influence professional standards and the quality of educational generally."[194] Stackpole saw this as an area for making significant contributions: "This is ... a relatively neglected [field]. It is one in which the RF [Rockefeller Foundation] is not active. FF [Ford Foundation] has done quite a bit, but this has represented only a part of their total program. It is a field in which one may usefully make both large grants and small. The important thing to my mind would be an identification of CC [Carnegie Corporation] with progressive ideas and action in this area, for this would help to focus public attention on it."[195]

After considerable internal discussion and board review, the trustees and leadership of the Corporation agreed with the thrust of Stackpole's arguments and decided to focus on the human capital component of education. This case offers an example of the Corporation staying in the same overall area for grant-making—namely, higher education in Africa—but paying close attention to the results of its grantees and the changing context in the field, especially the funding context, in order to target a specific component of the core problem.[196]

With the new thrust of the Corporation and the recognition of increasing African leadership in all the fields of education across the continent, the Corporation and the leaders of the Afro-Anglo-American Program for Teacher Education agreed that there had to be change. Despite the continuing support from the Corporation for the program through Teachers College, Karl Bigelow raised the issue of how African educationalists could take more control of the work of the association.

The Conference on the African University and National Educational Development, held at Lake Mohonk in September 1964, marked the turning point. About one-fifth of the participants were African educationalists, academics, and ministry staff, more than had participated in any of the prior meetings. Over the two-week conference, participants reviewed thoroughly all the issues in education, and specifically teacher education, on the continent. This meeting was the first to prominently feature African educators.[197] From 1964 on, more participants would be drawn from African institutions and, more frequently, they would have leadership roles. For example, at the 1967 meeting of the AAA program, out of the sixty-six participants, twenty-nine were Africans from Africa, and soon they were in the majority. Two leading participants, also associated with Corporation grantee institutions, were Professors W. Senteza Kajubi from Makerere University, director of the National Institute of Education (and later vice chancellor of the University), who was actively promoting education in Uganda and the East Africa region, and A. Babatunde Fafunwa, who was doing the same in West Africa from his base at the University of Ife's (now Obafemi Awolowo University) Institute of Education. (The first Nigerian recipient of a doctorate in education, Fafunwa later became acting vice chancellor of the University of Nigeria, Nsukka). In April 1969, the Association for Teacher Education in Africa (ATEA) was launched in Nairobi, Kenya. Bigelow remained a consultant, but the leadership was now fully ensconced in African institutions.

Across West and East Africa, the Corporation pursued its strategy. Grants helped strengthen the capacity of several institutions: the Institute of Education at Ahmadu Bello University in Zaria, Nigeria, in its coordination of teacher training activities with the fifty-three teacher training colleges in northern Nigeria; Makerere University College in Kampala, Uganda, in its work with thirty-one teacher training colleges in Uganda; University College in Dar es Salaam, Tanzania, primarily in its development of tests for selecting students for secondary school; University College Nairobi, in Kenya, in its effort to develop an education library; the University of Basutoland, Bechuanaland Protectorate, and Swaziland program to hold in-service courses for teachers for all three territories and at all levels; and the efforts of the University of Nigeria to open its contacts with other African universities.[198]

The grant to former Ashby commissioner Professor Kenneth Dike at the University of Ibadan in Nigeria—to study African history concerning the Benin Empire—resulted in a new set of examinations on African history for secondary students in Nigeria, Ghana, Sierra Leone, and the Gambia. For the first time the exams were developed locally and concentrated on local history rather than on European history. Not only did the Corporation support the development of the new curriculum, but it also gave support for a workshop for history teachers from West Africa and historians from West Africa and foreign universities to work together to develop the teaching materials. In-service training programs were also held for teachers so that they could learn the new materials.[199]

The Corporation maintained limited but significant interest in its traditional area of grant-making in Africa—libraries and the training of librarians. The Corporation provided support for specific kinds of library programs at Fourah Bay College in Sierra Leone[200] and for the first Institute of Librarianship at University College in Ibadan, Nigeria.[201] These grants mirrored the Corporation's concern that professional education was too often taking place outside the continent. By 1966, sixty-nine qualified librarians had graduated from the Institute, and they were all employed. The Institute was soon fully integrated into the education faculty at the university. It was an experiment that "had become an established institution [and was] considered a national asset to Nigeria, a training center of potential importance for other West African countries, and a model for other areas."[202]

In the increasingly fraught southern part of the continent, the Corporation continued its grants to strengthen the University College of Rhodesia and Nyasaland through consultations and the funding of manpower requirement studies. Although the Corporation had much earlier provided support for the libraries in this part of the continent, with the indications that Southern Africa would not have a peaceful transition to independence, the Corporation did not want to invest scarce resources where they might be wasted.[203]

FROM TEACHERS TO CHILDREN

WHILE THE CORPORATION was narrowing the lens of its grants program to focus on the quality of teacher training and educational planning geared toward improved teacher training at the primary and secondary school levels, its interest in understanding the local attributes of child development began to surface. With the participation of Frederic Mosher, a social/cognitive psychologist, in the Commonwealth Program, understanding child development and child psychology from an African perspective was increasingly viewed as a promising area for grant-making. Based on the results from initial studies, the Commonwealth Program began to fund child development study institutes located at the institutes of education in selected universities.[204]

As pointed out in the 1965 Annual Report, "Teacher training in Africa is almost completely dependent on materials, texts, and knowledge drawn from studies of children in the West. It is essential that there be similar studies of child development in Africa."[205] The recognition that educational materials needed to be grounded in the local culture opened a whole new area of activity for the Corporation's Commonwealth grants programs in the former African colonies, now new nations. In 1966, Pifer noted the high value in supporting educational systems in developing countries, along with a key caveat:

> But in transporting educational methods from developed to less-developed areas allowances must be made for local variables. One of these may be fundamental: children may actually learn differently in different societies. A group of social anthropologists and psychologists concerned that present theories of learning are based almost entirely on experiments with white children raised in industrialized nations have recently formed the International Child Development Committee to study whether and to what extent differences in learning and other aspects of development do exist.[206]

The International Child Development Committee members were interested in conducting studies on a global basis to show the differences and similarities in social structures, child-rearing patterns, and learning skills and styles. The Corporation participated in testing the soundness of these ideas by funding American researchers to develop collaborative activities in two African institutions, the Institute of Education at Ahmadu Bello University in Zaria, Nigeria, and the East African Colleges of Makerere and Nairobi. With Roy D'Andrade of Stanford University at the first site and Robert and Ruth Munroe of Pitzer College at the second, grants enabled them, with their African colleagues, to work on "developing child study materials, conducting their own research on these questions, and exploring the possibility of setting up permanent research centers at these colleges' institutes of education."[207] These studies served as the basis for the Corporation's grant-making related to strengthening the capacity for work on child development through the institutes of education, the major activities of the Commonwealth Program in the next era.

TRANSATLANTIC SUPPORT OF AFRICA: THE ANGLO-AMERICAN-CANADIAN PARLIAMENTARIAN CONFERENCES

J. WAYNE FREDERICKS was instrumental in establishing a long-term program of transatlantic meetings in the Gardner era that were reminiscent of the London conferences in the 1930s and continued for many years during the Pifer presidency. From 1965 through 1980, the Corporation supported the American participants (through Johns Hopkins University) in the Inter-Parliamentarian Study Group on Africa—formally known as the Anglo-American-Canadian Parliamentarian Conferences—and the Ariel Foundation based in the United Kingdom supported the British participants. The Ford Foundation joined in this effort after a couple of years.

Fredericks, with his US State Department experience, realized that meetings as usual would not sustain the necessary congressional interest in providing the funding required for assistance programs in Africa. There were congressmen committed to assistance programs in Africa, but only a handful. With George Thompson, then minister of state in the Foreign Office of the United Kingdom, Fredericks developed a plan for conferences devoted initially to Africa and Latin America, but soon Africa dominated the discussions. Vernon McKay, a former colleague of Fredericks at the State Department and at the time professor of African studies and director of the program of African studies at Johns Hopkins University School of Advanced International Studies, provided the intellectual heft for the meetings.[208] Canadian parliamentarians were also invited to participate as the Corporation became more interested in strengthening relations between Canadian institutions and those in the former colonies.[209] These meetings did not end when support came to a close in 1980. The organizer changed, the organizing institution changed, and the purposes were recalibrated, but Thompson and Fredericks's brainchild has had staying power far beyond its fifteen active years. This activity was the progenitor of the Aspen Institute Congressional Program, designed and led by former senator Dick Clark, a participant in these discussions when he was a young senator.[210] This new program, which continues to this day—funded by Carnegie Corporation and the Ford Foundation, among many others—has sustained the spirit of the parliamentarian conferences.

BUILDING ON THE AFRICAN EXPERIENCE IN THE CARIBBEAN

THE WORK IN THE CARIBBEAN also concentrated on strengthening universities and their connections with their societies, much as had happened with Corporation-funded activities at African universities. With the encouragement of the Inter-University Council for Higher Education Overseas, the Corporation enabled the University of Guyana, following national independence in 1966, to enlarge its role in teacher training. This entailed assistance for a new faculty member to plan courses and develop in-service training activities with the Ministry of Education; a follow-up grant enabled Guyanese staff to travel to meet counterparts at the University of the West Indies in Jamaica, Trinidad, and Barbados; in turn, staff from those branches visited the university in Georgetown. The Corporation's interest in building collaboration across universities in the United States and in Africa also shaped the grant-making in the Caribbean, albeit on a much more limited basis.[211]

The University of the West Indies also featured in the Corporation's continued grant-making in the region. Following the Corporation's new concerns about children and education, a grant in 1967 enabled Jamaican investigators at the Institute of Education at the University of London to evaluate a new approach to primary school education and to identify solutions to providing for more and better-trained teachers, better facilities, better instructional materials, and a redesign of the rigid school organizational patterns. The innovative approach of the Jamaican scholars involved working with available human resources and available technologies to develop the program "for disrupting the 'class-by-class' arrangement" so that "teachers can concentrate their teaching on subjects in which they are most proficient and inexperienced teachers receive help in planning their lessons in the basic subjects."[212] Even as the Corporation focused its efforts primarily on Africa, grants continued in the Caribbean through the next era.

IN THE DOMINIONS,
THE OLD AND NEW COMMONWEALTH

THE CORPORATION'S ACTIVITIES IN AUSTRALIA, Canada, New Zealand, and South Africa were almost overshadowed by those in the about-to-be new nations of Africa and the Caribbean, but were not yet eliminated. Pifer and Stackpole still sought to explore opportunities for grant-making throughout the dominions beyond the continuation of the travel grants. The abiding concern was what to do in South Africa.

South Africa—earlier a dominion, not a colony—had garnered major support from the Corporation up through 1940; the country still featured in the grants program, despite the concerns about the harsh apartheid regime—the increasingly destructive restrictions on black and colored citizens that restrained their effective functioning in their own society. The Corporation's post–World War II grants included training fellowships in the field of psychometric testing and funding for field research in the Eastern Cape for researchers at Rhodes University, as well as additional psychological testing support for the South Africa Council for Scientific and Industrial Research.[213] The intent of these grants was to open opportunities for the entire population, but as staff members soon realized, the situation was beyond repair and morally unacceptable. By 1958 the Corporation had

ended its institutional and fellowship grant-making to South African institutions, although travel grants would still be awarded to South Africans
until 1968, when the travel grants program as a whole was closed. The travel
grants still primarily supported white South Africans, either of British or
Afrikaner origin. Only a few Africans were included.

Canada, Australia, and New Zealand began to feature less frequently
in the Corporation's grant-making portfolio. As in South Africa, fellowships were provided for psychometric researchers in Australia and New
Zealand to study at the Educational Testing Service (ETS) in Princeton,
New Jersey.[214] The University of Malaya also received support via ETS for
a program in testing.[215] The University of Hong Kong, a first-time grantee,
and the University of Sydney received support to reach out to their local
constituencies.[216]Australia still received the bulk of the travel grants, and
New Zealand about half as many.[217]

A different focus for the work in Canada developed, even as a few grants
for Canadian universities and the Maritime Provinces Higher Education
Commission continued.[218] In 1961 the Corporation began to encourage
Canadian collaboration with African institutions, particularly in the field of
adult education. The Corporation funded visits to the University of Ghana
and its extramural department by North Americans from the United States
and Canada to discuss issues and approaches in adult education for Africa.
The Corporation also enabled North Americans, including university leaders, to visit other African universities.[219]

CONCLUSIONS

THIS ERA ILLUSTRATES Gardner's precept of "stability in motion" as a prerequisite for an innovating institution. In the international programs based
in the United States, the Corporation maintained the area studies and
national security focus but expanded to include brand-new areas: economic
development theory, modernization and development (including critical
analyses of these concepts), the underlying causes of internal conflict, the
economics of disarmament, nuanced comparative studies of communism,
and new thinking on world order and peace.

In the overseas grant-making, the Corporation focused many of its efforts on the newly independent nations in Africa. A major aim that succeeded was to bring in new donors; as a result, the Corporation concentrated on the themes of higher education and teaching. For nearly two decades, this field enjoyed vigorous partnership across African universities, national and international governments, foundations, and international donor agencies. In all of its international endeavors, even with financial resources more limited than those of its peers, the Corporation managed to continue pursuing agendas that took programmatic risks, especially as the agenda narrowed; the trustees and Gardner fully endorsed this pursuit.[220] Building on the prior thirty years of activities in the British dominions and colonies, the Corporation developed these activities in close consultation with new national governments and aimed to strengthen the relationship between local universities, local government, and local communities. Demand-driven, pragmatic actions resulted from the overseas grant-making.

Two less positive conclusions emerge from the US-based internationally oriented work in this era. More than his predecessors, John Gardner was involved in personally advising American leadership, particularly at the presidential level. His development of the idea of the White House Fellowships, for example, was one way of offering opportunities to young people to work in government. Despite Gardner's extensive connections in Washington, however, and despite grantees' attempts to train future employees or current employees of the State Department and even the Defense Department, clearly the critical studies on technical assistance, civilian-military relations, and national security did not penetrate into national policymaking. Moreover, the twenty years of commitment to promoting American understanding of international affairs through area studies, language training, and public outreach, along with significant support from other foundations and the government, did not seem to inform a nuanced understanding on the part of the public or policymakers. Analyzing what worked and what did not work from this active period might yield productive guidance for philanthropic emphasis on achieving such understanding in the early twenty-first century.[221]

At the same time, although John Gardner as president and later Alan Pifer as acting president during this period were both knowledgeable about the work undertaken in the domestic part of the program on international issues—in particular, the effectiveness of technical assistance, new theories of economic development, and the political dimensions of modernization—none of this internal knowledge influenced the directions taken in the Commonwealth Program, and vice versa. The lack of explicit connection between the ideas being worked on domestically that affected international development and the actual work on international development abroad illustrated a key decision premise: the issues funded nationally in the United States were ones that were pressing for both the academic and policy communities in this country, whereas the issues and the work funded throughout the Commonwealth, and particularly in Africa and the Caribbean, were pressing ones for those countries. Following the perspective of Keppel and Shepardson, the Corporation continued its emphasis on supporting those activities that made the most sense in the countries where they were working rather than designing grant-making to address what mattered most from an American point of view. Only in the area of psychometric testing and manpower/human capital did there seem to be an active intersection of the domestic and international development thrust of the Corporation. This raises questions about internal collaborative opportunities missed, such as those related to the technical assistance studies.

These missed opportunities extended into future eras. That is, Corporation amnesia affected the long-term institutional memory about the international work undertaken from 1945 to 1967. The programs and knowledge gained—especially on civilian-military relations, studies of economic theory, comparative studies of communism, and sources of internal conflict—did not surface in the 1980s or later, when these topics regained prominence in the international agenda of the Corporation, both in its domestic and overseas-funded activities. This era and the prior one highlight the challenges in achieving internal cross-generational learning.[222]

One particularly positive trait that predominated—along with and perhaps reflecting the intellectual risk-taking of the Gardner era—was the nurturing of staff members, who were empowered to take the lead in their program areas and in the field. In 1963, even before he thought that he would be going to Washington on a permanent basis, Gardner appointed Alan Pifer as vice president. With this appointment, he brought the international perspective to the very top of the Carnegie Corporation. When selected as president to succeed Gardner, Pifer had the most extensive international experience of any Corporation president until that time. Pifer had a very different perception, however, of the compelling issues in American society and the role of philanthropy and foundations. He slowly began to implement that vision, bringing fundamental shifts in the Corporation's program in both the United States and the Commonwealth.

6

CALIBRATING THE FOCUS, 1967–1982

W HEN STUDENTS at the University of California at Berkeley launched the Free Speech Movement in October 1964, they sparked antiwar demonstrations across the United States.[1] The protests ignited a movement that extended the civil rights struggle into student activism and would witness the use of violence both by and against student protesters. The closing years of John Gardner's presidency and the start of Alan Pifer's unfolded against this background of social and political upheaval. Gardner resigned in 1966 to become secretary of health, education, and welfare under an American president who was about to undermine remarkable gains in social justice for all Americans with his persistent prosecution of the Vietnam War. Pifer, first as acting, then as elected president, grabbed hold of the social justice agenda and infused it into all of Carnegie Corporation's domestic and international programs, and within the Corporation as well. A staff member for twenty-nine years, including his service as president from 1967 to 1982, Pifer transformed the worldview of the institution and, as a consequence, the grant programs. This chapter focuses on these institutional transformations and their influence on overseas grant-making and internationally oriented activities within the United States.

Although Pifer brought a distinct perspective to the Corporation's work, his underlying philosophy in some respects harkened back to Andrew Carnegie. In reflecting on his life and his work at the Corporation, Pifer remarked that he had been "guided by a single motivating force—a lifelong belief in social justice and the equality of all people under the law." Comparing his motivation to Andrew Carnegie's commitment to ensuring access to education for all, Pifer's goal during his leadership at the foundation was *"increasing access to education by overcoming barriers of discrimination and poverty."*[2]

The new directions internationally and domestically emerged not only from Pifer's personal convictions but also from trustee and staff consultations and retreats, informed by recognition of the changing mores in the United States. As a consequence, the scope and thrust of the international grants program differed fundamentally at the end of Pifer's tenure from its direction at any other period of the Corporation's history. When he stepped down in 1982, the overseas program was making grants primarily in Southern Africa, with a cluster in the Caribbean. Social justice and social action in response to persistent, egregious race and gender discrimination in Southern Africa had displaced, with a couple of notable exceptions, the traditional focus on universities, teaching, and libraries. International affairs grants in the United States no longer addressed a wide range of foreign policy issues and educational activities, despite the opening of China and the continuing ups and downs of the Cold War, nuclear weapons proliferation and control, the potential international impacts of presidential impeachment proceedings, and domestic as well as international economic dislocations due to the elimination of the gold standard and oil price rises. Rather, over time the core US-based international grants focused on Southern Africa and on bolstering anti-apartheid activities; these, in turn, influenced the Corporation's investment decisions for its assets.

Not surprisingly, there was an internal cost to these transformative actions. Pifer's focus on social justice related to the domestic issues at the forefront of the national debate nearly eliminated the Corporation's broader international affairs activities, which were arguably also important and necessary considering the increasingly complex international economic and political conditions, including the potential conversion of the Cold War to a hot one. The Corporation maintained only a limited set of its traditional activities aimed at educating the American public and policymakers about international affairs and those centered on Africa. The period from 1967 to 1982 was a transformative one for developing countries, especially those in

Africa. The optimism of the decolonization and independence era and the positive growth in many parts of the developing world, including African countries, dramatically changed from the end of the 1960s to the beginning of the 1980s. From 1960 to 1975, economic growth across African countries, as measured by gross domestic product, was 4.5 percent; by 1981, estimates had fallen to zero or negative economic growth.[3] The effects of two oil price shocks, in 1973 and 1979, plus increasing debt placed most African countries in dire economic situations. Outstanding debt obligations, for example, went from $9.9 billion in 1973 to $29.2 billion in 1978, to $51.4 billion in 1981.[4] African countries were not the only ones having to confront this downward trajectory, but they were the hardest hit because of a negatively reinforcing combination of economic, political, environmental, and historical factors.[5]

Carnegie Corporation did not actively tackle the economic or political development conditions in the Commonwealth Program, although many of the internationally oriented studies conducted in the previous era foreshadowed these issues, including the critical examinations of modernization theories and practices. By 1976, however, as part of the commitment to achieving social justice in South Africa, the Corporation had initiated its grant-making to counter the adverse effects of apartheid in South Africa and was participating vigorously in debates about the policies of the US government and business community. The actions against apartheid drew together in close partnership in South Africa the Corporation, the Ford Foundation, and the Rockefeller Brothers Fund; in the United States, the Rockefeller Foundation addressed the policy issues in partnership with the other foundations.

The gradual shift in the on-the-ground Commonwealth Program grant-making that was attempting to ameliorate the cruel and morally debilitating conditions in South Africa and neighboring countries in Southern Africa effectively halted three decades of effort devoted to strengthening the contributions of universities and other educational institutions to national development in other parts of the African continent. Modest efforts toward that latter aim, however, continued elsewhere in the Commonwealth. The Corporation was at the forefront of approaches to the new theme of the role of women in developing countries, primarily at the regional and international levels, with limited local-level activities.[6]

For Alan Pifer, the trustees, and the staff, the ethical and societal benefits of responding to the challenges posed by racial and gender discrimination in the United States and Southern Africa far outweighed the costs. The social justice ethic that guided Pifer and his colleagues realigned the themes for grant-making and remains, at varying levels of intensity, the leitmotif for Carnegie Corporation.

ALAN PIFER: RIGHT PERSON, RIGHT PLACE, RIGHT TIME

ALAN PIFER joined Carnegie Corporation in the fall of 1953, after spending five years as executive secretary of the US Fulbright Commission in London.[7] To promote the Fulbright Commission in Commonwealth countries, he had spent several weeks in the Caribbean, meeting with people throughout the region to identify promising sites and people. In 1952 and 1953, as he was planning to return to the United States from London, the Fulbright commissioners asked him to undertake a six-month tour of Africa to meet all the key people in universities and government and to ascertain promising opportunities for Fulbright activities in the African Commonwealth countries, including South Africa.[8]

On his return to the United States in August 1953, he decided to seek out a position at one of the foundations, first contacting Rockefeller, then Ford, and finally Carnegie Corporation. Even more than employment, he wanted to promote an idea for funding: an institute in the United States that would focus on increasing American understanding of Africa through fellowships for American students. He wanted to ensure that American students were properly trained before they left the United States to study in an African country. As he later recalled, "I felt there was a need for somebody in this country to act as a sort of counterpart to some of the research institutes, particularly the one at Makerere College in Uganda."[9] At the same time, Stephen Stackpole, who had been promoted to take Whitney Shepardson's place, was desperately searching for a colleague with knowledge of Africa. After Pifer had met with Dollard, Gardner, Perkins, and Stackpole, the Corporation team all agreed that he was just the kind of person they were looking for.

Like Whitney Shepardson, Pifer knew the British colonial staff in London well. Immersed in the decolonization debates and developments,

he had made contact in the African colonies with African leaders and academics, as well as British Colonial Office staff in London and in the region.
When he joined the Corporation to work in the British Dominions and
Colonies Program, he was able to back up Stackpole and harness the energies of change in the British colonies for new grant-making. When he joined,
he was the only member of the Carnegie staff who had been to Africa.[10]
He originally helped to identify an intellectually sound yet pragmatic set of
grants around the key issue of education for development. He was acutely
aware of the positive and negative ramifications of rapid social, economic,
and political change propelled forward by decolonization. Moreover, he had
seen firsthand the early stages of destructive change from the apartheid policies in South Africa.

His African experience gave him a special role to play in introducing
other donors and the foundation community to the potential contributions of grant-making under conditions of political, social, and economic
upheaval. The success of the Greenbrier and Mohonk conferences and the
Ashby Commission (described in Chapter 5) reflected his effectiveness in
building support with his African, British, and American colleagues.[11]

In 1963 John Gardner promoted Alan Pifer to vice president. It was clear
to Pifer that he needed to learn about the rest of the Corporation's work,
not only the international affairs grant-making but also the domestic activities to which he had been exposed in proposal review sessions but in which
he had certainly not worked before.[12] He then served as acting president
during Gardner's leaves in Washington in 1965 and 1966. Gardner resigned
on April 18, 1967, and the board elected Pifer president on May 18, 1967.[13]

EXTERNAL INFLUENCES ON INTERNAL DECISIONS AND
ACTIONS: THE US CONGRESS AND THE ECONOMY

AT THE SAME TIME that the Pifer era was marked by compelling social justice concerns in the United States and in the Commonwealth, the geopolitical situation in Vietnam was threatening international peace and stability
and political travails were roiling the Commonwealth, notably in Southern
Africa. Besides these external influences, a different set of influences was
also affecting the work of the Corporation. The combination of a domestic

economic situation weakened by the Vietnam War and a global economy weakened by oil price rises led to severe resource constraints for both the US and global economies. Domestically, the 1968–1969 US congressional investigations were potentially even more harmful for the Corporation and other American foundations than the economic conditions. Those hearings led to significant legislation that affected the work of foundations in perpetuity.

The impact of the Vietnam War on inflation and employment was considerable and certainly affected the resources available to the Corporation for grant-making: "Fiscal year 1974 brought the collapse of the 'Nifty Fifty'—the fifty most popular large-cap stocks traded on the New York Stock Exchange. The result was a devastating 40% drop in the Corporation's assets, from $338.5 million to $199.9 million.... The Corporation did not recover its real market value [adjusted for inflation] as of October 1, 1973 until 20 years later."[14] The precariously unstable economy resulted from the combination of the rise in oil prices, the declining value of the dollar, and a large balance-of-payments deficit, all on top of President Nixon's earlier decision on August 15, 1971, that "the gold window would be closed." While the economic challenges facing philanthropy were as considerable as the political ones, board management of the foundation's assets, despite the ups and downs, kept the resources available for grant-making fairly steady, although of necessity constrained.[15]

The political challenges emanating from Capitol Hill required considerable time, energy, and commitment by Pifer and the rest of the foundation community to ensure that Congress's concerns did not culminate in the demise of American philanthropic foundations. Soon into his presidency, Pifer found himself enveloped, like Dollard, in the murky cloud of congressional hearings that reopened discussions on the tax-exempt status of foundations.[16] Representative Wright Patman of Texas had been persistently questioning foundations since 1961 and had identified a series of abuses, including concerns about the overseas expenditures of foundations. His in-depth examinations led the Treasury Department to investigate private foundations. The report issued in 1965 identified six areas of potentially serious infractions: self-dealing, delay in making grants, ownership of business, control of corporate property, the nature of financial investments, and donor control. Nonetheless, the report's final comment acknowledged the positive contributions of foundations to American society. Despite that final comment, the investigations and report led directly to hearings of the House Ways and Means Committee. Those hearings, starting in January 1969 and drawing on Patman's hearings, continued to address the issues of payout, self-dealing, business holdings, and programmatic restrictions, such as support to individuals. Still, the resulting Congressional Tax Reform Act of 1969 was a shock to foundations. As Thomas A. Troyer writes, "Significant aspects of the 1969 legislation did appear abruptly, without foreshadowing, in the House Ways and Means proceedings of that year … however, the 1969 legislation was not a congressional bolt from the blue." He emphasizes that the concerns "had roots reaching back for more than two decades, and its core restrictions … had solid policy justifications."[17] The 1969 act included a 4 percent excise tax on foundations, regulation of grants to individuals, payout requirements from assets of 6 percent, new account- ing responsibilities for international grants, and limitations on political lob- bying and participation.

Even before the act was passed, two philanthropists had become exceed- ingly concerned about the debilitating effects on philanthropy that were looming. Alan Pifer had started writing, even as acting president in 1967, about the nature of nongovernmental organizations (NGOs) and their role in society; in 1968 he had written about foundations being at the service of the public, focusing on the obligations of foundations as well as the dilemma they posed for society and the limitations of governmental regulation. He also detailed the various approaches to internal and external accountability and concluded by articulating his fears for what would happen if founda- tions did not reform themselves:

> Perhaps the foundation field itself should set up an independent com- mission to review the present state of the field and make recommen- dations as to how foundations might more effectively serve the public interest … a constructive effort to help foundations attain the highest degree of social value of which they are capable.… For otherwise that great social invention which has done so much for American life and, indeed, for mankind over the past half century may find itself first fet- tered and then destroyed by a society which has lost faith in it.[18]

In his 1969 presidential essay, following his participation in the congressional hearings, Pifer addressed a concern that had been an issue in Washington, DC, since foundations were first established and that continues to this day: "I have seen alarming evidence both in the Congress and the Executive Branch of an astonishing lack of knowledge, and hence lack of concern, not just about foundations but about private organizations generally. Beyond that, there is a pervasive atmosphere of suspicion, even hostility, to the very idea of the independence of foundations, and this seems to extend in some measure to other private, tax-exempt institutions as well."[19]

At the same time, John D. Rockefeller III had been encouraging Peter Peterson, a prominent businessman, to establish a commission on foundations and private philanthropy.[20] Peterson did organize the commission, but its report was published after the act had been passed. Still, Rockefeller did not give up, and neither did Pifer. He continued to write, and Rockefeller continued to promote an idea similar to Pifer's in his 1968 essay: that a more extensive commission be established, one specifically charged with addressing the issues raised by the 1969 Tax Reform Act. Rockefeller established just such a new commission, with considerable support from President Nixon, the chairman of the House Ways and Means Committee, Wilbur D. Mills, and the Treasury Department, as well as from the philanthropic community.[21] The Filer Commission (the Commission on Private Philanthropy and Public Needs) reviewed all the issues raised by the act and issued its report in 1975. Pifer, one of the twenty-eight members of the commission, continued to write extensively on philanthropy.[22]

During his tenure, Pifer exerted effective leadership that not only promoted and reinforced social justice for society's marginal groups in both the United States and the Commonwealth but also protected the distinct role of foundations and the private nonprofit sector as a vibrant and indispensable part of American society. Although each Carnegie Corporation president—like any foundation president—brought a set of personal and professional values and passions to the position, Pifer's values and passions encompassed the field itself: his goal was to ensure the continued existence of foundations, albeit while also taking action to prevent foundation self-inflicted abuses.[23] He and his colleagues on the Filer Commission obtained important modifications of the 1969 Tax Reform Act: the original 4 percent excise tax on income was lowered to 2 percent, the payout

requirement was reduced from 6 percent to 5 percent, and the forty-year
sunset clause for the lifetime of a foundation was eliminated.[24]

Pifer's writings on the nature and responsibility of institutions and
the ethics of philanthropy helped shape the field of philanthropy in the
late twentieth century and earned him the Council on Foundations' first
Distinguished Grantmaker Award in 1984.[25]

INTERNAL TRANSFORMATIONS:
CHANGES THAT ENDURE

EVEN BEFORE PIFER transformed the grants programs, he introduced
changes in the way the Corporation worked and what it looked like, at both
the board and staff levels. Some of the changes resulted from issues raised
in Congress as well as Pifer's own concerns about the accountability of private foundations and social justice. Believing that John Gardner had kept
the trustees intrigued with his ideas but not engaged in the Corporation's
programs, Pifer set about having individual lunches with the trustees to
encourage them to dedicate more time to the work of the Corporation and
learn more about its activities, including the work in and on Africa. One
innovation he instituted was to invite new trustees to sit in on staff discussions of proposals in order to see how staff members conducted the grant
review process.[26] Another change was reminiscent of the role of the board up
to 1941: Pifer encouraged board members to take more of a leadership role
in introducing ideas and staying on top of programmatic developments.[27]

In 1970 Pifer began to introduce significant changes in the role and
responsibilities of the board as well as its composition, the latter changes
paralleling the changing program priorities that in turn reflected changing
American mores. In November 1971, after a committee of trustees reported
to the full board about the changing nature of board responsibilities, the
board resolved

> to focus its attention on the effectiveness of the Corporation's pro-
> gram as a whole, from a policy standpoint. While retaining final
> grant-making authority, the board should play a greater role in setting,
> reviewing, and revising the broad objectives of the Corporation then in

scrutinizing individual proposals for grants.... A proper and essential role of the board is to advise and support the president and staff in those areas where the more detached point of view and more diverse experience of trustees can add something to the in-depth analysis and specialized expertise of the staff.[28]

During Pifer's tenure, term limits for trustees resulted in a maximum period of service of eight years, with a few exceptions, such as for the trustee elected chair (by the other trustees). The cycling in and out of new people on the board was advantageous for introducing new ideas and new approaches, but at the same time term limits resulted in the downplaying or loss of historical knowledge of what worked and what did not for informing forward planning.

To increase the diversity of experiences on the board, and with the support of the trustees, Pifer resolutely began to change its composition. He and his fellow trustees increased the number of women, starting with Phyllis Goodhart Gordan, who in 1970 joined Margaret Carnegie Miller as the second female member of the board.[29] Gordan, a distinguished classicist and Renaissance scholar with extensive connections in Europe, assumed many leadership positions during her two terms on the board.

Also in 1970, Pifer and his board colleagues elected a new trustee, Franklin Thomas, a leading innovator in the African American community and the first head of the Bedford-Stuyvesant Restoration Corporation, one of the first major private-public-community initiatives to address black poverty. Thomas would chair important Corporation committees, including the 1974–1975 trustee review of the Commonwealth Program, play a major role on grants related to South Africa, and eventually serve as president of the Ford Foundation.[30] Another 1970 appointee was Francis Keppel, son of Frederick Keppel, who had been actively involved with the Corporation's work in Africa as one of the members of the Ashby Commission and who was at that time serving as dean of Harvard University's School of Education.[31]

Although Pifer's board reflected his commitment to social justice and human equality, this change did not come without a cost. Except for Francis Keppel, the trustees who joined during his tenure generally had considerable international experience, especially around the themes that the Corporation now embraced, but with the retirement of Devereux Josephs in 1967, no members with a deep awareness of the Corporation's history remained. Moreover, there were few surviving links to other Carnegie institutions.[32]

Pifer was true to his philosophy regarding staff. He hired women and promoted them.[33] He supported them after they left, even when they took whole program areas with them, as did Margaret Mahoney in 1972 when she took the Corporation's health program to the Robert Wood Johnson Foundation upon becoming its vice president in 1972.[34]

He also held firm convictions about what constituted the most appropriate background and approach for an outstanding staff member. Although he valued expertise, he was concerned that if staff were "too much wrapped up in their own specialization, they may try to develop more of an emphasis on their field than the foundation wants to have. Conversely, they may be unwilling to learn about new fields or lack the openness of mind to recognize and seize new opportunities when these appear." He concluded, "Most program officers must be jacks-of-all-trades—and, to the very best of their ability, masters of several."[35]

In the spirit of Andrew Carnegie's charge, and with acute awareness of the changing context for grant-making in the second half of the 1960s—with its movements, protests, riots, and assassinations and the Vietnam War's drain on social programs—Pifer initiated an intense program review at the start of his presidency in 1967. As he recalled in 1981:

> The Corporation began a review of its entire grants program in relation to the persistence of poverty in our national life…. It seemed to the staff that, in view of the slowdown of federal leadership for social change, the Corporation as a private organization had a constructive role to play in keeping alive the idealism that had so galvanized the nation to action a few years before. The trustees and staff agreed that the promotion of equal educational opportunity and rights should henceforth cut across all of its grants programs. In the 1970s, this commitment to a more equitable society broadened to include equal opportunity and rights for women, which grew naturally out of an earlier program involving the continuing education of women.[36]

Pifer maintained staff review of all program proposals, so that every staff member at the program level was familiar with what other staff members were doing and could weigh in with an opinion; he was also comfortable with debate about his own proposed grants. Possibly as a direct outcome of the Tax Reform Act of 1969, Pifer introduced the idea of formal programmatic evaluations. In 1971 he created an evaluation studies fund—later renamed the Program Development and Evaluation Fund—to encourage staff members to support outside evaluations of projects.[37]

At the October 1981 meeting, Alan Pifer informed the Board of Trustees of his desire to retire as president. He had been at the Corporation for slightly more than twenty-eight years. In his 1982 Annual Report essay, Pifer elaborated on why he had made the decision, even though he was relatively young. He talked about feeling the "distinct need of 'repotting.'"[38] He added that he had the "urge to be in a position to have fewer daily obligations and constraints on the use of my time for my remaining active years.... As for the Corporation, I felt that it would benefit from some new leadership. Change in the management of any institution is better made too soon than too late." Alan Pifer acted on his convictions about the necessity of social justice and worked to ensure the "broad development of all our people, and especially of our children, irrespective of race, sex, economic status, or any other consideration." The agenda for the Corporation he inspired and implemented remains relevant in the twenty-first century.[39]

THE METAMORPHOSIS OF CARNEGIE CORPORATION'S INTERNATIONAL GRANT-MAKING

IN JUST A FEW YEARS, the Corporation shifted its priorities in the United States by reducing the work on international affairs as well as developing new activities that differed considerably in approach from the usual grant-making. In the US domestic program, Pifer and his colleagues began sponsoring the major legal defense fund programs along with increasing access to legal training and careers for American blacks in the South.[40] This support included not only educational activities but, in a dramatic change for the Corporation, litigation activities as well. Carnegie Corporation was not only advancing and diffusing knowledge and understanding but through its grantees fighting in the courts to ensure that knowledge and understanding shaped better lives for marginalized populations in the United States.

Starting with the programs it supported in the United States, this shift dramatically affected the Corporation's international grant-making. Its grants to universities focused on international affairs in the United States had, by the early 1970s, been almost entirely overtaken by the new social justice agenda. As Pifer continued with the Commonwealth Program throughout his presidency, primarily in Africa and the Caribbean, the social justice focus in the United States led to a new set of priorities for the Africa-based grant-making.

Stackpole and Mosher had already narrowed the Africa component to continue the cross-cultural, field-based studies on child development, an area of increasing interest to the Corporation in its domestic programs, and the focus on teaching, including testing new technologies for training larger numbers of teachers and reaching more out-of-the-way places, along with supporting curriculum reform to reflect new teaching materials with more local content. This focus provided a special niche for the Corporation as international development assistance, including the programs of other foundations, increasingly focused on infrastructure, then on economic planning, basic needs, agricultural development, university development, family planning, and disease control.[41]

The Pifer era resulted in increasing, though not complete, connectivity between US-based international activities and those in the Commonwealth. The themes prior to and during the 1974–1975 trustee review of the Commonwealth Program covered education in the United States on international affairs; education and development in the United States, Africa, the Caribbean, and Asia; policy-related studies and outreach primarily in the United States, with some studies related to the Commonwealth as a whole and others to Anglo-American relations; and travel grants for Commonwealth countries and, increasingly, only for African countries. Following the trustee review, by 1976 the major thrusts comprised legal, economic, and national transformation activities in Southern Africa and global, regional, and national initiatives in the area of women and development.

As the following discussion of the grants illustrates, over the first eight years of the Pifer presidency the broadly focused international affairs activities in the United States essentially came to a close—sometimes grant activities ended as anticipated or grants were absorbed into other programs or institutions. Those related to Africa continued primarily through NGOs, such as the Council on Foreign Relations and the African-American Institute (now called the Africa-America Institute). Some succeeded beyond expectations, such as the Afro-Anglo-American Program for Teacher Education in Africa, which evolved from a tripartite institution to a fully African one; some failed as a result of unmet expectations, such as the Education and World Affairs (EWA) program; and others came to a close because of both life-cycle and other demands. A few out-of-Africa activities reflected the Corporation's comparative advantage and history, such as support for universities in other areas of the Commonwealth in the Caribbean and in Asia.

By mid-1975, the changes in the Corporation's international grant-making portfolio reflected three influences: changes in national and international contexts and mores; changes at the Corporation in program leadership and trustees; and changes resulting from the appearance of new and compelling actors. The following pages describe the limited continuity and considerable change that this era represents in the history of the Corporation.

CONTINUITY BEFORE CHANGE IN UNITED STATES– BASED INTERNATIONAL GRANT-MAKING

EDUCATION ON INTERNATIONAL AFFAIRS, particularly through support for universities, continued to feature in the Corporation's grant-making in the United States in the early years of Alan Pifer's presidency. Although the champions of US university–based international affairs grant-making, John Gardner and James Perkins, had departed, Pifer, Frederic Mosher, and soon Stephen Viederman and vice president Lloyd Morrisett maintained the work but with a tighter focus on the key themes of modernization, comparative studies, and, increasingly, African- and Commonwealth-related activities.[42] The latter area increased as the Corporation continued to pursue its goal of linking Americans with Africa and other parts of the Commonwealth through grants to the EWA program and the Overseas Liaison Committee and with new grantees such as the Africa-America Institute.

The main rationale for continuing these efforts centered on "trying to understand and help shape the various forces at work in this turbulent world" and, in the developing countries, figuring out "how to bring about much-needed social change without causing political chaos."[43] Phillip Foster and the Committee for the Comparative Study of New Nations at the University of Chicago received a third grant to examine issues in education related to economic, social, and political developments in new countries.[44]

In 1967 the Corporation extended the American Council of Learned Societies' efforts to conduct comparative studies on communist societies and refine techniques in comparative methodology. In addition, using the model developed in the 1950s for multi-university collaboration, the Corporation also in 1967 sponsored a five-college collaborative in the Pittsburgh area—bringing together the University of Pittsburgh, Carnegie Mellon, Duquesne University, Chatham College, and Mount Mercy College in a three-year study involving both graduate research and undergraduate teaching on communism with experts on China, the Soviet Union, Eastern Europe, and Latin America.[45] The courses included the comparative study of communist political and economic systems and comparative Marxist ideology; American and foreign scholars from other universities also participated in the program. Research conferences enabled the scholars to present papers and disseminate them beyond the participating colleges. The grants to the American Council of Learned Societies and the Pittsburgh-area institutions were matched by grants to Columbia University to examine the diversity of elites and interest groups in communist societies and to train graduate students in comparative research.[46] All of these grants served to enlarge the field of comparative communist studies and warrant further study for their impact on scholarship and policy.

The Corporation also promoted cross-national studies in citizen participation and political leadership across the United States and non-European countries. In 1969 a grant to the University of Chicago under the auspices of the Cross-National Program in Political and Social Change supported the work of political scientist Sydney Verba to participate in an international team of scholars from India, Japan, Nigeria, Yugoslavia, Austria, the Netherlands, and the United States. The project, completed many years later, was co-funded by the Ford Foundation and a variety of donors, including several from the participating countries.[47]

By the late 1960s, the Corporation's international affairs program for American universities included only a few new grants. Adam Curle, director of the Center for Education and Development at Harvard, was among the founders, along with Kenneth and Elise Boulding, of the field of peace studies. In 1969 Corporation support enabled Curle and his colleagues to conduct studies in Asia, Africa, and the United States on the relationship between development and social conflict as a consequence of modernization efforts such as education and urbanization.[48]

In 1968, Cornell University received continued support for its work in China and Southeast Asia in collaboration with the University of London so that American students could study in both England and Southeast Asia.[49] Northwestern University's program to delve into the relationship of conflict and hostility to modernization and nationalism, specifically through "cross-cultural study of ethnocentrism in premodern communities around the world," had been initially funded in 1962. In 1970 the study directors, psychologist Donald Campbell of Northwestern University and anthropologist Robert LeVine of the University of Chicago, received a final grant so that they could complete the analyses and publication.[50]

Although some grants were ongoing, after 1968 no new grants were made in the United States to bolster education and research at universities and colleges in the area of international affairs. At a time of increasing antagonism toward US foreign policy in Vietnam and intensifying Cold War concerns, fewer than a handful of grants spanning this period concentrated on national security and defense issues or public outreach on international affairs.

In 1968 an officer grant of $60,000 initiated an inquiry lasting several years and yielding major publications on the new era of the military-industrial complex related to national defense. Grant support, renewed several times to Columbia University, enabled the Institute of War and Peace Studies and other departments to organize study groups of British and American government administrators, scholars, and private-sector representatives. The researchers examined in depth the complex contract relationships across federal agencies, academic institutions, and NGOs. The first book covered the proceedings of a 1969 joint meeting in Ditchley Park, Oxford, England, that tussled with the questions of accountability, independence, and public contracts.[51] The Corporation renewed support for continued research and writing, particularly focusing on areas where British expertise might guide American policymakers. The example that best symbolized the complexity of the issue was the analysis of the Lockheed Tri-Star contract, an issue that received considerable media coverage in 1972. This issue was studied in depth at the Institute of War and Peace Studies to elucidate the lessons learned for government-industry relationships with national defense contractors. A follow-up grant in 1972 and 1973 enabled Professor Martin Edmonds, the British principal investigator, to stay in the United States, complete the research, and prepare a manuscript for publication.[52] The series of grants formed one of the few consistent areas of attention in the field of national defense by the Corporation in this era.[53] In addition to the accountability and independence dimensions of the contracting issues, the Corporation was increasingly interested in the role of nongovernmental organizations, foundations, and the private sector in relation to each other and to the federal government.[54]

The Council on Foreign Relations had received a small grant in 1967 to organize an Anglo-American Conference on Southern Africa, but soon that initiative was taken over by the Africa-America Institute. In 1970 the Corporation gave the Council $300,000, renewing the earlier requests from 1965 at a slightly lower level. In discussing the request, staff noted that the Council had been supported since 1934, particularly for its study groups in New York, Washington, and around the country, on a wide range of issues related to American foreign policy; for the publications that resulted from its research; and for its discussions with individuals both in and out of government. The agenda item indicated the high level of respect for the institution: "The officers believe ... that the Council continues to play a unique and valuable role in American foreign policy." Nonetheless, they also indicated that they did "not want to go on record as saying that the 1970 grant will absolutely be a final one, but ... additional funds for general support are not likely to be forthcoming from this source."[55]

Continuing the grants that started in 1957, the Corporation had regularly renewed funding for the Carnegie Endowment for International Peace. In 1969 another grant of $75,000 was approved to support its visiting scholars program for young non-Americans in the area of international affairs. "While this sort of activity is not part of the Corporation's present program, the officers, nevertheless, feel that the visiting research scholars plan is valuable both in itself and as a means of continuing collaboration with the Carnegie Endowment."[56] Despite the sentiment, this was the last grant to the Carnegie Endowment until the 1980s.

Keeping with the concern about disadvantaged populations, at the June 1974 board meeting the president referred to a confidential memo on a proposed commission to examine veterans' benefits, dishonorable discharges, and amnesty—all continuing problems related to the Vietnam War. The trustees recommended that there should not be a funding commitment for the time being, but that the president might want to participate in future meetings of the commission.[57] (In 1969 the Corporation had made a grant to the American Association of Community and Junior Colleges to develop a support program for servicemen attending college.[58]) In 1976 the Corporation underwrote a Georgetown University review of national military discharge policy.[59]

More than thirty years of support for scholars on issues of international security, international affairs, foreign policy, national defense, atomic energy, and the ubiquitous area studies came to a close. With the Ford and Rockefeller Foundations, along with the US government's Title VI program, spending millions of dollars on area studies and language training, the Corporation began to consider other opportunities for spending its relatively scarce resources. Its role in promoting broad-based international affairs had all but disappeared by 1976.[60]

However, the outwardly bound grant-making for connecting Americans to the Commonwealth continued, ever more focused on Africa but sporadically featuring other regions. The funding for Education and World Affairs— the institution dedicated to providing policy and institutional advice as well as teaching support to universities throughout the Commonwealth and other developing countries—continued through the end of the 1960s until its demise in 1970. The Corporation and the Ford Foundation, along with the US Agency for International Development, backed EWA, especially the work of its subsidiary the Overseas Educational Service, to recruit Americans to teach at universities in developing countries. But EWA faced considerable administrative challenges in meeting its mandate to coordinate and facilitate the linkages between universities in the United States and those in developing countries that might have benefited from such partnerships.[61]

Soon both Carnegie Corporation and the Ford Foundation saw the opportunity to reduce their commitments. Education and World Affairs had been instrumental in ensuring passage of the 1966 International Education Assistance Act.[62] Convinced that the act would lead to significant national resources for international education at American colleges and universities, both foundations reduced their grant-making commitments. As Joyce Hertko notes, "When the federal government announced its plans to fund programs previously funded by the foundations, the foundations left these programs and moved on to new priorities."[63] As foundations started withdrawing their funding, however, no monies were appropriated to implement the act, a consequence of budgetary demands for the Great Society programs and the Vietnam War. The government never took up the slack. Even Title VI, which was part of the 1958 National Defense Education Act and had been used to support academic area centers, language training, and research, as well as fellowships and the training of elementary and secondary language teachers, was significantly cut.[64] Corporation priorities began to change the focus to other pressing domestic concerns and to concentrate the US-based international activities on Africa, maintaining only a modicum of support for the earlier undertakings.[65]

Though Education and World Affairs itself received no further funding, the Corporation did modestly assist its successor institution, the International Council for Educational Development, which had been started by individuals, such as former Corporation vice president James Perkins (following his presidency at Cornell University), who were frustrated with EWA's administrative inefficiencies.[66] The Ford Foundation provided the core funding, and in 1975 and 1976 the Corporation provided small grants to cover participation in an International Council for Educational Development meeting on higher education bringing together American and foreign educators at Aspen.[67]

Far more support, both financial and through staff involvement, went to the American Council on Education and its Overseas Liaison Committee to build coordination and communication across American, British, and Canadian assistance efforts and to advise on US policy. Between 1959 and 1978, the Corporation gave approximately $1,330,000 to the Overseas Liaison Committee to bring American experience in higher education to bear in Africa. Because it proved to be so valuable in the African context, this assistance was expanded to cover other regions as well (hence the name change from "African" to "Overseas" Liaison Committee).[68] The committee maintained links with the Association of African Universities and brought together African and US experts in agricultural development and population as well as human resource planning. The committee also received significant funding from the US State Department and the Ford Foundation, with members representing a variety of American institutions and fields. In making the final grant in 1978, staff noted that the American Council would be covering 75 percent of the core costs and that specific contracts for connecting universities would cover the project activities.

In honing the US-based international activities to concentrate on American-African relations and exchanges, the Corporation maintained support for its longtime partner on work in African education, Teachers College at Columbia University. As the Afro-Anglo-American program in teacher education moved to the African continent, the Corporation continued the program of training promising potential education leaders to the master's or PhD level. Between 1961 and 1978, forty-six individuals completed the program and thirteen were still involved; all but four of the forty-six held leadership positions throughout English-speaking Africa in the field of education.

Staff members' assessment of the reasons for this success may be hard to replicate in other fellowship programs (staff called the program "unique"), but these factors are worth considering as design criteria, even for modern ones:

1. A strong sense of commitment on the part of both the fellow and the institution. The nominating African institution, for example, had a position in mind when the fellow returned and paid for all the travel costs.

2. The receiving institution (in this case, Teachers College) had "special interests and expertise in African education," along with long-standing collaborative relationships with institutions involved in African education and faculty across the continent.

3. The donor institution provided funds for field research in the home country and covered the costs of preparing the dissertation.

Moreover, the focus on doctorate-level support filled a real gap at that time.[69] This was the last grant to Teachers College until 1982, when a grant was awarded for a series of memorial lectures commemorating Karl Bigelow, the Corporation's main adviser, collaborator, and US grantee on the educational programs in Africa starting in 1942. The collaboration relating to Africa, however, had actually begun in 1928 and had lasted more than fifty years.[70]

THE AFRICA-AMERICA INSTITUTE:
A SPECIAL RELATIONSHIP

PERHAPS NO OTHER GRANTEE better captures Pifer's agenda in action than the African-American Institute (AAI).[71] During this period of transition in international grant-making at the Corporation, the Institute partnered with the Corporation on nearly every theme. Established in 1953, what was then known as the African-American Institute embodied the kind of institution that Pifer had in mind on his return to the States in that same year. After Pifer joined the Institute's board in 1956, he and fellow board members Dana Creel (president of the Rockefeller Brothers Fund) and Harold Hochschild (board chairman of American Metal Company) tried to sort out the finances of the institution and obtain considerable support from the foundations; subsequently, Waldemar Nielsen, from the Ford Foundation, became president in 1962–1963.[72]

Over time the African-American Institute (became the lead institution linking Americans and Africans not only around issues of education but also, more broadly, in their shared perspectives on development.[73] The Corporation had provided only small grants before Pifer became president (particularly to assist in scholarships for Nigerians in the United States), for a total of less than $100,000.[74] Starting in 1968, Carnegie Corporation provided support for travel grants for Africans to visit the United States, outreach on Africa for US congressmen through seminars, and, as the new Corporation agenda began in 1976, examination of external financial investments in South Africa and development of a new focus on women and development. Except for 1978, the Institute received support every year from the Corporation between 1968 and 1982, totaling $4,029,145. Although USAID was a major supporter of the Institute during this period and the

Ford Foundation also provided significant support, the Corporation was often the initiator of programs that then took off with funding from others. A snapshot of the variety of programs funded by the Corporation follows.

Travel Grants

Over these fourteen years, the Corporation provided $1,640,500 to AAI that enabled 180 men and women to visit the United States, the Caribbean, and other parts of Africa. In 1968 the Corporation had transferred the travel grants program to the African-American Institute for several reasons. The number of fellowship programs and exchanges had increased, including those offered by the Rockefeller Foundation, the Ford Foundation, the US government through the Fulbright Program, and many others. As the Corporation concentrated on African recipients for the travel grants, it brought to a close the Commonwealth-wide ones. Just as significant as these two reasons were two more: the questioning of individual grants by the foundations in congressional hearings, and the administrative burden of running the program. For these varied reasons, Pifer, Stackpole, and Mosher recommended to the board that the decision-making and administrative functions of the travel grants program be spun off and managed by an independent institution, namely, the African-American Institute.[75] In addition, AAI field offices could effectively backstop the grants to individuals, both from their home base and in their travels.

In 1968 the African-American Institute received $30,000 for travel grants, refocused so that academic and governmental employees in Africa could interact with their counterparts in both the United States and Canada.[76] Every other year, the Institute received a tranche of funds for the travel grants—with a maximum of $581,000 in 1977—that enabled the program to expand from its initial base of African educators to include Africans in government, media, and the private sector and to focus more intently on individuals from Southern Africa. Support over the years included not only the travel grants but opportunities for the grantees to meet in conferences in Africa and the United States. Informally, the African-American Institute was creating the network of African leaders in different sectors that it has maintained into the twenty-first century.

Information and Education on Africa for
Teachers and Congressional Aides

STARTING IN 1969, THE CORPORATION encouraged the African-American Institute, along with the Library of Congress, to become the major clearinghouses for African education, with the specific goal of reaching out to teachers and US congressional aides. Originally called the School Services Program, this program soon began to focus more intently on outreach to congressional aides. These grants together over the period 1969 to 1982 totaled $1,822,770.[77] Not only did the program involve collecting a considerable amount of material, but it also provided funding to organize conferences for legislators in the United States and for travel to Africa. The latter effort paralleled the Anglo-American-Canadian Parliamentarian Conferences that were supported concurrently throughout this era at Johns Hopkins University.[78] The African-American Institute's grants enabled members of Congress and their aides to meet with African leaders and discuss a wide range of policy issues related to conditions in Africa and American foreign policy toward Africa. Corporation staff members as well as trustees participated in the discussions at times. In 1982 the Corporation did not continue support for the Anglo-American-Canadian Parliamentarian Conference meetings but focused instead on the US congressional outreach activities of the African-American Institute, especially in Southern Africa. The Ford Foundation, particularly through the collaboration of program officer Melvin Fox, was a major partner in both the African-American Institute and the Johns Hopkins University congressional education initiatives.[79]

These discussions, including both congressional members and aides, should have led to greater interest in Africa by US policymakers. Although considerable attention had been paid during the apartheid era to sanctions as part of US foreign policy, the heyday of support prompted by the Greenbrier conferences and other meetings in the late 1950s and early 1960s clearly had waned. As J. Wayne Fredericks, the first deputy assistant secretary of state for Africa in the Kennedy years and an organizer of the parliamentarian conferences, noted in 1995, "In the early 1960s there was a constellation of political supporters for a new Africa policy which has not been equaled since."[80] Building interest among the public and policymakers for African assistance beyond the crisis mentality is the one area where success has continued to elude the Corporation and its usual partner in this endeavor, the Ford Foundation. This failure to build a constituency for development assistance—and in particular support for sound sustainable development in Africa beyond South Africa—remains a pressing concern.

Investments in Southern Africa

THESE GRANTS REFLECTED the Corporation's increasing concern, as apartheid seemed to become even more entrenched, about its social responsibility regarding both grant-making and its portfolio of investments in the region. In 1972, even before the Commonwealth Program's shift in focus to Southern Africa, the Corporation contributed $15,000 for an African-American Institute meeting with foundations and businesses as well as other investment organizations to discuss the issues and to prepare material for distribution to the public and individual policymakers.[81] In 1973 a couple of other research and education initiatives received funding, one of which complemented the African-American Institute grants in examining issues of external investment in South Africa and Namibia. Joseph Korbel at the Graduate School of International Studies at the University of Denver received a grant of $10,000 that enabled researchers there to conduct studies on the nature and impact of such investments in the region that could serve to guide investors.[82] Throughout the 1970s, the African-American Institute broadened its efforts to examine investments not just in South Africa but also across this complex region, including in Namibia, Angola, and elsewhere.

Women and Development

WHEN THE CORPORATION SHIFTED in 1976 to a focus on women and development (interchangeably called "women in development"), the African-American Institute was a logical place to turn to help extend the Africa-related work. Starting in 1979, the Institute developed a special program on this theme in Africa; funding to support this area continued for several years for a total of $469,500 between 1979 and 1982. With an initial grant of $132,500 from the Corporation and support from USAID, the African-American Institute staff reviewed training opportunities for women, developed programs to strengthen women's leadership capacity, and organized workshops to build their skills. The African-American Institute Women and African Development Program continued to receive support from the Corporation through the 1980s and into the 1990s.[83]

Over these years and since, the African-American Institute has played a significant role in bringing together academics and educational administrators, women activists and leaders, business leaders, and legislators. Its programs have contributed significantly to building a vibrant set of relationships focused on education and development across the continents.[84] Corporation funding of the African-American Institute for its work on these issues continued through the 1990s, until the Corporation changed its focus in the next century.

EDUCATION FOR DEVELOPMENT IN COMMONWEALTH COUNTRIES: A FOCUS ON AND IN AFRICA

THE 1966 ANNUAL REPORT, written by Alan Pifer as acting president, reflected the views that he, Stackpole, and Mosher shared about the changing nature of African universities and the role of the Corporation in supporting them. As Pifer and his colleagues noted, until the Commonwealth countries, particularly the colonies in Africa, achieved independence, African students eager to study at higher education institutions for undergraduate and advanced degrees needed to go abroad. Starting in the 1940s, this situation gradually changed for the better, with increasing support from the British Colonial Office for higher education at "university colleges" (the British term for what Americans call "colleges") on the continent. Nonetheless, the faculty was not African but consisted of British, American, and European teachers and researchers. The Corporation was involved from the beginning in transforming the leadership roles in African universities and in African education generally. By 1967, as Pifer remarked:

African scholars have increasingly assumed positions of leadership in the universities, which are on their way to becoming true centers of African intellectual life.... This trend is not just an expression of nationalistic pride, but reflects a well-founded belief that educational processes cannot be exported intact with good results, that in the end a nation must itself develop the educational system that suits it best. At the same time, Western universities have begun to realize that in many fields the work done by new teaching and research centers in other parts of the world can broaden and deepen their own basic knowledge.[85]

Grants in the early years of the Pifer era continued to focus on linking universities to their own environments, particularly by strengthening teacher education programs in institutes of education for secondary schools, primary schools, and training colleges. From 1967 to 1976, the Corporation's promotion of education for development in African countries included support for the field of child development; teacher training, especially primary school teachers; and curriculum reform that addressed the ways in which education could meet local needs, whether in the sciences, social sciences, or humanities.[86] In addition, the Corporation aimed to strengthen local capacity to evaluate these efforts, especially those related to curriculum reform.

The focus of the work to enhance research and curriculum development capacity in the field of child development continued from the mid-1960s through the early 1970s. These programs developed collaboratively between American and African investigators but drew on studies and approaches developed globally. Frederic Mosher, the responsible program officer, was particularly interested in different learning styles, that is, the possibility that children might learn differently in different societies.[87] The aim was to develop programs in both West Africa and East Africa to examine this question through researchers based at institutes of education, considered by university and Corporation staff the best-suited base from which to study the planning and development of new approaches in education, conduct research on a variety of education-associated issues, and test out the ideas. As described earlier (see Chapter 5), the work in West Africa did not progress as fully as that in East Africa owing to a combination of political and institutional constraints.[88]

In contrast, a more welcoming political situation in Kenya in 1966 facilitated a collaboration that had lasting results.[89] The project brought together researchers from University of Nairobi and their counterparts at Harvard University. John and Beatrice Whiting in the United States and Ruth and Robert Munroe in Kenya led this project together, with strong backing from the University of Nairobi vice chancellor Arthur Porter (from Sierra Leone). The project started in 1966 and resulted in the development of the university-based Child Development Research Unit, which housed the faculty and researchers from Harvard and Nairobi, with the first field station in Kisumu, on the shores of Lake Victoria in western Kenya. After six years of successful collaboration, Porter established the Bureau of Educational Research at the University of Nairobi to house the research unit and to build new ones, such as the Center for Education Research, in order to sustain educational research capacity for the university and for the country. The Center aimed to improve Kenyan universities' capacity for training teachers and coordinating their activities with the government. A series of grants from the Corporation provided nearly $1.4 million to sustain the work of the unit under the leadership of Professor Albert Maleche, a distinguished Kenyan educational researcher from the field of social psychology.[90] In a relatively short period of time, the Child Development Research Unit became a major training institution as well as a model for university-based comparative research on the developmental needs of children in East Africa.[91]

To strengthen teacher and education research around African-driven education initiatives, the Corporation made a series of grants to connect the universities with their local area or country. Two grants enabled the University of Ghana to establish a language center to assist students who had difficulties learning English and to examine language studies at all levels of the educational system.[92] Building on the early success of this program, Vice Chancellor Alexander W. Kwapong persuaded the Corporation to assist in establishing an institute to better train journalists in West Africa; as noted in the agenda item, "Such a grant is not central to the Corporation's program in Africa, but the University's vice chancellor ... places it among the University's own top priorities and has made a convincing case for its centrality to Ghana's educational goals."[93]

In 1971 the Corporation made a major grant to Makerere University to strengthen the National Institute of Education and enable it to continue to train primary teachers. Demand was high as the USAID project Teacher Education for East Africa was coming to a close; the Corporation responded to requests for support from its longtime partner in Uganda to improve and sustain the teaching and education efforts of this program.[94] Continuing the commitment to curriculum reform, the Corporation renewed support at the University of Nigeria in Nsukka to help it rebuild its academic programs after the Biafran War, starting with one of its top priorities: developing its Curriculum Development and Instructional Materials Resource Centre, with a focus on science and math, language skills in English and French, and social studies.[95]

The Corporation maintained its support for the Association for Teacher Education in Africa, established in 1969 as the follow-up institution to the Afro-Anglo-American Program for Teacher Education based at Teachers College and located in alternating years in Uganda at Makerere University and in West Africa at the University of Lagos. The Corporation made one last grant in 1974 of $260,860 for general support as the Association was developing plans for a central headquarters to consolidate its activities and costs.[96] Started by three founding institutions in 1960 (the University of Ghana's Institute of Education, the University of London's Institute of Education, and Columbia University's Teachers College), by 1974 thirty educators from eighteen universities across thirteen African countries regularly participated. As noted in the agenda item, in its various arrangements the Association received nearly $1.5 million from the Corporation beginning in 1960; by 1974 members were paying dues, another sign of the value that the institutions gave to the Association's efforts to share with them the comparative lessons in strengthening teacher education.

Sharpening the focus on developing curricula that both met local needs and celebrated local communities, the Corporation, in collaboration with the Ford Foundation, supported the African Social Studies Program and awarded a few grants to enhance the development of African histories. The African Social Studies Program developed a curriculum at the primary and secondary levels to give students a deeper understanding, based on their particular "traditions and heritage," of national social and historical developments, their own role in nation-building, and the international role of their country.[97] The funding underwrote activities in twelve countries, including workshops on the writing and teaching of history. In one of the few grants before 1976 to Southern Africa, the Corporation enabled the University of Zambia to organize a nine-day education workshop with the East African Regional Council for teachers of Central and East African history.[98]

EVALUATION

AN ESSENTIAL ASPECT OF EDUCATION, in whatever setting, is the capacity to evaluate whether programs make a difference for student learning. Corporation funding for curriculum development in the sciences and social sciences throughout Commonwealth Africa complemented the programs supported by other institutions in language skills and mathematics. Several universities were developing innovative curricula designed specifically for use in African schools along with in-service training. Mosher saw the opportunity to build capacity for educational evaluation to match the innovations in curriculum development.

The Science Education Program for Africa, initiated with Corporation support and based at the University of Ibadan, received a grant in 1972 to develop an experimental program in evaluation for African researchers and educators. The group's director, Hubert Dyasi, an educational measurement specialist from South Africa, and E. Ayotunde Yoloye, a Nigerian expert in measurement and psychological research at the University of Ibadan, were supported to conduct a one-year pilot training program with participants in the curriculum development program. The expectation was that the results of the pilot would "broaden into a more general concern for program and policy evaluation."[99]

As a consequence, the University of Ibadan administration encouraged the Corporation to support the newly created International Center for Educational Evaluation; the board approved funding at the level of $400,000 over three years. Dyasi and Yoloye aimed to develop nine-month comprehensive training courses for participants in positions of leadership at universities or ministries—who could then run appropriate courses as well as contribute to developing evaluation tools—and intensive three-month courses for support staff. The funds covered staff, equipment, research, fellowships, and refresher workshops for alumni.[100] This was the first international center on the continent focused on educational evaluation, and today it still serves a number of countries.[101]

Two grants in the early 1970s reflected the Corporation's earlier activities in the field of higher education. In 1969, nearly ten years after the Ashby Commission in Nigeria had issued its instrumental report, the government of Sierra Leone asked the Corporation to conduct a similar exercise. The government had established the University of Sierra Leone by combining Fourah Bay College, a traditional and historic liberal arts institution, with Njala University College, a relatively new land-grant college (developed with the help of the University of Illinois) and a new freestanding institute of education. The consolidation revealed the need to clarify roles and approach among the three preexisting institutions.[102] To accomplish this, the government, following the Ashby Commission model, appointed a commission composed of three members, one each from Sierra Leone, the United Kingdom, and the United States. Thirty-seven men and women, almost all from Sierra Leone, were members of the steering committee for the commission. Arthur Porter, the distinguished Sierra Leonean historian who had been the vice chancellor of the University of Nairobi and head of the UNESCO unit at the Kenyan Ministry of Education, had agreed to serve as vice chancellor of the new university and as a member of the commission.[103]

Like the Ashby Commission, this was an efficiently run review. All of the objectives were met by May 1974: the long-term strategy for educational development, with estimates of resource needs for implementation, had been prepared, following the vetting of various drafts in eight conferences. Corporation staff members who were at the May 1974 meeting recognized the potential for transforming the educational sector in Sierra Leone. In December 1975, the trustees approved a grant of $376,300 to establish a planning unit at the university, with the capacity to conduct additional studies and assist in implementing the recommendations in a partnership between the university and the government.[104]

For the first time, in 1972, the Corporation provided a modest grant for the Association of African Universities, a coordinating institution that had been established in 1967 to bring together vice chancellors from across the continent to discuss common issues. This first $15,000 grant to the Association contributed to the costs of a workshop and publication related to the function of higher education in Africa; the Association also received support from the Ford and Rockefeller Foundations, in collaboration with the Overseas Liaison Committee, for this activity.[105] The Association of African Universities remains in the twenty-first century the central body through which university vice chancellors and other higher education leaders can address higher education issues in Africa.[106]

UNIVERSITY SUPPORT IN THE COMMONWEALTH
BEYOND AFRICA: 1967–1976

ALTHOUGH FUNDING FOR INSTITUTIONS of higher education in Australia and New Zealand had come to a close, new universities entered into the Corporation's agenda as opportunities arose in the Commonwealth outside Africa in the late 1960s and 1970s. For example, in 1970 the Corporation assisted the Chinese University of Hong Kong in developing and implementing a secondary school curriculum in that city; this grant built on the Corporation's interest in teacher training, curriculum reform, and educational research. Corporation staff commented to the board that the university would be "a major force for change in educational objectives and practices."[107]

In the Caribbean, the University of Guyana remained the major university grantee of the Corporation in the period between 1966 and 1976. The Corporation helped the university to develop its curriculum development unit and in 1972 provided a grant to enable it to conduct research on a secondary-level curriculum comparable to that of the Chinese University of Hong Kong. These studies aimed to help the country obtain World Bank support for new types of secondary schools that would combine general and vocational education programs.[108]

The Corporation supported three types of geographically separated university systems: the University of Botswana, Lesotho, and Swaziland in Africa; the University of the West Indies in the Caribbean; and what was perhaps the most experimental of the three, given the timing and distance, the University of the South Pacific. That university—the most recent one launched by the British government—started receiving support from the Corporation in 1970. Headquartered in Suva, Fiji, the university covered seven island groups over a vast distance of "more than half a million square miles of ocean."[109] In 1970 the Corporation made what may have been its first grant in the area of technologically based distance education. The funds supported the university in its efforts to connect all the islands that it served by taking advantage of a new opportunity provided by a NASA satellite connection at the University of Hawaii. Support continued from 1970 through 1978 for this experimental initiative, which eventually was able to add another five islands covering 1.5 million square miles of ocean. By the end of the last grant, the university had incorporated the satellite project into its regular budget.

From 1966 to 1976, a cluster of activities maintained the Commonwealth connection and brought together British, American, and, occasionally, Canadian researchers to discuss common educational issues. Topics included mathematics curricula, the teaching of English, curriculum reform, new approaches to testing, and, with the new Open University started in 1971, new educational technologies. Meetings took place in the United States and the United Kingdom.[110]

Since the 1930s, the Corporation had been supporting gatherings of the heads of Commonwealth education institutions; the main continuing grantee was the Inter-University Council for Higher Education. In addition, the Corporation provided support in 1970 for the first meeting in Canada hosted by the Association of Universities and Colleges of Canada, including the major university associations, the Inter-University Council for Higher Education, the Overseas Liaison Committee of the American Council on Education, the UK Ministry of Overseas Development, the US Agency for International Development, the Canadian International Development Agency, the Ford Foundation, and the Corporation. The Corporation provided a follow-up grant for the next gathering in Hong Kong, enabling African vice chancellors to participate.[111]

THE TRUSTEE REVIEW: CHANGE OVER CONTINUITY
IN THE COMMONWEALTH PROGRAM

THREE YEARS INTO HIS PRESIDENTIAL TENURE, Alan Pifer introduced dramatic change at the Corporation. Responding to the concerns of trustees, and with the support of the staff, in 1970 he started to diversify the board; encouraged the board to take more leadership in introducing ideas and determining its own governance; instigated staff discussions on evaluation; and established a program evaluation and development fund.[112] Most dramatically of all, but well within the charge to the trustees from Andrew Carnegie, all levels of Carnegie Corporation began to work together to address issues of social justice in American society; intently concentrating on improvements in policy, the Corporation tackled issues ranging across a wide spectrum, from working toward achieving equal access to the law in the American South and for immigrants through new legal defense funds to defining a new field of public television, particularly to enhance the learning of all children. The one part of the Corporation where dramatic transformation had not taken hold, however, was the Commonwealth Program. As resources grew scarcer in the early 1970s economic downturn, as more actors took up the development initiatives where the Corporation had assumed an early lead role, including in education, and as longtime staff members retired or left the foundation, the conditions were in place for assessing the Corporation's overseas role, even considering the question of whether—or not—it should continue.[113] A fundamental change had also affected Pifer's role in philanthropy (as described earlier in this chapter): the Tax Reform Act of 1969 and all that entailed led Pifer to take on the challenge of clarifying the role of American philanthropy in American society for the American public and policymakers.

Pifer displayed his capacity for critical reflection on all these issues as the basis for moving forward in new directions in his presidential essay of 1973, "Twenty Years in Retrospect: A Personal View."[114] He addressed the lessons that he had learned over the previous two decades about defining and developing foundation programs. Given his and Stackpole's, and later Mosher's, extensive efforts to continually refine the grant-making in Africa, it is not surprising that Pifer would endorse the idea that carefully defined programmatic areas can lead to greater effectiveness. Rethinking the usual concerns of scatteration and superficiality, he nonetheless reached a different conclusion from the more standard embrace of focus:

> I have gradually reached the view that too rigid a definition of program can cause a foundation to become in-grown, stagnant and dull. To me a foundation's overall program should be a living organism. It should constantly be growing new cells and discarding old ones. New cells can be added by means of deliberate thought, study and debate by trustees and staff, and this is usually the case. Sometimes, however, it is a chance event or contact which produces an out-of-program proposal so interesting and important that it becomes a forerunner of a new program or subprogram. I see nothing to be ashamed of in this kind of opportunism; it goes naturally with an open, enquiring, undogmatic staff.[115]

Pifer pointed to the vital role that Africa had played in "absorbing my attention and interest during the initial years."[116] He highlighted the Commonwealth Program's accomplishments, particularly in Africa, under the leadership of Stephen Stackpole and with the two of them working as partners with their African, American, and British counterparts.[117] Yet even as he assessed the effectiveness of these initiatives, he also regretted his "unrealistically large" faith in "the power of education to promote social, political and economic development."[118] He saw that support for universities, for example, could not prevent the Biafra War; nor could the universities, despite their necessary role, work on their own to promote national development or end apartheid in South Africa. In highlighting "the commitment to social justice, widely shared today by both trustees and staff," and the fact that it "is a fundamental theme now running through all of the Corporation's programs and, indeed, through nearly every aspect of its work," Pifer signaled the attention to social justice issues on the African continent over the next few years.[119]

Despite his positive comments about its accomplishments, Pifer's comments implied that the Commonwealth Program seemed due for an evaluation. In 1973 Pifer asked E. Jefferson Murphy, a longtime colleague

from the African-American Institute and a historian of Africa, to undertake an in-depth review of the Corporation's Commonwealth Program,
with the main focus on Africa but also including activities elsewhere in
the Commonwealth and, as appropriate, pertinent activities in the United
States.

Although the evaluation was initially conceived of as no more than a
review for staff, Pifer proposed to the board that it was the right time to
consider the future of the program in light of Stackpole's announcement
that he would retire in early 1976. The thorough review that Murphy was
conducting would assist the trustees. Pifer recommended that the board
appoint a special committee "to consider whether the Corporation should
continue to operate in the Commonwealth and, if so, what geographic and
subject areas should have priority and how such a program should be administered."[120] The board agreed and established a review committee consisting
of Harding Bancroft, Caryl Haskins, Francis Keppel, Philip Lee, Howard
Samuel, Jeanne Spurlock, and Franklin Thomas (chair). Everyone on the
committee not only had wide-ranging general knowledge but had had some
experience with Africa. Murphy provided staff support to the committee.

The trustees were responsible for reviewing, assessing, and recommending new directions. Murphy was responsible for organizing the many meetings and polling the board with probing questions, starting with whether
there should be a Commonwealth Program and, if so, which areas it should
emphasize and whether an international dimension of the US program
should be reinstituted, possibly in close relation to the Commonwealth
Program. Another question was whether the Corporation should work
directly with institutions or through intermediaries such as the African-
American Institute and the Institute of International Education. The committee also discussed collaboration with other foundations and assistance
agencies and issues of staffing. After interviewing all the trustees, Murphy
crafted a detailed memo for the board that drew on his book to provide an
assessment of the work in Africa and the Caribbean in particular but also
in other regions of the Commonwealth.[121]

In addition to the Africa and Caribbean reviews, the process produced
a very detailed paper on potential problems and possibilities for the
Corporation if it enlarged its program in the Commonwealth Pacific and

extended it to Asia. The external reviews and board discussions emphasized that from 1953 to 1974 the Corporation had made significant contributions to education in the newly independent nations of Africa, in the South Pacific, and in the Caribbean. As Murphy noted in his summary for Pifer, the committee held seven meetings, read over eight hundred pages of material, heard from nine outside speakers, and took into account staff concerns and comments on the review process.

In concluding their review, the trustees recognized the program's contributions and recommended that its work be continued. At the same time, however, acknowledging that the Corporation did not have the resources or capacity to undertake large development projects, they recommended that it play a facilitative and communications role.[122] They further recommended targeting fields in which the Corporation had expertise, but also ones "which are generally of low priority in the programs of most other large foundations and aid agencies."[123] In considering the geographic focus, they urged that the program continue in tropical Africa but that it give "special attention to Southern Africa as a new area of concentration." They also recommended that serious consideration be given to projects in other regions, especially in the Pacific, Caribbean, and South and Southeast Asia.[124] They highlighted the importance of working in partnership with other foundations (although noting that on occasion the Corporation "must maintain its unique corporate identity"[125]), with appropriate US counterparts, and, most importantly, with and through institutions in the countries themselves.[126]

The review committee's recommendations, discussed at the trustee retreat in Atlanta, Georgia, in March 1975, led to the decision to seek new areas of concentration and a shift in the overseas program. But the board did not overdetermine what the Corporation should do; they recognized and urged that it was the staff's responsibility, under Alan Pifer's leadership, to develop the new program thrusts and approaches. Pifer issued a memo on the results of the review that was circulated widely.[127] He emphasized that university projects would gradually decrease; the program would continue in tropical Africa, with attention to Southern Africa, the Caribbean region, and the South Pacific. He stated that "emphasis in the future ... will be less on the support of substantial educational development and research projects and more on smaller, facilitative grants for a wider range of activities, in such fields as leadership development, social planning, regional and international communication, indigenous culture, and others."[128] Partnership with other donors and with local institutions and agencies would be encouraged; at the same time, promoting American understanding of these issues and countries would be of interest. Pifer closed by calling attention to the fact that these decisions represented "the outer limits" of the program boundaries. Over the next few years, the program focus would narrow both geographically and substantively.[129]

Even with the board encouragement and endorsement of program changes, all recognized the need for a gradual shift toward the new thrust. There would be no overnight dislocation of long-standing grantees, and earlier commitments would be maintained for a few years in Africa beyond Southern Africa, and elsewhere, such as to the University of the South Pacific. The last grant in Canada in this era enabled the Association of Universities and Colleges of Canada to publish a major work on the history of higher education in Canada by Robin Harris, which was seen "as putting a capstone on a significant 16-year endeavor" (earlier supported by the Corporation).[130]

For the last seven years of Alan Pifer's presidency (1975–1982), Corporation grant-making activities in the Commonwealth moved in new directions. In Africa, the staff concentrated on strengthening legal capacity, leadership development, and social and economic research in South Africa, investing in education in Southern Rhodesia (soon to be Zimbabwe) and building regional connections. Following the board decision, by 1978 Southern Africa featured as significantly in the Corporation's overseas program as it had in the 1930s.

In addition, a brand-new topic received special attention: the promotion of women in development, an increasingly prominent concern for all developing countries. Finally, a limited set of grants pursued the trustees' concerns about improving communication and outreach on these issues to increase American public and policymaker understanding.

LEGAL, ECONOMIC, AND NATIONAL TRANSFORMATION IN SOUTHERN AFRICA AND RELATED US ACTIVITIES, 1975 TO 1982

FOLLOWING THE TRUSTEE REVIEW of the Commonwealth Program, the Corporation began to shift the programmatic focus toward removing obstacles to the fair application of the law, especially for the black majority, in South Africa. Staff adapted the legal dimensions from the Corporation's work in the Southern United States to South Africa. Grants aimed to address the basic legal and structural constraints in South Africa by opening up access to university training and establishing a new type of law firm. In addition, Corporation grantees contributed to strengthening the evidence base about the social and economic structural constraints on those suffering under apartheid. Finally, in anticipation of a post-apartheid South Africa, the Corporation sought to contribute to building the leadership skills of black, colored, and Asian South Africans.

As a complement to the work in South Africa and Southern Africa, the Corporation also began to focus outreach and communications in the United States on conditions in the region.[131] These interrelated themes, with the increasing focus on South Africa and Southern Africa, began to feature in the grant-making as early as 1975. Paralleling the grant activity, the trustee finance and administration committee regularly reviewed and acted on the divestment and proxy vote issues associated with companies in the Corporation's equity portfolio invested in South Africa.

After a hiatus of twenty-six years, the South African Institute of Race Relations, founded in 1929 and a Corporation grantee from 1929 into the 1940s, received a modest grant of $2,500 to enable the director of the Institute, Quintin Whyte, to write the history of race relations in South Africa in preparation for the organization's forthcoming fiftieth anniversary.[132] In 1976 another earlier grantee from the 1950s reentered the agenda, the South African Institute of International Affairs in Johannesburg. With a grant of $14,000, the Institute put together a study group of South Africans, including businessmen, academics, and other specialists, to analyze the relationship between the United States and South Africa and to undertake exchange visits.[133]

A new grantee, one that would receive regular support for years to come, entered the portfolio at this time: the United States–South Africa Leadership Exchange Program. In the 1950s, Pifer had participated in its founding by a group of Americans and South Africans dedicated to exchanges between the two countries. The first grant in 1975 for $13,000 contributed to the planning of a career development program for blacks and other disadvantaged South Africans.[134] With this support from the Corporation and other foundations, the group's career development program began an extensive training program for disadvantaged South Africans and provided a varying number of fellowships each year for visits to the United States. In addition, the Corporation often provided modest support for the visits of American educators and lawyers to meet with their counterparts in South Africa and attend meetings there, for a total of $387,500 from 1975 through 1982.[135] Support for the exchange program continued in the 1980s and into the 1990s.

Complementing these efforts, the Corporation, in partnership with the Ford Foundation, USAID, and others, began to work more actively with the Institute of International Education to give specific attention to building leadership through fellowships to disadvantaged South Africans under the auspices of its South Africa Education Program. In 1980 the Institute received its first significant grant for some time from the Corporation, $75,000, which enabled it to identify opportunities for black, colored, and Asian South Africans, who together constituted 84 percent of South Africa's population at the time, to study in the United States.[136] The Institute identified the most appropriate host institutions and provided assistance to both the US institutions and the aid groups in South Africa to promote black leadership in education.

Another new grantee, the Centre for Intergroup Studies at the University of Cape Town, was funded in 1976 at the level of $13,500 to hold a workshop on the role of universities in Southern Africa. Even in the late 1970s, they were able to bring together representatives from the South African universities with university leaders from other African nations, Europe, the United States, and Canada. The Centre received renewed support over the next six years, for a total of $143,900, to continue its meetings and publication programs aimed at reducing discrimination without violating national laws.

By 1982, Corporation staff felt that there was sufficient local support from funders such as the Abe Bailey Trust, the University of Cape Town, and the Joseph Roundtree Charitable Trust to close the Corporation grants.[137]

Two months after Stackpole's retirement in April 1976, the Corporation hired David Hood, a civil rights litigation lawyer and dean of the University of Hawaii Law School, to take charge of the Commonwealth Program. Hood met with potential partners at the Ford Foundation and the Rockefeller Brothers Fund as well as with a wide range of advisers.[138] The Ford Foundation and the Rockefeller Brothers Fund had already been making grants in South Africa; all three foundations were interested in following up the 1973 meeting organized at the University of Natal and funded by the Ford Foundation on building the public interest bar.[139] One adviser, Kenneth Pye, chairman of the Duke University Committee on Commonwealth Studies, supported earlier by the Corporation, suggested that Hood meet with John Dugard, the dean of the University of the Witwatersrand Law School, and with Sidney and Felicia Kentridge, two barristers in Johannesburg. All three were prominent anti-apartheid activists.[140] Another adviser, Geoff Budlender, from the South African Institute of Race Relations, suggested that Hood meet with Francis Wilson at the University of Cape Town.[141] Dugard, the Kentridges, Budlender, and Wilson and their dedicated efforts to confront apartheid would feature in the Corporation's South Africa program for nearly twenty years.

Following these consultations, Hood visited South Africa several months after the June 1976 Soweto uprising and the reprisals that followed, but before the brutal September 1977 killing of Steve Biko, the prominent and popular anti-apartheid activist. Hood met with John Dugard during that first visit. Dugard convinced him about the value of the public interest bar in helping to rectify the situation in South Africa.[142] Hood, with support from Pifer, persuaded the Board of Trustees that the public interest bar was a promising opportunity for the Corporation. The intention was to develop a legal education program at the university and establish a public interest law firm.[143]

In March 1977, the board approved the initial, very modest grant of $3,865 to provide support for a consultant to advise on developing a program in public interest law, including the training of black lawyers at the University of the Witwatersrand Law School.[144] As noted in the 1977 Annual Report, ordinarily blacks would not be able to study at a white university, but an exception was made since this law course was not available at a black institution. (There were thirteen law schools in South Africa, nine for whites and four for blacks.) Columbia University law professor Michael Meltsner worked with the team at the law school; the result was the establishment of the Centre for Applied Legal Studies (CALS). CALS initiated a research program and organized public education for whites and blacks throughout South Africa. Dugard attributed the idea for CALS—that is, a legal research institution attached to the university—to David Hood. As he said, "I don't think there was any real precedent for such a structure. It was largely David Hood's idea."[145]

The law school, through CALS, incubated the Legal Resources Centre, a public litigation and legal education institution that would soon stand very firmly on its own two feet as an independent institution, benefiting from the leadership of the Kentridges, who persuaded Arthur Chaskalson, a highly respected lawyer, to take the directorship. The Legal Resources Centre was modeled after the American legal defense funds, following the advice of Jack Greenberg, then director of the NAACP Legal Defense Fund.[146]

Because of the complexity and sensitivity of the work in South Africa, Pifer and his colleagues recognized the importance of keeping the Board of Trustees fully engaged and informed about the situation. The first formal discussion of South Africa with external participants, in June 1978, focused on the potential for public interest bar grant-making in South Africa as well as the investment issues—that is, the disinvestment and proxy issues—concerning the Corporation's portfolio. (This was a major topic of discussion in the United States at this time.) Participants included Manas Buthelezi, Lutheran Bishop of Johannesburg; William Cotter, president of the African-American Institute; John Dugard, director of the Centre for Applied Legal Studies; Desaix Myers, associate director of the Investor Responsibility Research Center; William Sneath, chairman of the Union Carbide Company board; and Dwight Wait, chairman of Union Carbide Africa and Middle East. Each made presentations about working in South Africa and the Corporation's relations with South Africa, including its investment policies. The sense of the discussion was that the Corporation should continue to find useful projects in South Africa as long as feasible.[147] Following the meeting, the finance and administration committee of the Corporation continued to give close attention to the disinvestment aspects; Corporation treasurer David Z. Robinson took the lead on these discussions.[148]

The Centre for Applied Legal Studies at the University of the Witwatersrand was supported in 1978 at the level of $125,000, and the grant was renewed in 1980 at the level of $300,000; by the end of the Pifer era, CALS had become an autonomous unit within the university.[149] John Dugard and his colleagues brought public attention to the disparities embedded in South Africa's legal code and its application to blacks and other nonwhites. CALS remains vibrant to this day and continues to hold the South African legal system accountable to ensure that the rule of law prevails in South African society.[150]

But it was not enough simply to assist the university in developing public interest training for lawyers. Following the Legal Resources Centre's period of incubation at the university, and together with the Ford Foundation, the Rockefeller Brothers Fund, and South Africa's Anglo-American Trust, the Corporation awarded a new grant in 1979 to enable the Legal Resources Centre to spin off from CALS. Arthur Chaskalson, the first director, built its reputation for pursuing aggressively distinctive law cases, educating law students, engaging in public interest litigation, and providing advice for community members, particularly in Soweto. The Centre took the lead on public litigation for significant court decisions aimed at improving conditions for the black community, from housing to transportation. With legal aid clinics and assistance to the students who ran them, blacks throughout the country gained access to litigation advice and action. Grants for the Centre, under the auspices of its newly created entity, the Legal Resources Trust, were renewed in 1981 and 1982, for $100,000 and $180,000, respectively.[151] The Legal Resources Trust remained a Corporation grantee throughout the 1980s and 1990s.

Along with these two significant investments in building access to the law for blacks and other nonwhite groups in South Africa, Corporation staff members realized the importance of promoting other community-based initiatives. Small grants assisted in strengthening, for example, the nongovernmental organization Build a Better Society, which concentrated on providing social services to the colored population in Cape Town, South Africa.[152]

The University of Cape Town returned as a Corporation grantee in 1979, when it was awarded a small grant of $15,000 for the first international conference on human rights in South Africa; the conference also received support from the Ford Foundation, the Anglo-American Corporation, the Society of University Teachers of Law, and the British Council. This conference was an effort to stimulate interest in human rights and the law in South Africa among lawyers, academics, and journalists. It was an international meeting, and the Corporation helped to defray the costs for foreign participants.[153] In parallel, the Corporation, through a grant of $13,000, prompted another interracial dialogue organized by the director of the South African Institute of Race Relations and the deputy editor of one of the significant newspapers, the *Rand Daily Mail* in Johannesburg. The discussions focused on a nonracial South Africa, although not quite using that language; the emphasis was on reducing political and social inequities. To promote greater discussion of these issues in the United States, a comparable meeting was held at Goshen College in Indiana.[154]

By 1980, the Corporation had begun to focus on making grants to black-led groups for black lawyers, including a small grant of $34,000 to the Black Education and Research Trust to bring together a small group of black educators to discuss government policy on education for blacks. With a focus on urban communities, the funds enabled data collection, curriculum studies, analyses of school conditions and labor force needs, and a major conference of black leaders around the country.[155] By 1982, the Black Lawyers Association in Johannesburg had been formed. The Corporation provided support to enable Judge Leon Higginbotham, a distinguished American jurist, and other black lawyers and judges from the United States to visit South Africa and discuss the shared issues of social justice and the rule of law in their countries.[156]

The situation in the late 1970s prompted dedicated actions by the South African legal profession, academics, and activists, supported in part by the Ford Foundation, the Rockefeller Brothers Fund, the Anglo-American Trust, and Carnegie Corporation, to build the black legal profession and the public interest bar in South Africa. These efforts moved the South African respect for the rule of law from theory to practice, a significant contribution to the eventual transition to post-apartheid South Africa.[157]

In addition, the Corporation and the Ford Foundation supported a quite different activity that contributed to deepening the understanding of the social and economic structural constraints confronting both apartheid and post-apartheid South Africa. Following the suggestion of Geoff Budlender, Hood began to meet with Francis Wilson to discuss issues associated with the Corporation's work in South Africa. Monica Wilson, Francis's mother and a recipient of a Corporation travel grant, was a distinguished anthropologist; she became friends with Pifer, who then met Francis. In January 1980, during yet another conversation with Hood, Francis Wilson "decided to stop giving free advice"[158] and suggested a South African inquiry, much like the first one but focused on poor blacks.[159] When Pifer came to South Africa a few days later, the three of them talked about Wilson's research idea; Pifer and Hood agreed to provide a planning grant to Wilson to develop the scope for such a study.

In late 1980, through its Program Development and Evaluation Fund, the Corporation provided consultancy support, covering travel and related expenses, for Wilson to plan the study that led to the Second Carnegie Inquiry into Poverty and Development in Southern Africa. Over the next two years, he consulted widely around the country to ensure that there would be black and local participation, which was especially important with an American foundation funding the work.[160] Pifer and Hood reported to the board in 1981 on the political and economic conditions in South Africa that warranted such a study; the trustees expressed an interest in funding the inquiry and approved a planning grant of $56,000 to the University of Cape Town.[161] The trustees agreed to focus the board's December meeting on the possibility of the new inquiry.

At the meeting in December 1981, the morning was devoted to discussions with Wilson and Fikile Bam, a former political prisoner on Robben Island and an activist human rights lawyer who much later became the Judge President of the Lands Claims Court of South Africa.[162] They spoke in detail about the conditions in South Africa that warranted such an undertaking and how the inquiry would be conducted.[163] Following the discussions, the trustees asked for a full proposal, then voted to approve the first full grant at the February 1982 board meeting.[164] The Ford Foundation agreed to collaborate in sponsoring the inquiry, primarily by making it possible for a critical mass of black scholars and activists to participate. With support from the Ford Foundation and Carnegie Corporation, Wilson and co-organizer Mamphela Ramphele began to organize the study of the causes and conditions of poverty in Southern Africa.[165]

Following the model of both the Poor White Study and the Gunnar Myrdal study, Wilson and Ramphele organized a network of researchers, mainly but not only black South Africans, to conduct research on the many dimensions of poverty in South Africa and to explore opportunities in agriculture, business, and education. It took four years to complete the field research and another five years to analyze the data and write up the results. Commenting on the remarkable relationship between the Ford Foundation and Carnegie Corporation in backing this project, Wilson has said, "The relationship with Ford and Carnegie was incredibly powerful for the University of Cape Town. Carnegie provided the research support and Ford provided invaluable training support along with support for involvement of black researchers and overseas advisers."[166]

The Second Carnegie Inquiry into Poverty and Development in Southern Africa illuminated the conditions in South Africa by providing hard data that helped anti-apartheid activists strengthen the case for sanctions and political change. A volume consolidating all the studies was published in 1989.[167] Together with the effort to build the public interest bar, the Inquiry contributed to shaping and empowering black capacity through the engagement of black principal investigators and researchers throughout the country. The study not only led to the shaping of the national reconstruction work following the end of apartheid but also paved the way for many of the black participants to take significant leadership roles in post-apartheid South Africa.[168]

Although the Corporation did not begin providing grants to the anti-apartheid activist groups based in the United States until later in the 1980s and early 1990s, it did support a few grants for meetings to discuss ways to peacefully change conditions in South Africa as well as to build American constituencies for more activist American policies toward the country. The first grant contributed to the 1980 Seven Springs Conference Center symposium—organized with the United States–South Africa Leadership Exchange Program (USSALEP)—on "Where Is South Africa Headed?," a gathering that brought together a variety of South Africans and Americans to discuss the future of the country.[169] A 1981 grant of $75,000 to a prominent NGO based in Washington, DC, the TransAfrica Forum, founded by African American activist Randall Robinson in 1977, contributed to a program to engage more African Americans in developing a cohesive view on American foreign policy and examine the impact of American foreign policy on African and Caribbean countries.[170] Another small grant to the Massachusetts Institute of Technology in 1982 supported Fredrick van Zyl Slabbert, a prominent South African scholar and member of parliament who was one of the leading white proponents of anti-apartheid activities. While vociferously opposed to apartheid, he also was dedicated to finding a way to reduce the likelihood of confrontation and particularly violence. The funds enabled him to spend time in the United States at MIT and to meet with groups across the country to discuss the situation in South Africa with the hope of identifying ways to achieve a peaceful resolution of the situation there.[171]

Pifer had also participated in the 1979 Rockefeller Foundation Study Commission on US Policy Toward Southern Africa, chaired by Franklin Thomas. This commission and its final publication, *South Africa: Time Running Out*, both reinforced the on-the-ground efforts of the Ford Foundation, the Rockefeller Brothers Fund, and the Corporation and significantly influenced the South Africa policy debate in the United States.[172] As Thomas later noted, the work on and in South Africa during the apartheid era—building the public interest bar, addressing sanctions and US public policy, providing fellowships, and supporting the study of poverty—illustrated foundation collaboration "at its best."[173]

In his 1980 presidential essay, Pifer analyzed the Corporation's fifty-three years of involvement in South Africa, noting that "115 grants, totaling more than $2.5 million, were made to institutions and organizations in that country, and that travel grants were awarded to 324 South African citizens, to enable them to visit the United States, and to 41 Americans for visits to South Africa, at a further cost of about $1 million. Total expenditure, therefore, has amounted to approximately $3.5 million."[174] But he emphasized that it was not the money that mattered the most:

> Beyond simply the value of the funds granted, however, there is evidence that the nature of the Corporation—a nonpolitical, independent private organization, with no vested interests and answerable to no special constituency nor government (except of course meeting the requirements of the law)—has been of very great importance in strengthening its impact. This has been of special significance in South Africa, a country where, as a general matter, activity by private voluntary organizations has never been particularly encouraged by public authority.[175]

Pifer's concluding comments in the essay illustrate his convictions and his approach to work in another country as fraught as South Africa was in the late 1970s:

> As one becomes better informed about South Africa, one is more and more struck with how much its current problems are a product of its special history and how essential it is to know something about that history. Without this knowledge it is impossible even to begin to understand the character of the two great nationalist movements—African and Afrikaner—that are now locked in almost total confrontation. Even with such a background, it is presumptuous for outsiders to try to prescribe precisely what course South Africa should follow in trying to solve its racial problems. They should not, of course, refrain from expressing a concern about the probable consequences of the racial injustice that now afflicts the country nor leave unspoken their desire to see the process of change that has now begun to gather strength and become much more meaningful, but this is probably as specific as they can be about the future. Only South Africans themselves—South Africans of all races—can ultimately determine what new political arrangements will be necessary to allow the nation's varied racial groups to live in harmony and with justice for all.[176]

The activities discussed in this section underline the value of working in sometimes unpalatable conditions to effect a change for the better. The trustees heard the ethical qualms expressed by Pifer and Hood, and indeed they were already discussing the ethical dilemmas posed by South Africa in terms of proxy policies. They understood the risks and the considerable benefits to society from supporting this work. Moreover, they realized that with Pifer's leadership, the Corporation could work effectively under the complex conditions by drawing on his deep knowledge, his commitment to ensuring extensive interaction with all levels of society, and his proven talent for placing bets on the right people. Further analysis of the collaboration across the foundations in their support for the determined efforts of leading individuals from all walks of society in South Africa may provide a model for how American philanthropy can make a difference in other complex settings.[177]

TRANSFORMATIONS IN SOUTHERN AFRICA BEYOND SOUTH AFRICA

ALTHOUGH THE WORK IN SOUTH AFRICA was clearly the Corporation's major focus of attention, two other high-impact activities in the region, carried out in conjunction with other partners, featured during this period.

In 1979 the Corporation made a grant of $30,000 to the Joseph Roundtree Charitable Trust to convene a meeting in Rouges, Tanzania, at the behest of the president of Botswana, to discuss with development agency representatives, other ministries, and interested parties how best to foster economic cooperation and coordination in the region.[178] Additional Corporation grants contributed to establishing the Southern Africa Development Coordination Conference (SADCC), a pioneering effort to bring together the countries in Southern Africa to reduce their dependency on outside economic support and build a base for coordination and cross-boundary initiatives, as well as confront the issues of apartheid in South Africa.[179] Now called the Southern African Development Community (SADC), it has become a major institution for development initiatives in the region and on the continent over the ensuing decades.[180]

Given the volatile situation in Rhodesia and the plan to move to majority rule in 1980, the Corporation identified opportunities for constructive grant-making related to its efforts in South Africa. In 1978, through Corporation support, an economist from Rhodesia, Mudziviri Nziramsanga, at the Center for Research and Economic Development at the University of Michigan, gathered existing data and papers on social and economic conditions for use by the new government of Zimbabwe.[181] He returned from the United States to Zimbabwe to hold many high-level positions, and in 1990 Nziramsanga became the secretary of the Ministry of Industry and Commerce. He left the country in 1993 when the political situation became intolerable, to teach at the University of Washington in the United States.

In late 1979, in cooperation with Columbia University, the Corporation supported a meeting of the Seven Springs Center to bring African, American, and British development specialists together with Zimbabweans to discuss the country's economic future.[182]

In 1981, following the Zimbabwean Civil War and the destruction of many primary and secondary schools, the Corporation provided a grant of $104,000 to the Ministry of Education and Culture to rebuild the education system, with a focus on teacher training. The aim was to produce fully qualified teachers at the end of four years. The effort was co-funded by the United Nations and the Commonwealth Secretariat.[183]

Reminiscent of the earlier work in Africa, in 1981 the Corporation responded positively to a request from Walter Kamba, a former travel grant recipient, who would become the first black principal of the University of Zimbabwe, to support a conference to determine the role for the university in Zimbabwe's national development efforts. A wide range of participants from around Zimbabwe and representatives from other countries talked about the most effective ways in which higher education could contribute to meeting the nation's development goals and needs.[184] In 1982 a second grant of $50,000 supported Kamba's efforts to meet the increased demand for higher education through preparing and implementing a staff development plan and increasing the student body. Similar to what would happen later in South Africa, the University of Zimbabwe tackled the challenge of improving the balance of black and white faculty members and employees of the university to better reflect the changing nature of the student body.[185]

GLOBAL AND REGIONAL INITIATIVES
IN WOMEN AND DEVELOPMENT

AS EARLY AS THE 1920S in the US program, the Corporation had expressed interest in the education of women and provided support for women's colleges, ranging from endowments to libraries to specific academic programs.[186] Under Gardner and Pifer, this remained a special area of attention. As part of the social justice thrust of the late 1960s and early 1970s, the focus broadened to include not only education but also enhancing women's access to health care and income-generating activities.

Following the trustee review of the Commonwealth Program, in 1976 Pifer hired Kristin Anderson as a program associate to assume responsibility for grants related to improving conditions for women, including networks to bring women scholars together to develop targeted research and major international conferences on the theme. This was a new development for the Commonwealth Program, even though women from the Commonwealth had been participating from the beginning in the travel grants program, now in ever-increasing numbers. Anderson had been an assistant program officer at the Ford Foundation and had special expertise in the area of women in development. Her association with the Ford Foundation had facilitated the co-funding of many activities, which continued into the 1980s and 1990s. Since Anderson had already established ties to women activists in both Africa and the Caribbean, the Corporation would now rapidly develop grants on women's issues in these areas that also reflected the commitment in domestic grant-making to increasing attention to women's issues. In the international program, however, the focus was not so much on education and university issues with regard to women's access and participation, but rather on efforts to "assure the integration of women's interests and needs in national and regional development planning. Support of women's bureaus and their projects will be a likely expression of this concern."[187]

Corporation grant-making centered on three different sets of activities. First, efforts based in US institutions were designed to complement activities in other regions and pull together up-to-date data and articles to share with colleagues in the Caribbean and African countries who might not have such access. The first set of activities began with a grant for Anderson to work with consultants to gather pamphlets on successful projects run by women that dealt mainly with improving economic activities.[188] The Population Council published, with Corporation contributions, a special edition of its monthly journal, *Studies in Family Planning*, on programs to assist rural women; the edition targeted the policymakers responsible for development assistance programs to enhance women's economic opportunities.[189] In addition, the Corporation in 1980 enabled Martha Stewart Communications, an independent production company in New York City, to prepare a video about the relationship between feminism and issues of importance to women. This grant of $15,000 was co-funded by the Ford Foundation.[190] Significant financial support enabled the African-American Institute's Women and African Development Program, as discussed earlier in this chapter, to play a major role in promoting women's interests and creating linkages across African countries.

As part of an effort to provide additional information on issues related to women in development, the Corporation—following a grant from the US Agency for International Development—provided co-funding for the New Transcentury Foundation, a private voluntary organization based in Washington. With this support, the team there prepared an inventory of resources available for women's activities both in the United States and in Europe. The Corporation's $7,000 support enabled the Foundation to print five hundred additional copies of the publication and disseminate them throughout Africa and the Caribbean.[191]

A second set of Corporation-sponsored activities fostered regional and international networking and training, particularly for income-generating activities in the Caribbean. In 1980 the Corporation made its first grant in support of a UN conference, the 1980 World Conference of the United Nations Decade for Women.[192] The first conference had taken place in 1975 in Mexico City. The second one was held in July 1980 in Denmark, under the direction of Lucille Mair. The grant of $40,000 to the Secretariat enabled the UN to hire consultants from the Commonwealth countries of concern to the Corporation to write background papers reflecting the experiences of women in their countries and to attend seminars at the meeting. In addition, the UN Economic Commission for Africa and its African Training and Research Center for Women enabled twenty African women leaders to visit a variety of programs to observe what could be applicable in their own local settings.[193] The Eastern and Southern Africa Management Institute in Arusha, Tanzania, received support to design a course in management skills for women from the seventeen countries in the region, developed in conjunction with the Population Council.[194]

A special focus on regional networking in the Caribbean aimed to strengthen women's leadership in actively advocating to enhance the role of women in their societies. A major network- and institution-building activity in the Caribbean started in 1977. With a small grant of $15,000, the University of the West Indies at Barbados sponsored a meeting on women in development to understand better the conditions confronting women in the region and identify ways to improve their participation in economic development. The grant to the University of the West Indies was renewed in 1978 at the level of $225,000 to establish the Women and Development Unit (better known as WAND) under the leadership of Peggy Antrobus, who was becoming a leading spokesperson, both regionally and globally. The grant was focused on economic equality and leadership development; the intent was to develop a plan of action for women in the Caribbean. Substantial Corporation support continued over the years. In 1979 another small grant of $15,000, co-funded by USAID, to World Education, a private technical assistance agency based in New York, provided assistance to WAND to assess its general progress and to offer some training in evaluation.

WAND received a $200,000 grant in 1980 to conduct pilot programs throughout the region involving training, income-generating activities, and additional research surveys; a small grant of $15,000 in 1980 also supported a meeting organized by Antrobus following her participation in the UN meeting on women and development. With a grant of $200,000 in 1982, the group expanded its capacity to conduct workshops focused on enhancing vocational capacity for women throughout the region.[195]

From 1977 to 1982, the Corporation provided $645,000 to build WAND's capacity at the University of the West Indies. The Corporation continued to work with this organization for a few years—for as long as its grant-making continued in the Caribbean. Today WAND is still active as part of the Open University of the West Indies.[196]

A third set of activities, which included grants in Kenya, Rhodesia/

Zimbabwe, Jamaica, Belize, and the Dominica, were focused exclusively on the national level. To strengthen women's participation in development in Kenya, the Corporation provided a three-year grant of $68,000 to the National Council of Women of Kenya to bring together the thirty-three women's organizations and establish a strong liaison with the National Women's Bureau.[197] The support enabled the Council to hire a full-time executive director and to increase the sharing of information with all its members. A follow-up grant in 1982 of $15,000 enabled Kenyan anthropologist Achola Palo Okeye to review policies and material from government agencies concerned with women and their development in order to provide an analytical document with evidence drawn from the field as the basis for future planning.[198]

Complementing the efforts to strengthen higher education for national development in Rhodesia, in 1978 Anderson worked with representatives of women's organizations to establish a pilot women's bureau, the Zimbabwe Women's Bureau, and to link with a research unit at the Center for Interracial Studies at the University of Rhodesia. Grants in 1978 (for $60,000) and 1979 (for $81,500) contributed to the activities of both programs, enabling them to conduct surveys of urban black Rhodesian women and to hold a national meeting on the needs of women and development in the country.[199]

In the Caribbean region, the Corporation also supported women's bureaus. In Jamaica in 1977, the Corporation, together with the Ford Foundation, provided additional staff support, allowing the Jamaica Women's Bureau to institute income-generating activities.[200] In 1981 a grant of $15,000 provided support for the government of Belize to set up a development communications network as part of its newly established Women's Bureau.[201] And in the Commonwealth of Dominica, a comparable grant enabled the Women's Desk to conduct research and training programs to enhance women's productivity.[202]

Although Anderson was on the Corporation staff for only five years, she built a strong program with key national, regional, and international initiatives. Upon her departure, Jill Sheffield, a staff member of World Education, a Corporation grantee, was hired to take over the position. With a master's degree in international education from Columbia University's

Teachers College, Sheffield had extensive experience in family planning and had worked in Kenya. She would maintain the Corporation's activities on behalf of women into the 1980s.

CONCLUSIONS

THIS ERA REFLECTS the hard choices that the Corporation had to make under changing societal conditions and with increasingly limited resources. As major long-standing grant programs were brought to a close and new ones initiated, the Corporation's grant-making attention concentrated on one major overarching theme, namely, social justice. As indicated throughout this chapter, the Corporation not only pursued this program focus as part of its mission to advance and diffuse knowledge and understanding but also pushed out beyond the boundaries of the mission to follow Andrew Carnegie's charge to the trustees to change course as the times would require. This led Pifer, the trustees, and the staff to support, particularly in the United States and South Africa, advocacy and application, including litigation to ameliorate the conditions surrounding minority populations and their access to fair representation and a fair hearing under the law.

The period from 1975 to 1982 in the Commonwealth Program illustrates, moreover, a contrasting program strategy for the Corporation, when compared with earlier periods, in two respects. First, it was tightly focused—albeit with exceptions for special opportunities and a few continuing interests—on two thrusts: transformations in Southern Africa and women in development. In addition, for the first time, at least for Commonwealth efforts, specialists rather than generalists were hired; the usual practice had been what Pifer endorsed in 1973—hiring generalists who might become specialists in a particular field but who could move fluidly from one focus to another as needed because of their general analytical and programmatic skills. Now, with specialists on staff, the highly targeted programs drawing on their specialties could move very quickly from ideas into action. Of course, the strong endorsement from the president and the trustees also made that possible.

Given the limited resources available during this period for the work in the Commonwealth and the efforts to maintain activities both in the

Caribbean and in Africa, this targeting made sense and in many cases built enduring institutions, such as the Women and Development Unit at the University of the West Indies, the Centre for Applied Legal Studies, the Legal Resources Centre in South Africa, and the Southern African Development Coordination Conference. The Second Carnegie Inquiry on Poverty and Development in Southern Africa also informed social and economic planning in the early years of post-apartheid South Africa.

Nonetheless, the decision in 1975 to recalibrate the Commonwealth Program essentially brought to a close long-term support for universities elsewhere in English-speaking countries and their role in education for development. Ending these grants may have adversely affected these universities as they struggled with the economic downturn in the 1980s, when they also received increasingly limited support from their governments and other external donors.

Despite the adverse societal conditions in the United States of the 1960s and 1970s, which compelled attention and funding from the limited resources available to the Corporation, the Pifer era for several years maintained the Corporation's overseas grant-making throughout the Commonwealth. The 1975 "Trustees' Review of the Commonwealth Program" led the Corporation to recalibrate and refine its efforts and to move from its comparative advantage in higher education and libraries to the social justice themes and development initiatives (equality before the law and support for women). The review also resulted in a narrowing of the geographic focus in Africa to Southern Africa, a shift that concentrated energies and resources around a limited number of grantees, enabling them to make major contributions to redressing the wrongs of the apartheid era by forging a new legal and intellectual infrastructure. In turn, their legally oriented efforts facilitated the unexpectedly peaceful move toward post-apartheid South Africa, even when that possibility seemed like a distant dream.

The engaged social justice activism of this era, domestically and internationally, defined a distinctly different foundation that was inherited by Pifer's successor, David Hamburg, a trustee of the Corporation since 1979, who was elected at the June 1982 meeting to become president effective December 9, 1982. Hamburg's agenda, in turn, framed a new set of issues and actions. While endorsing the activities then under way, Hamburg was committed to promoting science and technology and, most passionately, to preventing harm to individuals across the life cycle, particularly children, and in the international arena. The extensive reviews of new opportunities for the Corporation began even before he became president. Once again, John Gardner's basic tenet for institutional renewal, stability in motion, informed a Corporation presidential transition.

7

GRAND EXPLORATIONS, 1982–1997

GLOBAL AND NATIONAL CONDITIONS in December 1982 replayed issues that had defined the political, economic, and social agendas over the prior thirty years. No hint lurked in scholarship or policy debate of the impending global upheaval.[1] When the Board of Trustees elected David A. Hamburg president of Carnegie Corporation in June 1982, the Cold War still dominated US foreign policy, with the Soviet Union and nuclear weapons the compelling concerns. The Soviets had invaded Afghanistan, and the United States was on the side of the Taliban.[2] The Iron Curtain was still drawn across Europe. Yet by 1986, unanticipated leadership changes in the Soviet Union through early deaths would reveal a new openness in Soviet leadership and society.[3] The Berlin Wall was about to crumble, and the dissolution of the Soviet Union soon followed. The Iron Curtain was drawn wide open by Solidarity in Poland and the 1989 Velvet Revolution in Czechoslovakia.[4] The 1981 release of fifty-two Americans held hostage in Iran had not diminished the allure of that nation's Ruhollah Khomeini; his influence continued to extend to Pakistan, Sudan, and beyond. And a new group in Saudi Arabia, Al-Qaeda, was drawing strength from this success.[5]

The US economy was barely out of recession; unemployment was high and the savings-and-loan crisis loomed. Black Monday (the stock market crash in October 1987) was about to strike, to be followed by an economic boom.[6] The first personal computer had been introduced for popular use, but the Internet was practically unheard of by ordinary consumers. And much more rapidly than predicted, "globalization" was soon to be a commonplace term for both the economy and communications.[7]

Apartheid, in full force since the late 1940s, still dominated life in South African society. In parallel to that fundamentally destructive policy, economically productive but socially predatory policies had been introduced throughout most of Africa and Latin America, a consequence of the fiscal structural adjustment policies of the World Bank and the International Monetary Fund (IMF). The economic crises in the 1970s resulted in the even more challenging situation of the 1980s, leading to that decade's discouraging epithet, "the Lost Decade for Africa."[8] Apartheid policies in South Africa would crumble soon after the fall of the Berlin Wall and the breakup of the Soviet Union, but the impact of the structural adjustment policies would persist throughout the 1990s.[9]

Child survival was a major concern of the international health community, and HIV-AIDS had just been named but was not widely recognized. Primary health care and tropical disease control, prominent on the global health agenda in the late 1970s and early 1980s, were soon to be balanced by a focus on reproductive health and behavioral measures. After initial recognition of only a few cases in 1980, mainly US-based, HIV-AIDS would rapidly become a global phenomenon by the 1990s.[10] Increasingly, issues of human resource development and science and technology for development became priorities for development assistance.[11]

Terrorism, not a new tactic, became more prominent as attacks occurred in Lebanon, Lockerbie, Oklahoma City, and Lebanon again, the underground garage of the World Trade Center was bombed, and Indira Gandhi was assassinated.[12] The United States invaded Grenada. And then Iraq invaded Kuwait and the UN coalition went in to turn back Saddam Hussein's army.[13]

The leadership of Presidents Ronald Reagan, George H. W. Bush, and William J. Clinton, with alternating Democratic and Republican majorities in both the House of Representatives and the Senate, shaped the US policy agenda: deregulation at home, pragmatism abroad. David I Iamburg, recently the director of the Institute of Medicine in Washington, was attuned to the variety of ways in which scholarly research could inform and influence these policies.

By the end of Hamburg's nearly fifteen years as president of Carnegie Corporation, the American economy had ballooned, but not yet burst. As a result, the Corporation's assets had soared to over $1.5 billion in the last year of the Hamburg presidency (1996–1997), enabling the annual grants budget to grow from $13 million to a new height of $59 million.[14] With the endorsement of the Board of Trustees and the greatly increased asset base, reinforced by Hamburg's experience and worldview, this era revived the international commitment of the Corporation in its US-based grant-making and extended the geographic and substantive focus of the overseas grant-making.

DAVID HAMBURG: A CHOICE FOR A CLEAR COMMITMENT TO NEW PROGRAMS

IN SELECTING DAVID HAMBURG, the Board of Trustees agreed to his main condition: that the board be willing to enlarge the focus and tackle the intractable problem of avoiding nuclear war, which he saw as the greatest threat facing human civilization.[15] While Hamburg had been on the board for three years and on several committees (new trustees committee, committee on policies and procedures, and the search committee), the previous three presidents had been longtime staff members prior to becoming president (Dollard for ten years, Gardner for nine years, and Pifer for fourteen years). Hamburg was the first medical doctor to head the foundation. Not only a psychiatrist but also a policy and field researcher, he was committed to promoting a worldview based on prevention of harm to nations, communities, families, women, men, and children.[16] To this end, he drew on input from scholars across the fields of policy research, science, technology, and behavioral sciences. With these scholars, he sought to ensure that policies were based on sound evidence, not opinion or political machinations. The dual determining thrusts—prevention of harm and evidence-based scholar-policymaker linkages—informed all Corporation activities during this period.

The internationally related activities in the United States in the 1980s and 1990s were for the most part targeted at national and international security issues, with a major emphasis on the Soviet Union and weapons of mass destruction; as the global and national policy concerns became more broadly related to conflict prevention, the scope broadened. In contrast, the developing countries program pursued a mix of development-oriented initiatives. Actions consistent with the previous era related to ameliorating the impact of apartheid in Southern Africa and supporting anti-apartheid work in the United States, along with strengthening the health and well-being of women in a variety of dimensions. For the first time since the 1960s, the development of locally conducted, policy-oriented research on sound national policies was related not to education and development, as in the past, but to science, technology, and health; by the 1990s, researchers had begun in-depth examinations of the transitions to democracy in Africa, approaches to conflict resolution, and new designs for development assistance.[17]

Adding to the significance of changing global conditions, the fairly rapid increase in assets led to a significant increase in grant-making. "For example," Hamburg wrote in his final Annual Report essay about the changes he had encountered, "annually the number of proposals received has grown from approximately 2,000 to about 5,100; the number of grants has increased from 85 to 343.... Indeed, 51 percent of all the dollars awarded in the Corporation's history since 1911 were granted during this period."[18] To implement his broad-based agenda of prevention of harm and tackling of real-world issues, Hamburg entered his presidency committed to bringing "universities, scientific academies, and research institutes" together to "share information, ideas, and technical abilities widely across traditional barriers and systems." As he promised, "Carnegie Corporation will attempt to foster conditions under which these broadly based competencies can be linked over an extended period. A particularly valuable undertaking will be the development of intelligible, credible syntheses of research related to important policy questions."[19] Hamburg sought to bring together individuals from across the disciplines and encourage them to work together; he was convinced about the value of "a mutually beneficial interplay between social concerns and basic inquiry."[20]

To build the basis for preparing syntheses, evaluating them, and connecting researchers and policymakers both in this country and elsewhere, Hamburg proposed more extensive use of the Corporation's "art form" of commissions and task forces as a complement to grant-making. He also realized that partnership was essential, not simply for bringing additional resources to bear but also for extending the impact of the work; thus, collaboration became a hallmark of the Corporation in this era—with other foundations, with the federal and state governments, with the United Nations and its range of agencies, and with the World Bank.[21] The newly created Special Projects Committee, in reaching across the grants programs and seeking collaboration not only in the review of its proposals but also for joint grant-making around the range of international activities, exemplified a new mode of internal collaboration.

To enhance the second half of the Corporation mission—the diffusion of knowledge and understanding—the Public Affairs Department, in an effort to reach the public and policymakers, began to play an even greater role, as a grant-making arm of the corporation, in identifying and developing opportunities for television programs and public television series, in working with journalists and, more traditionally, in extending assistance to the grants program (with special assistance for the outreach from the work in South Africa and the Caribbean) and maintaining the regular publications of the Corporation.

THE BOARD OF TRUSTEES

IN 1981 THE SEARCH COMMITTEE that selected Hamburg sought to continue the innovations in diversity of membership that Pifer had introduced. Under Hamburg, board diversity was sustained and enhanced through the expertise of new members in foreign policy, international affairs research, science and technology, and international outreach, especially in South Africa with the intensification of anti-apartheid concerns. Engaged in the South Africa activities, Helene Kaplan chaired the board from 1984 to 1990, serving as the first woman board chair; she also had chaired the search committee.[22]

A few board members brought to the table considerable foreign policy-making experience from serving in positions reminiscent of those held by trustees in the early decades.[23] Several members were involved in international issues as part of their work in finance or law.[24] Other board members were educators, philanthropists, and journalists, drawn from a range of fields related to the agenda of the Corporation: early childhood education, education reform, liberal arts education, African studies, and science and technology with a focus on minorities and women. Almost all were active in national and international research or networks.[25]

Hamburg sought to involve the board members in the work of the Corporation through their participation on commissions and task forces as well as in meeting regularly with staff members. Building on Alan Pifer's commitment to staff engagement with the board, Hamburg often had staff members presenting and introducing speakers; he also invited board members to speak at Corporation meetings and co-chair Corporation events. One board trip was organized to South Africa in 1984, at the time of the 1984 conference on the Second Carnegie Inquiry into Poverty and Development in Southern Africa. Annual retreats, held offsite, brought together trustees and senior staff to delve into existing program areas and explore new ones. When Hamburg announced in 1995 his intention to retire, the retreat in June of that year reviewed in-depth all the programmatic work during this era as the basis for setting priorities for the search committee and future grant-making.[26]

INSTITUTIONAL CHANGES IN FUNCTION AND FORM

IN HIS 1983 INAUGURAL PRESIDENTIAL ESSAY, Hamburg summarized his worldview: his commitment to achieve prevention of harm to human society through carefully designed research, policies "that respect evidence," and positive societal change through the promotion of healthy behaviors.[27] An internationalist president, Hamburg's premise was that American contributions to peace and development around the world would emerge from national strength in science and technology; at the same time, he emphasized, Americans had much to learn from connecting with others in other countries through active participation in international meetings and networks.

As the main corollary to concerns about avoiding nuclear war, Hamburg identified the vital necessity of building a stronger program focus on the Soviet Union. The Cold War obsession with communism dominated not only US policy but also academic discourse. Hamburg was determined to make a contribution so that the phrase "peaceful coexistence" could become a firm reality, not a smokescreen; he would do so by enhancing scientific, scholarly, and military contacts with the Soviets. This was an additional condition for his accepting the presidency.

Although Hamburg was fully committed to the work in Africa and the Caribbean, he also wanted the program related to international development to address issues in Mexico because of its common border with the United States. His work with the US Institute of Medicine, the World Health Organization, and the Pan American Health Organization had deepened his awareness of the disparities along that border and the pragmatic and academic advantages of promoting binational and international collaborations to tackle them.

He also saw the importance of connecting Africans and citizens of the Caribbean and the United States to broader global networks. Thus, his worldview was expansive in an era when imaginative, global approaches were needed to deal with the "intractable" problems of the Cold War, the dire economic conditions brought on by structural adjustment in developing countries, the aftermath of the Iran hostage debacle for the United States, and the declining educational standards in the United States.

Hamburg made it very clear that he had no intention of introducing major changes in staffing, in keeping with past practices at the Corporation. He offered a challenge to all current staff, whatever their area of expertise: he wanted them to work with him on developing program areas that either already were of interest to them or might become so. Over the review year of 1983, staff members held meetings, held discussions with experts, and wrote background papers for extensive internal discussion.[28]

As Hamburg explained in his presidential essay on the new programs:

The foundation has in the past year undertaken an institutional renewal leading to the development of four new grant programs. The programs reflect fundamental continuity in values as well as substantial change. Their objectives are to foster conditions under which young people everywhere may get a decent start in life, to deepen understanding of the rapidly changing world we live in, and to advance the cause of peaceful international relations.... Having identified several hotspots, we then tried to map the terrain of each.... Four of these "terrain maps" were presented to the board of trustees ... and became the basis upon which the trustees approved staff recommendations to modify and enlarge the foundation's scope of activities.[29]

In the fall of 1983, the board agreed to go forward with these four new programs: the Avoiding Nuclear War Program, the Education, Science and Technology, and the Economy Program, the Prevention of Damage to Children Program, and the Human Resources in Developing Countries Program, along with a formal Special Projects Committee to handle the out-of-program grants. In addition, the Public Affairs Department was considered a special part of the grant-making program as well as the dissemination and communications arm for the Corporation; a dissemination fund enabled that department to make specific grants related to the Corporation's programs and activities.

Hamburg elaborated on the premises undergirding the work of the Corporation:

> The need for us to take the long view has never been more evident. We live in an era of rapid, far-reaching transformation.... The particular approaches and strategies the foundation takes will doubtless undergo continuing evolution and evaluation. The formative concepts are clear, however. They are considered ... with full recognition of the limitations of what the Corporation—or for that matter any single institution—can do, but with the hope that the foundation can at least try to clarify the nature and scope of these great problems and engage others in the search for constructive responses.[30]

The Avoiding Nuclear War Program and the Human Resources in Developing Countries Program were the primary sites of international grant-making; the Special Projects Committee and the Public Affairs Department also promoted international activities, both through connections with these two grants programs and independently. Hamburg, with board approval, was moving the Corporation to a different model of work.

By establishing departments, boundaries were built around the program areas, similar to academic departments. Although program coherence was greatly strengthened by this organizational framework, staff members would now share ideas and activities only through informal conversation, by reading grant material in board books, or by listening to board discussions, not through reading and commenting on all grant requests, the practice introduced by Devereux Josephs in the 1940s.

In keeping with his policy on staff appointments—that is, to maintain as much as possible the current staff but offer them new opportunities and responsibilities as needed—Hamburg asked Frederic Mosher, a longtime staff member (about twenty years at the time of Hamburg's appointment in 1982) with training in social psychology and experience in both the Corporation's domestic and international programs (particularly the educational and child development issues in Africa), to take responsibility for the Avoiding Nuclear War Program.

Hamburg asked Vivien Stewart (hired in 1972), who also had experience with both the domestic and international programs—most relevantly with Barbara Finberg and Mosher on some of the early childhood education grants—to chair the Prevention of Damage to Children Program. Alden Dunham (hired in 1966), who had been working on higher education, was asked to head the Education, Science and Technology, and the Economy Program. In June 1983, David Hood, director of the international program, stepped down; Jill Sheffield (hired in 1981), who was also in the international program, assumed responsibility for the Strengthening Human Resources in Developing Countries Program, maintaining her focus on the women and development activities. Hood remained a consultant advising on the South Africa grants. Hamburg also brought with him an associate from his work in Washington and at Harvard, Dr. Elena O. Nightingale, to work on, inter alia, the program on and in Mexico and on activities in South African health and human rights, early childhood and adolescent health, and education.[31]

Besides bringing a significant number of internationalists onto the Corporation board, Hamburg made the first non–North American or non-European international hire for a leadership position at the Corporation by appointing, in 1986, Dr. Adetokunbo O. Lucas as the first chair of the Program on Strengthening Human Resources in Developing Countries.[32] Lucas, a distinguished and globally recognized public health leader, was originally from Ibadan, Nigeria, and may have been the first New York–based program director in any of the major foundations to come from a developing country.

THE US-BASED INTERNATIONAL PROGRAM: GLOBAL PREVENTION OF HARM

HAMBURG'S LIFELONG PASSION for preventing harm gave vision and structure to the international grant-making in the United States. He had been working on these issues for many years before taking the helm at the Corporation. In his first essay on the new programs, he elaborated on the scope for addressing the nuclear and US-Soviet issues:

> The overriding problem facing humanity today is the possibility of nuclear holocaust. The present moment in history is so decisive for the human future that the Corporation will work vigorously through its grants to increase the chances that good ideas for managing and preventing crises involving the risk of nuclear war will be subjected to constructive critical examination; it will try to engage the ablest and best-informed minds over a wide range of perspectives in generating new options; and it will work to build a broad public understanding of ways in which the risk of nuclear war can be diminished. The foundation will also explore possible contributions of the behavioral sciences to the conduct of negotiations, decision-making, and conflict resolution. Finally, it will look at possibilities for fundamental, long-term change in the relationship between the United States and the Soviet Union.[33]

Engaging informed minds from the United States, the Soviet Union, and other countries, Hamburg and his colleagues, led by Mosher, began to plan how best to address the high-stakes issues, the existential challenges, and to define the initial work of the program.[34] Because of the immediacy of the work that was funded by the Corporation through this program in this era, the thematic focus shifted as the context required. Although the fundamental principles remained the same, different areas of emphasis arose as compelling gaps to be filled were identified. The program would have three names that reflected the principal concerns arising from changing global conditions: Avoiding Nuclear War (1983 to 1990); Cooperative Security (1990 to 1994); and Preventing Deadly Conflict (1994 to 1997). Organized by these programmatic phases, the following discussion highlights the rationale, grants, meetings, commissions, and, where possible, results.[35]

AVOIDING NUCLEAR WAR, 1983–1990

THE INITIAL FOCUS of this program was to build a partnership of trust with the United States and the Soviet Union, paralleling and sometimes intersecting with official channels, to avoid nuclear war. The rationale for this program related in large part to the buildup of new weapons and the increasingly belligerent tone (such as the labeling of the Soviet Union as "the evil empire") under the presidency of Ronald Reagan. Four main lines of work, described in the 1983 program paper, shaped the activities: applied research to identify new ideas and understanding about ways to reduce the chance of nuclear war, linking closely the policymaking and policy advising communities; efforts to educate the public and policymakers, drawing on the best research results, to build broad nonpartisan interest; exploration of the role of the behavioral sciences in negotiations, decision-making, and conflict resolution, as well as in deepening understanding of the basis of human conflict and its resolution; and identification of the possibilities for fundamental, long-term changes in the relationship between the United States and the Soviet Union.[36]

To build a research base for all further work in the program, the first set of grants went to a cluster of seven institutions that had demonstrated capacity, many having been established earlier by the Ford and Rockefeller Foundations' international security programs. Two grants went to Harvard University for the Project on Avoiding Nuclear War, led by Joseph Nye, Graham Allison, and Albert Carnesale and based at the John F. Kennedy School of Government, for seminars, workshops, research fellowships, and review committees.[37] Stanford University received two grants: one for the research of Alexander George on the interplay between coercive diplomacy and crisis management in averting conflicts; and the second, under the leadership of John Lewis and Alexander George, for fostering policy-oriented research and training for scientists. A third project was funded in 1984 at the Massachusetts Institute of Technology under the leadership of Jack Ruina at the Defense and Arms Control Studies Program to home in on the scientific—including social scientific—and technological aspects of security issues.[38] Three multidisciplinary grants supported university programs in Soviet studies: the RAND/UCLA Center for Soviet Studies, the W. Averell Harriman Institute for the Study of the Soviet Union at Columbia University, and the Berkeley-Stanford Program in Soviet International Behavior.[39] Staff further described the expectations: "The analytical studies of university groups and centers are likely to be more useful if they take into account policymakers' perspectives, and policymakers can benefit greatly from ready access to new ideas, a wider range of options, and deeper insights."[40] Moreover, several of these institutions could educate the next generation of scholars who would have the capacity to analyze and inform national policy, a pressing need that had emerged since the Corporation ended its related grants in the late 1950s and the Ford Foundation, which in the early 1970s had established many of the centers now of interest to the Corporation, was no longer providing core support.

Two think tanks were also supported in 1984. The Carnegie Endowment for International Peace received funding to publish a report on the state of nuclear weapons proliferation called *Nuclear Proliferation Today*, co-funded by the Rockefeller Brothers Fund and the Endowment.[41] The International Research and Exchanges Board (IREX) received the first of several grants during this era for $394,125 over two years for holding meetings involving Soviet, American, and Eastern European scholars and policymakers.[42] In 1985 the Brookings Institution, with a grant of $750,000 over three years, introduced an explicit focus on Soviet relations into its work on foreign policy and international security under the Foreign Policy Program, led by John Steinbruner.[43]

An article in the *Carnegie Quarterly* in the spring of 1985 provided more detail on the rationales and intentions of these and many other grantees that were contributing to more nuanced understandings of the nuclear issues, including those related to US-Soviet relations, in the early years of the program.[44] With support from 1983 to 1984 of $5 million, and then $5.5 million in 1985, the Corporation was infusing new resources and energy into the field of Soviet studies, benefiting from the extensive investments in the 1970s by, inter alia, the Ford Foundation, the Rockefeller Foundation, and the Rockefeller Brothers Fund.[45]

As the 1980s progressed and the Ford and Rockefeller Foundations began to shift their international security studies work into other areas, new foundations entered the field, including the William and Flora Hewlett Foundation, the Pew Charitable Trusts, and the Ploughshares Fund. Significantly, the John D. and Catherine T. MacArthur Foundation sought to build up its grants program in this area, particularly in response to Roderick MacArthur's strong feelings about war and peace and the Cold War. In 1985 the MacArthur Foundation "announced a three-year $25 million program to promote international security studies."[46] This was the beginning of a long-term, mutually productive and beneficial partnership between the MacArthur Foundation and Carnegie Corporation for work on Soviet and security studies in the United States. Rather than jointly fund the same activities, the result of the discussions was a division of labor. The MacArthur Foundation focused on building research and training capacity in the social sciences through major grants to the Social Science Research Council for pre- and postdoctoral research. Carnegie Corporation continued its focus on bringing together scientists, scholars, and policymakers through the large institution grants, including bringing together behavioral sciences and security studies scholars to examine the problems related to nuclear policy and decision-making through the Committee of Behavioral and Social Sciences at the National Academy of Sciences and at the University of Michigan, under the leadership of Harold Jacobson at the Institute for Social Research.[47]

Staff believed that, to reach policymakers, it was essential that the policy research be conducted by scholars "who could not be faulted for lack of technical competence and real-world experience, who would not be dismissed as naive or ideologically soft. Scientific standing was an essential component. So too was international stature."[48] Corporation staff members suggested that, bolstered by the involvement of the MacArthur Foundation, this work had made the hoped-for contributions: "While MacArthur has taken a broader view of the nature of international security and the priority issues, it has been a substantial partner in supporting our program's grantees, giving a total almost twice ours over the same period."[49]

From 1983 to 1989, as Mosher noted in his 1989 report, the part of the program related to security and Soviet studies received 38 percent of the funding to support nineteen field-building or field-strengthening grants, for a total of $15,626,475.[50] Mosher commented on two important publications, the first two from the Harvard team. These shaped the discussions about the field and had considerable uptake in the policy community: *Hawks, Doves, and Owls: An Agenda for Avoiding Nuclear War* and *Fateful Visions.*[51]

At the same time the program was moving forward to develop the analytical capacity to address international security and Soviet studies in the country, on March 23, 1983, President Reagan announced a new defense policy called the Strategic Defense Initiative (SDI).[52] Agreeing with the scientific and policy research concerns, the Corporation saw this initiative and the required weapons system, popularly called "Star Wars," as a red flag to the Soviet Union. The program responded with a new set of grants. According to Mosher, the SDI called into question all the existing arms control agreements and the policy of deterrence.[53] There was little basis for understanding what was involved and whether it would work. Neither policymakers nor the public had much depth of knowledge about this subject. He noted that over the six years of the program, work on "high priority topics," including SDI, had involved about 30 percent of the total budget and 104 grants, for a total of $12,482,775.[54]

A key aspect of arms control that concerned the program was the complex process of negotiations, verification, and compliance. The major project in this area, Roger Fisher's Harvard Negotiation Project, examined in both theoretical and pragmatic terms the concept and process of negotiations between the United States and the Soviet Union; the intent was to demonstrate how to arrive at a win-win situation. Another grant to the American Academy of Arts and Sciences, linked with the International Institute of Applied Systems Analysis, studied the range of international negotiations, analyzing different cultures and different approaches. In both of these grants, the experts participating were not only American but Soviet and non-Western.[55]

With the ups and downs of the nuclear treaty discussions between the

Soviets and the Americans, the Corporation made a series of grants to the Committee on International Security and Arms Control of the National Academy of Sciences to work with Soviet scientists toward building a shared understanding of the concepts underlying an arms control regime and how to implement them. David Hamburg was a member of this committee.[56]

Grants grappled with the complicated subject of US-Soviet cooperation on verification. One grant, for example, brought together the Natural Resources Defense Council (NRDC) and the Soviet Academy of Sciences to examine the premise of permitting verification by Americans through seismic techniques on Soviet soil; this project was "the first time the Soviet government ... permitted American specialists and technology to monitor seismic activity in the USSR."[57] The Natural Resources Defense Council, a nongovernmental organization, and the Academy arrived at an agreement for such verification, to the embarrassment of the official negotiators.[58] Several foundations supported the Natural Resources Defense Council, along with the Corporation.

Early grants also delved into the issues of crisis management, with an increasingly sharp focus on crisis prevention.[59] The studies served as the basis for the continuing dialogue supported through the US-Soviet Study Group at Harvard University, which brought together Soviet and American experts in these fields.[60] The result was a major publication, *Windows of Opportunity: From Cold War to Peaceful Competition in US-Soviet Relations.*[61] The Soviet contributors were drawn from the leadership of major institutes in Moscow, and one was the personal aide to General Secretary Mikhail Gorbachev. The American contributors were drawn from a range of programs at Harvard, as well as from Columbia and Stanford. Hamburg was also part of the study group.

Another set of projects were precursors to the next phase of the program. Leonard S. Spector at the Carnegie Endowment for International Peace prepared a series of annual reports and publications on the spread of nuclear weapons from 1980 to 1989.[62] A prescient grant in 1987 supported the work of the Nuclear Control Institute on the capacity of non-nuclear countries and terrorist groups to obtain and use nuclear weapons; this work led to the publication of *Preventing Nuclear Terrorism* by the Institute's director, Paul Leventhal.[63] Also in 1987, Admiral Stansfield Turner, former director of the US Central Intelligence Agency (CIA), was supported to examine issues regarding the use of conventional weapons by terrorists. Turner and Sherman Teichman, director of Tufts University's Experimental College Project on International Terrorism and Political Violence, wrote about "the nature and extent of the terrorist threat to the United States and the American people," resulting in the book *Terrorism and Democracy*.[64]

One long-term grantee and two relatively new grantees rounded out the major grants in this first phase of the program. The Council on Foreign Relations and the American Committee on US-Soviet Relations assessed the US-Soviet relationship as a key focus for avoiding nuclear war.[65] At the Center for Strategic and International Studies in Washington, DC, Thane Gustafson studied military developments in Soviet society, particularly in relation to broader policy issues.[66]

As Corporation staff pointed out, the salient and vital feature of most of these grants was the collaboration across Soviet and American scholarship in the hard sciences, technology, and social science. Although the studies and publications advanced understanding, staff posited that the relationships established during these six years of grants were even more fundamentally important for keeping lines of communication open in the complex post-Soviet era.[67] One set of grants that focused on connecting policymakers and scholars from the United States and the Soviet Union revived the earlier focus, developed under Gardner and Pifer, on connecting parliamentarians. Mosher, on staff when these policies were developed in the 1970s, suggested this approach to Hamburg as a model for bringing together scholars and policymakers.[68]

Former US senator Dick Clark, a participant in the Anglo-American-Canadian Parliamentarian Conferences, established the Aspen Institute Congressional Program, with Corporation support of $25,000 in 1983, in order to provide more in-depth education for US senators and representatives by holding discussions on the Soviet Union with experts from both the United States and the Soviet Union. Corporation grantee Michael Mandelbaum, then a fellow at the Council on Foreign Relations, worked with Clark in preparing the background material for these meetings.[69]

The linkage idea—that is, connecting scholars with policymakers and practitioners—led to a second activity at the Aspen Institute, the Aspen

Strategy Group; formed in 1974 and funded by the Ford and Rockefeller Foundations, it was originally called the Arms Control Consortium. This program enabled scholars, both senior and junior, to meet with members of the US Congress, officials from the Soviet and American executive branches and the Soviet Duma (parliament), and others to review together the scholarly findings about key policy questions.[70]

At the American Association for the Advancement of Science, in Washington, DC, the Corporation supported the Center for Security and International Studies, a project directed by Barry Blechman with Senators Sam Nunn and John Warner as co-chairs, to review the work on crisis prevention and ways to prevent a nuclear war. According to Mosher, "their report and related efforts played a key role in decisions to upgrade the U.S.-Soviet "Hotline" and to establish Nuclear Risk Reduction Centers in Moscow and Washington."[71]

Mosher commented on the vital importance of the Aspen projects to ensuring

> access to well-informed, reliable bases for making judgments about the Soviet Union and the changes under way there. All of our major Soviet studies grantees have had a chance to participate in the Aspen meetings, and it seems clear from the testimony of the members of Congress themselves that this contact has had an important effect in deepening their understanding of what is happening and in exposing them to resources to which they can turn when specific questions and specific hearings come before them.[72]

From all the commentary, it is evident that the meetings were always informative, but one of Clark's Aspen meetings in 1988 was especially dramatic. On March 11, 1988, the participants had what must have been a "pinch me, I can't believe what I'm hearing" meeting with Mikhail Gorbachev at the Kremlin. Senior Soviet officials were there as well as the US ambassador to the Soviet Union, Jack Matlock, and members of Congress from both houses and parties, including Alan Cranston, Alan Simpson, Sam Nunn, William Cohen, and Carl Levin. The discussion with the general secretary focused on the improvements in US-Soviet relations and what was still needed; there was ample opportunity to ask questions and have them directly answered. In the trip report of program officer Deana Arsenian, David Hamburg noted that Gorbachev was positive about his visits to the United States, and that "he expressed his hope that the relationship between the Soviet leadership and the US Congress will continue to develop and improve." The group was able to ask Gorbachev about such sensitive issues as Afghanistan, human rights, emigration, and the arms race, and the general secretary discussed all of these issues fully. The trip report ended with an encouraging conclusion by Gorbachev, as quoted by Arsenian: "He welcomes Soviet and American scholars getting together and discussing these matters. The United States and the Soviet Union carry great responsibility in the world and must have the intellectual integrity to serve the interests of all mankind."[73]

This was not a confidential meeting. A press release issued after the meeting drew on the trip report, "The purpose of this trip to Moscow was to visit with General Secretary Mikhail S. Gorbachev and high ranking officials of the Soviet government about a broad range of issues in the U.S.-Soviet relationship. There was no specific agenda for discussion. Each participant was free to raise whatever issues most interested them … on political, economic, military, arms control and human rights issues among others."[74] The *Washington Post* covered the meeting the next day. Hamburg fully reported to the Corporation board in April, and Senator Alan Simpson made a report to Congress.[75]

Agreeing that the education of policymakers needed to be complemented by public education, the staff and trustees decided to support two television series. Co-funded by the Aaron Diamond Foundation, *Global Rivals*, shown in 1986 on WNET (New York's public television station), aimed to shape understanding of US-Soviet relations.[76] The second grant, in 1989, supported the production by WGBH (Boston's public television station) of *Inside Gorbachev's USSR*, with the host C. Hedrick Smith, then a two-time Pulitzer Prize winner and former *New York Times* Moscow bureau chief, and the producer Martin Smith, an Emmy winner. That production was also co-funded by the W. Alton Jones Foundation, as well as by others.[77] The Corporation continued to fund public outreach work through other media-focused activities.[78]

Another set of grants attempted to reach the public more directly. The Scientists' Institute for Public Information specifically reached out to journalists and media gatekeepers. At the Center for War, Peace, and the News Media at New York University, David Rubins and Robert Karl Manoff received grants to examine how to achieve greater media coverage of international security and US-Soviet relations. All the grantees, including the university-based ones, were encouraged to step up their efforts to reach out to a broader public and to share their research findings.[79]

Public education took on a very different dimension following discussions between Corporation staff members and officials of the Soviet Academy of Sciences in Moscow. The topic was using computers in early elementary education, an area of interest in both the United States and the Soviet Union. Corporation staff members thought that this project would bring complementary strengths from both countries to the task of learning more about this educational tool, as well as build yet another basis for collaboration and cooperation. Several discretionary grants enabled Michael Cole, head of the Laboratory of Comparative Human Cognition at the University of California at San Diego, to work closely with Alexandra Belyaeva, director of the Communications Laboratory of the Soviet Academy of Sciences' Institute of Psychology, to develop the framework for the grant and then launch the collaboration. The participating scholars and scientists produced papers on the design and use of the new educational software; the study findings also informed training in mathematics.[80]

This project, which continued for several more years, has been described as the "VelHam" or "Vega" ("ham" in Russian is *ga*) Project, reflecting the leadership of Evgeny Velikov, the deputy secretary of the Soviet Academy of Sciences, and David Hamburg. It resulted not only in greater knowledge about computer use in elementary school–level mathematics education but also greater examination of the role of telecommunications in scholarly collaboration and networks, demonstrating the viability of "carrying out generally reciprocal and mutually beneficial joint research between scholars in the two countries."[81] It ultimately became an extensive program linking scholars, public interest groups, and local governments in the Soviet Union to broader international networks.[82]

1989: Annus Mirabilis

A January 1989 board review covering the changing context for the Corporation's international grant-making activities and their results was positive about the range of work that had been funded over the past six years and the approaches that had been taken.[83] Indeed, it was the changing context that prompted the review. Opening the discussion, Hamburg described the scope of the program: "to involve credible institutions; select critical issues for focus; link scholars and policymakers for the mutual benefit of each community; to educate the public, with indirect effects reaching beyond the campus and with direct grants to media organizations; and to assess the needs in a post-Gorbachev relationship." He "noted that this time is an historic opportunity for Carnegie [Corporation] to make significant contributions as a nongovernmental institution. This is a time of testing and exploring the Soviet Union on issues—Central America, terrorism, Eastern Europe—and ensuring that agreements will last beyond Gorbachev—through arrangements comparable to the nuclear risk reduction centers, the International Atomic Energy Agency, confidence and security building measure[s] in Europe, etc."[84] Appealing to the board for guidance in determining the direction for the program's next phase, Hamburg framed the challenge, or the "paradoxes of success," in considering that next phase: it was still fraught with danger as well as the opportunities emerging in "the shift to a multicentric world, no longer ... dominated by the two superpowers." Nevertheless, he cautioned, the dangerous possibility of the "erratic or regressive behavior of the superpowers," as well as nuclear proliferation at many levels, could not be overlooked.[85]

Mosher reminded the board of the positive developments including the 1987 Intermediate-range Nuclear Forces Treaty. "One of the key aspects of this treaty," described in a later news article, "was a mutual inspection and verification process, which improved trust between the two countries over the reduction of their nuclear stockpiles."[86] Mosher also provided grant data: since the beginning of the program in June 1983, the Board of Trustees had approved $41,585,846 for a total of 212 grants.[87] But Mosher, a social psychologist, added a word of caution:

We would not dare to assert causality. Credit for the changes certainly goes to reality, particularly nuclear reality, and the ability of these leaders and their advisors to appreciate reality, to understand their interests, and to have the courage to change accordingly—to be realistic and not to be complete prisoners of their past rhetoric. Still it is certainly time to ask what role the Corporation's program has played and to consider what the changed situation implies for what it should do now.[88]

The trustees responded to the questions, discussed the potential for additional work related to US-Soviet relations, and raised other themes. At the end of the discussion, the trustees endorsed continuing both the lines of grant-making and the approaches, as stated by the board chair in her summation: "There is complete Board support for continuation of the efforts of the Avoiding Nuclear War program. This critical period in the US-Soviet relationship affords the Corporation opportunity to maximize its investment in this area."[89]

Scarcely eleven months later, by the end of 1989, the geopolitical situation was in ferment. Few had envisioned the radical transformations in Eastern Europe over the course of that year, or the dramatic effect on the Soviet Union. Here, rather than in Indochina, was where the domino theory was applicable: instead of spreading communism, the domino effect was spreading glasnost and democratization. Solidarity in Poland, the Velvet Revolution in Czechoslovakia, and then the opening of the German border in November 1989, allowing East Germans to cross immediately, all led to the demise of the Iron Curtain. The Berlin Wall cracked, and the bricks were suddenly on sale as souvenirs in capitalist markets. Seemingly instantaneously, the Cold War—which had so dominated East-West relations, US-Soviet relations, and the work of the Corporation—evaporated.[90]

Although the tumult had positive outcomes—the removal of the Iron Curtain and the dissolution of the Soviet Union—it created a dilemma for the Corporation. It was not quite "back to the drawing board"—institutions and mechanisms were in place to move forward in this new world order—but in addition to the global changes, at home there was a new president, George H. W. Bush, who had new concerns. It is no surprise that for a few years the Corporation, along with many others, displayed uncertainty as to the most productive responses to the new directions. The security-threatening concerns about nuclear weapons persisted, and, as the board had predicted, more conventional weapons as well as biological and chemical ones entered the agenda. The world organized by the Cold War was in disarray, not just in Russia but throughout the new states of the former Soviet Union and Eastern Europe. The question persisted: what kind of program strategy design could best weave together the tattered loose ends attending these transformations?

COOPERATIVE SECURITY: 1990–1994

THE PEACEFUL CATASTROPHIC EVENTS of 1989 and 1990 brought opportunities for cooperation instead of the confrontation and competition of the Cold War decades. Yet in August 1990, a few months after the dramatic changes—possibly as a result of the end of the Soviet Union and the Cold War and the loss of the checks and balances provided by the two superpowers—Iraq invaded Kuwait. Taking a diplomatically constructive approach to crisis management, the United States asked the UN to organize a coalition to push the Iraqis back across the border.[91]

Hamburg and his colleagues redesigned the Avoiding Nuclear War Program with the aim "to consolidate and spread the kind of thinking that has led to the incipient cooperative security system in Europe, and to support scholarship that will contribute to working out the details of such systems."[92] A prevailing concern was "the extent to which the organization of international security is driven back to nineteenth-century balance of power politics, or whether it can move instead to a more cooperative structure evolving into some kind of genuine collective security."[93] Recognizing the potential for new institutional arrangements for peace and cooperation, the board approved the change in name and strategy: on October 1, 1990, the Avoiding Nuclear War Program became the Cooperative Security Program.[94] The change in nomenclature was not meant to be taken as a statement that nuclear war had been avoided but rather, somewhat more positively, to highlight issues of security as the basis for new ways to work across national borders.

The uncertainty about which directions to pursue affected the work of

policymakers as well as academics, so the program staff decided that a productive way to define the new program would be to organize task forces
and commissions to explore new ideas and directions. By participating in
a task force, for example, scholars, practitioners, and policymakers could
debate and pool existing knowledge, build a framework for assessing that
knowledge, identify new or persistent gaps, arrive at recommendations for
focused research to fill those gaps, and, where appropriate, suggest recommendations for new policies.

Program staff also continued a focus on institutional grants for research,
analysis, and dissemination, maintaining support for the Corporation's
long-standing grantees and introducing new ones to work on the new
theme.[95] The concern about achieving successful communications with the
public and between scholars and policymakers led to continued support
for the Aspen Institute programs and the American Association for the
Advancement of Science (AAAS), for the work maintaining open access
to information at the Fund for Peace's National Security Project and the
American Civil Liberties Union (ACLU), and for the public education
activities of the Scientists' Institute for Public Information (SIPI).[96]

Developing a brand-new program strategy while maintaining many of
the same grantees has many benefits but also some downsides. The close
relationship between funders and grantees can lead either to an atmosphere
of high-level creative risk-taking (which is often given as one of the reasons
for providing endowment support for freestanding institutions) or to "business as usual," even with the new contextual conditions. In this instance,
the Corporation did not need to shake up its grantees—the domino chain
reaction shook up the world one more time. Over the years 1990 and 1991,
as the Soviet Union dissolved, it became clear that the program needed to
rapidly reappraise its strategy.[97]

In the 1991 to 1992 program budget paper, staff emphasized, as the overall
aim, "the application of cooperative security principles to the avoidance of
catastrophic conflict."[98] That paper presented the three primary areas and a
fourth cross-cutting one on outreach:

1. *Research and education on ways to reduce and restructure US and Soviet
   nuclear forces in accordance with the principles that nuclear weapons cannot*

be used and that the only reason to have them at all is to deter their use by others. The lead activity in this area was the Carnegie Commission on Reducing the Nuclear Danger, co-chaired by McGeorge Bundy, former national security adviser under President Lyndon Johnson and then president of the Ford Foundation; Sidney Drell, a professor of physics and deputy director of the Stanford Linear Accelerator Center at Stanford University; and Admiral William Crowe, former chairman of the Joint Chiefs of Staff and a professor of geopolitics at the University of Oklahoma. The Commission was funded through officer-assisted grants from 1991 to 1993 for about $500,000. The commissioners consulted with other Corporation-supported programs at Harvard, Stanford, the Brookings Institution, and MIT to examine in depth "the nature of the nuclear danger in the twenty-first century."[99] Its monograph *Reducing Nuclear Danger: The Road Away from the Brink* was published by the Council on Foreign Relations in November 1993.[100]

2. *Research and education on the applicability of cooperative security principles to restricting the supply of and reducing the demand for weapons of mass destruction and other modern weapons in regions of the world with a high risk of war.* There were two main activities, both started in 1991: the Task Force on the Prevention of Proliferation, organized by John D. Steinbruner and Janne Nolan of the Brookings Institution "to examine whether cooperative security principles can be applied" to control the use "of modern weaponry in unstable regions," with initial support of $331,520; and a program on "operational aspects of cooperative security" that brought together fourteen senior fellows, with support of $1.2 million over three years (co-funded by the MacArthur Foundation). Steinbruner and Nolan conducted briefings, ran discussion groups, and organized joint research and consultations. Both activities resulted in publications and, as discussed later, a significant piece of legislation.[101]

3. *Support for efforts to help the Soviet Union and its former allies become more reliable and stable partners in cooperative security efforts by successfully negotiating their political and economic transitions to freer and more responsive systems.* There were several lead activities in this area,

including a two-year, $735,000 project with Graham Allison and his team at Harvard's John F. Kennedy School of Government on strengthening democratic institutions in the Soviet Union. The Corporation also supported Ambassador Robert Blackwill and Kurt M. Campbell in offering a series of seminars to enable American specialists to consult with Soviet military and civilian officials, for $177,250 over fourteen months. Herbert Okun's research at Columbia University to organize a three-year study on the structure of European politics, economics, and security was funded at the level of $506,100. Allan Kassof at the International Research and Exchanges Board was awarded $300,000 to plan and implement a five-year program to develop a regional community of researchers and policymakers in the field of ethnic relations. Condoleezza Rice and her team's two-year effort to build a scholarly program at Stanford University for examining the democratic transitions in Eastern Europe, including rule of law, human rights, and freedom of speech, was funded in the amount of $250,000.[102]

4. *Continuing interest in helping policymakers and the attentive public understand these issues and have ample access to the information needed to make responsible decisions.* The grants continued to the Aspen Institute Congressional Program, for $505,350 over one year, and the Aspen Strategy Group, for $250,000 over two years. A range of small, short-term grants—of $25,000 each, for example—supported the Congressional Roundtable on Post–Cold War Relations at the Peace Through Law Education Fund and World Priorities, Inc., to prepare the publication *World Military and Social Expenditure.*[103]

The Task Force on the Prevention of Proliferation led to more than a publication, meetings, and grants to the Aspen Institute, the Brookings Institution, and Harvard and Stanford Universities. Under the auspices of the Brookings grant, a policymaker steering committee, co-chaired by Senators Sam Nunn and Richard Lugar, worked in a consultative fashion with the other working groups.[104] The Aspen meetings provided additional opportunities to work through these complex ideas. One of the most dramatic results of these activities was the Nunn-Lugar Cooperative Security Program, which was "designed to safeguard weapons material in the former

Soviet Union."[105] As Ashton B. Carter, who participated with William J. Perry in these discussions, noted in a 2005 speech, "The principal successes ... were ... the denuclearization of Ukraine, Kazakhstan, and Belarus; and the stabilizing and initial dismantlement of the Russian military and military-industrial-nuclear complex during a dangerous period of turmoil."[106]

Over the period of the Cooperative Security Program from 1990 to 1994, another political election in 1992 led to a new president, William J. Clinton, who as governor of Arkansas had been actively involved in the Corporation's education programs. Clinton appointed William J. Perry as his secretary of defense, and as assistant secretary of defense for international security policy he chose Ashton B. Carter; both were longtime grantees, leaders of the Task Force on the Prevention of Proliferation, and part of the consortium examining cooperative security regimes based on the work in Europe but applicable elsewhere. The program staff, however, realistically recognized that even though Perry and Carter had been longtime collaborators whose work funded by the Corporation might help shape policy, "this is not assured. Policymaking is a political undertaking; at the end of the day, policy is cobbled together to accommodate a variety of practical concerns. And the real world problems policymakers face may not always lend themselves to cooperative solutions."[107]

In the period 1993 to 1994, when it was not clear whether cooperative security or conflict would dominate the world's agenda, the Corporation continued to give support to strengthening democratic institutions, ensuring ways to build strong civil societies in post-Communist nations, and finding new approaches to conflict prevention. IREX, for example, developed a new Project on Ethnic Relations, with a focus on Eastern and Central European conflicts. The Conflict Management Group examined the effectiveness of early warning systems in Eurasia reinforced by continued support for human rights monitoring through the Lawyers Committee on Human Rights and Helsinki Watch in the region. With the hypothesis that cultural and economic development was the solution, the Institute for East-West Studies conducted studies in the Carpathian Mountain region of Poland, Slovakia, Hungary, Romania, and Ukraine, "a remote area whose borders have changed more than a hundred times in recorded history." The team explored different approaches to achieving greater economic security.[108]

As the prevalence of these conflicts trumped the potential for achieving cooperative security, the Corporation began once again to reconsider its programmatic direction.[109]

Preventing Deadly Conflict

The presidential essay in the 1993 Annual Report, "Preventing Contemporary Intergroup Violence," signaled the pervasive global changes that were provoking a reconfiguration of the Corporation's US-based grant-making, as the threat of nuclear holocaust and the fall of the Soviet Union had done just a few years earlier. As Hamburg observed,

> The world of the next century will be different in profound respects from any that we have ever known before—deeply interdependent economically, closely linked technologically, and progressively more homogenized through the movement of information, ideas, people, and capital around the world at unprecedented speed. At the same time, it will be more multicentric in the devolution of economic, political, and military power to smaller adaptable units. Some nations will undergo a perilous fragmentation, as the centralizing forces that once held people together are pulled apart and traditional concepts of national sovereignty and nationhood are contested, sometimes violently. How these tendencies will be reconciled is far from clear.[110]

To address the changing global conditions, the Corporation—Hamburg, the trustees, and the staff—determined that the responsible course would be to refocus the work of the US-based international program on a new set of concerns that threatened harm to individuals, communities, and nations. Unlike the tidy framework provided by the Cold War agenda or the hopeful one of cooperative security, the new theme of ethnic violence and deadly conflict was messy, unpredictable, and potentially deadly. To handle these truly intractable and uncertain situations, grants and task forces, no matter how well staffed and funded, would not suffice. In Hamburg's judgment, the conditions required a major initiative with global reach beyond what could be achieved with even the most extensive grants.

To pool knowledge, assess what had worked and what had not, embark on a major campaign to promote values of comity and community to reduce the use and threat of violence, and provide a global—not just American— imprimatur, Hamburg proposed to the board that the Corporation establish the independent, international Commission on the Prevention of Deadly Conflict, which would be intertwined with the grants program.[111] This was the first time in the Corporation's history of international grant-making that there had been such an intricate, intimate relationship between an entity like a commission or task force and the concurrent grants program. Although the Commission on the Prevention of Deadly Conflict, like some of the others—especially the domestic Carnegie Council on Adolescent Development—would take on the life of an operating agency, the grants program would maintain both parallel and intersecting lines of activity, drawing on and contributing to the Commission's work. The program chair of the grants program effectively was the program officer for the Commission, and the Commission's executive director reported to the Corporation.[112] With the selection of Jane E. Holl as executive director in May 1994 and the grant development work undertaken by the program team led by David Speedie, the Commission launched into action in June 1994.[113]

The Commission's work gave significant visibility to the wide range of issues associated with the prevention of deadly conflict at the highest policy levels. Over its more than three years of work, the Commission produced eight books and twenty-five reports and held meetings all over the world. The total cost from start to launch of the final report was just under $8 million. The Corporation disseminated the Commission's publications for several years; some of its recommendations informed the program in the next era (see Chapter 8).

The Commission's recommendations resulting from the participation of the sixteen commissioners led to detailed differentiation among the deadly conflicts of the 1990s—those within states and those between states—as well as comparison with historical experiences. The findings detailed the roles that international institutions, regional organizations, state agencies, and more informal coalitions could all play in prevention. A series of analytic tools for early warning, integrating political, military, economic, social, and other measures, was also developed and disseminated widely.[114] Although some criticism of the Commission's final report pointed out that these concerns were not new, it was precisely the fact that these concerns were familiar but remained unaddressed that had motivated the Commission and the follow-up activities. The question that drove the entire process was how to arrive at a new understanding of institutional arrangements and mechanisms to transform and channel the all-too-familiar persistent tendency toward violence and conflict in human society into more peaceful and constructive aims. Andrew Carnegie had devoted the last twenty years of his life to this quest, and the Commission on Preventing Deadly Conflict reshaped the knowledge base on ways to accelerate toward peace in the twenty-first century.[115]

While the Commission on Preventing Deadly Conflict scrutinized global conditions and the potential for policy change, drawing on the policy analyses prepared by a wide range of advisers from around the world, Corporation staff, along with scholars and senior UN officials such as Secretary General Boutros Boutros-Ghali, examined the potential for conflict growing out of the changed political world as internal conflicts spread within states. The Corporation's grants program, called Preventing Deadly Conflict, addressed related but distinctive issues, drawing as well on the previous ten years of grant-making through the prior programs, Avoiding Nuclear War and Cooperative Security.

First, staff sought grantees who would examine cases of conflict, whether ethnic, nationalist, or religious, whether between or within states, and identify early warning systems for preventing deadly conflicts, explore the potential for partnerships between government and nongovernmental organizations, and draw on evidence-based assessments, including building capacity "to analyze international disputes, understand international negotiation techniques, and practice negotiation skills in disputes."[116]

Second, recognizing the potential for conflict in the former Soviet Union and Eastern and Central Europe, the program continued the ongoing examination of the potential for cooperative security and strengthening democratic institutions in these regions.[117]

Third, with 30,000 nuclear weapons remaining among the Soviet republics of Russia, Ukraine, Belarus, and Kazakhstan, the problem of proliferation added the intrastate dimension to the interstate one. The program sought to support more "robust" ways to curb such proliferation, as well as the weapons of mass destruction that fuel regional and domestic conflicts, by bringing together Russian, American, and other expertise, including many of the same grantees that had been associated with the Corporation since the early 1980s. Projects addressed the horizontal proliferation from Cold War arsenals to rogue states or groups, a continuing concern throughout the early twenty-first century.[118] New areas focused on chemical and biological weapons agreements, such as work at Harvard and Sussex Universities and the Henry L. Stimson Center. China reentered the Corporation's agenda for the first time since the 1970s; the issue was arms control.[119]

To promote the next generation of scholars in international peace and security, new grantees entered the program. At the University of Maryland, the Women in International Security Program (WIIS) attracted and retained women and minorities in the field of security studies. At the Monterey Institute of International Studies, early- to mid-career professionals worked on the project on nonproliferation in the Commonwealth of Independent States (CIS). Harvard's Program on New Approaches to Russian Security (PONARS) and its Project Liberty, for enhancing women's leadership in Eastern and Central Europe, connected young American and Russian scholars.[120]

During the final year of the Hamburg presidency, 1996 to 1997, as the work of the Commission drew to a close, the Preventing Deadly Conflict Program maintained grant-making around the same themes explored by the Commission, namely, examining alternative ways of preventing mass intergroup violence and rebuilding disintegrating states. These themes, along with the abiding concern about the proliferation of nuclear weapons and other weapons of mass destruction, continue to resonate in the Corporation's grant-making in the twenty-first century.

Commentary on the US-Based International Program

In assessing the outcomes of this work over fourteen years, staff highlighted three substantial achievements: the Cooperative Threat Reduction Act of 1992, co-sponsored by Senators Sam Nunn and Richard Lugar as a result of their participation in the Task Force on the Prevention of Proliferation; the Chemical Weapons Convention analyses by the Henry L. Stimson Center, which became essential to obtaining the ratification of such weapons; and the collaborative US-Russian Project on Biological Weapons Elimination, which built on ten years of investment by the Corporation and the National Academy of Sciences and was led by grantee John Steinbruner and Corporation trustee Joshua Lederberg.

Another clear impact—though it may not have been visible in the assessment by staff members at the time—was the strengthening of enduring academic centers for the work on international and national security, especially by bringing together a range of scientific and social scientific perspectives to focus on the proliferation of nuclear weapons and other weapons of mass destruction. Along with the networks that encouraged participation in next-generation policy research, such as WIIS and PONARS, these investments reinforced the commitment to ensure that American scholars, linked with European and Russian scholars, could contribute "credible analyses" as conditions changed but the same policy dilemmas remained—such as in the next era when the prevailing global context shifted from the concern about state to nonstate actors in the proliferation of nuclear and other weapons. The impact of the work on preventing deadly conflict, on the other hand, remained elusive given the spread of terrorism and continuing intractable conflicts in Central Africa and the Middle East.

External independent analysts John Tirman and Sada Akasatova have both commented on the fact that the Corporation and other foundations did not focus on the role of civil society organizations in promoting peace-building.[121] In light of the aims and objectives of the Corporation's program, this was not a central theme of its work. The focus was on prevention of harm, not peace building per se. With the increased focus on Track II negotiations, global engagement, and other on-the-ground components of constructive cooperative security and preventing deadly conflict, peace and peace-building became a more central concern in the next era.

STRENGTHENING HUMAN RESOURCES
IN DEVELOPING COUNTRIES

DAVID HAMBURG SET THE CONTEXT and tone for the Corporation's work in the Commonwealth in his first presidential essay:

> Why are there still widely prevalent threats to survival when modern science and technology have made such powerful contributions to human welfare?... Can technically advanced countries do more to strengthen their ties with the developing world and work cooperatively with them toward the reduction of poverty, illiteracy, and ill health? Can a private foundation make a contribution toward these goals? Certainly the Rockefeller and Ford foundations have done so.... So, too, Carnegie Corporation.... Foundations can help to alert, inform, and stimulate others throughout the United States and elsewhere to give higher priority to developing-country needs. For the Corporation, this means drawing upon a strong tradition of emphasis on human resources.[122]

With his commitment to strengthening human resources in developing countries, Hamburg highlighted the main thrusts:

> The program on strengthening human resources in developing countries will ... emphasize healthy maternal and child development, broadly defined to include basic education, education for nutrition and health, and family planning ... the seamless web of factors that bear heavily on human resource capability and economic development. The program will be organized into two complementary parts. The largest effort will be conducted through U.S.-based institutions. It will emphasize international collaboration in applying science and technology to human resource development, and especially projects that heighten American understanding of human resource issues. The other part of the program will involve on-site activities that make a special contribution in several countries or regions to build knowledge based on firsthand experience and to foster long-term collaborative efforts.[123]

He added that the program would give geographic priority to "sub-Saharan Africa and the Caribbean. Grants in the United States will also focus on Mexico, the only developing country that shares a border with the U.S. All these regions are intrinsically important, have special meaning for substantial minorities in our nation, and have high significance for U.S. international relations."[124] Harking back to the comments of Henry Pritchett in the early 1920s on grant-making and perpetuity, Hamburg added, "The time span for development must be seen without wishful thinking. Significant progress will have to be measured not in years but in decades, and it will not be automatic ... in each country or region very good relations will be needed to foster the articulation of technical competence with distinctive cultural traditions. Sensitivity to local conditions and authentic spirit of collaboration are essential for success in such enterprises."[125]

Over the course of Hamburg's presidency, the name of the program remained the same, Strengthening Human Resources in Developing Countries (HRDC); the subprogram names and themes, however, changed regularly, reflecting the changing international context, as happened with the US-based international program. Two distinctive phases defined the program. The first phase, from 1983 to mid-1986, covered the transition from the Pifer era to the Hamburg one, with program leadership by David Hood, then Jill Sheffield. The next phase, from mid-1986 to mid-1997, was the main phase of the program: the building blocks were set in place for the different thematic emphases, which were then refined, consolidated, and changed over the next eleven years.[126] The following sections describe these two phases, the staff involved, the themes, the approaches, and highlights of selected grants and outcomes.

CONTINUATION AND EXPLORATION: 1983–1986

THE CORPORATION INITIALLY MAINTAINED THE WORK of the international program from the earlier era—that is, from 1976 onward—on South Africa (the public interest bar and the Second Carnegie Inquiry); women and development, now primarily with a health focus; and international communication, especially coverage of development and anti-apartheid issues in the United States.[127]

The early South Africa activities provide insight into Hamburg and his leadership of the Corporation. Originally skeptical about working in such a morally egregious situation, he solidified his commitment to maintaining activities in South Africa, particularly as follow-up to the important work of the Second Carnegie Inquiry into Poverty and Development in Southern Africa, after a crucial meeting took place. In April 1984, the inquiry investigators held a meeting at the University of Cape Town in Cape Town, South Africa, with a team of seven from Carnegie Corporation participating.[128] As described by Francis Wilson and Mamphela Ramphele in their preface to the major book resulting from the Inquiry, *Uprooting Poverty: The South African Challenge*, the meeting followed two years of intensive research: "Some 450 people participated. Although it was by no means the main object of the Inquiry, the conference itself was a happening of some significance. Those who came, all in their individual capacities, had thought deeply about poverty and represented a wide spectrum of all South African society.… There was a sense in which it was itself, for six brief but hectic days, a small model of what South Africa could be."[129]

In a November 1984 memo to the board, Hamburg also underlined the significance of the conference and his change of perspective on South Africa, reflecting his exposure to material prepared by staff and grantees as well as his discussions with Archbishop Desmond Tutu, Reverend Allen Boesak, and industrialist Harry Oppenheimer. He noted that although members of the board had been as ambivalent as he was about maintaining activities in South Africa, the "paradox of success" of the Inquiry argued against withdrawal. He added: "Many dedicated and courageous people— committed to democratic, non-violent change—are counting on our encouragement and moral support. I conclude with mixed feelings that we cannot let them down. The symbolism of a Carnegie (Corporation) pullout would be all wrong." He also envisioned the global impact of the situation in South Africa, with its "worldwide symbolism of prejudice and ethnocentrism, and emotionally-charged efforts at democratic reform and conflict resolution.… It is just barely possible that the world will learn a lot from South Africa in the next few decades about ways of dealing with the most intense human predicaments."[130]

Hamburg suggested that the work in South Africa focus on support of

black-led programs and that activities in South Africa "be placed in the context of the larger program involving other countries in Africa."[131] For extending the work elsewhere in Africa, he informed the board that staff members
were already attempting to identify grants in the field of maternal and child
health.[132] For the work in Africa, he identified a major need to engage with
a wide range of media to inform both the American public and American
policymakers.[133]

The grants in South Africa reinforced the work of organizations that
had also been prominent in earlier years, the US–South Africa Leadership
Exchange Program, the Centre for Applied Legal Studies at the University
of the Witwatersrand, and the inquiry at the University of Cape Town. New
organizations were also added to the portfolio, responding to Hamburg's
desire to identify and fund black-led organizations, such as the Black
Lawyers Association's Legal Education Center and the Center for Adult
and Continuing Education at the University of the Western Cape.[134]

Refocusing the area of women and development, the Corporation began
to make grants focusing on maternal and child health care, nutrition,
education, family planning, and the status of women.[135] The Women and
Development Unit at the University of the West Indies received continued
support, and a new grantee, the University of Minnesota, was funded to
assist NGOs as they prepared to participate in the final conference of the
UN Women's Decade, held in Nairobi in 1985.[136]

As part of the outreach to US policymakers on foreign assistance, the
program supported two sets of outreach activities, one set related to Latin
and Central America and the Caribbean, and the other related to Africa.
A grant to the Aspen Institute hosted the Inter-American Dialogue, a new
program responding to the crisis in Central America.[137] The Community
Television Foundation of South Florida received a modest planning grant
of around $13,000 to develop a telecourse and associated educational mate-
rials on Latin America and the Caribbean in conjunction with Florida
International University and Columbia University.[138] A range of more
modest grants focused on communication and outreach, including the
Africa News Service, which produced a newsletter on African affairs.[139]

When Dr. Adetokunbo O. Lucas joined as the first chair of the
Strengthening Human Resources in Developing Countries Program in July
1986, his mandate was to develop strategies for the program that would

address the concerns articulated by Hamburg and the trustees as well as through these early grants.[140] Although he oversaw all elements of the program, he assumed specific responsibility for sharpening the focus of the women and development theme.[141]

Developments in the Commonwealth Nations of Africa and the Caribbean: 1986–1997

The external context for the program in 1986 differed only slightly from that at the end of the 1970s. Throughout Africa, economic pressures from the structural adjustment programs had created a policy environment that was increasingly disabling for positive social change; over the period 1980 to 1987, GDP growth rates averaged 0.4 percent per annum and "per-capita income declined by about 2.6 percent per annum."[142] The weakness of institutions (academic, nongovernmental, and national), magnified by the pre-Internet isolation of African scholars and scientists and their limited access to policymakers, also shaped programmatic approaches to enhancing individual capacities. The intent was to bolster African expertise by developing a basis for shared problem-solving on issues of common concern within and across countries.

Approaching the end of the 1980s, the deplorable conditions in South Africa increasingly came in for international scorn and sanctions, reinforced by internal discontent. Significant change still seemed far off. Yet, in 1989, as the walls came tumbling down in Europe, political change in South Africa made the impossible possible. The harsh rule of P. W. Botha gave way to that of F. W. de Klerk, a segregationist former minister of education. Electrifying the country and the world, "in his first speech after assuming the party leadership, [de Klerk] called for a nonracist South Africa and for negotiations about the country's future." Soon "he lifted the ban on the ANC [African National Congress] and released Nelson Mandela [from prison]. He brought apartheid to an end and opened the way for the drafting of a new constitution for the country based on the principle of one person, one vote."[143] By early 1990, another part of the world, this one of long-standing engagement with the Corporation, tore down what had seemed to be a permanent edifice of oppression.

The changes in South Africa, combined with the fall of the Berlin Wall and Gorbachev's policies leading to the end of the Cold War, ignited dramatic political and economic change throughout the African continent, leading to democratic transitions and increasingly more positive economic conditions. At the same time, the more negative reverberations from the end of the Cold War lifted the lid to reveal deeper internal tensions in some African countries—internal fault lines that countered the hope and optimism.[144] The HRDC program, much like its counterpart in the international program at the Corporation, responded to these crosscurrents; with support from Corporation leadership and the trustees, by the mid-1990s it had revised its subprograms accordingly.

Putting the Building Blocks in Place

Hamburg and the trustees requested that Lucas and his team present the proposed new program strategy at the February 1988 board retreat in Washington, DC. The program paper stated, "The priorities of the program … are based on a view of development as a process of expanding indigenous human capacity to identify and solve social and economic problems and on the conviction that scientific research provides knowledge and technologies that can help societies achieve development that is sustainable—economically, environmentally, and socially."[145] The program maintained the geographic focus on the Commonwealth countries of Africa and the Caribbean and on Mexico and the US-Mexico border.[146] Grants would also be made in the United States for outreach to the American public and policymakers and as part of networks linked with the primary geographic foci. Approaches to grant-making, like those already informing the Corporation's work in other areas, would be interdisciplinary and based on partnerships, capacity-strengthening linkages, and outreach. One hallmark of this era was the emphasis on funding programs in partnership with other donors, both American and international, both because of limited resources compared to the scope of the problems being tackled and as a way to counter the possibility of grantees building dependency on a single funding agency.[147]

Staff recommended organizing the work around four major subprograms, building on the programmatic emphases from 1983 and even earlier:[148]

1. *South Africa:* Encouraging activities to enhance the legal, educational, and health status of black South Africans.

2. *Maternal and child health:* Reducing levels of maternal mortality and morbidity through conducting operational research; strengthening researcher-policymaker linkages nationally, regionally, and internationally; enhancing provider skills; and building NGO capacity. In 1994 this subprogram was renamed Women's Health and Development, extending the work on health to include improvement of women's legal status, access to education, and leadership opportunities.

3. *Science and technology for development:* Strengthening local, individual, and institutional capacity to conduct policy research and facilitating the linkages between policymakers, policy researchers, and scientists across Commonwealth African and Caribbean countries and between those countries and other developing and developed countries.

4. *Public understanding of development:* Communicating the lessons learned from development experience to American audiences, both public and policymaking, with a special focus on improving science and health reporting on and in sub-Saharan Africa, the Caribbean, and Mexico. By 1993 the subprogram was focusing on constituency-building for Africa, transitions to democracy in Africa, and new approaches to development assistance.

The goals, strategies, and expected outcomes for each of the subprogram areas (summarized here) provided the framework for continuity, consolidation, and change throughout this era.

South Africa

This was the one section of the program that in its early years could not present clear goals, objectives, and expected outcomes beyond "the aim is to study and test both the limits of what is possible now and ways that certain sectors of society can be organized in a majority-ruled South Africa of the future."[149] The Corporation continued supporting the legal training and litigation efforts of, inter alia, the Centre for Applied Legal Studies at the University of the Witwatersrand and the national network of Legal

Resources Centres. With increased funding for their efforts and other work both within and outside of South Africa, these grantees not only remained vibrant but would be crucial in shepherding South African society into its new future.[150]

The major effort in 1988 and 1989—before the exhilarating opportunity to redesign the program following the release of Nelson Mandela as South Africa moved toward a democratic, open, post-apartheid society—was the dissemination of the work of the Second Carnegie Inquiry.[151] The Inquiry produced over three hundred papers and monographs. The first major publication, *South Africa: The Cordoned Heart*, prepared by South African photographer Omar Badsha and Francis Wilson along with the Center for Documentary Photography at Duke University, illustrated the extent of the poverty in apartheid South Africa, along with reserved optimism for progress.[152] The final publication, *Uprooting Poverty: The South African Challenge*, co-authored by Francis Wilson and Mamphela Ramphele, further revealed the state of poverty in South Africa and recommended solutions to manage it. The Inquiry also resulted in a special report on children that was published in 1987 by UNICEF as *Children on the Front Line*.[153] From a policy perspective, the Inquiry's findings had an impact at the highest level, as Wilson reported: "The government White Paper on Reconstruction and Development, published in November 1994, proclaimed that, 'At the heart of the Government of National Unity is a commitment to effectively address the problems of poverty and the gross inequality evident in all aspects of South African society.'"[154]

The Inquiry highlighted, for example, the field of community health in South Africa for productive investment. The Kaiser Family Foundation was supporting a network of progressive community health doctors, outside of the official health care system, to determine the gaps in the delivery of health services to underserved South Africans and "to draw together a coherent framework for future health policies."[155] The Corporation supported the National Progressive Primary Health Care Network and other nongovernmental health institutions, along with demonstration projects.[156]

Before the ending of apartheid, the Corporation had contributed to efforts to inform American policymakers about the conditions in South Africa by supporting the Aspen Institute Congressional Program in 1988 in creating the Southern African Policy Forum. The Forum provided one of the rare settings where blacks and whites in South Africa could meet to discuss the range of issues confronting them.[157]

Program staff members recognized that with the February 2, 1990, dismantling of apartheid policies and the February 11, 1990, release from Robben Island prison of Nelson Mandela, "opportunities for grantmaking in South Africa changed radically."[158] They determined that the program needed to maintain its flexibility and focus on areas where the Corporation had a comparative advantage. Following a series of site visits to South Africa, Richardson determined that the Corporation could contribute to improving the status of women and girls through a focus not only on health but also on legal rights and leadership. As highlighted by Francis Wilson, "Gender and unemployment are the two big issues of the 1990s in South Africa. If Carnegie [Corporation] decides to focus on women, it can make a tremendous difference."[159]

The board in 1992 approved the two major objectives for the new thrust in South Africa: "to improve the health and legal status of women ... and to increase women's participation in civil society."[160] The Corporation funded policy research, education, and monitoring of women's rights; supported intermediary organizations to improve women's ability to participate in society, including their leadership development; and backed selected women's organizations. Partnership with the Ford Foundation, and on occasion the W. K. Kellogg Foundation, the Charles Stewart Mott Foundation, and the Rockefeller Brothers Fund, created a community of scholars, practitioners, and organizations dedicated to women's issues in South Africa and a critical mass of women leaders who became effective advocates for women's issues. The first grants in 1992 went to the University of the Western Cape to establish the first Resource Center on Gender and the Law and the University of the Witwatersrand for the Centre for Applied Legal Studies, a longtime grantee, to establish a program to research gender issues.[161]

The Women's National Coalition, the Women's Development Foundation, and other women's networking projects, as well as the support for the Women's Charter, illuminated the issues of women's rights as part of the elections.[162] Frene Ginwala became the speaker. From all of these efforts, the South African constitution incorporated the Women's Charter, the first constitution anywhere in the world to include such explicit recognition of women's rights.[163]

This cluster of grants, focused on women's legal rights and status, women's health and development, and women's leadership, particularly in the not-for-profit community, had ramifications for the Corporation beyond South Africa. These grants helped to shape a new theme for the Corporation, one that melded the work elsewhere in Africa and the Caribbean on maternal and child health with the work in South Africa to revive and redesign the earlier focus on women's health and development.

Maternal and Child Health

The excessive death and disability experienced by pregnant women in the developing world demonstrated the largest public health problem separating developed and developing countries.[164] Yet the conclusion reached at the Safe Motherhood Conference, held in Nairobi, Kenya, in February 1987 and co-sponsored by the Corporation, was that, despite the scope of the problem, existing knowledge, procedures, and tools made most maternal deaths preventable.[165] The challenge was to ensure that women and health services had access to this information and used it so that life-saving care could become a reality. Given the persistence of the problem, staff members made it clear that grants alone would not achieve "measurable change in rates of maternal mortality and morbidity in large populations."[166] Nonetheless, a carefully defined focus that supported the testing and implementation of both existing and new interventions at the grassroots level and strengthened training for specialists and community workers could make strides toward that goal. The Corporation became a lead donor at the global level, the first major foundation to undertake work specifically focused on reducing maternal mortality.

Expected outcomes for the four major program components—research, training, technology, and women's status—were: increased institutional and individual capacity for operational research in this area, the accumulation of new knowledge on the multiple dimensions of the health of pregnant women, and demonstrations of life-saving interventions. All these outcomes would provide the basis for national and international policy change to reduce the levels of maternal mortality and morbidity.[167]

Operational research was undertaken by the Prevention of Maternal

Mortality Network, with teams working in Nigeria, Sierra Leone, and Ghana.[168] Over nearly ten years of support, the network produced a strategic program design for implementation by services and agencies, along with an evaluation framework.[169] Their findings on the importance of emergency obstetric care and the reduction of delay in seeking treatment for women at the time of delivery became the main thrust for the Joint Program for Reduction of Maternal Mortality of the UN Development Program, WHO, the UN Fund for Population Activities, and UNICEF. The new indicator, the need for emergency obstetric care, was added to the short list of international indicators of safe motherhood by the WHO Technical Working Group.[170] As the Network support from the Corporation was drawing to a close, the Bill and Melinda Gates Foundation was getting under way and provided a grant of $50 million over five years for the Network to maintain its program and expand its work across the continent. This support enabled the Network to move the locus of activities from Columbia University in the United States to Ghana and to establish the Regional Prevention of Maternal Mortality Network, with over eighty members.[171]

To address the complementary issue of the professional training of obstetricians and gynecologists, in 1988 the Corporation supported an innovative addition to the medical residency programs at the medical schools of the University of Ghana in Accra and the University of Science and Technology in Kumasi. This entailed developing a fourth-year community rotation so that residents could learn problem-solving skills in the local communities, instead of receiving more advanced training in either the United Kingdom or the United States, which usually contributed to extensive brain drain.[172] As of this writing, the program is still going strong and is considered a model by other West African medical schools and elsewhere in Ghana, even for training in other fields of medicine.[173]

Complementing the research and training grants, the Sierra Leone Home Economic Association and the US-based Program for Appropriate Technology in Health evaluated new and improved technologies specifically for improving the chances of a healthy delivery for women at the tertiary or specialist hospital and at the community level. A partnership between the American Red Cross and the government of Uganda piloted a new approach to ensuring safe blood supplies at the time of delivery, which was then applied countrywide.[174] Starting in 1987, studies were conducted through the World Health Organization by local teams in Zimbabwe, Ghana, Nigeria, and Zambia, coordinated by Dr. Aleya El Bindari Hammad, to examine the impact on women's health of functional literacy programs and to determine how best to increase this impact.[175]

As the work was getting under way in Africa, the Corporation also supported a program of research and action on maternal and child health, linking universities and researchers across the US-Mexico border. This effort led to major cross-border university collaboration and the identification of important issues for policy consideration, such as women's health in the maquiladoras.[176]

Drawing on the status of women activities in South Africa and elsewhere in Africa, the program officer Yolonda Richardson prepared the request to change the subprogram name to Women's Health and Development; the board approved it in 1994. The program then concentrated on supporting projects and networks that promoted women's involvement in health and development policymaking and focused on conducting research and advocacy with respect to education and legal issues. The ongoing work on the prevention of maternal mortality was also incorporated into this subprogram.

In addition to the women's legal and health activities supported by the Corporation in South Africa at the University of the Witwatersrand, another longtime partner, the University of Cape Town, provided opportunities for women's leadership in education and other areas. In 1991 the university's vice chancellor, the anti-apartheid activist Stuart Saunders, appointed Corporation grantee Mamphela Ramphele deputy vice chancellor, directly in line to succeed him.[177] In 1996 Ramphele became the first black woman university vice chancellor in South Africa. There, among many other innovations, she would launch the African Gender Institute, the first on the continent, with the support of the Ford Foundation, the government of Norway, and the Corporation.[178]

In extending the work from South Africa, in 1994 the Corporation supported the Women's Action Group in Zimbabwe to enhance its advocacy work on women's health and legal status. In 1996 Bisi Adeleye-Fayemi, the director of the London-based group Akina Mama wa Afrika, and her team received support to plan an African women's leadership institute in Uganda.[179] Both groups were still playing significant roles as of 2012.

With its experience in South Africa in work to enhance the legal status of women, the Corporation became a major supporter of a continent-wide network for training and advocacy on women's rights, Women in Law and Development in Africa (WiLDAF), based in Zimbabwe.[180] A comparable pan-African network, the Forum of African Women Educationalists, initiated by senior African women ministers of education and university vice chancellors, developed and implemented projects to improve girls' access to education; it also established national chapters. As of this writing, the Forum of African Women Educationalists remained the main network promoting women's education in Africa.[181]

In 1995 the Fourth World Conference on Women in Beijing, China, offered an opportunity for the Corporation to build on its earlier support for the women's conferences in Copenhagen and Nairobi. A Corporation grantee, the African Women's Development and Communication Network (FEMNET), was selected by the African NGOs to serve as a regional nongovernmental coordinator for African involvement. Corporation support enabled many of the African grantees to participate; additional support assisted the Conference secretariat.[182] One of the most important developments resulting from the conference was the endorsement of the UN Platform of Action, with regular monitoring by the Commission on the Status of Women. Nearly twenty years later, these issues remain at the forefront of the global agenda.[183]

SCIENCE AND TECHNOLOGY FOR DEVELOPMENT

THE PREMISES UNDERLYING THIS SUBPROGRAM recognized the value of a vibrant scientific research community for increasing economic productivity and the critical role of national policies in sustaining such research as well as encouraging the use of the results.[184] Although they paid much lip service to the importance of science and technology, the governments of African countries never invested more than 1 percent of GNP in science and technology over the period 1973 to 1986, and indeed, in 1990 average investment languished at 0.25 percent. In 2011 it was 0.03 percent.[185] Complementing the efforts of other donors that were promoting scientific or technological research and training projects, the Corporation focused on investments that contributed to building and sustaining a scientific community, including linkages between scholars and policymakers so that the latter might use the knowledge generated by scholars and researchers to enact more supportive policies.[186] Another factor limiting the promotion and conduct of sound science and technology policy research was the isolation, in that pre-Internet period, of African researchers, who did not have easy access to each other or to up-to-date publications in their fields.

Four expected outcomes, identified by Corporation staff in consultation with key in-country and donor partners—primarily in and across sub-Saharan African countries but also, to a more limited extent, in the Caribbean and Mexico—comprised the interrelated subprogram priorities:[187]

1. Creating and/or strengthening the interdisciplinary policy research capacity of individuals to improve science and technology policymaking, with a focus on applied research in science and technology, health (including social sciences and health), and trade policy
2. Developing plans for science and technology information systems, focusing on health information systems, at the regional, national, and institutional levels
3. Fostering institutional arrangements for science and technology policymaking and assessing mechanisms for setting research priorities in these areas
4. Building linkages locally, nationally, regionally, and internationally across different levels of involvement in science and technology, policy research, and policymaking

Science and Technology Policy Research

Grants related to strengthening policy research capacity supported networks working on health policy, science and technology policy assessment, and trade policy. As in other parts of the Strengthening Human Resources in Developing Countries Program, the networks engaged individuals, not institutions, as members or participants; on occasion, policymakers also participated, enhancing the likelihood that research findings would influence policy decisions.[188] In the fields of health policy and science and technology policy research, the activities paralleled institutional developments that either sustained or built on the findings of the policy research networks. To reinforce the connectivity across the interrelated approaches in the field of health policy and science and technology policy—namely, supporting research networks, supporting policy dialogues, strengthening institutional capacity, and promoting global connections—all four elements are discussed together here.

Health Policy Research, Institutional Strengthening, and Outreach

Over the period 1986 to 1997, the Corporation invested in the support of the interdisciplinary international health policy research network, a mid-career training program, and an international commission that resulted in the establishment of a global institution. Given the limited scale of international health policy research in the late 1980s, there was considerable overlap in the key grantee individuals and institutions. In 1986 the Corporation joined with Pew Charitable Trusts, the World Bank, and the World Health Organization in support of the International Health Policy Program (IHPP), an initiative to bring together policymakers and researchers from Asian and African countries to conduct joint research projects. With researchers and policymakers working as a team to develop and implement projects, the expectation was that the findings not only would address high-priority health care needs but would also be used to inform policies and programs on a range of issues associated with the design, delivery, and assessment of health care services.[189] In addition to the viable policy recommendations that emerged, the IHPP signaled the value of local researchers contributing to local policies and problem-solving; this program was the first to support local health policy researchers based in local institutions to conduct this kind of work (instead of the usual practice of bringing in research consultants from the United Kingdom and the United States to advise on national policies).[190] Over time the IHPP Secretariat leveraged the foundation support to obtain $1 million from the World Bank that significantly strengthened the activities of its last few years.

The Corporation provided funding for another health policy research initiative, the Taro Takemi Fellowship Program in International Health, based at the Harvard University School of Public Health, to enhance the interdisciplinary research and policy skills of midlevel professionals, primarily from developing countries. The program was designed to enable students to draw on all academic resources at the university. Inspired by Dr. Takemi, an internationally recognized medical and scientific leader, the program was funded primarily by a variety of donors from Japan, with fellowship support also forthcoming from the Merck Corporation.[191]

To promote increased investment in health research in developing countries, reinforcing the basic IHPP premise about linking researchers and policymakers, along with promoting greater external donor commitments, the Corporation joined the UN Development Program (UNDP), the Edna McConnell Clark Foundation, the International Development Research Centre, and a handful of other agencies and foundations in support of the international Independent Commission on Health Research.[192] The Commission was based at the Harvard University School of Public Health under the leadership of David Bell (formerly at the Ford Foundation and before that an administrator at USAID) and Lincoln Chen (formerly the Ford Foundation representative in India and for many years closely associated with UNICEF), with John Evans chairing this initiative. Adetokunbo O. Lucas was a member of the commission and played a significant role in promoting the idea of essential national health, that is, "research on country-specific problems ... based on the evolution of research capacity in developing countries," as well as research on global health problems whose solution required international partnerships.[193] The Commission's recommendations on applied research in developing countries over the past two decades have shaped the work of the Council on Health Research for Development.[194]

As part of the focus on interdisciplinary health policy research, both research and institution-strengthening activities linking the health and social sciences were funded for a number of years by the Corporation, both separately and in collaboration with the continuing partnership of the Rockefeller Foundation, the Ford Foundation, and the International Development Research Centre (IDRC). An inter-institutional, interdisciplinary program joining Harvard University with the University of Dar es Salaam in Tanzania and the University of Nairobi in Kenya aimed to build a critical mass of interdisciplinary expertise through a collaborative mid-career program for physicians and social scientists.[195] The program involved not only taking courses at Harvard University but also conducting field-work in Kenya and Tanzania.[196]

The Harvard–Dar-es-Salaam–Nairobi Universities' collaborative program opened a new field of activity for the Corporation. Over the year 1989 to 1990, with encouragement from David Hamburg, the interdisciplinary field of health and human behavior was incorporated as a special theme in the program. The launch in 1992 of the International Forum on Health and Social Sciences made the program a global one, drawing together associated regional networks and task forces to share ideas, experiences, and findings across disciplines and countries.[197] Colleagues from the International Health Policy Program network and Harvard University promoted the establishment of the African regional network SOMA-Net (Social Sciences and Medicine in Africa Network).[198]

Three outreach activities contributed to building linkages between the United States and developing countries in the area of health research and policy. A distinguished visitors program brought health experts from African Commonwealth countries to the United States, based at Johns Hopkins University, to conduct research, writing, and outreach on international health to the general public and other academics.[199] A small cluster of grants turned the tables on development assistance efforts and examined how findings from health-promoting research and actions in developing countries might contribute to improvements in health programs in the United States through the National Council for International Health and the Board on International Health of the Institute of Medicine.[200] Specifically, through the Medical and Health Research Association, under the leadership of Commissioner Dr. Margaret A. Hamburg (David Hamburg's daughter), New York City applied approaches from developing countries to refine strategies for immunization, tuberculosis control, and maternal and child health care.[201]

Science and Technology Policy:
Enhancing Research, Institutional Capacity, and Linkages

Two major activities addressed the goal of strengthening capacity in Africa for science and technology policy research and building linkages between policy researchers and policymakers. The main research initiative, the African Technology Policy Studies Network (ATPSN), based in Nairobi, Kenya, is still active in the twenty-first century; it promotes research, organizes meetings to review and recommend support of the research proposals, brings the researchers together to debate their findings, and assists with publishing the findings.[202] The initiative was originally funded by the IDRC; the Corporation joined in with support for the coordinating institutions and individual researchers from 1989 to 2000.[203] Also in partnership with the IDRC, the program responded to a promising opportunity in the field of economic planning to enhance African participation in the significant negotiations on the General Agreement on Trade in Services (GATS). Together, the IDRC and the Corporation funded, from 1992 to 1999, the Coordinated African Program of Assistance on Services (CAPAS), an eighteen-country network of economists and policymakers coordinated by UN offices in Geneva and New York.[204] As trade negotiations became subsumed under the World Trade Organization, new challenges for African country participation emerged; the CAPAS had closed by 2000.[205]

Akin Adubifa, the network coordinator for West Africa, joined Carnegie Corporation as program officer for science and technology for development in January 1994. Adubifa worked with the new executive secretary, K. Y. Amoako of the UN Economic Commission for Africa (UNECA), and ATPSN colleagues to host over several years pan-African roundtables on ways to enhance the role of science and technology in economic policymaking.[206] At the country level, with the assistance of the UN African Institute for Economic Development and Planning, the Corporation promoted science policy roundtables in Ghana, Nigeria, Tanzania, and Zimbabwe, bringing together local scientists and policymakers.[207]

A major institutional capacity strengthening activity of the Corporation responded to the African Academy of Sciences initiative proposed in 1987–1988 by Thomas R. Odhiambo, the senior biological scientist in Africa at the time.[208] Odhiambo was concerned about the limited support for science and technology in Africa, the low uptake of research results, and the need for greater visibility of African scientists in their own countries, regionally and internationally. With colleagues at the Third World Academy of Sciences, he planned and then established the African Academy of Sciences. Odhiambo partnered with the Rockefeller Foundation, the MacArthur Foundation, and the Corporation for more than ten years in support of a variety of Academy activities to build support for science in African societies, and with African leaders as well as a range of donors.[209] A noteworthy accomplishment of the Academy is the peer-reviewed publication *Discovery and Innovation*, which it is still publishing and which continues to bring wide recognition to the work of the African scientific community.[210]

Three additional institution-focused activities linked the women's health and development subprogram with the program for science and technology development. First, the Gender Working Group of the UN Commission on Science and Technology for Development established, following the 1995 Beijing Conference, the Gender Advisory Board, which still advises the United Nations.[211] Second, the Third World Organization of Women in Science (TWOWS), an offshoot of the Working Group, still actively promotes women in science throughout the developing world.[212] Third, the Association of Women for Research and Development, based in Dakar, Senegal, works to strengthen its institutional capacities to bring together African women scholars across disciplines and countries and is also still active today.[213]

With the encouragement of Hamburg and the board, Corporation staff members promoted three initiatives specifically aimed at bringing the developments in science and technology in Africa to the attention of the American public and policymakers: the American Association for the Advancement of Science "Science in Africa" meeting series,[214] the Connecting Science-Rich, Science-Poor States Program of the New York Academy of Sciences (NYAS),[215] and the World Bank's "Knowledge and Development" activities.[216] The first two resulted in several publications, circulated through the membership of both scientific organizations. The World Bank support for the third initiative led to an ongoing partnership grants program, InfoDev, focused on promoting information-based innovations and partnerships throughout the developing world.

Science and Technology Information Systems

Under the Science and Technology for Development Program, a continuing commitment aimed to reduce the isolation of African scientists and
researchers through improved access to modern, up-to-date communications systems. A multipronged set of activities addressed the range of issues
in building capacity and enhancing access. As a first effort to address the
pressing concern about access to up-to-date scientific information, in 1987
the American Association for the Advancement of Science developed, with
Corporation support, an extensive journal distribution program.[217] At its
peak, the program provided over three thousand subscriptions to two hundred journal titles in over thirty-eight African countries; the program also
held workshops on CD-ROM technologies and the advanced use of electronic networking and examined prospects for the future of libraries.

Over the period 1987 to 1989, three modestly funded grants—that is, at
the level of $25,000 or less—initiated an entirely new and unanticipated
set of activities in science and technology information systems, beyond
the hard-copy journal subscriptions in the areas of scientific information
management systems in Kenya, CD-ROM technology in Zambia, and
health information systems in Zambia.[218] These three grants, along with the
work of the American Association for the Advancement of Science, led the
Corporation to support a wide range of initiatives across universities and
institutes, both nationwide and Africa-wide.[219]

Of the two continent-wide initiatives, one resulted in instructive lessons
for the Corporation about the timing of network-building in the life cycle of
grants, and the other led to a series of activities that remain ongoing as of this
writing. In 1992 the Corporation supported the African Regional Centre for
Technology and the National Academy of Sciences Board on Science and
Technology for International Development (BOSTID) to work with a wide
range of information systems grantees to develop an agenda for a network
or partnership.[220] The grantees, who were at varying stages of development
and were focused on distinctive elements, could identify no compelling
reason for establishing a network, and the Corporation did not pursue this
idea. More positively, a major challenge voiced by the grantees, the difficulty
of sustaining information systems without supportive national policies, led

to extensive support for the UN Economic Commission for Africa to create a receptive policy environment.

Starting in 1994, the Corporation supported UNECA's Pan-African Development Information System (PADIS), whose mission was to harmonize and standardize information systems and databases across the continent. To enlarge the constituency for its efforts and ensure continuity, PADIS launched the African Information Society Initiative in May 1996, with the mandate to ensure that information policies remain central components in national social and economic development. The Initiative, endorsed by telecommunications ministers and heads of state, still forms an integral part of UNECA's work in this area.[221]

Initially, the only donor partner in support of these efforts was the International Development Research Centre. Over time the Ford Foundation, the Health Foundation, the Rockefeller Foundation, and other bilateral and international organizations became more engaged in this work. One of the unexpected outcomes from the grants on this theme has been the creation of receptive environments at universities for the information systems initiatives undertaken in the Corporation's next era.

Science and Technology for Development in the Caribbean and Mexico

Outside of the work in Commonwealth Africa, the Corporation adopted a modified strategy of promoting networks and strengthening institutions in the Caribbean and Mexico.[222]

THE CARIBBEAN

Responding to Caribbean Cooperation in Health, a new initiative of the Pan American Health Organization (PAHO), and after consultations with health, education, and scientific leaders from the region, the Corporation supported three distinct activities in this period. In 1989 its support to the University of the West Indies fostered a program on intra-Caribbean technical cooperation for maternal and child health, co-sponsored by Pew Charitable Trusts, that included networking across Caribbean institutions, professional exchanges, workshops and courses, and a special experiment in distance teaching.[223]

Two Caribbean-wide science networking institutions also received support.[224] Linked to the Corporation's strategic interests in giving visibility to the work of local scientists (including social scientists), the Corporation contributed to the May 1988 launch of the Caribbean Academy of Sciences, still active today with over two hundred members.[225] A series of grants from 1988 to 1994 enabled leaders of the Commonwealth Caribbean Medical Research Council to prepare a strategic plan and build strong ties within and outside the region.[226] The Council continues its regional networking and research-promoting activities.[227]

With limited resources, it was not feasible to advance the same level of activity in this region as in the African countries. Despite the Corporation's engagement with the Caribbean since the 1930s, over the fiscal year 1992 to 1993 the board asked the program staff to bring that part of the program to a close. The last grant directly to the region was approved in 1994 for the Commonwealth Caribbean Medical Research Council.

MEXICO

The focus on Mexico extended beyond the US-Mexico border.[228] The Fundación Mexicana para la Salud, or the Mexican Health Foundation, had been launched in 1985 as a grant-making foundation endowed by the Mexican business community. Over a ten-year period, following the charter review that it inspired, and with Corporation backing, the Foundation planned, developed, and implemented its grant-making and internal research programs; organized local and international meetings; and disseminated its work through an active publications program, including English-language publications, across the United States. The Mexican Health Foundation remains a thriving, well-funded philanthropic institution for promoting essential national health research.[229]

PUBLIC UNDERSTANDING OF DEVELOPMENT

CORPORATION LEADERSHIP ENDORSED the theme of educating Americans about developing countries and the value of development assistance, but recognizing the enormity of this task, they also urged staff to look for high-impact grants, to not aim at "kindergartners."[230] The staff agreed and proposed the following approaches: shaping education messages that reflected developing-country perspectives and the complexity of sustainable development; strengthening US-based development education coalitions and their linkages with nongovernmental development organizations in the Third World; and improving reporting about development in the United States, strengthening health and science reporting in Africa, and connecting American journalists with those from Africa and other regions of interest.[231]

Continuing core grantees for public outreach included television stations, such as WGBH, and, for policymaker outreach, the Aspen Institute Congressional Program, the African-American Institute, the Overseas Development Council, and the Council on Foreign Relations.[232] A mix of new and continuing grantees—for example, the Global Tomorrow Coalition, the International Development Conference, the Curry Foundation, the National Council of Returned Peace Corps Volunteers, the Consortium for International Cooperation in Higher Education, the Overseas Development Network, and Michigan State University—aimed to reach specific public and academic constituencies on broader issues of development assistance.[233] Specific work focused on the Caribbean included a symposium on US development assistance organized by the Development Group for Alternative Policies.[234] Another set of grantees, such as the TransAfrica Forum and the Africa Fund, specifically focused during the period before the ending of apartheid on disseminating accurate information about the conditions in South Africa.[235]

Building on the continuing concerns about the need for more effective outreach on Africa in the United States, the Corporation and its major partner in these efforts, the Ford Foundation, under the leadership of John Gerhart, director for Africa, began to think of a more focused effort to promote more effective constituency-building. In 1989 the Ford Foundation and the Corporation undertook an extensive review of the range of Public Understanding of Development (PUD) activities. Following the results of the 1989 evaluation, both foundations focused their efforts less on broad themes and more on policy outreach—especially the congressional staff seminars—and specific areas of interest.[236]

CONSTITUENCY-BUILDING FOR AFRICA AND THE
UNITED STATES: A SPECIAL FOCUS

THE RELEASE OF NELSON MANDELA in 1990 prompted several organizations involved in anti-apartheid activities to rethink the ways in which they
could use the knowledge they had gained to build a broader constituency
for Africa in the United States and move beyond the earlier compelling
conditions in South Africa. A particular effort aimed to enhance African
American understanding of developments on the continent, drawing on
the increasing interest of African Americans in deepening their connections
with Africans, across a wide range of African countries. These considerations reinforced the recommendations from the external evaluation and
led the Corporation, in continuing partnership with the Ford Foundation,
to narrow the public and policymaker outreach efforts to understanding
developments across the African continent.

To reach policymakers and their staffs, the Corporation and the Ford
Foundation supported building a base of scholarship targeted at informing
the American foreign policy community's understanding of developments
in African countries. Starting in 1995, the two foundations provided grants
to the Brookings Institution for the research and writing project of former
representative Howard Wolpe, who had served as chairman of the House
Foreign Affairs Committee's Subcommittee on Africa.[237] He also served as
one of the main organizers for the March 1997 American Assembly on Africa
that brought together scholars, current and former policymakers on Africa,
and foundation staff.[238] The Assembly resulted in several policy-oriented
volumes that were circulated widely.

To galvanize the public, Africare, the oldest and largest development
organization working throughout Africa led by African Americans, brought
together forty NGOs. All agreed to nurture the development of a national
network, the Constituency for Africa, with the aim of strengthening outreach on Africa to Americans, especially the African American community,
and building connections with American policymakers to deepen their
understanding about the continent and the opportunities there.[239] Following
the launch of the Constituency, the Ford Foundation and the Corporation
recognized the increasing overlap in aims, objectives, and activities of the

constituency-building efforts. Staff members agreed to co-sponsor a second review on the possible approaches for consolidation and coordination in order to enhance the likelihood of success for the new outreach efforts.[240]

One result of the review led to backing by the Ford Foundation and Carnegie Corporation of a brand-new approach developed by C. Payne Lucas of Africare, Melvin P. Foote of the Constituency for Africa, Imani Countess of the Africa Policy Information Center, Randall Robinson of TransAfrica Forum, and others to organize a National Summit on Africa, requiring extensive outreach across the United States and culminating in a summit-like meeting in Washington, DC. The Corporation made a grant to the Africa Policy Information Center to bring together all the different summit participants to review effective constituency-building approaches and come to agreement on joint actions for such advocacy.[241] Organized as a campaign, the institutions responsible for the summit organized large and small meetings around the country (in colleges, at business gatherings, and as regional convenings), conducted national polls, and prepared policy briefs and other publications. The centerpiece, the National Summit on Africa, took place February 16–20, 2000, in Washington, DC.[242] About eight thousand participants attended the summit, including a contingent from Africa. The UNECA executive secretary K. Y. Amoako spoke, emphasizing connections between African countries and the United States. President Clinton spoke with enthusiasm about the initiative. A follow-up activity, the Africa Society, has maintained the mission of the summit and remains dedicated to building an informed constituency for Africa in the United States.[243]

Despite all these efforts, with the prominent media attention given to diseases and poverty, persistent internal conflicts, and continuing political leadership concerns, achieving more positive and better-informed American public attitudes and official policies remains a challenge.[244]

TRANSITIONS TO DEMOCRACY IN AFRICA

THE ELECTION OF NELSON MANDELA as president of South Africa in 1994 ignited transformative thinking around the continent and, indeed, around the world. At the same time, countervailing forces destabilized other

African countries, as exemplified by the early 1990s experience in Sierra Leone. Corporation grantees were directly affected by local destructive internal conflicts, and institutions of governance were not strong enough to withstand them. The juxtaposition of transitions to democracy in Africa alongside increasing internal conflicts led Corporation staff members to request board approval for a new subprogram, to be called Transitions to Democracy in Africa, to identify and assess evidence-based approaches to maintaining peace, stability, and democracy, and, accordingly, reform development assistance in Africa.[245] The board agreed in October 1993 and approved the following themes: advancing knowledge on and strengthening individual and institutional capacity in conflict management and democratic transitions, and experimenting with and building constituencies on behalf of Africa in the United States.[246]

With the overarching goal of contributing to knowledge on the key elements for stable societies in Africa, the staff proposed two expected outcomes from this work that were notably ambitious given the three-year time frame: to promote new approaches to conflict management that could reinforce democratic transitions, and to recommend ways in which external actors could bolster African-led efforts to achieve peaceful and sustainable societies, including by identifying promising reforms to development assistance and actions to reinforce constituency-building in the United States.

Six major organizations and their projects shaped the core of the work under the first theme, linking conflict management and democratic transitions: the Africa Leadership Forum; the Southern Africa/Sub-Saharan African Security Project; the International Peace Academy; the Brookings Institution for the research and writings of Francis Deng; the Council for the Development of Social Science Research in Africa; and the African Association of Political Science.

The Africa Leadership Forum, established in 1988 by General Olusegun Obasanjo, the military head of Nigeria who peacefully stepped down in 1979 to return the country to civilian rule, aimed to bring together scholars and high-level government officials to discuss all the developments affecting the continent.[247] This initiative was put on hold in 1995 when Obasanjo was imprisoned by Nigeria's military government on unproven charges.[248] Obasanjo was finally released in 1998. The changing political situation in

Africa and in Nigeria enabled him to stand for election as president, and he won.[249]

The Southern Africa Security Project, initiated in 1992 and led by Ambassador Joseph Garba, a senior Nigerian diplomat, military leader, and policy scholar, was based at the Institute of International Education and then at the International Peace Academy. Initially, it focused on the reentry of military forces into the newly democratic South Africa.[250] Over the years 1992 to 1997, Garba and his colleagues brought together generals, military chiefs of staff, researchers in military studies and defense politics, and key political leaders in defense ministries in meetings throughout the continent, leading to recommendations on ways to restructure forces so that they could embark on productive civilian life not only in South Africa but in West Africa and the Great Lakes region of east-central Africa.[251] The volumes were widely circulated to the political leaders, military leaders, and scholars.[252]

Under the leadership of Olara Otunnu, former foreign minister of Uganda and former president of the UN Security Council, the International Peace Academy (IPA) in 1992 proposed an activity that would be complementary to those of Garba and Obasanjo and would focus on addressing mechanisms for conflict resolution and prevention at the highest political levels on the continent. The Academy, the lead NGO working on peacekeeping, had organized a meeting with African leaders in Tanzania to consider ways to resolve and prevent internal conflicts in Africa.[253] The meeting report urged the Organization of African Unity (OAU), the highest-level political body on the continent at that time, to establish "a mechanism for the prevention, management, and resolution of conflict in Africa."[254] With support from the Corporation and the governments of the Netherlands and Sweden, the Academy attempted to win acceptance for the mechanisms of the Organization for African Unity and to work with a wide range of civil society organizations—NGOs, universities, business organizations, and the media—to engage them in monitoring the Organization's willingness to undertake conflict management, for both interstate and intrastate conflicts.[255]

Francis Deng at the Brookings Institution and then Johns Hopkins University, drawing on his work funded by the Special Projects Committee on the origins of conflict in Africa and through his appointment by UN Secretary-General Boutros Boutros-Ghali as his special representative for internally displaced persons, embarked, with Corporation support, on a new project to illuminate his increasing concern about the responsibility and accountability of national sovereignty in the face of internal conflicts. Others shared that concern about the conditions that allowed internal conflicts to fester and explode out of control. Deng's work developed the conceptual framework for a new international paradigm, which was eventually called "responsibility to protect." For the first time there were norms for the international community to follow when internal conflicts arose and national sovereignty was no longer responsible and accountable.[256]

With the aim of promoting serious scholarship on the subject of democratic transitions and disseminating the results widely, not only to scholars but to policymakers, the Corporation extended support to two institutions that represented broad networks of scholars.

The Council for the Development of Social Science Research in Africa, headquartered in Dakar, Senegal, was the premier networking and scholarship institution for the social sciences in the region. It prepared a synthesis of existing knowledge on democratization and governance, political and economic reforms, and popular participation in Africa, under the direction of Thandika Mkandawire, the executive director and a political economist, and Mamadou Diouf, head of the Council's Research, Information, and Documentation Department and an African historian.[257] The African Association of Political Science, headquartered in Harare, Zimbabwe, the only pan-African institution solely for political science researchers, was examining the range of political issues confronting the continent. Its aim was to strengthen itself as an institution and build national chapters where researchers would present their work in forums and engage in policy dialogues with the public and policymakers.[258]

With donor fatigue, that is, the continual challenge to maintain external development assistance flows to African countries, an issue seen to be both a cause and result of the increase in internal conflict, staff members and their African colleagues explored together ways to improve the effectiveness of development and technical assistance.[259] One promising approach was to design and test more collaborative development assistance models and identify local sources of support rather than rely on external aid.[260] Consequently, the second theme in this subprogram, new forms of development assistance, was approached with a three-pronged strategy: backing the development of a brand-new model for national-level development strategies; supporting analytical case studies on the development assistance experience in Africa; and assisting with the creation of new, local grant-making institutions in developing countries.

The Task Force on Development Organizations chaired by President Jimmy Carter under the auspices of the Carnegie Commission on Science and Technology for Government led to a radical new approach to development assistance: the Global Development Initiative, developed, piloted, and enacted in Guyana and then adapted in Mali, Mozambique, and Albania, promoted the building of country capacity for designing and implementing national development strategies.[261] From 1993 to 1997, the Corporation contributed to the team's development of the plan and organization of debates about the plan, from the local village level to the ministerial level. Released in January 1997, the Guyana National Development Strategy has been national policy since 2000.[262]

With the ongoing general critiques of development aid effectiveness in the 1980s and 1990s, the Overseas Development Council conducted in-depth case studies in eight countries in sub-Saharan Africa, with teams comprising local researchers, representatives of aid agencies, and council staff.[263] One of the most salient lessons from all of the studies was closely related to the findings of the Carter Center efforts; as reported in congressional hearings by the Overseas Development Council team leader, Nicholas van de Walle, "Aid recipients must clearly articulate their own priorities for assistance, assume the primary role in aid management, and integrate all aid flows into a national budgetary planning process. The study further recommends that the African press sponsor public debates about aid in order to promote greater accountability."[264]

In explicit recognition of the limitations of overseas development assistance and even the role of external foundations, the Corporation considered seriously the idea, already demonstrated in Mexico by the Fundación Mexicana para la Salud, that local resources could be tapped for local initiatives in African countries. In 1992 Synergos, a nongovernmental organization dedicated to promoting poverty alleviation in developing countries, including through philanthropy and volunteerism, proposed to identify promising local philanthropic institutions in Africa. In Zimbabwe, following several studies and planning efforts, the partnership between Synergos and the Organization of Rural Associations for Progress resulted in the 1997 launch of the Western Regional Foundation of Zimbabwe.[265] The Foundation continues to play a leadership role in the region and has maintained its own endowment based on *qogelela*, a community group savings practice.[266]

Responding to the international community's continuing consideration of global issues related to economic and social development and development assistance, with the encouragement of David Hamburg and the trustees, the Strengthening Human Resources in Developing Countries Program, instead of recommending that the Corporation organize its own commission, supported a variety of dissemination activities for three international commissions: the World Commission on Environment and Development,[267] the South Commission,[268] and the Commission on Global Governance.[269] For the first two commissions, the Corporation also contributed to establishing the institutions dedicated to implementing the recommendations.[270]

Commentary on the Strengthening Human Resources in Developing Countries Program

Given the extent of the activities discussed here, the "Commonwealth" program of the 1980s and 1990s displayed many tendencies of a quasi-mini-foundation. Although all programmatic decisions and grants were thoroughly vetted by foundation leadership and the Board of Trustees, the extent of the work stretched the boundaries of grant-making, covering as it did nearly all countries in Africa and the Caribbean that were members of the British Commonwealth as of 1948, and even making grants in non-Commonwealth countries such as Mexico, Ethiopia, Senegal, and Thailand, albeit for charter-approved purposes supporting regional institutions engaged with Commonwealth countries. A longtime International Development Research Centre partner, Rohinton Medhora, now IDRC's vice president for grants and programs, raised provocative questions about funding levels for grantees and about the level of activity, which was quite comparable to the Centre's. "In many cases, the ideas were ahead of their time," Medhora noted. "They [the grantees] were working in tough environments and had no constituencies. Without doubt they were underfunded."[271] With the array of challenges, the fact that many of the networks created in this period are still thriving today is a testimony to the effectiveness of their leadership and programs.[272] The institutions that the Corporation and its donor partners helped to establish—the African Academy of Sciences, the Mexican Health Foundation, the Western Regional Foundation of Zimbabwe, the Caribbean Academy of Sciences, the Caribbean Health Research Council, and the Council on Health Research for Development— are all active in the early twenty-first century, and their astute leadership and notable accomplishments continue to attract sustaining support from other donors.

In commenting in 2000 on the work of the program, John Tirman, executive director of the Winston Foundation for World Peace during this period, provided a perspective that differs from Medhora's:

Intentionally or not, Carnegie's funding in a program for developing countries perhaps did more to build civil society and the kinds of NGO networks that contribute to stability. Much of this funding was for science and education in Africa, for example, and quite a bit of it was for in-country capacity building: $250,000 for a Forum for African Women Educationalists, several large grants to the African Academy of Sciences, and other major gifts for women's health issues. In this mode, Carnegie seemed to parallel the civil society effect of the Ford Foundation grants, which long emphasized the nurturing of intellectual capacity in the Third World.[273]

Yet the pressing questions for the Corporation still persisted: should the "Commonwealth" program continue into the twenty-first century with so many grants, in so many areas, and at such low-dollars-per-grant funding levels? With the range of subprograms and grants, even if focused on strategic issues, these probing questions, posed in response as well to changing conditions in African countries, led the Corporation in the next era to revisit its earlier focus on institutions rather than on projects and networks.

THE SPECIAL PROJECTS COMMITTEE

THE SPECIAL PROJECTS COMMITTEE established in 1984 and chaired by Barbara Finberg supported out-of-program grants, incubated new ideas for the grants programs, and occasionally supported cross-program initiatives.[274] For several years, the international focus of the committee included the nexus of conflict prevention, conflict resolution, the transition to democracy and the strengthening of democratic institutions, education of the public about the US role in global affairs, philanthropy, and components of its overall work on science policy.[275]

Four activities stand out in the work of the Special Projects Committee in conflict resolution and democracy.[276] The first set of grants enabled the Carter Center to launch the International Negotiations Network Council, chaired by former president Carter, as a complement to the conflict resolution activities of the United Nations and other official bodies. The network was able to assist in the Ethiopian-Eritrean conflict, as well as in Haiti, Nigeria, Sudan, and southern Sudan.[277] The network is still active today, and President Carter continues to maintain his extensive international mediation efforts.[278]

The Special Projects Committee provided support through the Duke University Center for International Development Research for the International Commission on Central American Economic Recovery and Development, a major effort to effect a new phase of development in Central America.[279] In the 1995 retreat paper, staff members commented that "the extent to which the commission's efforts brought about change in the area has not, to the Corporation's knowledge, been assessed, but members of Congress acknowledged that the commission's existence helped to forestall US armed intervention in the conflicts in the region."[280]

A third cluster nurtured the work of Francis Deng at the Brookings Institution.[281] In 1988—a time when brutal internal and cross-country conflicts were increasingly prominent in Africa—Deng proposed the development of an agenda for research on conflict and conflict resolution in Africa. A network of researchers and scholars prepared, reviewed, critiqued, and then assisted in publishing and disseminating the case studies that addressed conflict resolution in Southern Africa, the Horn of Africa, and

West Africa. The final two volumes not only summarized the case studies but indicated the contours of the new work on sovereignty, responsibility, and accountability, which shaped the next phase of Deng's research.[282]

The other conflict resolution activity for the Special Projects Committee was related to facilitating nongovernmental efforts to resolve conflicts. Small grants to George Mason University and the Northern Ireland Inter-Group Relations Project, for example, supported research and a workshop on the future of Northern Ireland that provided background material for the eventual negotiations leading to the Good Friday Peace Accords.[283]

The component on educating Americans about global affairs joined the Special Projects Committee with the Strengthening Human Resources in Developing Countries and Preventing Deadly Conflict Programs. The major international activities funded by the Special Projects Committee included the Inter-American Dialogue,[284] the Citizens Network for Foreign Affairs,[285] and the Pacific Council for International Affairs.[286] All three continue to contribute to disseminating new thinking about international affairs in their areas to the public and policymakers.

Complementing the efforts of the HRDC program to promote philanthropy outside the United States, the Special Projects Committee helped launch CIVICUS: World Alliance for Citizen Participation in 1993. CIVICUS by 1997 had 260 members; it continues to focus on strengthening civil society throughout developing countries.[287]

The Special Projects Committee served as the institutional home for the Carnegie Commission on Science and Technology for Government, another major commission organized in this era, to examine this theme in-depth with a wide range of scholars, scientists, and policymakers.[288] For the Commission, President Carter chaired the Task Force on Development Organizations, which, as mentioned earlier, spawned the Carter Center's Global Development Initiative, a brand-new approach for reforming development assistance. The follow-up to the Task Force and the work of the initiative were supported by the Corporation through the HRDC program.[289]

A Special Project of the Special Projects Committee

One of the very few examples in the Corporation's history of a three-way cross-program activity (involving the Special Projects Committee, the Preventing Deadly Conflict Program, and the Strengthening Human Resources in Developing Countries Program) was support for the UN Studies Program at Yale University under the leadership of Bruce Russet, professor of international relations and political science. The program was established in 1993 to increase undergraduate understanding and respect for the work of the United Nations, especially in an era of threats to security ranging from war to poverty and environmental damage. Toward that end, the Corporation contributed support over the period 1994 to 1997 for seminars and special studies, particularly on restructuring the UN Security Council; linkages with UN officials, current and former; and building the curriculum. Over time the program garnered funding from the Ford Foundation, the Center for Global Partnership of the Japan Foundation, the Korea Foundation, and the Kemp Fund of Yale University. A book on the Security Council, *The Once and Future Security Council*, was published in 1997.[290]

Commentary on the Special Projects Committee

Recognized as a vital component of Carnegie Corporation for most of its one hundred years, the special project remains firmly ensconced in the Corporation's portfolio. The Special Projects Committee in this era pursued an agile balancing act between funding the truly special out-of-program grants, such as the UN Studies Program, and incubating those activities that had the potential for shaping new subprograms or even entire new programs at the Corporation. The grants to the Carter Center on both international negotiations and international development, for example, contributed significantly to the work of both the Preventing Deadly Conflict and the HRDC Programs.[291] The results of the Special Projects Committee efforts effectively demonstrated the importance of such a committee—one informed by the mission but not limited to the main programmatic strategies of the Corporation.

PUBLIC AFFAIRS

CORPORATION PRESIDENT JAMES ANGELL, IN preparing the first Annual Report in 1921, emphasized that public dissemination of the work of the Corporation was integral to fulfilling the mission. Hamburg maintained this commitment and encouraged the Public Affairs Department, working with colleagues throughout the Corporation, to diffuse the work of the Corporation in a variety of ways, not only through publications disseminating the work of grantees but also through specific grants to extend outreach to the public.[292]

Avery Russell, hired from the Asia Society in 1970, was the first public affairs staff member appointed program officer for media grants.[293] Media-related grants had always been of interest to the Corporation, starting with Frederick Keppel's attraction to radio and film as forms of public education.[294] From 1983 to 1995, nearly $47.8 million was spent on a wide range of media activities, from computer-based information, education, and research services to improvements in the institutional capacity of the media. A small percentage was devoted to international activities, including the work of the HRDC Program.[295]

With the Avoiding Nuclear War Program, Russell assisted, inter alia, with the publications related to the 1987 report of the American Physical Society on directed energy weapons, funded jointly with the National Science Foundation. One result of the considerable publicity about the challenges of the Strategic Defense Initiative was a call to the Reagan administration to clarify for the public the issues involved in this undertaking. The Harvard University study on control of the nuclear arsenal in the disintegrating Soviet Union in 1992 resulted in broad public attention to the nuclear danger posed by the rapid breakup of the Soviet Union and led to federal legislation. The Public Affairs Department worked with the staffs of the Program on Preventing Deadly Conflict and its grantee-partner, the Commission on Preventing Deadly Conflict, to enhance national and international coverage, including use of the Corporation's new website.[296]

For the program on Strengthening Human Resources in Developing Countries, Russell led the efforts to develop a cadre of reporters with special knowledge of development issues and to encourage editorial gatekeepers to support articles on development issues in Africa and Latin America. Russell designed and managed the multipronged dissemination activities of the Second Carnegie Inquiry into Poverty and Development in Southern Africa, with grants in the United States and South Africa. Not only were the publications well received by reviewers and the public, but they were highly visible statements of the situation in South Africa and the opportunities for change in a post-apartheid nation.[297]

CONCLUSIONS

WITH EXTENSIVE SUPPORT for international activities both in the United States and in the Commonwealth countries of Africa and the Caribbean, the Hamburg presidency revived Carnegie Corporation's strong international commitment, which had been subsumed by the intense focus on social justice in the United States and Southern Africa in the second half of the Pifer presidency.

The internationally related activities in the United States in the 1980s and 1990s were for the most part targeted at national security issues, with a major emphasis on Russia and weapons of mass destruction. As the concerns became more broadly related to conflict prevention, the scope broadened. Even so, the majority of direct grants to institutions in the United States, including many universities and think tanks, maintained a consistent focus on national security and associated foreign policy concerns.

In contrast, the Strengthening Human Resources in Developing Countries Program pursued a mix of strategic initiatives. Throughout the period, the consistent focus, building on the work of the Pifer years that began in the late 1970s, was on activities related to strengthening the health and well-being of women in a variety of dimensions and, for the first time, enhancing the development of sound national policies related to science, technology, and health. The Corporation remained responsive to developments, particularly on the African continent, and over time supported initiatives related to the unfolding challenges of development, namely, democratic transitions and the rise in the number of conflicts within states.

In the area of disseminating knowledge and understanding, the second half of the Corporation's mission, the international program, reinforced by the active participation of the Special Projects and Public Affairs teams, achieved success in reaching American policymakers on critical issues. In the HRDC Program, policymakers at the country level in Africa were reached more effectively than policymakers in the United States. Almost all the international activities, in the United States, Africa, the Caribbean, and elsewhere, resulted in advances in knowledge, and sometimes the findings directly influenced policy. The historical challenge, however, remained: achieving comparable success in educating a broad swath of the American public on international issues, whether national security or economic and social development.

The successes and challenges from these years served as the basis for refining and redefining the frame of action for the Corporation and its new leadership as they responded to the increasingly complex global political, security, and economic interactions of the next era.

8

WORK IN PROGRESS, 1997 TO THE PRESENT

Each president of carnegie corporation has confronted major disruptions with international ramifications during his tenure.[1] The Corporation's one-hundred-year history has encompassed world wars; economic depressions; new and old weapons of mass destruction; the end of empires and the birth of new nations; conflicting ideologies and virulent responses; the intractable interactions of demographic, agricultural, health, and environmental changes; and the emergence of inexorable economic and informatic globalization.[2] Yet, soon after the trustees selected Vartan Gregorian as the twelfth president of Carnegie Corporation in June 1997, the world was confronted by even newer threats, starting with the terrorist attacks of September 11, 2001—leading to further attacks outside the United States and to more than a decade of lengthy and costly preemptive wars—and the global reach of the Great Recession of 2008. Efforts to combat terrorism in particular have dominated the national and international policy agenda in this era. In addition, numerous major natural catastrophes—the 2004 Indian Ocean earthquake and tsunami, the Pakistan earthquake in 2005, Hurricane Katrina on the Gulf Coast of the United States the same year, the Haitian earthquake of 2010, and the global threat in March 2011 of radiation from the earthquake-damaged nuclear reactor in Fukushima, Japan—have fueled the controversy about planetary climate change.

All these perturbations have contributed to widening inequality between rich and poor around the world, including in the United States. The information revolution, with the not yet realized promise of bridging the information divide across rich and poor populations and nations, also solidified these economic distinctions and created a new level of Midas-like wealth, since information innovations "touched" by technologists or financial service leaders tended to turn to gold. The polarization was magnified by the Asian financial crisis of 1997, the crash of the dot-com industry in 1999 and 2000, the defaults of the investment banks in 2007 and 2008, and the sovereign debt crisis of 2010 and 2011. The wealthy continue to thrive, while conditions for the poor and middle class decline.[3]

Moving up the economic ladder, a favorite theme of Andrew Carnegie's, became ever more challenging in this era as the rungs spread farther and farther apart for those at the bottom and even for those midway up. The challenge for nationally and internationally oriented philanthropic foundations of responding to economic inequity led to the questioning of fundamentals about decision-making strategies and impact assessment. With the adverse economic conditions, should grant-making foundations include more social service programs and focus on giving to the poor rather than understanding the root causes of social and economic conditions? Should program design tighten around narrow, bottom-line strategies with narrower, shorter-term, and more easily measurable outcomes? Or should grant-making foundations hold the course as social risk-taking institutions and continue to tackle the intractable, longer-term challenges, banking on ideas for a better future?[4] Although these are not new questions for American foundations, the continuing fiscal difficulties for national and local governments have revived debates about the appropriate role of foundations as part of the private nonprofit sector.

And closely related to the Cold War conditions that had influenced Corporation priorities in the 1980s, the tragic, costly ramifications of the World Trade Center calamity—two major wars in Iraq and Afghanistan, along with the spillover in Pakistan—heightened the potential for the spread of nuclear weapons to nonstate actors. The enhanced risk of nuclear warfare and the use of other weapons of mass destruction, compounded by the continued debate in US politics about nation-building versus isolationism as well as by the expansive threat of terrorism, provided a strong rationale for programmatic developments on these themes at the Corporation.[5]

At the same time, the mixed economic and political conditions in African countries offered a contrast between the economic success and societal improvements in some countries and sectors, the stable political conditions in a handful of countries, and the persistent internal and cross-border conflicts in several others.[6] Corporation leaders and staff members in the Commonwealth Program redesigned grant-making to return to the Corporation's long-standing focus of the decades before the mid-1970s on universities and public libraries as institutional providers of access to knowledge and integral components of economic and social development.[7]

One significant side effect of this era for the field of philanthropy, including the Corporation, stemmed from the financial successes of investors and entrepreneurs in the United States and around the world. Media innovator Ted Turner may have been responding to Andrew Carnegie's admonition that "the man who dies thus rich dies disgraced" when he contributed $1 billion in September 1997 to create the UN Foundation and challenged his fellow billionaires to make their own contributions. This period is similar to the period when Carnegie established the Corporation in that Turner's challenge has been one contribution to a dramatic increase in the number of private philanthropists and new grant-making foundations active both in the United States and overseas.[8]

In June 1997, the Foundation Center estimated that there were 44,146 foundations with assets of $330 billion (current dollars) whose annual giving amounted to about $16 billion.[9] By 2010, the Center's estimates had increased to 76,000 grant-making foundations with assets of $622 billion that granted nearly $46 billion, even with the effects of the Great Recession that began in 2008.[10] One indication of the growth in foundation assets, despite the economic conditions, is the change in the Corporation's ranking. With assets in 1997 of $1.54 billion, the Corporation's ranking among American foundations by level of assets was number nineteen; in 2012, even with its increased assets of $2.8 billion, it had fallen to twenty-second place.[11]

VARTAN GREGORIAN:
THE COMPASS POINTS OF A NEW ERA

VARTAN GREGORIAN was the first historian to be selected as president of Carnegie Corporation. In light of the Corporation's commitment since 1911 to librarianship, library science, and library investments, it is noteworthy that he also was the only president of the Corporation to have headed a public library: Gregorian served as president of the New York Public Library for eight years. As a scholar, faculty member, dean, provost, and president, he was the third president with a career at major research universities. Gregorian was distinctively the first president since James Angell in 1920 who had no prior board, staff, or direct grant connections with the Corporation. His abiding research interests centered on democracy, the power of ideas, and nationalism, and he had in-depth knowledge about Afghanistan, a nation and a part of the world that would feature significantly in American foreign policy during Gregorian's presidency.[12] As he pointed out, because of his birth outside of the United States and his diverse cultural background, he saw developments in America through a different filter.[13]

In addition, Gregorian brought a particular sensitivity to the position concerning the obligation to give away money. As he wrote, "Having been embroiled for so many years in the arduous though rewarding business of raising money for one's own institution, it is quite sobering to find oneself in the position of giving it away responsibly and creatively to *other* institutions."[14] He maintained the ethos shared by all Corporation presidents—an openness in meeting with a wide variety of people to listen to their ideas, to try to fund them if their work fit the mission and program, and if it did not, to advise them on where else they might seek support.

In embracing the values of his predecessors, Gregorian elucidated his vision of the societal role of philanthropic foundations:

As Andrew Carnegie saw himself as a trustee of public wealth, I see foundations as stewards of public trusts. After all, philanthropies have historical, legal and moral obligations to society as well as to their founders. They are entrusted with the administration of considerable wealth—totaling some $385 billion in 1999.... Philanthropies bear heavy societal responsibilities by virtue of their wealth, their central role in our civil society and their power to help or, unintentionally, to harm. They have a moral responsibility to see that this power is used openly, wisely and responsibly in upholding society's values rather than subverting them.[15]

The desire to reach the public led the Corporation to expand the dissemination activities beyond grantee publications and the Annual Report by publishing analyses of its grant-making clusters; the overall aims, objectives, and outcomes of Corporation programs; and the field of philanthropy.[16]

THE TEAM: THE BOARD OF TRUSTEES AND THE STAFF

THE CARNEGIE CORPORATION BOARD that selected Vartan Gregorian as president was international in composition, reflecting the priorities of the Hamburg era. Composed of nineteen full members and one honorary trustee, many of the members had worked extensively overseas or had major international ties.[17] For the first time in the Corporation's history, some board members lived overseas, not in the United States, and in countries where the Corporation was not active.[18] Although all were supportive of the international thrust of the Corporation—that is, grant-making based in the United States on international affairs, including Russia and elsewhere in Eurasia, as well as in Commonwealth African countries—they were also open to changes in topics, approaches, and locales.[19]

In October 1998, the trustees also agreed to a new approach to reviewing the work of the four programs by establishing four new standing committees of the board, with each board member serving on one of the program committees. The program committee meetings would take place before the full board meeting and provide an opportunity for the board members to question closely each program's staff members and, as appropriate, suggest promising approaches. (In the international area, for example, this opportunity led to work on bandwidth access in Africa, as discussed later.) Eventually, almost all board members would participate in almost all committees, although that level of participation was not formally mandated. The program committee meetings continued from 1999 until the Corporation's grant-making was reorganized in 2007.[20]

THE CONTEMPORARY INSTITUTION: DIFFERENCES AND SIMILARITIES WITH EARLIER ERAS

GREGORIAN'S FIRST PRESIDENTIAL ESSAY, "Some Preliminary Thoughts," provided insight into the philosophies that shaped him, the kinds of questions he was going to ask of his colleagues, the themes that motivated him, and his approach to the work of philanthropy and Carnegie Corporation.[21] Much like other presidents, he put forth his overall agenda and principles. As Gregorian explained, however, he was not focused on a single theme:

> Other than … unshakable convictions about the special role of foundations, I have come to the Corporation with no preconceived ideas— certainly not about the specific purposes toward which our funds should be spent; my mind has been open to the wise, expert guidance of others, including most importantly the Corporation's experienced program staff and trustees. What I have done is to ask provocative questions, with the intent to challenge and evoke a thoughtful response, and to set in train a process that will help me understand this institution, before forwarding any recommendations to the board about future directions.[22]

The questions Gregorian raised in 1997 remained the same ones that informed his program and proposal review discussions throughout this period, including at the several staff and board retreats held after he assumed the presidency.[23]

With about a $60 million grants budget in 1997, Gregorian noted the importance of forging "a cohesive grant program that will do justice to the foundation's historic purposes … finding the right relationship between programmatic and administrative expenditures … achieving more integration, information sharing, and synergy among our somewhat disparate program areas; and clarifying our policies and the foundation's expectations of both program staff and grantees."[24] In meetings held with grantees and outside experts over the year 1997 to 1998, staff reviewed progress and results on the grant-making themes continuing from the prior era around democracy, education, and international security. Along with the historical focus on African countries and on Russia and the other nations of the former Soviet Union, new topics were also considered: "higher education, telecommunications policy, the state of Islamic studies, and foundation strategies and impact."[25]

The trustees approved the new programmatic strategy for the Corporation at the October 1998 board meeting.[26] The structure of separate programs, with priorities refreshed for this era, was maintained for the following areas: education, international peace and security, international development, and democracy, with special projects for out-of-program requests. In addition, the board approved the Carnegie Fellowship Program (soon changed to Carnegie Scholars) and a new portfolio, the 21st Century Fund, for one-time-only initiatives.

Gregorian presented the newly defined programs in the February 2, 1999, document "New Directions for Carnegie Corporation of New York: A Report to the Board": "The plans ... maintain a balance between continuity and change, and stress our comparative advantage in certain areas. The new programs are intended to serve as a catalyst for change while taking the long view; they will seek partnerships in implementing programmatic objectives and priorities and incorporate a credible evaluation system and dissemination scheme. Internally, the structures for decision making will encourage maximum interaction and cooperation among the staff."[27] To make concrete the commitment to accountability and implementing, Gregorian encouraged the staff to develop new approaches to evaluating the work of the Corporation. These new evaluation methods, as well as the intense continual questioning of strategy, objectives, design, and results, ultimately led to a restructuring of the Corporation's programs in 2007.

Gregorian, like his predecessor, was not seeking to make major staffing changes despite some of the new approaches. He also retained for many years the program management structure of the previous era, namely, one with program chairs, officers, associates, and assistants.[28] He also kept all the senior administrative staff.[29] The trustees approved another governance change by revising the constitution and bylaws to permit new vice presidential positions: alongside the existing program vice president position, the three new positions included vice president for administration, vice president for investment, and vice president for public affairs.[30] One major difference from earlier periods was that an investment team was staffed, under the vice president for investments, to work closely with the board investment committee. Previously, the treasurer and one or two staff members had worked with the board committee.[31]

With the team in place and new programs approved, the foundation was poised to move forward.[32] Gregorian and his leadership team agreed on the value of introducing the idea of evaluation from the very beginning of the grant-making process. He empowered the vice president for program, Neil Grabois, to take on this challenge and build capacity for program evaluation across the institution.

EVALUATION: A TEAM EFFORT ACROSS THE PROGRAMS

IN RESPONSE TO THE REQUEST from the president, by November 2001 Grabois had established the Council on Evaluation, with the charge "to guide evaluation plans and activities."[33] Council members were representatives from each of the programs and two senior leaders: Grabois, the vice president for administration and corporate secretary, and Gregorian, the president.[34] The Council's major contribution to the work of the Corporation was not, however, in the grant-related evaluation but rather at the program level.[35]

The main outcome of a staff retreat held in June 2002 was an agreement to prepare detailed program strategy papers, following guidelines developed by the Council on Evaluation. These would make explicit the implementation plans for each program, facilitate review by the leadership and trustees, and provide the basis for eventual evaluation of the program or subprogram areas.[36] The program strategy and budget papers put forward in October 2003, as discussed later, served to structure proposal review meetings and later program updates, including the ten-year program assessment held in December 2006.[37]

As a result of that assessment by the board and leadership of the Corporation, institutional structural changes were implemented with the intention to reduce scatteration (that is, to reduce the spread of grants across too many themes, thereby increasing depth and focus) and encourage collaboration among program officers, even across international and domestic lines. President Gregorian summarized the review process and the outcomes from the trustee retreat in a document issued on October 1, 2007, "Meeting the Challenges of the 21st Century": "As a result of our efforts, I am confident that we have created an integrated and more effective structure that organizes the foundation's programs under two major categories: International and National programs. The programs and subprograms will work collaboratively, building on each other's strengths, learning from each other's experiences and sharing knowledge."[38] Gregorian situated these internal changes at the Corporation as responses to the contemporary global context:

> In an era when the forces of globalization sometimes seem to be pulling humanity apart at the same time that they are pushing world markets and economies closer together, Andrew Carnegie's vision of a world of potentialities—the potential for peace, for shared knowledge, for education and democracy to enlighten the lives of men, women and children everywhere—is one that Carnegie Corporation of New York continues to envision as well.... Andrew Carnegie saw the world as One. He saw America as One. So do we.[39]

With this integrating vision, Gregorian, the trustees, and the staff embarked on creating a very different structure for the foundation; that process remains a work in progress.[40]

With a new team in place, a revitalized effort to design one evaluation strategy for both the national and international grants programs started in 2009.[41] Several staff meetings helped to refine the plan, another work in progress. In the final plan, Corporation leadership noted,

> Many of the Corporation's activities address issues where the stakes are high, the duration long, and the problems vast in scale.... The risk of failure is always present, as is the likelihood that, even when the strategy is successful, a foundation's particular contribution will be difficult

to trace. Despite these challenges, many agree that philanthropy has a crucial and unique role to play in finding solutions to global, long-term problems … we have an obligation to use all reasonable means to assure that our investments are making a difference and to measure progress toward our objectives.[42]

In this chapter, the discussion of the programmatic activities of the first fourteen years of the Gregorian era follows the same format as other chapters, with the sections corresponding to Corporation programs and activities (and incorporating the later structural changes): the two main international programs, International Peace and Security (the international grant-making in the United States) and International Development (in the Commonwealth countries in Africa); and the other program and activities, Strengthening US Democracy, Immigrant Integration, the Special Projects/Special Opportunities Fund, the Carnegie Scholars Program, and Public Affairs (Journalism Initiative and Dissemination).[43]

INTERNATIONAL GRANT-MAKING
BASED IN THE UNITED STATES

GREGORIAN CONTINUED, WITH SOME MODIFICATIONS, the grant-making themes of his predecessor, David Hamburg, in the newly named International Peace and Security Program. The major international initiative of the prior three years, the Commission on Preventing Deadly Conflict, had issued its final report in December 1997, six months after Gregorian had been elected president. The trustees and the new president determined that with this investment of intellectual and financial resources, and as importantly, because of the state of the world, the Corporation had an opportunity to move forward on the Commission's major recommendations.

At the same time, continuing concerns about the proliferation of nuclear weapons and other weapons of mass destruction, particularly in relation to conditions in Russia and the states of the former Soviet Union, provided an important rationale for Gregorian and his colleagues to continue to focus the work in these areas.[44] Moreover, the Corporation, in partnership with the MacArthur Foundation and others, had been investing for a decade in the creation of scholarly institutions, both academic and freestanding, that were dedicated to policy research on critical international affairs issues; cadres of knowledgeable colleagues and former grantees had been appointed to various policymaking positions in the federal government. Gregorian and his team, with encouragement from the board, refined and reshaped the existing lines of US institution-based international grant-making on the nonproliferation of weapons of mass destruction, with intensified and tightly focused Track II activities; Russia and the former states of the Soviet Union; conflict prevention and resolution, including an abiding concern about the internal conflicts that were increasing the number of states at risk; and, by 2008, the Islam Initiative.[45]

INTERNATIONAL PEACE AND SECURITY

FOLLOWING PROGRAMMATIC REVIEWS IN 1997, the Prevention of Deadly Conflict Program broadened its scope and was renamed the International Peace and Security Program. The program development paper presented to the board in 1998 defined the program's objectives:

> The primary objective of Carnegie Corporation's program on international peace and security (IPS) in all its phases since 1983 has been to identify the gravest threats to world peace and security and explore ways to diminish them.... The Corporation will concentrate its efforts on three specific objectives: (1) Arms Control and Nonproliferation of Weapons of Mass Destruction; (2) Stability in Russia and the Post-Soviet States; and (3) Examination of New Dimensions of Security. In promoting those objectives, the IPS program will build on the work accomplished to date, incorporating the findings of the Carnegie Commission on Preventing Deadly Conflict.... A fourth focus of activity, Strengthening Higher Education in the Former Soviet Union (FSU), is aimed primarily at safeguarding post-Soviet intellectual capital. This will be a cross-program initiative between the IPS and Education divisions.[46]

The principles for grant-making, approved by the board, included:

Continued support for important work by current grantees, while being vigilant in seeking out new centers of excellence.... Emphasis on a smaller number of long-term grants to institutions that have credibility with, and access to, policymakers and the media.... Emphasis on project, rather than institutional support, attention to project evaluation, and, if possible, a clear work plan and 'exit strategy' identified at the point of entry into the relationship with the grantee.... A willingness to collaborate, wherever possible, with other funders.[47]

The team emphasized that the aim was not to make policy but to help inform policy—the traditional role of the Corporation and, indeed, other philanthropic institutions—by amplifying the findings of a credible group of policy analysts so that they could reach receptive policymakers in the executive branch, the US Congress, and the United Nations.[48] The unpredictability, the lack of order in world events, and the complexity of international and global relations required a flexible program strategy using the approaches that worked best, that is, "enlisting the clearest thinkers and most knowledgeable scholars on the issues to guide us."[49]

One concern that has surfaced over the years with this program is the continuing engagement with the same cluster of US educational and policy research institutions, for example, Stanford University, Harvard University, Massachusetts Institute of Technology, the University of Georgia, the Monterey Institute of International Studies, the Brookings Institution, the Center for Strategic and International Studies, the Carnegie Endowment, the Council on Foreign Relations, and the Henry L. Stimson Center. These ongoing grantees, some with deep historic ties to the Corporation, illustrated the time-tested partnership approach of the Corporation: harness the results from building the capacity of individuals and institutions dedicated to addressing the current, imminent, or persistent thorny problems that bedevil foreign policy, as indicated by the themes of the program.

With continuing Corporation backing, long-term grantees also contribute to future policy analyses by training the next generation of scholars, a vital contribution to keeping the field vibrant through the introduction of fresh perspectives from new scholars, who might become new practitioners.[50] By supporting the work of experts outside of government, the intellectual capital accumulated in the out years can be expended when these experts assume positions in government, which has frequently happened.[51] Concurrently, as program staff continued to seek differing perspectives and attributes, new institutions and their teams would enter the portfolio, as evidenced in the following section related to the component areas under the International Peace and Security Program.[52]

NUCLEAR SECURITY AND THE NONPROLIFERATION OF WEAPONS OF MASS DESTRUCTION

THE NUCLEAR SECURITY CONCERNS of the late 1990s and the first decade of the twenty-first century have remained high on the priority list of the Corporation, both during this period and as of this writing.[53]

Despite the fall of the Soviet Union and the reduced threat of inadvertent use of nuclear weapons, new issues compounded the complexity of nuclear proliferation. Economic problems in Russia resulted in opportunities to lose control of the nation's nuclear materials and arsenal; the new Chinese nuclear program raised concerns, as did those of India, Pakistan, North Korea, and, later, Iran.

As the Corporation expanded its grant-making in this area, scholar and policymaker attention was drawn to the threats from both national and nonstate actors. At the same time, the spread of chemical and biological weapons across states and nonstate actors kept those weapons on the Corporation's agenda to explore ways to limit their proliferation. Finally, the concern about the weaponization of space, an offshoot of the missile defense program of the US government, featured in the Corporation's grant-making.

In all these areas, the Corporation considered seriously the potential of treaties as an internationally accepted mechanism to obtain sovereign-state buy-in to control proliferation. The Corporation remained, for example, deeply involved in promoting policy-relevant research and outreach to the policy community and the public on the relevance of the Nuclear Nonproliferation Treaty.[54] By 1999, the program had expanded the long-time focus on the nuclear threat to reintroduce biological and chemical weapons, paying special attention to the nonproliferation of all weapons of mass destruction. As in other areas, the program often brought together researchers from the United States, Europe, and Russia to share experiences and expertise. Treaty ratification and implementation were also targets for grant-making on non-nuclear weapon systems.

The shared anxiety about "loose nukes" on the part of US foreign policy shapers, Corporation staff members and advisers, the Russian Ministry of Atomic Energy, Princeton University's Center for Energy and Environmental Studies (integrated into the Princeton Environmental Institute in the early 2000s), and the US Department of Energy resulted in the Nuclear Cities Initiative in Russia, with the aim to prevent sales of nuclear material from Russia's formerly closed nuclear cities and develop a new economic base in those cities.[55] The Russian-American Nuclear Security Council (RANSAC) became the private-sector NGO that helped to launch the initiative; the Corporation supported RANSAC from 1999 until 2006, for a total of $743,000.[56]

With the changing US administrations, it was a challenge to open "the crown jewels in the Soviet defense establishment" and to retrain the "precious assets"—namely, the nuclear scientists—even in post-Soviet Russia.[57] As Princeton scholar Sharon Weiner noted, despite the problems with the initiative, "NCI [the Nuclear Cities Initiative] gets kind of a bum rap in my opinion.... It didn't do exactly what it was supposed to. But it never got a lot of money and it really did do some important things."[58] RANSAC helped to create analytical centers in Russia for scientists to work on "non-threatening research projects" and build analytical NGOs; the program also led to relationships of trust between Americans and Russians on the sensitive issues of the nuclear cities. In addition, there were open publications of bulletins from previously totally secret centers.[59] Nonetheless, as the analysts described the results, each of the partners in the Initiative bore some responsibility for its inability to fully meet the objectives of downsizing the nuclear stockpiles, job creation, and community development.[60]

In 2006, as part of the Corporation's accomplishment assessment reports, the International Peace and Security team flagged the problems with the RANSAC initiative, but also highlighted other nuclear security grants that were yielding more positive results, such as the studies from the University of Georgia's Center for International Trade and Security, which recommended strategies for controlling trade in nuclear materials that were eventually adopted by the US government.[61] The 2006 report also mentioned the benefits derived from the continuing support for the centers at Stanford, Harvard, MIT, and the Monterey Institute of International Studies: "IPS [International Peace and Security program] has contributed to maintaining strong academic and policy capacity in the United States."[62] The Corporation's support of the Center for Nonproliferation Studies at the Monterey Institute, moreover, led to the establishment of the Center for Policy Studies in Russia, the first indigenous NGO working on nuclear security issues in that country. As noted in the report, "In 2006, eighteen graduates received a Certificate in Nonproliferation Studies, the only credential of its kind. A nonproliferation training program has also been developed for Russian faculty and nuclear specialists in the Siberian region."[63]

The accomplishments report also described the continuing collaboration with partners of then nearly eight decades, such as the National Academy of Sciences, the Brookings Institution, the Council on Foreign Relations, and the Carnegie Endowment for International Peace, as the specifics changed with changing context. In this era, the concern shared by the Corporation and its partners was how to find ways to prevent further proliferation of nuclear weapons. Discussions with program staff resulted in grants that contributed to the Academy's efforts to facilitate exchanges of American, Russian, and Chinese scientists on nuclear weapons and safety, creating the basis for open discussions on a wide range of nonproliferation issues.[64] The Brookings Institution and the Council on Foreign Relations continued their programs to share research findings on nuclear policy implementation with policymakers and a wide range of institutions, Corporation grantees among them, enabling the latter to home in on specific elements.[65]

The Carnegie Endowment for International Peace examined issues in compliance and alternatives to existing proliferation controls. The Carnegie Endowment's 2005 report, *Universal Compliance*, presented a new blueprint for nonproliferation.[66] It made waves then and continues to do so, having prompted numerous articles and testimonies before the relevant Senate and House committees.[67]

Another partner from the prior era, the Center for Strategic and International Studies, assisted by a Corporation grant, contributed $500,000 toward the establishment of fifteen policy research centers focused on nuclear security throughout Europe, North America, and Asia, leveraging "nearly $20 million over the next 10 years from G-8 nations to work toward threat reduction measures in Russia, possibly expanding to other countries."[68]

New players, some of them brand-new, also began to work in close association with the Corporation. In 2001 former senator Nunn (who was at the time a Carnegie Corporation trustee), in collaboration with Ted Turner, funder and founder of the United Nations Foundation, established the Nuclear Threat Initiative.[69] As highlighted in the 2006 programs and accomplishments report, "NTI [Nuclear Threat Initiative] extends the impact of Corporation-supported efforts in generating greater public support, understanding and governmental attention to the subject of threat reduction and bringing greater resources to bear on these problems. It also addresses the issue of safety, security and accountability for weapons of mass destruction in Russia and the former Soviet states and addresses the issue of terrorism in this regard."[70] Since 2001, the Nuclear Threat Initiative has been a major partner of the Corporation's nuclear security efforts, as both grantee and collaborator.[71] Through the NTI, Nunn and his colleagues have continued to promote a nuclear weapon–free world.[72]

As noted in Gregorian's 1999 "New Directions" paper, the proliferation of nuclear weapons was not the only concern. Years before anthrax-filled letters illuminated the potential dangers of non-nuclear and nonconventional weapons of mass destruction, Gregorian called attention to the changing nature of the threat from chemical and biological weapons: "Where such weapons were once viewed as the exclusive property of advanced nation-states, they are now available in a virtual global supermarket, in which the most eager potential customers are states that threaten world security and nonstate actors such as terrorist groups."[73] Increasingly in the late twentieth century, international treaties addressed the use of biological and chemical weapons, with varying degrees of effectiveness.[74] The Corporation, with its commitment to legal remedies that bound states to right actions, had pursued that line of grant-making in an earlier era; the International Peace and Security Program enlarged the scope, particularly in the area of biological weapons. Several grantees, some also supported for their work on nuclear security, such as the Stimson Center and the Federation of American Scientists, combined the control of chemical and biological weapons under one program rubric; the Harvard-Sussex program, for example, was dedicated to biological weapons.[75]

With the ratification of the Chemical Weapons Convention in 1997, the relevant industry partners took up implementation in a significant way, making it possible for the Corporation to focus its limited resources on reducing the proliferation of biological weapons, an area to which other funders and the corporate sector had paid much less attention. Over the ten years of support for efforts to reduce the use of biological weapons, from 1999 to 2009, the Corporation shifted its initial focus on obtaining compliance through global agreements to enhancing international capacity for responding to biological weapon use and adopting codes of conduct for scientists.[76] From the early efforts, staff members learned, "it was not possible to adapt a successful model from the nuclear nonproliferation area to biological arms control ... there simply wasn't enough political will for an international treaty."[77] Consequently, starting in 2000, the program adapted the other success from the nuclear nonproliferation area, namely, "to integrate bioscience and biotechnology expertise within national security by funding education programs that inform postgraduate biologists about the rigors of policymaking as well as introducing influential biologists into the policymaking realm."[78]

Propelled to action by the events of September 11, 2001, the Corporation intensified its efforts in this area.[79] Responding to the recommendations from the National Academy of Sciences' Fink Committee (undertaken with support by the Nuclear Threat Initiative and the Sloan Foundation) concerning the need for educating bioscientists and policymakers about the interactive nature of their work, the Corporation created in 2002 the Biosecurity Integration Initiative, which brought together five longtime grantees.[80] As Karen Theroux wrote, "Since 2003, the Initiative has produced upwards of 200 scientifically competent experts versed in both policy formation and security concerns, some of whom have already entered the policy realm."[81]

One series of grants that directly forged the policy skills of scientists and connected them with policymakers, the Jefferson Science Fellows Program, initiated by the MacArthur Foundation and the Corporation in 2004 and funded through 2008, was institutionalized by the US Department of State.[82] In 2003 the efforts of George H. Atkinson, science and technology adviser to two US secretaries of state, Colin Powell and Condoleezza Rice, resulted in establishing the program for senior scientists under the auspices of the National Academy of Sciences, complementing a similar program but for more junior scientists at the American Association for the Advancement of Science. The fellows worked with Foreign Service officers at the State Department on key foreign policy issues in Washington, DC, and overseas.

Atkinson's creative energy made this program a success. He persuaded the State Department to find the most appropriate assignments for the fellows and convinced the department to provide five-year consultancies following their assignments to ensure their continuing advice. Atkinson worked hard to convince foreign policy specialists that there was a role for the scientists.[83] The MacArthur Foundation provided total support of $1,150,000 over five years, and the Corporation $1,050,000; now the program is fully supported by the State Department.[84] As of 2011, sixty-six fellows have gone through the program, and several remained involved once they completed their fellowship.[85] As Joyce Baldwin concluded: "Though it faces ongoing challenges, the Jefferson Science Fellows program stands as a workable model for 'how to get the job done,' not only within the State Department but potentially, within other U.S. departments and agencies.... It has clearly already made a great deal of progress in striving to meld the world of scientists and engineers with that of diplomats."[86]

In addition to building educational opportunities for scientists and policymakers and a network to connect them, the Corporation's efforts, as noted in the 2006 report, led to "adopting codes of conduct for scientists … educating and training life scientists whose apparently benign research could be used to develop weapons, the so-called 'dual use' problem."[87] This concern prompted the Nuclear Threat Initiative to build on the work of the Corporation and create a multiplier effect internationally through its Global Health and Security Initiative.[88]

A distinctive concern related to the earlier ones about the Strategic Defense Initiative (SDI), the ballistic missile defense shield policy under President Reagan related to the weaponization of space. As noted by the staff, "Many experts view the issue of missile defense as a prelude to the larger issue of the militarization of space.... The prospect of weaponization brings a plethora of related issues dealing with the nature of the threat, possible responses to the threat, and alternatives to space militarization."[89] In 2003 the conditions for the weaponization of space came close to being realized when the United States withdrew from the Anti-Ballistic Missile (ABM) Treaty.[90]

Encouraged by the program's academic advisers, Corporation staff tackled this theme by developing in 2003 a new (but short-lived) subprogram, Technological and Scientific Advances, to examine "emerging risks and opportunities" as well as the weaponization of space initiatives.[91] With a budget of $1 million, the aim was to spend half that amount on issues related to the weaponization of space and half on new initiatives. The importance of collaborative efforts between security policy experts and members of the scientific and technological communities became a central emphasis.[92] The MacArthur Foundation remained the foundation's funding partner in this area.

A working group convened by the American Academy of Arts and Sciences examined, in light of the September 11, 2001, attacks in New York and Washington, DC, the impact of the deployment of weapons in space on international cooperation.[93] The Center for Defense Information assessed ways to prevent another tragedy through the use of, for example, nuclear reactors in orbit, and focused especially on providing information to policymakers, the media, and others.[94] The Dwight D. Eisenhower World Affairs Institute, under the leadership of Corporation academic adviser and grantee Susan Eisenhower, brought together a similarly wide range of stakeholders to try to arrive at an agreement against deploying weapons in space.[95] Eisenhower made the case for continuing to hold consultations: "This is a subject to get out in front of because nothing substantial has happened yet. The cost of putting weapons in space is prohibitive relative to the net gain in security—besides the fact that the technical capability isn't there. Even defining what a space weapon is, is challenging."[96] In December 2002, the Arsenault family established the Secure World Foundation to support work on weaponization of space issues.[97] By 2005, recognizing the work of the Secure World Foundation and concluding that the work on the weaponization of space had met the initial goals of building awareness and connections, Corporation staff brought the grant-making to an end.[98]

AN ALTERNATIVE APPROACH: TRACK II

A CLUSTER OF ACTIVITIES related to the Track II process as an alternative to official diplomacy formed an integral part of the International Peace and Security Program's efforts to introduce credible evidence and analyses into negotiations over nuclear security issues.[99] Hussain Agha, Shai Feldman, Ahmad Khalidi, and Zeev Schiff, scholar-practitioners with in-depth experience with the Track II meetings that were undergirding the official Middle East negotiations, received a grant from the Corporation to write about the lessons learned from those experiences and to provide an analysis of Track II as a practice.[100] These authors conclude: "Backed by suitable sponsors, Track-II talks can achieve a wide range of objectives: from the consolidation of an ongoing peace processes [*sic*], to the creation and generation of new peace networks; and from the stimulation of public debate on basic issues, to the creation of new and dramatic political realities."[101]

The first set of Track II–type efforts supported by the program addressed, not nonproliferation, but rather water management in South Asia.[102] However, the most systematic grant-making in support of Track II discussions (and even Track 1½ meetings, with a mix of unofficial and official participants) concerned three complex situations related to nuclear nonproliferation: India-Pakistan, Iran, and North Korea.[103] Two grantees received support to undertake Track II dialogues on the South Asian security issues. The Henry L. Stimson Center was supported for several years in undertaking unofficial trilateral dialogues on South Asian security issues between India and Pakistan and addressing the issues of Kashmir.[104] The US arm of Pugwash International was also funded in 2004, for two years at approximately the same level of $335,800, to work through Pugwash groups in India and Pakistan to hold meetings and workshops with senior officials covering the scientific matters as well as military and policy matters.[105] As noted in the 2006 accomplishment report, these Track II efforts "were implicated in, and perhaps even led to, the notification agreement for ballistic missile test launches between India and Pakistan."[106]

The Track II diplomacy efforts concerning Iran had more mixed results, partly as a consequence of the difficulty in engaging consistently the relevant interlocutors on the Iranian side. Nonetheless, some progress was made in engaging Iranians, both government officials and nongovernmental experts with ties to the government.[107] Building on the efforts of the Rockefeller Brothers Fund, the United Nations Association of the United States of America and the Stockholm International Peace Research Institute, the Carnegie Endowment for International Peace, under the leadership of Rose Gottemoeller at the Endowment's Moscow Center, received a grant to organize multinational approaches to meet Iran's energy needs.[108] For various reasons, it was difficult to engage appropriate Iranian counterparts in this work, although Gottemoeller was able to involve Russians in expert discussions about the Iranian nuclear program. In addition, with Corporation support, the Council on Foreign Relations attempted to launch a Track II dialogue on Iran under the leadership of foreign policy scholars Ray Takeyh and Vali Nasr.[109] Similar difficulties in engaging the appropriate Iranian participants prevented this effort from succeeding.

Notwithstanding the challenges, a variety of other Track II efforts concerning Iran, through the Asia Society, the International Institute for Strategic Studies, the National Academy of Sciences, Princeton University, and Pugwash International, have had some success in bringing Iranians, including high-level government officials, into the conversation.[110] Given the lack of formal diplomatic relations between Iran and the United States since 1979, these Track II dialogues have, at a minimum, allowed channels of communication to remain open where none otherwise existed.[111] On both sides, the results of these unofficial deliberations were shared with policymakers in Teheran and Washington, DC.

In September 2009, the Corporation hosted a meeting of the Iran Track II grantees to assess the opportunities to continue with this work.[112] The UN Association of the USA and the Stockholm International Peace Research Institute presented the idea of "sending some of the low-enriched uranium from Iran to other countries in return for higher-enriched uranium to fuel Iran's research reactors; and internationalizing Iran's enrichment facility under the supervision of IAEA [International Atomic Energy Agency]."[113] This idea and others developed during Corporation-supported

Track II dialogues have been reflected in various official policy proposals considered by Iran and the "P-5 plus one" (the five permanent members of the UN Security Council—China, France, Russia, the United Kingdom, and the United States—plus Germany) and by other interested countries, such as Brazil and Turkey.[114]

Unfortunately, the combination of increasing regional tensions, uncertainties over the trajectory of the political transitions following the "Arab Spring," and continuing disputes have limited the frequency and scope of Track II–type discussions with the Iranians. This does not mean, however, that those that did take place lacked resonance in the policy arena. An inherent challenge with this type of work that limits definitive assessments of its efficacy is that, in some important instances, the most useful and consequential Track II–type discussions occur outside of the official negotiating sessions and, in light of concerns about confidentiality and political sensitivity, are not publicly touted.[115] Notwithstanding these constraints, the Corporation remains committed to examining—and, where feasible, pursuing—the possibilities in this area, given the high stakes involved, the improved, though still tentative, prospects, and the mixed record of progress (at the time of this writing) on the Track I front. Corporation grantees have worked to support these Track I efforts, through multiple channels in the media as well as less publicly. Moreover, if and when official diplomatic negotiations with Iran resume, Track II could provide an opportunity to delve more deeply and freely into issues than is often allowed in the time-constrained, more structured format of official diplomacy.[116]

Despite the equally complex situation in North Korea, there has been more commitment by North Koreans to continue the Track II efforts, even when official dialogue (in the "Six Party Talks" involving representatives of China, Japan, the Democratic People's Republic of Korea, the Republic of Korea, Russia, and the United States) has been stalled. Arguably, the very on-again/off-again nature of the official talks has provided an incentive for all parties, including the North Koreans, to participate in more regular Track II dialogues to exchange, test, and critique ideas without the constraints imposed in official negotiations, as in the Iranian talks. A framework for discussion involving representatives from multiple regional powers is often used in this work. A six-party framework, however often in abeyance, also offers the potential for moving forward once some level of consensus from all sides is reached.[117] Grantees involved in Track II efforts related to North Korea include the University of California at San Diego's Institute on Global Conflict and Cooperation, the National Committee on American Foreign Policy, the Johns Hopkins University School of Advanced International Studies, the National Committee on North Korea, the Social Science Research Council, the Institute for Foreign Policy Analysis, Stanford University's Center for International Security and Cooperation, and the Pacific Forum/Center for Strategic and International Studies.[118]

Despite the vagaries inherent in both the scheduling and conduct of these unofficial dialogues, persistent efforts, much like those in the official talks, on occasion yield positive results. Through the National Committee on American Foreign Policy, under the leadership of George Schwab and Donald Zagoria, the Corporation has supported a series of Track 1½ discussions. A successful Track 1½ session, held in New York on June 30 and July 1, 2005, one day at the Asia Society and the next at Carnegie Corporation, brought together North Korean officials and other representatives of the six parties as well as officials from the White House, the National Security Council, the US State Department, and the Senate Foreign Relations Committee. This meeting, with its highly productive conversations, open atmosphere, and opportunities for private discussions, contributed in some measure to the resumption of official talks between North Korea and the five other parties.[119] Michael Zuckerman makes the crucial point, however, that "it was not a single set session that yielded success. NCAFP [National Committee on American Foreign Policy] ... conducted similar sessions, in 2003 and 2004, that organizers now say provided important 'confidence building'... Nor was it a single organization that worked towards a renewal of talks. Several organizations, again, many of them Carnegie Corporation grantees, have maintained a steady flow of meetings, encouraging all parties to the talks to come together in the more informal settings of Track 1½ where ... they can glean some better understanding of the other's needs and the perspectives that shape their positions."[120] Recent (at the time of this writing) difficulties in establishing official dialogue between the United States and North Korea and uncertainties about developments in North Korea following the rise to power of Kim Jong-un underscore the role of nongovernmental organizations in facilitating channels of communication and information sharing between experienced, knowledgeable Americans and their North Korean counterparts.[121]

Recognizing the challenges of assessing success in the North Korean situation, the Corporation supported an external evaluation and then a meeting with advisers and experts to review the results. Despite the difficulties in this particular set of negotiations, the meeting participants not only reviewed the evaluation results but also took into account the on-the-ground context. Given the continued political commitment to achieving success in the North Korean negotiations, the group recommended that the Corporation continue its grant-making in this area.[122]

After so many years of investing in the complex effort of relationship-building, the president, trustees, and staff now recognize the role that a neutral institution, such as a philanthropic foundation, can play in supporting this activity, which is crucial for success in the long run yet often confronted with limited results in the short run. Even with the internal restructuring, the Corporation continues to make grants in support of unofficial Track II talks.

Increasingly by 2008, the program returned to a concentration on a carefully delineated range of nuclear nonproliferation efforts, clearly the threat that animated the abiding concern of all who worked on this program. In the 2010–2011 program strategy paper, Deana Arsenian and her colleagues elaborated further: "Having devoted sustained attention to the nuclear weapons problem since the 1980s, we have kept the analytical and expert community engaged with the nuclear security agenda, leading to many of our grantees (fourteen at the time of this writing) holding high-level positions within the Obama administration in policy areas that deal with nuclear security.... The United States spends $50 billion on nuclear security each year, compared to about $25 million of independent spending by foundations. In order to have an impact, we focus on a few specific interventions, both immediate and long-term, that can leverage resources much larger than our investments ... specifically directing our resources toward analysis, outreach and policy action ... strengthening expertise in nuclear security, and resolving regional disputes involving North Korea and Iran."[123]

RUSSIA

IN THE EARLY 1990S, the exuberance resulting from perestroika and glasnost, the emergence of Russia, the formation of the Commonwealth of Independent States (CIS), and the democratic election of Boris Yeltsin led to world expectations that Russia would take its place alongside the other democracies of the world, bolstered by a vibrant market economy.[124] By 1998, as described in the International Peace and Security Program paper, a different reality had emerged:

> Russia finds itself on the verge of economic collapse, political stalemate, military breakdown, and national identity crisis. Russia's economy is nearly insolvent ... its democratic institutions are fragile and impotent. Russia's military establishment is disintegrating, threatening the basic coherence of the military forces and their control over weapons ... one Russia [is] trying to step into the Western camp, the other into the East, and the third reaching out to the South ... while Russia must take the lead in solving its problems, it cannot do it alone. In any case, the country's size, resources, nuclear arsenal, regional influence, and ability to project global power through intercontinental delivery means make Western disengagement from Russia a nonviable option. Indeed, the greater the magnitude of Russia's crisis, the greater the global consequences and the greater the need for Western involvement in reversing Russia's decline.[125]

To contribute to reversing that decline, the Corporation sought to work with the World Bank and the US government in supporting the Russian link to the American business community, policymakers, military, and intelligentsia.[126] The intent was to strengthen the partnership between the Russians and the West and to identify solutions through the sharing of ideas and experiences rather than directives. A main grantee identified to bring these different groups together was the Aspen Institute, both the Congressional Program for connecting members of the Russian parliament (the Duma) with members of the US Congress, headed by Dick Clark, and the Aspen Strategy Group and its US-Russia dialogue providing expert advice for wider foreign policy, headed by Coit D. Blacker.[127] The program at Harvard University's Kennedy School of Government, led by Robert D. Blackwill, continued to facilitate the sharing of ideas between high-level American and Russian military personnel as well as their counterparts in Great Britain, the countries of the former Soviet Union, and elsewhere in Eurasia.[128] A parallel program, along with the US-Russia one, was later developed by the Kennedy School program to focus on the Black Sea region, including Ukraine, Moldova, Georgia, Armenia, Turkey, Greece, Romania, and Bulgaria.[129]

A special initiative designed to last a decade aimed to support the intelligentsia and reduce brain drain; the grants linked universities, scholars, and administrators across Russia, Ukraine, Georgia, Armenia, and Azerbaijan with counterparts in Europe and the United States through joint research projects and scholarly exchanges, as well as by upgrading university libraries.[130] Recognizing the importance of American understanding of the developments in Russia and the post-Soviet states, the Corporation program staff determined that reinforcing research and training in the United States, along with continued efforts to disseminate the research findings, was needed to rebuild and keep American scholarship up-to-date on developments in Russia and the former Soviet states.

Working closely with Gregorian and the program's academic advisers (Thomas G. Weiss, John D. Steinbruner, and Rajan Menon), David Speedie, Deana Arsenian, and their colleagues developed an extensive cross-national program, with US, European, and Russian scholars and policymakers, to build interdisciplinary thinking and analysis on Russia and share those analyses with appropriate policymakers.[131] Under the auspices of the Russia Initiative, starting in 1999 and budgeted at $1 million per year, lead investigators organized studies and held regular meetings that ensured the sharing of ideas and analyses; programmatic recommendations emerged for the Corporation on education about Russia in the United States and policymaker-scholar connections between the United States, Russia, and Europe.[132] These complemented another Corporation effort that brought together younger, university-based scholars from Russia and the United States into a research network through the Program on New Approaches to Russian Security (PONARS).[133]

The Russia Initiative's final report, issued in 2001, identified the challenges to Russia's societal dynamics, from the interconnectedness of its economic, political, and social spheres to the impact of globalization; these challenges reinforced the Corporation's perspective that "helping Russia today is not a matter of altruism, but an issue of self-interest and a national security imperative for the United States."[134] The extensive materials prepared by the initiative participants were shared with policy officials, including the secretary of state, Condoleezza Rice, a former trustee and grantee. Three interrelated objectives formed the basis for the grant-making in response to the initiative's recommendations: strengthening "Russia's capacity to deal with its challenges"; facilitating "Russia's integration with the West"; and exploring "new paradigms for U.S.-Russian relations."[135]

The Corporation's strategy of building and sustaining American institutional and individual capacity for understanding the changing conditions in Russia and the region, on the one hand, and connecting American scholars with key scholars and policymakers in those areas, on the other, facilitated its continuing ability to disseminate grantee contributions that could inform American foreign policymaking. For example, when a stronger Russia emerged over the period 2000 to 2001 under Vladimir Putin and with his implementation of new economic policies, then-president Clinton began highlighting US-Russian relations.[136] The Corporation team saw the opportunity to consider with its grantees how best to share findings with policymakers and also the opportunity to build on the Russia Initiative by connecting with Russian research institutions and more senior researchers. Core grants continued over this time, although each year a few new grantees received support as well, all aiming to elucidate the most effective ways to work with their Russian counterparts on strengthening the Russian capacity to meet internal challenges and engage with global issues, while sustaining US-Russian connections.[137]

The range of grantees continued to include those overseas, such as the Moscow School of Political Studies, the Carnegie Moscow Center, and the UK-based International Institute for Strategic Studies.[138] Analyses at Rutgers University of Russia's relationships with the United States, for example, were broadened to include Europe.[139] Three of the core grantees dedicated to connecting scholars and policymakers received renewed support for their US-Russia-specific activities: the Aspen Strategy Group, the

Richard Nixon Library and Birthplace Foundation, and the Aspen Institute Congressional Program.[140]

By 2002, with the increasingly positive conditions in Russia and between the United States and Russia, staff members raised some pertinent questions:"Why should the Corporation continue to be concerned about Russia and U.S. policies toward Russia; and, just as importantly, why should the Corporation retain a focus on Russia when so many negative trends are taking place in the rest of the world.... The answers rest on Russia and on the Corporation's comparative advantage in the field of international peace and security."[141] The Corporation's long-term investments had resulted in networks of scholars and policy researchers in settings that could both deepen understanding of the nature of the Russian transformation and identify ways to address such key policy issues as the proliferation of weapons of mass destruction, the role of Russia as a partner in negotiations in tough situations such as with Iran, and increasing Russian involvement in multilateral projects.[142]

The program concentrated more intently on strengthening multifaceted US-Russian cooperation through partnerships around key issues, including the possession of weapons of mass destruction by state and nonstate actors, technological advancement, regional and economic conflicts, and other areas of common interest. Noting that other foundations, even though limited in number, were contributing about $30 million for initiatives related to democracy and economic issues, staff commented that only a modest percentage went to encourage US-Russian relations. In addition, the US Agency for International Development, which had been supporting work on and in Russia at approximately $70 million annually, was considering a reduction in its commitments.[143] Reflecting these changing conditions, the overall goal of the Carnegie grants program on Russia by 2003 was "to strengthen U.S.-Russian cooperation in addressing pressing global challenges."[144] The objectives changed as well, including work on integrating Russia into European regional institutions, identifying shared interests, building the capacity of Russian citizens to participate in their nation's transformed relationship with Europe and the United States, and maintaining "the attention of the U.S. public and policymakers on Russia and on the potential for U.S.-Russian cooperation."[145]

The shift in goals and objectives tended to reinforce the work of existing grantees; in some cases, with Corporation encouragement through redirect-ing grant resources, grantees included new dimensions related to coopera-tion. For example, the Carnegie Endowment's policy outreach work in Russia and the United States continued.[146] Working groups such as at RAND and the Atlantic Council emphasized multilateral relations.[147] Again, main-taining support for longtime grantees whose work fit with the new thrust, the Corporation continued to fund the Harvard University program that connected military officers and security specialists from the United States, Russia, and the Black Sea countries.[148] The Aspen Institute programs expanded to bring together members of Congress with US, Russian, and European experts and parliamentarians as part of the Corporation's out-reach to the American public and policymakers.[149]

Corporation staff members also encouraged local initiatives aimed at reinforcing internal political, economic, and social developments in Russia. The Moscow-based New Eurasia Foundation, led by Corporation adviser Andrey Kortunov, emphasized building democratic institutions through citizen engagement and fostering connections in Europe and elsewhere.[150] The Corporation provided grants to the international NGO Mercy Corps to provide a leadership training program for young decision-makers from Russia, Armenia, and Georgia and to the Moscow School of Political Studies for seminars on democracy for Russian legislators.[151]

In an effort to focus the many working groups that had been sup-ported under the Russia subprogram—on internal Russian developments, post-Russian states, and US-Russian-European-Eurasian cooperation—by 2007 program staff were concentrating on nurturing cooperative rela-tionships between American and Russian counterparts, as well as with new participants from Eurasia and China, aimed at *promoting multilateral solu-tions to security challenges through effective and responsible U.S. global engage-ment.*"[152] The program encouraged long-term grantees based in think tanks and universities to continue their research to advance knowledge on issues related to US foreign policy; renewed support that facilitated connections between these investigators and scholars in Europe; and disseminated find-ings to policymakers.[153]

With a change in national leadership in both Russia and the United States from 2007 to 2008—from Vladimir Putin to Dmitry Medvedev in

Russia, and from George W. Bush to Barack Obama in the United States—Corporation staff members considered it timely to organize another major initiative to rethink US policy toward Russia, this time under the auspices of the American Academy of Arts and Sciences and with the expert guidance of Russia specialist Robert Legvold from Columbia University.[154] The studies underlined both the role of Russia as a major player on global issues and the vital necessity of a sound US policy toward Russia. Corporation staff emphasized that "a new relationship needs to be built on parity, mutual respect and appreciation of national interests."[155]

By 2009 global engagement had become a major organizing theme for the Corporation's efforts to connect American, Russian, Eurasian, and other European scholars, practitioners, and policymakers to collect and analyze data, share information, and disseminate findings on the themes related to crucial security challenges.[156] As part of the multilateral thrust, the trustees, president, and International Program staff were increasingly committed to finding ways to work with, and even in, China, cognizant of its ever-expanding global political, economic, and cultural presence.[157] The Corporation supported the new China program of the Carnegie Endowment for International Peace, with a grant of $3 million, and the work of the National Academy of Sciences to bring together experts in the United States, Russia, and China around foreign policy, security, and economic issues.[158]

At the end of the Corporation's first century of international philanthropy, the International Peace and Security Program sustained the commitment to "supporting research, outreach, and international linkages of leading American think tanks and university-based centers that serve as authoritative sources for policymakers, the media, and the public both in the United States and abroad."[159]

For the Corporation, the consistency of focus on Russia, through the lens of US-Russia relations and that of multilateral relations, conferred a clear comparative advantage in terms of depth of knowledge of the issues, institutions, and individuals; these pivotal relationships remained an area of focus. Still co-funding many of these initiatives were the MacArthur Foundation, the Ford Foundation, the Open Society Institute, the Compton Foundation, the Ploughshares Fund, the Nuclear Threat Initiative, and new philanthropies such as Google.org and Skoll Foundation, along with European and multinational donor agencies. Given the global geopolitical challenges, the persistent threat of nuclear proliferation, and the opportunity for collaborative approaches, all of the partners remained convinced that networks linking scholars, practitioners, and policymakers across pivotal powers would keep discussions going, build trust, and produce creative documents with solid policy recommendations.

HIGHER EDUCATION IN THE FORMER SOVIET UNION

IN "SOME PRELIMINARY THOUGHTS," his 1997 presidential essay, Vartan Gregorian introduced the topic of higher education in the former Soviet Union:

> I am concerned about the state of educational and scientific institutes in the countries of the former Soviet Union—in particular the condition of higher education and the drain of high-level scientific expertise to other regions.... What opportunities can we pursue through cooperation with our sister foundations, nongovernmental organizations, the World Bank, the U.S. Agency for International Development, and other instruments in order to prevent the collapse of institutions of learning in countries that are so crucial for the maintenance of world peace and for the success of democracy?[160]

The journalist Sophia Kishkovsky, in a 2000 article for the *Carnegie Reporter*, reinforced these concerns but also highlighted more positive changes, particularly in the flagship institutions of higher education around Russia that were urging that an atmosphere of freedom and intellectual creativity be fostered.[161] Still, she acknowledged the problems of adjustment to a new era, the tension between research and teaching, and the institutional arrangements between the scientific academies and universities, along with the high level of bureaucracy.

Gregorian and the trustees encouraged the program staff, in particular, Deana Arsenian, the senior program officer, and David Speedie, the program chair of the International Peace and Security Program, to identify the role that the Corporation could play in strengthening Russian higher education through developing a set of arrangements that would enable the Russian intelligentsia—those who fueled the creativity of that society—to flourish. A grant in 1998 to the American Council of Learned Societies for $1 million helped launch a special program for Russian scholars in the humanities, directly related to rebuilding the Russian intelligentsia.[162]

Earlier in the 1990s, the Corporation program staff members were involved with the Russian higher education activities of the MacArthur Foundation and the Ford Foundation. The MacArthur Foundation, working with the US Civilian Research and Development Foundation, had been supporting, with considerable resources, the basic scientific research centers across Russia in the post-Soviet Union, co-funded by the Ministry of Education and Science of Russia. The Corporation joined this initiative in 1999 with an initial grant of $1 million and stayed engaged with the program throughout its duration. These training and research centers were intended "to narrow the gap between research and teaching and to help transform Russian universities into institutions that do both."[163]

Together the MacArthur Foundation and the Corporation established an advisory group, composed of Russian and American experts, to review the state of disciplines, scholarship, and university programs in the social sciences and humanities. The intent was to identify appropriate models for the universities and for collaboration. The foundation staff asked Blair Ruble and his colleagues at the Kennan Institute of the Woodrow Wilson International Center for Scholars to undertake an extensive review of the needs of higher education in the former Soviet Union.[164] Drawing on their recommendations and the understanding of what was feasible in Russia, Corporation and MacArthur Foundation staff endorsed the support for individual scholars under the auspices of a new type of institution, based at regional universities: the interdisciplinary Centers for Advanced Study and Education (CASEs). Paralleling the MacArthur Basic Research in Higher Education (BRHE) program, the CASEs were to concentrate on the social sciences and the humanities.[165]

The Kennan Center study, the site visits undertaken by Arsenian and her Moscow colleagues, and the strong recommendations from Russian leadership to focus on the regions, not the usual urban centers, helped shape the Corporation's approach, which was to "develop a network of scholars beyond the main academic hubs of St. Petersburg and Moscow who will be able to continue to advance in their disciplines, conduct research and also teach a new generation of scholars."[166]

Because of the Corporation's charter, the grants could not be made directly to the institutions, as was possible in the Africa program. Instead, the Kennan Institute served as fiscal agent; an initial grant of $2.4 million to support the CASEs was launched with partnership support from the MacArthur Foundation, the Open Society Institute, and the Russian Ministry of Education and Science.[167] Nine Russian centers were supported to conduct research, hold conferences and workshops, prepare publications, engage in international projects, and strengthen their libraries: Immanuel Kant State University of Russia, Kaliningrad; Voronezh State University; Far East State University, Vladivostok; Irkutsk State University; Novgorod State University; Rostov State University; Saratov State University; Tomsk State University; and Ural State University, Yekaterinburg.[168] By 2003 the Corporation was also funding CASE-like centers in Belarus through a grant to the American Councils for International Education intended to serve academics from Belarus, Ukraine, and Moldova. In the South Caucasus, through a grant to the Eurasia Foundation in Washington, DC, three additional centers, designated as the Caucasus Research Resource Centers, were established in Georgia at the International School of Economics at Tbilisi State University, in Armenia at Yerevan State University, and in Azerbaijan as an independent center in Baku.[169] To ensure effective implementation of the grants, a governing board was organized for the Russia program that included the program administrators and donor representatives.[170] To ensure the work's quality, the Council of Academic Curators was also established by the Russian NGO administering the Russian CASE program, the Center for Innovation, Technology, and Education based in Moscow.

Mark Johnson, historian of Russian higher education, was commissioned in 2009 to conduct an extensive review of the program.[171] As he noted, by the end of the CASE program, the Corporation had expended over $50 million of grant support and the accomplishments were significant.[172] While identifying successes, he also noted that some centers had struggled to be consistent in achieving high-quality research results or building and sustaining partnerships. Johnson highlighted the range of institutional results: "The single most important issue in the relative intellectual vitality and institutional adaptability of each CASE seems to be the quality of leadership and the style of governance within and around each interdisciplinary center."[173]

As described by the program staff, the HEFSU program led to "Thirteen university-based centers for the advancement of study and education in the social science disciplines in Belarus, Armenia, Azerbaijan, Georgia and Russia.... Sixteen university-based centers for the advancement of research and education in the sciences in Russia.... Humanities research and writing fellowships for over 650 post-Soviet academics and close to 5,000 research, writing and travel grants for social scientists, scientists and university administrators.... Strengthened university leadership and educational policies.... Implementation of pilot reforms at select universities in Russia and other countries in post-Soviet Eurasia."[174]

One of the most promising developments has been the agreement between the Russian Ministry of Education, the CASEs, and the BRHE program to provide either complementary or additional support. Concerning the BRHE program, the government created fifteen new research centers entirely funded by the Russian institutions. The program has leveraged many millions of dollars of support from the Russian government.[175]

The Corporation, as of 2011, continued to focus on enhancing the capacities of academics, researchers, and university leaders in the region, including the work in Eurasia.[176] As Johnson concluded, the success in strengthening intellectual life through the CASE approach "will leave behind some potentially transformative legacies and institutional structures, which local interest groups, other donors, and international partners could—and perhaps should—continue to build upon in the future."[177]

NEW DIMENSIONS OF SECURITY: SELF-DETERMINATION, RESOURCE CONSTRAINTS, AND STATES AT RISK

DRAWING ON THE RECOMMENDATIONS of the Carnegie Commission on Preventing Deadly Conflict, Vartan Gregorian and the leadership of the International Peace and Security Program in 1999 identified four problem domains "that are in critical need of attention by policymakers and the analytic research community."[178] These domains were: resource scarcity, with a special focus on water; self-determination and territorial integrity, particularly where violence had not yet occurred; peacebuilding to consolidate and prevent the reoccurrence of violence; and the controversial role of sanctions and incentives, particularly with respect to what works, why, and how.[179] Initial grants in this area continued some of the themes that had been supported in the prior period, particularly the work of Alexander George on international relations at Stanford University and the United Nations Institute for Training and Research for its program on peacemaking and preventive diplomacy, as well as the work related to war-torn societies, conflict management in the post-Soviet region and the Balkans, and the general area of strengthening democratic institutions in the former Soviet Union.[180]

After a series of consultations and discussion papers, two areas were selected from the initial four: self-determination and the sanctity of existing borders, and the perils and promise of competition over water.[181] As in the approaches used by other areas of the International Peace and Security Program, staff members in this subprogram sought to identify established scholars as well as emerging ones across different disciplines; to form networks across the different scholars to enable them to learn from each other's work and arrive at policy-oriented findings; and to connect those scholars with policymakers.

Program staff members, led by Stephen Del Rosso, broadly defined self-determination as "greater political, economic and cultural autonomy, federalism and other power-sharing arrangements—up to and including the establishment of a separate state."[182] Recognizing the complexity of this area, they identified three themes to further define the grant-making: internal political structures, implications of globalization, and external interventions. Because self-determination was a relatively new area for the Corporation's attention, staff members circulated RFPs widely to identify the most promising grantees.[183]

In response to the initial RFP, the program received more than one hundred proposals; with funding available for the year, reviewers selected thirty-nine projects.[184] From this process, the Corporation homed in on three specific grant-making objectives: "To examine the efficacy of various power sharing arrangements in multiethnic societies ... to assess the role of external actors and internal conflicts ... [and] to better understand and evaluate the impact of globalization on international peace and security."[185] Concurrent with the review process, program staff identified sovereignty as a concept that could bridge the two distinct themes of self-determination and water. "As extensively chronicled, the ability of states to control developments both within and between their borders has changed dramatically. Although never as secure and sacrosanct as sometimes assumed, state sovereignty has been increasingly undermined from above by the myriad forces of globalization, and from below by the proliferating challenges of restive groups demanding greater self-governance."[186]

After initial grant-making was under way on self-determination and water issues, program staff sought to link the two under a coherent conceptual framework that reflected key aspects of both. The result was a focus on the concept of evolving notions of sovereignty and a redefinition of the grant-making areas under the rubrics of: (1) contested borders in a globalized world and (2) resource scarcity: competition and cooperation over freshwater.[187]

Cognizant of the extant work on freshwater, Corporation staff determined that linking water issues to emerging conceptions of sovereignty would fill an important gap.[188] Riparian rights, boundary disputes, control over the scarce resource—all of these issues were clearly related to issues of sovereignty, as addressed in one of the early grants to Johns Hopkins University for Track II talks over water rights between India and Pakistan.[189] Staff adapted the Russian Initiative model and proactively identified water-related experts, other scholars, and practitioners, along with participants drawn from the field of international security, to help define the grant-making opportunities.[190] From the meeting recommendations, program staff considered that a three-year time frame would be sufficient to arrive at research recommendations and policy connections around the themes of sovereignty in contentious areas in time for the next World Water Forum, the key global meeting in the field scheduled for Japan in April 2003.[191]

The terrorist attacks of September 11, 2001, reinforced the crucial role of sovereignty, especially in relation to contested borders: "The events of September 11 have magnified the increasingly precarious nature of sovereignty and its role on the emerging security agenda ... well-established notions of sovereignty are being increasingly eroded by a wide range of groups that 'transcend the nation-state' and operate in the interstices of what has been the traditional purview of the state-dominated 'international community.'"[192] The concept of preemptive war, buoyed by the "war on terrorism," created new sources of conflict in Afghanistan, Iraq, and Pakistan and continuing concerns in areas explored by program grantees in Kosovo, Bosnia, and East Timor.[193] A 2002 *Carnegie Challenge Paper* by David Callahan, scholar and political commentator, further emphasized the vital importance of concern about self-determination in light of 9/11; he reinforced the program's focus on building the field of study and actively sharing research results with policymakers.[194]

Given the magnitude of these emerging issues and the relatively limited number of donor partners, Corporation leadership and program staff determined that, among the array of issues identified as new dimensions of security, grant-making related to self-determination and sovereignty presented the most promising opportunities for the application of scarce financial resources. Staff acknowledged that in the broader area of conflicts over water rights, multiple solutions had been proposed over many decades; at the same time as the program started, an international freshwater commission was under way and about to make major recommendations highlighting the international dimensions.

During the three-year time frame envisioned at the initial water experts' meeting, the program supported a focused cluster of water-related grants.[195] Given the considerable work already funded by others, particularly at the intergovernmental level, some of the tangible outcomes from Corporation-supported grants (such as from the Track II water dialogue in South Asia), and the Corporation's relative lack of comparative advantage in this area, staff agreed with Corporation leadership not to invest further.[196]

To concentrate the efforts related to conflict prevention, early warning systems, and the relationship between the global and local potential for conflict, the program determined that the focus over the next few years would converge around the theme of preventing failed states under the revised rubric of "Global Engagement." The goal highlighted the positive possibilities for preventing failed states: "To advance new conceptions of global engagement and multilateral cooperation by providing expert, policy-relevant assistance to official efforts to prevent failed states, and advancing other IPS program interests, as appropriate."[197] The United States was clearly involved in massive "nation-building" efforts in Afghanistan, as were other international agencies, and the topic was of concern to foundations such as the Rockefeller Brothers Fund and the Rockefeller Foundation. Concurrent with program developments, the George W. Bush administration, at the time, had also declared that the United States "is threatened less by conquering states than we are by failing ones," a sentiment echoed in policy pronouncements by other Western and international organizational leaders.[198] The Corporation planned to draw on its networks of scholars and practitioners in studies on self-determination to prompt new scholarship, build dialogue among stakeholders to address the problem of failing states, and step up the dissemination of recommendations to policymakers and the public by publishing in major media outlets.[199]

For example, the City University of New York, under the leadership of Susan Woodward, created an ever-increasing database of young scholars.[200] Through grantees such as the International Peace Academy, New York University's Center for International Conflict and the NYU Law School, the Stimson Center, the Center for Security and International Studies (CSIS), and the International Crisis Group, over one hundred policy-relevant, evidence-based articles, reports, and books were published on state failure, the crisis of government, the future of UN state-building and human development, peace-building reform, and action strategies for a number of countries with internal conflicts.[201] Moreover, these grantees, from 2003 to 2005, held over seventy-five policy-level conferences, bringing together representatives from the UN, the US Department of Defense, NGOs, UN mission staffs, the World Bank, and the International Monetary Fund with scholars and policymakers.[202] Grantees not only contributed to the Post-Conflict Reconstruction Essential Task List Matrix used by the US Department of State Office of the Coordinator for Reconstruction and Stabilization but also provided information on the Matrix following requests from the Department of State, the National Security Council, congressional staff, and the UN Department of Peacekeeping Operations.[203] CSIS and RAND, among other grantees, also contributed to the establishment of the Office of the Coordinator and, later, its successor, the Bureau of Conflict and Stabilization Operations.

Grantees Stephen Stedman and Bruce Jones made a significant contribution to the UN secretary-general's influential High-Level Panel on Threats, Challenges, and Change when they were seconded from their home institutions to serve as deputy research director and deputy special adviser to the secretary-general (Stedman) and research director to the assistant secretary-general responsible for implementing the panel's recommendations (Jones). The work of the panel resulted in the report *A More Secure World: Our Shared Responsibility*.[204] On the basis of this report, with the input of a wide range of Corporation grantees, and after many years of discussion, the UN, through Secretary-General Kofi Annan and the General Assembly, established the United Nations Peacebuilding Commission in December 2005. Unusually, the report connected the areas of states at risk and development, pointing to the opportunity for collaboration across the two programs at the Corporation as well as elsewhere.[205]

By 2006, the results related to the New Dimensions of Security subprogram covered a wide range of activities—from the early Track II dialogues that had led to regional water agreements in South Asia and reduced tensions in the Caucasus to the more than sixty grants in the area of self-determination that had served to "build a body of policy-relevant scholarship on the design of political systems satisfactory to existing states and potentially secessionist national groups, the complex role of external interveners, and implications of globalization on self-determination."[206] Staff noted that findings from grantees were used by negotiators in internal conflict situations; for example, "the East-West Center … study of the separatist movement in Aceh province, Indonesia, was the primary resource for the U.N. mediation team that brokered the peace treaty."[207] The Fund for Peace developed and fine-tuned the State Failure Index Series in *Foreign Policy* magazine referred to by policymakers and other researchers.[208]

Staff determined that these accomplishments warranted recasting the program: rather than a late-stage focus on the challenges of failed states, the program would address concerns at an earlier stage by adopting the concept of "states at risk" (specifically, at risk of instability or collapse).[209] Moreover, Del Rosso and his colleagues had long recognized that the term "failed state" reflected a freighted, inapt characterization of a complex phenomenon that required a more nuanced treatment.[210] Toward that aim, in 2007 the Corporation began to broaden its scope of activity by bringing in a few new grantees, ranging from those that examined the role of preventive community action in states at risk, such as Future Generations (an international NGO), to those that confronted state-building challenges, such as the Center for Cultural and Technical Interchange Between East and West (the East-West Center in Hawaii). The Corporation also brought back prior grantees working on postwar state-building, such as the University of California at San Diego, the International Peace Academy, and the University of Denver.[211] The total annual budgets for this area averaged about $4 million.[212]

From 2007 to 2011, staff continued to build the field of knowledge and foster connections among scholars across disciplines and countries through the networking and database activities of the City University of New York, New York University, the University of Denver, Columbia University, and the University of Cambridge/University of Reading, each addressing a different set of issues associated with states at risk. The program encouraged the country-specific work in Afghanistan, Iraq, and Pakistan. The reports from the International Crisis Group's work on Afghanistan, for instance, contributed to shaping both American and international policy debates.[213] Rather than focusing solely on the threats and failures, some efforts directly considered the potential for progress in Afghanistan, such as Future Generations' programs on community empowerment, Princeton University's Lichtenstein Institute on Self-determination, and the Century Foundation's high-level task force on Afghanistan co-chaired by then-trustee Thomas Pickering and Lakhdar Brahimi.[214] The country-specific work featured the critical role of local capacity in the area of peace-building and postconflict reconstruction as a complement to that of international experts.[215]

Many of the grantees have been working closely with international and national agencies to assist in strengthening their programs and policies, especially with fragile states. The report from the Council on Foreign Relations' Conflict Prevention Program on enhancing US preventive action appeared to have influenced the high-level policy review on the subject within the US government.[216] The International Peace Institute (formerly the International Peace Academy) has not only contributed to the peace-building efforts of the UN but also worked with the Security Council on specific situations, such as in Uganda.[217]

With a cluster of nearly thirty grantees and having expended over this particular period around $24 million, the Corporation and other foundation partners—notably, the MacArthur Foundation, the Compton Foundation, and the United States Institute of Peace—contributed to building the field around the concept of states at risk. Other foundations, such as the Stanley Foundation, have been creating an NGO-foundation coalition; the Corporation and others developed a foundation affinity group as a subset to the Peace and Security Funders Group to facilitate the sharing of ideas and results and to build collaboration.[218]

Yet the area of states at risk remains a complex one where lessons drawn from site-specific situations provide guidance on approaches but often not specific interventions, since each new situation has its own defining characteristics. Nevertheless, the approach can be crucial: the comparative advantage of a foundation is that it can identify and provide funding on both the local and international levels for the most relevant research, the most promising younger and more seasoned scholars, the most productive way to convene stakeholder dialogues, and the most effective way to disseminate findings. Following the 2007 structural changes at the Corporation that resulted in the International Program, the states at risk and Africa components developed an intraprogram partnership to build local-level policy research capacity on conflict and development.[219] Organized by the Social Science Research Council in collaboration with African partners, this new approach, started in 2011, aimed to contribute to more successful conflict prevention policies and the building of sustainable peace in African countries and beyond.[220]

THE ISLAM INITIATIVE

WHEN VARTAN GREGORIAN became president in 1997, he illuminated an issue that was being given scant attention by foundations. As he wrote in his "Preliminary Thoughts" essay of 1997:

Islam is the fastest-growing religion in the United States—a phenomenon that few recognize but that will have a profound impact on American society in the future. As America develops a viable Muslim community, our understanding of Islam will be important for the harmony of our democracy. Of fundamental importance is that this country maintain its strong tradition of religious tolerance and religious freedom in the years to come.[221]

Over the next nine years, several programs made grants related to enhancing knowledge and, especially, public understanding about Islam and Muslim societies. The democracy and special projects programs, along with the Public Affairs Department, funded a series of projects, meetings, and media efforts. Starting in 2005, the Carnegie Scholars Program focused entirely on supporting the research of public scholars on Islam and Muslim societies. In late 2006, Gregorian and the trustees determined that sufficient groundwork had been developed so that a special Islam Initiative could develop institutional grants to make more systematic inroads on both public and policymaker understanding. They decided to hire a staff member with deeper expertise in the field specifically dedicated to this area. Hillary Wiesner, a scholar of religion, philosophy, and Islam, had most recently served in the cabinet of the director-general of UNESCO. Drawing on all the disparate efforts at the Corporation, she developed the Islam Initiative, approved by the president and the board in 2007.[222] The program's three-pronged thrust comprised educating Americans on the diversity of Islam, strengthening lines of communication between experts on Islam and the public policy community, and building international partnerships.[223]

The first set of activities addressed public outreach by scholars by introducing "public engagement functions into ... [university-based] national centers for area and international studies that were created in 1958 through Title VI of the National Defense Act."[224] Staff determined that the Social Science Research Council (SSRC) was best placed to design and implement a competition to encourage public outreach by scholars beyond their centers and universities.[225] By 2012, forty-nine grants had been awarded under this program, entitled "Academia and the Public Sphere: Islam and Muslims in World Context," with funds from the Corporation totaling $3.4 million.[226] The National Endowment for the Humanities complemented the initiative through its "Bridging Cultures" competitive grants program.[227] A special grant to the American Council on Education promoted the fiftieth anniversary of the Title VI international education programs, highlighting the centers engaged in study and outreach on Islam.[228]

A historically oriented effort with potentially distinctive contemporary policy impact focused on bringing to light "significant writings of scholars of the past, from the 18th to early 20th centuries, writers in Muslim societies who analyzed issues including nationalism, modernity, science, law, constitutionalism, and the status of women. Relevant to their time and shedding some light on current debates and controversies, these works require modern editions and translations with interpretive prefaces to enable today's researchers, students and the public to take full advantage of the intellectual inheritance of this creative period."[229] A cluster of grants were awarded in support of the modernization project, for selecting the publications, translating them for contemporary audiences, and publishing them, including online, through the Bibliotheca Alexandria (the Library of Alexandria in Egypt), the Institute for Advanced Study in Princeton, and Yale University Press.[230] Complementary projects extended this effort: one with the Oxford Centre for Islamic Studies for publication of the *Historical Atlas of the Islamic World*, a multinational, multivolume atlas aimed at attracting both scholarly and wider readership; and a project with the Friends of the British Council to examine Euro-Muslim identities in both historical and modern contexts, with extensive transatlantic dissemination of the findings.[231]

Relating directly to the strengthening of academic expertise and outreach in the field, the Corporation also funded George Washington University under the leadership of Marc Lynch to establish an international network of experts, bringing together specialists in areas of international relations and political science to focus on the Middle East.[232] As in other parts of the international program, the Islam Initiative staff facilitated connections between American scholars and overseas scholars. Rami Khouri, an adviser from the American University of Beirut, emphasized building "structural, long-term collaborations among academics, nongovernmental and other private sector organizations, educators, researchers, journalists, and others." As a result, the staff emphasized "the building of contacts and communications between university centers and think tanks in the United States and abroad by promoting exchanges and institutional partnerships."[233] Partners included the Ford and Henry L. Luce Foundations. A follow-up grant to the Council of American Overseas Research Centers linked their centers and local scholars with US-based academic institutions.[234]

Working closely with the Corporation's Public Affairs Department, three direct public outreach programs received support. The New York Public Library organized a series of programs and exhibits on the Abrahamic faiths.[235] *The Charlie Rose Show* broadcast a series of interviews on the theme of Islam, and the Paley Center for Media held a symposium with media experts and American Muslim specialists to examine ways to improve the coverage of these issues.[236] One of the outcomes was a Web-based resource site providing the results of the symposium.[237]

A recent event of potent historical magnitude, the Arab Awakening of 2011, illustrated the contributions that can result from a foundation's multifaceted focus on a central theme. The combination of support for networks (such as the one housed at George Washington University linking scholars and policymakers, including for its dissemination on the website ForeignPolicy.com), public outreach via a television news interview show (such as *The Charlie Rose Show*), and funding of individuals (namely, both academic and policy scholars committed to public outreach on Islam, such as through the Carnegie Scholars Program and the program on States at Risk)[238] led to the widespread involvement of well-grounded, knowledgeable grantees who were sought out by print and broadcast media as commentators and analysts. As noted by program staff, "The [Tunisian and Egyptian] revolutions created an unprecedented demand for genuine expertise in Middle East studies. World events turned out to be the ultimate 'news hook' for the dissemination of Corporation-supported knowledge production."[239] For example, scholars who had spent years studying the Muslim Brotherhood or constitutional democracy in Egypt were in particular demand, and grantees were consulted frequently by the National Security Council and the Department of State throughout the period. Moreover, other grantees testified before Congress at the 2011 hearing on the American Muslim community.

With support of $4 million to $6 million a year since 2007, the Corporation still faces the dual challenge of sustaining grantee access to the public and policymakers, once the crisis has subsided from the news agenda, and assessing whether that access and outreach have improved social relations and public policy by sufficiently advancing public and policymaker knowledge and understanding.[240]

INTERNATIONAL DEVELOPMENT

GREGORIAN, IN HIS FIRST ESSAY AS PRESIDENT, "Preliminary Thoughts," explicitly stated his concerns about American perceptions of Africa and the state of higher education and accessibility to up-to-date information in African countries:

> I am concerned that sub-Saharan Africa remains low in the American consciousness and last on its political agenda. I am especially concerned about the fate of African universities and research libraries, given the exodus of great talent from that continent to other parts of the world and given the environment of political instability and the severe economic hardship that prevail in many countries. How can we as a nation support African leadership in the university realm? Which are the institutions that should be strengthened? How can we, collectively and in a sustainable way, build model universities in Africa and support leadership training that will enhance the development process?... Much of donor attention has been directed to achieving a market economy or privatization in Africa, but support for scholars within institutions of higher learning there would contribute substantially toward African development.[241]

The thrust of the efforts in international development in this era soon evoked comparable premises that informed the work of Stephen Stackpole and Alan Pifer in the 1950s and 1960s in Commonwealth African countries (see Chapters 5 and 6). Over those years, the Corporation worked closely with selected African universities to help them make significant contributions to national development at independence. With the focus on universities and libraries as two prominent knowledge-conveying institutions in African countries, and including the theme of enhancing opportunities for women in higher education, the International Development Program was transformed to meet these recurring needs in the new century.[242]

Staff members reviewed the Corporation's efforts in the 1950s and 1960s, along with those of the Rockefeller Foundation in that period through its extensive University Development Program. (Although unmentioned in the program paper, the Ford Foundation was also involved in higher education in Africa.[243]) Staff members also reviewed the impact of limited internal and external financing combining almost simultaneously in the mid-1980s with the World Bank's focus on primary education, which had led to the dire condition of African universities.[244] As a response to the concerns expressed by African university vice chancellors, the World Bank established the Donors to African Education Program, which became the Association for the Development of Education in Africa (still active as of this writing). In the 1990s, the bank also agreed to host the Working Group on Higher Education led by William Saint, a former Ford Foundation staff member; that group, along with the Association of African Universities, continued to promote the vital role of higher education in African development.[245] The 1997 publication *Revitalizing Universities in Africa: Strategies and Guidelines*, issued jointly by the World Bank and the Association of African Universities, detailed the more than twenty universities that were preparing strategic plans, reinforcing the viability of a focus on university strengthening by the Corporation and other donors.[246]

That document served as background for a Roundtable on Africa held at the Corporation in November 1997 with grantees and advisers from around the continent. Participants recommended three principles to guide the future work: development is a national responsibility that should be initiated by those being developed; development must be participatory and responsive to the local cultural, social, political, and economic environment; and development initiatives, if they are to succeed, must build on national structures, values, and institutions as the primary sources of ideas. Participants uniformly agreed that investments in Africa should take place in the spirit of partnership—partnership based on transparency, accountability, and clear expectations of roles, time frames, and resources.[247]

A follow-up meeting held in 1998 at the Corporation with representatives from key African organizations (the Association of African Universities, national library associations, the Forum of African Women Educationalists, and the UN Economic Commission for Africa), the Working Group on Higher Education, and the American Library Association, along with potential foundation partners, emphasized the vital importance of continuing to focus on access to knowledge, improving the availability of skilled human resources, and strengthening the institutions responsible for education and knowledge production and dissemination.[248] The participants reinforced the Corporation's intention to enhance the sustainability of its investments in university strengthening by encouraging proposals developed around activities that were already part of institution-approved strategic plans. In this way, the Corporation would not be introducing new programs and projects; instead, the grants would serve to reinforce areas that needed piloting or testing before they could be fully funded through university budgets and other national sources.

Drawing together all the recommendations from reviews of context, meetings, grantees, and foundation colleagues, and with encouragement from the president and trustees, the new program addressed "strengthening innovative African universities and university leaders, enhancing opportunities for women to participate in higher education, and assisting public libraries in becoming more effective and more accessible learning centers for African people."[249] The program would also explore a few university-based projects addressing issues of the rule of law and private-sector development in Africa, both considered crucial for sustaining successful investments in economic development.

The focus on women continued the Corporation's commitment since the late 1970s to strengthening their role in development. Women's impeded access to higher education limited their capacity to participate in and contribute to national development at higher leadership levels. The prevailing family and institutional tendency was to fund men to go to university, not women. At the time when the program was being planned, women "constitute[d] less than 20 percent of university entrants in Africa."[250] Many women attending university dropped out before graduation because the environment was simply not conducive for retaining them. To help remove these obstacles, Corporation leadership and staff worked with university leadership to examine ways to provide scholarships for undergraduate women and to make the university environment more conducive for women to succeed.[251]

With increasing recognition of the information and digital divide and the impact of this gap on people at lower income levels and outside of universities with no access to information technologies, the program revived the early commitment of Andrew Carnegie and Carnegie Corporation to public libraries, including those in Africa and other Commonwealth countries. Program staff began to consider ways to reinforce the role of public libraries in enhancing access to information for all members of the community. Kay Raseroka, senior librarian at the University of Botswana, pinpointed the crux of the issue: "The crucial question faced by all African public libraries is how to justify themselves to government. Studies to find what role public libraries play in supporting education have shown they are in decline because of lack of government commitment towards their funding."[252] Clearly the Corporation was tackling a challenging question, and up-to-date information was a prerequisite to start the program.

Recognizing that pursuing the three new themes would require extensive efforts, staff members decided not to enter into new grant-making in the other areas noted in the program paper, the rule of law and entrepreneurship. They proposed "a three-stage approach in each program area: a diagnostic phase aimed at synthesizing existing knowledge, assessing institutional capacity, and identifying specific opportunities for grantmaking; an intervention phase to support a few selected institutions that have shown the will and the commitment to institute significant reforms; and a replication phase through targeted dissemination of program results by putting structures and resources in place that will identify points of leverage and opportunities for successful adoption in other settings."[253]

Following the discussions at the 1998 meeting, Corporation and Rockefeller Foundation staff members began considering a foundation-university partnership in support of a few specific initiatives (comparable to other collaborative activities undertaken in the 1990s, as described in Chapter 7).[254] The first idea was that together the two foundations would support the mapping of universities in Commonwealth African countries and conduct case studies to identify the most promising institutions engaged in reform.[255] Although unanticipated at that early stage, the partnership plan of the two foundations to strengthen African universities evolved into a ten-year, multimillion-dollar model partnership linking several foundations in several countries with a multitude of universities.

Regarding women's educational opportunities, the Corporation intended to support studies examining university life at all levels and to develop model programs along with a planned scholarship program. Corporation staff members considered it important to identify universities that had created an institutional climate where women undergraduates could flourish. Two institutions at the forefront of this effort were the University of Dar es Salaam in Tanzania and Makerere University in Uganda. Their programs were clearly thought through and well positioned for appropriate external support.[256] The exploratory work assessed not only the feasibility of a scholarship program but also the level of leadership and investment that would be required to ensure the successful retention of women undergraduates even with the scholarships.[257]

In the area of revitalizing public libraries, grants to the UK-based International Network for the Availability of Scientific Publications led to a series of baseline studies on the state of public library services and systems in Commonwealth African countries.[258] The results were disseminated widely in Africa and at international meetings. Moreover, from these studies Corporation staff members determined that "there is solid evidence that a dynamic system of library services can emerge in three countries in southern Africa: South Africa, Botswana, and Zimbabwe."[259] The Corporation considered a number of strategies, including a partnership across the countries and building out from that partnership to other countries and areas in the region. It was anticipated that professional training programs would be necessary to reinforce the library systems, but also that after five years grants would result in models for reforming public library systems to encourage other donors, and especially governments, to maintain support for such investments.

Gregorian and the board wished to make the overall program more manageable by limiting its geographic scope. Staff members recommended concentrating on six countries where the Corporation had deep experience in education, women in development, and information systems: Nigeria and Ghana in West Africa, Uganda and Tanzania in East Africa, and Zimbabwe and South Africa in Southern Africa. Staff members also identified a number of potential partners, both continuing and new ones, including foundations, bilateral and multilateral assistance agencies, and the United Nations.[260]

To implement the new program on strengthening African universities and the intended close cooperation with university vice chancellors, the Corporation sought a program officer from the leadership level of African universities. To develop the new public library thrust, the Corporation also decided to bring into the program a trained librarian who could work with counterparts on the continent to develop new approaches to public libraries. A leader in African education, Narciso Matos, was selected by the Corporation in late 1999 both to chair the International Development Program and to direct the university-strengthening efforts.[261] To manage the library work, Gregorian encouraged Gloria Primm Brown, a longtime staff member in the Education Program who had been trained as a librarian, to develop the library program in Africa and design the new grants program. Andrea Johnson, already a member of the International Development Program, was promoted to program officer; she worked directly with Matos on the university grants and developed the women's undergraduate scholarship program.

With the new staff configuration, the program strategies moved rapidly from development to implementation, building in evaluation as a critical element in each area to encourage adoption by other institutions and to attract new resources.[262] Infusing each area was the theme of partnership: between foundation and university leaders for university-strengthening and women's scholarships, and between governments and the Corporation in revitalizing public libraries.

THE PARTNERSHIP FOR HIGHER EDUCATION IN AFRICA: UNIVERSITIES, WOMEN, AND CONNECTIVITY

NOTWITHSTANDING THE CONSTRAINTS, the magnitude of the opportunities for strengthening African universities led other foundation leaders to express interest in the partnership under development between the Rockefeller Foundation and Carnegie Corporation. President Susan Berresford of the Ford Foundation and President Jonathan Fanton of the MacArthur Foundation soon joined Gregorian and President Gordon Conway of the Rockefeller Foundation in preparing and finalizing a memorandum of understanding defining the partnership. In April 2000, with Kofi Annan, secretary-general of the United Nations, and Andrew Siwela, former president of the Association of African Universities, the four presidents of the four institutions with their staffs launched the Partnership for Higher Education in Africa (PHEA). The presidents framed their announcement with optimism and enthusiasm about investing $100 million over five years to strengthen African universities, building on national reforms already under way and the commitment of African university leaders to tackling and overcoming the adverse conditions of the past decades. To clarify the criteria as expressed in the memorandum of understanding, the press release issued jointly by the four foundations specified the selection process so that it would be open and transparent.[263]

Although all four foundations had been supporting African universities prior to this announcement, it was agreed by the presidents that under the Partnership they would follow the terms of the memorandum of understanding and contribute to strengthening those institutions that met the criteria and were in the countries where reforms were well under way. The initial six countries focused on by the Partnership were Ghana and Nigeria in West Africa, Tanzania and Uganda in East Africa, and Mozambique and South Africa in Southern Africa. Carnegie Corporation was active in five of these countries; because of charter constraints, it could not make grants in Mozambique.[264]

By 2002, the foundation leaders agreed that establishing a small office with a coordinator specifically dedicated to the Partnership could play a synergistic role to ensure careful monitoring of Partnership implementation, including selected joint initiatives. Established at the New York University Steinhardt School of Education, the office played a coordinating role until the end of the Partnership in 2010.[265] The Partnership coordinating committee, comprising at least two representatives from each foundation, met regularly and identified a range of joint initiatives related to advancing Internet connectivity and use, higher education research and advocacy, publications and dissemination, university leadership, and the next generation of scholars and faculty.[266]

According to an evaluation in 2004, one of the most effective of the Partnership activities resulted from recognizing that it was vitally important for African universities to reduce the isolation of their students and faculty by improving access to less expensive bandwidth. Several of the Corporation's university grantees included investments related to university-wide information systems as integral components in their strengthening plans.[267] Unreliable connections and prohibitively high access costs, however, limited the use of those systems. Affordable increased bandwidth would enhance connectivity and reduce the time required to access the Internet, download documents, and communicate outside the continent.[268]

After studies, assessments, and negotiations with bandwidth providers and university systems, by 2005, as part of the Partnership's Information, Communications, and Technologies (ICT) subcommittee, the foundations agreed to support a grant to the African Virtual University "to function as sole agent and negotiator with Intelsat—a satellite bandwidth provider— on behalf of partnership universities. This consortium will enable universities to reduce the unit cost of bandwidth and buy, on average, three times the quantity of bandwidth that universities could buy individually."[269] During 2005 and 2006, with an initial investment of $5 million, the group helped provide bandwidth for twelve universities in six countries and achieve greatly reduced costs. The Corporation then specifically invested in the Nigerian ICT Forum, which took over the work from the African Virtual University for the Bandwidth Consortium.[270] As a result of all these efforts, the universities could purchase bandwidth and share Internet capacity at a greatly reduced rate. This focus on bandwidth and the improvements in the IT infrastructure of each of the universities allowed earlier investments to be sustained. Still, Corporation staff remained realistic about the results, recognizing that, for the MIT I-Labs (see note 267), for example, "some successes notwithstanding, bandwidth constraints, especially within the least well-resourced institutions, continue to inhibit uptake of the labs on a broader scale, keeping this a programmatic priority for our work."[271]

The Partnership sponsored an evaluation in 2004 to assess the feasibility of renewing support. The results affirmed the significant difference in resource levels and approach brought about by the Partnership: since 2000, it had "tripled the annual investment of the four foundations in African higher education over what they had invested in the 1990s; shifted the balance of investments in favor of institutional transformation rather than simply 'using' universities to conduct and manage projects; increased collaboration between the Partnership foundations, bringing about greater synergy of grantmaking for some key initiatives, such as the bandwidth proj-ect in Nigeria and Uganda; and contributed significantly to the production and distribution of knowledge on higher education in Africa." The evalua-tion team identified some areas for improvement related to strengthening the Partnership itself. These included "'more sharing of information within the Partnership and with donors; more collaboration planning within the Partnership; greater focus in specific strategic areas; a higher profile to reap the benefits of the Partnership's symbolic value; and better engagement with governments in the region.' In light of this, the evaluators recommended a higher profile for the Partnership; strengthening organizational and oper-ating modalities of the Partnership's work; and tighter and better coordina-tion among foundations to achieve greater efficiency and effectiveness."[272]

The foundation presidents at their meeting in November 2004 reviewed the results of the evaluation and agreed to work on the issues related to the profile for the Partnership and to continue the Partnership for another five years. The Partnership was re-launched in September 2005 at a widely attended meeting at the Ford Foundation. With the visibility of the early accomplishments of the Partnership and the increasing recognition of the importance of higher education for national economic and social develop-ment in African countries, other foundations and countries also asked to join. The only condition was that they agree to the criteria and provide staff involvement and support for the Partnership office. Starting in 2005, the Hewlett Foundation and the Mellon Foundation joined the Partnership, and in 2007 the Kresge Foundation did as well. With their collaboration, two new countries, Kenya and Egypt, were added.

The original four partners contributed a total of $191 million over the first five years, considerably more than their initial pledge of $100 million. With the new foundation partners, an additional $200 million was pledged for the next five years. When the Partnership came to a close in 2010, it had directly generated a total of $440 million, nearly $140 million more than anticipated.[273] It is impossible to estimate how much that support leveraged over the ten years. The accomplishments review prepared by the Partnership coordination team in 2010 underlined the point that the com-mitment to provide direct support to African universities greatly influenced the nature of the grant-making:[274]

$370 million of support (84%) went directly to African grantees, including $243 million in direct support to African universities and colleges.... In responding to university demands, grants for institutional development usually supported priority areas identified by the universities themselves. Of the 65 African universities and colleges supported, a subset of 27 received $1 million or more, with seven universities receiving over $10 million each. African regional networks for postgraduate training and research were the second largest type of grantee, receiving $60.5 million in total. Thirteen networks received over $1 million each.... Two University Leaders' Forums, numerous consultative meetings, and several task forces over the ten-year span highlight the PHEA's commitment to consultation. Finally, the considerable support for individual fellowships, scholarships, and leadership training was generally administered by universities and their faculties, in line with their institutional and staff development plans.[275]

Although the money was surely important, perhaps even more significant, as highlighted by the 2004 evaluation, was the principle of putting the universities and their leaders in the driver's seat so that most of the investment supported the identified needs of the institutions, not the specific interests of the foundations beyond the institutional support. The future challenge for all the partners will be to find ways to maintain this innovation and apply the lessons learned.

In comparison with other impressive formal foundation partnerships, this may have been the first planned international initiative with multiple foundations agreeing to carefully delineated goals and milestones along with funding commitments that combined both specific institutional grants made by each partner and joint partnership grants.[276] In over ten years of working in close collaboration with university leaders in Africa, the Partnership for Higher Education in Africa ultimately included "nine African countries: Egypt, Kenya, Uganda, Tanzania, Madagascar, Mozambique, South Africa, Nigeria, and Ghana. These countries have a combined population of 459 million. In a continent with a tertiary education enrollment ratio of only 3%, the PHEA has, directly and indirectly, improved conditions for 4.1 million African students enrolled at 379 universities and colleges."[277]

The PHEA endeavor could lead the way to new forms of international partnerships that engage not only the donors at all levels but also the institutional leaders. The vice chancellors participated in discussions and meetings with the Partnership participants as well as with other institutional constituencies. The one missing element, albeit sensitive for external actors to engage in actively, was advocacy at the national and international levels for continued support beyond the ten-year initiative of the foundations. Later activities promised to begin to fill that gap by holding stakeholders' meetings and policy dialogues, such as those organized by the Association of African Universities, the Higher Education Research and Advocacy Network in Africa at the South Africa–based Centre for Higher Education Transformation, Higher Education Policy Dialogues at the Senegal-based TrustAfrica, and the partnership-convened University Leaders Forum.[278] As Suzanne Grant Lewis noted, these activities, at the least, "helped change the terms of the debate on educational investment in Africa."[279] The World Bank would probably have issued a report different in tone and recommendations than the one it published in 1988 if it could have taken into account the depth and scope of the changes in African higher education institutions over the past decade as a result of the Partnership. Nonetheless, given the history of the last sixty years, African universities, even as strengthened, face continuing challenges to sustain and build on their accomplishments— including the challenge, discussed in the next section, of replenishing faculty.

STRENGTHENING AFRICAN UNIVERSITIES: CARNEGIE CORPORATION'S EFFORTS

OVER THE TEN YEARS of the Partnership for Higher Education in Africa, the Corporation provided direct support for both individual institutions and university systems, as well as for PHEA activities; new staff was also brought on board.[280] As estimated by Lewis, the Corporation's investment over this period was $125,509,354, or 29 percent of the total Partnership funding.[281]

The case studies initiated by the Partnership at Makerere University in Uganda and the University of Dar es Salaam in Tanzania, along with subsequent planning grants from the Corporation, resulted in initial institution-strengthening programs of approximately $3 million at each of these institutions. The specific activities, defined by the university leaders, all related directly to each university's strategic plan.[282] The focus for the University of Dar es Salaam was on computerization of the library, development of databases, improved access to library facilities, and introduction of smart cards—all efforts to bring the university rapidly into the electronic information age. At Makerere University, the plans involved not only improving the library but also developing programs for distance education, strengthening overall research capacity, and building stronger science departments.

With extended university sectors in South Africa and Nigeria, the partnership and the Corporation began considering ways to work with both individual institutions and the system. In South Africa a series of planning grants explored two areas highlighted by the national plan for higher education: national quality assurance and accreditation. To contribute to these key elements in the national plan, with Corporation funding, the South African Council on Higher Education, the South African Ministry of Education, and the South African Universities Vice Chancellors Association conducted studies and shaped policy recommendations for the main decision-makers.[283]

From the reviews, additional site visits, and consultations, the first round of university-strengthening grants in South Africa centered on developing partnerships between historically advantaged and historically disadvantaged universities. After circulating a request for proposals in 2001 and 2002, the program staff and reviewers recommended three partnerships, involving seven institutions and covering a wide range of topics, for the board's approval: the University of Pretoria and the University of the Western Cape (international trade); the University of Cape Town and the University of the Western Cape (structural biology), Rand Afrikaans University and the University of Fort Hare (accounting); and the University of Stellenbosch and Medical University of South Africa (HIV/AIDS management in the workplace).[284]

Following a study of higher education opportunities in Nigeria by the Social Science Academy of Nigeria and consultations with colleagues at the MacArthur Foundation, which had a special program in Nigeria, the

Corporation supported planning grants at three universities.[285] From these, three were selected to receive institution-strengthening grants at the level of approximately $2 million each: Ahmadu Bello University in Zaria, Obafemi Awolowo University in Ile-Ife, and the University of Jos in Jos.[286]

In addition, exploratory reviews and site visits in Ghana undertaken by the Corporation with the Ford and Rockefeller Foundations led to support for two institutions: the University College of Education at Winneba, the main teacher training college, and the University of Ghana at Legon, the flagship educational institution for the country.[287] In support of the national systemwide review under way, the National Council for Tertiary Education and the Committee of Vice Chancellors received grants to review plans and develop stronger advocacy and advisory capacity for the universities related, in part, to improving access to ICTs, the development of management information systems, and strengthening libraries.[288]

From site visits, discussions at the universities, and the ongoing evaluations, Corporation staff, in collaboration with their nine institutional partners, developed a technical assistance portfolio to reinforce the main grants by building, for example, "capacity for fundraising and financial, grants, and research management.... Activities may include proposal development workshops, participation in relevant management training courses and conferences, study visits, consulting advice, and external auditing services."[289] Peer-to-peer evaluation was also included so that universities could work with each other on assessment and evaluation. The Board of Trustees approved the first request at the level of $550,000, but recognized that additional monies would be required as more opportunities became available.[290]

A national higher education plan, approved in South Africa in 2002, necessitated major programmatic revisions. The plan reduced the number of universities by consolidating weak and strong institutions.[291] As a result, the university partnerships funded by the Corporation were no longer viable, especially since some of the university grantees were now combined with others. With the new national policy, Corporation staff consulted extensively with South African educators to consider the most appropriate new grants strategy. The preeminent need identified by many advisers was to change policy so as to increase gender, ethnic, and racial equity at the universities; this change would lead them "to undertake changes in the demographic composition of their faculties and student bodies, as well as to make the content of their programs and their institutional culture more democratic and equitable."[292]

Returning to the request for proposal model, the Corporation asked five universities to prepare full proposals. Given the resources available to the Corporation and the anticipated long-term commitment, the preference was to identify two universities, with the option of a third if the proposal warranted it. Staff members cited the revised objectives and approaches in the 2005 program paper. They were explicit about the selection criteria and transparent about the universities under consideration: the University of Cape Town, the University of the Witwatersrand, the University of Pretoria, the University of the Western Cape, and the University of KwaZulu-Natal.[293] Three main program areas, reflecting national priorities and the advisers' recommendations, were considered appropriate for support:

1. Training and mentorship programs of a new generation of faculty members, especially black and female academic staff development, in areas such as research and teaching

2. Programs that encourage new graduates, female and black graduate students, as well as junior faculty members to remain at the university, following the completion of their doctoral degree

3. The planning, development, and delivery of programs designed to develop and support a non-racial and non-sexist university culture[294]

In 2005 the board approved the requests from three universities, each to receive up to $2 million over three years, with a planned renewal for another three years: the University of Cape Town, the University of the Witwatersrand, and the University of KwaZulu-Natal.[295]

For the fifth year of the partnership, in 2005, Corporation staff members highlighted the diverse results for the institutions outside of South Africa and presented them in the next year's accomplishments report:[296]

+ Significant improvement at most universities in information and communications technology infrastructure and utilization, as well as access to "broader and cheaper broadband." In four countries—Nigeria, Ghana, Tanzania, and Uganda—National Research and Education

Networks increased access to and assisted with bandwidth management for improved access to the Internet. In Nigeria, "at Obafemi Awolowo University, 70 percent of the campus is now covered by fiber optic cable, while improvements in emergency power supply, provision of additional computers, installation of LANs, and staff training have improved coverage and reliability of the network."[297] Internet laboratories were also established at Makerere University, Obafemi Awolowo University, and the University of Dar es Salaam, and Makerere University introduced e-learning capacity.

- A variety of new degree programs were established—in quantity surveying at Makerere University, in international trade law at the University of Pretoria and the University of the Western Cape, in structural biology at the University of Cape Town and the University of the Western Cape, and in computer engineering at Obafemi Awolowo University—and a new Graduate Studies program for faculty trying to finish their PhDs was established at Makerere University.

- Laboratory facilities were improved at several universities in Nigeria. The Central Science Lab at Obafemi Awolowo University became a national resource for users from across the country. "The facility has also attracted an additional infusion of about $1 million from the government to add to the stock of equipment and the lab was instrumental in the university's designation by the National Universities Commission in 2004 as the country's top research university."[298] Ahmadu Bello University's biotechnology project was jointly funded with the university and the Central Bank of Nigeria.

- A project at the University of Jos undertaken by students to improve the quality of life at the university provided a reliable water supply to student hostels for the first time, serving almost six thousand students. (The municipal water supply system serving the hostels was unreliable.)

- In South Africa, improvements in university management followed the development of quality assurance and accreditation systems.

- Community service and contributions to economic development were enhanced through new programs such as the diploma in HIV/AIDS management at the University of Stellenbosch and the Medical

University of South Africa and the rural dentistry program developed at Obafemi Awolowo University.[299]

On the other hand, staff noted, the distance education programs, some of the other university-wide programs for quality assurance, and support for research and staff development were showing little progress; more attention would be paid to these areas in the future.[300]

Three developments following the accomplishments review informed the priorities of the university-strengthening program. First, after structural changes at the Corporation in 2007, the new International Program served as the umbrella for both the International Peace and Security Program and the International Development Program. In an effort to bring the programs closer together, the work on higher education was placed under a subprogram entitled Higher Education in Africa and Eurasia. To ensure sustained attention to the issues of gender equity, the activities to promote women's educational opportunities were maintained as part of the African university-strengthening activities.[301] Second, the program continued to build the next generation of scholars as part of the university-strengthening activities under the framework developed during the last two years of the Partnership for Higher Education in Africa, in response to the request of the African university vice chancellors. In addition, again in response to the concerns expressed by the vice chancellors, the Corporation and other members of the Partnership (the Ford, Rockefeller, and Kresge Foundations), through the South African–based Centre for Higher Education Transformation, in 2007 initiated support for a network to strengthen academic leadership and advocacy: the Higher Education Research and Advocacy Network in Africa (HERANA).[302] Finally, in 2008, Matos returned to Mozambique to become executive director of the Foundation for Community Development, one of the first major grant-making community foundations in Africa, initiated by Graça Machel, the widow of the late president of Mozambique and now the widow of Nelson Mandela. By the end of 2008, the Corporation had appointed Omotade Akin Aina, at the time the Ford Foundation's regional representative in East Africa, to be the next program director.[303]

In examining the types of successes at the African universities, the

Corporation recognized the importance of strengthening capacity for high-level scientific research on the continent, increasingly made possible by improved bandwidth access. Staff members considered opportunities to branch out from the direct support to universities. The Science Initiative Group at the Institute for Advanced Study in Princeton, New Jersey, requested a planning grant for developing with African partners a new scientific networking initiative for universities, the Regional Initiative in Science and Education (RISE).[304] It has served as a meta-network comprising five competitively selected, graduate-level, scientific research–oriented regional networks, some of which were newly created around key scientific themes relevant to national development in African countries.[305] Each network initially received a three-year grant of up to $800,000 via the Institute for Advanced Study, which has played a coordinating role and added value by connecting these networks to the broader scientific community and developing postgraduate research and training programs. Starting in 2008, RISE received $5 million over three years.[306]

Also in 2008, the program responded to the vice chancellors' fears that with the limited number of faculty members eligible to replace the many senior professors retiring in the next few years, the intellectual vibrancy of their institutions would be compromised. The missing element they identified was a sufficiently strong critical mass of doctoral degree holders who were also excellent teachers and who could both inspire students and contribute to the production of knowledge in their institutions. The losses in the broad area of the humanities—the core disciplines for strengthening a sense of nationhood and culture in both the university setting and the country at large—were singled out as potentially severe. The trustees approved a program organized by the American Council of Learned Societies at the level of $5 million over two years to offer research and writing fellowships to African scholars in Ghana, Kenya, Nigeria, South Africa, and Tanzania for the study of culture, history, art, philosophy, languages, and other humanities disciplines. While the Council administers the fellowships, the fellowship award selection is the responsibility of a network of senior scholars in the humanities from the continent.[307] All the selected scholars have been based at universities in African countries with a high likelihood of maintaining their academic commitments.[308]

Following the Corporation's consultation with African educators, stakeholders throughout the continent, and international funding agencies, the Corporation's board approved a new initiative in September 2010 to complement the Council's initiative by strengthening MA and PhD programs at the University of Cape Town, the University of Ghana, Makerere University, and the University of the Witwatersrand.[309] The intent was to foster the retention of well-trained faculty with advanced degrees and create a vibrant environment for research and training. TrustAfrica, a pan-African foundation based in Dakar, Senegal, received support to make small grants and hold dialogues with local stakeholders and donors for strengthening the constituency for higher education reform and mobilizing new resources to support these reforms.[310] A second pan-African organization based in Dakar, Senegal, the Council for the Development of Social Science Research in Africa, began to plan, with Corporation support, for a network to promote social science analysis of higher education in Africa, including models of effective governance.[311]

In 2010 and 2011, three more networks aimed at building the next generation of academics in African universities received support. The first involved strengthening training in interdisciplinary research across public health and population sciences through the Consortium for Advanced Research Training in Africa, based at the African Population and Health Research Center. Through 2011, the Corporation had provided $1 million to enable the Consortium to strengthen interdisciplinary graduate training.[312] With colleagues in the International Peace and Security Program, the Strengthening African Universities Program formed an intraprogram partnership to build the next generation of scholars in peace, security, and development via support for three different approaches: Kings College at the University of London and the University of Nairobi have collaborated in support of the Nairobi-based African Leadership Centre to promote the next generation of scholars working in these areas; the New York–based Social Science Research Council (SSRC) and the African Leadership Centre have partnered in support of the African Peacebuilding Network, which brings together practitioners and academics; and the SSRC has organized a PhD-level fellowship program, also focusing on peace, security, and development.[313] An interdisciplinary, international network, this project also began to meet the needs identified by the 2011 *World Development Report* and UN Assistant Secretary-General Carolyn McAskie when the UN Peacebuilding Commission was established.

This recent phase of the university-strengthening programs has aimed to sensitize university leaders; strengthen the institutional capacity for promoting and managing networks, especially to increase the likelihood of retaining more highly trained academics; and enhance universities' overall capacity to engage in outreach in the community and more significant fund-raising activities. As described by the program staff, the Corporation aims "to build a critical mass of Africa-based practitioners and researchers, improve their retention prospects ... and connect African academics and researchers to each other and to international communities as contributors to global debates and processes concerning their disciplines. This is a long-term goal as there are many impediments that need to be overcome at the level of institutions and governmental policies."[314]

The ten years of investment by the seven foundations in a wide variety of countries cutting across the continent should enhance the likelihood of continued success.[315] Although the Partnership for Higher Education in Africa came to a close in 2010, its demise has not meant the end of the Corporation's support for higher education in Africa. Nonetheless, as noted by program staff, sustaining these institutional, networking, and individual initiatives, including the retention of highly trained academics in more vibrant universities, remains the challenge, further underlining the role of advocacy in support of higher education nationally in African countries as well as internationally.

ENHANCING WOMEN'S OPPORTUNITIES IN HIGHER EDUCATION

FUNDING WOMEN'S SCHOLARSHIP was distinctly different from anything the Corporation had pursued in Africa before, and in doing so it acknowledged the vital importance of financial barriers to undergraduate education, especially for women.[316] From studies on women's access to higher education, moreover, universities had emerged as less than welcoming to women students. Corporation staff members realized that cultural, institutional, and psychological barriers for women students were likely to negate any benefits that would accrue from being awarded a scholarship.

Concentrating on the universities that were receiving institution-strengthening grants (except initially in South Africa, as discussed later), the Corporation entered into discussions with university leaders on providing scholarships as a way to attract many more women students. The objectives of the program, approved by the Corporation leadership and endorsed by the universities' leadership, covered the financial and other barriers and included: "1) undergraduate scholarship programs in selected universities to increase women's access to university education; 2) interventions in those universities to remove some of the barriers that prevent women from successfully participating in higher education; and 3) partnerships with selected organizations that have a comparative advantage in analyzing women's higher education issues and advocating for institutional policy change."[317]

With the prior investments made by the University of Dar es Salaam and Makerere University to increase the number of women students and enhance the environment for women students at their institutions, the vice chancellors had welcomed discussions about the women's scholarship program. The institution-strengthening requests from both institutions included actions to improve the learning and living environments for women students.[318] The Corporation initiated the women's educational scholarships program with $1 million for each of these institutions.[319]

In reviewing the situation in South Africa, including the new national plan for higher education and enrollment figures, it was clear that women students were present in these institutions but that, as noted in the prior section, equity of opportunity across race and class was the issue. Moreover, Corporation-supported studies revealed that "women's enrollment lags behind men's in such critical fields as science and technology, engineering and commerce."[320] Keeping these concerns in mind, and with anticipated support of $2.6 million, the Corporation determined that the most effective way to proceed was to work with the South Africa Department of Education. In June 2002, the Board of Trustees approved the Department's request of $3.15 million for a national scholarship program that would focus on scholarships for 150 women over three years in the sciences, engineering, business, and education.[321]

Ghana and Nigeria presented yet another situation: university students in these two countries did not pay tuition fees. Discussions with the academic leadership led to planning grants to examine the other constraints that might limit the participation of women at the undergraduate level to reduce dropouts and enhance retention. Scholarships to cover other costs, such as housing and additional fees, became the focus.[322]

In the 2003 program strategy paper, program officer Andrea Johnson and colleagues assessed the situation regarding the education of women and girls in Africa. They noted that the percentage of women undergraduates had increased from the 1970s to the 1980s: "Today [2003] the average is probably closer to 30 percent, although accurate data are hard to obtain."[323] While the situation varied from country to country, only in South Africa did women constitute about 50 percent of the student body, although as mentioned, relatively few were in the sciences and engineering. Despite the constraints, Corporation staff members predicted the anticipated long-term results of this initiative: "By the end of the full 10-year relationship with each university, Corporation staff expects to see evidence of transformation in gender relationships in the university, leading to increased involvement of and improved outcomes for women. This will be the legacy of the strategy, difficult to measure but largely sustainable because of the focus on changing policies, procedures, and attitudes."[324] The Corporation also instituted a tracking program with each institution to assist in documenting and analyzing the results of what was working and what was not, both for continued implementation in each setting and for sharing with others.[325]

By 2005, the scholarship support for the universities in Nigeria, Tanzania, and Uganda was concentrated on women majoring in the sciences, similar to the national focus in South Africa. At the same time, with the new university-strengthening strategy in South Africa, the program staff ended support to the Department of Education. In consultation with institutional leaders at the universities selected, the Corporation reconfigured the scholarship program so that students at those universities would be eligible for support. The section of the program that addressed barriers to retention, performance, and career development was incorporated into the university-strengthening grants in South Africa.[326]

As of 2010, the Corporation's support for female undergraduates at the universities had led to scholarships for over three thousand women, for a total of $19,507,814; additional support of $5.9 million had contributed to strengthening the institutional commitment to gender equity; and over $2 million in grants had enhanced women's educational leadership capacity in higher education. The total investment in support of women and their educational opportunities in Africa over the ten years came to $27.7 million.[327] One sign of success with this part of the program was that some of the universities were beginning to find ways to sustain the scholarship program. Makerere University, one of the early recipients of the scholarships, instituted in 2011 the Makerere University Female Scholarship Foundation to continue the program with local resources.[328] In 2010 and 2011, ten women students received scholarships and another ten were awarded tuition waivers. In 2011 and 2012, twenty scholarships were awarded.[329] The university's intent is to increase these numbers every year with contributions from individuals, businesses, and the government. Here, too, a greater emphasis on advocacy could encourage other institutions to adopt comparable approaches.

REVITALIZING PUBLIC LIBRARIES IN AFRICA

THE PLANS for the public library component of the International Development Program were developed in 1998 and 1999, before the university partnership got off the ground.[330] Gloria Primm Brown, the responsible program officer, prepared the plans based on the assessments and diagnostic work conducted for the Corporation by the International Network for the Availability of Scientific Publications.[331]

The reviews ultimately identified four countries that offered promising conditions: Botswana, Kenya, Zimbabwe, and South Africa. The first three countries prepared planning grants; following a peer review process, the proposals from Botswana and Kenya were accepted and supported.[332] The plans were ambitious. At the level of $2 million each over three years for the National Library Services of Kenya and Botswana, the activities aimed to improve the library systems, with a special focus on rural areas, technology, and fund-raising. Similar to the broader institution-strengthening support provided by the university-strengthening part of the program, the public library funding included technical assistance in such areas as fund-raising.

From the reviews, Corporation staff saw the opportunity in South Africa, given its extensive library system, to build a stronger network across all the library systems in the nine provinces, and they identified a limited number of provincial systems for targeted support, including training in librarianship. Staff decided the newly formed Library and Information Association of South Africa, with some additional support, could be an effective advocate for public libraries in the country. Given the range of activities, staff anticipated that over the next three years a special library initiative in South Africa would be funded at the level of $1,750,000.[333]

To complement other activities in the program, in 2001 and 2002 staff members began exploratory work in West Africa, starting in Ghana with an anticipated planning grant and follow-up activities.[334] With the International Network, efforts were under way to introduce information and communication technology capacity in the grantee library systems in Botswana and Kenya and to build on the Mellon and Kresge Foundations' support in South Africa. The International Network also began to adapt the International Federation of Library Associations and Institutions guidelines to undertake an audit evaluation of the library systems funded by the Corporation.

Over the year 2002 to 2003, however, questions arose from the foundation leadership about the escalating costs of systemwide expenses in the three countries and the feasibility of expanding the reach of the program.[335] Gregorian and the library program officer, Rookaya Bawa, along with program chair Matos, decided to return to the original goal of developing a few model libraries, testing innovations, and sharing the results widely with libraries elsewhere on the continent. Using the benchmark of innovative model libraries, Bawa reviewed the public library system grants in Botswana and Kenya, the provincial and urban grants in South Africa, and the discussions about Ghana, as well as some of the other support activities, including linkages with the university grantees to improve their libraries. The 2003 program strategy paper reflected the program's revised scope:

> The Corporation's first grants were thus to revitalize library systems, with grants made to many service points and to system-wide organizations. Especially in South Africa, we have since learned that support for systemic interventions and for a large number of library service points

requires an enormous investment of financial resources, supervision, and monitoring that are beyond the capacity of IDP [International Development Program]. The progress made thus far, or in some cases, the lack of it, led IDP staff to refocus the strategy on a few selected projects that will build models that can be successfully replicated.... Hence, the library subprogram will now focus on three sets of interventions: developing national libraries, revitalizing selected public libraries and developing academic libraries in universities that receive support under the university strengthening program.[336]

For all three countries, the program worked with the grantees to reduce the scope to strengthen essential services related to top-priority activities (for example, reducing the number of service points, that is, the number of staffed desks to assist the library users, in South African libraries, or reducing the number of library sites in Botswana and Kenya).[337] Support for national libraries was reinforced in each setting. Technical assistance for training in librarianship and the use of information, communications, and technologies (ICTs), along with participation in networks, continued. Staff also aimed to enhance training, the development of databases, and other activities comparable to those already under way in the partner university libraries. The Corporation made new commitments of approximately $2 million each over three years to transform the following South African municipal libraries into centers of library excellence: Pietermaritzburg in the province of KwaZulu-Natal; Cape Town City Library in Western Cape; and the City Library in Johannesburg. A similarly sized grant supported modernization of the National Library of South Africa on the premise that the national library of a country was crucial for maintaining the national cultural heritage and strengthening the entire system.[338]

By 2005, despite some of the earlier concerns about sustainability, some of the library grants were beginning to show results.[339] In South Africa, library systems had been computerized in the provinces of Mpumalanga and Northern Cape to effect cross-system borrowing, and the more recent grants to Cape Town City Library and Pietermaritzburg City Library had leveraged government commitments for new facilities. Because of changes in leadership and the uncertainty about completing the program, the grants to Botswana and Kenya had been terminated (although in Kenya the National Library Service, with government funding, had renovated the National Library and developed four model district libraries).[340]

At the same time, staff began to discuss with those responsible for strengthening universities a new strategy to tie together the university-strengthening grants and the library subprogram activities, particularly a strategy to upgrade university libraries by drawing on the experiences of the public library grantees. Following those discussions, a new library plan was submitted for 2006. For the public library component, staff determined that focusing on one country and enhancing support for a carefully focused model library program would provide an in-depth experience for sharing with other systems. Given the extent of the work in South Africa, along with the potential for close partnership with the government, South Africa was selected for the public library focus. For the university library work, staff recommended working with university leadership to develop model university library systems, one in South Africa and one outside South Africa. The new goals were set forth as follows:

> Create models of excellent national, public and academic libraries that attain the quality and standards set by the International Federation of Library Associations. Share and disseminate the experience of institution-building and quality service provided by these libraries with libraries, governments, donor agencies and other stakeholders, thus encouraging the replication of these models. These libraries will provide access to information and knowledge to users who in turn use knowledge and information for personal advancement and contribute to community or social development.[341]

Over the nine years of the library program, from 2002 to 2011, South Africa had developed a model program, and one that also demonstrated a constructive working relationship between Corporation staff members, the South African government, and local leaders in the South African library community.[342] The Corporation had contributed to the development of seven model public libraries in South Africa with skilled librarians in significant positions, the digitization of holdings, and the publication of online periodicals. In the tradition of Andrew Carnegie's insistence that his library investments be matched by community support, the government not only matched but surpassed the Corporation's contributions; as staff noted, "To date, our investment of about $24 million into this program has yielded about $80 million from South African local, provincial and national governments. These state-of-the-art libraries are transforming the role of public libraries as resources for information and services, including for underprivileged communities, and as anchors in larger efforts to revitalize cities and towns."[343] By 2011, three libraries were fully completed and officially open, two were under construction, and two were in the planning phase.[344]

As part of the strategy to strengthen academic libraries in Corporation-supported universities, the program had focused on a "research commons initiative ... which *strengthens and connects university research libraries.* Reflecting a revised and integrated strategy, the information and research commons and portals linking university libraries aims [*sic*] to improve access to information and knowledge geared toward postgraduate training and research."[345] The research commons and associated portals for linking the libraries, initiated in 2009 at the University of Cape Town library, was extended to the libraries at the two other universities receiving support in South Africa, the University of the Witwatersrand and KwaZulu-Natal. The research commons approach not only enabled the pooling of material but also facilitated training programs and interlibrary loans. In 2011 three other universities joined the portal: the University of Pretoria, Rhodes University, and Stellenbosch University.[346] The University of Ghana received support to develop a research commons and portal in 2010.[347]

Also by 2011, over 1,200 librarians had attended courses run jointly by the Mortenson Center for International Development in Illinois and the Library Association of South Africa. The digitalization of collections also proceeded with SABINET (South African Bibliographic Network) for over 250 leading African journals from the past ten years. The partnership built between the US Library of Congress and several libraries in Africa and in post-Soviet Eurasia introduced the latter to the Library of Congress's global digitization program and contributed to advancing digitization activities in those libraries.[348] The University of Pretoria in South Africa offered, as of 2010, a formal master's degree program on academic librarianship and a second program on leadership skills for public librarians.[349]

In 2012, with the increased responsibility by the government of South

Africa for the public libraries and with the return of Rookaya Bawa to South Africa, the Corporation decided to end the public library program in order to devote more resources to nurturing postgraduate research capacities with the partner universities in South Africa and elsewhere in West and East Africa.[350] As the Corporation now begins to evaluate the grant clusters, its analysis of the concept of model libraries, both public and university, will be instructive in assessing approaches to building sustainability and adopting innovations. For example, one critical element in the university program that merits special attention both in evaluation and forward planning is the strong support from the vice chancellors for all elements of the institution-strengthening grants, especially around the institution's strategic plan.[351]

"GLOBAL" DIMENSIONS: INTERNATIONAL ACTIVITIES IN NATIONAL PROGRAMS

WITH GREGORIAN'S VISION of one Carnegie, issues of global importance also entered into the grant-making agendas of three national programs: the Strengthening US Democracy Program, the Carnegie Scholars Program, and the Special Projects Committee (soon to be renamed Special Opportunities Fund). The Public Affairs Department, in its dissemination and public outreach role, also contributed substantially to all the international activities throughout the Corporation. In addition, the Journalism Initiative of the Public Affairs Department included a modest amount of international reporting. Most of the international activities in these programs revolved around issues related to Islam, seeking to reorient American understanding and tolerance through a wide variety of approaches.

STRENGTHENING US DEMOCRACY

ANDREW CARNEGIE'S DEVOTION TO DEMOCRACY stemmed from many sources, but primarily from his abiding enthusiasm for "Democracy's 'gift of welcome' to the new comer" and his analytical passion for the "foundation upon which the political structure rests, the equality of the citizen."[352] A persistent concern for the newcomer also informed Corporation activities over the century. Only in the era covered by this chapter, however, has there been a program explicitly entitled "Strengthening US Democracy." Bringing together the democratic strands that Carnegie saw as woven into the very fabric of this country, the program recognized that some of these strands were at risk, such as the welcome to all newcomers, the equal application of the law to all, and the level playing field of democracy as represented by voting, elections, and political participation.

Gregorian highlighted in his initial essays the importance of a program on democracy and noted that a "source of deep concern for our society is the condition of religious, ethnic, and racial relations."[353] He stressed his pressing concerns about religious diversity and interreligious tolerance, observing that "our understanding of Islam in all its facets will be important for the harmony of our democracy."[354]

The program, led by Geri Mannion, continued the efforts of the Special Projects Program begun under David Hamburg and Barbara Finberg in the 1980s and 1990s, and even earlier under Alan Pifer in the 1970s, to address the Corporation's long-standing commitment to work on a variety of pressing social justice issues in the American context; in this era, the program also paid attention to religious tolerance and Islam, as well as the long-standing concerns about immigrant integration.

In 1998 and 2001, the Corporation held meetings specifically on Islam, organized by Mannion and her colleagues and with a diverse group of Muslim leaders and scholars from around the United States in attendance to discuss how best to develop "a better understanding of the growing impact that this great religion was having on the nation and the world."[355] The 2001 meeting, held on June 28, sought, primarily with scholars, "to help define the state of Islam in America and the complex range of concerns the Muslim community confronts as the fastest growing religion in the United States."[356] The meeting participants, including African American Muslims, concluded that the issues surrounding the integration of Muslims required greater examination and that "America must overcome the demonization of Islam, and study, understand and accommodate the reality of Islam to set an example of contemporary pluralism for the rest of the world."[357]

Following September 11, 2001, the program supported activities that addressed how the fears of another terrorist attack would influence the integration of newcomers, especially Muslim newcomers, into American civic life. In 2003 the Corporation, for example, supported the Arab Community Center for Economic and Social Services (ACCESS), the preeminent organization "committed to the economic and cultural development of the Arab American community."[358] The intention was to "provide technical assistance to Arab-American community-based organizations, with the goal of building a national infrastructure designed to foster the acculturation of Arab Americans into American civic life."[359]

The program funded efforts to examine the domestic security considerations related to immigrants, "in particular those who are Muslim, Sikh, and/or of Middle Eastern background, with respect to legal services, pursuit of citizenship and the right to vote and participate in electoral processes."[360] The program staff, concerned about increasing public understanding about the impact of new domestic security laws and the impact on democratic practice and civil liberties, worked collaboratively with a number of other national foundations to establish at Public Interests Projects a new donor collaborative, the Four Freedoms Fund, to encourage state and regional funders to address these and other issues.[361]

The program has also addressed international issues of migration and immigration, particularly through its support of the TransAtlantic Council, managed by the Migration Policy Institute.[362] Consciously harking back to the Americanization studies of the 1920s, the Corporation began to address, more specifically, educational opportunities for immigrants and to develop linkages with European scholars and policymakers, on occasion through partnership with the Sutton Trust in the United Kingdom, to build an international base for the work on these issues.[363]

Under the restructuring of the Corporation into the National and International Programs, the Strengthening US Democracy Program was placed under the National Program with the mandate to develop programs on immigrant integration through education, including identifying ways to assist Muslim immigrants and other groups, both in the context of intergroup relations and in their participation in American education and national life.[364] The program also continued its support of citizenship issues (the naturalization of legal immigrant residents), a long-standing concern of the Corporation following World War I. It has also maintained the theme of immigration with its inherent international connections, a context in which both its positive and negative valences have only increased in the twenty-first century: the contradictory forces of the push toward porous borders from globalization and the pull for local control through hardened identities show no sign of abating.

SPECIAL PROJECTS

VARTAN GREGORIAN CONTINUED the long-standing practice at the Corporation of having a special—that is, uncommitted—projects portfolio and asked Geri Mannion, chair of the democracy program, to chair this as well.[365] As noted in the "New Directions" paper, Special Projects would continue to encompass grants awarded outside of major program areas and would encourage "interprogram grantmaking, support a limited number of important 'special initiatives,' and continue to make grants for strengthening the nonprofit and philanthropic sectors of our country."[366] Whereas the Democracy Program addressed Islam under the thematic work on immigrant integration, a series of Special Projects grants focused on educating Americans about Islam in its broadest context. Documentaries for television were supported to provide greater understanding of contemporary Muslim culture.[367] The American University of Beirut was supported to bring together scholars and educators in the Islamic world to visit the United States to teach short courses in this country.[368] Shireen T. Hunter, a scholar at the Center for Strategic and International Studies, directed a study on modernization and democratization in the Muslim world.[369] Search for Common Ground, a nongovernmental organization based in Washington, DC, received support to assist Partners in Humanity, an initiative of Crown Prince Hassan of Jordan that was also aimed at building greater understanding of and respect for the Muslim world.[370] With the John D. and Catherine T. MacArthur Foundation, a special grant through the United Nations Assistance Mission to Afghanistan supported the Kabul Public Library.[371] An innovative program to connect undergraduate students in US universities with students in Israel and Palestine, called Soliya Net, was also funded in 2007; starting with about twelve universities in 2003 (the year it was established), by 2011 it had become a global program involving over one hundred universities in twenty-seven countries.[372] Over the last ten years, Special Projects, renamed the Special Opportunities Fund, has continued to support research, case studies, and dialogues to address issues related to the United States and the Muslim world, such as religious pluralism and religious tolerance.[373]

Practically for the first time in its history, the Corporation, through the Special Opportunities Fund and at the initiative of the board and the president, began to make modest but targeted grants following man-made and natural catastrophes, both in the United States and internationally. These grants went toward rebuilding after September 11, 2011, the Asian tsunami, Hurricane Katrina, and the earthquake in Haiti.[374]

Although the grants often are opportunistic, the Special Opportunities Fund opens windows that allow world issues to enter into the Corporation's portfolio; the chance that these grants might sow seeds for new efforts is always present. This flexibility has been an integral part of Corporation grant-making since James Angell formalized the idea in 1921, and it is likely to persist.

CARNEGIE SCHOLARS PROGRAM

GREGORIAN IN HIS 1999 "New Directions" essay signaled his intention to revive support for independent individual scholarship at the Corporation.[375] Although each of the programs was funding topic-related scholarship, these grants went to institutions to support work by individuals often working in teams. Gregorian identified the opportunity to organize a separate fellowship program (with grants directly to individuals, not through their institutions and not for teams), with the aim "to support fundamental research by young scholars and established experts with outstanding promise to contribute significantly to the advancement of knowledge and scholarship. Up to twenty fellowships will be awarded annually in those realms that reflect the current program priorities of the Corporation: Education, International Peace and Security, International Development, and Democracy."[376] Gregorian and his colleagues identified an initial list of six hundred nominators from around the United States.[377] Over the first five years, even with its specific attention to both domestic and international topics, the latter dominated the submission and selection of Carnegie Scholars.[378]

By 2004, with sixty-seven Carnegie Scholars covering a wide range of distinctive research related to the Corporation programs, Gregorian raised with staff the idea of focusing the program on a specific but capacious theme. Acknowledging the efforts under the democracy program and the Special Projects/Special Opportunities Fund around the theme of Islam, Gregorian, in consultation with the trustees and staff, moved to redirect the Carnegie Scholars Program from its broad range to a more concentrated focus on Islam as a religion and on Muslim communities around the world and in the United States.[379]

The focus on Islam as a religion and on Muslim communities in the United States and around the world lasted five years, from 2005 to 2009, and supported over 101 scholars.[380] The total of 117 Carnegie Scholars working on this theme (over the full ten years of the program) addressed issues in predominantly Muslim states and examined the practice and interpretation of Islam in both Muslim-majority and -minority countries, including constitutional and legal issues, the impact of globalization on the religion, historical studies on the spread of Islam by trade and exploration, the celebration of Islam as a religion in nineteenth-century Europe, and burgeoning contemporary conversion to Islam among youth in the United States and the Caribbean.

With a focus on public scholarship around issues related to Islam and Muslim communities, the Carnegie Scholars Program worked closely with the Public Affairs Department.[381] The program also worked with the International Development Program to increase the number of submissions from scholars working on Africa,[382] with the International Program to build connections across the Carnegie Scholars and scholars in Russia,[383] and with the Islam Initiative specifically.[384] Starting in 2005, to expand the number of donors funding projects and individual scholars in this field, program staff, with colleagues at the Rockefeller Brothers Fund and the Open Society Institute, organized a series of informal meetings with a focus on Islam and Muslim societies.[385] Complementing the dissemination activities of the Public Affairs Department for the Carnegie Scholars, the program supported three efforts to reach a broader range of scholars through the New York Times Knowledge Network to reach public universities and colleges,[386] the Center for Law and Security at New York University's Law School on the theme of law and Islam,[387] and the Carnegie Council on

Ethics in International Affairs for those scholars whose work related to the mission of the council.[388]

An assessment of the impact of the Carnegie Scholars Program on informing the field, public opinion, and public policies has yet to be conducted.[389] When the program came to a close with the last round of awards in 2009, the Islam Initiative remained the central focus for work on these issues at the Corporation. With a more systematic approach to funding public scholarship, deepening understanding of Muslim contributions to scholarship, and working to build international connections, that program has extended and deepened the earlier work.[390]

PUBLIC AFFAIRS:
DISSEMINATION AND THE JOURNALISM INITIATIVE

THE PUBLIC AFFAIRS DEPARTMENT, renamed the External Affairs Department in 2007, assisted all elements of the Corporation with fulfilling the second part of the Corporation's mission, namely, the diffusion of knowledge and understanding.[391] Although always a part of the Corporation's mandate, the communications revolution of the 1990s made it imperative for the Corporation to rethink its communications strategy for grantees, Corporation leadership, and Corporation staff members.[392]

For the international activities at the Corporation, the department assisted with organizing special outreach efforts, such as for the Russian Initiative and the Carnegie Scholars Program. The department continued the Corporation's tradition of identifying opportunities to support specific programs through public radio and public television, particularly news programs, such as the PBS *NewsHour*. In addition, the department assisted in enlarging outreach efforts for the Scholars Program through the Women's Foreign Policy Group for a special series of discussions on Islam by Carnegie Scholars. Support to the *Boston Review* for a special series of articles on Islam by Carnegie Scholars also contributed extensively to shaping public scholarship in this area.[393] For both the work in Africa and the work on Islam, the department organized a communications consultation for the grantees and Scholars to enhance public outreach. The younger, emerging Carnegie Scholars benefited from assistance with the preparation of op-ed pieces, longer but publicly oriented articles, and media appearances.[394]

Directly related to the concerns expressed by Gregorian about the state of journalism education, the Public Affairs Department under its dissemination program developed a special initiative to improve the training of journalists on the complex issues and challenges faced by the media in the twenty-first century.[395] In 2005 the Corporation and the Knight Foundation established the Carnegie-Knight Initiative on the Future of Journalism Education, a five-year partnership aimed at advancing journalism education in a new media-savvy environment.[396] One area that brought international concerns to the program was a focus for some of the students on reporting on religion, although as stated by department staff, "the one piece of unfinished business for the Carnegie-Knight initiative is the internationalization of the network."[397] Strengthening the capacity of journalism schools to improve coverage of global issues and other countries should contribute to increasing the in-depth international understanding of Americans—the long-sought-after goal of the Corporation.

CONCLUSIONS

THIS PERIOD of continually disruptive national and international events—politically, economically, and culturally—resulted in grant-making programs that were responsive to both the dynamic global disequilibria and the traditional themes of the Corporation. Overall, the last fourteen years at the Corporation bringing the Corporation up to its one-hundredth year represented, yet again, what John Gardner called a period of "stability in motion." Stability was embodied in Corporation leadership and staff, who built on the previous decade's work in Russia, foreign policy, and national security. Motion was represented by the leadership's redirection of the developing-countries program toward its traditional, comparative advantage in Africa to work with universities and libraries to enhance access to knowledge for all, with a special focus on increasing opportunities for women in education. Gregorian introduced areas and approaches that reflected former activities but were newly designed for this era: the Carnegie Scholars Program of individual grants, the Islam Initiative, the Journalism Initiative, and the Andrew Carnegie Medal of Philanthropy.

Along with the seemingly disparate cultural, intellectual, and geographical initiatives in Russia, Eurasia, Africa, and the United States, the

Corporation's internal structural changes, starting in 2007, have moved the foundation toward new arrangements of institutions and individuals, enabling it to maintain the initiatives in nuclear security and states at risk, enhance access to knowledge for all in Africa, and remain committed to scholarship and connecting scholars with policymaking. The lines of connectivity across the disparate fields and regions, however, are still dotted, not filled in. The focus on Islam may provide one way of drawing on many of the disparate dimensions. Another promising opportunity for collaboration and coherence lies in the strengthening of science, social sciences, and humanities in institutions of higher education in Russia, Eurasia, and selected African countries, as evidenced by new program thrusts. As mentioned in the section on the Strengthening Democracy Program, the crucial areas of identity and migration might form promising connections across the National and International Programs, drawing together this work with work related to conflict, development, and education.

In addition to continuing in many areas informal partnerships with foundations and other donor partners, the formal partnerships across foundations and African universities ensured not only significant new resources for the universities but also the sharing of ideas, information, and experiences between the partners. Importantly, the foundation partnership did not become a barrier that impeded grantee access to the array of relevant donors. More time is needed to assess whether these partnerships of the Corporation and others in Russia and Eurasia and in the United States will result in greater sustainability for the work.

A new and distinctly different partnership was also instituted by Gregorian. Struck by the lack of contact between the Carnegie institutions despite their shared heritage, in 2000 Gregorian discussed with his counterparts in the Carnegie family of institutions the possibility of a collective activity. From these discussions, on December 10, 2001, the sister institutions launched the Andrew Carnegie Medal of Philanthropy. Working together, the more than twenty Carnegie institutions selected representatives of the best in modern philanthropy (the field their good ancestor had helped to spawn)—philanthropists who embodied the spirit and promise of Andrew Carnegie.[398] This activity has revived connections across the Carnegie family of institutions that had existed in the early part of the Corporation's history (as board members and persistent grant-seekers). Additionally, new modes of collaboration may emerge from the Carnegie Medals program to build complementary as well as synergistic programs around the mission shared by many of them: to advance and diffuse knowledge and understanding.[399]

Although the impact of the contemporary programs cannot yet be assessed, the central themes of this era have been explicitly guided by the founder's avid embrace of the practice of providing access to knowledge for all, as embedded in libraries and educational institutions, matched by his fervent pursuit to end war and build a peaceful world. Andrew Carnegie's vision and mission serve as the intellectual and institutional momentum for Carnegie Corporation's second century of international philanthropy.

CONCLUSIONS:
LOOKING AHEAD TO A SECOND CENTURY OF
INTERNATIONAL GRANT-MAKING

W HEN ANDREW CARNEGIE founded Carnegie Corporation in 1911, he dedicated his fortune, not to building monuments, not to acts of kindness, and not to hospitals or universities, but to a mission intended to guide actions across a long span of time: the advancement and diffusion of knowledge and understanding. In doing so, he was trusting in the decisions of others. His "chief happiness," as he declared in his deed of gift to his first trustees, rested in his confidence that his "welth ... is to continue to benefit humanity for generations untold."[1]

Andrew Carnegie complicated the pursuit of the Corporation's mission by charging his trustees, then and in perpetuity, with the "full authority to change policy or causes hitherto aided," and he stipulated that they "shall best conform to my wishes by using their own judgment." This charge has encouraged the trustees to engage with societal challenges as they arise, while remaining committed to the mission in perpetuity. True to mission, the trustees have endowed enduring institutions and funded research with long-term implications. They have also respected Carnegie's injunction to remain alert to contemporary conditions by fostering activities with shorter-term objectives in response to changing societal priorities. For over a century, Carnegie's dual directive has kept Carnegie Corporation both on course and finding new territory to explore.[2]

With the trust Andrew Carnegie placed in the trustees to exercise "their own judgment," he gave the Corporation's stewards the self-assurance they needed to take intellectual risks. Carnegie rarely hesitated to move ahead when he saw a good idea in practice, even if it was not yet widely implemented, such as using iron, not wood, to build bridges and train tracks, introducing the Bessemer steel process into his steel mills, or adapting for his philanthropic efforts the approach of scientific philanthropy (rather than charitable giving) to address the root causes of social problems, as promoted by the mid-nineteenth-century Boston donor George Peabody in his programs.[3]

Carnegie took risks that paid off in long-term results. He provided pensions for retired university faculty, an effort that resulted in TIAA-CREF, a major pension investment organization that continues to serve millions of people in the academic, foundation, medical, cultural, governmental, and research fields. Requiring that communities provide matching funds for the libraries he built both in the United States and abroad, to demonstrate their commitment to their library, is arguably one of the reasons why, decades later, many of these institutions in developing countries (as well as in the United States) still provide access to knowledge. The institutions he established to promote peace and end war, the Carnegie Endowment for International Peace and the Carnegie Council for Ethics in International Affairs (originally the Church Peace Union), continue to serve as knowledge and policy leaders in the area of international affairs.[4] When Carnegie put the bulk of his remaining fortune into Carnegie Corporation of New York in 1911, entrusting control of the foundation's grant-making not to his family but to his trustees, he helped launch the first century of American grant-making foundations.

FINDINGS FROM THE FIRST CENTURY OF CARNEGIE CORPORATION'S INTERNATIONAL GRANT-MAKING

FROM THIS STUDY of Carnegie Corporation's international activities both in the United States and overseas, four intertwined attributes emerge as integral to effective grant-making. These attributes, considered together, define the contours of the answer to the question asked over the last one hundred years about foundations by congressional investigations, government regulators, and public critics, as well as by supporters and institutional leaders themselves: how can privately endowed foundation resources of money and effort be put to best use so that they make a lasting difference in understanding and ameliorating the root causes of social problems? These four attributes are:

1. Significance of mission
2. Openness to risk-taking
3. Willingness to make long-term investments
4. Openness to collaboration and partnership

The interplay of these attributes over the decades has enabled the Corporation's leadership to navigate between the untested and the proven with respect to both ideas and partners. There have been many successes, but the lessons learned from the failures have also contributed to the Corporation's ability to tackle new themes and adopt new approaches. The evidence of the effects of these interacting attributes on the history of Carnegie Corporation compellingly suggests how the Corporation and other foundations might address the causes of both persistent and emerging societal problems in the twenty-first century.

Significance of Mission

The fundamental attribute from which the others follow is the commitment to the centrality of the institution's founding mission. The vision and purpose elaborated in the Corporation charter, along with Andrew Carnegie's charge to the trustees to change the focus, when necessary, to accommodate changing conditions, provided a mission capacious enough both to encompass a wide array of activities and to guide the Corporation's decision-makers. An early example was the Corporation's support for the American Red Cross during World War I, as described in Chapter 1. With legal advice, and recognizing the importance of the work, the trustees were able to stay within the charter by directing the grant toward support of the educational activities of the Red Cross, not its non-mission-related relief work.

Responsive to the mission, program development and grant-making for both domestic and international activities led to extensive support over the decades for formal educational activities, from preschool through postgraduate, as well as nonformal education, which encompassed not only libraries but also extension programs and many aspects of adult education. Research programs in a wide array of areas, along with support for individual fellowships, travel grants, and grants-in-aid, encouraged the exploration of ideas and the publication of findings. Starting with the 1919 Americanization Study (see Chapter 2), commissions and large-scale surveys aimed to inform specific topics or fields, make policy recommendations, and identify gaps in knowledge requiring further research.

The Corporation's dedication to mission also informed the analysis and discussion about the allocation of resources for its international grant-making. Starting as early as 1913 in Canada, and then in the 1930s throughout the other British dominions (South Africa, Australia, and New Zealand), universities received support from the Corporation for endowments, library-strengthening, extension programs, and departmental grants in multiple fields covering the sciences, social sciences, and the humanities. Community-based education initiatives similar to those funded in the American South to improve educational conditions in poor communities formed the basis for many of the nonformal educational activities in the colonies in Africa, although toward the end of the 1930s some higher educational institutions there also received support.[5] In both the dominions and the colonies, free public libraries remained a central investment to provide public access to knowledge. The support for individual scholars and practitioners reflected in the four-decades-long travel grants program established in 1928 for residents of the British Empire resulted from the trustees' endorsement of Andrew Carnegie's premise that knowledge and understanding can result from the encouragement of individuals as well as from support for institutions.

In the first third of its history, the Corporation established the pattern of grant-making that draws on the mission and the charge. Succeeding trustees, presidents, and staff continued to balance ongoing support for established programs with grants that addressed new developments. In Africa, over the decades following World War II, as more donors stepped in to help build the field of higher education and respond to the needs expressed by the leaders of the newly independent countries, the Corporation reshaped its grant-making and identified specific niches to fill gaps in knowledge and contribute to improving conditions. The overseas grants programs, primarily in the African and Caribbean context but occasionally elsewhere, included support for a wide array of activities related to university strengthening, teacher education, child development and health, the status of women (legal, educational, and health), science and technology policies and programs, and access to knowledge through libraries and information systems. These grants included support for institution-strengthening activities, research for new programs and policies, and educational initiatives. The international grants program implemented in the United States worked with universities, think tanks, research councils, and individual scholars to identify and explore new ideas and approaches and share results widely with the public and policymakers. The activities were not centered on delivering services but rather on strengthening institutional and individual capacity to conduct research and use research results to advocate for improving existing policies and programs and developing new ones—all efforts that were consistent with the Carnegie Corporation mission.

Openness to Risk-taking

The propensity to take risks—that is, to act when outcomes, whether positive or negative, are difficult to predict—features as a significant topic of research in the social and management decision sciences.[6] Risk-taking in the public and private corporate sectors—such as launching space exploration, establishing new health programs, or promoting technological innovations—often garners much attention. Risk-taking on the part of private grant-making foundations has received less attention, however, except when grant-makers and critics call on foundations to take greater risks.[7]

Privately endowed foundations have a greater degree of freedom to innovate with fewer constraints wrapped around their decision-making than other kinds of institutions and organizations. The decision to take risks has fewer costs than it does in other sectors; jobs, market share, and bottom lines are not a concern, nor is re-election to office. Foundations that make safe choices are not taking advantage of their special status in American society. Openness to risk-taking goes hand in hand with the recognition that the protected resources of philanthropy can be used to explore new ideas when the outcomes are uncertain and when methods are unproven. This freedom to innovate and to take the risk to invest in the unknown enables foundations to contribute to the public good by funding for the long term—for example, by providing endowment support for new institutions and funding exploratory research in new areas of knowledge.

Over the course of the century, the Corporation's presidents, in consultation with the trustees, have shown little hesitation to take risks. Frederick Keppel, the Corporation's fifth president, described his attitude toward risk-taking in his 1930 book *The Foundation:* "One can trace a growing tendency to insist less and less on clean-cut proposals, and a growing tendency to undertake what might be called speculative ventures."[8] John Gardner, the Corporation's ninth president, summed up the role of foundations in American society and how they succeed in achieving results:

> How could the foundations ... have achieved such a reputation for influence and accomplishment?... I believe most serious students of the subject would say that it is due to the effectiveness of the modern foundation as a device for fostering innovation. It is designed to make money go a long way in the service of creativity and constructive change. It is one of the few institutions in our society that can keep itself free to act quickly and flexibly in the support of the talented individual or the institution that wishes to undertake an experimental program ... one of the great barriers to new developments is that the conventional institution rarely has funds for innovation. Its funds are committed to normal operating expenses. The modern foundation keeps money explicitly for innovation.[9]

At the same time, however, one of the conclusions drawn from the analysis of Carnegie Corporation's international grant-making is that for risk-taking to be an effective component of successful grant-making, it has to be undertaken in the context of the other attributes, such as the foundation's mission and the evidence base drawn from its history. Taken together, these other attributes can make risk-taking more responsible.

Positive innovations have resulted from the Corporation's risk-taking throughout its history, but on the downside, there have been two negative outcomes as well. The first, and most obvious, is failure. As described by several Carnegie Corporation presidents in their Corporation-related writings and elsewhere, a foundation's assets serve as the social-risk capital in American society, whether for grants made in this country or for those overseas, and as with almost any undertaking aimed at improving societal conditions, these grants carry the potential for failure as well as success. Accepting the likelihood of failure is an integral part of high-risk/high-potential-yield philanthropic undertakings, as well as of for-profit entrepreneurial investments. It is also important to acknowledge that failure can lead to harm, both physical (as when tests of a new medical technology fail or are inconclusive) and psychological (as when the expectations of the people affected are dashed). But failure is more acceptable if it produces useful knowledge. With due diligence informing funding decisions—that is, if both the design and any prior knowledge that might relate to the grant have been carefully reviewed—foundation staff members can learn from the failure about what to avoid or what to focus on and strengthen in future activities.[10]

When, starting in 1927, the foundation expanded its overseas activities to work in Africa, Australia, New Zealand, and the Caribbean (see Chapter 3), the Corporation's experience with the failure to establish the Federation for Higher Education in the Maritime Provinces had already taught the trustees and presidents the importance of listening to local leaders and potential beneficiaries.[11] With that lesson as a guide, they concentrated on creating conditions for success, for example, by working with local committees that would identify suitable grantees. Keppel, then president, also identified key consultants in different fields to undertake site visits, meet with those committees, and review, in dialogue with local stakeholders, the results of grants and opportunities for new funding. Keppel also responded to trustee concerns about the risks of working in the British colonies and arranged the London Conference Series, held under the auspices of the Royal Institute of International Affairs, where academic leaders, key intellectuals, and policymakers reviewed the Corporation's work and plans and suggested promising opportunities. Consultation with other foundations active in a particular region, such as the Rockefeller Foundation and the Phelps Stokes Fund, also helped mitigate risks and identify areas for new grant-making.

Gaining additional perspectives on local conditions by working with and listening to local partners and having either staff or consultants make site visits enabled the Corporation leadership to blend firsthand knowledge, evidence drawn from past efforts, and consideration of how a field might develop to enhance the likelihood of success. Problems could be identified and addressed, as well as taken into account in future grants. These approaches have remained essentially the same throughout the international overseas efforts of the Corporation.

A second corollary, rarely discussed, is the unexpected consequences of risky grant-making. The Poor White Study of 1928–1932 in South Africa offers a poignant case in which the Corporation's high-risk grant-making had significant unexpected consequences (see Chapters 3, 6, and 7). The intention of the Corporation was to contribute to understanding and improving the conditions of poverty for one segment of the South African population, the poor Afrikaners. (Local advisers had also raised the need for a comparable study on poverty in the African population.) Initially, the welfare-related recommendations and their role in the establishment of academic departments of sociology seemed benign. The study, however, published in 1932, contributed to strengthening Afrikaner intellectual leadership in a period of white-nationalist ascendency. Sixteen years later, many of those academic leaders had become the political leaders of the Nationalist Party, partly as a consequence of their use of the findings from the Poor White Study. When they came to power in 1948, they made apartheid policies official. The result was decades of suffering for the black, colored, and Asian members of South African society.

Five decades later, the Corporation had the rare and unanticipated opportunity to help redress the harm to which its earlier choices had contributed. In the late 1970s, under the still-pervasive conditions of apartheid, the Afrikaner national leaders remembered the Corporation's past support for that earlier study, and this enabled the Corporation to fund a new investigation into the poverty of nonwhite South Africans and their neighbors: the Second Carnegie Inquiry into Poverty in Southern Africa. The team, this time fully integrated in terms of race, ethnic group, gender, and discipline, examined in-depth the conditions surrounding the poverty of the black and other poor populations in South Africa and surrounding regions. This is one example of institutional perpetuity making it possible for grant-makers in a later generation, aware of their history, to positively transform the negative consequences, however unintended, of a grant made by a past generation.[12]

This example further illustrates the value of drawing on knowledge from past activities, assessing where progress has been made or why failure occurred, building on what has been learned, and taking the next steps. Such an iterative process deepens and extends the learning that results from innovative grant-making, reducing the risks and enhancing the likelihood of success. Such learning can provide the basis for revising existing programs and establishing new programmatic themes.[13]

Effective risk-taking activities can often challenge prevailing scholarly or policy opinions.[14] Lloyd Morrisett, Corporation vice president in the late 1960s, spoke about the Corporation taking risks by embracing the rising wave that was lifting a new idea, such as public television, and thus helping to shape "the direction of the wave."[15] Foundations also have "to know when to ride it all the way onto the shore," as Sara Engelhardt, Corporation secretary in the 1970s and 1980s, elaborated on this momentum metaphor in her "surfer theory of foundations."[16] The choppy seas of the twenty-first century will provide ample opportunity for foundations to maintain their openness to taking risks as they navigate uncharted waters and arrive at new shores.

Willingness to Make Long-Term Investments

As vital as long-term investments have been for building new institutions and fields of endeavor, foundations are finding it even more challenging in this modern era to make such investments. The widespread acceptance of metrics-focused impact evaluations often leads to decisions that seek results in the shorter term of one to three years. The drive to achieve shorter-term expected outcomes has been motivated in part by the frustration on the part of critics, as well as leaders in the field, with philanthropic foundations that seem to be complacent about doing the same thing or not absorbing enough risk with their protected philanthropic resources, at least in the United States.[17] As foundation leaders continue to tackle the challenges of grant-making under the complex set of dynamic conditions that confront philanthropy and its grantees in the early twenty-first century, they are revisiting the benefits of providing long-term, multiyear funding for grant-ees, with conditions agreed to in advance. Long-term investments can offer the opportunity to provide core stability for the grantee institutions and encourage them to take risks, confident that they have a funding partner that backs their approach to social change.

Whatever label is given to philanthropy today—scientific philanthropy, venture philanthropy, shared-value philanthropy, or public-private philan-thropy—the approaches all indicate an attempt to answer the question posed earlier: what is the optimum way to make a positive societal differ-ence with resources that are protected from taxes and dedicated to alle-viating social problems and achieving public good? As many foundation leaders recognize, a commitment to institutions over the long term, rein-forced by a willingness to take risks to support new lines of inquiry and new approaches, is the basis for effective philanthropy.

The current attention to outcome-based evaluation in nearly all foun-dations might also include more explicitly the pros and cons of the longer-term perspective, especially relevant for foundations established in perpe-tuity. In this regard, the comment about evaluation made in 1922 by Henry Pritchett, then acting president of the Corporation, resonates ninety years later: "The real test of the great foundations ... can be made only after a rea-sonable lapse of time. More than one generation must pass before thought-ful men will be in a position to assess the relative good and the possible harm that such trusts can affect."[18] Two different areas, as noted earlier, illustrate results from the Corporation's long-term strategic grant-making: endowing institutions and establishing new fields of knowledge and study.

ENDOWMENTS

The Corporation's first Board of Trustees embraced support for institu-tional endowments, responding to the donor's commitment to the notion of grant-making in perpetuity. Over his lifetime, Andrew Carnegie had endowed some twenty-two organizations from Pittsburgh to Scotland, each with a specific mission.[19] The trustees were keen to fund endowments as a way of ensuring the longevity of the institutions that they thought would contribute to improving both policy and public understanding of the crucial issues facing Americans, especially those related to economic policy. Meticulously drawn-up conditions for these, which entailed considerable reporting and monitoring, served to give the trustees confidence about the long-term use of Corporation resources.

The heyday of endowment support extended from Andrew Carnegie's era through the mid-1920s; the Corporation provided such funding for universities and freestanding policy research institutions, that is, the early think tanks. In the international arena, in Canada, Queen's University in 1913, McGill University in 1918, St. Francis Xavier in 1919, and Acadia University in 1920 all received endowment grants for general support or specific departments. Institutions in the United States with international orientation also received endowment grants. The Corporation endowed the Church Peace Union in New York City with $2 million in 1914.[20] In partnership with the Carnegie Endowment for International Peace, the Corporation established the Institute of International Education, also in New York City, in 1919. From 1919 to 1922, a distinctive feature of the grants that endowed free-standing institutions, such as the National Research Council, the Stanford Food Research Institute, the National Bureau of Economic Research, the Institute of Land Economics at the University of Wisconsin, and the Institute of Economics (which became the Brookings Institution), was that the institutions agreed to put plans in place that would allow them to grow their endowments and/or sustain themselves without expectations of further Corporation funding (see Chapter 2).

The increasing diversity of programs leading to greater demands on resources resulted in a reluctance to make long-term endowment commitments. Later presidents and staff began to recommend grants with shorter time horizons, more often one to three years. While not intended as long-term endeavors at the beginning, as positive results were demonstrated these grants were often renewed for two additional three-year rounds and sometimes for significantly longer. As many examples have shown, however, the practice of short-term renewals, even on a regular basis, rarely leads to the building of enduring institutions, as occurred in the earlier era. With the uncertainty of renewal, grantees may tend to work toward short-term objectives and miss key opportunities for more significant research or educational activities. Flourishing investments such as those for the Brookings

Institution or the National Research Council, grantees that continue to succeed in meeting the objectives set nearly one hundred years ago, demonstrate one of the most potentially effective results of strategic grant-making. The open question for results-based philanthropy today is whether the short-term agenda, even when renewals are likely, yields results that can be sustained, that strengthen the home institution, or that have influence on policy or on a field.

FIELD-BUILDING

The Corporation's experience illustrates that foundations can play a singular societal role when they award grants in support of a new field of knowledge, often through support for an institution and for individuals in the new field. Foundations are uniquely situated to make a long-term commitment to build or develop a field of knowledge or activity, whether in one discipline, across disciplines, in one sector, or across sectors.[21]

Corporation leadership has frequently embraced field-building, and the themes, given both the mission and the charge, have varied considerably: adult education; museum studies; library science and librarianship studies; the social sciences, including social relations; early childhood development and teacher education in the United States and in the Commonwealth, especially in Africa; public interest law in the United States and in South Africa; women and development in the Caribbean and across Africa; and information systems in Commonwealth Africa. Field-building support in library studies and adult education entailed building academic institutions, developing professional associations, and providing training support. The Corporation provided nearly twenty years of reinforcing grants, both in the United States and overseas, to build the field of adult education. Support for building the field of library science and librarianship has featured in the Corporation's grant-making for nearly one hundred years.

To build the fields of area studies (see Chapters 4, 5, and 6) and international security studies (see Chapters 7 and 8), the Corporation provided long-term support for new academic departments, research centers, curricula, field-related meetings and study groups, fellowships, publications, and travel.[22] In both areas, the Corporation did not work alone. A variety of collaborative approaches with other foundations made it possible to develop and sustain these fields; in area studies, the US government also became a major player.

In contrast to the provision of endowment support, where individual philanthropists play an active role, field-building support may be one of the few areas where foundations can play a central role, especially at the earliest stages. Few other sectors in society are flexible enough to assume the risks involved in such initiatives. The government can assist these efforts through agencies such as the National Science Foundation, the National Institutes of Health, the National Endowment for the Humanities, and the National Endowment for the Arts, but often that support becomes available only after the initial, risk-embracing work of foundations. In area studies, for instance, government agencies have played an essential role in extending the results of the early phases of the work, as well as scaling it to cover a wider range of institutions and individuals.[23] Success in establishing and sustaining field-building activities depends on the diversity of the partnerships across time.

Openness to Collaboration and Partnership

As prominent as discussions about risk-taking are in the foundation literature in the twenty-first century, the topic of partnerships and collaboration dominates the discourse.[24] Yet the foundations have never eschewed external partnerships or collaboration, as reflected throughout this book. Since early in the twentieth century, many foundations have worked jointly to support a grantee, worked in complementary fashion to support different dimensions of a project, or supported a grantee sequentially, with one foundation responsible for initiating the work and another for sustaining it. Occasionally, such partnerships have included government agencies, but usually that occurs at a later stage, once the foundations have taken the risks and tested new ideas. The role of government has been to sustain tested ideas or take them to scale, as happened with area studies. In addition, the foundations have initiated partnerships at the local level, as with the local committees discussed earlier, local universities, or nongovernmental organizations.[25]

The Corporation's earliest partnership for its grant-making outside the United States was the joint matching grant to Dalhousie University in 1920 (Chapter 2). The Rockefeller Foundation and Carnegie Corporation agreed to grants of $500,000 each if the provincial government of Nova Scotia would match foundation support. Using private resources to attract local government support for overseas grants was not a regular strategy, but happened on occasion. Recently, the Corporation's efforts to contribute to reviving the public library sector in South Africa were matched by governmental support, and two different types of multi-foundation partnerships illustrated both formal and less formal approaches to inter-foundation collaboration (see Chapter 8).[26] For ten years (2000 to 2010), a multi-member foundation collaborative known as the Partnership for Higher Education in Africa linked Carnegie Corporation with the Rockefeller, Ford, MacArthur, Hewlett, Mellon, and Kresge Foundations through a formal memorandum of understanding to guide grant-making and joint activities. Extending the scope of the partnership, university vice chancellors in nine countries worked with foundation leadership and staff to determine priority activities. The Corporation's eight-year program (from 2000 to 2008) known as Higher Education in the Former Soviet Union (HEFSU) centered on a foundation-government partnership linking Carnegie Corporation, the Ministry of Education of the Russian Federation, the MacArthur Foundation, and the Open Society Institute to support Centers for Advanced Study and Education (CASEs) in thirteen universities in Russia and Eurasia. In both programs, the agenda for university grant-making was informed by the priorities of the partners: in the African partnership program, the institution's approved strategic plans shaped the basis of the grants, and in Russia, for the HEFSU program, the government's priorities informed the scope of grants.

The lessons drawn from the experiences of Carnegie Corporation of New York are proffered as a guide to new and existing institutions. These four integral attributes of effective grant-making have reinforced each other in the work of the Corporation and other foundations over the decades. While the focus on mission underlies decisions about program priorities and subsequent grant-making, it is the openness to pursuing opportunities in new and emerging themes, reinforced by the confidence to take risks and to fund for the long term, that enables foundations, particularly those established in perpetuity, to be effective partners with each other and with other sectors of society.[27]

GOING FORWARD: POTENTIAL CONSTRAINTS

GOING FORWARD, pressures from both the public and private sectors may affect the historical flexibility of philanthropic institutions to adhere to mission, take risks, fund for the long term, and even work in partnership. Following the economic crisis of 2008, much as happened during the Great Depression of the 1930s, the US federal government and local governments have urged private foundations to partner in the funding of heretofore publicly supported social services, including service delivery programs overseas. This kind of partnership with government, to help maintain public and nonprofit service agencies, could compromise a foundation's mission and capacity to undertake risk. New initiatives responding to economic conditions, such as social impact investing, have developed from the premise that partnership with the corporate sector will enable private foundations to respond positively to the requests from government and contribute to sustaining and going to scale with these formerly public initiatives.[28]

Not only could such investments detract from the capacity to examine the root causes that underlie the need for these social services, but they also could begin to blur the lines between charity and philanthropy. Several studies have examined, in depth, the downside for nonprofit organizations working in partnership with government, as well as with the private sector.[29] As the concept of private-public partnerships is endorsed in other countries,[30] more systematic examination will shed light on the opportunities realized and opportunities forgone when those partnerships are not aimed at taking new ideas to scale but rather at using private philanthropic resources to fill the gaps in public financing.

The pressure to introduce business perspectives and metrics into foundation processes, such as strategic planning and quantitative evaluation, may also affect a foundation's propensity for risk-taking, its long-term grant-making, and its partnerships. Approaches that involve specifying the quantitative expected outcomes in advance of making a grant can often favor a shorter time frame to ensure that the outcome predictions remain reliable. Measures of financial effectiveness used in bank loans, such as rates of return, are now applied to assess the difference that a grant or a grant program is expected to achieve; the rate of return calculation favors safe predictable investments over uncertain, risky ones.[31] While some positive social change is likely to result from the use of such models and metrics, the cost to the field of philanthropy is that it reduces the impetus for making long-term investments, for taking risks, and for entering into partnerships.

Corporation president Henry Pritchett explained, in terms that reverberate across the eras, the premises that set private philanthropy apart from the electorate-driven pressure of government and the shareholder-driven metrics of the business sector. Writing in 1922, he emphasized that the Corporation was an agency equipped to "work with time."[32] This long-view perspective enabled the trustees to build on both the mission and the charge to change by recognizing, as Pritchett declared, "that their efforts will be more fruitful and more likely to be cumulative, if, taking up a particular cause, they assist it over a term of years long enough to try out the conception which lies back of its claims for usefulness and for support."[33] Favoring the long view, however, did not imply complacency with the original decision. According to Pritchett, and as practiced over the decades, "it is likewise the judgment of the trustees that their funds should not be permanently pledged to one or another of these causes, but that they should be free at all times to give up the support of an enterprise which has either become well-established, which has shown only mediocre results, or which for one reason or another seems less significant at the time than other projects to which their attention may be directed."[34]

Going Forward: From International to Global Philanthropy

The swift spread of local, private grant-making foundations around the world, often inspired by philanthropists invoking Andrew Carnegie and his precepts, offers an unprecedented opportunity for international grant-makers to engage in partnership at a different level with local grant-making institutions.[35] Outside the United States, philanthropies are burgeoning throughout Europe, Asia, the Middle East, Latin America, and Africa.[36]

In China, an estimate from 2011 suggests that nearly 1,200 private grant-making foundations have been established.[37]

With the increase in the number of private foundations throughout the world, a new approach is possible that will greatly facilitate working effectively in other settings.[38] This approach recognizes that local foundations, as culturally derived institutions, offer insight and knowledge into local persistent social problems as well as the capacity to delve beneath the surface of political and economic issues to support individuals and communities as they work toward renewal or advancement. Rather than make grants directly in other countries, foreign foundations could work in tandem with like-minded partners, that is, local grant-makers aiming to address local issues in the same or complementary priority areas.[39] This kind of partnership could also address the concern raised in the introduction to this volume, namely, that a foundation chartered in the United States that then works in another country needs to consider special questions concerning its role in that society, such as how to take into account the concerns of that society, its historical background, its diversity, and its current development and growth trajectory.[40]

Working as funding partners with local foundations may change the nature of grant-making. Decisions would be made jointly, with local actors shaping and funding the agenda for local action and with some additional resources coming from the outside. Such a partnership need not detract from the attributes for effectiveness of staying true to mission, taking risks, and investing for the long term. Over the Corporation's history, steps in this direction were taken as early as the 1930s; other foundations established full-fledged regional offices to better respond to local conditions. This suggestion draws on a different model, namely, the support of national, regional, and international networks by foundations. With networks, the research or action is usually defined by the local actors while the external partner provides funding and, at times, some operational guidance. The model could productively be adapted for partnership with local grant-making institutions. The historian Akira Iriye has observed that such partnerships could contribute as well to meeting the challenges of contemporary global developments that transcend local boundaries.[41]

While many might characterize the last one hundred years as the

Century of American Philanthropy,[42] given current trends, the next one hundred years may well be more accurately defined as the Century of Global Philanthropy. In that regard, Andrew Carnegie's observations from his 1884 trip around the world seem remarkably prescient: "When the circle has been completed ... the parts fit into one symmetrical whole and you see humanity wherever it is placed working out a destiny tending to one definite end."[43] Through a world of giving, Andrew Carnegie's vision of humanity working together for the common good can be achieved.

AUTHOR'S NOTE AND ACKNOWLEDGMENTS

In 1960, Robert H. Bremner wrote one of the first histories of American philanthropy. His publication, along with Merle E. Curti's articles in the late 1950s, brought respectability to philanthropy as a field of historical study. As a practitioner for over twenty-five years, but trained in the social and physical sciences rather than history, I have long appreciated the path modeled by Bremner and Curti. As they did with their work, I hope to stimulate students, scholars, and practitioners to study this vibrant sector of American and global society.

I have benefited also from the availability of the historical record in the archives of both Carnegie Corporation and its frequent grant-making partners, the Rockefeller and Ford Foundations. Investigating these records through a practitioner's lens enabled me to situate letters, reports, grant recommendations, minutes, and even annual reports in the context of practice as well as the times. Able archivists have brought to light connections with and among other philanthropic and nonprofit institutions and the roles they have played in American and world history. As a beneficiary of these remarkable records and modest contributor to some, I am grateful for the wisdom of the foundation leaders who ensured in perpetuity the presence of professional archivists and the open availability of these records for the public.

When Vartan Gregorian was named the twelfth president of Carnegie Corporation of New York in 1997, it was the first time a historian had served in that role. From the very beginning, Gregorian has invoked the legacy of Andrew Carnegie and the Corporation for contemporary policies and programs. In that spirit, in 2008, as the Corporation's centennial approached, Gregorian and Ellen Bloom, the vice president, chief administrative officer, and corporate secretary, asked me to write a history of the Corporation's work in the international arena. I remain profoundly grateful to Vartan for not only offering me this unusual opportunity, but also for providing me with unfettered access to all of the Corporation's files and encouraging me to draw my own conclusions from the material.

In addition to deep research into original Carnegie Corporation records, this book benefited from consultations with colleagues in philanthropy, grantees of the Corporation and other institutions, scholars in the United States and around the world, and others associated with the Corporation either through family or institution. It is only possible to thank here those who contributed directly to researching, editing, reviewing, and publishing this volume. While I cannot recognize everyone individually, I am nonetheless indebted to so many for the considerable time they gave to this project. Notwithstanding all the thoughtful assistance, I am, of course, solely responsible for any errors of fact and interpretation.

Ellen Bloom, new to the Corporation at the start of this process, deserves great thanks for supporting my work on the book as it progressed. Readily engaging with the Corporation's history, her sound counsel on administrative matters was crucial throughout the entire effort. The talented Jeanne D'Onofrio, chief of staff to the president, offered much-appreciated comments on the first draft, especially regarding other Carnegie institutions. Eleanor Lerman, the Corporation's director of public affairs and publications, was a dedicated supporter and partner in the process of preparing this manuscript. I am pleased to acknowledge her considerable contributions to its development and completion.

Three former leaders of Carnegie Corporation directly and indirectly contributed to this project. In 1987, David A. Hamburg, the eleventh president of the Corporation, hired me to serve as program officer in the recently formed Strengthening Human Resources in Developing Countries Program, under the new program chair, Adetokunbo O. Lucas (for whom I had worked at the World Health Organization). Dr. Lucas has been my valued mentor since 1978, and Dr. Hamburg since the early 1980s. Both gently and frequently nudged me to bring this book to completion. A third leader of the Corporation, the late Barbara D. Finberg, ultimately its executive vice president, became a cherished mentor and friend who provided continual encouragement over eighteen years.

In 1987, Barbara asked me to serve on the Special Projects Committee, where she, along with Corporation leaders David Z. Robinson, Sara L. Engelhardt, Dorothy W. Knapp, Geraldine P. "Geri" Mannion, and Avery Russell shared a deep understanding of the role that the Corporation played in American society and overseas. My writing has benefited immensely from the many years of those discussions and the notes I took during the committee meetings.

The support I have received from the trustees of the Corporation for this and my other activities over the years has been essential. In particular, Helene L. Kaplan, the longest-serving trustee in recent history and now honorary trustee, was always available for consultation on strategy and people to contact, as well as for general reflections on the state of American philanthropy. Mary Patterson "Pat" McPherson, a mentor since college, also deserves great thanks. As a philosopher, educator, vice president of the Andrew W. Mellon Foundation, and executive officer of the American Philosophical Society, Pat has provided invaluable advice about philanthropy and scholarship in the humanities.

Paul Sager, an astute young historian of colonial France, joined the Corporation as a research consultant for the project in late 2009 and brought to the project meticulous persistence and his superb grasp of historiography. His talents were particularly valuable as we tackled the complicated era of the 1930s and the Corporation's efforts in South Africa and in World War II. Paul is also a fine editor, with a discerning eye and ear.

Once drafts began to see the light of day, Joyce Baldwin, an insightful writer and editor, expertly wielded her track-changing scythe to pare down the original manuscript and then assist with editing later versions of the manuscript and associated articles. Paul Berk, a talented editor and patient proofreader, read text and footnotes rapidly and accurately. Several other colleagues contributed at various editing stages, and I am most grateful for all of their special efforts: Anne Phelan, Nick Mirra, Elina Aleyeva, Kimberly Hafner, Kendra White, Ashley Davis, and Julia Cheung.

The history of an institution cannot be written without an extensive exploration of its archives. The Corporation's archives are at Columbia University's Rare Book and Manuscript Library, where Jane Gorjevsky, who served as the Corporation curator when I began writing this book, not only shared her in-depth knowledge of the archives and context, particularly of the area studies activities, but also provided, with her students, assistance with searching and copying. Moreover, Jane generously contributed her time to a critical review of the manuscript, corrected all the archival references, and provided me with copies of her own papers, published and unpublished. Jennifer Comins, who succeeded Jane, has been equally generous in the final stages. Mary Marshall Clark, director of the Columbia Center for Oral History, and her terrific team provided special assistance in making available the Corporation's oral histories. Gladys D. McQueen, the Corporation's on-site records manager, facilitated access to all of the necessary files and assisted in finding those that were difficult to locate; it is with deep appreciation that I acknowledge her efforts over the last five years.

In 2011, James Allen Smith, vice president and director of research and education of the Rockefeller Archive Center, and Jack Meyers, RAC president, offered me the opportunity to become a Carnegie scholar-in-residence at RAC. This wonderfully productive period deepened my understanding of the relationship between Andrew Carnegie and John D. Rockefeller Sr. and the interplay between their foundations and across time and geography. The savvy archival assistance I received there—in particular from archivists Nancy L. Adgent and Tom Rosenbaum and RAC's assistant director and head of reference, Michele Hiltzik—along with RAC's many other expert staff and its high-quality facilities, made the process of exploration especially rewarding and amiable. I want to thank my colleagues Barbara Shubinski and Teresa Iacobelli for their willingness to impart their knowledge about the Rockefeller Foundation. In my role as senior fellow at RAC—where, now through the generosity of the Ford Foundation, I have had the opportunity to elucidate the Foundation's history to inform its current and new activities—I also want to express my appreciation to my RAC colleagues Rachel Wimpee, Lucas Buresch, and Marissa Vassari for sharing their time and ideas related to both Carnegie Corporation and the Ford Foundation.

Twenty-five years of working at Carnegie Corporation and being associated with a variety of foundations enabled me to partner in strategy setting and grant-making with a wide variety of especially talented individuals. One practitioner in philanthropy stands out. The late Francis X. Sutton avidly and frequently shared his astounding knowledge of so many fields and the profound challenges in writing such a book as this. A longtime staff member and leader at the Ford Foundation and at the Social Science Research Council, and an adviser, inter alia, to the Aga Khan Foundation, Frank called regularly with enouragement, sharing anecdotes and stories about the Corporation from the 1950s and 1960s, hard-to-find references, and tales from his unpublished memoirs. His capacity for kindness while insisting on rigorous attention to the matter at hand added depth to my work. I treasure his special mentoring friendship and am saddened that he did not live to see me "slay this monster," one of his favorite Winston Churchill quotes.

Frank was not the only practitioner of philanthropy who contributed to this work. Daniel M. Fox, president emeritus of the Milbank Memorial Fund, scholar of philanthropy, and policy practitioner, kindly offered advice and insight on a variety of issues. Even more generously, he critically read every single page as an expert reviewer before I showed the document to anyone else. His corrections of assertions, facts, and interpretations added to the book's accuracy, balance, depth, and scope.

Elizabeth J. McCormack, the doyenne of American philanthropy, became a wise guide as she shared her deep experience and her increasing concerns about present-day foundations during my writing and research. Franklin A. Thomas, former president of the Ford Foundation and trustee of Carnegie Corporation in the pivotal period of the early to mid-1970s, spent several hours with me providing insights from the trustee review he chaired of the Corporation's Commonwealth Program as well as the remarkable period of anti-apartheid foundation collaboration. His successor, Susan V. Berresford, former president and longtime staff member at Ford, amply shared time, meals, and advice about the entire field of philanthropy. William D. "Bill" Carmichael, also from the Ford Foundation, where he was vice president for developing countries, has deep global experience and provided his insights about the Corporation, especially about his programmatic leadership at Ford.

My closest colleagues and partners at the Rockefeller Foundation, Kenneth Prewitt, senior vice president, and Joyce Moock, associate vice president, have always unselfishly provided strategic guidance about philanthropy, particularly about partnerships across foundations and with institutions and grantee institutions. I want to express my gratitude for their discerning contributions to a variety of discussions throughout this book. I am also deeply appreciative of Ken's critical reading of the manuscript and his astute comments. Gerry Salole, chief executive of the European Foundation Centre and a colleague during his work at the Ford and Bernard Van Leer Foundations, shared his distinctive understanding of evaluation from the community perspective. I am particularly grateful to him for taking the time to carefully read the manuscript and provide thoughtful comments. Two other longtime partners, Brent Herbert-Copley, formerly at the International Development Research Centre in Canada and now vice president of the Canadian Social Science and Humanities Research Council, and Rohinton Medhora, president of the Canadian Centre for International Governance Innovation, contributed additional perspectives on partnership with this American foundation. Joan E. Spero, former president of the Doris Duke Charitable Foundation and author of the most recent analysis of American foundations' international grant-making, kindly shared her ideas and comments as both our projects were under way and generously provided timely comments on the manuscript.

I benefited enormously from the wise expertise of Stanley N. Katz, Princeton University professor and author of many distinguished publications on the history of philanthropy, which often feature the Corporation. Stan offered his own commentary and critique as well as the opportunity to undergo tough questioning by his graduate policy class. I am grateful also to his longtime colleague, the late Barry D. Karl at the University of Chicago, who gave me insights about the role of the trustees of the Corporation, especially around World War II. Marian Z. Stern, historian of philanthropy at New York University, has kindly invited me to share drafts for critique with her history of philanthropy class for the past five years.

Four historians have significantly influenced the thinking underlying this work. Stephen R. Graubard, for many decades the editor of *Daedalus*, served as adviser to the Carnegie Scholars Program and then provided wise guidance when I began working on the early drafts of this book. I cherish his continuing friendship and sage advice. John G. Reid, the distinguished Canadian historian of the Maritime Provinces at St. Mary's University, opened my eyes to the failure of the Corporation's early major activity in Canada. I am in his debt for his in-depth understanding of the local dynamics and the reasons for the failure. David Ekbladh, first mentee, then mentor, and always a colleague, shared his insights, particularly his exciting findings on the origins of foundation support for international security in the 1930s. Dave took time away from his own research to provide an extensive review of the final draft manuscript, noting some important lacunae, particularly on South Africa. He also gave me a critically important introduction to Professor Akira Iriye, whose classic book on cultural internationalism provided intellectual grounding for my study. Discussions with Professor Iriye have deepened my understanding of transnational history. I am especially grateful for his willingness to discuss his ideas with me and to read and comment extensively on the entire manuscript.

Five scholars who specialize in the history of Carnegie Corporation have been profoundly knowledgeable guides. The late E. Jefferson "Pat" Murphy, a social anthropologist, was the first scholar to give serious attention to the history of the Corporation's overseas grant-making. He extensively shared with me his deep knowledge of the Corporation and other foundations working in Africa from 1950 to 1975 at the Africa-America Institute (he was the first staff member, then became vice president) and teaching at the University of Fort Hare in South Africa in the 1950s. Along with Pat, Michael J. Birkner of Gettysburg College, Richard Glotzer of the University of Akron, and Maribel Morey of Clemson University contributed their insights, in particular about Frederick Keppel (Birkner), the Corporation's work in Africa and Australia (Glotzer), and the support for Gunnar Myrdal (Morey). All deepened my understanding of the Corporation in the 1930s and the implications for the Corporation's future. Inderjeet Parmar of Manchester University has studied the Corporation's history alongside the histories of the Ford Foundation and the Rockefeller Foundation. Although our conceptual and analytical approaches differ, Inderjeet was more than willing to discuss our findings and our differences. I am most appreciative of our lively conversations and informal debates.

I also had the pleasure of talking with Terry Keppel Albright, Frederick Keppel's granddaughter, and learning more about Keppel's personal life and how it influenced his leadership at the Corporation. I thank D. Ellen Shuman, then the Corporation's vice president for investments, for making this contact possible.

A special note of thanks goes to presidential historian Richard Norton Smith for our conversations at the Rockefeller Archive Center over the past few years. Richard shared with me his approach to archival research and interviews, and he kindly considered book titles with me. I am especially grateful for his help in crafting the final title for this book.

Although I would like to thank every member of the Corporation's staff, especially over the last five years, for reasons of space I cannot. I want particularly to thank Michele Cahill, vice president for national programs, who generously hosted the Carnegie Scholars Program and this writing project, while asking constructive questions related to education about the Corporation's role at various points in its history. Deana Arsenian, vice president for international programs, provided expert critique, not only from her current leadership role but also from her past involvement in the programs on Russia and on weapons of mass destruction. Susan King, at the time vice president for external relations, with great élan and creativity, provided guidance and support for this work. Her successor, Deanna Lee, chief communications and digital strategies officer, has given equally strong support. Several Carnegie Corporation staff members (current and former), generously proffered their time and advice, some patiently letting me share the latest findings and others providing documents that they had fortuitously preserved in their files. Some also critically reviewed the more recent chapters for accuracy and any breaches of confidentiality. In addition to the colleagues already mentioned, I always will be grateful for the friendship and collegiality of Corporation staff members Omotade "Tade" Aina, Stephen Del Rosso, Eli Evans, Barbara Gombach, Andrea Johnson, Heather S. McKay, Frederic "Fritz" Mosher, Patricia Moore Nicholas, and Hillary Wiesner.

For thoughtful conversations about the Corporation's history, including identifying key hard-to-find references and sharing their own files, I also wish to thank the following past and present Corporation colleagues:

Patricia Aquino-Macri, Rookaya Bawa, Randy Brett, Deborah Cohen, Natasha Davids, Lynn Di Martino, Paula Douglas, Claudia Fritelli, Veronica "Ronnie" M. Garwood, Andrew Gerhaghty, Mirela Geprifti, Neil Grabois, Idalia "Dee" Holder, Nicole Howe-Buggs, Zoe Ingalls, William R. Louis, Kathy R. Lowery, Anne MacKinnon, Virginia Mallon-Ackermann, Michelle Napoli, Kate Newburger, Evelyn Nieders, Patricia Pagnotta, Carl Robichaud, Courtenay Sprague, Robert J. Seman, Ronald Sexton, David Speedie, Rikard Treiber, and Sara K. Wolpert. I also want to thank Kirk Thomas and Rosa Cabrera for their kind encouragement during this project.

Information and knowledge can only be conveyed if the technology works. I want to give special thanks to the expert team of information technology specialists at the Corporation: Loretta Harris, Rick Brown, Yotaro Sherman, and former IT staff member Maud Darucaud-Bates. Their support over the several years of writing this book, both during the week and on weekends, went far beyond the call of collegiality. In addition, the office management staff, formerly led by Ruth Frank and continuing now under José A. Rivera and Damon Roundtree, all provided continually appreciated support via facilities, photocopying, and daily camaraderie.

Several scholars who also have been grantees verified or critiqued my interpretations and provided additional historical material: Francis Wilson, University of Cape Town; Tatiana Carayannis, Social Science Research Council; Nancy Bodurtha and her team at the Council on Foreign Relations; the late John Temple Swing, formerly of the Council on Foreign Relations; Mary Coyle, former director of the Coady International Institute, Nova Scotia, Canada; Shibley Telhami, University of Maryland; and Thomas Weiss, City University of New York.

I thank the following advisers, scholars, and friends from the field of philanthropy who were actively involved in discussions about this book and about new directions in the field: Alberta Arthurs, Thomas Asher, Jennifer Barsky, Howard W. Buffett, Elizabeth Campbell, Martha Choe, Elan Garonzik, Claire Gaudiani, Peter Geithner, the late Margaret Mahoney, Kathleen McCarthy, Gail McClure, Janice Nittoli, Michael Seltzer, Joe Short, Darren Walker, and Derek Yach.

For all the aforementioned efforts to see the light of day, the manuscript had to become a book. PublicAffairs has provided its expertise at every level of this transformative process. Susan Weinberg, group publisher, provided overall leadership. Robert Kimzey, consultant to PublicAffairs, spearheaded editing, design, and formatting with humor, creativity, and dedication. Cynthia Buck, the tireless and gifted copy editor, not only improved lines but ensured appropriate attention to detail in text and notes. The book benefited from the exquisite taste of Janet Tingey, the designer. I also greatly value the creative judgment of Pete Garceau, the Art Director at PublicAffairs. Other colleagues and friends in publishing provided much appreciated feedback: Tina Bennett, Catherine Carlin, Azzurra Cox, Marc Favreaux, the late Ann Hawthorne, Nicolas Liu, and Alane Mason.

Demonstrating depth of friendship as the writing season turned into years, I deeply appreciate the understanding and flexibility of Sue Block-Tyrrell, Jason Calder, Chris Cluett, Aditi and Nitin Desai, Constance Freeman, Helen Freeman, Aleya El Bindari Hammad, Jean Herskovits and John Corry, John Good Iron, Angela and William Kane, Anne and Charles Lieberman, Socrates and Susan Litsios, David Matz, Agnes and James Metzger, Prue Bach Mortimer and Jay Mortimer, Bettye Musham, Barbara Paley, Sandra Priest Rose, Deborah Rose and Jan Stolwijk, Betsy Rosenfield and Norman Samet, Daniel C. Taylor, Jesse O. Taylor, the late Joanne Troy and Bill Troy, Caroline and Douglas Van, and Sharon, Robert, and Gregory Zimmer. Grace Goodell deserves special mention for her inspiration, including as I tackled the complex subjects of development and modernization. Ann-Marie and Tommy Farrelly enabled me to juggle multiple responsibilities across writing, work, and home seven days a week. Dr. Flavia A. Golden and Dr. Thomas P. Sculco, treasured physician-friends, have helped me sustain energy and well-being, as has Phyllis J. Steinberg. Last but never least, I want to thank Frank Kessel, my writing partner for ten years in other areas, and Marion Kessel, his graceful wife, for their perfectly timed humor and Frank's willingness to pick up the slack in our other projects during this venture.

My graduate school mentors who continued to provide wise advice over the decades, the late M. Gordon Wolman and the late Carl E. Taylor, each a professor emeritus at Johns Hopkins University, did not live to see the hard copy of this book, but infuse every page that I write.

My immediate family, with great good humor, tolerated the deluge of research material filling every nook and cranny of our home and monopo-lizing our conversations. My gratitude and love are limitless for my father Herbert and my late mother Audrey Rosenfield, my daughter Victoria Shuster, my brothers and their families: Tom and his daughters Danielle, Jessica, and Vanessa, and Nelson, Nelson's wife Ruth, and their daughters Elaine and Julie.

In closing, the most fundamental acknowledgment and the dedication of this book belong to Andrew and Louise Carnegie. Andrew knew for most of his life that he wanted to give away all his money. In agreeing to marry him, Louise made that possible. David Nasaw recounted the teamwork in philanthropy of Andrew and Louise: "She knew precisely what she was doing. Her husband was going to give away his fortune during his lifetime and she was going to help him."[1] Thus the story of Carnegie Corporation of New York.

NOTES

NOTES FOR INTRODUCTION

1   See the sidebar to this chapter for a list of his endowments, including his last foundation, the Carnegie United Kingdom Trust, established in 1913.

2   As Andrew Carnegie wrote in his 1889 essay *Wealth*, "This, then is held to be the duty of the man of Wealth: ... to consider all surplus revenues which come to him simply as trust funds, which he is called upon to administer, and strictly bound as a matter of duty to administer in the manner which, in his judgment, is best calculated to produce the most beneficial results for the community—the man of wealth thus becoming the mere agent and trustee for his poorer brethren ... returning their surplus wealth to the mass of their fellows in the best form calculated to do them lasting good." Andrew Carnegie, "Wealth," *North American Review* CCCXCI (June, 1989) available at www.swarthmore.edu/SocSci/rbannis1/AIH19th/Carnegie.htm. (accessed June 30, 2014)

3   Robert H. Bremner, *American Philanthropy*, 2nd ed. (Chicago: University of Chicago Press, 1988), 5–39. Starting in the early 1900s, philanthropic entities more familiar to twenty-first-century philanthropists were established—for example, the Carnegie Foundation for the Advancement of Teaching in 1905, the Milbank Memorial Fund in 1905, and the Russell Sage Foundation in 1907.

4   Burton Jesse Hendrick, *The Life of Andrew Carnegie*, 2 vols. (Garden City, NY: Doubleday/Doran, 1932), vol. 2, 141–142. Carnegie was worth $312 billion in 2009 dollars, calculated using the website Measuring Worth, www.measuringworth.com.

5   "Carnegie's dazzling gifts attracted much public attention. Box scores began to appear in the press comparing Carnegie's gifts with those of his most important convert to the Gospel of Wealth, John D. Rockefeller. In 1904, the London *Times* reported Carnegie's gifts to have totaled $21 million, Rockefeller's $10 million.... Most discouraging of all [to Carnegie] was the fact that no matter how fast he had run ... he had not run fast enough.... By 1911 he had given away $180 million, but he still had almost the same amount left." Joseph Frazier Wall, ed., *The Andrew Carnegie Reader* (Pittsburgh: University of Pittsburgh Press, 1992), 126 127.

6   As Robert Lester writes in his analysis of Carnegie's giving over the period 1901 to 1941, in 1911 "Carnegie ... was tired of the constant strain of giving.... Root asked him, Why not set the trust up now, transfer to it the bulk of his fortune and prepare for others to do the work. This suited Mr. Carnegie. He would create a new trust, not limited in purpose as were his others, but with the broad aim of advancing and diffusing knowledge." Robert M. Lester, *Forty Years of Carnegie Giving, 1901–1941* (New York: Charles Scribner's Sons, 1941), 57.

7 Carnegie Corporation of New York (CCNY), Minutes of the Board of Trustees, I, 7, November 10, 1911, Carnegie Corporation of New York (CCNY) Records, Rare Book and Manuscript Library, Columbia University Libraries (RBML-CUL); Andrew Carnegie, letter to CCNY trustees transmitting the deed of gift, November 10, 1911.

8 Despite a century of grant-making, the Corporation's assets as of June 2012 equal $2.67 billion. For current details, see www.carnegie.org.

9 For more details about the family of Carnegie organizations and institutions, see CCNY, "The Carnegie Trusts and Institutions," 2007, available at: http://carnegie.org/fileadmin/Media/Publications/PDF/carnegie_trusts_Inst_small_low.pdf.

10 "Conditions upon the erth inevitably change; hence, no wise man will bind Trustees forever to certain paths, causes or institutions. I disclaim any intention of doing so." Carnegie, letter to CCNY trustees transmitting the deed of gift, November 10, 1911. Starting in 1906, Carnegie used phonetic spelling in his personal and professional transactions; Hendrick, *Life of Andrew Carnegie*, 262.

11 Most of the 75,000 foundations in the United States and overseas make grants in their home countries. In 2008, however, nearly one-quarter of all grants by American foundations supported international programs; for more discussion, see Joan Spero, *The Global Role of US Foundations* (New York: Foundation Center, 2010). The Foundation Center data for 2010 show that 24.4 percent of grants made in the United States supported international programs, a substantial increase from the slightly over 10 percent in 2000; Steven Lawrence and Reina Mukai, *International Grantmaking Update* (New York: Foundation Center, 2010), 2.

12 Akira Iriye, *Cultural Internationalism and World Order* (Baltimore: Johns Hopkins University Press, 1997), 3. For a different perspective on cultural internationalism and international institutions, including American foundations, see Mark Mazower, *Governing the World: The History of an Idea* (New York: Penguin Press, 2012), esp. 419–421. For additional discussion of the international role of American foundations, see Helmut K. Anheir and David C. Hammack, eds., *American Foundations: Roles and Contributions* (Washington, DC: Brookings Institution Press, 2010). For a more detailed discussion of globalisms, see Robert O. Keohane and Joseph S. Nye Jr., "Globalization: What's New? What's Not? (and So What?)" *Foreign Policy* 118 (Spring 2000): 104–119.

13 CCNY, Minutes of the Executive Committee, 1, 3, February 16, 1912, CCNY Records, RBML-CUL.

14 The Church Peace Union was endowed by the Corporation at the request of Mr. and Mrs. Carnegie. In 1986 it was renamed in their honor as the Carnegie Council on Ethics and International Affairs. In 2005 the Council changed its name to Carnegie Council for Ethics in International Affairs. For details, see Carnegie Council for Ethics in International Affairs, "Carnegie Council History," available at: http://www.carnegiecouncil.org/about/info/history.html.

15 Elihu Root, acting president, 1919–1920; James S. Angell, president, 1920–1921; and Henry Pritchett, acting president, 1921–1923.

16 Keppel had been dean at Columbia University, had served in the War Department during World War I, and had represented the American Red Cross and the American International Chamber of Commerce in Paris for several years before returning to the United States to run the New York City Regional Plan Initiative for the Russell Sage Foundation.

17 CCNY, "The Carnegie Trusts and Institutions"; see also the Carnegie Medal of Philanthropy website, http://www.carnegiemedals.org.

18 See note 14.

19 When John Gardner was appointed secretary of the US Department of Health, Education, and Welfare in 1965, Alan Pifer served as acting president of Carnegie Corporation from 1965 to 1967.

20   This tax-reducing feature did not benefit Andrew Carnegie in founding Carnegie Corporation or John D. Rockefeller Sr. in founding the Rockefeller Foundation.

21   Ellen Lagemann's *The Politics of Knowledge: The Carnegie Corporation, Philanthropy, and Public Policy* (Middletown, CT: Wesleyan University Press, 1989), which covers the years 1911 to 1983, explicitly excludes the overseas programs and international grants. Stephen Stackpole's *Carnegie Corporation: Commonwealth Program, 1911–1961* (New York: Carnegie Corporation, 1961) provides not only a brief analytical section but a valuable list of grants made under the Commonwealth Program in the first fifty years. E. Jefferson Murphy's *Creative Philanthropy: Carnegie Corporation and Africa, 1953–1973* (New York: Teachers College Press, 1976) analyzes in-depth the twenty years cited in the title and includes a very useful introductory chapter that summarizes the earlier grant-making.

22   Akira Iriye, *Global Community: The Role of International Organizations in the Making of the Contemporary World* (Berkeley: University of California Press, 2002), 209.

NOTES FOR CHAPTER I

1   As listed in the sidebar to this chapter, many of these trustees were already leading other Carnegie philanthropies.

2   See the sidebar in the introduction for a listing of those institutions and their founding dates.

3   Other foundations that were primarily operating in nature—that is, they ran their own programs by supporting the work of their staff members—had been established earlier, including the Milbank Memorial Fund, established in 1905, and the Russell Sage Foundation, established in 1907, as well as the earlier Carnegie and Rockefeller entities. These foundations only occasionally made grants to nonstaff members. The Corporation, established as a general-purpose foundation, only made grants to others, both in the United States and overseas, and was the first foundation that did so as its sole practice. For a different perspective, see William T. R. Fox, *The Reminiscences of William T. R. Fox: Oral History, 1968* (New York: Oral History Collection of Columbia University, 1968), 2 (hereafter "Fox, COHC"). For more discussion of the differences between private operating foundations and private non-operating grant-making foundations, see IRS, "Life Cycle of a Public Charity/ Private Foundation," available at: http://www.irs.gov/ Charities-&-Non-Profits/Charitable-Organizations/Life-Cycle-of-a-Public-Charity-Private-Foundation (last updated November 6, 2013); and Council on Foundations, United States International Grantmaking, "International Grantmaking Basics: US Foundation Types," available at: http://www.usig.org/legal/Types-of-gm-orgs.asp.

4   Lester, *Forty Years of Carnegie Giving*, 170.

5   Ibid., 168.

6   Carnegie Corporation of New York (CCNY), Minutes of the Board of Trustees, I, 7, November 10, 1911, Carnegie Corporation of New York (CCNY) Records, Rare Book and Manuscript Library, Columbia University Libraries (RBML-CUL).

7   Robert E. Kohler, *Partners in Science: Foundations and Natural Scientists, 1900–1945* (Chicago: University of Chicago Press, 1991), 58.

8   Frank Pierce Hill, *James Bertram: An Appreciation* (New York: CCNY, 1936), 19–22.

9   For further information about Andrew Carnegie, the reader is referred to the four most extensive biographies of Andrew Carnegie (in order of publication): Burton J. Hendrick, *The Life of Andrew Carnegie*, 2 vols. (Garden City, NY: Doubleday, Doran & Co., 1932); Joseph Frazier Wall, *Andrew Carnegie* (Pittsburgh: University of Pittsburgh Press, 1989); Peter Krass, *Carnegie* (Hoboken, NJ: John Wiley & Sons, 2002); and David Nasaw, *Andrew Carnegie* (New York: Penguin, 2006).

10   Barry Werth, *Banquet at Delmonico's: Great Minds, the Gilded Age, and the Triumph of Evolution in America* (New York: Random House, 2009), 206.

11   Carnegie, "Wealth."

12   CCNY, Minutes of the Board of Trustees, I, 9, November 10, 1911, CCNY Records, RBML-CUL.

13   Ibid., 3. The constitution uses the modified spelling practiced by Andrew Carnegie.

14   Dwight Burlingame, *Philanthropy in America: A Comprehensive History* (Santa Barbara, CA: ABC-CLIO, 2004); Barry D. Karl and Stanley N. Katz, "The American Private Foundation and the Public Sphere, 1890–1930," *Minerva* 19 (1981): 236–270.

15   As Andrew Carnegie wrote to the trustees on August 11, 1913: "I am enabled to relieve you of administering that portion of the income of Twenty million dollars ($20,000,000) of Bonds transferred to the Corporation with a letter of January 16, 1912, which is required for the needs of Library Buildings and Church Organs in Great Britain and Ireland, thus increasing your resources." The Executive Committee then turned over to the United Kingdom Trust all the obligations in those areas except for ones where the work had already started. CCNY, "Report of the Executive Committee of Carnegie Corporation of New York to the Adjourned Annual Meeting of the Board of Trustees," 24, December 6, 1913, CCNY Records, RBML-CUL.

16   Henry Smith Pritchett, *The First Twenty Years of Carnegie Corporation* (New York: CCNY, 1931), 17–18.

17   In May 1913, the Rockefeller Foundation held the first meeting of its board of trustees. John D. Rockefeller Sr. had been working since 1910 to obtain a federal charter to establish a foundation. When that option proved unfeasible, he went the Carnegie route of obtaining a charter from the New York State Legislature, which approved it in the spring of 1913. Rockefeller initially funded his foundation with a gift of $35 million. The mandate, "to promote the well-being of mankind throughout the world," more than matched that of Carnegie Corporation, whose mission was "to advance and diffuse knowledge and understanding." Even though its resources, for the moment, were less than those available to the Corporation, the Rockefeller Foundation's mission was clearly broader, and it functioned differently as well. It set up its own boards or brought existing boards (for example, the China Medical Board and the International Health Board) under its ambit. In the words of Raymond Fosdick, president of the Rockefeller Foundation in the late 1930s and 1940s, "these groups were direct agencies of the Foundation, financed and operated by the Foundation"; Fosdick, *The Story of the Rockefeller Foundation* (New York: Harper & Brothers, 1952), 21, 25–26. Rockefeller Foundation historian Robert Shaplen notes that "Rockefeller, who was much impressed by Carnegie's philosophy and by his clarion call—'I would that more men of wealth were doing as you are doing with your money,' he wrote the steel magnate—was already thinking of ways to distribute his own acquired oil fortune for worth-while ends"; Shaplen, *Toward the Well-Being of Mankind: Fifty Years of the Rockefeller Foundation* (Garden City, NY: Doubleday, 1964), 3.

18   As Burton Hendrick noted, "These foundations, twenty of which disperse not far from fifty million dollars a year, the two largest being Carnegie Corporation with resources of $160,000,000 million, and the Rockefeller Foundation with $147,000,000, have really become a new estate in the American realm"; Hendrick, *Life of Andrew Carnegie*, 354. However, once the Rockefeller Foundation merged with other existing Rockefeller philanthropies, completing that process by 1928, the enormous consolidation of resources enabled it to surpass the Corporation in assets.

19   CCNY, Minutes of the Executive Committee, I, April 30, May 17, July 13, August 17, September 14, September 27, and October 29, 1912, CCNY Records, RBML-CUL.

20   CCNY, Minutes of the Executive Committee, II, August 11, 1913, RBML-CUL. Although it aimed to support only 275 "Chinese Government Indemnity Students" (who were receiving scholarships through the Imperial Qing Boxer Indemnity Scholarship Program), it is possible

that the Corporation funded most if not all of the 852 Chinese students who studied in the United States between 1912 and 1925, perhaps through the Chinese Office for Students Going to the United States, which supported over 500 men and hundreds of women at about $480 annually, totaling a bit more than $200,000; T. K. Chu, "Translator's Preface," in Ning Qian, *Chinese Students Encounter America* (Seattle: University of Washington Press, 2002), xviii. See also Stacey Bieler, *"Patriots" or "Traitors"? A History of American-Educated Chinese Students* (Armonk, NY: M. E. Sharpe, 2004), 67. Bieler mentions that a Chinese "American Returned Students Society" solicited funds from the "Carnegie Foundation" in 1914 to create a political science library in Beijing (164). Another source shows the number of Chinese students in the United States increasing from 650 in 1911 to 1,600 in 1926 and asserts that they were largely self-funded; Yeili Ye, *Seeking Modernity in China's Name: Chinese Students in the United States, 1900–1927* (Stanford, CA: Stanford University Press, 2001), 9–10.

21 Interestingly, these monies came out of the general-purpose fund, not the fund set aside for international activities; perhaps because Canada had been included in the mandate for the Carnegie Foundation for the Advancement of Teaching, the Corporation trustees at this early stage apparently saw this support more as an extension of US-related work. CCNY, Minutes of the Executive Committee, II, March 14, 1913, CCNY Records, RBML-CUL.

22 CCNY, Minutes of the Board of Trustees, I, 50, November 16, 1916, CCNY Records, RBML-CUL; Lester, *Forty Years of Carnegie Giving*, 128; for charter change, see Lester, 171.

23 Niall Ferguson, *Colossus: The Price of America's Empire* (New York: Penguin, 2004), 15.

24 CCNY, Minutes of the Board of Trustees, III, 84, March 12, 1918, CCNY Records, RBML-CUL.

25 CCNY, Minutes of the Executive Committee, II, unpaginated, January 31, 1913, CCNY Records, RBML-CUL.

26 Franklin Parker, "George Peabody, 1795–1869: His Influence on Educational Philanthropy," *Peabody Journal of Education* 49, no. 2 (January 1972), 143.

27 Andrew Carnegie, *A League of Peace: A Rectorial Address Delivered to the Students in the University of St Andrews, 17th October, 1905* (Boston: Ginn, 1906), reprinted by CCNY (2012), 48. Joseph Frazier Wall, one of Carnegie's major biographers, wrote, "Carnegie was one of the first to use the term 'League of Nations.' In an article in *Outlook*, in 1907, he wrote, 'I believe the next step to universal peace to be the formation of a League of Nations similar to that formed recently in China for a specific object.'" Wall, *Andrew Carnegie* (Oxford: Oxford University Press, 1970; reprint, Pittsburgh: University of Pittsburgh Press, 1989), 920–921.

28 Wall, *Andrew Carnegie*, 921–940.

29 Although this effort, too, would ultimately fail, and Taft would lose the next election to Woodrow Wilson (for a variety of reasons), Carnegie still had confidence in these efforts and lobbied hard for the treaties in the United States and with European and British leaders. Wall, *Andrew Carnegie*, 976–996; see also David Nasaw, "The Continuing Relevance of Andrew Carnegie's Legacy," lecture at the Peace Palace, The Hague, Netherlands, August 30, 2012, Carnegie Corporation of New York, available at: http://carnegie.org/fileadmin/Media/Publications/David_nasaw_hague_lecture_aug12_peace.pdf (accessed December 11, 2013).

30 Andrew Carnegie, *Autobiography* (Garden City, New York: Doubleday, Doran & Co., 1920), 264.

31 Notwithstanding the difficulties of Carnegie Corporation's institutional relationship with the Carnegie Endowment for International Peace, until 1983 most of the Corporation's work for the promotion of peace was through grants to the Endowment.

32 CCNY, Minutes of the Board of Trustees, III, 139, November 21, 1918, "Report of the Executive Committee," CCNY Records, RBML-CUL. On the Lichnowsky Memorandum, see Edward Mandell House and Charles Seymour, eds., *What Really Happened at Paris: The Story*

of the Peace Conference, 1918–1919 (New York: Charles Scribner's Sons, 1921), 401; and William Mulligan, *The Origins of the First World War* (New York: Cambridge University Press, 2010), 5.

33   As David S. Patterson suggests, "emotionally he sympathized with the more ardent advocates of peace and after 1910 became even more outspoken in support of their continuing efforts to reduce international tensions." Patterson, "Andrew Carnegie's Quest for World Peace," *Proceedings of the American Philosophical Society* 114, no. 5 (October 20, 1970): 381.

34   David Nasaw, *Andrew Carnegie* (New York: Penguin, 2006), 772–773, 777–780.

35   Akira Iriye describes the cultural internationalism of that era as "a vision of an international community in which nations and peoples gained a more mature understanding of one another than had been possible when commerce was combined with military conquest and seen in terms of sovereign states' struggles for power. Distant parts of the world were being brought closer together through modern shipping, trade, and marketing organizations, and it seemed possible to expect the growth of mutual knowledge and, as a result, a greater sense of shared concerns and interests across national boundaries." Iriye, *Cultural Internationalism and World Order*, 26.

36   CCNY, Minutes of the Executive Committee, II, 123, March 11, 1914, CCNY Records, RBML-CUL.

37   Carnegie Council for Ethics in International Affairs, "Carnegie Council History," available at: http://www.carnegiecouncil.org/about/info/history.html.

38   John Frederick Woolverton, *Robert H. Gardiner and the Reunification of Worldwide Christianity in the Progressive Era* (Columbia: University of Missouri Press, 2005), 155–156; Wall, *Andrew Carnegie*, 114–117.

39   Hendrick, *Andrew Carnegie*, 345.

40   Nasaw, *Andrew Carnegie*, 782, 784–785.

41   Louise Carnegie, preface to Carnegie, *Autobiography*, v; *New York Times*, November 25, 1915; both reprinted in Patterson, "Andrew Carnegie's Quest for World Peace," 382.

42   CCNY, Minutes of the Executive Committee, II, 256, 261, May 3 and June 8, 1917, CCNY Records, RBML-CUL.

43   The resolution was made "subject to securing from counsel an approval of the legality thereof"; CCNY, Minutes of the Executive Committee, II, 263, June 20, 1917. By the end of the summer of 1917, it was reported to the Executive Committee that Pritchett had obtained a report from the Red Cross on its planned activities and counsel had approved the grant as within the charter; CCNY, Minutes of the Board of Trustees, I, unpaginated, September 14, 1917, CCNY Records, RBML-CUL.

44   CCNY, Minutes of the Board of Trustees, I, unpaginated, September 14, 1917, CCNY Records, RBML-CUL.

45   CCNY, Minutes of the Board of Trustees, III, 90, May 20, 1918, CCNY Records, RBML-CUL.

46   CCNY, Minutes of the Board of Trustees, III, 87, March 25, 1918, CCNY Records, RBML-CUL.

47   Andrew Carnegie suggested, for example, that the church organ grants should be reduced to a minimum. Bertram offered that this could be done by refusing to provide organs to churches that were in debt or being constructed; CCNY, Minutes of the Board of Trustees, I, 28, November 19, 1914, CCNY Records, RBML-CUL. The trustees also took their cue from Carnegie in discussing the deficit in the library-building program. With fewer and fewer grants, they began to discuss the value of this program and the influence of the war on the decline in requests.

48   CCNY, Minutes of the Board of Trustees, I, 28, 35, November 18, 1915, CCNY Records, RBML-CUL.

49   CCNY, Minutes of the Executive Committee, II, 256–257, May 3, 1917, CCNY Records, RBML-CUL.

50   Lester, *Thirty Years of Carnegie Giving,* 144.

51   Hendrick, *The Life of Andrew Carnegie,* 354.

52   Henry Pritchett made the most definitive comment about the situation in a 1931 paper: "Mr. Carnegie was too keen a man to lose sight of the fact that the set-up of the Corporation board left the five institutions in practical control. The five ex-officio members formed a majority and could at any time, by agreement upon a common policy, carry out such measures as they might deem wise. This consideration gave him some food for thought, and at one time he had in mind to insert the condition that no ex-officio member should propose a grant to his own institution. He decided, however, that it was wiser to trust to the integrity and broad-mindedness of all of the trustees." Pritchett, *The First Twenty Years,* 23.

53   Hendrick, *The Life of Andrew Carnegie,* 351.

54   These were the Carnegie Institute of Pittsburgh, the Carnegie Institution of Washington, the Carnegie Hero Fund Commission, the Carnegie Foundation for the Advancement of Teaching, and the Church Peace Union. Funds for the war-related analyses of the Carnegie Endowment for International Peace were granted in 1917.

55   CCNY, Minutes of the Board of Trustees, I, 3, December 3, 1915, CCNY Records, RBML-CUL.

56   Lester, *Thirty Years of Carnegie Giving,* 144.

57   James Allen Smith, "Congressional Investigations and the Legitimacy and Accountability of Foundations," presentation to the Rockefeller Foundation staff (unpublished), October 23, 2012. See also Thomas C. Reeves, *Foundations Under Fire* (Ithaca, NY: Cornell University Press, 1970). For more details on the 1950s hearings, see Chapter 4, and on the 1960s hearings, see Chapter 6.

58   In these hearings the Rockefeller family had to confront public concerns over the Ludlow Massacre, an attack by the Colorado National Guard on coal miners and their families during a 1914 strike. The Rockefellers owned the largest companies involved in the attack.

59   Matthew Bishop and Michael Green, "Carnegie & Co.," bonus chapter to their book *Philanthrocapitalism: How the Rich Can Save the World* (New York: Bloomsbury, 2008), available at: http://www.philanthrocapitalism.net/bonus-chapters/carnegie-co (accessed September 24, 2010).

60   Quoted in Nasaw, *Andrew Carnegie,* 788.

61   A year earlier, in his April 15, 1916, memorandum to the board, Pritchett had listed as his top suggestion "The Problem of the Alien." He noted: "Some of them do not find out for years that the public schools are free, that the police do not have the same power as in Russia, that citizenship is possible under certain conditions. The function of the government in dealing with this mass of incoming human beings has been merely to act as a screen for shutting out the most objectionable. No agency attempts to deal with the immigrant's needs after he has left Ellis Island … a private agency, in good relations with the government, could put into each newcomer's hands a brief statement in his language, of his rights and privileges." Henry S. Pritchett, "Fields of Activity Open to the Carnegie Corporation," April 15, 1916, 3, CCNY Policy and Program Files, Folder 1, Box 1, Series 1.D, CCNY Records, RBML-CUL.

62   CCNY, Minutes of the Executive Committee, 259, May 3, 1917, CCNY Records, RBML-CUL. Note the continued use of Carnegie's phonetic spelling.

63   CCNY, Minutes of the Board of Trustees, III, 67, January 9, 1918, CCNY Records, RBML-CUL.

64   Frank V. Thompson, foreword to *Schooling of the Immigrant* (New York: Harper and

Brothers, 1920), available at: https://archive.org/stream/schoolingofimmioothom_djuu.txt (accessed June 30, 2014).

65 The themes were: "Schooling of the Immigrant," "The Press," "Adjustment of Homes and Family Life," "Legal Protection and Correction," "Health Standards and Care," "Naturalization and Political Life," "Industrialization and Economic Amalgamation," "Treatment of Immigrant Heritages," "Neighborhood Agencies and Organizations," and "Rural Developments"; see CCNY, Minutes of the Board of Trustees, III, 75–82, March 12, 1918, CCNY Records, RBML-CUL. Burns was initially recommended to the Corporation by John M. Glenn of the Russell Sage Foundation. A nationally recognized leader in the field of social work, following his work on the Carnegie Americanization Study, he contributed significantly to the extensive growth of the community chest movement in the United States; Scott M. Cutlip, *Fundraising in the United States: Its Role in American Philanthropy* (New Brunswick, NJ: Rutgers, The State University, 1965; reprint, New Brunswick, NJ: Transaction Publishers, 1990), 222.

66 For further discussion, see J. M. Beach, "What Is Americanization? Historiography of a Concept, Social Movement, and Practice," August 3, 2011, available at: Dare to Know: An Inquiry into Human Experience, Education, and Enlightenment: http://jmbeach.blogspot.com/2011/08/what-is-americanization-historiography.html (accessed December 2, 2011). In the 1920s, the reports were issued even as Congress was passing restrictive legislation, the 1921 and 1922 Quota Acts and the Immigration Act of 1924 (the Johnson-Reed Act). Their aim was to influence domestic conditions for immigrants, not immigration policy. This theme has resonated across the Corporation's history and is again prominent in the twenty-first century, albeit with considerably more attention to policy reform, as noted in Chapter 8.

67 Thompson, *Schooling of the Immigrant*, Publisher's Note.

68 Amy D. Rose, "Challenging the System: The Adult Education Movement and the Educational Bureaucracy of the 1920s," in *Breaking New Ground: The Development of Adult and Workers' Education in North America: Proceedings from the Syracuse University Kellogg Project's First Visiting Scholar Conference in the History of Adult Education (March 1989)*, ed. Rae Wahol Rohfeld (Syracuse, NY: Syracuse University Kellogg Project, 1990).

69 For an interview with Menken about his life, see M. C. Sammon and Geoffrey T. Hellman, "Talk of the Town: Fast Traveller," *The New Yorker*, June 21, 1952.

70 CCNY, Minutes of the Board of Trustees, III, 72–74, March 12, 1918, CCNY Records, RBML-CUL.

71 CCNY, Minutes of the Executive Committee, IV, 323, 343–344, 352, 370, February 21 and November 17, 1919, February 9 and May 17, 1920 (respectively), CCNY Records, RBML-CUL.

72 CCNY, Minutes of the Executive Committee, IV, 333, September 26, 1919, CCNY Records, RBML-CUL.

73 CCNY, Minutes of the Executive Committee, IV, 411–412, May 2, 1921, CCNY Records, RBML-CUL.

74 Butler had much earlier urged Andrew Carnegie to establish the Endowment; when the Corporation was established, he became a persistent seeker of support. Butler recognized the urgency of increasing the availability of international education and exchanges for Americans to sustain peace.

75 CCNY, Minutes of the Executive Committee, IV, 319, January 28, 1919, CCNY Records, RBML-CUL.

76 Institute of International Education, "A Brief History of IIE," available at: http://www.iie.org/en/Who-We-Are/History (accessed January 13, 2013).

77 According to its 2010 annual report (p. 24), the Institute of International Education's total annual revenues in 2010 were $337,404,000.

78 See, for example, E. Richard Brown, *Medicine and Capitalism in America* (Berkeley: University of California Press, 1979), 44. John D. Rockefeller Sr. explicitly acknowledged this cooperation in his memoir: "The general idea of cooperation in giving for education, I have felt, scored a real step in advance when Mr. Andrew Carnegie consented to become a member of the General Education Board." John D. Rockefeller Sr., *Random Reminiscences* (1909; reprint, New York: Sleepy Hollow Press/Rockefeller Archives Center, 1984), 165.

79 Jones was originally from Wales and came to the United States in 1884 for his education at Washington and Lee University. He received a PhD from Columbia and also studied at the Union Theological Seminary. His detailed but controversial survey for Phelps Stokes and the US Education Department of the education of blacks in the South, published in 1917, recommended closing schools in the South that he considered substandard but were often all that was available. The study was criticized for the standards against which the schools were judged. One of the strongest negative statements about Jones and his approach is the obituary written by Carter G. Woodson, "Thomas Jesse Jones," *Journal of Negro History* 35, no. 1 (January 1950): 107–109, available at: http://www.jstor.org/stable/2715572 (accessed January 13, 2013). Nonetheless, Jones's survey led to investment in different approaches to education, including the Jeanes Foundation community-based vocational approach.

80 Du Bois graduated from Harvard in 1895, Woodson in 1912. Both received doctorates in history. The controversy centered on American philanthropic support for basic education, rather than providing opportunities for rural blacks to move up the education ladder. An indication of the controversy is provided in Beverley Guy-Sheftall, "The American Negro Academy," and Jennie Carney Smith, "Anna T. Jeanes Foundation," in *The Encyclopedia of African American Education*, ed. Kofi Lomotey, vol. 1 (Thousand Oaks, CA: Sage Publications, 2010), 47–48. The community-based approach and the so-called Jeanes teacher provided significant support for the poorest families in the South and employment for black women. See William A. Link, "Jackson Davis and the Lost World of Jim Crow Education," Jackson Davis Collection of African American Educational Photographs, Albert and Shirley Small Special Collections Library, University of Virginia, available at: http://www2.lib.virginia.edu/small/collections/jdavis/resources/linkar-ticle.html (accessed December 7, 2011).

81 In his autobiography, Andrew Carnegie acknowledged Washington's contributions to improving opportunities for African Americans and avidly embraced his educational philosophy and approach: "My connection with Hampton and Tuskegee Institutes … has been a source of satisfaction and pleasure, and to know Booker Washington is a rare privilege." Carnegie, *Autobiography*, 265.

82 For a good overview of the work, see Robert Lester, *The Corporation and the Jeanes Teacher*, CCNY Review Series 27, May 15, 1938, CCNY Records, RBML-CUL.

83 CCNY, Minutes of the Executive Committee, II, 245, April 3, 1917, CCNY Records, RBML-CUL.

84 Ibid., 246.

85 CCNY, Minutes of the Executive Committee, IV, 298, April 16, 1918, CCNY Records, RBML-CUL. The trustees also gave another grant for this purpose on November 17, 1919; CCNY, Minutes of the Executive Committee, IV, 341, November 17, 1919, CCNY Records, RBML-CUL.

86 CCNY, Minutes of the Board of Trustees, III, 71–72, March 12, 1918, CCNY Records, RBML-CUL.

87 John G. Reid, "Health, Education, Economy: Philanthropic Foundations in the Atlantic Region in the 1920s and 1930s," *Acadiensis* 14, no. 1 (Autumn 1984): 64–83.

88 Hendrick, *Andrew Carnegie*, 383.

89 Wall discusses correspondence from November 1918; Wall, *Andrew Carnegie*, 1013–1037. Carnegie had donated $1.5 million to build the Peace Palace in 1903.

90 CCNY, Minutes of the Board of Trustees, III, 191, November 28, 1919, CCNY Records, RBML-CUL.

91 CCNY, Minutes of the Board of Trustees, III, 167–168, March 28, 1919, CCNY Records, RBML-CUL.

92 Although Andrew Carnegie was originally not interested in the building for the National Academy of Sciences and the National Research Council, the leadership of George Ellery Hale, the astronomer and beneficiary of the Carnegie Institution of Washington and Carnegie's support for the Mt. Wilson Solar Observatory, and the support of trustees Pritchett and Root, led to the eventual approval of the request. See Kohler, *Partners in Science*, 82–87.

93 CCNY, Minutes of the Board of Trustees, III, 227–228, December 19, 1919, CCNY Records, RBML-CUL.

NOTES FOR CHAPTER 2

1 Elihu Root served as president for two months in December 1919 and January 1920, then began a term as chairman of the Board of Trustees in February 1920. James S. Angell was Corporation president in 1920–1921, and Henry Pritchett served as acting president from 1921 to 1923.

2 Kohler, *Partners in Science*.

3 Frederick Keppel, soon to be president of Carnegie Corporation, was the American representative at the International Chamber of Commerce from 1920 to 1922. See Lewis Galantiere, "France After the First World War," in *Appreciation of Frederick Paul Keppel*, ed. Harry J. Carman et al. (New York: Columbia University Press, 1951), 39–40.

4 Iriye, *Cultural Internationalism and World Order*, 55–56.

5 "The postwar internationalists believed that what was really novel about their movement for peace was the stress on cultural, intellectual, and psychological underpinnings of the international order; that at bottom, peace and order must depend on a habit of mind on the part of individuals in all countries—a mindset that looked beyond security, legal, and even business issues and was willing to link national to world interests … cultural internationalism was, at one level, an intellectual proposition. The cultural internationalists agreed that the key to peace lay in cross-national understanding, which in turn had to be built solidly upon active cooperation of cultural elites. Intellectual cooperation, the term that came to be used widely in the 1920s, was as important as cooperation in security, political, or economic issues." Ibid., 59–60.

6 Ibid., 66–67.

7 These institutions include think tanks such as the Brookings Institution and the National Bureau of Economic Research; scholarly organizations such as the National Research Council, the Social Science Research Council, and the American Council of Learned Societies; and other institutions specifically geared to keeping international communications flowing, such as the Council on Foreign Relations, the Foreign Policy Association, and the Institute of International Education. The Corporation's work with these institutions is described in this and subsequent chapters. For a succinct history of the Rockefeller Foundation and its support for several of these institutions over the last one hundred years, see Rockefeller Archive Center, "100 Years: The Rockefeller Foundation," available at: rockefeller100.org.

8 David Ekbladh, *The Great American Mission: Modernization and the Construction of an American World Order* (Princeton, NJ: Princeton University Press, 2010), esp. 23–25.

9   See Lions Clubs International, "Our History," available at: http://www.lionsclubs.org/EN/about-lions/mission-and-history/our-history/index.php.

10   Joining the group of foundations established earlier—the Milbank Memorial Fund (1905), Russell Sage Foundation (1907), Carnegie Corporation (1911), the Phelps Stokes Fund (1911), and the Rockefeller Foundation (1913)—were, for example, the Commonwealth Fund (1918), the Dayton Fund (1918), the Century Fund (1919), the Duke Endowment (1924), the Kresge Foundation (1924), the Daniel and Florence Guggenheim Foundation (1924), the John Simon Guggenheim Memorial Foundation (1925), the Charles Stewart Mott Foundation (1926), the Danforth Foundation (1927), the John and Mary Markle Foundation (1927), the Buhl Foundation (1927), and the Julius Rosenwald Fund (1928). See Burlingame, *Philanthropy in America*, xxxii–xxxiii.

11   Karl and Katz, "The American Private Philanthropic Foundation and the Public Sphere," 260.

12   Burlingame, *Philanthropy in America*, xxxiii.

13   Thomas E. Woods Jr., "Warren Harding and the Forgotten Depression of 1920," First Principles: ISI Web Journal, October 20, 2009, available at: http://www.firstprinciplesjournal.com/print.aspx?article=1319&loc=b...1.

14   Lynn Dumenil, *The Modern Temper* (New York: Hill and Wang, 1995), 207.

15   Kenneth T. Jackson notes, for example, that "the primary target of this crusade [between 1920 and 1925] were Catholics, eastern and southern European immigrants, African-Americans, and Jews." Jackson, *The Ku Klux Klan in the City, 1915–1930* (Chicago: Elephant Paperback, 1992), viii.

16   Also known as the Emergency Immigration Act of 1921 and the Immigration Restriction Act of 1921.

17   In 2007 the Carnegie Institution of Washington was renamed the Carnegie Institution for Science (see carnegiescience.edu).

18   Karl and Katz, "The American Private Philanthropic Foundation," 263–264; Lagemann, *The Politics of Knowledge*, 61.

19   Lagemann, *The Politics of Knowledge*, 60.

20   Henry Smith Pritchett, *The First Twenty Years of Carnegie Corporation* (speech delivered November 19, 1931), 28–29, Carnegie Corporation of New York (CCNY) Records, Rare Book and Manuscript Library, Columbia University Libraries (RBML-CUL).

21   In James Rowland Angell the trustees selected a true scientific star. A scientist without a PhD, Angell had studied with William James, the father of modern psychology, and worked closely with John Dewey, the father of modern educational principles. Angell was perhaps James's preeminent student in helping him to establish the field of functional psychology. Angell's research in the early twentieth century led to the recognition of the importance of mind-body interactions and laid the groundwork for the vibrant field of neurological and psychological interdisciplinary research in the twenty-first century. For more details, see W. S. Hunter, *James Rowland Angell 1869–1949: A Biographical Memoir* (Washington, DC: National Academy of Sciences Press, 1951), available at: www.nasonline.org/publications/biographical-memoirs/memoir-pdfs/angell-james-r.pdf (accessed December 26, 2013).

22   CCNY, Minutes of the Board of Trustees, III, 244–246, April 8, 1920, CCNY Records, RBML-CUL.

23   CCNY Annual Report (hereafter "CCNYAR"), 1921, 12, CCNY Records, RBML-CUL.

24   Ibid., 13.

25   CCNY, Minutes of the Board of Trustees, III, 245, April 8, 1920, CCNY Records, RBML-CUL.

26 These categories and allocations were universities and colleges (60 percent), institutions of secondary education (5 percent), scientific research (10 percent), institutions of art, literature, and science (10 percent), and organizations other than schools and colleges doing social and educational work (15 percent).

27 Lagemann, *The Politics of Knowledge*, 62–63.

28 Kohler, *Partners in Science*, 62–63; see also Lagemann, *The Politics of Knowledge*, 62–63.

29 Martin Bulmer and Joan Bulmer, "Philanthropy and Social Science in the 1920s: Beardsley Ruml and the Laura Spelman Rockefeller Memorial, 1922–1929," *Minerva* 19, no. 3 (September 1981): 347–407.

30 CCNYAR, 1921, 10.

31 John C. Merriam, secretary of the National Research Council and a distinguished paleontologist from the University of California at Santa Barbara, had been responsible for the excavations at the La Brea Tar Pits, among other accomplishments. In his capacity as president of the Carnegie Institution of Washington, he became a member of the Board of Trustees of the Corporation; see Chester Stock, *John Campbell Merriam, 1869–1945: A Biographical Memoir* (Washington, DC: National Academy of Sciences Press, 1951), available at: www.nasonline. org/publications/biographical-memoirs/memoir-pdfs/merriam-john.pdf (accessed December 27, 2013). William J. Holland, a butterfly expert, had been born in Jamaica. He served on the Corporation's board in his capacity as head of the Carnegie Institute of Pittsburgh; see Robert J. Gangewere, *Palace of Culture: Andrew Carnegie's Museums and Library in Pittsburgh* (Pittsburgh: University of Pittsburgh Press, 2011), and the website accompanying the book, http://www.carnegiespalaceofculture.com/.

32 CCNYAR, 1921, 13–14 (all quotes in this paragraph).

33 Yale University, *Inauguration of James Rowland Angell, LLD, as Fourteenth President of Yale University, on June 22, 1921* (New Haven, CT: Yale University, 1921), 5. Angell served as Yale's president for the next sixteen years, building it into a world-class university. At Yale he set in stone the appearance of the campus by erecting thirty-seven Gothic buildings, and despite the Depression, he raised the endowment from $25 million to $95 million. In addition to many other innovations, including instituting an interdisciplinary curriculum, he built the Institute of Human Relations into one of the most prominent psychology research programs in the country. "Education: Yale-Builder," *Time*, March 14, 1949, available at: www.time.com/time/magazine/article/0,9171,794682,00.html (accessed May 18, 2010).

34 CCNY, Minutes of the Board of Trustees, III, 311, June 6, 1921, CCNY Records, RBML-CUL.

35 Ellen Lagemann suggests that one reason Angell might have departed for Yale was a continued conflict between him and some board members—as well as among board members—over the direction he had proposed for the Corporation; Lagemann, *Politics of Knowledge*, 62. The most likely reason for his departure, however, as Pritchett hinted, was that Angell found it hard to refuse being "offered a seat among the high gods at Yale"; Pritchett, *The First Twenty Years of Carnegie Corporation*, 29. Pritchett's dismay is evident in his letter of March 15, 1921, to the head of the General Education Board: "Mr. Root reaches Santa Barbara this afternoon and we are to hold some conferences ... as to the question of Angell's successor. We are both desolated that Yale has captured him and feel rather forlorn in going into the process of finding another man. Can you make us a suggestion?" Henry S. Pritchett to Dr. Wallace Butterick, March 15, 1921, Carnegie Corporation 1921–1954, Folder 2783, Box 269, Series 1.2, FA058, General Education Board (GEB) records, Rockefeller Archive Center (RAC).

36 Pritchett was the first leader to be president of both the Carnegie Foundation for the Advancement of Teaching and Carnegie Corporation; this overlap led to a very close working

relationship between the two philanthropies. Over the years, either the Carnegie Foundation president was also president of Carnegie Corporation or a Carnegie Foundation vice president was also a program staff member for the Corporation. For example, when Pritchett became acting president, William S. Learned, vice president of the Carnegie Foundation, joined him at the Corporation. Following Pritchett and Keppel was Walter Jessup, president of both institutions in the 1940s; Oliver Carmichael was vice president of the Foundation and executive officer of the Corporation in the 1940s and 1950s; John Gardner and Alan Pifer were also presidents of both institutions. It was only when Ernest Boyer became president of the Foundation in 1979 that a real separation of staff occurred. Offices were also shared until the Foundation moved to Princeton, New Jersey. It is now located in Stanford, California. See Carnegie Foundation for the Advancement of Teaching, "Foundation History" available at: http://www.carnegiefoundation. org/about-us/foundation-history (accessed December 27, 2013).

37   It was not the first time that the Corporation in its short history had turned to a board member for leadership (Root having been the presiding officer as chairman of the board in the year between Carnegie's death and the selection of Angell), and it would not be the last time either. Other foundations might turn immediately to outside leadership, but the Corporation tended to turn to staff or other board members to take over when there was an unexpected change in the executive, and even when there was a planned one. Only three presidents had not previously been associated with the Corporation: James Angell, Frederick Keppel, and Vartan Gregorian. Devereux Josephs had been the head of the Teachers Insurance and Annuity Association before becoming president; he was not technically on the board, but that group was a major recipient of Corporation funds and the offices were shared with the Corporation.

38   Pritchett, however, was research-oriented, while Carnegie had tended to seek specific, tangible results—hence, the dual mission of the Carnegie Foundation for the Advancement of Teaching, encompassing both teaching and learning; see www.carnegiefoundation.org.

39   Annual reports have been issued every year since (with the exception of two that were issued biennially in 2002–2003 and 2004–2005), and electronically since 2006.

40   CCNYAR, 1922, 7.

41   Ibid., 13.

42   Ibid., 19–20.

43   Ibid., 20.

44   CCNYAR, 1923, 14–15.

45   CCNYAR, 1922, 8.

46   The Brookings Institution was formed in 1927 when the Institute of Economics joined with the Rockefeller Foundation–funded Institute for Government Research and the Robert S. Brookings Graduate School of Economics and Government. See James Allen Smith, *Brookings at Seventy-Five* (Washington, DC: Brookings Institution, 1991).

47   CCNYAR, 1922, "Part II: Summary of Expenditures Made by the Corporation," 74.

48   Charles C. Mierow, "Book Review: *Henry S. Pritchett, A Biography* by Abraham Flexner," *Popular Astronomy* 52 (1944): 108, available at: http://articles.adsabs.harvard.edu/full/gif/ 1944PA.....52..107S/0000108... (accessed December 27, 2013).

49   CCNYAR, 1922, 42.

50   For in-depth discussion of the Corporation's early support for science, see Lagemann, *Politics of Knowledge*, 29–50; on the often collaborative efforts by the Corporation and the Rockefeller Foundation, see Kohler, *Partners in Science*, 1–129.

51   CCNY, Agenda Book of the Board of Trustees, 1922–1923, Henry Pritchett, confidential memo for the trustees, November 9, 1922, 4, CCNY Records, RBML-CUL; CCNYAR, 1922, 32–44.

52 CCNYAR, 1922, "Part II: Summary of the Expenditures Made by the Carnegie Corporation, Analysis of Annual Expenditures Since Establishment, 1911," unpaginated.

53 Rockefeller Foundation, "Moments in Time, 1913–1919," available at: http://www.rockefellerfoundation.org/about-us/our-history/1913-1919.

54 Hoover, highly respected by many Americans for his outstanding job as chairman of the Commission for Relief in Belgium, was also head of the US Food Administration during World War I and director of the American Relief Administration from 1919 to 1923. See comments in CCNYAR, 1922, 42; and Miller Center, University of Virginia, "American President: A Reference Resource: Herbert Clark Hoover: Life Before the Presidency," available at: http://millercenter.org/president/hoover/essays/biography/2 (accessed December 27, 2013).

55 Bruce F. Johnston, "Creating Stanford's Food Research Institute: Herbert Hoover, Alonzo Taylor, Carl Alsberg, J. S. Davis, and M. K. Bennett," available at: http://www.stanford.edu/group/FRI/fri/history/bruce.html (accessed May 20, 2010). Perhaps even more attractively, the institution would be located at Stanford University, an institution specifically mentioned by Andrew Carnegie in his Gospel of Wealth. Carnegie indicated that he envied Senator Leland Stanford for founding the university, which he called "a noble use of wealth." Carnegie, *Gospel of Wealth*, 21.

56 CCNY, Minutes of the Board of Trustees, III, 295, January 27, 1921, CCNY Records, RBML-CUL.

57 CCNYAR, 1921, 19–20.

58 Johnston, "Creating Stanford's Food Research Institute."

59 CCNY, Minutes of the Board of Trustees, IX, 6, October 13, 1931, CCNY Records, RBML-CUL.

60 Johnston, "Creating Stanford's Food Research Institute," essay 1.

61 As Johnston notes, "The original directors were keenly aware of the urgent need 'to formulate a manageable and fruitful program' because the Carnegie Corporation's decision about future funding of the Food Research Institute was to be made at the end of ten years"; ibid., 4. Nearly fifteen years later, the Rockefeller Foundation, with its major commitment to agricultural research, began to provide nearly $1 million in support to the Food Research Institute, and in the 1950s the Corporation made two new grants to the Institute, totaling $350,000, for research on economic development in Africa; see Stackpole, *Carnegie Corporation*, 59.

62 Andrea Johnson, "Softening the Painful Path to Goodbye," *Alliance*, June 1, 2004, available at: http://www.alliancemagazine.org/en/content/softening-painful-path-goodbye.

63 For a detailed discussion of these decisions, see Lagemann, *The Politics of Knowledge*, 51–70. For a comprehensive discussion of the origin and role of social science policy research institutes, see James Allen Smith, *The Idea Brokers: Think Tanks and the Rise of the New Policy Elite* (New York: Free Press, 1991).

64 Solomon Fabricant, "Toward a Firmer Basis of Economic Policy: The Founding of the National Bureau of Economic Research" (Cambridge, MA: NBER, 1984), 2, available at: http://www.nber.org/nberhistory/sfabricant.pdf.

65 See correspondence of Jerome D. Greene, secretary of the Rockefeller Foundation, with Wesley Mitchell, Edwin F. Gay, J. Laurence Laughlin, W. L. Mackenzie King, and others, Folders 290–293, Box 26, Series 200, Record Group 1.1, FA386, Rockefeller Foundation records, RAC.

66 Frederick T. Gates, letter to John D. Rockefeller Jr., March 19, 1914, Folder 292, Box 26, Series 200, Record Group 1.1, FA386, Rockefeller Foundation records, RAC;. see also Fabricant, "Toward a Firmer Basis," 5.

67 CCNY, Minutes of the Executive Committee, IV, 413, May 2, 1921, CCNY Records, RBML-CUL.

68   CCNY, Minutes of the Executive Committee, V, 17, November 9, 1922, CCNY Records, RBML-CUL.

69   See Rockefeller Foundation board action, grant recommendation memo, "Minutes of the Rockefeller Foundation Board Regarding the National Bureau of Economic Research, May 22, 1929," NBER 1928–1931, Folder 4351, Box 367, Series 200S, Record Group 1.1, projects, FA386, Rockefeller Foundation records, RAC.

70   National Bureau of Economic Research, "About NBER," available at: http://www.nber.org/info.html (accessed May 18, 2010).

71   Lambda Alpha International—London Chapter History, "The Story of Lambda Alpha International," http://www.lailondon.org/publications/lai_history.htm (accessed Jan. 31, 2012).

72   CCNY, Agenda Book of the Executive Committee, 1922–1923, 27, May 24, 1922, CCNY Records, RBML-CUL; CCNY, Minutes of the Executive Committee, V, 16–17, November 9, 1922, CCNY Records, RBML-CUL.

73   Marc A. Weiss, "Richard T. Ely and the Contribution of Economic Research to National Housing Policy, 1920–1940," *Urban Studies* 26 (1989): 116.

74   Robert M. Lester, *A Thirty Year Catalog of Grants* (New York: CCNY, 1942), 80, "List D: Other Institutes and Operating Agencies, Institute of Land Economics, 1922, $72,500." "This is the simplest of several titles used," Lester notes, adding that the "total here does not include $37,500 to Northwestern University for this agency."

75   Wisconsin Historical Society, "Dictionary of Wisconsin History: Richard Theodore Ely, 1854–1943," available at: http://www.wisconsinhistory.org/dictionary/index.asp?action=view&t (accessed January 29, 2012).

76   Folders 290–297, Box 26, and Folders 298–300, Box 27, both Series 200, Record Group 1.1, Rockefeller Foundation records, RAC.

77   CCNY, Minutes of the Board of Trustees, V, 64–67, February 9, 1922, CCNY Records, RBML-CUL.

78   The Corporation provided support over ten years: $200,000 annually for the first five years, $150,000 annually for the following three years, and $100,000 for each of the last two years, at which point the Corporation's initial financial commitment ended.

79   CCNY, Minutes of the Board of Trustees, V, 64, February 9, 1922, CCNY Records, RBML-CUL.

80   "The work of the Institute of Economics shall be conducted in the interest of the common good … and shall be administered … without regard to the special interests of any group in the body politic, whether political, social, or economic." Ibid., 65–66.

81   Smith, *Brookings at Seventy-Five*.

82   US Department of State, "The Role of Think Tanks in US Foreign Policy," *US Foreign Policy Agenda* 7, no. 3 (November 2002), available at: http://photos.state.gov/libraries/korea/49271/dwoa_120909/ijpe1102.pdf. See also Smith, *The Idea Brokers*.

83   The trustees recognized that the work of the Institute of Economics more than justified the commitment and the approach. After reviewing the work on international commercial policies, international economic reconstruction, agriculture, labor, industry, finance, taxation, transportation, public utilities, and natural resources, Pritchett commented in his last president's essay in 1923: "A serious effort is to be made by the staff of the Institute, under the direction of the trustees, to obtain the actual facts of economic causes and effects and to lay these before the public in a clear and concise fashion. If the Institute succeeds in this effort, it will have made one of the greatest possible contributions, not only to the commercial prosperity of the nation, but also to that satisfaction of spirit which can be gained only by facing the facts of existence and dealing with them intelligently and courageously." CCNYAR, 1923, 38.

84   From 1919 to the early 1920s, the Corporation paid the interest on the $5 million endow-ment that was on the books of the Corporation for the credit of the National Academy of Sciences for use by the National Research Council. The way the Corporation finally agreed to arrange this in 1923 was "to make payments monthly in advance, as needed, to the extent of $182,500 per annum on certificates of the Chairman of the National Academy of Sciences and the Chairman of the National Research Council." CCNY, Minutes of the Board of Trustees, V, 159, May 18, 1923, CCNY Records, RBML-CUL. For more details on the relationship of the National Academy of Sciences and the National Research Council, see "Welcome to the National Research Council," available at: www.nationalacademies.org/nrc.

85   At the same time that the Corporation was focusing on economics and science in the early 1920s, its sister foundations, the Rockefeller Foundation (in addition to its support for the Institute for Government Research) and the Laura Spelman Rockefeller Memorial were estab-lishing complementary institutions with global reach in foreign policy studies and the social sci-ences: the Council on Foreign Relations in 1921 and the Social Science Research Council in 1923. Over the century, these institutions have played a significant role as grantees of several founda-tions, becoming leaders in both national and international applied and policy-oriented research. See Rockefeller Archive Center, 100 Years: The Rockefeller Foundation, "Social Sciences," avail-able at: rockefeller100.org/exhibits/show/social_sciences.

86   CCNYAR, 1921, 28.

87   J. M. Beach, "What Is Americanization? Historiography of a Concept, Social Movement, and Practice," August 3, 2011, Blog: Dare to Know: An Inquiry into Human Experience, Education, and Enlightenment, available at: http://jmbeach.blogspot.com/2011/08/what-is-amercianiza-tion-historiography.html (accessed December 16, 2013).

88   CCNY, Minutes of the Executive Committee, V, 16, November 9, 1922, CCNY Records, RBML-CUL.

89   While a detailed discussion of the anti-immigration legislation in the early part of the twentieth century is beyond the scope of this book, its relation to the international ramifications of the work on intelligence testing is discussed in the next chapter.

90   CCNY, Minutes of the Executive Committee, IV, 208, May 2, 1921, CCNY Records, RBML-CUL. Inflamed by the popularity of D. W. Griffith's *The Birth of a Nation*, the Ku Klux Klan had become increasingly brutal, engaging in cross-burnings and lynchings and egregious destructive behavior throughout the American South and elsewhere. See, for example, Wyn Craige Wade, *The Fiery Cross: The Ku Klux Klan in America* (Oxford: Oxford University Press, 1987).

91   Korey Bowers Brown, "Carter G. Woodson," Association for the Study of African American Life and History, available at: http://asalh.org/woodsonbiosketch.html (accessed December 28, 2013).

92   Lester, *The Corporation and the Jeanes Teacher*. For more details on the work of the Corporation in this area, see chapters 1 and 3.

93   A thoughtful discussion of the controversies surrounding all these perspectives may be found in Kenneth James King, *Pan-Africanism and Education: A Study of Race Philanthropy and Education in the Southern States of America and East Africa* (Oxford: Clarendon Press, 1971). See also Donald Johnson, "W. E. B. Du Bois, Thomas Jesse Jones, and the Struggle for Social Education, 1900–1930," *Journal of Negro History* 85, no. 3 (2000): 71–95.

94   "General Education Board, Purpose and Program" (pamphlet), Folder 145, Box 15, Series O, FA324, Office of the Messrs. Rockefeller records, RAC; this document and others related to the General Education Board are available at Rockefeller Archive Center, 100 Years: The Rockefeller Foundation, Rockefeller100.org/exhibits/show/education/general_education_board.

95   George Gray, *Education on an International Scale* (New York: Harcourt, Brace, 1941), 91.

96   Patricia L. Rosenfield, Courtenay Sprague, and Heather McKay, "Ethical Dimensions of International Grantmaking: Drawing the Line in a Borderless World," *Journal of Leadership and Organizational Studies* 11, no. 1 (2004): 53–56.

97   CCNY, Minutes of the Board of Trustees, V, 149, April 16, 1923, CCNY Records, RBML-CUL.

98   Thorndike received a Corporation grant in 1922 to conduct research in the theory and practice of measurements of intellect and capacity at his Institute for Educational Research at Teachers College. CCNY, Minutes of the Board of Trustees, V, 66, February 9, 1922, CCNY Records, RBML-CUL.

99   Much of this debate, covered in an extensive literature, stemmed from the study of human differences as defined by genetics and heredity versus the role of social, environmental, political, and economic influences on human development. A brief biography of Thorndike succinctly presents the issues in the context of education; see "Edward L. Thorndike (1874–1949)," available at: http://education.stateuniversity.com/pages/2509/Thorndike-Edward-L-1874-1949.html. For a perspective on race, see, for example, Louis Kushnick, "The Political Economy of White Racism in the United States," in *Impact of Race on White America*, ed. Benjamin P. Bowers and Raymond G. Hunt (Thousand Oaks, CA: Sage Publications, 1996), 61–62.

100   CCNYAR, 1921, 27.

101   Lester, *A Thirty Year Catalog of Grants, 1911–1941*, 264.

102   Gray, *Education on an International Scale*, 71–93.

103   See also Abigail Deutsch, "Women in Higher Education," *Carnegie Results* (Winter 2012).

104   CCNYAR, 1921, 17–19.

105   CCNYAR, 1923, 6.

106   Lester, *A Thirty Year Catalog*, 146. This total is about 14 percent of the total $184,371,246 spent during this period.

107   CCNY, Minutes of the Board of Trustees, III, 246, April 8, 1920, CCNY Records, RBML-CUL.

108   CCNY, Minutes of the Board of Trustees, III, 297, January 27, 1921, CCNY Records, RBML-CUL.

109   Arthur Berriedale Keith, *War Government of the British Dominions* (Oxford: Clarendon Press, 1921). A reviewer noted that "Professor Keith has, then, made a contribution to the Carnegie History that is not only prefatory to the volumes of its British series, but also valuable for an understanding of how the Great War has hastened the evolution of the United States of Britain." Francis J. Tchan, "Keith, *War Government of the British Dominions*" (book review), *Catholic Historical Review* 11, no. 4 (January 1926): 713.

110   Neither the board minutes nor the biography of Mrs. Carnegie mentions her opinion on the decision. Burton Jesse Hendrick and Daniel Henderson, *Louise Whitfield Carnegie: The Life of Mrs. Andrew Carnegie* (New York: Hastings House, 1950).

111   CCNY, Minutes of the Board of Trustees, V, 131, November 16, 1922, CCNY Records, RBML-CUL.

112   Ibid.; see resolution B127, also on p. 131.

113   While all the Carnegie institutions received regular support until 1941, as evidenced in the Board of Trustees and Executive Committee minutes (CCNY Records, RBML-CUL), the Carnegie Institution of Washington and the Carnegie Foundation for the Advancement of Teaching (separate from the pensions) were often supported without any qualms. Support for the other institutions often entailed prolonged discussion. For more details and a different perspective, see Kohler, *Partners in Science*, 118–129.

114   For McGill, see CCNY, Minutes of the Board of Trustees, III, 71, March 12, 1918, CCNY Records, RBML-CUL. The two Nova Scotia–based grants were awarded to St. Francis Xavier University in Antigonish as a $50,000 matching grant for a French professorship (CCNY, Minutes of the Board of Trustees, III, 217, November 20, 1919, CCNY Records, RBML-CUL) and to Dalhousie University in Halifax, which received a matching grant of $40,000 for the science department (CCNY, Minutes of the Executive Committee, II, unpaginated, April 19, 1915) and a little more than $20,000 to repair damage following a fire (CCNY, Minutes of the Executive Committee, IV, 289, March 11, 1918, and 333, September 26, 1919, CCNY Records, RBML-CUL). A third grant in Ontario provided general support of $250,000 for Queens University, once it made a major match (CCNY, Minutes of the Executive Committee, IV, 336, September 26, 1919, CCNY Records, RBML-CUL).

115   Newfoundland was a British dominion from 1907 to 1949, when it became Canada's tenth province.

116   The most detailed discussion of the grants in this region may be found in Robert M. Lester, "Review of Grants in the Maritime Provinces of Canada and in Newfoundland, 1911–1933," March 15, 1934, CCNY Review Series 15, 7, CCNY Records, RBML-CUL.

117   CCNY, Minutes of the Board of Trustees, III, 248–249, May 20, 1920, CCNY Records, RBML-CUL.

118   CCNYAR, 1921, 15.

119   Lester, "Review of Grants in the Maritime Provinces," 8.

120   Carnegie Foundation for the Advancement of Teaching (CFAT), *Education in the Maritime Provinces of Canada*, May 15, 1922, Bulletin 16, CFAT records, RBML-CUL.

121   These were Acadia University (Baptist), University of King's College (Anglican), Mount Allison University (Methodist), the college at St. Francis Xavier University (Roman Catholic), and Dalhousie University (independent, with Presbyterian influences). The commission did not propose integrating tax-supported institutions such as the University of New Brunswick, Nova Scotia Technical College, Nova Scotia Agricultural College, and Prince of Wales College in Prince Edward Island. Newfoundland had no college or university, a situation that the Corporation would help remedy in later grant-making. Lester, "Review of Grants in the Maritime Provinces," 10.

122   Ibid.

123   John G. Reid, "Health, Education, Economy: Philanthropic Foundations in the Atlantic Region in the 1920s and 1930s," *Acadiensis* 16, no. 1 (Autumn 1984): 72.

124   CCNYAR, 1923, 47.

125   John G. Reid, "Health, Education, Economy," 74.

126   Ibid., 72. Local opinion, however, was far from unanimous: Acadia was not interested, Mount Allison was unsure, Dalhousie and King's College were in, and St. Francis Xavier ultimately declined. Lester noted some of the issues: "Do students fare better in large colleges or in small, in strictly denominational or in liberal, in large cities or in towns and villages?... Should students pursue courses under denominational and university auspices at the same time?... In addition to denominationalism, local pride and economic considerations ... were involved"; Lester, "Review of Grants in the Maritime Provinces," 13. The board did not want to commit itself without having firm assurances from all the institutions involved that they would participate; ibid., 11–12.

127   Reid, "Health, Education, Economy," 73.

128   Ibid.

129   CCNY, Minutes of the Board of Trustees, V, 143, January 12, 1923, CCNY Records, RBML-CUL.

130   Lester, "Review of Grants in the Maritime Provinces," 12. For more details, see CCNY, Minutes of the Board of Trustees, V, 144–145, January 12, 1923, CCNY Records, RBML-CUL.

131   Lester, "Review of Grants in the Maritime Provinces," 15.

132   Ibid., 15–16.

133   CCNYAR, 1923, 49.

134   Michael Redmon, "Q: Who Was Nathaniel Potter?" *Santa Barbara Independent*, July 6, 2006, available at: http://www.independent.com/news/2006/jul/06/question-who-was-nathaniel-pot/.

135   Between 1922 and 1924, the Corporation awarded $45,000 to the Potter Metabolic Laboratory and Clinic and $19,000 to the Macleod and Banting laboratory at the University of Toronto. The Corporation supported later work on the treatment of diabetes at the California Institute of Technology, the University of Alberta, and Johns Hopkins University, bringing the total supported over the period from 1922 to 1928 to $114,000. Complementing this work was support for nutritional research at the Potter Metabolic Laboratory and Clinic between 1916 and 1928 for a total of $90,000. Robert M. Lester, "Summary of Grants Primarily for Research in Biological and Physical Sciences," January 2, 1932, CCNY Review Series 4, 61–62, CCNY Records, RBML-CUL.

136   CCNYAR, 1922, 55.

137   For example, when funding difficulties led the Carnegie library in Muizenberg, Cape Province, South Africa, and in Hastings, New Zealand, to charge fees, the trustees, while reluctant, were realistic and did "not wish the capital cost of the building returned." CCNY, Minutes of the Executive Committee, V, 37, April 13 ,1923, CCNY Records, RBML-CUL.

138   Smith, *The Idea Brokers*.

NOTES FOR CHAPTER 3

1   Carnegie Corporation of New York (CCNY) Annual Report (CCNYAR), 1930, 11–12, CCNY Records, Rare Book and Manuscript Library, Columbia University Libraries (RBML-CUL). As Keppel further explained, "A foundation grant once made is likely to be forgotten; the organization, absorbed in new projects, fails to conduct a running audit of its experience which would prove most valuable both as a historic record and as a guide to its own future policy.... The object of the inquiries instituted is not to exercise control but to guide future actions."

2   These are referred to as the "CCNY Review Series" in the various chapters of this book. While they have been published as separate monographs, they are also all available from CCNY Records, RBML-CUL.

3   CCNYAR, 1924, 6–7.

4   As Gourley and Lester acknowledged, this was not a complete list. Most of the entries were not published by the Corporation but were "made possible wholly or in part by funds provided by Carnegie Corporation of New York. As such, it is a record of Corporation stewardship in aiding the diffusion of knowledge to the printed page.... As it stands the compilation is, we believe, the first comprehensive list of its kind ever prepared and made public by a general foundation." James E. Gourley and Robert M. Lester, *The Diffusion of Knowledge: A List of Books Made Possible Wholly or in Part by Grants from Carnegie Corporation of New York and Published by Various Agencies During the Years 1911–1935* (Philadelphia: Press of W. F. Fell Co.).

5   "Frederick Keppel" (obituary), *New York Times*, September 10, 1943.

6   Russell Leffingwell, "Postscript," in *Appreciations of Frederick Paul Keppel* by Harry J. Carman, Ralph Hayes, Lewis Galantière, et al. (New York: Columbia University Press, 1951), 116–124.

7   Lewis Galantière described Keppel's "ceaseless concern to educate himself in everything that related to man in his time. He was the exact contrary of the specialist, and it is this that makes … him … a humanist. He wanted passionately to know how things work"; Lewis Galantière, "France After the First World War," in Carman, Hayes, Galantière, et al., *Appreciations of Frederick Paul Keppel*, 38–39. Raymond Fosdick, however, had a more critical assessment. In 1927, writing to John D. Rockefeller Jr. with an overall critique of the state of philanthropy, he declared that "men are not as easily attracted as they were [to philanthropy] … a dozen years ago. Consequently, the Carnegie Corporation has to appoint a Fred Keppel as president, and other foundations are wobbling along under even more mediocre leadership"; quoted in Kohler, *Partners in Science*, 69.

8   Frederick Keppel, *The Foundation: Its Place in American Life* (New York: Macmillan Co., 1930; reprint, New Brunswick, NJ: Transaction Publishers, 1989).

9   New foundations that arose at this time included the Kresge Foundation in 1924, the John Simon Guggenheim Foundation in 1925, the Daniel Guggenheim Foundation in 1926, the Kellogg Foundation in 1930, and the Ford Foundation in 1936. See Burlingame, *Philanthropy in America*, xxxiii–xxxiv.

10   CCNYAR, 1933, 14.

11   Edwin L. Shuman, "Broad Scope of American Philanthropy," *Current History* 33, no. 5 (1931): 702.

12   Ibid., 702, 704.

13   For details, see Rockefeller Archive Center, 100 Years: The Rockefeller Foundation, available at: rockefeller100.org.

14   For more discussion of the importance of the Pacific Rim countries to American foreign policy in the 1930s, see George Blakeslee, "The Foreign Policy of the United States," in *Interpretations of American Foreign Policy: Lectures on the Harris Foundation 1930*, ed. Quincy Wright (Chicago: University of Chicago Press, 1930), esp. 26–27.

15   David Ekbladh, "Present at the Creation: Edward Mead Earle and the Depression-Era Origins of Security Studies," *International Security* 36, no. 3 (Winter 2011–2012): 107–141; Rockefeller Foundation, Board of Trustees meeting, December 15, 1936, "Statement of Program 1936," 11–12, Folder 171, Box 23, Series 900, Record Group 3.1, FA112, Rockefeller Foundation records, Rockefeller Archive Center (RAC).

16   The Inter-Imperial Relations Committee reported in 1926 to the Imperial Conference the change in status of the British dominions: "*They are autonomous communities within the British Empire, equal in status, in no way subordinate one to another in any aspect of their domestic or external affairs, they are united by a common allegiance to the Crown, and freely associated as members of the British Commonwealth of Nations.*" Balfour Declaration 1926, available at: http://foundingdocs.gov.au/resources/transcripts/cth11_doc_1926.pdf (emphasis in original).

17   Corporation counsel offered other justifications at other times, but this was the reason given in the 1930s. IndiaNetzone, "History of India: Government of India Act of 1935," available at: http://www.indianetzone.com/14/government_india_act_1935.htm; for a copy of the act, see "Government of India Act, 1935," available at: http://www.legislation.gov.uk/ukpga/1935/2/pdfs/ukpga_19350002_en.pdf; Stackpole, *Carnegie Corporation*, 4–6.

18   Shuman, "Broad Scope of American Philanthropy," 705–706.

19   Keppel, *The Foundation*, 105.

20   Robert M. Lester, "Summary of Grants for Visitors, Grants-in-Aid, Scholarships and Fellowships, 1921–1934," September 30, 1934, CCNY Review Series 17 (67 pages), CCNY Records, RBML-CUL. When the United States entered World War II in December 1941, it became clear that the travel grants and international exchange activities had to come to a halt. It was one of the first programs reinstated when the British dominions and colonies program resumed in 1946, as discussed in later chapters.

21 See, for example, Inderjeet Parmar, "The Carnegie Corporation and the Mobilization of Opinion in the United States' Rise to Globalism, 1939–1945," *Minerva* 37 (1999).

22 Keppel, *The Foundation*, 94.

23 In 1933 the Board of Trustees voted to amend the constitution of the Corporation, article 3, to bring it into alignment with a charter change approved in 1917 that enabled the Corporation to support work outside of the United States in charter countries on the same priority topics as within the United States. The constitution was amended to read: "This corporation is also empowered to hold and administer any funds given to it for use in Canada or the British colonies for the same purposes in Canada or the British colonies as those to which it is by law authorized to apply its funds in the United States." CCNY, Minutes of the Board of Trustees, X, 110, March 21, 1933, CCNY Records, RBML-CUL.

24 One complicated example, however, is Frederick Osborn, who joined the board in 1936. He came from a family of scientists, although they had the increasingly questionable distinction of having been major proponents of eugenics. Osborn maintained some of that support in his own personal life, and professionally became deeply concerned about population and family planning. He went on to become a leader of the Population Council. He also was one of the strongest proponents of social science research as a major factor in understanding family planning and later during World War II in conducting the war.

25 Following is a list of the trustees under Keppel and their years of service: James Bertram (secretary of the board and the Corporation, Andrew Carnegie's former private secretary), 1911–1934; Robert A. Franks (treasurer of the board and the Corporation, Carnegie's finance assistant), 1911–1935; Henry S. Pritchett (president, Carnegie Foundation for the Advancement of Teaching [CFAT]), 1911–1930; Elihu Root (president, Carnegie Endowment for International Peace [CEIP]), 1911–1937; Samuel Harden Church (president, Carnegie Institute of Pittsburgh), 1914–1943; John A. Poynton (Carnegie's private secretary), 1916–1934; Mrs. Andrew (Louise W.) Carnegie (Carnegie's wife), 1919–1929; John C. Merriam (president, Carnegie Institution of Washington [CIW]), 1921–1938; William J. Holland (director, Carnegie Museum of Pittsburgh, and president, Carnegie Heroes Commission), 1922–1932; John J. Carty (trustee, CEIP, inventor/engineer, vice president, American Telephone and Telegraph [AT&T], and board chair, Bell Laboratories), 1923–1932; Russell C. Leffingwell (vice chairman, J. P. Morgan & Co., Inc.), 1923–1959; Nicholas Murray Butler (president, CEIP), 1925–1945; Henry James (chairman, Teachers Insurance and Annuity Association [TIAA], biographer), 1928–1947; David F. Houston (former US treasury secretary, former US agriculture secretary, president, Bell Telephone Securities), 1929–1934; Henry Suzzallo (president, CFAT), 1930–1933; Newton D. Baker (former US War secretary [World War I], lawyer, member of the Permanent Court of Arbitration, The Hague), 1931–1937; Thomas S. Arbuthnot (president, Carnegie Hero Commission), 1933–1952; Walter A. Jessup (president, CFAT), 1934–1944; Arthur W. Page (vice president of AT&T, founder of the field of corporate public relations), 1934–1958; Margaret Carnegie Miller (Carnegie's daughter), 1934–1959; Lotus Delta Coffman (president, University of Minnesota), 1936–1938; Nicholas Kelley (lawyer, US Treasury assistant secretary, vice president, Chrysler Corporation), 1936–1961; Frederick Osborn (anthropologist, eugenicist, American Museum of Natural History, founder of the Eugenics Society and the Office of Population Research, Princeton University, led US Selective Service Commission), 1936–1962; Elihu Root Jr. (lawyer, painter, son of Elihu Root Sr.), 1937–1960; Vannevar Bush (president, CIW), 1939–1955; and W. Randolph Burgess (president, Academy of Political Science, vice chairman, National City Bank of New York), 1940–1957. Dates from Lagemann, *The Politics of Knowledge*, 317.

26 David Ekbladh, personal communications to the author, August 23, 2010, and June 11 and 13, 2011.

27 Daniel T. Rodgers, *Atlantic Crossings: Social Politics in a Progressive Age* (Cambridge, MA:

Belknap Press of Harvard University Press, 1998); Encyclopedia of the New American Nation, "Internationalism: Interwar Isolationism and Internationalism," available at: http://www.americanforeignrelations.com/E-N/Internationalism-Interwar-isolationism-and-internationalism. html.

28 CCNYAR, 1930, 9.

29 For example, the two board members who joined in 1929 were David F. Houston, who had broad national experience, having served as secretary of agriculture and secretary of the treasury, and Henry Suzzallo, president of the Carnegie Foundation and director of the National Advisory Committee on Education. Houston, who had been president of several institutions, including the University of Texas and the University of St. Louis, originally came from North Carolina and was educated in South Carolina. Keppel pointed out that "their combined educational experience includes membership in academic communities in seven States of the Union." Lotus Coffman, elected trustee in 1936, also brought a broad national and international network of contacts to the board, particularly from his long service as president of the University of Minnesota.

30 CCNYAR, 1925, 27–29. This report lists more than two hundred advisers and the different advisory committees, including adult education, the arts, engineering education, library service, modern foreign language study, and Canada.

31 Richard Glotzer, "Frederick Keppel and Carnegie Corporation's Interwar Overseas Experts," American Educational History Journal 33, no. 1 (2006): 47–56; Richard Glotzer, "A Long Shadow: Frederick P. Keppel, the Carnegie Corporation, and the Dominions and Colonies Fund Area Experts, 1923–1943," History of Education, 38, no. 5 (September 2009): 621–648; Gerald Jonas, Circuit Riders: Rockefeller Money and the Rise of Modern Science (New York: Norton, 1989).

32 The Corporation's approach is reflected in the 1967 oral history of New Zealand key man and grantee Clarence Beeby, who noted that Keppel responded to his question about the Corporation's policy by writing: "'My dear Dr. Beeby: the Corporation most certainly has a policy, and our policy is that you should do whatever you think is best for education in New Zealand. But if you'll take an older man's advice, you won't go for quick results.'" According to Beeby, "And that, to me, really was for many years the essence of the Corporation, that it chose men that it could trust. It didn't choose me; it chose the people who chose me. But it chose men it felt it could trust and then it trusted them. And I just don't know a better way of making slaves of people than that." Clarence Edward Beeby, The Reminiscences of Clarence Edward Beeby: Oral History, 1968, interviewed by Isabel Grossner, Carnegie Corporation Project: Oral History, 1966–1970, Columbia Center for Oral History (CCOH), Columbia University Libraries (CUL), 4 (hereafter "Beeby, CCOH").

33 In South Africa, Keppel relied heavily on Charles Templeton Loram, said to be a "South African liberal in race relations" who had trained at Teachers College and written the definitive book on the education of the African population in South Africa; see Richard D. Heyman, "C. T. Loram: A South African Liberal in Race Relations," International Journal of African Historical Studies 5, no. 1 (1972): 41–50. As quoted by Richard Heyman, Thomas Jesse Jones, educational director of the Phelps Stokes Fund, as a result of Loram's membership on the Phelps Stokes Commission investigating education in Africa, considered him "the leading authority on Native education" (41). A point of clarification: in the South African context, the term "colored" has a technical, quasi-legal definition as well as complex cultural, social, and political definitions. Technically, a colored person is someone who "has one grandparent who is white and one who is not"; see definition in Macmillan Dictionary, available at: http://www.macmillandictionary. com/thesaurus/british/coloured. For a discussion of the term's complexity, see, for example, L. Bloom, "The Coloured People of South Africa," Phylon: The Atlanta University Review of Race and Culture 28, no. 2 (1967): 139–150.

34   For work in East, West, and non-Union Southern Africa, Keppel and his colleagues relied, in part, on colonial educators and governments as well as missionaries. The major adviser was grantee Thomas Jesse Jones, the director of education for the Phelps Stokes Fund. Mabel Carney from Teachers College, one of the few "key women," not only worked with African students at Teachers College but also helped identify areas for Corporation grant-making in her travels throughout the continent. See Richard Glotzer, "Mabel Carney and the Hartford Theological Seminary: Rural Development, 'Negro Education,' and Missionary Training," *Historical Studies in Education* 17, no. 1 (2005): 55–80.

35   Furthermore, significant proportions of the approved grants were conditional: steps had to occur before the board could give final approval. The implication was that payout for these grants would come at unpredictable times; it would be difficult to know how much money would be available for new grants. One conditional loan of $8 million had been made to the Carnegie Institute of Pittsburgh, payable in 1946, for which the Institute needed to set up a permanent endowment fund. The details for this loan and other loans to the Institute are fully discussed in CCNY, Minutes of the Board of Trustees, III, 300–303, May 12, 1921, and 307–308, June 6, 1921, CCNY Records, RBML-CUL; the fund is discussed in CCNYAR, 1924, 2 and 33. In addition, the trustees had earlier ordered major payments for buildings, such as new ones for the Johns Hopkins Medical School, the Pan American Union, and the New York Academy of Medicine. In fiscal year 1923, there were $40 million of outstanding obligations. Keppel had to introduce new policies to reduce these obligations so that new grants could be made. Two thorough discussions of endowment may be found in CCNYAR, 1922, 7–14, "Uses and Abuses of Endowments," and 1924, 2–3 and 7–10.

36   CCNYAR, 1924, 7–8.

37   Ibid., 8–10.

38   Ibid., 4–14.

39   CCNY, Minutes of the Executive Committee, X, 54, December 1, 1932, CCNY Records, RBML-CUL.

40   CCNY, Minutes of the Executive Committee, X, 96, February 21, 1933; and Minutes of the Board of Trustees, X, 114, March 21, 1933, CCNY Records, RBML-CUL.

41   CCNYAR, 1929, 33, and 1934, 61.

42   Keppel's first assistant, Cartwright, left by 1926 to run the American Association for Adult Education and was not involved in the overseas initiatives. Keppel hired Robert M. Lester, who had an extensive background in education, to take Cartwright's place. Lester later assumed the role of Corporation secretary when James Bertram died in 1935. John Russell was the son of James Russell, dean of Teachers College, Columbia University and a major key man for the Corporation. He joined in 1932 when Lester was asked to prepare the audit of experiences. Russell left in 1946 to become president of the John and Mary R. Markle Foundation. Charles Dollard joined in 1938 as a second staff member and became president of the Corporation in 1948.

43   CCNYAR, 1924, 13.

44   Frederick P. Keppel, "Memorandum on the Activities of Carnegie Corporation of New York in the British Colonies and Southern Dominions," January 26, 1942, 3, CCNY Program Files, Box 4, Series I.D, CCNY Records, RBML CUL. For more details on the music and arts grants, see Abigail Deutsch, "Investing in America's Cultural Education: The Carnegie Art and Music Sets," *Carnegie Reporter* (Fall 2010): 19.

45   Keppel, "Memorandum on the Activities of Carnegie Corporation in the British Colonies and Southern Dominions," 3. These figures differ from those given by Lester (*A Thirty Year Catalog of Grants*, 265–271, 286, 318–333), who uses a different start date, and by Stackpole (*Carnegie Corporation*, 23–59), who uses different start and end dates. Lester's figures for overall

overseas grant-making, minus the overseas funds for library buildings and church organs, for example, equal $12,991,897 (see 269, 286, and 332–333).

46 For more details, see Murphy, *Creative Philanthropy*, 19–32; Stackpole, *Carnegie Corporation*, 6–14.

47 Additional activities that were consistently pursued in Canada, as they were in the United States and around the British Commonwealth, included museum development, the teaching of art and music, reinforcement of the study of foreign languages, sponsorship of international meetings (especially around Commonwealth relations), support for Canadians to travel to international meetings, and other travel grants.

48 Lester, *A Thirty Year Catalog of Grants*, 47, 110–111.

49 Lester, "Review of Grants in the Maritime Provinces," 12.

50 Stackpole, *Carnegie Corporation*, 8, 42; Lester, "Review of Grants in the Maritime Provinces," 26–27. In 1974 the Central Advisory Committee became the Maritime Provinces Higher Education Commission (MPHEC), and it continues to promote and strengthen higher education institutions for the region; see MPHEC, "The Maritime Provinces Higher Education Commission Mandate," available at: http://www.mphec.ca/about/mandateandact.aspx; for an update on the Maritime Provinces Higher Education Commission Act as of January 31, 2005, see www.gov.pe.ca/law/statutes/pdf/m-02_01.pdf (accessed December 29, 2013).

51 Lester, "Review of Grants in the Maritime Provinces," 29.

52 John G. Reid, "Health, Education, Economy: Philanthropic Foundations in the Atlantic Region in the 1920s," *Acadiensis* 14, no. 1 (1984): 75–77.

53 Ibid.

54 Stackpole, *Carnegie Corporation*, 47; Lester, "Review of Grants in the Maritime Provinces," 22–23.

55 As Mary Coyle, then president of Coady International Institute, wrote recently: "Following World War II, global attention began to focus on the plight of newly emerging nations. Men and women from these countries came to St. Francis Xavier University to study and examine the approach and methods that had been so successful in the region. In 1959, the University established the Coady International Institute, named after Rev. Dr. Moses Coady, and gave it the mandate to train leaders from around the world in the principles and practice of this people-based approach to development. Over the past five decades, the global reach of the Institute has grown immensely. More than 5,000 development professionals from 130 countries have taken part in the Institute's campus-based programs, and many others have benefited from Coady training overseas." Mary Coyle, personal communication to the author, June 2010.

56 Florence Anderson, *Carnegie Corporation Library Program: 1911–1961* (New York: CCNY, 1963), 17, 103.

57 In addition, the Corporation supported several Canadian educational associations: the Canadian Council for Educational Research, the Canadian Educational Association, and the Canadian Library Association. Grants went to the Canadian Social Science Research Council for work on population studies and the Canadian Institute of International Affairs to organize and hold conferences on British Commonwealth relations and to establish its information service. See Stackpole, *Carnegie Corporation*, "Canada," 39–59.

58 CCNY, Minutes of the Executive Committee, VI, 167, November 8, 1926, CCNY Records, RBML-CUL.

59 The crucial role of higher education in the development of African countries and the work of the Corporation have been addressed in detail in several key texts, including three supported by the Corporation: Stephen H. Stackpole's *Carnegie Corporation Commonwealth Program, 1911–1961* (1963); E. Jefferson Murphy's *Creative Philanthropy: Carnegie Corporation and*

Africa, 1953–1973 (1976); and a book cowritten by three former African university vice chancellors, J. F. Ade Ajayi, Lameck K. H. Goma, and G. Ampah Johnson, *The African Experience with Higher Education* (Accra, North London, and Athens, OH: Association of African Universities, James Currey Ltd., and Ohio University Press, 1996). See also King, *Pan-Africans and Education*; Richard Davis Heyman, "The Role of Carnegie Corporation in African Education, 1925–1960," EdD diss., Teachers College, Columbia University (1970); and Patricia Rosenfield, "A Noble Use of Wealth: Carnegie Corporation's Commitment to African Higher Education," *Carnegie Reporter* (Spring 2011): 32–39.

    60 These higher-level secondary schools—Gordon Memorial College in Khartoum, Sudan; Makerere Government College in Kampala, Uganda; Yaba Higher College in Lagos, Nigeria; and Prince of Wales School and College, Achimota, Ghana—could offer certain degrees through the University of London. Fourah Bay College, established in 1826, had since 1876 been able to confer a full degree through Durham University.

    61 In total, they visited 124 institutions and talked with 439 people, including governors, high commissioners, principals, faculties, and students, garnering more than 90 grant applications and setting the stage for future investments.

    62 The Rockefeller Foundation, for instance, had public health projects in some parts of Africa. See Raymond Fosdick, *The Story of the Rockefeller Foundation* (New York: Harper & Brothers, 1952), 58–70.

    63 As James Bertram wrote in his separate memorandum on the trip, further illustrating their understanding of the complex situation, "There is a feeling that Africa has been overlooked in world movements, and with some basis. What has become of the upwards of 125,000,000 or more natives of Africa, how they are to develop, what will be their attitude toward the white race of Europe and America, when such development takes place, it would appear will depend largely on the line followed during the next few years by those now dealing with the question of white and natives in Africa." Frederick Keppel and James Bertram, "Report of the President & the Secretary as to an Educational Program in Africa," December 1, 1927, 9, 46, CCNY Miscellany Volumes, Series VIII.A.3, CCNY Records, RBML-CUL.

    64 Ibid., 9; CCNY, Minutes of the Board of Trustees, VII, 5, October 20, 1927, CCNY Records, RBML-CUL.

    65 This program included scientific research; a major cooperative research project on the question of the poor whites; development of public and academic library services; encouragement of native education and culture through support of Jeanes schools, educational research, educational testing, and aid to agencies concerned with interracial relations; improvement of training for other non-Europeans; music and archaeology publications; development of adult education; and a limited number of social service projects.

    66 Over fourteen years, the Corporation's grant-making in Africa largely reflected the recommendations from the Keppel-Bertram 1927 trip report. Corporation activities encompassed a mix of initiatives: Jeanes education training and establishment of what was said to be the first teacher training school for all teachers on the continent; libraries, including continuing support for the Johannesburg public library and libraries elsewhere in South Africa, Nyasaland, Southern and Northern Rhodesia, Kenya, Uganda, and later Nigeria and Ghana; grants providing music and arts curriculum materials for secondary schools and higher education institutions, such as the East Africa Institute in Uganda (later to become Makerere University), the University of Cape Town, and the University of the Witwatersrand in South Africa; traveling fellowships; and major poverty- and race-related initiatives in South Africa. Lester, *A Thirty Year Catalog of Grants*, 266–267, 270–271, 322–327, and 332–333.

    67 Lester, *Grants for Visitors, Grants-in-Aid, Scholarships, and Fellowships*, 9. Lester listed

the committee members for these grants: "Mr. Justice Feetham, Chairman, Supreme Court, Transvaal; Professor Edgar H. Brookes, University of Pretoria; Mr. Charles Christie, Principal Clerk, Public Works Department, Pretoria; Dr. E. G. Malherbe, Chief of National Bureau of Education, Pretoria: Professor R. B. Young, Chairman, Union Government Research Grant Board; Mr. Langham Murray, Honorary Secretary, Assistant Registrar, University of South Africa. Former members … Dr. C. T. Loram, Dr. S. F. N. Gie, and Mr. C. C. Grant." Ibid., 9–10.

68   Malherbe established in 1929 the forerunner to the South African National Bureau for Educational and Social Research, under the auspices of the Department of Education in South Africa. In 1934 the Corporation provided a significant grant of $62,500 that "enabled the Bureau to sponsor, conduct, and publish social science research as well as build a national library and education and the social sciences." Brahm Fleisch, "American Influences on the Development of Social and Economic Research in South Africa, 1929–1943," paper presented at the annual meeting of the American Educational Research Association, Atlanta, April 1993, abstract available at: http://eric.ed.gov/?id=ED370843.

69   "The financing of a research into the Poor White problem is a stroke of genius, both for its own sake, and also as a sound tactical move to prevent any criticism of the expenditure proposed for Native development." Edgar Brookes to Frederick Keppel, December 8, 1927, Folder 4, Box 5, Series I.D, CCNY Records, RBML-CUL.

70   Marita Golden, "Carnegie Corporation: A Difficult Past Leads to a Commitment to Change," *Carnegie Results* (Winter 2004): 2.

71   The most thorough paper, with excellent references, is by Morag Bell, "American Philanthropy, the Carnegie Corporation, and Poverty in South Africa," *Journal of Southern African Studies* 26, no. 3 (September 2000): 481–504. The Corporation itself discusses the Poor White Commission in Golden, "Carnegie Corporation in South Africa." For more on the controversy associated with the commission and on other controversies in South Africa, the United States, and elsewhere, see: Lagemann, *The Politics of Knowledge*, 30, 81; Ann Laura Stoler, "Tense and Tender Ties: The Politics of Comparison in North American History and (Post) Colonial Studies," in *Haunted by Empire: Geographies of Intimacy in North American History*, ed. Ann Laura Stoler (Durham, NC: Duke University Press, 2006), 50 and 66, n71; Kate Rogers, untitled paper delivered at the Academy of Social Sciences in Australia (ASSA) workshop "Philanthropy and Public Culture: The Influence and Legacies of the Carnegie Corporation of New York in Australia," University of Melbourne, February 24–25, 2010.

72   Another example, albeit highly positive, of unintended consequences from high-risk grant-making is the Corporation-sponsored, multi-year, multi-authored, multidisciplinary study of black poverty in the United States undertaken by Gunnar Myrdal from 1937 to 1942. In Myrdal scholar Maribel Morey's view, the intention of trustee Newton Baker and Keppel in supporting the study was to broaden the focus on blacks away from the narrow one on education and to examine the full range of conditions they confronted. While Keppel applauded the study and its work, neither he nor the trustees expected that it would return the focus to education in the 1954 landmark Supreme Court decision in *Brown v. Board of Education*. Their intention in supporting the study had been to provide the data and analyses to effect deeper social and economic change. The Supreme Court decision was, of course, a distinctively positive outcome, and later legislation began to address the broader societal issues. Maribel Morey, "A Reconsideration of *An American Dilemma*," *Reviews in American History* 40 (2012): 686–692.

73   Robert Miles and Malcolm Brown, *Racism*, 2nd ed. (London: Routledge, 2003), 170.

74   The discussion here draws heavily on independent research prepared for use by the author by Paul Sager, the research assistant for this book. His unpublished draft of an analytical literature review covering articles ranging from the 1930s to contemporary studies in the 2000s,

"The Question of Racism in Carnegie Corporation History: Carnegie Corporation and South Africa: A Reassessment" (2010), is available on request from the author.

75 The innovative study design used by the Poor White Commission involved teams fanning out over the country, collecting and analyzing a wide range of information, and then publishing in several volumes with credit to multiple authors; Johann Friedrich Wilhelm Grosskopf, Raymond William Wilcocks, Ernst Gideon Malherbe, J. R. Albertyn, and Mrs. M. E. Rothmann, *The Poor White Problem in South Africa: Report of the Carnegie Commission* (Stellenbosch, South Africa: Pro Ecclesia, 1932). Sager's 2010 review ("The Question of Racism in Carnegie Corporation History") refers to recent work on the social welfare aspects of the study; see Jeremy Seekings, "The Carnegie Commission and the Backlash Against Welfare State–Building in South Africa, 1931–1937," *Journal of Southern African Studies* 34, no. 3 (September 2008): 515–537.

76 Golden, "Carnegie Corporation," 3.

77 Ibid.

78 For example, as noted by Sager, "all South African governments intervened in one way or another on behalf of unemployed or otherwise impoverished Afrikaners." He further noted that "South African civil society, the government and Afrikaner nationalists had already held two conferences on white poverty in 1916 and 1917"; Sager, "The Question of Racism in Carnegie Corporation History," 26. Sager drew his comments from works by David Berger, "White Poverty and Government Policy in South Africa, 1894–1934," PhD diss., Temple University (1983); John Bottomley, "Public Policy and White Rural Poverty in South Africa, 1881–1924," PhD diss., Queen's University (1990); Robert Morrell, ed., *White but Poor: Essays on the History of Poor Whites in Southern Africa, 1880–1940* (Pretoria: University of South Africa, 1992).

79 Steffen Jensen, *Gangs, Politics, and Dignity in Cape Town* (Chicago: University of Chicago Press, 2008), 41; Deborah Posel, "The Meaning of Apartheid Before 1948: Conflicting Interests and Forces Within the Afrikaner Nationalist Alliance," *Journal of South African Studies* 14, no. 1 (October 1987): esp. 123–124 and 139.

80 Saul Dubow, *Racial Segregation and the Origins of Apartheid in South Africa, 1919–1936* (New York: St. Martin's Press, 1989), 177.

81 A later effort by the Corporation in its larger commitment to supporting intelligence testing also included the more controversial aspect of ascertaining biological differences between racialized groups. Grants were made to support testing in Kenya (Chloe Campbell, *Race and Empire: Eugenics in Colonial Kenya* [Manchester: Manchester University Press, 2007], 148–156), South Africa (Johann Louw, "Social Context and Psychological Testing in South Africa, 1918–1939," *Theory and Psychology* 7, no. 2 [1997]: 235–256; Saul Dubow, *Scientific Racism in Modern South Africa* [Cambridge: Cambridge University Press, 1995], ch. 6), and Australia (David McCallum, *The Social Production of Merit: Education, Psychology, and Politics in Australia, 1900–1950* [New York: Falmer, 1990]; Rogers, untitled paper delivered at ASSA workshop "Philanthropy and Public Culture"). Although the Corporation did fund a number of studies interested in testing whether entire "races" differed in levels of intelligence, grant money also went to researchers who determined that this goal was not scientifically possible; see Dubow, *Scientific Racism in Modern South Africa*, 219–221.

82 Sager, "The Question of Racism in Carnegie Corporation History," 21; Dubow, *Scientific Racism in Modern South Africa*, 157; see also Christoph Marx, *Oxwagon Sentinel: Radical Afrikaner Nationalism and the History of the "Ossewabrandwag"* (Berlin: Lit Verlag, 2008), 126; and Judith Tayler, "'Our Poor': The Politicisation of the Poor White Problem, 1932–1942," *Kleio* 24, no. 1 (1992): 61.

83 Sager, "The Question of Racism in Carnegie Corporation History," 23; quotes from Tayler, "'Our Poor,'" 48, quoting a Rothmann article in *Die Burger*, November 13, 1936, and citing

Rothmann's *My beskeie deel* (Kaapstad & Johannesburg, 1972), 229. Sager also notes that Mrs. Rothmann was later situated as a member of an ultra-right-wing party; see Marx, *Oxwagon Sentinel*, 126.

84   On Verwoerd, Sager ("The Question of Racism in Carnegie Corporation History") cites Roberta Balstad Miller, "Science and Society in the Early Career of H. F. Verwoerd," *Journal of Southern African Studies* 19, no. 4 (December 1993), 643; and Henry Kenney, *Architect of Apartheid: H. F. Verwoerd—An Appraisal* (Johannesburg: Jonathan Ball, 1980).

85   Miller, "Science and Society," 659; Francis Wilson, *The Reminiscences of Francis Wilson: Oral History, 1999*, interviewed by Mary Marshall Clark, August 3, 1999, Carnegie Corporation Project, Part 2: Oral History, 1996–2004, CCOH, 118 (hereafter "Wilson, CCOH").

86   See note 33 for details. Loram accompanied Keppel and Bertram in South Africa from July 25 to September 2, 1927, and helped to make their stay "as useful as possible." As they wrote in their Africa report, "Dr. Loram, a graduate of Cambridge in Arts and Law and of Columbia in Education, is a recognized leader in British Africa, a man of wide experience, unbounded energy, and with a host of devoted friends. We feel that not only are we personally but the Corporation as a whole is under a deep sense of obligation to him." Keppel and Bertram, "Report of the President & Secretary as to an Educational Program in Africa," 7.

87   Charles T. Loram to Frederick Keppel, January 24, 1929, and February 8, 1929, Folder 8, Box 295, Series III.A, CCNY Records, RBML-CUL. Keppel replied that he was "much interested" and that he thought Jones could go to Africa in 1930; Frederick Keppel to Charles T. Loram, March 4, 1929, ibid. It is possible that this study never materialized not only because of the increasingly sensitive political conditions but also because Loram emigrated in 1931 to the United States to teach at Yale. Undiscussed, however, was the fact that in the 1920s William M. Macmillan, a British-born South African historian, had undertaken a limited survey of black poverty; see Hugh Macmillan, "The Travels and Researches of W. M. Macmillan in Southern Africa, 1915–32," paper presented at the colloquium "A Hundred Years of History at Rhodes University," September 2011, available at: www.ru.ac.za/media/rhodesuniversity/content/conferences/documents.

88   Golden, "Carnegie Corporation," 3.

89   Ernst Gideon Malherbe, "Education and the Poor White," *South African Journal of Science* 26 (1929): 892, quoted in C. J. Groenewald, "The Methodology of Poverty Research in South Africa: The Case of the First Carnegie Investigation, 1929–1932," *Social Dynamics* 13, no. 2 (1987): 72.

90   Wilson, CCOH-CUL, 119.

91   Briefly, the Corporation was able, again through its grant-making, to contribute to advancing knowledge and understanding about sensitive social and economic conditions for highly marginalized and deeply discriminated against members of a society. In both inquiries, the study populations benefited from subsequent policies that drew on the findings. The second time, however, as described later, the study results—again, among many other inputs—contributed to positive political change that removed barriers of societal discrimination rather than imposed them. BBC News, "South Africa Bans Discrimination," January 26, 2000, BBC News Online, available at: http://news.bbc.co.uk/2/hi/africa/619337.stm (accessed January 28, 2013).

92   "Verwoerd publicly cautioned the South African Institute of Race Relations that if it showed prejudice in favour of the Africans, it would evoke opposition from the country's white population. To avoid this, he suggested that the Institute initially concentrate on gathering scientific data, which he considered innocuous, rather than on research, which could be used to promote particular views"; Miller, "Science and Society," n60. Miller cites Verwoerd's presentation to the second annual general meeting of the South African Institute of Race Relations in

Race Relations 1 (1934): 37. Already by 1935, however, the Institute had become involved in the controversial urban segregation question, or urban control of the native population, "which has formed the basis of modern apartheid"; Paul B. Rich, "Administrative Ideology, Urban Social Control, and the Origins of Apartheid Theory, 1930–1939," *Journal of African Studies* 7, no. 2 (Summer 1980): 72.

93   CCNY, Agenda Book of the Board of Trustees, October 15, 1929, "South African Institute of Race Relations" (agenda item), 58–59, CCNY Records, RBML-CUL; see also Anna M. Cunningham, Records of the South African Institute of Race Relations: Part II, Library of the University of the Witwatersrand, June 1990, available at: http://www.historicalpapers. wits.ac.za/?inventory/U/collections&c=AD843RJ/R; James Aggrey, a Ghanaian "key man" for the Corporation, joined Loram in urging this support, as described in these records. For more about Aggrey, see Sylvia M. Jacobs, "James Emman Kwegyir Aggrey: An African Intellectual in the United States," in "80th Anniversary Year: Vindicating the Race: Contributions to African-American Intellectual History," ed. V. P. Franklin and Bettye Collier Thomas, *Journal of Negro History* 81, nos. 1–4 (1996): 47–61.

94   Stackpole, *Carnegie Corporation*, 8–11, 28–32.

95   R. Alain Everts, "The Pioneers: Herbert Isaac Ernest Dhlomo and the Development of Library Service to the African in South Africa," *World Libraries* 3, no. 2 (Spring 1993): 1–2.

96   Ibid., 2; see also, Maxine K. Rochester, "The Carnegie Corporation and South Africa: Non-European Library Services," *Libraries and Culture* (now *Information and Culture*) 30, no. 1 (Winter 1999): 27–51.

97   Ibid., 8–9.

98   See Chapter 6; see also Golden, "Carnegie Corporation," 4–7.

99   Information and quotations in this section come from "Primitive Peoples, Education," Grant Files, 1932–1960, Folder 1, Box 298, Series III.A, CCNY Records, RBML-CUL. This quotation from the 1937 section is undated.

100   Loram brought students to the University of Colorado, Duke University, Harvard University, Hampton Institute, Tuskegee Institute, and the Bishop Museum in Honolulu, Hawaii. The summer study visits included trips to Haiti, the Dominican Republic, Puerto Rico, and the Virgin Islands. The Corporation between 1933 and 1937 provided over $40,000 in scholarships and $30,000 for the conferences. The General Education Board provided $20,000 for the conferences, and Phelps Stokes provided $1,500 each for scholarships and special grants. The Agricultural Mission Foundation provided grants for travel; Yale eventually provided $800 for fellowships each year.

101   Frederick Keppel, unsigned memo, January 7, 1937, "Primitive Peoples, Education," Grant Files, 1932–1960, Folder 1, Box 298, Series III.A, CCNY Records, RBML-CUL.

102   Among those on the trip were a student from New Zealand who had taught in a Maori village, an Afrikaner from a distinguished family of Christian missionaries, a Zulu from South Africa, a Southern American librarian, a native of Nigeria, and Strong, who was assistant secretary of the International Missionary Council and worked in India.

103   Esther Strong, trip report, sent to CCNY by Helen Frost, July 19, 1940, 1, CCNY Program Files, Folder 2, Box 4, Series I.D, CCNY Records, RBML-CUL.

104   Ibid. One lasting impact of this program was the work of a faculty member, George Murdoch, who, with modest support from the Corporation, went on to establish the Human Relations Area Files (HRAF) now based at Yale, funded and maintained by a number of institutions. These files provide a wealth of material for any scholar who wishes to delve into ethnography, anthropology, and cultural studies in a wide variety of populations covering multiple time periods.

105 Gunnar Myrdal, preface to the 1962 edition, *An American Dilemma*, vol. 1, *The Negro Problem and Modern Democracy* (1944; reprint, New Brunswick, NJ: Transaction Press, 1966), xxxv.

106 Clark Wissler, "Report of a Visit to Research Institutions in New Zealand and Australia During the Year 1925," report received by Rockefeller Foundation, March 10, 1926, Folder 42, Box 4, Series 410D, Record Group 1.1, FA386, Rockefeller Foundation records, RAC (68 pages).

107 CCNY, Agenda Book of the Executive Committee, November 8, 1926, "Special Fund Applicable Elsewhere Than in the United States, (a) African Trip and Australasian Projects" (agenda item), 2, CCNY Records, RBML-CUL.

108 These visitors included, in 1931–1932, Lotus Coffman, president of the University of Minnesota (soon to be a Corporation trustee); in 1932, C. O. G. Douie, an adult education expert from the United Kingdom; in 1934 Ralph Munn, director of Carnegie Library of Pittsburgh, paired first with Ernest R. Pitt of the Melbourne Public Library and then with John Barr of the Auckland Public Library; and in 1937 Isaac Kandel, director of the Institute of International Education, Teachers College. Two Corporation visits were also undertaken; a formal visit by Keppel in 1935 and an informal one by John Russell in 1938. Russell, Keppel's assistant, was the son of the first visitor, James Russell, and had accompanied his father on the 1928 trip.

109 Frederick Paul Keppel, "The Southern Dominions of the British Empire," in Keppel, *Philanthropy and Learning with Other Papers* (New York: Columbia University, 1936), 139.

110 Ibid., 140.

111 Michael White, "Carnegie Corporation Travel Grants to Australian Educators in the 1930s," Paper delivered at the joint conference of the Australian Association for Research in Education and the Singapore Educational Research Association, Singapore (November 24–29). Available at: http://publications.aare.edu.au/96pap/whitm96274.txt (accessed September 15, 2013); and Michael White, "Carnegie Philanthropy in the Nineteen Thirties: A Reassessment," *History of Education Review* 26, no. 1 (1997): 1–24.

112 W. F. Connell, *The Australian Council for Educational Research, 1930–1980* (Hawthorn, Victoria: Australian Council for Educational Research Ltd., 1980), 2.

113 Ibid., 3. Connell further commented, "From Russell's diagnosis of Australia's educational needs and his suggestive prodding of selected educators, it was to be shaped, staffed, and directed by local people according to their own views of what was practicable and desirable in an Australian situation." Ibid., 3.

114 Ibid.

115 Ibid., 6.

116 Ibid., 1.

117 Ibid., 23.

118 Ibid., 22, 49–51. "With more than a decade of support from the Corporation, programs designed and implemented to make a difference, and careful shepherding of funds by Cunningham to take them through the funding lulls of World War II, and with increasingly strong backing from other institutions, but never being taken over by the government, the Australian Council of Educational Research is one of the leading educational research institutions in the world today," according to Caroline Milburn. The Council "generated $60 million [in 2009] from various research grants and contracts for developing and running services, from scholarships and student entry test for schools and universities to professional development materials for teachers and schools. Internationally it has carved a reputation as a leader in survey research. The Council operates the world's best-known student testing regime—the Program for International Student Assessment (PISA)—for the Paris-based, international Organization for Economic Co-operation and Development (OECD). It won the contract to manage PISA in 2000, translating the tests into 20 languages and working with 60 countries to analyze, compare,

and report on their students' 'results.'" Caroline Milburn, "Taking Research to the Top of Its Class," *The Age*, available at: http://www.theage.com.au/national/education/taking-research-to-the-top-of-its-class-20100409-rxja.html.

119 The freestanding Australian Institute of International Affairs had been established in 1924. These travel grants increased Australian exposure to more distant as well as more accessible international issues. James Cotton, "Carnegie, Rockefeller, and the Role of American Soft Power in the Emergence of International Studies in Australia," paper delivered at the ASSA workshop "Philanthropy and Public Culture: The Influence and Legacies of the Carnegie Corporation of New York in Australia," University of Melbourne, February 24–25, 2010.

120 Institute of Education, University of London, "DC/WEF World Education Fellowship" (formerly New Education Fellowship), 1920–1995, Records of the World Education Fellowship, reference code GB/366/DC/WEF, available at: http://www.ioe.ac.uk/services/1013.html (accessed December 29, 2013).

121 Connell, *The Australian Council for Educational Research*, 111.

122 Maxine Rochester, "American Philanthropy Abroad: Library Program Support from Carnegie Corporation of New York British Dominions and Colonies Fund in the 1920s and 1930s," *Libraries and Culture* 31, no. 2 (1996): 342–363. Rochester also describes some of the grants for innovations in library service, such as the country lending service in New South Wales and South Australia. A recent article analyzes the role of the Corporation's advisers on libraries in Australia and New Zealand; see Michael J. Birkner, "'The Wisest Help': Frederick Keppel and His Consultants' Impact on Australian and New Zealand Libraries," *Library and Information History* 29, no. 4 (November 2013): 258–271.

123 White, "Carnegie Philanthropy in Australia," 15.

124 Birkner, "'The Wisest Help,'" 261–263.

125 Larry Amey, "When Libraries Made Headlines," *Australian Library Journal* 50, no. 3 (2001): 229–234. In contrast to the constructive working relations that Munn established with local advisers, Professor Isaac Kandel, director of Teachers College International Institute, had a much less positive outcome. Keppel sent Kandel, one of his more iconoclastic key men, to assess education developments in Australia in the late 1930s. Despite considerable efforts undertaken since 1930 by the Australian Council on Education Research, Kandel was quite critical of what he saw in Australian education, particularly at the higher education level. Rather than share his findings with the local committee, he issued reports to the press and, privately, to others. He was scathing about what he encountered at the universities. He also named names. When word of this reached Keppel in New York, he immediately initiated a fairly testy correspondence with Kandel, saying that Kandel did not grasp the sensitivity of his outsider role.

126 Michael J. Birkner, "'Not Yet Ready': Australian University Libraries and Carnegie Corporation Philanthropy, 1935–1945," in *Collections, Characters, and Communities: The Shape of Libraries in Australia and New Zealand*, ed. B. J. McMullin, 77–93 (Melbourne: Australian Scholarly Publishing, 2010).

127 For outcomes of Douie's work, see CCNY, Agenda Book of the Board of Trustees, October 19, 1933, "Adult Education Program: British Dominions and Colonies" (agenda item), 11–13, and "Maori Purposes Board" (agenda item), 14, CCNY Records, RBML-CUL.

128 Over the period 1932 to 1933, Miers and Markham conducted, with Corporation support, an Empire-wide study of museums under the auspices of the British Museum Association; see CCNY, Minutes of the Executive Committee, XI, 3–4, October 5, 1933, CCNY Records, RBML-CUL. On the continued value of all their surveys, see Lisa M. Given and Liane McTauris, "What's Old Is New Again: The Reconvergence of Libraries, Archives, and Museums in the Digital Age," *Library Quarterly* 80, no. 1 (January 2010): 7–32.

129 The first exhibit took place at the National Museum of Victoria in 1929. The North

American tour began at the National Gallery in Washington, DC, and the Metropolitan Museum of Art in New York City. For more information on the exhibits, see Daniel Thomas's *tour d'horizon* on the visibility of aboriginal art, "Aboriginal Art: Who Was Interested?" *Journal of Art Historiography* 4 (June 2011), available at: http://arthistoriography.files.wordpress. com/2011/05/daniel-thomas-document.pdf.

130   Cotton, "Carnegie, Rockefeller, and the Role of American Soft Power"; White, "Carnegie Philanthropy in Australia in the Nineteen-Thirties."

131   Scholars from a wide range of disciplines and areas of interest met at the conference "Philanthropy and Public Culture: The Influence and Legacies of the Carnegie Corporation of New York in Australia" to examine in-depth the many elements of the Corporation's program in Australia. The conference was held at the University of Melbourne, where the Corporation between 1927 and 1954 had supported adult education programs, an adult education library, a survey of the university, different lectureships, the vice chancellor's fund, and faculty-related travel in 1954 to Indonesia. The rationale for foundations, particularly American-based philan- thropies (notably the Carnegie Corporation, Rockefeller Foundation, and Ford Foundation), to make grants overseas varies enormously—ranging from donor intent and foundation mis- sion to programmatic thrusts to, simply, opportunities to make a difference. The scholars at the Australia meeting brought much greater poignancy to the analysis than is usually the case when the international grant-making analyst is American, British, or European. The Australian schol- ars saw the impact of the Corporation and other foundations in shaping their history and their culture. Their analyses merit detailed study by American-based international philanthropies to gain a greater understanding of why good intentions do not always lead to good results in the long run. To their credit, the Australian scholars were balanced in their analysis, recognizing that while some harm was done by the activities of foundations, some good—and in some cases significant good—resulted as well.

132   White, "Carnegie Philanthropy in Australia in the Nineteen-Thirties," 21.

133   Ibid.

134   Ibid., 19, 21.

135   Kate Darian-Smith, Julie Mcleod, and Glenda Sluga (ASSA workshop convenors), "Philanthropy and Public Culture: The Influence and Legacies of the Carnegie Corporation of New York in Australia," *Dialogue* 29, no. 2 (February 2010), available at: http://www.assa.edu. au/publications/dialogue/2010_Vol29_No2.pdf.

136   Keppel, "Memorandum on the Activities of Carnegie Corporation in the British Colonies and Southern Dominions," 3; Lester, *A Thirty Year Catalog of Grants*, 267–268 and 326–327; and Stackpole, *Carnegie Corporation*, 34–39.

137   CCNY, Agenda Book of the Board of Trustees, October 19, 1933, "New Zealand Council for Educational Research" (agenda item), 21–22, CCNY Records, RBML-CUL.

138   Ibid., 5–6.

139   As Beeby stated in his oral history, he felt a great deal of appreciation for the Corporation and Keppel. Through their support, his life changed from being a professor of philosophy at Canterbury University to holding a major position that enabled him to shape education not only in New Zealand but around the world through his work as the first assistant director-general at UNESCO in 1948. He also highlighted a special aspect of working with the Corporation: "Somehow or other, if you really want to get to the core of it, what really distinguished the Corporation, I think, in those early days, and since as far as I'm aware, was its extraordinary personal character. If you came to New York, you never felt that here was an organization with a vast mass of card indexes or with everything tucked away neatly, a computer somewhere that knew all about you … you found *somebody* who knew all about you." Beeby, CCOH-CUL, 6.

140   Ibid., 8.

141   Ibid., 13.

142   Ibid., 14–16.

143   Ibid., 8.

144   Maxine K. Rochester, "Wise Philanthropy: The Carnegie Corporation and Libraries of the British Commonwealth in the 1920s and 1930s," paper presented at the 68th International Federation of Library Associations and Institutions (IFLA) Council and General Conference, Glasgow (August 18–24, 2002). This paper and Rochester's many books provide the most extensive analyses of the Corporation's multifaceted support for libraries overseas; Stackpole, *Carnegie Corporation*, 12–13.

145   CCNY, Minutes of the Board of Trustees, VII, 119, February 13, 1929, CCNY Records, RBML-CUL; see also Maxine Rochester, "American Philanthropy Abroad: Library Program Support from the Carnegie Corporation of New York British Dominions and Colonies Fund in the 1920s and 1930s," *Libraries and Culture* 31, no. 2 (Spring 1996): 352.

146   Keppel, "Memorandum on the Activities of Carnegie Corporation in the British Colonies and Southern Dominions," 3; Lester, *A Thirty Year Catalog of Grants*, 268, 328; Stackpole, *Carnegie Corporation*, 52–54.

147   "Institute of Pacific Relations Fonds," compiled by Kate McCandless, Philip Holden, and Laurenda Daniells (1981), revised by Jane Turner (1990), Marnie Burnham (1996), and Erwin Wodarczak (2004, 2012), University of British Columbia Archives, available at: http://www.library.ubc.ca/archives/u_arch/ipr.pdf (accessed December 30, 2013). The last grant to the Institute in this period was made in 1941; CCNY, Minutes of the Executive Committee, XVIII, 121, April 7, 1941, CCNY Records, RBML-CUL.

148   Fosdick, *The Story of the Rockefeller Foundation*, 198.

149   Frederick P. Keppel, "The Effect of the Machine Age on Occidental and Oriental Culture," undated memorandum, 9–10, Box 14, Series I.E, CCNY Records, RBML-CUL.

150   Keppel, "Memorandum of the Activities of the Carnegie Corporation in the British Colonies and Southern Dominions," 2; see also CCNY, Minutes of the Executive Committee, XIX, 83, March 9, 1942, CCNY Records, RBML-CUL. For an example of the Corporation's early rationale, see CCNY, Agenda Book of the Executive Committee, September 29, 1933, "London Conference" (agenda item), 5–6, CCNY Records, RBML-CUL.

151   Rockefeller Foundation board action of April 13, 1932, provided an appropriation of $150,000 over five years, starting May 1, 1932, Folder 1012, Box 77, Series 401S, Record Group 1.1, FA386, Rockefeller Foundation records, RAC; see also Peter Grose, *Continuing the Inquiry: The Council on Foreign Relations from 1921 to 1996* (New York: Council on Foreign Relations Press, 2006/1996), 8–9, available at: http://www.cfr.org/history-and-theory-of-international-relations/continuing-inquiry/p108 (accessed December 30, 2013).

152   Glotzer, "Frederick Keppel and Carnegie Corporation's Interwar Overseas Experts," 50.

153   CCNY, Agenda Book of the Executive Committee, September 29, 1933, "Agricultural Researches in British Dominions and Colonies" (agenda item), 8, CCNY Records, RBML-CUL; see also Keppel, "Memorandum on the Activities of Carnegie Corporation in the British Colonies and Southern Dominions," 3 (Imperial College of Tropical Agriculture in Trinidad); 4 (East African Agricultural Research Station, Amani, Tanganyika); 5–6 (Empire Marketing Board). Mainly in the form of one-year grants ranging from $300 to $7,500, the Corporation also supported a few projects in the smaller colonies, particularly the island ones in the Pacific, Atlantic, and Mediterranean: museum development in Fiji, Singapore (a large grant to the Raffles Museum of $25,000), Ceylon, Bermuda, and the Falkland Islands; library development in the Malay States; and monument preservation in Cyprus and Malta; Lester, *A Thirty Year Catalog*

of Grants, 330, and Stackpole, *Carnegie Corporation*, 52, 55. Professor Benoit Challand of New York University kindly informed me (personal communication, December 19, 2013) of a longer-term, more extensive activity in Cyprus supported through the Near East Foundation from 1936 to 1941, for $21,500 that worked with Thomas Jesse Jones to introduce the Jeanes approach of village education for development schemes; CCNY, Minutes of the Board of Trustees, XIII, 89, January 16, 1936, and CCNY, Minutes of the Executive Committee, XVIII, 121, April 7, 1941, CCNY Records, RBML-CUL.

154 Stackpole, *Carnegie Corporation*, 57; Richard Glotzer, "Sir Fred Clarke: South Africa and Canada Carnegie Corporation Philanthropy and the Transition from Empire to Commonwealth," *Educational Research and Perspectives (Australia)* 22, no. 1 (1995): 1–21.

155 The first request was conditionally approved on October 13, 1931, for $75,000. The funds were not released until an organization plan was submitted and approved; see CCNY, Agenda Book of the Board of Trustees, October 19, 1933, "Study of Equatorial and Southern Africa" (agenda item), 7–8, CCNY Records, RBML-CUL. The Rockefeller Foundation was also unsuccessfully approached to provide support; memorandum of conversation between Tracy B. Kittredge and Dr. J. H. Oldham, London, September 22, 1933, Folder 1012, Box 77, Series 401S, Record Group 1.1, FA386, Rockefeller Foundation records, RAC. According to Helen Tilley, the Rockefeller Foundation funded a more scientific component of the study; Helen Tilley, *Africa as a Living Laboratory: Problems of Scientific Knowledge, 1830–1950* (Chicago: University of Chicago Press, 2011), 91. Tilley also describes in her chapter on the Survey the more than three hundred participants and the three-volume, three-thousand-page final product.

156 Stackpole, *Carnegie Corporation*, 24; Keppel, CCNYAR, 1939, 30.

157 Andrew Roberts, *The Colonial Moment in Africa: Essays on the Movement of Minds and Materials, 1900–1940* (New York: Cambridge University Press, 1990), 74. For more details on the African survey in context, see Andrew Roberts, "The Imperial Mind," in *The Cambridge History of Africa*, vol. 7, *1905–1940*, ed. J. D. Fage and Roland Oliver (Cambridge: Cambridge University Press, 1986), 73–76; for a detailed discussion of the debates prompted by the Africa Survey, see Barbara Bush, *Imperialism, Race, and Resistance: Africa and Britain, 1919–1945* (Florence, KY: Routledge, 1999), 262–264.

158 Rohland Schuknecht, *British Colonial Development Policy After the Second World War: The Case of Sukuymaland, Tanganyika* (Berlin: Lit Verlag, 2010), 14–15.

159 Tilley, *Africa as a Living Laboratory*, 72.

160 Keppel, "Memorandum of the Activities of the Carnegie Corporation in the British Colonies and Southern Dominions," 8–9. Recognizing the opportunities provided by the Corporation's travel grants program, the Chatham House group was particularly keen that the Corporation provide such grants for colonial officers as refreshers during or after their period of service overseas, and Keppel may have been referring to this cluster of grants, for which the Corporation spent $108,000 over the period 1932 to 1936. One unexpected outcome of these discussions, as Keppel noted, was the considerable amount of money spent on Empire-wide grants based in London. The Empire Marketing Board, established in 1926 to promote trade in goods produced around the Empire, was one of the largest grant recipients, at a level of $160,000. An even larger sum of money went toward constructing Dominions Students Hall Trust, at $200,000, as a residence at the University of London for dominion students studying at the university.

161 Keppel comments, Tuesday, June 27, 1939, CCNY Admin. Records Policy and Program Files, BDC, London Conferences, 1939, Box 6, Folder 6, CCNY Records, RBML-CUL.

162 CCNY, Agenda Book of the Executive Committee, February 26, 1932, Frederick P. Keppel, "Report on Recent Trip to Caribbean and Certain Recommendations" (agenda item), 34–35, CCNY Records, RBML-CUL.

163   Alma Jordan, "Public Libraries in the Caribbean I," *Library Quarterly* 34, no. 2 (April 1964): 143–162.

164   Keppel also provided one telling example of the value of personal contacts: "The Governor, Sir Edward Denham, is an old acquaintance, as Mr. Bertram and I were his guests when he was Colonial Secretary of Kenya … [he] is still deeply interested in education.… With the funds at their disposal, however, they can do little to improve conditions in the Colony." Keppel, "Report on Recent Trip to Caribbean and Certain Recommendations," 30–31. These grants in British Guiana paved the way for Corporation efforts in the late 1960s and the 1990s, as discussed in Chapters 6 and 7.

165   Cecilia McAlmont, "History of the Week: Developments During the Forty Years Before Independence," *Starbroek News*, April 27, 2006.

166   Macmillan was a distinguished South African historian recognized for his studies of poverty among blacks and whites in South Africa. For a more detailed narrative on his contributions to the study of impoverished South Africans—starting around 1915 with his study of poor whites and poor blacks—along with his radical approach to South African society as a society for all its people in the 1920s, see Hugh Macmillan, "The Travels and Researches of W. M. Macmillan in Southern Africa, 1915–32," paper presented at the colloquium "A Hundred Years of History at Rhodes University," September 2011, available at: www.ru.ac.za/media/rhodesuniversity/content/conferences/documents; and Paul Maylam, "A Hundred Years of History at Rhodes University: Some Reflections on the Department's Centenary Colloquium, September 2011," *Historia* (Durban) 57, no. 1 (May 2012), available at: http://www.scielo.org.za/scielo.php?pid=S0018-229X2012000100009&script=sci_arttext.

167   Malcolm Gladwell, "Epilogue: A Jamaican Story," in *Outliers: The Story of Success* (New York: Little, Brown, 2008), 270–286.

168   These institutions included the Carnegie Endowment for International Peace, the Church Peace Union, the Council on Foreign Relations, the Institute of International Education, the Institute of Pacific Relations, the American Council for Education, and the International Commission for Intellectual Cooperation (American branch).

169   In 1934 the Institute of International Education, for example, received a grant of $300,000, payable at $60,000 annually for five years, to promote international exchanges and enable Americans to attend international conferences. It also included support to promote the study of foreign languages in the United States. This grant reinforced the role of the Institute as one of the major partners of the Corporation in building and establishing international connectivity for Americans. It also was a result of a 1927 agreement between the Rockefeller Foundation and the Corporation that the former would support the American University Union in London and Paris and the latter would support the US-based Institute; see CCNY, Agenda Book of the Board of Trustees, October 19, 1933, "Institute of International Education" (agenda item), 30–31, CCNY Records, RBML-CUL.

170   Joseph Barber, *These Are the Committees* (New York: Council on Foreign Relations, 1964).

171   Ekbladh, "Present at the Creation."

172   Council on Foreign Relations, "CFR History," available at: http://www.cfr.org/about/history/cfr/index.html; see also Grose, *Continuing the Inquiry*, 1–9.

173   Lester, *A Thirty Year Catalog of Grants*, 296–297. For the first grant for this activity, see CCNY, Agenda Book of the Board of Trustees, January 20, 1938, "Council on Foreign Relations: Cooperative Adult Education Scheme" (agenda item), 12–13, CCNY Records, RBML-CUL; see also Grose, *Continuing the Inquiry*, 15–16.

174   Inderjeet Parmar, *Think Tanks and Power in Foreign Policy: A Comparative Study of the Role and Influence of the Council on Foreign Relations and the Royal Institute of International Affairs, 1939–1945* (Hampshire: Palgrave Macmillan, 2004), 142–147.

175 CCNY, Minutes of the Board of Trustees, XVII, 3, October 19, 1939, CCNY Records, RBML-CUL.

176 Office of the President, "Informal Meeting of the Trustees at Mr. Leffingwell's House" and "Organizations Interested in Peace and War" (records of interviews), October 17, 1939, CCNY Trustees Meetings, Informal: 1931–1939, Folder 1, Box 11, Series I.E.2, CCNY Records, RBML-CUL.

177 For a detailed report on the planning and the resulting program, see the draft paper prepared for the author by Paul Sager, "Summary of the Carnegie Corporation's National Emergency Program," April 2010, available on request from the author. Sager points out that Root did not achieve the results he intended for stimulating major new programs at the Corporation to address the implications of the national emergency; see also Ekbladh, "Present at the Creation," 120–123.

178 Sager, "Summary of the Carnegie Corporation's National Emergency Program," 15–17.

179 Ekbladh, "Present at the Creation," 115–118.

180 Ibid., 9.

181 CCNY, Agenda Book of the Board of Trustees, February 1, 1940, "Institute for Advanced Study, US Military and Foreign Policy, $6,500" (agenda item), 28, CCNY Records, RBML-CUL.

182 CCNY, Agenda Book of the Executive Committee, November 7, 1940, "Institute for Advanced Study, Study of Military and Foreign Policies of United States, $10,000" (agenda item), 17, CCNY Records, RBML-CUL.

183 Out of the $184,371,246 granted between 1911 and 1941, $71,855,011 went to fund the full range of Carnegie institutions, along with the Professors' Annuities Fund, the Teachers Insurance and Annuity Association, and the Church Peace Union. Lester, A Thirty Year Catalog of Grants, 366–367.

184 The Church Peace Union today thrives as the Carnegie Council for Ethics and International Affairs; after a hiatus that lasted decades, in 2011 it once again became a grantee partner of the Corporation.

185 The long-standing question of the relationship between the Corporation and its sister organization, the Carnegie Endowment for International Peace, was resolved, first in 1928 and then more firmly in 1931, by legal counsel, who advised "that the Corporation was free to use its best judgment at all times under its charter; that it could justly expect information as to specific purposes of proposals regardless of source." From then on, the Endowment submitted highly targeted requests: to fund a disarmament conference and enhance public opinion about it; to advocate ratification of the World Court protocol by the US Senate and the United States; and to undertake studies that provided information about the financial and economic problems threatening world peace and examined ways to solve those problems. Although it did not come close to meeting the Endowment request of $5 million as either capital grant or annual payments equaling that, the Corporation supported the specific studies in 1932 for $100,000; Robert M. Lester, "Review of Grants to Carnegie Endowment for International Peace 1911–1933," CCNY Review Series 13, October 1, 1933, CCNY Records, RBML-CUL. Despite the entente cordiale, the Endowment continued to receive only limited funding from the Corporation until the early twenty-first century, when mutually reinforcing programmatic objectives have resulted in a much more active partnership, as will be seen in Chapter 8.

186 The last overall general grant to the Carnegie Endowment for International Peace during the Keppel era was made at the Board of Trustees meeting on November 18, 1941; see CCNY, Minutes of the Board of Trustees, XI, 46, November 18, 1941, CCNY Records, RBML-CUL. The total of $2,523,824 cited here is calculated from all the grants made in this era, including the ones for Canadian-American studies. Lester gives the total from the Corporation over the period

1912 to 1941 as $2,949,823.75; Lester, *Forty Years of Carnegie Giving*, 51–52. A third amount, also reported by Lester, gives the total from the Corporation to the Endowment from 1917 to 1941 as $2,919,824; Lester, *A Thirty Year Catalog of Grants*, 366–367.

187   Keppel, "Memorandum on the Activities of Carnegie Corporation in the British Dominions and Colonies," 4–7. In an earlier report, Keppel conveyed his understanding of the key to successful grant-making: "The contribution of money, from whatever source, is, in effect, only secondary in importance to the work of men and women of creative minds and devoted lives"; CCNYAR, 1932, 5.

188   Keppel seemed unaware of the negative impact of the Poor White Study, with its contributions to the Afrikaner nationalist cause. He called it a "strike" and even claimed it as "an idea of my own." He added the following caveat, however, when discussing the question of race in the African colonies and South Africa: "It must always be remembered that the whole treatment of the Natives is red hot politically—this is particularly so in the Union of South Africa—and what might be regarded as outside interference would accomplish more harm than good." Keppel, "Memorandum on the Activities of Carnegie Corporation in the British Dominions and Colonies," 4, 6.

189   Ibid., 4.

190   Ibid., 5

191   Ibid., 6–7.

192   Ibid., 6.

193   Ibid., 7.

194   Harvie Branscomb, "Report to President Jessup," received at CCNY on October 20, 1943, 3, Program and Policies, Commonwealth: General, 1921–1955, 4–6, CCNY Records, RBML-CUL.

195   Ibid., 5.

196   Ibid., 3, 4.

197   Ibid., 5.

198   Ibid., 10–12.

199   Keppel, "Memorandum on the Activities of Carnegie Corporation of New York in the British Colonies and Southern Dominions," 7.

NOTES FOR CHAPTER 4

1   Carnegie Corporation staff and trustees served at the front during World War II and especially in Washington, DC. When asked in 1966 about having left the Corporation to serve in the war, Charles Dollard remembered: "I finally concluded you wouldn't have anybody to talk to if you didn't go and participate in what was so galvanizing. Everybody was there; everything that was going on was there." Charles Dollard, *Reminiscences of Charles Dollard: Oral History, March 1969*, interviewed by Isabel S. Grossner on February 15, 1966, Carnegie Corporation Project: Oral History, 1966–1970, Columbia Center for Oral History (CCOH), Columbia University Libraries (CUL), 18 (hereafter "Dollard, CCOH").

2   Ekbladh, *The Great American Mission*, ch. 3.

3   "Post World War Two Domestic Affairs: The United States at Home, 1945–2001," available at: http://www.sageamericanhistory.net/postww2domestic/index.html. The US economy, as measured by gross national product (GNP), grew from "about $200,000 million in 1940 to $300,000 million in 1950 and to more than $500,000 million in 1960." US Department of State, "The Post War Economy: 1945–1960," available at: About.com: Economics, http://economics.about.com/od/useconomichistory/a/post_war.htm (accessed September 20, 2012).

4   For an overview of the period, see James T. Patterson, *Grand Expectations: The United States, 1945–1974* (New York: Oxford University Press, 1996).

5   See L. J. Butler, *Britain and Empire: Adjusting to a Post-Imperial World* (London: I. B. Tauris, 2002). The shrinking of the British Empire exacerbated the British economic problems resulting from World War II.

6   David McCartney, "Jessup, Walter Albert (August 12, 1877–July 5, 1944)," in *The Biographical Dictionary of Iowa* (University of Iowa Press, 2009), available at: http://uipress.lib.uiowa.edu/bdi/DetailsPage.aspx?id=195 (accessed January 3, 2014).

7   The Corporation's wartime grant-making in the United States continued to help "mobilize scholarship and science in the interest of the nation as whole" through grants to universities, institutes, and agencies, both separate from and under the auspices of the trustee-inspired National Emergency Program. The program, which expended a total of nearly $3 million in grants, was in effect from 1940 to 1947.

8   Carnegie Corporation of New York (CCNY) Annual Report (CCNYAR), 1942, 28–29, CCNY Records, Rare Book and Manuscript Library, Columbia University Libraries (RBML-CUL).

9   CCNY, Minutes of the Board of Trustees, XIX, 70, January 15, 1942, CCNY Records, RBML-CUL.

10   CCNY, Minutes of the Board of Trustees, XIX, 90, March 19, 1942, CCNY Records, RBML-CUL.

11   Charles Dollard said in his oral history that the BDC program was "optional": "That whole business about the British Dominions and Commonwealth Program is interesting because it's not mandatory upon the trustees; it's permissive. As I read the charter, any time the trustees want to stop giving it [protected status] to the Dominions and Colonies, they could. But they could not take money from the basic endowment and spend it in the British Dominions and Colonies; that is, they could decrease the fund but they couldn't increase it. This never came to a test because they always did, in fact, reserve that money for the British Dominions and Colonies. [*Interviewer: They were 'empowered' to use the income, but not 'enjoined' to use it?*] That's right. That's typical lawyer's language, where every word has been argued about for three or four days. My recollection is that this [charter change to make the BDC capital $12 million] is something the counsel just did, and said, 'We have to do this to be in the clear,' and we said, 'Fine,' and went along with it." Dollard, CCOH, 171.

12   For the 1941–1942 amounts, see CCNYAR, 1942, 72, 110, and for the 1945–1946 amounts, see CCNYAR, 1946, 68, 82, and 83.

13   CCNYAR, 1943, 38–39. For Keppel's role in the State Department, see Arthur Ringland, *The Organization of Voluntary Foreign Aid: 1939–1953*, State Department Economic Cooperation Series (Washington, DC: US Government Printing Office, March 15, 1954), 2.

14   The trustees were eager to find a president fairly soon. Unlike in 1919 and 1921, this time no board members were willing to assume the presidency. The committee on the presidency was appointed by the board chair in September 1944, with Russell Leffingwell as chairman, and members included Nicholas Murray Butler, Henry James, Nicholas Kelley, and Elihu Root Jr. Taken together, these board members had served a total of seventy-one years. They surely would have had a sense of the right president to follow the deeply loved Keppel and the much-admired Jessup. Instead, according to the biographer of AT&T public relations guru and Corporation trustee Arthur Page, Jessup's death "touched off a battle over naming a successor," with Butler campaigning for Brown University president Henry Wriston, while most other trustees opposed Wriston as "too controversial." For more details, see Noel L. Griese, *Arthur W. Page: Publisher, Public Relations Pioneer, Patriot* (Tucker, GA: Anvil, 2001), 270. The board minutes reflected a

more measured approach; the committee "surveyed a wide field of possibilities, had taken counsel with competent persons and with the Trustees, and, after full consideration, decided to recommend that Mr. Devereux C. Josephs be appointed President of the Corporation." CCNY, Minutes of the Board of Trustees, XXII, 62, May 17, 1945, CCNY Records, RBML-CUL.

15   "The Morgan Guaranty Trust," "Bank History, Morgan Guaranty Trust Company of New York," available at: http://www.smokershistory.com/MorganGT.html.

16   Dollard, CCOH, 320–321, 326.

17   Pendleton Herring, *Reminiscences of Edward Pendleton Herring: Oral History, 1967*, interviewed by Isabel S. Grossner, Carnegie Corporation Project: Oral History, 1966–1970, CCOH-CUL, 3, 5, 10, 39 (hereafter "Herring, CCOH").

18   John Gardner, *Reminiscences of John Gardner: Oral History, 2000*, interviewed by Sharon Zane, Carnegie Corporation Project, Part 2: Oral History, 1996–2004, CCOH-CUL, 9–10, 18, 60, 69–70, 83 (hereafter "Gardner, CCOH, 2000"); John Gardner, *Reminiscences of John Gardner: Oral History, 1971*, interviewed by Isabel S. Grossner, Carnegie Corporation Project: Oral History, 1966–1970, CCOH-CUL, 9–10, 124 (hereafter "Gardner, CCOHC, 1971"); and Devereux Josephs, *The Reminiscences of Devereux Colt Josephs: Oral History, 1969*, interviewed by Isabel S. Grossner, Carnegie Corporation Project: Oral History, 1966–1970, CCOH-CUL, 23–24 (hereafter "Josephs, CCOH").

19   Josephs presented ideas on how to reorganize the board's membership, that is, how to reduce the number of ex officio trustees (those serving in their capacity as head of a Carnegie institution and for as long as they held that position) and increase the number of term members (members appointed in their own right, not because they held a seat on the board as president of a Carnegie institution). Eventually the board agreed. CCNY, Minutes of the Board of Trustees, XXIII, 44–46, January 17, 1946, CCNY Records, RBML-CUL.

20   CCNYAR, 1941, 83, and 1946, 61.

21   The Foundation Center estimates that before 1940 there were 640 large foundations (each with assets equivalent to $1,000,000 in 2006–2007). That number increased to 794 in the 1940s, then jumped to 1,915 in the 1950s; Steven Lawrence and Reina Mukai, *Foundation Growth and Giving Estimates: Current Outlook*, Foundations Today Series (New York: Foundation Center, 2009), 4. Many were working in the field of education, and some were making grants overseas as well. As Josephs commented in 1946, "It may be of interest to note here that the total value of three of the larger foundations with which educational institutions and agencies have had extensive dealings decreased during the period 1911–1941, while the permanent funds of colleges and universities increased from $260,000,000 to $1,760,000,000." CCNYAR, 1946, 50.

22   Michael Warner, *The Office of Strategic Services: America's First Intelligence Agency* (Washington, DC: Public Affairs, Central Intelligence Agency, 2000), available at: https://www.cia.gov/library/center-for-the-study-of-intelligence/csi-publications/books-and-monographs/oss/index.htm (posted March 15, 2007).

23   CCNYAR, 1945, 15. Josephs's "Inaugural Report," as he called it, also noted that "foundations do not distribute largess. They search hard for intelligent ways to use their money and are indebted to the wise and skillful who accept grants and do the work." Furthermore, he talked about the basic premise of the Corporation: "This is an American foundation most of whose resources are dedicated to the service of the American people. It is operated to promote the American way of life. Foundations are conscious of criticism leveled at them for influencing public opinion. Such sensitiveness is proper in respect to some conflicts in American life, but should never apply to the primary concepts of that way of life. This Corporation should not hesitate to provide funds to those who can show better ways to democracy, to the freedoms of thought, race, religion, and enterprise. These are purposes to be openly avowed.... It is not the

function of this fund simply to give money in the order of application to those whose plans are acceptable. Such projects, large or small, as may be selected for support must be not only of public interest but, because the Corporation income is limited, they must have great possibility of public benefit." Ibid., 14–16.

24 CCNYAR, 1945, 22–23.

25 Robert Lester, who was hired as Keppel's assistant and then became Corporation secretary in 1928, was the longest-serving staff member under Keppel. In 1934 Keppel hired Florence Anderson, the first woman to handle grants (in the arts and music), in addition to the administrative and secretarial duties for which she had been originally hired. In 1938 he hired another assistant, Charles Dollard, to help his main staff assistant, John Russell (hired in 1931). Keppel hired Stephen Stackpole in 1940 to help primarily with the work in Canada. When Walter Jessup became president, he was already quite familiar with Lester, Dollard, Anderson, and Stackpole because he had served for twelve years on the Corporation's board, filling the seat reserved for the president of the Carnegie Foundation for the Advancement of Teaching.

26 "I don't want an assistant. I want a partner," Devereux Josephs, as quoted in Dollard, CCOH, 100. In his second essay, Josephs described his approach to hiring and working with staff: he sought staff who were talented generalists and could move across a variety of fields without being tied to a particular area. As he had earlier explained to Dollard, Josephs wanted staff to "operate more in the manner of general partners than as corporate officers with defined hierarchies or restricted departments." CCNYAR, 1946, 17.

27 Oliver Carmichael had become president of the Carnegie Foundation for the Advancement of Teaching, had been a Rhodes Scholar at Oxford, and had served in World War II with the British in India and South Africa as well as with the US Army. He was deeply involved in the education system of the United States, and as a Southerner—he hailed from Alabama—he was especially concerned about education in the South. He agreed to serve not only as president of the Foundation and trustee of the Corporation, but also as a full staff member for the Corporation. Pendleton Herring, a political scientist from Harvard, was hired to explore issues related to problems of government; he was then still on leave as director of the Atomic Energy Commission of the United Nations. John Gardner came in to interview while on his way home to California after serving in Europe with the Marines. Josephs recalled thinking that Gardner was "the perfect person to hire for Carnegie Corporation." After a quick consultation with Dollard, Josephs offered Gardner the job on the day of his interview. Gardner, a psychologist with a degree from Stanford University, had been teaching at the University of California, Connecticut College, and Mount Holyoke. He, too, was hired to work on issues related to government. CCNYAR, 1946, 14–18.

28 Ibid., 16. In helping to found the CFR, Shepardson had worked closely with the Council's UK counterpart, the Royal Institute of International Affairs, one of the UK institutions that Keppel often visited; the Corporation had supported it in the 1930s. Thus, his contacts in the United Kingdom with the British Foreign Office and the Colonial Office were comparable to those of the Corporation. In his work with the Rockefeller Foundation in the 1930s, he had helped organize meetings around agriculture and strengthening US universities in this area. Although he had very limited relations with the dominions and colonies, his familiarity with his British counterparts and the Rockefeller Foundation made him an attractive choice to revive the Corporation's overseas grant-making in the British Commonwealth. See Franklin D. Roosevelt Library, "The Papers of Whitney Hart Shepardson, 1910–1966: A Descriptive List," available at: http://www.fdrlibrary.marist.edu/archives/pdfs/findingaids/findingaid_shepardson.pdf.

29 "The opportunity, following the war, for service to the welfare of mankind will be unprecedented in the history of the Foundation"; President Raymond B. Fosdick, "Agenda of Suggested

Topics for Discussion at the Board of Trustees of the Rockefeller Foundation" (memo to the Rockefeller Foundation Board of Trustees), April 4, 1945, Folder 174, Box 23, Series 900, Record Group 3.1, FA112, Rockefeller Foundation records, Rockefeller Archives Center (RAC). Both foundation presidents, Fosdick and Josephs, clearly saw the role their institutions could play in strengthening America's role in sustaining peace, and they saw how the two institutions could reinforce each other's efforts. Hence, this period reflects unusually close collaboration on the profound international challenges confronting the country and the citizenry immediately following the war.

30   These included the Institute of Pacific Relations, the Council on Foreign Relations, the Foreign Policy Association, and Brookings Institution, all Corporation partners for most of the previous two decades.

31   Glenn Edwin Hoover, *Twentieth Century Economic Thought* (1950; reprint, New York: Philosophical Society, 1970), 524.

32   As Josephs wrote in his 1946 presidential essay, "Foremost of those welcomed back is Charles Dollard.... The competence which he brought to his Army assignment and which won for him the award of the Legion of Merit is again at the disposal of the Corporation and its constituency at this most important time." CCNYAR, 1946, 14. For a more critical assessment, see Lagemann, *The Politics of Knowledge*, 159.

33   Dollard hired James Perkins (vice president of Swarthmore College on leave as chairman of the Research and Development Board of the Department of Defense) in 1950 as executive associate; William Marvel (with the State Department and the Army in Latin America and China, Marvel had also taught international relations at Princeton, Yale, and the US Military Academy), primarily to assist with international relations and area studies work; and Eugene Burdock, a classicist and psychologist from the University of Illinois. He retained Whitney Shepardson as head and Stephen Stackpole as assistant head of the British Dominions and Colonies Fund. When Shepardson left in 1953, as discussed later in the chapter, Dollard changed the status and name of the BDC Fund from a fund to a program, and asked Stackpole to head the program; in 1953 he hired Alan Pifer (with experience in the Fulbright Commission office in London and Africa) as Stackpole's assistant. Dollard broke a barrier in 1951 by appointing Florence Anderson the Corporation's first female officer (associate secretary) and promoting Margaret Mahoney from assistant to the secretary to assistant secretary of the Corporation. Dollard's only other new hire was Robert Wert (on the presidential staff at Stanford University), who joined the Corporation toward the end of Dollard's tenure; Dollard also appointed Gardner as vice president. Commenting on writing the Annual Report, for example, he made it clear that he regarded his colleagues as close collaborators: "The record should show, however, that, like the quarterback of any other team, the President's role is to call plays which are part of the total strategy perfected in collaboration with the other officers of the Corporation and the members of the board." CCNYAR, 1950, 13.

34   CCNYAR, 1948, 23; for a detailed discussion of the Corporation's grant-making in the social sciences during this period, see Lagemann, *The Politics of Knowledge*, ch. 7.

35   As Dollard noted, the Ford Foundation had been chartered by the state of Michigan in 1936. As a result of a study group organized by the Ford trustees in 1948, the Gaither Study Committee, the Foundation expanded its scope to become a truly international foundation; see Ford Foundation, "History," available at: www.fordfoundation.org/about-us/history (accessed January 3, 2014), and Gaither Study Committee, *Report of the Study for the Ford Foundation on Policy and Program* (Detroit: Ford Foundation, November 1949), available at: www.fordfoundation.org/pdfs/about/gaither-report.pdf (accessed January 3, 2014). The trustees asked Paul Hoffman, the remarkable businessman and public servant who had spearheaded the Marshall

Plan, to be the president of the newly constituted foundation. Practically from day one in 1950, its budget for grants exceeded $25 million per year; see Francis X. Sutton, "The Ford Foundation: The Early Years," *Daedalus: Philanthropy, Patronage, Politics* 116, no. 1 (Winter 1987): 41–91. The National Science Foundation was the brainchild of Vannevar Bush, a Carnegie Corporation board member and president of the Carnegie Institution of Washington. His report "The Endless Frontier" prompted congressional action that raised the NSF endowment to $3.5 million. Comparing the NSF and Ford in that order, Dollard wryly observed that the funding levels were David and Goliath in reverse. Yet he was confident that the NSF would become a significant grant-making institution. For the Gates Foundation comparison, see Stanley N. Katz, "The Chronicle Review: Beware Big Donors," *Chronicle of Higher Education* (March 25, 2012), available at: http://chronicle.com/article/Big-Philanthropy-Role in/131275 (accessed October 7, 2012).

36 CCNY, Agenda Book of the Board of Trustees, November 14, 1950, "This Brave New World" (agenda item), 8–9, CCNY Records, RBML-CUL.

37 CCNYAR, 1951, 31 (emphasis in original).

38 CCNYAR, 1954, 38.

39 CCNYAR, 1954, "Appendix: Charles Dollard, Introductory Statement to Special Committee to Investigate Tax-Exempt Foundations," 79–98.

40 CCNYAR, 1954, 38–39.

41 Dennis McIlnay, "Philanthropy at Fifty: Four Moments in Time," *Foundation News and Commentary* 39, no. 5 (September–October 1998), available at: www.foundationnews.org\CME\article.cfm?ID=1053, 3 of 7.

42 CCNY, Agenda Book of the Board of Trustees, January 17, 1952, "For the Information of the Trustees" (agenda item), 5, CCNY Records, RBML-CUL. In succinctly presenting the issues associated with the conduct of evaluation and the challenges of effective communication, this memo remains apt in the twenty-first century.

43 In the twenty-first century, as described in Chapter 8, the *Carnegie Quarterly* was replaced by a series of publications dedicated to meeting the Corporation's dissemination mission. One specific publication, for example, *Carnegie Results*, concentrates on analyses of the results of the grants programs.

44 Gardner, CCOH, 2000, 69–70, 83.

45 The board remained stable through the many years of service of Nicholas Murray Butler (1925–1945; chair, 1937–1945), Samuel Harden Church (1914–1943), Russell Leffingwell (1923–1959), Elihu Root Jr. (1937–1960), and Frederick Osborn (1936–1962). Keppel's long tenure of nineteen years had also reinforced the sense of purpose even when disagreements arose over specific activities. Keppel and his fellow trustees set a standard for future boards.

46 Marshall (1947–1949) had served as Army chief of staff throughout World War II and would soon become US secretary of state, in which role he initiated the European Recovery Plan (the "Marshall Plan"), an international program of unprecedented scale for rebuilding war-torn Europe. He stepped down from the board in November 1950. While a man of Marshall's international stature would have been difficult to replace, the board attempted to fill his shoes with another military man, Charles Spofford (1953-1973), an accomplished attorney and a brigadier general during the war.

47 Charles Allen Thomas (1951–1965) was the author of the 1946 "Report on the International Control of Atomic Energy" (the Acheson-Lilienthal Report), a topic of increasing concern to the Corporation; this was the first statement to call for establishing a US atomic energy policy and an international agency that would "own the fissile materials." In 1953 the board elected Gwilym Price (1953–1967), an Andrew Carnegie–like individual who was born in Pittsburgh, the son of a tin mill worker who died when Price was sixteen. A high school dropout (ironically,

it was Carnegie High School that he quit to support his widowed mother), Price went on to become the youngest graduate of the University of Pittsburgh Law School and then the CEO of Westinghouse Corporation. *Time* magazine called him "Mr. Expansion" for his expansionary views of business and the economy. Balancing the appointment of internationally oriented board members, however, was the departure in 1931 of Dr. Nicholas Murray Butler, Nobel Laureate and longtime president of the Carnegie Endowment for International Peace. His resignation from that position, at the age of eighty-three, also concluded his ex officio membership on the Corporation board, after twenty years as a trustee. By the time Gardner became acting president, the board had changed in another important respect: only Vannevar Bush (the Carnegie Institution of Washington) and Oliver Carmichael (Carnegie Foundation for the Advancement of Teaching) represented Carnegie institutions. Three other board members during this period were William Frew, president, Carnegie Institute of Pittsburgh (1943–1948); Morris Hadley, a lawyer and president of the New York Public Library (1947–1967); and Leroy A. Wilson, president, American Telephone and Telegraph (1948–1951). Dates from Lagemann, *The Politics of Knowledge*, 317.

48   CCNYAR, 1946, 20. He added at the end: "Knowledge of other cultures, the economic aspirations of other countries, European tensions, and Asiatic ambitions are only a few of the many related subjects that suddenly belong in the consciousness of every voter. In this country there is no longer any room for 'foreign' affairs." Ibid., 22.

49   As Josephs and the joint committee reported to the other trustees, "It is certain that peace cannot be continued unless this country shoulders its responsibility towards it. We are a nation grown great because of the isolation that most of us still subconsciously cherish. We Americans are not to become permanently world-minded by listening to the tales of our returning veterans. We have got to learn and to learn we have got to study. We will never move from a negative to a positive force for peace until the Mississippi Valley, the State of Texas, the sea coasts, and all the other parts of the country equally grow familiar with the rest of the world, admire what they can of it, understand what they cannot admire, and resolve to contribute patience and judicious compromise to every point of friction. And, if we are not a positive force for peace, it cannot endure." CCNY, Agenda Book of the Board of Trustees, November 20, 1945 (agenda item), 2, CCNY Records, RBML-CUL.

50   Ibid., 3.

51   Participants included Executive Committee members Josephs, Kelley, Leffingwell, and Root; invited board members Burgess, Bush, Carmichael, James, and Page; and invited staff members Dollard, Herring (newly appointed), Shepardson (newly appointed), and C. Herbert Lee, the investment officer since 1937.

52   CCNY, Minutes of the Executive Committee, XXIII, 91, September 17, 1946, CCNY Records, RBML-CUL.

53   CCNY, Agenda Book of the Executive Committee, April 18, 1946, "International Relations and the Corporation" (agenda item), 2, CCNY Records, RBML-CUL.

54   Ibid., 3.

55   Ibid., 3–4.

56   Ibid.

57   CCNY, Agenda Book of the Executive Committee, April 18, 1946, "International Relations and Carnegie Corporation: An Introduction" (agenda item), 1, CCNY Records, RBML-CUL.

58   CCNY, Agenda Book of the Board of Trustees, May 21, 1953, "For the Information of the Trustees: The Corporation Program in International Affairs" (agenda item), 9–20, CCNY Records, RBML-CUL.

59   Rockefeller Archive Center, 100 Years: The Rockefeller Foundation, "Area Studies,"

available at: rockefeller100.org/exhibits/show/social_sciences/area-studies (accessed January 3, 2014); Sutton, "The Ford Foundation: The Early Years," 41–91; Francis X. Sutton, "Nation-Building in the Heyday of the Classic Development Ideology," in *Nation-Building Beyond Afghanistan and Iraq*, ed. Francis Fukuyama, 42–63 (Baltimore: Johns Hopkins University Press, 2006), 9.

60 The Rockefeller Foundation focused on educating Americans about Latin America, the Far East, the Near East, the Soviet Union, and the Slavic region, concentrating in the 1930s primarily on language training and some broader coursework while also extensively aiding academic programs in anthropology in US universities and field studies in developing countries. The pioneering anthropologist Franz Boaz, for example, who used a scientific approach in his studies, was one of Rockefeller's major grantees; in the 1930s, he also received multiple grants from the Corporation. Starting in the mid- to late 1940s, the Rockefeller Foundation renewed its aid to Princeton University's Near Eastern Studies program and to the Hoover Institute at Stanford University for its program in Slavonic studies. In 1945 it began funding Russian research and language training at Columbia University. As discussed in Chapter 3, both the Rockefeller Foundation and the Corporation had contributed to the Institute of Pacific Relations' extensive program of meetings. The Laura Spelman Rockefeller Memorial helped to found the University of Hawaii–based Institute in 1925, and the Corporation modestly funded its American branch and supported some of the meetings. As further discussed in Chapter 3, the Corporation's earlier support of foreign language training and Charles Loram's revealing field research on different population groups—which led to the cross-cultural studies undertaken by George Murdoch and others also at Yale—evolved into a major new Corporation effort that in 1949 created the Human Area Relations Files. For more details, see Rockefeller Foundation Annual Report, 1946, 32–34, 39–40; CCNY, Agenda Book of the Executive Committee, April 18, 1946, "International Relations and Carnegie Corporation" (agenda item), 1–4, and two exhibits; CCNY, Agenda Book of the Board of Trustees, September 17, 1946, "A Long Term Program: A Statement by the President of the Corporation" (agenda item), 3–6; CCNYAR, 1946, 20–24; all in CCNY Records, RBML-CUL.

61 Waldo G. Leland, letter and proposal to Rockefeller Foundation (identical letter sent to Carnegie Corporation), December 7, 1942, "The Ethnogeographic Board, 1942–1947," 1, Folder 3936, Box 331, Series 200S, Record Group 1.1, FA386, Rockefeller Foundation records, RAC.

62 Matthew Farish, "Archiving Areas: The Ethnogeographic Board and the Second World War," *Annals of the Association of American Geographers* 95, no. 3 (2005): 663–679; Lagemann, *Politics of Knowledge*, 173–174; David H. Price, *Anthropological Intelligence: The Deployment and Neglect of American Anthropology in the Second World War* (Durham, NC: Duke University Press, 2008), 91–116.

63 Lagemann, *The Politics of Knowledge*, 174–175; Rockefeller Foundation, Annual Report, 1947, 43–45, 225–235; Charles B. Fahs, "Area Studies: An Outline of Humanities Concern," December 3, 1946, Folder 165, Box 31, Series 900, Record Group 3.2, Rockefeller Foundation records, RAC (also available as Charles B. Fahs, "Definition of Area Studies," Rockefeller Archive Center, 100 Years: The Rockefeller Foundation, available at: http://rockefeller100.org/items/show/1794 (accessed January 9, 2014).

64 The broad curriculum for area studies had its parallel in domestic grant-making, under both Josephs and Dollard—first for liberal studies, then for general studies and programs on citizenship—so that Americans could also receive in-depth exposure to American values in the context of the responsibilities of citizenship. Citizenship and international activities were linked in the minds of staff. For a thoughtful discussion of this rationale, see Akira Iriye, "The Role of Philanthropy and Civil Society in US Foreign Relations," in *Philanthropy and Reconciliation:*

Rebuilding Postwar US-Japan Relations, ed. Yamamoto Tadashi, Akira Iriye, and Iokibe Mahota (Tokyo: Japan Center for International Exchange, 2006), 46–47.

65   Rockefeller Foundation Annual Report, 1945, 13–15. Even in the early twenty-first century, the Corporation's experience with Russian studies continues to attract scholars, analysts, and journalists. David Engerman in 2009 published a detailed and balanced analysis of the field, including the Corporation's efforts, *Know Your Enemy: The Rise and Fall of America's Soviet Experts* (New York: Oxford University Press, 2009); see also Lagemann, *The Politics of Knowledge*, 172–175.

66   Paul Buck, *The Reminiscences of Paul Buck: Oral History, 1967*, interviewed by Isabel S. Grossner, Carnegie Corporation Project: Oral History, 1966–1970, CCOH-CUL, 3 (hereafter "Buck, CCOH").

67   CCNY, Agenda Book of the Board of Trustees, March 18, 1948, "Harvard University: Support for the Russian Research Center—Preliminary Statement Following Planning Grant of $100,000 Made in October 1947" (agenda item), 23–25, CCNY Records, RBML-CUL.

68   Clyde Kluckhohn was well known for his in-depth work with the Navajo and his cultural studies on Japan during World War II, which had been used by the War Department. He had never worked on Russia and did not speak Russian, but as Engerman points out, this fit with the results from his wartime studies of Japan, when he had produced compelling insights about Japanese culture that had decisively influenced military decisions without having ever visited Japan and without speaking the language. With the selection of this controversial grant, the Corporation expanded the scope of area studies. For a full recounting, see Engerman, *Know Your Enemy*, 44, 53; see also, generally, Buck, CCOH, esp. 17–30.

69   Sigmund Diamond, *Compromised Campus: The Collaboration of Universities with the Intelligence Community, 1945–1955* (New York: Oxford University Press, 1992), 50–110; see also Engerman, *Know Your Enemy*, and Buck, COHC.

70   Buck, COHC, 45. Buck also felt that the Center should even be restricted from contracting with the US Air Force for a study on the Russian economy (36–37).

71   Ibid., 46.

72   Arthur Schlesinger Jr., "Who Was Henry A. Wallace? The Story of a Perplexing and Indomitably Naive Public Servant," *Los Angeles Times*, March 12, 2000.

73   Buck, CCOH, 39–46. Buck commented that Hughes became very important in the field of history and even ran for the Senate later on; see also Diamond, *Compromised Campus*, 74–76; For a more nuanced perspective from the viewpoint of the post–Cold War twenty-first century, see Engerman, *Know Your Enemy*.

74   In 1952, at the Corporation's request, Harvard put together a seven-"gentlemen" member external review committee, including Henry Wriston, president of Brown University; Francis Plimpton, a lawyer-scholar at Debevoise and Plimpton; and J. Douglas Brown, dean of the faculty at Princeton. CCNY, Minutes of the Board of Trustees, 4, January 17, 1952, CCNY Records, RBML-CUL.

75   CCNY, Agenda Book of the Board of Trustees, May 21, 1953, "Foreign Area Studies" (agenda item), 9–12, CCNY Records, RBML-CUL; a more critical perspective on the interdisciplinarity of the work is given in Lagemann, *The Politics of Knowledge*, 175.

76   The board meeting agenda item describing the project observed that the Soviet Union was graduating more than twice as many scientists and engineers as the United States: "It is clear that Russia is making an heroic effort to achieve technological superiority." MIT was studying the quality of this education and sought a fuller understanding of the role of science in Soviet society. Corporation staff members recommended providing the last-mile funds, and the board agreed, all concerned being certain that this was an important subject. CCNY, Agenda Book of

the Board of Trustees, November 16, 1954 , "Massachusetts Institute of Technology: Grant of $20,000 for the Study of Scientific Education" (agenda item), 15, CCNY Records, RBML-CUL.

77   Although there have been variations in numbers, reflecting the end of the Cold War, a recent low estimate puts the number of Russian study and language programs in North America at 161. Russkiy Mir Foundation, "Dynamics of Russian Language Programs in USA: Recent Trends," November 15, 2011, available at: http://www.russkiymir.ru/russkiymir/en/publications/articles/article0222.html (accessed April 6, 2012).

78   CCNY, Agenda Book of the Board of Trustees, January 16, 1947, "A Program in Area Studies: Grant of $1,100,000 to Be Allocated to Twelve or More Universities" (agenda item), 8, CCNY Records, RBML-CUL; CCNY, Agenda Book of the Board of Trustees, March 20, 1947, "Program of Area Studies in Universities: Report of Progress" (agenda item), 5, CCNY Records, RBML-CUL. The Rockefeller Foundation had been funding work in Latin American studies since the 1930s, first through the American Council on Learned Studies and then through universities—Michigan, Texas, Duke, Tulane, and North Carolina—as well as through grants in Mexico; for a detailed discussion, see Helen Delpar, *Looking South: The Evolution of Latin Americanist Scholarship in the United States, 1850–1975* (Tuscaloosa: University of Alabama Press, 2008), 112–118. During the war years, both foundations also linked with the Council on Inter-American Affairs, run by Nelson Rockefeller; see ibid., 118.

79   CCNY, Minutes of the Board of Trustees, 7, January 16, 1947, CCNY Records, RBML-CUL.

80   CCNY, Minutes of the Board of Trustees, 5–6, March 20, 1947, CCNY Records, RBML-CUL; CCNY, Agenda Book of the Board of Trustees, November 14, 1950, "University of Washington: Grant of $75,000 in Support of Research on Inner Asia and Asiatic Russia" (agenda item), CCNY Records, RBML-CUL.

81   An omnibus agenda item in 1952 reviewed the centers and provided the rationale for several of the centers that had been receiving support for several years. CCNY, Agenda Book of the Board of Trustees, May 15, 1947, "Review of Corporation Activities" (agenda item), 11–13, and March 20, 1952, "Area Study Centers" (agenda item), 2–5, CCNY Records, RBML-CUL.

82   CCNYAR, 1953, 31, 37.

83   CCNYAR, 1949, 41; 1947, 29; and 1948, 41.

84   CCNY, Agenda Book of the Board of Trustees, May 21, 1953, "University of Toronto: Grant of $42,000 for Development of East-Asiatic Studies" (agenda item), 38–39, CCNY Records, RBML-CUL.

85   CCNYAR, 1952, 39.

86   CCNY, Agenda Book of the Board of Trustees, May 20, 1948, "Columbia University: European Area Studies" (agenda item), 14, and March 17, 1949, "Columbia University: Grant of $100,000 for (a) Courses in Asiatic Civilization" (agenda item), 14, CCNY Records, RBML-CUL.

87   Robert D. Calkins, record of interview with John Gardner, December 19 and 20, 1950, Folder 2785, Box 267, Series 1.2, FA058, General Education board records, RAC.

88   CCNY, Agenda Book of the Board of Trustees, November 21, 1951, "Institute of International Education: Grant of $30,000 for Reconnaissance in Africa" (agenda item), 26, CCNY Records, RBML-CUL.

89   See, for example, Leonard W. Doob, "Information Services in Central Africa," *Public Opinion Quarterly* 17, no. 1 (1953); Leonard W. Doob, "The Use of Different Test Items in Nonliterate Societies," *Public Opinion Quarterly* 21, no. 4 (1957–1958).

90   Corporation staff members had considerable respect for Herskovits because he was the first author to get his book out as part of the Myrdal study, and also because they valued his

position that African cultures needed to be understood separate from African American culture. CCNY, Agenda Book of the Board of Trustees, October 21, 1948, "Northwestern University: Grant of $30,000 Toward Support of Its African Research Program" (agenda item), 13, CCNY Records, RBML-CUL.

91　CCNY, Minutes of the Board of Trustees, XXVI, 20, January 18, 1951, and XXVII, 53, November 20, 1951, CCNY Records, RBML-CUL.

92　"Obituary: Caryl Haskins, 93; Scientific Renaissance Man," *Los Angeles Times*, October 13, 2001.

93　CCNY, Agenda Book of the Board of Trustees, May 21,1953, "For the Information of the Trustees: the Corporation's International Affairs" (agenda item), 9–20, CCNY Records, RBML-CUL.

94　Ibid., 19.

95　Richard D. Scarfo, "The History of Title VI and Fulbright–Hays," in *International Education in the New Global Era: Proceedings of a National Policy Conference on the Higher Education Act, Title VI, and Fulbright-Hays Programs*, ed. John N. Hawkins, Carlos Manuel Haro, and Miriam A. Kazanjian, et al., 23–25 (Los Angeles: International Studies and Overseas Programs, 1998), available at: www.international.ucla.edu/pacrim/title6/Over2-Scarfo.pdf; US Department of Education, Office of Postsecondary Education, International Education Programs Service, "International Education Programs Service: Fulbright-Hays Programs: The World Is Our Classroom: Archived Information," available at: http://www2.ed.gov/about/offices/list/ope/iegps/fulbright-hays.html (accessed April 18, 2012).

96　Frank Sutton, "US Strengths: Non-Western Area Studies to 1956: The FAFP," July 15, 1988, 2, unpublished, available from the author.

97　Ibid.; see also Frank Sutton, "The Ford Foundation's Development Program in Africa," *African Studies Bulletin* 3, no. 4 (December 1960): 1–7; Sutton, "The Ford Foundation: The Early Years"; and Sutton, "Nation-Building in the Heyday of the Classic Development Ideology." As some programs continued, their breadth overshadowed their depth and academic respect for them gradually declined, along with funding. In the 1990s, the Ford Foundation would attempt to rebuild area studies through what it called its "cross-border programs." Rockefeller and Ford, the two foundations that had maintained these investments, did some important work to strengthen the field in the 1990s. New approaches to area studies that involved working in cross-disciplinary global and world systems studies evolved from the earlier approach. In the twenty-first century, these programs have taken on increasing significance, and some of the early ones that the Corporation helped to initiate, such as Princeton's program in Near Eastern Studies and others around the country in Eurasian and Central Asian studies and in Asian and Chinese studies, have been revived and greatly enlarged, with increased student demand and faculty interest along with some increase in foundation funding; David S. Wiley and Robert S. Glew, eds., *International and Language Education for a Global Future: Fifty Years of US Title VI and Fulbright-Hays Programs* (East Lansing: Michigan State University Press, 2010), 1, 47–148. Gilbert Merkx notes that Ford Foundation's investments in the 1950s and 1960s were larger than those of the federal government; Gilbert Merkx, "Gulliver's Travels: The History and Consequences of Title VI," in Wiley and Glew, *International and Language Education for a Global Future*, 5. In addition to the Wiley and Glew publication, an excellent review of the Ford Foundation's work is Ford Foundation, *Crossing Borders: Revitalizing Area Studies* (New York: Ford Foundation, 1999).

98　CCNY, Agenda Book of the Board of Trustees, October 21, 1948, "Social Science Research Council: Grant of $130,000 for Area Research Fellowships and Travel Grants" (agenda item), 12, CCNY Records, RBML-CUL. The Council also received support to organize a separate working group on Near East and Middle East studies; the Rockefeller Foundation had supported a working group on Latin American studies for years with the American Council of Learned Societies and then the Social Science Research Council. As mentioned in the previous chapter and earlier in this chapter, Professor George P. Murdoch at Yale had worked with Charles Loram in the education of primitive peoples program and accumulated extensive files on different regions of the world. That information was put to active use during the war, and afterwards, in 1949, Yale and four other universities created the Human Relations Area Files (HRAF), which the Corporation helped launch with a grant of $62,500. As noted in the renewal grant—which provided support for a reserve fund and for assistance with the backlog of work—eleven more universities joined the HRAF project, and the files were used extensively by scholars as well as by the military. Today the HRAF remains a resource for scholars in the social sciences and continues as an inter-university nonprofit consortium; CCNY, Agenda Book of the Board of Trustees, March 18, 1954, "Human Relations Area Files: Grant of $100,000 Toward Support" (agenda item), 21–22, CCNY Records, RBML-CUL; for more recent details, see "Human Relations Area Files: Cultural Information for Education and Research," available at: http://www.yale.edu/hraf/.

99 US Department of State, Bureau of Education and Cultural Affairs, "Fulbright: The Early Years: An Informal History of the Fulbright Program," 2, available at: http://eca.state.gov/fulbright/about-fulbright/history/early-years (accessed February 25, 2012).

100 US Department of State, "Diplomacy in Action: The United States Information and Exchange Act of 1948 (Smith-Mundt Act)," passed January 27, 1948, available at: http://www.state.gov/pdcommission/library/177362.htm (accessed January 6, 2014).

101 Steven Schindler, "Case 25. Facilitating Global Knowledge Creation: University Area Studies Program Ford Foundation 1952," in *Casebook for the Foundation: A Great American Secret*, ed. Joel L. Fleishman, Scott Kohler, and Steven Schindler (New York: Public Affairs, 2007), 73. As Sutton noted, there was great growth in this area, with "spreading enthusiasm for international studies and for non-Western studies in particular. The foundation … could follow the Rockefeller and Carnegie examples in starting and stimulating expanded area studies, and it was quickly engaged in doing so." The Ford Foundation provided over five hundred Foreign Area Fellowships over the period 1952 to 1956. Frances X. Sutton, "US Strengths: Non-Western Area Studies to 1956," 4.

102 Rockefeller Foundation, Board of Trustees meeting, December 15, 1936, "Social Sciences and Humanities: Statement of Program 1936," 11–12, 14, Folder 171, Box 23, Series 900, Record Group 3.1, FA112, Rockefeller Foundation records, RAC; for Carnegie Corporation, see Ekbladh, "Present at the Creation," 118–125.

103 Ekbladh, "Present at the Creation"; CCNY, Agenda Book of the Board of Trustees, November 16, 1954, "Council on Foreign Relations: Grant of $500,000 for Research, Regional Committees, and Fellowships" (agenda item), 5, CCNY Records, RBML-CUL.

104 CCNY, Agenda Book of the Board of Trustees, May 21, 1953, "For the Information of the Trustees: The Corporation Program in International Affairs" (agenda item), 13–14, CCNY Records, RBML-CUL.

105 Leo Pasvolsky, a longtime Brookings staff member, was a senior figure in the wartime State Department and a major influence in drafting the United Nations Charter; see Anita Nolen, "Leo Pasvolsky: A Register of His Papers in the Library of Congress," 2008, revised by Patrick Kerwin, available at: http://lcweb2.loc.gov/service/mss/eadxmlmss/eadpdfmss/2008/ms008035.pdf. "Leo Pasvolsky … was probably the foremost author of the UN charter," according to Stephen Schlesinger, director of the World Policy Institute; see CNN: Transcripts, "Diplomatic License: Current Events at the United Nations," Richard Roth interviewing Stephen Schlesinger, December 24, 2004, available at: http://transcripts.cnn.com/TRANSCRIPTS/0412/24/i_dl.01.html; see also CCNY, Agenda Book of the Board of

Trustees, January 16, 1947, "Brookings Institution: Grant of $35,000 for Summer Conference to Improve Teaching of International Affairs" (agenda item), and January 19, 1950, "Grant of $100,000 for Regional Conferences on Teaching of International Relations" (agenda item), CCNY Records, RBML-CUL; see also Rockefeller Foundation Annual Report, 1947, Social Sciences Division, 207, CCNY Records, RBML-CUL.

106 CCNY, Agenda Book of the Board of Trustees, May 21, 1953, "International Affairs" (agenda item), 14, CCNY Records, RBML-CUL.

107 The Corporation was not clear about what the most productive next steps might be. Staff members were convinced that more focus and depth in research, rather than broad lines of research, were needed: "Indiscriminate interest in all current events in the international field is an intellectual cul-de-sac and is responsible for much shallowness in current research and teaching." This review led them to identify continuing concerns about President Truman's Point Four Program and "their uneasiness at some of the uncritical assumptions implicit in many of the public pronouncements on Point Four." They also pointed to the limited "range of political alternatives open to backward peoples," in particular to the alternative of "leadership which will enable such peoples to resist Soviet subversion." While this rationale was never explicitly made in Corporation support for the work on technical assistance described in the following section, it illustrates how the changing atmosphere in Washington was beginning to seep into Corporation discussions. All quotes from CCNY, Agenda Book of the Board of Trustees, January 18, 1951, "For the Information of Trustees: A Review of Corporation Activities in the Field of International Affairs" (agenda item), 4–6, CCNY Records, RBML-CUL.

108 CCNY, Agenda Book of the Board of Trustees, May 15, 1952, "Problems of Civilian-Military Relations" (agenda item), 39–43, CCNY Records, RBML-CUL. The questions flowed from those two framing issues: how to better define the military and military policy, the extent of civilian concern for military policy, the organization of the Defense Department and its relation to civilian control, how to coordinate military and civilian policy, civilian and judicial control of the military, and the role of the civil service versus the military—all with a number of sub-questions. The secretary of the army and the secretary of the air force supported further work on these issues; they especially focused on the role of the civilian secretaries and their military departments.

109 Ibid., 41.

110 Ibid., 40–41.

111 According to the Columbia University website, Fox was the first person to use the phrase "superpower." See "William T. R. Fox," Wikipedia, available at: http://www.wikicu.com/William_T.R._Fox.

112 In 1945, 1946, and 1947, the Corporation had supported the Council at a fairly modest level for war-related grants. (SSRC had received continuing annual support since 1926.) CCNY, Agenda Book of the Board of Trustees, October 18, 1945, "Social Science Research Council, for Administrative Expenses, $16,000" (agenda item); October 17, 1946, "Discretionary Funds: Social Science Research Council, for a Popular Book on the Wartime Contribution of the Social Sciences (Chase) for $7,500" (agenda item); and October 16, 1947, "Social Science Research Council; Grant of $34,000 for Analysis of Wartime Studies of Soldier Attitudes" (agenda item), CCNY Records, RBML-CUL.

113 CCNY, Agenda Book of the Board of Trustees, March 18, 1954, "Social Science Research Council: Grant of $75,000 for Studies on American Military Policy" (agenda item), 15–16, CCNY Records, RBML-CUL. In 1956 the committee consolidated work under the rubric of national security studies and was funded by the Corporation for another several years, as discussed in Chapter 5.

114 As Fox later recalled, Dwight D. Eisenhower had conceived the idea of the Institute of

War and Peace Studies when he was president of Columbia (1948 to 1953) and had insisted that Fox take the lead in establishing and directing the Institute. Building on Earle's international security studies seminars, Fox created the field of national security studies, together with the Institute of War and Peace Studies and the Social Science Research Council committee, all with Corporation sponsorship; Fox, COHC, 2. For the grant details, see CCNY, Agenda Book of the Board of Trustees, May 21, 1953, "Columbia University: Grant of $63,000 for a Study of Civil-Military Relations" (agenda item), 23–24, CCNY Records, RBML-CUL.

115 Fox, CCOH, 4.

116 CCNYAR, 1953, 38.

117 CCNY, Agenda Book of the Board of Trustees, March 21, 1946, "Program on Public Understanding of Atomic Energy" (agenda item), 20, CCNY Records, RBML-CUL; "Rockefeller Foundation Program and Policy Report on Grants Made to Date: The Atomic Bomb," July 9, 1946, Folder 167, Box 31, Series 900, Record Group 3.2, FA112, Rockefeller Foundation records, RAC.

118 Rockefeller Foundation, "Minutes of the Rockefeller Foundation Regarding the Social Science Research Council's Investigation into the Social Implications of Atomic Energy," Rockefeller Archive Center, 100 Years: The Rockefeller Foundation, available at: http://rockefeller100.org/items/show/5525; see also "Social Science Research Council," Rockefeller Archive Center, 100 Years: The Rockefeller Foundation, available at: http://rockefeller100.org/exhibits/show/social_sciences/social-science-research-counci (accessed January 4, 2014).

119 James P. Delgado, "Operations Crossroads," in *The Archaeology of the Atomic Bomb: A Submerged Cultural Resources Assessment of the Sunken Fleet of Operation Crossroads at Bikini and Kwajalein Atoll Lagoons, Republic of the Marshall Islands*, ed. James P. Delgado et al. (Santa Fe, NM: US Department of the Interior, National Park Service, Submerged Cultural Resources Unit, National Maritime Initiative).

120 Rockefeller Archive Center, "Social Science Research Council."

121 CCNY, Agenda Book of the Board of Trustees, March 18, 1954, "Social Science Research Council" (agenda item), 15, CCNY Records, RBML-CUL.

122 These activities included graduate schools and area institutes; the Council of Foreign Relations and its twenty-four committees; the Foreign Policy Association in its coordination of the World Affairs Councils and special projects; the Brookings Institution bringing together teachers, US State Department officials, and representatives of the military to discuss foreign relations; and the Carnegie Endowment for International Peace for work on public understanding, particularly of the United Nations. CCNYAR, 1950, 24–26.

123 Ibid., 25.

124 Ibid., 24.

125 Ibid., Dollard closed his somewhat gloomy assessment on an upbeat note. Despite the dark days, the recognition of American strengths, particularly the increasing role that universities and colleges were playing in American intellectual life, left him hopeful: "Yet one need not be mad to be optimistic as to the long view." Ibid.

126 CCNY, Agenda Book of the Board of Trustees, January 17, 1946, "Institute of Pacific Relations" (agenda item), 4, CCNY Records, RBML-CUL.

127 CCNY, Agenda Book of the Board of Trustees, January 16, 1947, "Institute of Pacific Relations" (agenda item), 28, CCNY Records, RBML-CUL. The Institute suffered fatal damage from the McCarthy Era witch hunts. For an informative account of the Institute, its demise, and its lasting impact, see Paul F. Hooper, ed., *Remembering the Institute of Pacific Relations: The Memoirs of William L. Holland* (Tokyo: Ryukei Shysha, 1995).

128 The Council on Foreign Relations, for example, had received support from different Rockefeller family members and entities for its launch in 1921; see "Council on Foreign

Relations—Research," Folder 889, Box 98, Series 100S, Record Group 1.1, FA386, Rockefeller Foundation records, RAC. In 1954 a CFR proposal to the Rockefeller Foundation indicated the range of support from Rockefeller, Carnegie Corporation, and, increasingly, the Ford Foundation; document from November 12, 1954, Folder 883, Box 98, Series 100S, Record Group 1.1, FA386, Rockefeller Foundation records, RAC; CCNY, Agenda Book of the Board of Trustees, November 16, 1954, "Council on Foreign Relations: Grant of $500,000 for Research, Regional Committees, and Fellowships" (agenda item), 5–6, CCNY Records, RBML-CUL. Peter Grose also notes the $500,000 awarded in support of the Council by the Rockefeller Foundation as well as the $1.5 million provided by the Ford Foundation; Grose, *Continuing the Inquiry*, 29.

129 CCNY, Agenda Book of the Executive Committee, September 17, 1946, "Carnegie Endowment for International Peace" (agenda item), 12, CCNY Records, RBML-CUL.

130 CCNY, Agenda Book of the Board of Trustees, May 15, 1947, "Carnegie Endowment for International Peace: Grant of $30,000 for United Nations News" (agenda item), 19, CCNY Records, RBML-CUL. The Corporation renewed support at this modest level periodically for several years.

131 For the Church Peace Union, see, for example, CCNY, Agenda Book of the Board of Trustees, March 21, 1945, "Church Peace Union" (agenda item), 6, CCNY Records, RBML-CUL. The Union, like the Endowment, always sought significant funding from the Corporation and was similarly rebuffed continuously. For the Federal Council, see CCNY, Agenda Book of the Board of Trustees, May 16, 1946, "Discretionary Fund" (agenda item), 15, CCNY Records, RBML-CUL.

132 CCNY, Agenda Book of the Board of Trustees, May 21, 1953, "International Affairs" (agenda item), 18–19, CCNY Records, RBML-CUL.

133 See, for example, CCNY, Agenda Book of the Board of Trustees, May 15, 1947, "World Affairs Council (San Francisco): Grant of $16,000 for Support" (agenda item), 28, CCNY Records, RBML-CUL.

134 CCNY, Agenda Book of the Board of Trustees, January 19, 1950, "Institute of International Education: Grant of $32,000 (BDC) for Supervision of African Students in the United States" (agenda item), 20, CCNY Records, RBML-CUL.

135 CCNY, Agenda Book of the Executive Committee, April 18, 1946, "International Relations and Carnegie Corporation: II. The Area of International Contacts" (agenda item), 3, CCNY Records, RBML-CUL.

136 CCNY, Agenda Book of the Executive Committee, September 17, 1946, "Institute of International Education" (agenda item), 13, CCNY Records, RBML-CUL; CCNY, Agenda Book of the Board of Trustees, May 21, 1953, "International Affairs" (agenda item), 18–19, CCNY Records, RBML-CUL; as an example, see CCNY, Agenda Book of the Board of Trustees, May 15, 1947, "World Affairs Council (San Francisco): Grant of $16,000 for Support" (agenda item), 28, CCNY Records, RBML-CUL; CCNY Agenda Book of the Board of Trustees, January 19, 1950, "Institute of International Education" (agenda item), 20, CCNY Records, RBML-CUL.

137 CCNY, Agenda Book of the Executive Committee, March 14, 1950, "Institute of International Education: Grant of $150,000 Toward Support" (agenda item), 7–8, CCNY Records, RBML-CUL.

138 Even while the studies were under way, the Corporation still supported the Institute. In a 1952 effort to bolster it and expand exchanges beyond the usual academic ones, the Corporation made a grant to fund visits by the staff of the State Department and the National Security Agency, along with delegations of leaders in labor, journalism, industry, agriculture, and educational activities.

139 CCNY, Agenda Book of the Board of Trustees, January 15, 1953, "Institute of

International Education: Grant of $450,000 Toward Support" (agenda item), 20, CCNY Records, RBML-CUL.

140 Ibid., 21.

141 CCNY, Agenda Book of the Board of Trustees, March 20, 1952, "Social Science Research Council: Grant of $75,000 for Evaluation of Student Exchanges" (agenda item), 6–7, CCNY Records, RBML-CUL.

142 Carol Lancaster, *Foreign Aid: Diplomacy, Development, Domestic Politics* (Chicago: University of Chicago Press, 2007).

143 Ringland, *The Organization of Voluntary Foreign Aid: 1939–1953.*

144 Dennis Bilger and Randy Sowell, "Point Four Program of Technical Assistance to Developing Nations" (archival materials prepared February 1999), Harry S. Truman Library and Museum, available at: http://www.trumanlibrary.org/hstpaper/point4.htm.

145 Starting in 1950, the Rockefeller Foundation staff began to address concerns similar to those of the Corporation about technical assistance programs and approaches; see, for example, discussion of the Cornell project supported by Carnegie Corporation, Folder 4275, Box 500, and Folders 4454, 4455, and 4456, Box 521, Series 200S, Record Group 1.2, FA386, Rockefeller Foundation records, RAC. In 1950 the Corporation made a small grant, with the agreement of the Brazilian government, to Harvard University's Research Center in Entrepreneurial History and Vanderbilt University's Institute for Brazilian Studies to study the role of businessmen in economic development in underdeveloped countries, as part of an examination of the assumptions underpinning the Point Four Program; CCNY, Agenda Book of the Board of Trustees, November 14, 1950, "Harvard University: Grant of $11,750, in Support of Research on the Role of the Businessman in Brazil" (agenda item), CCNY Records, RBML-CUL.

146 CCNY, Agenda Book of the Board of Trustees, October 16, 1947, "Cornell University, Grant of $180,000 for a Program in Anthropology" (agenda item), 4, CCNY Records, RBML-CUL.

147 Ibid., 4–5.

148 CCNY, Agenda Book of the Board of Trustees, November 16, 1954, "Cornell University: Grant of $40,000 as a Final Grant for Studies of the Impact of Technological Change on Nonindustrialized Countries" (agenda item), 9, CCNY Records, RBML-CUL.

149 Ibid., 10. See letters and proposals between the Rockefeller Foundation staff and Cornell staff, Folders 4275 and 4276, Box 500, Series 200S, Record Group 1.2, FA386, Rockefeller Foundation records, RAC. See also, for example, Rockefeller Foundation Annual Report, 1954, 239–240.

150 CCNY, Agenda Book of the Board of Trustees, November 15, 1949, "Michigan State College, Grant of $34,500 for a Study of Some Problems Involved in Technical Assistance to Backward Peoples" (agenda item), 28, CCNY Records, RBML-CUL.

151 CCNY, Agenda Book of the Board of Trustees, November 16, 1954, "Michigan State College, a Grant of $150,000 for Research on Technical Assistance in Underdeveloped Areas" (agenda item), 7–8, CCNY Records, RBML-CUL. The focus on differences in conditions on the two sides of the border is nearly the same rationale as that given for a set of similar activities that the Corporation funded related to health and development programs, including women's health, on both sides of the US-Mexican border in the 1990s; see Chapter 7.

152 Corporation staff had hired Aannestad to do a survey on "education for values, especially American values." The report was "excellent." CCNY, Agenda Book of the Board of Trustees, March 16, 1950, "For the Information of the Trustees: Memorandum on Special Studies" (agenda item), 2, CCNY Records, RBML-CUL.

153 The memos, correspondence, and reports from Aannestad are available in Folders 1 and 3, Box 1, Series 100, Record Group 1.2, FA386, Rockefeller Foundation records, RAC.

154 Aannestad, "Basic Questions on Aid to Underdeveloped Countries" (table) and "Background Notes to Preceding Questions," December 5, 1951, Folder 3, Box 1, Series 100, Record Group 1.2, FA386, Rockefeller Foundation records, RAC.

155 Rockefeller Foundation annual report, 1954, 25–26.

156 See, for example, the final publication of research results from one set of grants, Nicolas van de Walle and Timothy A. Johnston, *Improving Aid to Africa*, Policy Essay 21 (Washington, DC: Overseas Development Council, 1996).

157 CCNY, Agenda Book of the Board of Trustees, January 21, 1954, "For the Information of the Trustees: British Dominions and Colonies Program" (agenda item), 5, CCNY Records, RBML-CUL.

158 CCNYAR, 1946, 34.

159 Shepardson, at age thirty, was part of the team that created the Council on Foreign Relations, modeling it on the Royal Institute of International Affairs. In World War II, he had headed the Secret Intelligence Branch of the Office of Strategic Services based in London.

160 Following a 1948 conference of British Commonwealth ministers, Canada, Australia, and New Zealand changed their status from dominion to nationhood. India became a dominion and then a republic. For the Corporation, given its charter, the change from dominions to nation-states made it necessary to legally clarify where grant-making could take place and which funds could be used where.

161 All quotations in this paragraph are from Stackpole, *Commonwealth Program*, 4–6.

162 CCNYAR, 1946, 35.

163 Ibid.

164 The travel grants program reopened when in late 1945 twenty medical doctors from Australia received support from the Corporation to travel to the United States. As a postwar goodwill effort, the program's aim was to update their knowledge of medical techniques and provide a respite from the suffering that some of them had endured during World War II in Japanese prisoner-of-war camps and in frontline service. Shepardson had supported travel grants earlier but formally made the case in CCNYAR, 1951, "Report of the Director of the BDC," 36–37. All quotes are from these pages.

165 Shepardson's trip reports are nearly publishable as monographs; in addition to his assessment of political conditions, he provided extensive details on cultural activities and took excellent photographs. His trip reports provide insightful records of developments at that time. He traveled by road and various sorts of vehicles, by river and canoe, and of course, by this time, by airplane to move across continents.

166 The British Colonial Office response to such demands was to enable Makerere Government College, established in 1922, to become a full university college. Located in Kampala, Uganda, and well known to the Corporation from earlier grants, it was now called Makerere University College and was the seat of higher education for East Africa, a school attended not only by Africans but by a large number of British settlers. In 1942, at the colonial government's request, the Corporation made an exceptional wartime grant for the library at Makerere. Ever since, Makerere has featured in every era of the Corporation's grant-making related to teaching, research, and university extension work. Makerere led the way for the other British colonies in Africa. Starting in 1943, the Colonial Office began upgrading the other university colleges so that they could "promote research, be wholly residential, and emphasize global arts and science above professional/vocational studies." The resulting special relationship between the University of London and the newly named university colleges in Sierra Leone, Nigeria, Ghana, Uganda, Kenya, and Sudan not only began to meet African demands but also to give focus to the Corporation's reengagement in African higher education once the war was over.

167 CCNY, Minutes of the Board of Trustees, 34, May 21, 1953, CCNY Records, RBML-

CUL. The director of the project, Dr. Audrey Richards, invited Professor Leonard Doob from Yale, who had been part of the earlier team of American faculty visiting the region, to participate, reinforcing Doob's commitment to African studies and to building a strong program in this area at Yale. CCNY, Agenda Book of the Executive Committee, January 21, 1954, "Yale University: Grant of $15,000 (BDC) for Research in East Africa" (agenda item), 23, CCNY Records, RBML-CUL.

168 This was one of the few grants related to the concern about the response of communities in developing countries to new technologies and new approaches in health and education that went directly to a local institution rather than through a US-based institution. Even before the Ford Foundation developed its extensive programming on community development—but building on the approaches of the Rockefeller Foundation to community development and the earlier Carnegie Corporation work in this area as well—this grant aimed to strengthen local capacity for community-based programs; CCNY, Agenda Book of the Board of Trustees, March 15, 1951, "Rural Training and Demonstration Centre, Asaba, Nigeria: Grant of $60,000 (BDC) for Village Community Development" (agenda item), 25–26, CCNY Records, RBML-CUL. For more on the Fund, see Rosaleen Smyth, "The Roots of Community Development in Colonial Office Policy and Practice in Africa," *Social Policy and Administration* 38, no. 4 (August 2004): 418–436.

169 CCNY, Agenda Book of the Executive Committee, September 24, 1953, "Stanford University: Grant of $150,000 for Research on Economic Development of Africa Conducted by the Food Research Institute" (agenda item), 10–11, CCNY Records, RBML-CUL.

170 CCNY, Agenda Book of the Board of Trustees, November 16, 1948, "For the Information of Trustees" (agenda item), 11, and "Economic Aspects of the South African Race Problem" (agenda item), 37–39, CCNY Records, RBML-CUL. At this meeting, Shepardson proposed a fairly radical approach to examining the economic aspects of the race problem. It was never funded because it required a willingness by the Corporation trustees to engage directly with a South African committee that, although multiracial, would be led by whites, including representatives from the party of apartheid, the Nationalist Party. Clearly the trustees did not want to invest in such an initiative, as the situation was becoming ever more egregious; ibid., 36–37.

171 CCNY, Minutes of the Board of Trustees, XXVI–XXVIII, 2, May 21, 1953, "Summary of Executive Committee Actions," CCNY Records, RBML-CUL.

172 Francis Wilson, *Dinosaurs, Diamonds, and Democracy: A Short, Short History of South Africa* (Roggebai, South Africa: Umuzi, 2009), 81.

173 Ibid., 88.

174 CCNY, Agenda Book of the Board of Trustees, January 15, 1948, "Natal University College: Grant of $15,000 for the Purchase of Books" (agenda item), 35, CCNY Records, RBML-CUL.

175 Jan Smuts, distinguished general and scientist, was a senior Afrikaans political leader with inconsistent views on the role of the different population groups in South Africa. Nonetheless, he was opposed to the 1948 developments concerning apartheid: "The idea that the natives must be removed and confined in their own *kraals* is in my opinion the greatest nonsense I have ever heard." South African History Online: Towards a People's History, "General Jan Christian Smuts," available at: http://www.sahistory.org.za/people/general-jan-christiaan-smuts.

176 R. W. Johnson, "The Wrecking of a University," December 5, 2008, available at: http://www.politicsweb.co.za/politicsweb/view/politicsweb/en/page72308?oid=111909&sn=Marketingweb%20detail (accessed July 5, 2014).

177 Stackpole, *Carnegie Corporation*, 28.

178 CCNYAR, 1948, 35; Stackpole, *Carnegie Corporation*, 31.

179 CCNYAR, 1949, 48, and 1950, 34.

180 Stackpole, *Carnegie Corporation*, 28, 32; see also CCNYAR, 1952, 32.

181 CCNYAR, 1952, 45; CCNY, Agenda Book of the Board of Trustees, May 21, 1953, "Social Science Research Council of Australia: Grant of $40,000 for Grants-in-Aid" (agenda item), 45–46, and January 21, 1954, "University of Western Australia: Grant of $40,000 for Teaching and Research in Psychology and Social Anthropology" (agenda item), 22, CCNY Records, RBML-CUL.

182 Stackpole, *Carnegie Corporation*, 35. Grants were made to the Carnegie Institution of Washington in support of this activity in 1950, 1953, and 1954, for a total of $17,000.

183 CCNY, Agenda Book of the Board of Trustees, May 21, 1953, "University of New Zealand: Grant of $60,000 for Research in the Social Sciences" (agenda item), 43–44, CCNY Records, RBML-CUL.

184 CCNYAR, 1948, 35.

185 CCNY, Agenda Book of the Board of Trustees, January 19, 1950, "Australian Council for Educational Research and New Zealand Council for Educational Research: Grants of $3,000 for Coordination of Work" (agenda item), 65, CCNY Records, RBML-CUL.

186 Stackpole, *Carnegie Corporation*, 54.

187 CCNYAR, 1951, 31.

188 CCNYAR, 1953, 43.

189 McCallum, *The Social Production of Merit*.

190 CCNY, Agenda Book of the Board of Trustees, May 30, 1954, "South African Council for Scientific and Industrial Research: Grant of $11,200 for Mobile Testing Laboratory for Research on Mentality and Aptitude of Africans" (agenda item), 85, CCNY Records, RBML-CUL.

191 Louw, "Social Context and Psychological Testing in South Africa," 2; Johann Louw and Kurt Danziger, "Psychological Practices and Ideology: The South African Case," in *History of Psychology and Social Practice*, ed. Adrian C. Brock and Johann Louw, special issue of *Social Practice/Psychological Theorizing*, no. 1 (2007): 6–22, available at: http://www.kurtdanziger.com/Joahnn&Kurt.pdf.

192 Dollard's report on educational conditions in Canada was of such general interest to the US public that the *New York Times* covered his trip and report on the impact of the war on Canadian higher education: "The war in Canada has not, as it has in this country, led to a redefinition of education as a 'cluster of immediately useful skills.'... The country is still operating on the assumption that trained minds are a national resource and is still conscious of the fact that war presents problems which cannot be solved with a slide rule." "Canada Stresses Educational Aims," *New York Times*, April 4, 1942; CCNY Minutes of the Executive Committee, XIX, 83, March 9, 1942, CCNY Records, RBML-CUL.

193 Both were supported during the war years, with the former continually through 1954. Stackpole, *Carnegie Corporation*, 41, 49.

194 Ibid., 44, 45, and 47; see, for example, CCNY, Agenda Book of the Board of Trustees, May 19, 1947, "McGill University: Grant of $15,000 for the Service Center for Community Programs at Macdonald College" (agenda item), 33–34, CCNY Records, RBML-CUL.

195 Stackpole, *Carnegie Corporation*, 39–49 (for all the grants funded in Canada during this period, including work on international law and social sciences).

196 CCNYAR, 1952, 45. The University of British Columbia was funded in 1951 to develop research and training in the social sciences; CCNYAR, 1951, 38.

197 CCNYAR, 1948, 34.

198 These included the Canadian Citizenship Council, the Canadian Institute of International Affairs (including support for a conference on contemporary Canadian, UK, and US relations), the Canadian Mathematical Congress, the Canadian Mental Health Association,

the Humanities Research Council of Canada, the Canadian Bar Association, and the Canadian Foundation (for a publication on the French-Canadian mind). See, for example, CCNY, Agenda Book of the Board of Trustees, January 15, 1948, "Canadian Organizations: Grants Totalling $24,500 Toward Support of Four Organizations" (agenda item), 36–38, CCNY Records, RBML-CUL.

199   There are now fifty Canadian studies programs in the United States and more than five hundred courses on Canada, along with an Association for Canadian Studies in the United States. Québec, "Québec and Canadian Studies in the United States and Québec," available at: www.gouv.qc.ca/portail/quebec/international/usa/etudes/etudesquebecois/quebec_canadian_studies/ (updated November 29, 2011).

200   CCNY, Agenda Book of the Board of Trustees, May 18, 1950, "Cornell University: Grant of $75,000 for Research on Social Factors in Mental Health" (agenda item), 17–18, CCNY Records, RBML-CUL.

201   See, for example, CCNY, Agenda Book of the Board of Trustees, November 16, 1954, "University College of the West Indies; Grant of $64,000 (BDC) for Faculty Research and Study in the Caribbean Area" (agenda item), 24–25, CCNY Records, RBML-CUL.

202   Stackpole, *Carnegie Corporation*, 15.

203   Ibid., 15–16.

204   CCNY, Agenda Book of the Board of Trustees, January 15, 1948, "Universities Bureau of the British Empire: Grant of $40,000 Toward Travel Expenses of Dominion and Colonial Delegates to Commonwealth Universities Congress" (agenda item), 33–34, CCNY Records, RBML-CUL.

205   Stackpole, *Carnegie Corporation*, 56.

206   See, for example, Robert R. Kuczynski, *Demographic Survey of the British Colonial Empire*, vol. 1, *West Africa* (Oxford: Oxford University Press, 1948); Nicholas Mansergh, *Survey of British Commonwealth Affairs: Problems of Wartime Cooperation and Post-war Change, 1939–1952* (Oxon, UK: Routledge/New Impression, 1968).

207   CCNYAR, 1952, 32.

208   CCNY, Agenda Book of the Board of Trustees, March 18, 1948, "International African Institute: Grant of $12,000 Toward a Study of Documentary Material Relating to the Impact of White Civilization on African Family Life" (agenda item), 35, CCNY Records, RBML-CUL.

209   CCNY, Agenda Book of the Board of Trustees, November 16, 1948, "Columbia University, Teachers College: Grant of $50,000 for Conference on Educational Problems of Special Cultural Groups" (agenda item), 32–33, CCNY Records, RBML-CUL; Murphy, *Creative Philanthropy*, 28.

210   CCNY, Agenda Book of the Board of Trustees, January 21, 1954, "For the Information of the Trustees: British Dominions and Colonies Program" (agenda item), 5, CCNY Records, RBML-CUL.

211   Alan Pifer, another Harvard graduate (having been a scholarship student in prep school), had won a Harvard fellowship to study at Cambridge and then served in the military. Following the war, he served for five years in London as secretary of the US Education Commission (the Fulbright Commission); one of his responsibilities was to identify opportunities for Africans to receive these same awards. Before he returned to the United States, he traveled extensively throughout sub-Saharan Africa. After Dollard interviewed Pifer, who had literally walked in off the street to see if there might be a job, he declared that Pifer was just what the Corporation needed—a generalist who, as the Fulbright program's man in London since the end of the war, had worked in and on Africa. Stackpole and Pifer were perfect complements. Through his travel

on behalf of the Corporation, Stackpole knew the dominions, while Pifer knew the colonies, and both knew the key players in London.

212 All quotations are from CCNY, Agenda Book of the Board of Trustees, January 21, 1954, 6, CCNY Records, RBML-CUL.

213 "Canada … received approximately $930,000; Australia $510,000; the Union of South Africa $240,000; New Zealand $110,000; and the Colonies $290,000 (largely Africa and the West Indies). Grants totaling about $350,000 and $140,000 have been made to institutions in the United Kingdom and the United States, respectively, for studies or projects related to the Commonwealth generally or to a particular colonial area or dominion." CCNY, Agenda Book of the Board of Trustees, November 16, 1954, "British Dominions and Colonies Program" (agenda item), 17–18, CCNY Records, RBML-CUL.

214 Ibid., 18.

215 Ibid., 19.

216 Ibid., 21.

217 Ibid., 21–22.

218 Ibid., 22–23.

219 Ibid., 21.

220 See Ekbladh's "Present at the Creation" for the first critical, non-ideological reassessment of the field and the work in the 1930s. Since these issues persist even more tenaciously in the twenty-first century, in-depth critical assessment of the difference these grants made and how and why they did so would be an invaluable aid to understanding current strategies. Such analyses would yield insightful findings about the successes and failures of efforts to educate the public about global affairs, help develop appropriate interdisciplinary educational programs at the undergraduate and postgraduate levels, and reveal mechanisms for ensuring that this scholarship has an appropriate role in informing policymakers about the most effective ways to provide foreign assistance.

NOTES FOR CHAPTER 5

1 The 1960–1961 recession led to a period of sustained growth throughout the 1960s. Although the United States was not involved in a hot war, Cold War proxies detracted from peace and security in Africa, such as in the Congo, and Indochina throughout this period.

2 William G. Hyland, "Foreign Affairs at Seventy," *Foreign Affairs* (Fall 1992): sect. IV, available at: http://cfr.org/world/foreign-affairs-70/p8277.

3 "Military-Industrial Complex Speech, Dwight D. Eisenhower, 1961," *Public Papers of the Presidents, Dwight D. Eisenhower, 1960*, 1035–1040, available at: http://coursesa.matrix.msu.edu/~hst306/documents/indust.html.

4 According to Tom Smith, a result of the crisis was that "foreign policy was now viewed as the most important area." For more details, see "Kennedy Library Releases New Report on Cuban Missile Crisis—Study Documents Impact of Crisis on American Public Opinion" (news release), John F. Kennedy Presidential Library and Museum, October 16, 2002, available at: http://www.jfklibrary.org/About-Us/News-and-Press/Press-Releases/Kennedy-Library-Releases-New-Report-on-Cuban-Missile-Crisis-Study-Documents-Impact-of-Crisis-on-Amer.aspx.

5 Earlier, the 1954 *Brown v. Board of Education* decision (which cited the Corporation-funded Myrdal study) outlawing racial desegregation "served as a catalyst for the modern civil rights movement" in the United States. The Leadership Conference, "*Brown v. Board of Education*," available at: www.civilrights.org/education/brown (accessed January 19, 2014). The passage of

the Civil Rights Act of 1964 prompted the Corporation to reinforce its commitment to strengthening historically black colleges and universities in the South and to work with organizations such as the National Urban League. As discussed in Chapter 6, the pull of domestic social forces gradually led to a shift in the Corporation's grant-making, internationally as well as in the United States.

6 Burlingame, *Philanthropy in America*, 111. Burlingame reports IRS estimates of more than 45,000 tax-exempt institutions in 1960; Carnegie Corporation of New York (CCNY) Annual Report (CCNYAR), 1960, 92, CCNY Records, Rare Book and Manuscript Library, Columbia University Libraries (RBML-CUL).

7 CCNYAR, 1964, 7–8.

8 Ibid., 8.

9 McIlnay, "Philanthropy at Fifty," 4–6.

10 Josephs, CCOH, December 16, 1966, 140–141.

11 Within the Corporation, Gardner was regarded with admiration and affection from day one, starting with his 1945 interview with Devereux Josephs and Robert Lester, both of whom felt that "he is the right kind of stuff"; record of interview with Robert Lester, December 13, 1945, CCNY Records, RBML-CUL. Charles Dollard's assessment when he promoted Gardner to vice president was that "he is one of the really first rate social scientists of his generation and also one of the most capable executives in the foundation business." Dollard added, in a 1949 letter to Lewis Terman, "I rather think I would have gone and enlisted in the French Legion if he hadn't been on the premises this year"; Charles Dollard, letter to Lewis Terman, April 5, 1949, CCNY Records, RBML-CUL. His Ford Foundation colleague Frank Sutton commented that he was an outstanding figure at the Corporation, "with admirable political and organizational and intellectual strengths"; Francis X. Sutton, personal communication with the author, April 19, 2012.

12 William Carmichael, the Ford Foundation's representative in Brazil in the 1970s and 1980s, and then the Corporation's vice president for developing countries responsible for co-funding its work in South Africa, commented, "Gardner had developed the habit of thought where he could see the critical missing area and where with limited resources, the foundation could make a difference. Areas that come to mind include disarmament and selecting the economics of disarmament as a focus, as well as teachers and teachers' training in Africa. I'd always thought of Carnegie Corporation as having consequence. I saw it as America's most prestigious foundation but certainly not the richest. If you don't have the millions, you find the critical part where you can make a difference"; William Carmichael, personal communication with the author, April 24, 2010. Carmichael was a close observer of the foundation under Gardner because his uncle, Oliver Carmichael, was on the Carnegie Corporation board, president of the Carnegie Foundation for the Advancement of Teaching, and a staff member under both Dollard and Gardner. Young Carmichael often visited the foundation and was able to observe its work firsthand.

13 His father died when Gardner was one year old; he was raised by his mother and had to work throughout school. He became a champion swimmer in college at Stanford, studied psychology at Berkeley, and accepted teaching positions at two women's colleges. At various times in his first twenty-seven years, he saw firsthand the issues associated with trying to achieve both equity and excellence, from his summer jobs in the fields of California as well as from teaching undergraduates. These observations would later be central to his intellectual contributions to the study of educational and other organizations. Trained as a psychologist, he achieved his PhD at the University of California at Berkeley in 1938. In World War II, he served first with the Foreign Broadcast Intelligence Services, focusing on Latin America, where he could put his fluent Spanish to work. Then, as a captain in the Marines, he was sent to Italy for the Office of Strategic Services in Europe to review the suitability of field staff through personality assessment tests.

During this period, he discovered his management skills: "When I first arrived in Washington in 1942, I was asked to head the Latin American section of the Foreign Broadcast Intelligence Service (FCC). Since I had a good knowledge of the Spanish language and of Latin America I had no doubt of my intellectual capacity to handle the job. But I was astounded when I began to receive good marks on my management skills. It was wholly contrary to my image of myself, wholly at odds with my plans for the future. I was 29 years old and had never run anything. I had no ambition to run anything. From my earliest years, I had thought of myself as a student, an observer, pleasantly detached from the mainstream of the world's action. From that point, on my life was to be governed by constant conflict between the life of action and the life of reflection." Jean and Irving Stone, eds., *There Was Light: Autobiography of a University: A Collection of Essays Written by Alumni of the University of California, Berkeley, 1868–1996*, 2nd ed. (Berkeley: University of California Press, 1996). Quoted on www.pbs.org/johngardner/sections/writingshtml.

14 Gardner's crisp writing also contributed to the efforts of other foundations. For example, in 1958 Gardner helped the Rockefeller Brothers Fund prepare a major report, *The Pursuit of Excellence: Education and the Future of America*. Nelson Rockefeller, president of the Fund, served as chair of the task force, and Henry Kissinger was the staff director. After highlighting the question, How "may we best prepare our young people to keep their individuality, initiative, creativity in a highly organized, intricately meshed society?" the report concluded that "our conception of excellence must embrace many kinds of achievement"; Rockefeller Brothers Fund, *The Pursuit of Excellence: Education and the Future of America* (New York: Doubleday, 1958). These involvements, along with his grant-making responsibilities for education at the Corporation, led Gardner to consider even more deeply the relationship between excellence and equity. The Rockefeller Brothers Fund report not only helped to shape grant-making in education, especially with respect to its psychological testing component, but also brought him to the attention of President John F. Kennedy, who asked Gardner—a Republican—to edit *To Turn the Tide*, a collection of Kennedy's writings and speeches from his first year in office.

15 John Gardner, *Self-Renewal: The Individual and the Innovative Society* (New York: Harper & Row, 1963), 6–7.

16 In this period, the Corporation, under the rubric of creativity, provided funds for pioneering work on cognitive development, finding and supporting gifted children of every background, and refining the role of testing and assessment. These activities plus considerable work on higher education comprised much of the Corporation's domestic grant-making not related to international issues. Related to dissemination, see CCNY, Agenda Book of the Executive Committee, April 25, 1957, "Dissemination Fund: Appropriation of $50,000 for Experimentation in Disseminating Results of Corporation Grants" (agenda item), 11–12, CCNY Records, RBML-CUL.

17 CCNY, Minutes of the Executive Committee, XXIX–XXXI, 31, June 18, 1959, CCNY Records, RBML-CUL. This was the beginning of introducing support for the education and professional growth of staff.

18 For example, the White House Fellowships, a program he developed that has continued into the twenty-first century, offers opportunities to young people to work in government; CCNY, Minutes of the Executive Committee, XXXII–XXXIV, 72, September 25, 1964, CCNY Records, RBML-CUL. At that meeting, the Executive Committee approved $225,000 to cover the costs of the fellowships, with the government covering all other costs.

19 In 1964 Gardner chaired the National Task Force on Education; that year President Johnson recognized his service to the nation by awarding him the Presidential Medal of Freedom.

20 Over his twelve years at the helm, Gardner recommended fourteen new members who were then voted onto the board; five of them joined as he was taking leave to work in Washington. The board consisted of such internationally minded members as Chairman of the Board Russell

Leffingwell, a longtime board member, a childhood friend of Keppel's, and a former president of the Council on Foreign Relations who had fully backed Josephs and his international agenda; Frederick Osborn of the Population Council; Randolph Burgess, then undersecretary of the treasury for monetary affairs; Gwilym Price, CEO of Westinghouse; Arthur Page, the public relations guru; Charles Allen Thomas, the president of Monsanto Chemical Company; Charles Spofford, a distinguished international lawyer and brigadier general in World War II, and one of the US representatives to the North Atlantic Treaty Organization (NATO); Morris Hadley, senior partner in the law firm Milbank, Tweed, Hadley and McCloy, and president of the New York Public Library; Nicholas Kelley, a lawyer active in labor relations and civil service reform and a board member since 1936; Vannevar Bush, science adviser to presidents and the remaining representative of the Carnegie family of institutions as president of the Carnegie Institution of Washington; and the two members with the closest links to Andrew Carnegie—Elihu Root Jr., son of Carnegie's attorney and himself Corporation counsel since the beginning, and Margaret Carnegie Miller, Andrew Carnegie's only daughter. An early appointment was Frederick Sheffield, a lawyer who had won a gold medal for rowing in the 1924 Olympics. Gardner's appointments also included distinguished scientists, like Caryl Haskins, who had a deep interest in Africa and was selected as president of the Carnegie Institution of Washington (the one remaining Carnegie institution represented on the board), and Manhattan Project participant Robert Bacher, provost at the California Institute of Technology. He chose business leaders like Walter Wriston, then executive vice president of National City Bank; David Shepard, vice president of Standard Oil Company of New Jersey; Malcolm MacIntyre, who had been undersecretary of the air force and president of Eastern Airlines; and Amyas Ames, who helped found the Lincoln Center in New York City. Frederick Eaton, a lawyer and a leader in the disarmament movement, was also a trustee. General Charles Jackson, an aide to President Eisenhower and vice president of *Time* magazine, was also appointed a trustee during this period; he brought to the board a very strong focus on American-European relations. Toward the end of Gardner's tenure, two new board members were appointed who also reflected strong international connections: Harding Bancroft, then executive vice president of the *New York Times*, had served with the lend-lease program, the US State Department, the International Labor Office (ILO), and various American delegations to the UN; Louis Cabot was involved in international conservation issues and served on several commissions of the Defense Department and also as a US representative to the UN in Europe.

21 Lagemann, *The Politics of Knowledge*, 147–151; Waldemar A. Nielsen, *Inside American Philanthropy: The Dramas of Donorship* (Norman: University of Oklahoma Press, 1996), 263. During Gardner's tenure, the annual grant expenditures ranged from $7.1 million for 1955–1956 to a high of $13.9 million in 1966–1967. The overseas grants budget, as discussed later, was higher than usual in the mid-1950s because of carryover from unspent funds; it ranged over this period from $440,000 to around $1 million. The detailed grants data are available in the Secretary's Report in each Annual Report. See, for example, CCNYAR, 1956, 73, and 1967, 95.

22 CCNYAR, 1956, 29.

23 The titles and themes for the public and international affairs area illustrate not only a mélange of programs and interests but the evolution of the Corporation's postwar commitment to prepare Americans to play a significant role in the new world following World War II: American universities and world affairs; public education and international affairs; international scholarly communications; higher education on the world scene; universities and overseas relationships; education for international affairs; education for international relations; research for international affairs; modernization and the emerging nations; international studies; undergraduate study and work abroad; national security policy; the non-Western civilizations program;

public and international affairs; education and world affairs; improvement in foreign language teaching; education and national development; political factors and modernization; national security and international research; research on China and Southeast Asia; Anglo-American cooperation; foreign languages and foreign studies; and international education and research.

24   Starting as early as 1951 and continuing into the twenty-first century, the field of area studies has generated a significant literature, including, for example (and in order of date of publication): Wendell C. Bennett, *Area Studies in American Universities* (New York: Social Science Research Council, 1951); Richard D. Lambert, *Language and Area Studies Review* (Philadelphia: American Academy of Political and Social Sciences, 1973); David L. Szanton, ed., *The Politics of Knowledge: Area Studies and the Disciplines* (Berkeley: University of California Press, 2004); Jody Shepherd, "Bibliography of Area Studies in Relation to Higher Education: The Past, Present, and Future," Indiana University, 2005, available at: http://www.libraries.iub.edu/index.php?pageId=1000308 (accessed May 19, 2012); Gilbert W. Merkx et al., "Comparative Education, Area Studies, and the Disciplines," *Comparative Education Review* 501 (2006): 125–148; and Wiley and Glew, *International and Language Education for a Global Future* (2010). The Corporation's grant-making in area studies was not constrained by the charter limitations for the direct grants to overseas institutions; those could only be made to countries of the British Commonwealth.

25   For an overview, see CCNYAR, 1959, 28–29, 34.

26   CCNY, Minutes of the Executive Committee, 23, April 21, 1959, CCNY Records, RBML-CUL.

27   CCNY, Agenda Book of the Board of Trustees, May 21, 1959, "University of Kansas: Grant of $80,000 in Support of Faculty Exchanges with the University of Costa Rica" (agenda item), 13–15, CCNY Records, RBML-CUL.

28   CCNY, Agenda Book of the Board of Trustees, May 21, 1959, "Cornell University: Grant of $250,000 for a Program of Training and Research on South America" (agenda item), 11–12, CCNY Records, RBML-CUL.

29   CCNY Agenda Book of the Executive Committee, September 29, 1959, "Undergraduate Study Abroad, Allocations Totaling $115,300 with $40,500 for Columbia University's Program" (agenda item), 23, CCNY Records, RBML-CUL; CCNY Agenda Book of the Board of Trustees, November 15, 1960, "Columbia University, Grant of $160,000 for an Inter-University Program for Undergraduate Study Abroad" (agenda item), 19, CCNY Records, RBML-CUL.

30   CCNY Agenda Book of the Executive Committee, April 18, 1961, "Undergraduate Study Abroad, Allocation of $11,500, for the MIT Program" (agenda item), 19, CCNY Records, RBML-CUL; CCNY Agenda Book of the Board of Trustees, May 17, 1962, "Massachusetts Institute of Technology, Grant of $250,000 for an Inter-American Program in Civil Engineering" (agenda item), 15–16, CCNY Records, RBML-CUL.

31   CCNY Agenda Book of the Executive Committee, December 20, 1960, "University of Wisconsin, Grant of $100,000 for a Junior Year Program for Engineering Students at the Instituto Tecnologico de Monterrey" (agenda item), 7–8, CCNY Records, RBML-CUL.

32   CCNY Agenda Book of the Executive Committee, April 19, 1960, "Undergraduate Study Abroad, Allocations Totaling $101,600, for Arizona, $12,100" (agenda item), 26, CCNY Records, RBML-CUL.

33   CCNY Agenda Book of the Board of Trustees, March 15, 1962, "Vanderbilt University, Grant of $150,000 for Research and Graduate Training on the Process of Modernization in Latin America" (agenda item), 14, CCNY Records, RBML-CUL.

34   CCNYAR, 1960, 34. The Rockefeller Foundation had been providing support for Latin American studies since the mid-1930s through the American Council of Learned Societies and then the Social Science Research Council (SSRC). That support had ended by the late 1940s.

The field was in the doldrums until the SSRC organized a meeting in 1958, with support from the Corporation, which also supported the follow-up activities at the Council through 1962. At that point, the Ford Foundation came in with major support and became the main funder of the work on Latin American studies. Bennett, *Area Studies in American Universities*, 26–27; Paul W. Drake and Lisa Hilbink, "Latin American Studies Theory and Practice," in Szanton, *The Politics of Knowledge*, 34–73.

35 CCNY, Agenda Book of the Board of Trustees, May 19, 1960, "Institute for International Education: Grant of $200,000, for Support of the Council on Higher Education in the American Republics" (agenda item), 17–18, CCNY Records, RBML-CUL.

36 Robert Myers, "Brain Drains and Brain Gains," *International Development Review* 5, no. 4 (1967): 4–9.

37 CCNYAR, 1966, 58. Herbert Grubel refers to Myers's paper as having prompted two US government reports. Herbert Grubel, "The Reduction of the Brain Drain: Problems and Policies," *Minerva* 6, no. 4 (1968): 541–558.

38 For the rationale, see CCNYAR, 1955, 38.

39 CCNY, Agenda Book of the Board of Trustees, May 17, 1962, "University of Wisconsin: Grant of $115,000 for a Program of Undergraduate Study in India" (agenda item), 17–18; Agenda Book of the Executive Committee, April 25, 1957, "University of Chicago: Grant of $48,000 for Expansion of Undergraduate Program on Non-Western Civilizations" (agenda item), 7–8; Agenda Book of the Executive Committee, December 18, 1957, "University of Chicago: Final Grant of $25,000 Towards Support of the Philippine Studies Program" (agenda item), 3–4; Agenda Book of the Board of Trustees, November 17, 1959, "University of Michigan: Grant of $140,500 for Development of the Undergraduate Asia Course and Related Training and Research" (agenda item), 20–21; Agenda Book of the Board of Trustees, April 17, 1963, "Grinnell College: Grant of $50,000 for Curriculum Experimentation" (agenda item), 8–9; Agenda Book of the Board of Trustees, March 15, 1962, "Cornell University: Grant of $450,000 for Research and Graduate Training on China and Southeast Asia" (agenda item), 12–13. CCNYAR, 1962, 42–43. The support "included graduate studies and field research on the social, economic, and political subdivisions in China and Southeast Asia and [would] help train a new generation of scholars able to carry on such studies. Special emphasis will be given to social anthropology, economics, political science, and modern institutional history." This was part of a "significant joint venture," as Gardner described it, "to study the societies of China and Southeast Asia … by Cornell University and two schools of the University of London—the London School of Economics and Political Science and the School of Oriental and African Studies." Carnegie Corporation supported the Cornell part, and the Nuffield Foundation supported the London-based institutions; CCNYAR, 1960, 45–46, and 1957, 53. The University of Pennsylvania received continued support for its work on South Asian studies in 1957. In the agenda item, the Corporation noted that many of its graduates held responsible government as well as academic positions. UPenn also had a special focus on Indian languages, an area of continuing excellence; CCNY, Agenda Book of the Board of Trustees, January 24, 1957, "University of Pennsylvania: Grant of $85,000 Toward Support of South Asian Studies" (agenda item), 17. A renewal grant to Columbia University supported its plan to give undergraduate courses on Asian civilization to complement its general education courses on the Western world, hold an annual conference, and train faculty from Columbia and other universities. The agenda item notes with enthusiasm program developments since the first grant in 1949, including the preparation of teaching materials and source books; CCNY, Agenda Book of the Executive Committee, January 16, 1958, "Columbia University: Grant of $185,000 Toward Strengthening the General Education Program in Asian Civilization" (agenda item), 14–15. All at CCNY Records, RBML-CUL.

40   CCNYAR, 1957, 53, CCNY, Agenda Book of the Executive Committee, April 25, 1957, "University of Arizona: Grant of $54,000 for Undergraduate Studies on Asian Civilizations," (agenda item) 5–6, CCNY Records, RBML-CUL.

41   CCNY, Agenda Book of the Executive Committee, December 18, 1957, "Massachusetts Institute of Technology: Grant of $25,000 for a Study of the Political Process in Burma" (agenda item), 1–2, CCNY Records, RBML-CUL (emphasis in original).

42   CCNYAR, 1962, 42.

43   CCNYAR, 1966, 58–59. Since 1985, the Committee has maintained an office in Beijing to facilitate the exchanges. See China Development Brief (English), "NGO Directory," available at: http://www.chinadevelopmentbrief.com/dingo/Province/Nationwide/1-58-0-48-0-0.html.

44   CCNYAR, 1966, 59.

45   Corporation staff noted, "The Russian Research Center has proved itself a major national resource … precisely when the nation needed it most…. The new grant … will be spent chiefly for research on other strategic areas of the world … to have an ample fund of the verified knowledge concerning such regions." CCNYAR, 1955, 37–38.

46   CCNYAR, 1956, 47. A supplemental grant was made in 1957. In 1960, after the Inter-University Committee on Travel Grants was "handsomely funded by the Ford Foundation," the Corporation also contributed to the US-USSR Exchange Agreement between the American Council of Learned Societies (ACLS) and the USSR Academy of Sciences for exchanges of scholars in the social sciences and humanities. Staff noted in the agenda item that the US government did not provide funds for the actual exchanges, on the assumption that private money would support them; CCNY, Agenda Book of the Board of Trustees, March 17, 1960, "American Council of Learned Societies: Grant of $50,000 for Support of American Scholars on Visits to Russia Under the US-USSR Exchange Agreement" (agenda item), 10–11, CCNY Records, RBML-CUL.

47   CCNYAR, 1956, 47. In 1959 the Center for International Studies at MIT embarked on a three-year study of economic development and social change in sub-Saharan Africa, applying "all the tools of modern economic analysis for examining the real potential for economic growth," CCNYAR, 1959, 30. The Stanford Food Research Institute was funded again, after several years' hiatus, to conduct studies of food security and supply in Africa from the perspective of African economic development; CCNYAR, 1958, 33.

48   The issues rankling scholars at the time in all international fields—anthropology in particular—included "McCarthyism and CIA infiltration." For this reason, a College of Fellows was formed to review the election of officers and selection of fellows, a decision that later became controversial but was deemed essential then. Many articles have been written about the field of African studies and the ASA; all quotes come from Gwendolen M. Carter, "The Founding of the African Studies Association," *African Studies Review* 26, nos. 3-4 (1983): 5–9, available at: http://www.jstor.org/pss/524159 (accessed May 19, 2012). In the most comprehensive recent review of African studies in the United States, Pearl Robinson, with exquisite documentation, presents the checkered history, illustrating not only the role played by the Corporation and to some extent the Rockefeller Foundation, but also the major role played by the Ford Foundation, starting with Ford's Foreign Area Fellows Program, which, along with Title VI, had a great influence on the area studies field; Pearl T. Robinson, "Area Studies in Search of Africa," in Szanton, *The Politics of Knowledge*, 82–122.

49   See African Studies Association, "About the ASA," available at: www.africanstudies.org/about-asa (accessed July 6, 2014).

50   CCNY, Agenda Book of the Executive Committee, September 25, 1957, "The American Assembly, Columbia University: Grant of $85,000 for Expenses of an Assembly on 'the United States and Africa'" (agenda item), 8–9, CCNY Records, RBML-CUL.

51 CCNY, Agenda Book of the Board of Trustees, November 20, 1962, "African-American Institute: Grant of $290,000 Toward Support and Scholarship Administration" (agenda item), 7–8, CCNY Records, RBML-CUL. For more details on CCNY-Ford-RBF efforts, see Murphy, *Creative Philanthropy*, 87–88.

52 CCNYAR, 1955, 39. In the interest of maintaining exchanges with their British counterparts also engaged in Commonwealth studies, the Corporation made a modest grant to the University of Wisconsin to bring professors from England to teach in its program on British Commonwealth history.

53 CCNYAR, 1960, 29.

54 For more details, see CCNYAR, 1957, 48–50.

55 CCNYAR, 1959, 28.

56 For example, foreshadowing a major area of Corporation activity in the 2000s and complementing its support for Near East and Arabic language studies (the latter including study in Lebanon) at Princeton, staff members recognized the need for a more complete history of the Muslim world in English. In 1960 Gustave von Grunebaum at the University of California at Los Angeles received a grant to prepare a comprehensive history of the Muslim world: He will "treat Islam as it has appeared in various parts of the world, not just in the Middle East which was its home, and intends to explain the inter-relations among ideological, social, economic, and cultural as well as military and political events"; CCNYAR, 1959, 35; for the Princeton Arabic-language grant, see CCNYAR, 1962, 34–35. An unusual grant for this era went to Vassar College to bring together "leading women from various parts of the world to discuss problems of common interest." Another aspect of the meeting would resonate in the twenty-first-century grant-making of the Corporation (see Chapter 8): "In many of the underdeveloped countries, the education of women is a critically important problem because—as the Muslim world is discovering to its dismay—the attitudes which youngsters of both sexes have toward going to school are apt to be heavily influenced by the enlightenment (or ignorance) of the mother"; CCNY Agenda Book of the Executive Committee, June 18, 1959, "Vassar College: Grant of $20,000 Toward Support of an International Conference on Education" (agenda item), 6, CCNY Records, RBML-CUL.

57 CCNYAR, 1966, 59. The Corporation for many years was committed to refining comparative study methods in a variety of fields, as discussed elsewhere in this chapter. See also, for example, CCNY, Agenda Book of the Executive Committee, April 25, 1957, "Yale University: Grant of $41,600 for Research on Comparative Field Administration" (agenda item), 9–10, CCNY Records, RBML-CUL.

58 For more details, see CCNYAR, 1967, 60–61.

59 Ibid., 61.

60 The theme of comparative studies across a multitude of disciplines shaped the agenda of a conference sponsored by the Institute of War and Peace Studies at Columbia University and the American Academy of Arts and Sciences, with the support of Carnegie Corporation and the W. K. Kellogg Foundation. Scholars were drawn from fields such as political science, history, social psychology, psychiatry, anthropology, and economics. Here, too, the interest was in content and methods; at the meeting, "they explored ways in which their concerns and methods of study overlap or complement each other." Ibid., 62.

61 CCNY Agenda Book of the Executive Committee, June 14, 1954, "University of Chicago, Grant of $75,000 for Courses on Non-Western Civilizations" (agenda item), 11, CCNY Records, RBML-CUL. An important rationale for the continuing work in this area was to provide support for scholars preparing textbooks—William H. McNeill was working on a new textbook on world history, and L. S. Stavrianos was preparing a new world history course; CCNYAR, 1957, 39–42.

62 CCNYAR, 1965, 47.

63   In an effort to expand beyond those undergraduates who wanted to focus on international affairs, Northwestern University faculty embarked on a new approach to developing the international content of the introductory courses in basic subjects. It was similar to Stavrianos's world history program (see note 61), an innovative program focusing on literature, art, government, sociology, philosophy, and economics training for faculty members studying a culture with which they were not familiar. The aim was for faculty to learn new fields, teach introductory courses, and then make new syllabi and text material available to other US universities; CCNY Agenda Book of the Board of Trustees, January 24, 1957, "Northwestern University: Grant of $250,000 for Research and Training in International Affairs" (agenda item), 9–10, and November 14, 1961, "Grant of $150,000 for Development of the International Content of Introductory Courses" (agenda item), 12–13. In 1959, Percy Bidwell, a retired staff member of the Council of Foreign Relations, received renewed support to continue to compare the course offerings, textbooks, and teacher training on international relations in US universities and colleges. The staff justified support by noting: "It is an interesting fact that no such comparable study has ever been done"; CCNY Agenda Book of the Executive Committee, June 18, 1959, "Study of International Content of Undergraduate Courses: Appropriation of $47,000" (agenda item), 7–8. All at CCNY Records, RBML-CUL.

64   CCNYAR, 1959, 33.

65   For the University of Oregon, see CCNY, Minutes of the Executive Committee, 27, June 22, 1961; for Southwestern University and Western College, see CCNYAR, 1956, 45–46; for San Francisco State, see CCNY, Minutes of the Executive Committee, 50, January 16, 1958, CCNY Records, RBML-CUL.

66   CCNY Agenda Book of the Executive Committee, October 16, 1963, "University of Denver: Grant of $80,000 for an Inter-University Program in International Relations" (agenda item), 8–9, CCNY Records, RBML-CUL.

67   CCNYAR, 1960, 45–46. The University of Michigan was funded for two years at $144,000, the University of Arizona for two years at $100,000, and Western Michigan University for three years at $144,000.

68   For the rationale, the program, and the cluster of grants made over the year 1962–1963 for enhancing language training for high school and college students, see CCNYAR, 1963, 21–25. The Rockefeller Foundation had been supporting foreign language learning at the college level for decades, but gaps still persisted there and at the high school level. The Rockefeller Foundation had also been funding the Modern Language Association for several years to promote the teaching of foreign languages, and the Corporation later added its support; CCNYAR, 35.

69   CCNYAR, 1963, 22. The Corporation brought on a new grantee in 1961, Indiana University, to strengthen its program of Russian language learning along with an overseas language program for Indiana high school students, at the level of $200,000. Oberlin College received a grant ($90,000) for an overseas language program open to students from different institutions in Austria, France, and Mexico. Bryn Mawr College received a grant for its program in French language training and French culture, which took place each summer in Avignon. In 1960 the Corporation's continuing focus on foreign language training in the United States extended to supporting programs for American honors students to study French in the summer language schools run by McGill University in Montréal and Laval University in Québec City. Oberlin also expanded its programs in Mexico, Austria, and France to include students from other academic institutions; CCNYAR, 1960, 30–32. As noted, both the Corporation and the Rockefeller Foundation funded the Modern Language Association to promote foreign language teaching throughout the United States; CCNY, Minutes of the Board of Trustees, XXXII–XXXIV, 52, March 19, 1964, CCNY Records, RBML-CUL.

70   CCNYAR, 1963, 21–24. Seeking additional ways to expose American secondary school

students to new languages, the Corporation identified a gap in language teaching for American students in the international schools in countries where their parents were based. Experimental programs took place in the Japanese language and civilization in Japan and in Chinese language and civilization in Taipei; CCNYAR, 1960, 45–46.

71　CCNYAR, 1960, 22. Princeton University received five years of support for its program on the study of Arabic, the only one with a study abroad component (at the Middle East Center for Arabic Studies in Lebanon); CCNY Agenda Book of the Board of Trustees, November 14, 1961, "Princeton University: Grant for a National Undergraduate Program of Overseas Study of Arabic, $136,500" (agenda item), 14–16; and CCNY Agenda Book of the Executive Committee, December 16, 1964, "Princeton University: Grant for a National Undergraduate Program of Overseas Study of Arabic, $100,000" (agenda item), 12–13. In 1966 one of the last language study grants was extended to nearly forty colleges in New York State for a special effort over five years to teach "neglected" languages, such as Arabic, Chinese, Hindi, Japanese, Portuguese, and Swahili; CCNY, Agenda Book of the Board of Trustees, March 17, 1966, "University of the State of New York: Grant of $167,750 for a Program of Independent Study of Neglected Languages" (agenda item), 11–13. All at CCNY Records, RBML-CUL.

72　Neither short-term nor long-term ex-post analyses have been conducted of the reach and impact of the area studies, language, and international affairs programs. Clearly, given the geographic extent and the fact that many of these programs lasted for five or more years, they must have reached several thousand students and teachers. Did they create a critical mass of Americans informed about international affairs in a specific region, through courses on the area, training in one or two pertinent languages, and research-oriented visits to the region or country? Did students' experiences in these programs make a difference in their choice of college major, or their postgraduate work or career choices? Deeper studies might reveal lessons relevant for international education even in the twenty-first century. One of the few analyses of the foundation-specific impact on individuals was done by Francis X. Sutton, who assessed the results strictly from a Ford Foundation perspective; his analysis showed that fellowship programs can influence the choice of careers and leadership in the field; Sutton, "US Strengths." Analyses of area studies and language learning have focused on assessing the impact of Title VI. As noted earlier, two excellent and recent books provide a useful set of analyses and references to the earlier literature on the investments in both area studies and foreign language learning, as well as a brief commentary on foundation support: Szanton, *The Politics of Knowledge*, and Wiley and Glew, *International and Language Education for a Global Future*. The classic review, prepared after many years of research under the auspices of the Social Science Research Council, is Lambert, *Language and Area Studies Review*.

73　Sutton in his unpublished 1988 piece, however, states that the Ford Foundation "could follow the Rockefeller and Carnegie examples in starting and stimulating expanded area studies, and it was quickly engaged in doing so." Sutton, "US Strengths," 10.

74　A different, and more critical, analysis, related to the direct support for work in other countries, features Carnegie Corporation along with its two main partner foundations. See, for example, Inderjeet Parmar, *Foundations of the American Century: The Ford, Carnegie, and Rockefeller Foundations in the Rise of American Power* (New York: Columbia University Press, 2012), and Edward H. Berman, *The Influence of the Carnegie, Ford, and Rockefeller Foundations on American Foreign Policy: The Ideology of Philanthropy* (Albany: State University of New York Press, 1983), both of which question the motives and implications of the foundations' promotion of area studies and overseas work in terms of American political values, power, and economic interests. Much earlier, Curti provided an extensive, non-ideological review of foundation and voluntary agency overseas activities; Merle Curti, *American Philanthropy Abroad: A History*

(New Brunswick, NJ: Rutgers University Press, 1963). Ekbladh (*The Great American Mission: Modernization and the Construction of an American World Order*) and Szanton (*The Politics of Knowledge*) situate the foundations' work in broader policy and educational contexts. For a crisp, thoughtful analysis of the field of Latin American studies and the downside of foreign policy involvement, see Jesse Hoffnung-Garskoff, "Latin American Studies and United States Foreign Policy," *International Institute Journal* 2, no. 1 (Fall 2012), available at: http://hdl.handle.net/2027/spo.11645653.0002.103 (accessed January 20, 2014). Additional studies that undertake more in-depth and extensive on-the-ground analysis are still needed to assess the sustained impact of foundation support for area studies in the United States and elsewhere.

75 CCNYAR, 1962, 40–41.

76 CCNY, Agenda Book of the Board of Trustees, March 20, 1958, "Columbia University: Grant of $138,000 for Research in the Field of National Security Policies" (agenda item), 12, CCNY Records, RBML-CUL.

77 For the Dartmouth and Wisconsin grants, see CCNYAR, 1962, 41. The School for Advanced International Studies at Johns Hopkins University, reflecting the changing nature of international relations, conducted research through the lens of national security policy research on the new nations of Africa and Asia in order to consider appropriate Western policy responses; CCNY, Minutes of the Board of Trustees, XXIX–XXXI, 47, January 18, 1962, CCNY Records, RBML-CUL. The Corporation also regularly supported the policy-oriented studies on "the interplay between military and political policy" of Hans Morgenthau and his colleagues at the Center for the Study of American Foreign Policy at the University of Chicago; CCNYAR, 1957, 52–53. The Social Science Research Council was supported for many years on the topic of national security, as discussed in the following pages. Originally called the Committee on Civil-Military Relations, it then focused on the history of American military policy, defense mobilization, and then, for several years, national security policies. The funds provided for committee meetings and for a research grants program; see, for example, CCNY, Agenda Book of the Executive Committee, September 20, 1961, "Social Science Research Council: Grant of $42,000 for Grants-in-Aid for Research on National Security Policies" (agenda item), 9, CCNY Records, RBML-CUL.

78 The grant provided for analyses of existing knowledge, promotion of new studies, and conferences; CCNY, Agenda Book of the Board of Trustees, March 21, 1957, "Columbia University: Grant of $127,000 for Support of the Council for Atomic Age Studies" (agenda item), 21–22, CCNY Records, RBML-CUL. From 1966 to 1972 (the year it closed), the Council was called the Institute for the Study of Science in Human Affairs; Annette Baker Fox, "The Institute of War and Peace Studies: The First Thirty-Five Years," Columbia University, 2001, 35–36, available at: http://saltzman.obiki.org/about.attachment/fox-manuscript/Fox%20Manuscript%201.pdf. In a few years, international law, including law related to space, featured in the grants portfolio. In the context of deepening understanding of the Soviet Union and its attitudes toward international law, Kazimierz Grzybowski, a Duke University specialist on Soviet and Eastern European legal affairs and doctrine working at Duke's World Rule of Law Center, was supported over several years to "chart the changes in Soviet doctrine that are relevant to such areas as space law and the law of war and disarmament"; CCNYAR, 1962, 43.

79 *Sputnik* was also responsible for a partial shift of focus in the Corporation's domestic program. This shift was not unexpected, given the strength of the scientists on the Corporation's board, such as Caryl Haskins, then president of the Carnegie Institution of Washington, and the continuing relationship with Vannevar Bush, a significant promoter of scientific developments in the United States, a presidential adviser during and after World War II, and a former Corporation board member from 1939 to 1950 when he served as president of the Carnegie

Institution of Washington. With *Sputnik*, more staff time and money were given to strengthening primary and secondary education in math, science, and teacher training in these areas. Special emphasis was given to reaching out to minorities in the country, especially to ensure that they received excellent math education. To accomplish these goals, the Corporation gave significant support for the development of the "new math," setting in motion an area of grant-making that has persisted until present times.

80   CCNY, Agenda Book of the Board of Trustees, March 17, 1960, "Harvard University: Grant of $75,000 Toward Support of the Defense Policy Seminar" (agenda item), 8, CCNY Records, RBML-CUL. Kissinger's reputation was also greatly enhanced by his eighteen-month stint directing the Special Studies Project for Nelson Rockefeller and the Rockefeller Brothers Fund, starting in 1956; *Encyclopedia of World Biography*, "Henry Kissinger Biography," available at: http://www.notablebiographies.com/Ki-Lo/Kissinger-Henry.html.

81   CCNYAR, 1959, 49.

82   CCNY, Agenda Book of the Executive Committee, December 16, 1958, "Social Science Research Council: Grant of $75,000 for Studies and Conferences on National Security Policies" (agenda item), 2. The Corporation noted that the Council, through its earlier work on civil-military relations, its publications, its support of scholars, and the connections it made between scholars and policymakers, had "defined and advanced a new field of research"; CCNY, Agenda Book of the Board of Trustees, March 19, 1956, "Social Science Research Council: Grant of $75,000 for Studies and Conferences on National Security Policies 1939–1955" (agenda item), 15.

83   In making this request, staff further noted: "Although these policies are affected at almost every point by economic considerations, it is a curious fact that the nation's ablest economists have given relatively little attention to this field.... Rewards of reputation and advancement are reserved for those economists who concern themselves with theory, mathematical economics, and with various other fields remote from the kinds of policy studies which are under discussion here." CCNY, Agenda Book of the Executive Committee, December 16, 1958, "Social Science Research Council" (agenda item), 3, CCNY Records, RBML-CUL.

84   CCNYAR, 1962, 40.

85   The Benoit-Boulding work has been called a "pioneering study." See Murray Weidenbaum, *The Competition of Ideas: The World of Washington Think Tanks* (New Brunswick, NJ: Transaction Publishers, 2009), 50; Sylvia Nasar, "Kenneth Boulding, an Economist, Philosopher, and Poet, Dies at 83," *New York Times*, March 20, 1993.

86   The main book is Emile Benoit and Kenneth E. Boulding, eds., *Disarmament and the Economy* (New York: Harper & Row, 1963). In his obituary on Boulding, Corporation grantee Richard Falk wrote: "Boulding was instrumental in bringing serious academic attention to conflict as a distinct subject, founding the Center for Conflict Resolution while on the faculty of the University of Michigan. His book *Conflict and Defense* (1962) developed a sophisticated and rigorous theory of security and conflict in international relations that linked, in an original manner, a concern with the viability of sovereign states with the distance separating them from their perceived enemies." Richard Falk, obituary for Kenneth Boulding, *The Independent*, March 18, 1993.

87   CCNY, Agenda Book of the Executive Committee, April 17, 1963, "University of Michigan: Grant of $245,000 for Research on Conflict Resolution" (agenda item), 2–3, CCNY Records, RBML-CUL. These issues are revisited in Chapters 7 and 8.

88   CCNYAR, 1960, 35.

89   CCNY, Agenda Book of the Executive Committee, April 19, 1960, "Princeton University: Grant of $90,000 for Research on Internal Warfare" (agenda item), 13, CCNY Records, RBML-CUL.

90   CCNYAR, 1962, 43. From the late 1960s to the early 1970s, Robert LeVine directed one of the main centers on child development in Kenya as part of the Commonwealth Program.

91 CCNY, Agenda Book of the Board of Trustees, June 15, 1966, "American Society for International Law: Grant of $54,000 for Studies of International Law and Civil Wars" (agenda item), 15–16, CCNY Records, RBML-CUL.

92 CCNYAR, 1966, 56.

93 CCNY, Agenda Book of the Executive Committee, December 20, 1960, "Carnegie Endowment for International Peace: Grants of $75,000 for Visiting Research Scholars" (agenda item), 14; CCNY, Agenda Book of the Executive Committee, April 21, 1965, "Carnegie Endowment for International Peace: Grants of $75,000 for Visiting Research Scholars" (agenda item), 11; both at CCNY Records, RBML-CUL.

94 Richard A. Falk and Saul H. Mendlovitz, *The Strategy of World Order*, 4 vols. (New York: World Law Fund, 1966).

95 CCNYAR, 1967, 62.

96 Ibid.

97 John Gardner, "The American University in World Affairs," CCNYAR, 1959, 20. The full essay presents clearly the Corporation's rationale for and experiences with this field of research.

98 CCNYAR, 1959, 20–21.

99 CCNY, Agenda Book of the Board of Trustees, March 17, 1960, "Council on Foreign Relations: Grant of $500,000 for Support of Research, Regional Committees, and Fellowships" (agenda item), CCNY Records, RBML-CUL. The Executive Committee renewed this grant in 1964 for $400,000, noting that the reduced level was to open up resources for new ideas by "modestly" lowering the commitments to longtime grantees; CCNY, Agenda Book of the Executive Committee, November 20, 1962, "Council on Foreign Relations: Grant of $400,000 for General Support" (agenda item), 17–18, CCNY Records, RBML-CUL.

100 CCNYAR, 1960, 47.

101 As raised in Chapter 4 and later in this chapter, the staff members working on overseas activities did not draw directly on these efforts, nor did the results from the overseas grants in the Commonwealth influence the work of the US-based teams.

102 Ibid., 23. Gardner introduced the essay by noting, "In 1950, 54 per cent of the world's land area, 63 per cent of its population, and 70 per cent of its national entities were contained in 'underdeveloped' areas."

103 For thorough discussions of the complex of issues surrounding development and modernization in this era, see Ekbladh, *The Great American Mission*, and Nils Gilman, *Mandarins of the Future: Modernization in Cold War America* (Baltimore: Johns Hopkins University Press, 2003).

104 As discussed in Chapters 2 and 3, the Corporation was involved in community development through the Jeanes education initiatives in the US South and Africa and the projects with St. Francis Xavier University in Antigonish, Nova Scotia, and the Rockefeller Foundation was involved in this work through the General Education Board in the United States and village-level work in China. The Ford Foundation briefly supported community development efforts in its overseas work in the 1950s, and more extensively in the United States in the 1960s. See Sutton, "Nation-Building in the Heyday of the Classic Development Ideology," and Richard Magat, *Ford Foundation at Work: Philanthropic Choices, Methods and Styles* (New York: Plenum Publishing, 1979).

105 There have been few analyses of the three foundations' contributions, both jointly and separately, to building the field of post–World War II economic development. Given the current state of both theory and practice in the field of economic development, with scholars and practitioners calling for new values, theories, and approaches, such analytical work could make a significant contribution to understanding how political, social, economic, and cultural pressures distort decision-making about economic development, both in developing countries and

in development assistance activities. Because the intervening years have yielded only a few sustainable, equitable country-level successes that are neither riven by conflict nor dependent on external resources, a fresh analysis of the beginning of the era—the period of decolonization and independence—might provide new insights that could shape more positive and productive futures to fulfill the still-unmet expectations raised in the 1950s; Ekbladh discusses these issues throughout *The Great American Mission*. Jeremy Adelman illuminates these issues through a biography of one of the leading scholars and practitioners in the field of economic development, *Worldly Philosopher: The Odyssey of Albert O. Hirschman* (Princeton, NJ: Princeton University Press, 2013). Drawing on extensive on-the-ground experience, Daniel Taylor, Carl Taylor, and Jesse Taylor provide an excellent overview of the field in *Empowerment on an Unstable Planet* (New York: Oxford University Press, 2011).

106 For the Rockefeller Foundation, see early reviews by the officers of program ideas, prompted by a memo from Norman Buchanan, "Further Notes on Social Science Program," April 24, 1955, Folder 333, Box 61, Series 900, Record Group 3.2, Rockefeller Foundation records, Rockefeller Archive Center (RAC). What would be the main focus for many years was put forward by President George Harrar at a Board of Trustees meeting, December 5–6, 1961, "Proposed University Development Program of the Rockefeller Foundation," Folder 331, Box 60, Series 900, Record Group 3.2, Rockefeller Foundation records, RAC. The full experience is described in James Coleman, with David Court, *University Development in the Third World: The Rockefeller Foundation Experience* (Oxford: Pergamon, 1993). For the Ford Foundation, see Sutton, "Nation-Building in the Heyday of the Classic Development Ideology" and "The Ford Foundation's Development Program in Africa."

107 Michael P. Collinson, ed., *A History of Farming Systems Research* (Wallingford, UK, and Rome, Italy: CABI Publishing and Food and Agricultural Organization, 2000). Collinson defines farming systems research as "a diagnostic process; a basket of methods for researchers to elicit a better understanding of farm households, family decisions and decision-making processes. Its applications use this understanding to increase the efficiency in the use of human and budgetary resources for agricultural development, including research, extension, and policy formulation"; ibid., 1. The field of farming systems research is a logical outgrowth of the work in Jeanes education and all that entailed in the American South, Africa, and the Caribbean, as well as the work in the 1930s funded by the Rockefeller Foundation in China and Carnegie Corporation in Nova Scotia. An important area for future research is connecting these areas through the technical assistance work of Cornell and Michigan State Universities in the 1950s and 1960s, along with the community development program of the Ford Foundation in the 1950s, especially in India, with its multifaceted approach to development and related extension services; Frank Sutton, personal communication with the author, April 27, 2012.

108 CCNYAR, 1957, 19. In the agenda item for the board, staff noted that the Peruvian government had passed a new law for small landholders; "under this new law, the Hacienda Vicos (which is owned by the Peruvian Government) will be broken up into individual plots, with the title to those plots going to the Indian families who now live and work on the hacienda"; CCNY, Agenda Book of the Executive Committee, June 27, 1957, "Cornell University: Grant of $16,800 for Studies of the Impact of Technological Change on Non-industrialized Societies" (agenda item), 16–17, CCNY Records, RBML-CUL. This was a final grant.

109 Illustrating some of the concerns about internal conflict discussed in this chapter, the situation with the Peruvian landowners culminated in a series of protests over the period 1956–1957; the landowners threatened to "store potatoes in Vicos school," said Francisco Sagasti, whose mother was a journalist writing about the conflict; personal communication with the author, May 4, 2012.

110   For the most recent publication that presents the many dimensions of the Los Vicos Project, see Tom Greaves, Ralph Bolton, and Florencia Zapata, eds., *Vicos and Beyond: A Half Century of Applying Anthropology in Peru* (Lanham, MD: AltaMira Press, 2011).

111   For both projects, see CCNYAR, 1962, 38.

112   Hoffnung-Garskoff, "Latin American Studies and United States Foreign Policy."

113   CCNYAR, 1964, 41.

114   Ibid. At the same time, the Corporation supported the political sociologist Seymour Martin Lipset, the director of the Institute of International Studies at the University of California, to review the many studies on development and see whether there were some principles emerging that could enhance understanding and management of national development programs and activities. The chair of the Department of Government at Indiana University, Walter Laves, in a complementary project, reviewed the United Nations and its agencies working on the development of political institutions (ibid., 41–42), and Professor Nicholas DeWitt, an expert on Soviet education, also at Indiana University, received a grant to analyze the relationship between education and development in developing nations (ibid., 41). The Corporation would support similar work in 1990—a series of studies led by political economist Nicholas Van der Walle, then at the University of Michigan and the Overseas Development Council, of the impact of development assistance projects in Africa—and again, in 2003, when it supported the research of economist and policymaker Carol Lancaster at Georgetown University, who, as a Carnegie Scholar, prepared an analytical history of fifty years of development assessment. One of the challenges with such a publication, even one as excellent and revelatory as Lancaster's, is whether the development agencies, the World Bank, or the technical assistance agencies of the different countries involved have a way of taking the findings into account. While all of these parties now take seriously the issue of evaluation, there is still often not enough interaction between serious academic policy analysts and the potential users of their results. Corporation staff have recognized this conundrum of development assistance—how to use knowledge gained in the field to make projects better and more effective—but even after nearly seventy years of research, funded by the Corporation and many others, a feedback loop that is both pragmatic and of high quality has not yet been effectively developed and used.

115   As Lloyd Rodwin wrote in 1994, "The new development agenda looks very much like Hirschman's old one, which is not surprising since Hirschman has had a major impact on it. His main ideas have been vindicated." Lloyd Rodwin, "Rethinking the Development Experience: Aims, Theories, and Theses," in *Rethinking the Development Experience: Essays Provoked by the Work of Albert O. Hirschman*, ed. Lloyd Rodwin and Donald A. Schon (Washington, DC, and Cambridge, MA: Brookings Institution and Lincoln Institute of Land Policy, 1994), 30–31.

116   Albert O. Hirschman, "Author's Preface: A Hidden Ambition," in *Development Projects Observed, with a New Preface by the Author* (1967; reprinted, with a new preface, Washington, DC: Brookings Institution, 1995), xii. See also Adelman, *Worldly Philosopher.*

117   CCNYAR, 1956, 44; CCNY, Agenda Book of the Board of Trustees, March 19, 1956, "Columbia University: Grant of $85,000 for Support of American Assembly on Representation of the United States Abroad" (agenda item), CCNY Records, RBML-CUL.

118   Eugene Burdick and William J. Lederer, *The Ugly American* (New York: W. W. Norton, 1958).

119   CCNYAR, 1961, 29. For a detailed discussion that situates this work in a broader context for the Corporation and the field, see Ekbladh, *The Great American Mission*, 254–259.

120   For Corporation discussion of the issues and grants, see CCNY, Agenda Book of the Board of Trustees, November 18, 1958, "Syracuse University: Grant of $150,000 for an Experiment in Training for Overseas Service" (agenda item), 21–22, and "Montana State College:

Grant of $90,000 for an Experiment in Training for Overseas Service" (agenda item), 23–24, CCNY Records, RBML-CUL; see also CCNYAR, 1959, 14–20. To interest a highly relevant cluster of educational institutions in becoming more involved in international development, the Corporation made a grant to the American Association of Land Grant Colleges and State Universities for its Centennial Convocation, which focused on the international responsibilities of land grant institutions. Given the Corporation's early and consistent support to two land grant institutions for this purpose, Cornell University and Michigan State University, this grant clearly fit into its agenda to make technical assistance more effective. Although this did not remain a significant area of interest for the Corporation, USAID picked up on it and worked closely with this cluster of institutions in implementing its programs; CCNY, Agenda Book of the Executive Committee, October 11, 1960, "American Association of Land-Grant Colleges and State Universities: Grant of $68,000 for Expenses of the Centennial Convocation on International Responsibilities of Land-Grant Institutions" (agenda item), 5–6, CCNY Records, RBML-CUL.

121 CCNYAR, 1962, 30; The Committee on the University and World Affairs, *The University in World Affairs* (New York: Ford Foundation, 1960).

122 CCNYAR, 1962, 30–31; CCNY, Agenda Book of the Board of Trustees, November 15, 1961, "New Organization Concerned with University Activities in World Affairs: Grant of $500,000 Towards Support" (agenda item), 5–7, CCNY Records, RBML-CUL. The foundation partnership leading to Education and World Affairs had its counterpart in the 2000s, the Partnership for Higher Education in Africa (see Chapter 8).

123 Gardner made the case in his 1962 annual essay: "Higher learning has never respected national boundaries. It has always been international in character. But education as an international concern has taken on new dimensions and new significance in the 1960s. Everyone now realizes that it is essential to economic development and political evolution, and the demand for education in the developing nations has become articulate, often clamorous, and sometimes unrealistic. This demand—and the expectation of its fulfillment—constitutes a radically new element in international affairs. Economists and manpower experts have popularized the notion of education as the development of human resources similar in many respects to capital investment in the development of natural resources. If this conception prevails, large sums to build and equip schools, colleges, and universities will be considered as capital expenditures, and loans will also be regarded as a normal rather than an exceptional way of extending educational assistance. This new conception of the educated man as a resource has drawn the universities of the more advanced nations into assuming ever-increasing responsibilities. But substantial as their efforts have been, educational development in the emerging nations appears capable of absorbing all the teachers and specialists that the advanced countries can supply and train. All of the many organizations and persons now active in educational assistance abroad—governments, international organizations and lending agencies, universities and colleges, teachers, research scholars, foundations, business and industry, and missionaries—have their own special and important functions to fulfill. They will seldom, if ever, act as one; but they should be aware of each other's roles and of the essential elements for an effective program of foreign assistance to educational development"; CCNYAR, 1962, 36–37. See also the Corporation's support in the 1960s for the work of Gary Becker at the National Bureau of Economic Research: Becker was developing a theoretical framework for human capital as integral to economic analyses, for which he won the Nobel Prize in 1992; see "Gary S. Becker—Biographical," Nobelprize.org, available at: www.nobelprize.org/nobel_prizes/economic-sciences/laureates/1992/becker-bio.html (accessed January 20, 2014).

124 EWA was a controversial institution from the beginning. An insightful dissertation written by Joyce Hertko detailed its ups and downs until its demise in 1970. The major entity for promoting and coordinating the international orientation programs for American universities, EWA

worked closely with the federal government to obtain passage of a pathbreaking bill to promote international education, namely, the International Education Assistance Act of 1966; unfortunately, this act passed as the Vietnam War costs were soaking up funds for domestic programs. The government never provided the promised significant support anticipated by the foundations and EWA staff. Joyce Mary Hertko, "The Internationalization of American Higher Education During the 1960s: The Involvement of the Ford Foundation and the Carnegie Corporation in Education and World Affairs," PhD diss., Indiana University School of Education, August 1996, UMI Microform 9716447. For an analysis of the field written closer to the time period, see Fred A. Sondermann, "Colleges, Universities, and World Affairs: A Review," *Journal of Conflict Resolution* 10, no. 2 (June 1966): 227–239.

125 CCNYAR, 1960, 24–25.

126 CCNY, Agenda Book of the Board of Trustees, January 21, 1960, "Princeton University, Grant of $200,000 for an Inter-University Study of the Role of Education and High-Level Manpower in the Modernization Process" (agenda item), 8, CCNY Records, RBML-CUL. Manpower studies became very popular with aid agencies and national governments in the 1960s (as discussed later in this chapter) but later fell into disrepute, largely because of the problem faced in many developing countries: too many educated citizens and not enough jobs.

127 CCNYAR, 1960, 25.

128 "Sol Tax, Anthropology" (obituary), *University of Chicago Chronicle*, January 19, 1995; CCNYAR, 1962, 38. The self-teaching materials were an important step forward in learning how best to teach English to people from other cultures. This work helped develop the techniques and principles that could be adapted for teaching any language to members of another culture while simultaneously teaching them about the culture in which the language is spoken. Tax's work also related at the time to the Corporation's long-standing interest in foreign languages and teaching them as a part of adult education, although it was not framed in that way when the grant was made.

129 CCNYAR, 1960, 23.

130 CCNYAR, 1966, 55.

131 Ibid., 55–56.

132 Robert D. Kaplan, "Looking the World in the Eye," *Atlantic Monthly* 288, no. 5 (December 2001); Samuel Huntington, *Political Order in Changing Societies* (New Haven, CT: Yale University Press, 1968).

133 CCNY, Agenda Book of the Board of Trustees, January 19, 1961, "MIT: Grant of $475,000 Toward a Program of Research and Training on the Politics of Transitional Societies" (agenda item), 4–6, CCNY Records, RBML-CUL. For several years the Corporation also supported interdisciplinary studies on the economic, social, and political factors associated with modernization; CCNY, Agenda Book of the Board of Trustees, January 19, 1961, "University of California: Grant of $200,000 for Research and Training on Social, Economic, and Political Developments of Transitional Societies" (agenda item), 7–8; CCNY, Agenda Book of the Executive Committee, December 16, 1964, "University of Chicago: Final Grant of $200,000 for the Research and Training Program of the Committee for the Comparative Study of New Nations" (agenda item), 8–9; both at CCNY Records, RBML-CUL. In addition, the Corporation provided support for several scholars and their individual research, including, for example: Karl Deutsch for his work on political communities (CCNY, Agenda Book of the Executive Committee, October 22, 1959, "Yale University: Grant of $55,000 for Research on Large-Scale Political Communities" [agenda item], 7); Henry Kissinger and his work on political developments (CCNY, Agenda Book of the Board of Trustees, March 16, 1961, "Harvard University: Grant of $45,000 for Support of Research on Political Development in Transitional Societies" [agenda item], 20);

Walter Laves and Fred Riggs for research on political factors (CCNY, Agenda Book of the Board of Trustees, January 18, 1962, "Indiana University: Grant of $105,000 for Studies of Political Development in New Nations" [agenda item], 9–10); and Charles Frankel for his work on the political-philosophical dimensions (CCNY, Agenda Book of the Executive Committee, April 24, 1962, "Columbia University: Grant of $57,000 for Research on Democratic Development in Transitional Societies" [agenda item], 10–11; all at CCNY Records, RBML-CUL. For a more expansive study of democracy, Charles Frankel, James Perkins, and Pendleton Herring were supported under the auspices of the Social Science Research Council to conduct field studies, hold meetings, and produce papers and books on the subject of democracy and development, a complement to their work on the United States for the Rockefeller Brothers Fund, *The Power of the Democratic Idea* (1960); CCNY, Agenda Book of the Board of Trustees, March 16, 1961, "Social Science Research Council: Grant of $37,500 for a Study of the Growth of Democracy in Transitional Societies" (agenda item), 17–19, CCNY Records, RBML-CUL.

134   Walt W. Rostow, *The Stages of Growth: A Non-Communist Manifesto* (Cambridge: Cambridge University Press, 1960).

135   Godfrey Hodgson, "Obituary: Walt Rostow: Cold War Liberal Adviser to President Kennedy Who Backed the Disastrous US Intervention in Vietnam," *The Guardian*, February 16, 2003.

136   Rostow, *The Stages of Economic Growth*, 4.

137   Barbara Ward Jackson, "Cutting Aid to Punish Pakistan: Why the United States Should Be Patient with Assistance," *Foreign Affairs* 41, no. 1 (1962). Sir Robert Jackson was a senior United Nations official and national development adviser, inter alia, in Ghana, India, and Pakistan.

138   CCNY, Agenda Book of the Executive Committee, October 21, 1958, "Radcliffe College: Grant of $88,000 for a Study of Economic Assistance Programs by Lady Barbara Ward Jackson" (agenda item), 1, CCNY Records, RBML-CUL.

139   Barbara Ward, *The Rich Nations and the Poor Nations* (New York: W. W. Norton, 1962), 15. In the agenda item for a follow-up grant, Corporation staff noted that this volume was a "best seller last spring and was distributed by the Book of the Month Club." Ward was considered "one of the most literate and experienced observers of the modernization process today"; CCNY, Agenda Book of the Board of Trustees, November 20, 1962, "Radcliffe College: Final Grant of $88,000 for a Study of Economic Assistance Programs by Barbara Ward" (agenda item), 13, CCNY Records, RBML-CUL.

140   Paul Brass and Ashutosh Varshney, "Remembering Wiener's Legacy," Rediff on the Net, September 23, 1999, available at: http://www.rediff.com/news/1999/sep/23us2.htm.

141   CCNYAR, 1966, 56.

142   Myron Weiner, *Party Building in a New Nation* (Chicago: University of Chicago Press, 1967).

143   CCNYAR, 1960, 25. Outside of grants in the 1930s to missionary institutions and in the 1950s to the Hartford Seminary to train missionaries for overseas work in the newly developing countries (see CCNYAR, 1956, 45), this was the only grant made explicitly to examine the issue of religion in the context of development. It would not be until the twenty-first century that the Corporation returned to examining the relationship between religion and development, in the context of studies related to Islam and Muslim communities.

144   CCNY, Agenda Book of the Executive Committee, April 17, 1963, "Columbia University: Grant of $33,400" (agenda item), CCNY Records, RBML-CUL; CCNYAR, 1963, 31; for discussion of Caplow's work, see CCNYAR, 1965, 47–48.

145   Morris David Morris, *Measuring the Conditions of the World's Poor: The Physical Quality of Life Index: Pergamon Policy Study 42* (New York: Pergamon Press for the Overseas Development Council, 1979).

146   CCNYAR, 1960, 27.

147   Having served as midwife at the birth of the Institute in 1919, the Corporation right away felt warm parental instincts, housing it for many years in the same offices, paying its rent, covering its overdrafts, and ensuring its stability through difficult times in the 1930s, 1940s, and even into the 1950s. Every time the Institute requested a major grant and was then supported by the Corporation, the same wording would be used: if the Corporation did not provide support, it would be detrimental to the health of the institution and would compromise the valuable services that it provided to connect Americans to the world in bringing foreign students and visitors to the United States. Even though this was to be a "terminal" grant, the Corporation was soon supporting the Institute of International Education again.

148   CCNY, Agenda Book of the Board of Trustees, January 19, 1956, "Institute of International Education: Grant of $1,500,000 Toward Support" (agenda item), 6–9, CCNY Records, RBML-CUL.

149   For example, CCNY, Agenda Book of the Board of Trustees, May 17, 1956, "Social Science Research Council: Grant of $250,000 for Faculty Research Grants" (agenda item), 22; CCNY, Agenda Book of the Board of Trustees, May 16, 1957, "Social Science Research Council: Grant of $150,000 for Travel Expenses of Scholars to International Meetings" (agenda item), 11–12; CCNYAR, 1960, 28; all at CCNY Records, RBML-CUL. The Corporation was extraordinarily strong in its support: "The Social Science Research Council, as the leading organization of social science scholars in this country, identifies important international meetings and selects outstanding scholars to attend"; CCNYAR, 1960, 28. See also "Social Science Research Council," 100 Years: The Rockefeller Foundation, available at: rockefeller100.org/exhibits/show/social_sciences/social-science-research-council (accessed January 20, 2014).

150   American Council of Learned Societies, "On Our History," available at: http://www.acls.org/about/history.

151   CCNYAR, 1960, 28.

152   CCNYAR, 1966, 59.

153   Laurence D. Stifel, Ralph K. Davidson, and James S. Coleman, "Agencies of Diffusion: A Case Study of the Rockefeller Foundation," in *Social Sciences and Public Policy in the Developing World*, ed. Laurence D. Stifel, Ralph K. Davidson, and James S. Coleman (Lexington, MA: Lexington Books, 1982); Coleman and Court, *University Development in the Third World*; on the Ford Foundation, see Sutton, "Nation-Building in the Heyday of the Classic Development Ideology."

154   As mentioned in Chapter 4, the change in the status of the British colonies led not only to significant programmatic changes for the Corporation but also to an amendment of the charter. Legal counsel was asked to seek an amendment that would approve "a redefinition which would include within the permissible scope of the Corporation's activities all countries and territories which were within the intended meaning of the act of April 3, 1948, without regard to changes in their political status which have occurred since that date or which may occur in the future"; CCNY, Agenda Book of the Executive Committee, September 29, 1959, "Amendment of Charter: Proposal to Amend the Corporation's Charter with Respect to Expenditures Abroad" (agenda item), 14–15, CCNY Records, RBML-CUL. The board agreed to this and also clarified the calculation of the annual amount available to the BDC program: rather than choose a dollar amount, the trustees agreed that 7.4 percent of the Corporation's general funds would be available for the program each year; as they pointed out, "the figure of 7.4% is merely another way of expressing the approximate ratio of $10 million to $135 million" (ibid., 15), that is, the original amount Andrew Carnegie made available for this work divided by the total amount he gave the Corporation. The New York State Legislature passed an amendment to the Corporation's charter on February 4, 1961; CCNY, Agenda Book of the Board of Trustees, March 16, 1961,

"Administration: Allocation of Income to British Commonwealth Program" (agenda item), 2–4, CCNY Records, RBML-CUL.

155 The work of the Commonwealth Program from the period 1953 to 1973 has been fully described and cogently analyzed by Jefferson Murphy in his 1976 book *Creative Philanthropy.* Although he focuses on Africa, Murphy also briefly reviews the work in the rest of the program, including some of the US-based activities. In addition, Murphy prepared two internal documents that amplified his publications on the Commonwealth Program and some of the international activities in the United States during this period. Three other publications perceptively analyze the development of higher education in Africa: Ajayi, Goma, and Johnson, *The African Experience with Higher Education;* King, *Pan-Africanism and Education;* and Heyman, "The Role of the Carnegie Corporation in African Education, 1925–1960." At an Australian Social Studies Association conference held in February 2010 to review the history of Carnegie Corporation's activities in Australia and New Zealand, scholars presented papers on activities during this period; see Darian-Smith, McLeod, and Sluga, "Philanthropy and Public Culture."

156 Stephen H. Stackpole, memo to Florence Anderson, September 17, 1962, Commonwealth Program (Africa), 1956–1975, Folders 4–7, Box 5, Series I.D, CCNY Records, RBML-CUL.

157 Murphy, *Creative Philanthropy*, 64.

158 Clive Whitehead, *Colonial Educators: The British Indian and Colonial Education Service, 1858–1983* (London: I. B. Taursis & Co., 2003), 202.

159 CCNYAR, 1956, 29.

160 Stephen H. Stackpole, memo to John Gardner and James Perkins, October 2, 1958, Commonwealth Program (Africa), Folders 4–7, Box 5, Series I.D, CCNY Records, RBML-CUL.

161 CCNYAR, 1959, 52.

162 Prosser Gifford and William Louis Roger, *Decolonization and African Independence: The Transfers of Power: 1960–1980* (New Haven, CT: Yale University Press, 1988), xxvii.

163 E. Jefferson Murphy, "Past Activities of the Commonwealth Program: 1953–1973," February 1975, 25–26, Staff and Trustee Files, Box 9, Series I.E, CCNY Records, RBML-CUL.

164 Murphy, *Creative Philanthropy*, 38.

165 Thirty years after the Greenbrier meeting, in 1995, the late J. Wayne Fredericks (appointed the first deputy assistant secretary of state for Africa in 1961, very early in the Kennedy administration) brought together many of the participants—still active "Africanists"—with support from the Corporation and the Ford Foundation under the auspices of the Institute of International Education. All had been instrumental in developing a new American relationship with the British Foreign Office and the new African countries. As noted by Fredericks, "In the early 1960s there was a constellation of political supporters for new African policy which has not been equaled since." The meeting summary provided insight into the issues that the Corporation and Fredericks faced in trying to develop sound policies toward Africa and promote funding for them: poor media coverage (the Cold War slant) and an absence of American expertise and public knowledge. They acknowledged that "these distortions complicated the efforts of policymakers" who were designing the first policies toward Africa; see J. Wayne Fredericks, *A Second Look: The Role of Africanists in US Policymaking During the Late 1950s and Early 1960s* (New York: Institute of International Education, 1995), which is a report on the conference, held at the Aspen Institute's Wye Woods Conference Center, Queenstown, MD, March 9–11, 1995.

166 Alan Pifer, "Report on Trip to Africa—December 19, 1959, to February 1960" (memo to staff), Folders 4–7, Box 17, Series I.E.4, CCNY Records, RBML-CUL. It should be noted that Pifer made trips to Africa annually, and sometimes more frequently.

167 An early success of the Africa Liaison Committee was assisting the University of Nigeria in Nsukka in its educational planning activities. Organized with the help of Michigan State University, this grant reflected a pragmatic land-grant approach to education, not the clas-

sical approach promoted by the British. The British Colonial Office expressed deep concerns that the Americans were entering their territory without due consultation. The Africa Liaison Committee, with its tripartite approach, negotiated this potential contretemps between the Americans and the British, enabling this experience to be a successful one for Nigeria; ibid., 104–106. For the first grant, see CCNY, Agenda Book of the Board of Trustees, May 21, 1959, "American Council on Education: Grant of $12,500 to Establish a Committee for Educational Liaison with African Countries" (agenda item), 23, CCNY Records, RBML-CUL.

168 Murphy, *Creative Philanthropy*, 121.

169 CCNY, Minutes of the Board of Trustees, May 19, 1960, 66, CCNY Records, RBML-CUL. One impetus for support was a concern raised by Tom Mboya, a student leader in Kenya who staged a dramatic airlift of eighty-one students in September 1959, after having made smaller-scale efforts to help Kenyan students go to the United States. Starting in 1956, Mboya had received support from American colleges and universities. After becoming frustrated with the educational requirements of the university colleges at Makerere and Nairobi, he tried to persuade American colleges to admit students from East Africa. As Murphy reported, "With the support of a specially organized African-American students foundation, he [Mboya] hit upon the idea of chartering flights from Nairobi to New York, thus greatly reducing the high travel costs handicapping many would-be students. Response from American colleges and universities was generous, and soon there were scores of offers of places, most of the scholarships covering tuition or even some living expenses.… The airlift was of some concern to many Americans— government officials, foundation staff, and university administrators." Although government, foundation, and university officials wanted the students to get an education in the United States, their concern was on administrative, educational, and placement grounds. Colonial officers were equally concerned: Mboya was a nationalist leader, and the airlift could not avoid being framed in anticolonial passions. Murphy, *Creative Philanthropy*, 104–107.

170 Murphy, *Creative Philanthropy*, 110–111. The Corporation provided a grant to the Provisional Council of the university to prevent duplication across the constituent colleges in Kenya, Tanganyika, and Uganda and to ensure that "core requirements should more closely reflect East African conditions." CCNYAR, 1962, 46; CCNY, Agenda Book of the Board of Trustees, March 15, 1962, "The Provisional Council of the University of East Africa: Grant of $50,000 for Travel Expenses for University Planning" (agenda item), 25–26, CCNY Records, RBML-CUL.

171 Teachers College, Columbia University, "Teachers for East Africa and Teacher Education in East Africa Hold Fortieth Reunion," *TC Today*, 26, no. 2 (January 1, 2002), available at: http://www.tc.columbia.edu/news.htm?articleID=3773&pub=7&issue=72.

172 CCNYAR, 1966, 61–62.

173 Alan Pifer, *The Reminiscences of Alan Pifer: Oral History, 1967*, interviewed by Isabel Grossner, August 22, 1967, Carnegie Corporation Project: Oral History, 1966–1970, Columbia Center for Oral History (CCOH), Columbia University Libraries (CUL), 68 (hereafter "Pifer, CCOH"); Murphy *Creative Philanthropy*, 72–81.

174 Pifer, CCOH, 69.

175 The commissioners included the distinguished historian Kenneth Dike, soon to be principal of University College Ibadan and the first Nigerian vice chancellor of the University of Ibadan; Francis Keppel, Corporation Board member, dean of the Graduate School of Education at Harvard University, soon-to-be US commissioner of education, and son of Frederick Keppel; and Eric Ashby, master of Clare College, Cambridge University. Ashby, who believed deeply in the need for African universities to be more relevant to the development experience, was asked to be the chair and thus lent his name to the commission.

176 CCNYAR, 1959, 53–54.

177   Murphy, *Creative Philanthropy*, 81.

178   One of the unforeseen consequences of the recommendation welcoming external funding was that it not only prompted investment by government but also led to considerable support
from external donors, increasing the vulnerability of Nigeria to the vagaries of donor interests.
Two decades later, that would have devastating consequences for the state of universities in
Nigeria and elsewhere on the continent.

179   CCNY, Minutes of the Executive Committee, 28, June 22, 1961; CCNY, Minutes of the
Executive Committee, 38, October 16, 1963; both at CCNY Records, RBML-CUL.

180   Murphy, *Creative Philanthropy*, 78.

181   Ibid., 81.

182   Ibid.

183   CCNYAR, 1960, 52.

184   See, for example, Andrew Taylor, ed., *Insights into African Education: The Karl W. Bigelow
Memorial Lectures* (New York: Teachers College Press, 1984).

185   For a discussion of the links between the Ashby Commission and these plans, see
CCNYAR, 1960, 51–54.

186   Rosenfield, "A Noble Use of Wealth," 35.

187   CCNY, Minutes of the Board of Trustees, XXIX–XXXI, 66, May 19, 1960, CCNY
Records, RBML-CUL.

188   Association for Teachers Education in Africa, "The Association," available at: www.afri-
ate.org (accessed January 25, 2014).

189   The program worked with joint support between the University of London's Institute of
Education, Teachers College at Columbia University, and six institutions in Africa: the Institute
of Education at University College, Ghana; University College of Ibadan, Nigeria; the Nigerian
College of Arts, Science, and Technology, Zaria, Nigeria; Makerere University College, Uganda;
University College of Rhodesia and Nyasaland, Rhodesia; and the Department of Education,
Fourah Bay College, Sierra Leone. All of these institutions had been Corporation grantees
over the past few years, and many of them would be grantees in the future. Earlier colleges had
been funded for library development and special research projects; now support was given for
strengthening institutions in order to meet the new teacher educational needs of the various
countries. CCNYAR, 1960, 52–53, and 1963, 37–41.

190   For a comparative discussion on this period, see Tade Akin Aina, "The State, Politics, and
Philanthropy in Africa: Framing the Context," in *Giving to Help, Helping to Give: The Context
and Politics of African Philanthropy*, ed. Tade Akin Aina and Bhekinkosi Moyo (Dakar, Senegal:
Amalion Publishing/Trust Africa, 2013), 19–27.

191   The undergraduate scholarship program was an anomaly. As part of the effort to jump-
start the enhancement of educational capacity of the African populations in the newly independent countries, the Corporation complemented its local and regional efforts with a cluster of
activities related to providing fellowships for undergraduates to study in American institutions.
Recognizing that students would be coming to study in the United States whether or not the
Corporation provided fellowships, staff members thought it was worth at least a modest effort
and chose to work with the African-American Institute. The Institute had been created in 1953
with the aim of enhancing African human resources through scholarships, training programs,
and other types of investments. The Corporation made its first grant to the Institute in 1960 to
provide scholarship aid to African students. The initial activity was a pilot scheme for Nigerian
students in twenty-one institutions, organized by the director of admissions at Harvard
College, David Henry. The reaction was so positive that the US International Cooperation
Administration provided additional support to involve other institutions, and the Corporation

agreed to continue to cover the administrative expenses. Nonetheless, the Corporation did not usually fund scholarships at the undergraduate level (for another successful, albeit also exceptional, effort, see Chapter 8); thus, this effort, while successful, did not stimulate similar ones for West Africa or other regions. Murphy, *Creative Philanthropy*, 88–91.

192   Stephen Stackpole, "First Memorandum on Commonwealth Program for the Period Ahead," September 18, 1963, 1–2, Folder 7, Box 4, Series Commonwealth Program (General), 1956–1968, CCNY Records, RBML-CUL.

193   Ibid., 5 (emphasis in original).

194   Ibid., 7.

195   Ibid., 8. This memo by Stackpole amply illustrates his leadership and analytical capacities, although he was often overshadowed by others at the Corporation.

196   As Gardner wrote in his 1962 presidential essay, reflecting studies that influenced the Corporation's decision: "Almost everyone closely associated with what is happening in Africa today recognizes that the economic development of the new nations depends ultimately on the strength of the educational base. African leaders know this, and as a result, their goals for higher education have risen spectacularly. In 1945 there were two institutions of university rank in Middle Africa [sub-Saharan Africa today]. Now there are more than 12 times that number and several others in the planning stages. The financial implications of this academic explosion are staggering. No less tremendous are the human resources required in terms of staff. Both problems were discussed at the UNESCO Conference on the Development of Higher Education in Africa, held at Tananarive in September 1962. A preparatory study done for the Conference on the dimensions of the staffing task was financed by Carnegie [Corporation] through a grant to the Inter-University Council for Higher Education Overseas (London). The findings provided the basis for the conclusions … that over the next 18 years some 14,000 Africans must be recruited and trained for university teaching and some 7,000 teachers must be recruited from abroad for short-term appointments if the development of higher education in Africa is to meet the goals set forth at the Conference. The study was directed by Sir Alexander Carr-Saunders." CCNYAR, 1962, 44–45.

197   CCNYAR, 1964, 44–46.

198   CCNYAR, 1965, 51–53. There was an unexpected development with the former Jeanes educational training center in Kabete, Kenya, funded originally by the Corporation in 1925. (It was the first Corporation grantee in Africa, besides those for libraries and church organs.) Building on earlier work with University College Nairobi, the Corporation renewed support for the Institute of Adult Studies to merge with the College of Social Studies and use the Kabete center to hold a variety of adult education courses for professionals and reach out to adult educators around the country. The intention was for the Institute to continue to work with adult educators throughout the country and to test the idea of using a variety of teaching aids, including television and correspondence courses, to upgrade adult education skills. The Institute would also work with the newly established National Board of Adult Education. "Like many Americans, adults in Kenya seem to find education habit-forming; the director of the extramural department reports:'The more courses we offer, the more we find that people are hungry to learn.'" CCNYAR, 1966, 63–64.

199   CCNYAR, 1965, 53.

200   CCNY, Agenda Book of the Board of Trustees, March 15, 1962, "University College of Sierra Leone (Fourah Bay): Grant of $110,000 for Library Development" (agenda item), 23–24, CCNY Records, RBML-CUL.

201   CCNYAR, 1959, 54.

202   CCNYAR, 1966, 62–63. See also Adam Gambo Saleh, "Educators' Perspective on

Library Education in Nigeria," *Library Philosophy and Practice* 2011, available at: http://www.webpages.uidaho.edu/~mbolin/gambo.htm.

203 Murphy, *Creative Philanthropy*, 113.

204 As the Corporation was developing this focus in the Commonwealth Program, a similar set of interests emerged in the US program under the leadership of Barbara Finberg and Frederic Mosher. Although the work mainly evolved along separate tracks, at times ideas were shared.

205 CCNYAR, 1965, 54.

206 CCNYAR, 1966, 57.

207 Ibid., 57–58.

208 UnCAP: Guide to the Vernon McKay (1912–1988) Papers 1935–1977, Northwestern University Library, available at: http://uncap.lib.uchicago.edu/view.php?eadid=inu-ead-afri-ar-chon-1067. McKay had also been president of the African Studies Association.

209 Pifer wrote eloquently about these events in 1966: "Political allies who speak a common language may not always recognize and understand each other's actions and attitudes in the arena of international affairs. For example, England and the United States share many goals in their relations with the developing nations of Africa and South America—the encouragement of democratic institutions would be one—but their economic and cultural ties with these areas, which grow out of different historical involvements, differ in many respects and can lead to policies that seem diverse. From one side of the Atlantic it is often difficult to comprehend fully thinking on the other side, even when ultimate objectives are similar." CCNYAR, 1966, 56–57.

210 As Clark wrote to Fredericks as part of the review: "My participation in the Anglo-American-Canadian Parliamentary Study Group on Africa was critical to my Congressional career and to my decision to successfully seek the chairmanship of the African Affairs Subcommittee of the U.S. Senate Foreign Relations Committee. Like virtual[ly] every Member of Congress, I knew nothing about Africa and had never given serious thought to U.S. policy prior to attending the series as a participant.... This meeting so stimulated my interest in the continent that I began to read much more on the subject, talk to experts and to visiting Africans. When I moved onto the Foreign Relations Committee I had a chance to apply for the Chairmanship of the African Affairs Subcommittee and I took it.... The fact is that almost no one elected to Congress has any special interest in Africa. It has not been a part of their formal education. Few have ever traveled there and few have ever thought about U.S. policy. It is not big on the policy agenda for most Members. Unless a special effort is made to introduce Members to Africa they will remain uninformed and uninterested. Meetings with other parliamentarians can be very stimulating and can lead to the creation of a cadre of members who will take leadership positions on important issues." Dick Clark, May 15, 1995, in J. Wayne Fredericks, *The Anglo-American-Canadian Parliamentary Study Group on Africa 1965–1980: A Preliminary Review* (New York: Institute of International Education, 1995), 10–11.

211 CCNYAR, 1967, 68. A singular grant supported the distinguished St. Lucian economist Sir W. Arthur Lewis (1979 Nobel Laureate) to examine the political issues in the region; CCNY, Agenda Book of the Board of Trustees, November 19, 1963, "Princeton University: Grant of $60,000 for a Study of the Disintegration of the Federation of the West Indies" (agenda item), 18–19, CCNY Records, RBML-CUL.

212 CCNYAR, 1967, 67–68.

213 One more grant was made in 1958 to continue these fellowships, including for two South Africans. CCNY, Agenda Book of the Executive Committee, June 18, 1958, "Educational Testing Service: Grant of $25,000 for Psychometric Fellowships for Commonwealth Students" (agenda item), 11–12, CCNY Records, RBML-CUL.

214 CCNYAR, 1959, 56.

215 CCNY, Agenda Book of the Executive Committee, September 19, 1956, "Educational Testing Service: Grant of $50,000 for Assistance to the University of Malaya in Developing Educational Testing" (agenda item), 8–9, CCNY Records, RBML-CUL.

216 CCNY, Agenda Book of the Executive Committee, February 21, 1957, "University of Hong Kong: Grants of $54,000 for Staff Training, Salaries, Library Development, and Extension Work" (agenda item), 11–12, and April 25, 1957, "University of Sydney: Grant of $12,000 for a Study of Community Attitudes Toward the University" (agenda item), 13–14, CCNY Records, RBML-CUL.

217 The "Table of Travel Grants, 1964–1966, prepared September 22, 1967," shows that over the three years Australia received fifty-three travel grants; New Zealand twenty-seven; South Africa twenty-four; the rest of Africa thirty-nine; Asia, the West Indies, etc., thirteen; and the United States and Canada six; Commonwealth Program (general), 1956–1968, Folders 4–7, CCNY Records, RBML-CUL; for earlier information, see CCNYAR, 1963, 42. In 1965 the Corporation noted that there was increased interest in American studies in Australia and New Zealand; separately from the travel grants, a grant to the American Council of Learned Societies provided fellowships for scholars from Australia and New Zealand to study American history and civilization in the United States; CCNYAR, 1965, 55.

218 See, for example, consistent with the focus on testing, CCNY, Agenda Book of the Executive Committee, December 18, 1957, "Central Advisory Committee for Education in the Atlantic Provinces: Grant of $82,000 for a Program of Testing High School Students" (agenda item), 12–13, CCNY Records, RBML-CUL.

219 CCNYAR, 1963, 42.

220 Frank Sutton, a Ford Foundation staff member and leader during part of the Gardner years, emphasized that "Carnegie Corporation always punched above its weight." Personal communication with the author, April 19, 2012.

221 See Chapter 7 for renewed concern about the lack of effectiveness of grants on this theme in the 1980s and 1990s.

222 Patricia L. Rosenfield, "Perspectives on Philanthropy: The Role of History as a Guide," *Carnegie Reporter* (Summer 2013): 32–41.

NOTES FOR CHAPTER 6

1 Glenn Howze, review of *The Free Speech Movement: Reflections on Berkeley in the 1960s*, edited by Robert Cohen and Reginald E. Zelnik, *Academe Online* 89, no. 5 (September–October 2003): 98–99, available at: htpp://www.jstor.org/stable/40253401 (accessed January 27, 2014).

2 Carnegie Corporation of New York (CCNY), Annual Report (CCNYAR), 1982, 5 (emphasis in original), CCNY Records, Rare Book and Manuscript Library, Columbia University Libraries (RBML-CUL).

3 Abdalla Bujra, "Pan-African Political and Economic Visions of Development from the OAU to the AU: From the Lagos Plan of Action (LPA) to the New Partnership for African Development (NEPAD)," Development Policy Management Forum Occasional Paper 13 (2004), 4, available at: http://www.dpmf.org/images/OccasionalPaper13.pdf (accessed September 14, 2013). This is an excellent overview of the main Pan-African official policy agreements from the 1970s to the 2000s.

4 Robert J. Berg and Jennifer Seymour Whitaker, eds., *Strategies for African Development* (Berkeley: University of California Press, 1986), table A.7.

5 The South Commission, "The State of the South: The Development Record of the South, 1950–1980," In *The Challenge to the South: The Report of the South Commission* (Oxford:

Oxford University Press,1990), 25–77; Tade Akin Aina,"Development Theory and Africa's Lost Decade: Critical Reflections on Africa's Crisis and Current Trends in Development Thinking and Practice," in *Changing Paradigms in Development—South, East, and West*, ed. Margaretha von Troil (Uppsala, Sweden: Nordiska Afrikainstitutet, 1993), 11–25. For a comparative review of the effects of aid over the period before oil price rises and heavy debt accumulation, see David Morawetz, *Twenty-Five Years of Economic Development, 1950–1975* (Washington, DC: World Bank, 1977).

6 Eva Rathgeber,"WID [women in development], WAD [women and development], GAD [gender and development]: Trends in Research and Practice," *Journal of Developing Areas* 24, no. 4 (1990): 489–502.

7 Pifer's background showed him to be an enterprising, principled, and energetic person. He enlisted in World War II when he was a sophomore at Harvard. After fighting in the Battle of the Bulge, he won a Bronze Star and was promoted from private to captain. He returned home after the war to finish his degree at Harvard with honors in general studies. On graduation, he returned to the United Kingdom for a fellowship at Oxford University before becoming executive secretary of the Fulbright Commission in London. Wolfgang Saxon,"Alan Pifer Is Dead at 84; Led Carnegie Corporation," *New York Times*, November 5, 2005.

8 Alan Pifer, *The Reminiscences of Alan Pifer: Oral History, 1969*, interviewed by Isabel Grossner, August 22, 1967, Carnegie Corporation Project: Oral History, 1966–1970, Columbia Center for Oral History (CCOH), Columbia University Libraries (CUL), 2 (hereafter "Pifer, CCOH").

9 Ibid., 1–5. It is not clear if Pifer was aware of the government effort to do just what he was proposing. That year government support established the Africa-America Institute, which became a major institutional player in the 1960s and ensuing decades, going far beyond the role that even Pifer had originally envisaged. See Africa-America Institute,"About AAI," available at: http://www.aaionline.org/about-aai/ (accessed May 26, 2012).

10 Pifer, CCOH, 9–10. Pifer commented in his oral history that neither Stackpole nor Gardner had been to Africa.

11 It is entirely possible that his leadership role with other foundations in the early 1950s through the mid-1960s in this area also made him a logical choice to be the spokesperson for the foundation community in the late 1960s and then throughout the 1970s, times that called for such leadership.

12 Pifer, CCOH, 202. Frederic "Fritz" Mosher was assigned to work with Stackpole; they built on the prior grants for higher education, institutes of education, and teachers to move in new directions in Africa and the Caribbean. Stephen Viederman, the executive assistant who had been working with Gardner on the international affairs grant-making, continued those efforts in this transition period. When Pifer became president in 1967, Mosher was still working with Stackpole but remained involved in other areas of grant-making at the Corporation. The international affairs grant-making in the United States was handled by Viederman.

13 CCNYAR, 1976, 73.

14 Karen Theroux,"Weathering the Financial Storms of a Century," *Carnegie Reporter* 5, no. 4 (Spring 2010): 28.

15 When Pifer took over fully as president in 1967, the Corporation was spending $13.8 million on domestic grant-making and $950,000 on international overseas grant-making. Domestic grant-making reached a high in 1973 (before things started tumbling down) of $16.4 million; the high mark for the overseas grant-making was $1.8 million in 1973. By the end of the Pifer presidency in 1981, the economic travails had led to only about $12.3 million being available for domestic grant-making and $536,400 for overseas. See CCNYAR, 1967, 77; 1974, 86, 100; and 1981, 29.

16 This was not the first time Pifer and his philanthropic career had experienced congressional

investigations. When he joined the Corporation in 1953, the president, the staff, and the trustees were toiling in the wake of the Reece Committee and the hurling of charges of anti-Americanism against the foundation community. In 1961 the Patman Subcommittee on Foundations of the Select Committee on Small Business started investigating tax exemption and alleged abuses by foundations; this effort continued from 1962 to 1972. The best concise summaries, from which much of this discussion draws, are found in McIlnay, "Philanthropy at Fifty," and James Allen Smith, "Introduction: The Foundation Center: Fifty Years On," in *Philanthropy in the Twenty-First Century*, ed. Mitch Nauffts (New York: Foundation Center, 2006), 1–12. The most accessible and complete technical discussion is by Thomas A. Troyer, "The 1969 Private Foundation Law: Historical Perspective on Its Origins and Underpinnings," *Exempt Organization Tax Review* 27, no. 1 (January 2000): 52–65. Troyer also clarifies and puts into the context of the overall hearings the role of the "fabled Ford Foundation grants" and Ford Foundation president McGeorge Bundy's testimony in prompting some aspects of the resulting legislation; ibid., 52, 60–61.

17 Troyer, "The 1969 Private Foundation Law," 52. The hearings throughout the 1960s took place despite the efforts of foundations, as Smith details. Following the Cox and Reece hearings of the early 1950s, foundation leaders like F. Emerson Andrews, president of the Russell Sage Foundation, and James Perkins, vice president of Carnegie Corporation, worked with other foundations to take "a necessary and decisive step toward improving foundation accountability" by establishing the Foundation Center in 1956. Smith, "Introduction: The Foundation Center," 2–8.

18 CCNYAR, 1968, 13–14.

19 CCNYAR, 1969, 3.

20 There is an extensive literature on these commissions; see Olivier Zunz, *Philanthropy in America: A History* (Princeton, NJ: Princeton University Press, 2012), 226–231; and Eleanor L. Brilliant, *Private Charity and Public Inquiry: A History of the Filer and Peterson Commissions* (Bloomington: Indiana University Press, 2000), 87–98.

21 In addition to Zunz, *Philanthropy in America* (232–241), and Brilliant, *Private Charity and Public Inquiry* (99–143), see Peter Frumkin, "Private Foundations as Public Institutions: Regulation, Professionalization, and Organized Philanthropy," in *Philanthropic Foundations: New Scholarship, New Possibilities*, ed. Ellen Condliffe Lagemann (Bloomington: Indiana University Press, 1999), 69–98; Carl Schramm, "Law Outside the Market: The Social Utility of the Private Foundation," *Harvard Journal of Law and Public Policy* 30, no. 1 (2006); and Ruth Lilly Special Collections and Archives, "Commission on Private Philanthropy and Public Needs Records, 1964–1980," Indiana University, Purdue University, and Indianapolis University Library, available at: http://www.ulib.iupui.edu/special/collections/philanthropy/mss024 (accessed May 28, 2012).

22 Pifer's 1970 presidential essay, "The Jeopardy of Private Institutions," elaborated on the distinctions between private and public institutions, as well as the kinds of threats posed by the congressional hearings and the 1969 act. He identified what he saw as one of the gravest concerns—that the damage to philanthropy happened "with so little protest from the public"—and again called for a national commission; CCNYAR, 1970, 13. Over the seventeen years that Pifer served as president or acting president of Carnegie Corporation, he wrote more than half of his presidential essays around the issues of private and public institutions. His 1970 essay generated a considerable reaction: over 50,000 copies were requested; CCNYAR, 1973, 14.

23 Such abuses were a persistent worry of Carnegie Corporation and other foundation leaders. As Smith writes, in establishing the Foundation Center, "they wanted to lift the veil from foundation activities and assure the public that organized philanthropy would continue to enjoy a legitimate place in American society." Smith, "Introduction: The Foundation Center," 7–8.

24 There are other perspectives on the 1969 act and the Filer Commission. "Although greeted

at the time with dismay among foundation executives," notes Daniel Akst, "the 1969 Act is seen today as a perfectly moderate approach to keeping foundations on the straight and narrow." Daniel Akst, "What Are Foundations For?" *Carnegie Reporter* (Fall 2004): 4; Elan Garonzik, review of *Private Charity and Public Inquiry: A History of the Filer and Peterson Commissions* by Eleanor L. Brilliant, *Alliance*, September 1, 2001, available at: http://www.alliancemagazine.org/node/3067 (accessed June 3, 2012).

25 For a summary of Pifer's vision for philanthropy, see the speech he made in 1984 when he received the award, reprinted in Alan Pifer, *Speaking Out: Reflections on Thirty Years of Foundation Work*, rev. ed. (Washington, DC: Council on Foundations, 2005).

26 Breaking with usual practice, Pifer changed the way staff and trustees interacted at board meetings. Starting when Devereux Josephs increased the size of the staff, the board would call in the responsible officer for a particular set of activities to make a presentation and stay for the discussion on that proposal; then that person would leave. This practice continued under Dollard and Gardner. Much as Josephs, Dollard, and Gardner had been committed to building a sense of teamwork among program staff on the grant-making side, Pifer was equally committed to making board members part of the team. Without blurring boundaries, he opened up board meetings by bringing staff into the meetings, whether or not they were making a presentation, and encouraged them to discuss issues with the board and even raise questions on areas for which they were not responsible.

27 Building on that role, Pifer and the board established a special committee that reviewed how the trustees went about their work. In 1972, after several months of deliberation, the committee recommended changes in the constitution and the bylaws concerning terms of membership, officers, the composition of board committees, and, most importantly, trustee responsibilities. This work on board policies and procedures led to a document defining the board's role as setting policy but not micromanaging. It remains the main guide for trustees forty years later and provides one of the clearest statements of how a board can work in relationship to the mission of the institution and the programs and with the president and staff. CCNYAR, 1972, 59.

28 CCNY, "Board of Trustees: Charter, Constitution, and Bylaws," April 21, 1988, 19–20, CCNY Board Meetings, Series I.A.3; and Alan Pifer, "The Management of Carnegie Corporation, 1911–1977: Part I," 30–31, Box 11, Series I.F; both at CCNY Records, RBML-CUL.

29 Louise Carnegie, who joined the board after her husband's passing in 1919, was the first female trustee (1919–1929). Her daughter, Margaret Carnegie Miller, joined in 1934 and remained until 1980. Of the twenty-eight board members appointed during Pifer's tenure, Pifer appointed eleven women who were pathbreakers from a variety of professions and fields, especially law and civil rights organizations, as well as distinguished academic leaders: Marta Valle (1971), an administrator of the recently created New York City Human Rights Commission and then director of the Columbia School of Social Work; Jeanne Spurlock (1971), an early African American leader in adolescent psychiatry; Madeline McWhinney (1974), founder of the Women's National Bank; Mary Louise Peterson (1976), president of the Iowa Board of Regents; Anne Firor Scott (1976), who established the field of Southern women's history; Judy Rosenstreich (1978), Vermont's youngest female state legislator and the first person from Vermont to win a White House Fellowship; Margaret Rosenheim (1979), professor of social welfare at the University of Chicago and one of the first scholars to combine studies of law and child welfare; and Ann Leven (1981), CFO of the Smithsonian Institution and a leading financier. Over this and the next two eras, Helene Kaplan (1980), a lawyer specializing in nonprofit law and the chair of the Barnard College Board of Trustees, became the longest-serving nonfamily woman trustee, twice serving full terms as board chair under two different presidents (David Hamburg and Vartan Gregorian), for a total of twenty years. Kaplan broke two traditions in that

capacity: she was the first woman board chair of the Corporation and the first person to serve two distinctive terms as chair. She was also the first board chair to be named an honorary trustee. In addition, she served on two of the Corporation's presidential search committees and was one of the board members most actively engaged in the foundation's anti-apartheid concerns. Many of the Corporation's women trustees, in contrast, have not had strong international experience, especially in the Commonwealth, with the exception of Ruth Simms Hamilton, a scholar of the African Diaspora, who was elected to the board in 1981, toward the end of the Pifer era.

30 Before 1970, Corporation precedent was maintained when in 1966 the board elected Harding Bancroft, executive vice president of the *New York Times*, and Louis Cabot, manufacturer, international conservationist, and chair of the Brookings Institution board, who was also involved with the United Nations. In 1967 a milestone was reached: Devereux Josephs retired after serving with the Corporation since 1939 as head of the Teachers Insurance and Annuity Association (now TIAA-CREF), as a trustee, as president, and then as a trustee again. He had been responsible for greatly deepening and expanding the focus on international grant-making in the United States, as well as for reopening the Commonwealth Program. When he stepped off the board, he took with him knowledge of the Corporation's history and an abiding commitment to international affairs grant-making in the United States.

31 The election to the Corporation board in 1967 of Frederick Adams, director of the Pierpont Morgan Library, and Aitken Fisher, chairman of Fisher Scientific and a member of the Carnegie Hero Fund Commission as well as chair of the board of Carnegie-Mellon University, added one member associated with another Carnegie institution. In 1972 the three board members elected reflected quite different types of trustees: Dr. Philip Lee, the first physician on the board, was chancellor of the University of California at San Francisco, after serving at the US Department of Health, Education, and Welfare and in USAID's Office of Technical Cooperation Research; Howard Samuel, the board's first labor unionist, was vice president of the Amalgamated Clothing Workers of America. Both Samuel and Lee were tangentially involved in international issues through their work on health and population. In 1977 Samuel was appointed deputy undersecretary for international labor affairs in the US Department of Labor. The board found a second labor leader, Thomas Donohue, to replace him in 1977. Donohue was executive assistant to the president of the AFL-CIO. Candido A. de Leon, the first Hispanic male trustee, was elected in 1976 and was president of Eugenio Maria dos Hostos Community College of the City University of New York. The election of more traditional candidates continued as well, such as Carl Mueller (1975), president of the investment company Loeb Rhodes & Company, and John Taylor (1976), a partner in the law firm of Paul, Weiss, Rifkind, Morton, and Garrison who was also involved in the American Field Service. John Gloster, president of the Opportunity Funding Corporation in Washington and formerly the State Department's assistant country director for Northeast Africa, joined in 1978. In 1979 two more internationally oriented trustees were elected. Jack Clark, an international lawyer, was senior vice president of Exxon Corporation and a trustee of the American Ditchley Foundation, the National Planning Association (an occasional Carnegie Corporation grantee), and the US Council of the International Chamber of Commerce. John Whitehead, at the time a senior partner at Goldman Sachs & Company with strong international connections, soon became deputy secretary of state under President Reagan. In 1980 Tomas Arciniega and David Hamburg joined the Corporation board. Arciniega was dean of the College of Education at California State University and soon became vice president for Hispanic affairs; he was one of the leading proponents of bilingual education and actively involved in Mexican-American relations. Hamburg, the second medical doctor on the board, was president of the National Academy of Sciences' Institute of Medicine and soon became a professor of health policy and education at Harvard's Kennedy School of Government while remaining

involved in international issues through his biomedical research and health policy work at the World Health Organization.

32   One such link was Caryl Haskins, a Gardner appointee who had conducted scientific research in Africa and was president of the Carnegie Institution of Washington from 1956 to 1971. Pifer himself provided another connection. Like several prior Corporation presidents, he simultaneously served as president of the Carnegie Foundation for the Advancement of Teaching and played a very active role in establishing the basis for joint grant-making between the foundation and the Corporation. During Pifer's tenure, however, there was no other formal linkage with the Carnegie family of institutions in the United States or in the United Kingdom.

33   Avery Russell, "The Second Fifty Years: A Personal View," *Carnegie Reporter* (Spring 2011): 28–29. Available at: www.carnegie.org.

34   CCNYAR, 1973, 9, and 1972, 61.

35   CCNYAR, 1973, 10–11.

36   CCNYAR, 1981, 6.

37   In a series of 1972 memos, Pifer and staff members considered the possibility of much more systematic reviews of all or some of the program areas and related those to trustee reviews. Pifer implemented this idea for the Commonwealth Program grants when he instituted a full-scale, full-year trustee review of the Commonwealth Program in 1974–1975 (discussed later in this chapter). In 1975 the Corporation extended the Fund's reach to cover program development that would enable the exploration of new programs. Starting in 1976, the Program Development and Evaluation Fund underwrote activities in both the United States and the Commonwealth.

38   CCNYAR, 1982, 3.

39   Ibid., 3–11.

40   Joyce Baldwin, "Promoting Social Justice: A Vision of Philanthropic Activism," *Carnegie Results* (Spring 2007). Greater continuity was maintained in the domestic grant-making—in the areas of early childhood and higher education, for example. However, this was a period when the Corporation embarked on more operational activities, particularly the Public Television Commission and, jointly with the Carnegie Foundation for the Advancement of Teaching, the Higher Education Commission. One of the domestic successes of this era was the funding of *Sesame Street*; see Lloyd Morrisett, *The Reminiscences of Lloyd Morrisett: Oral History, 1968*, interviewed by Isabel Grossner, August 1967, Carnegie Corporation Project: Oral History, 1966–1970, CCOH, CUL, 184 (hereafter "Lloyd, CCOH"). The Ford Foundation was a major partner in the social justice and public television activities in the United States.

41   For instance, it was during the late 1960s and early 1970s that the Ford and Rockefeller Foundations joined with the World Bank to launch a global program on agricultural research that included a program in Nigeria; see Uma J. Lele et al., *The CGIAR at Thirty-One: An Independent Meta-Evaluation of the Consultative Group on International Agricultural Research* (Washington, DC: World Bank, 2003, 2004). The Ford and Rockefeller Foundations, along with the Population Council, established a joint interdisciplinary fellowship program on population and development; the International Labor Office initiated its basic needs strategy as part of its World Employment Program in 1976 for development; and international partners launched two major disease research and control programs: in 1974, the Onchocerciasis Control Program, based in West Africa and in 1976, the UN Development Program/World Bank/WHO Special Program for Research and Training in Tropical Diseases, based in Geneva, Switzerland, with plans for a major center in Ndola, Zambia. For a review of the development assistance programs of the different donors, see Lancaster, *Foreign Aid.* For donors to Africa, see van de Walle and Johnson, *Improving Aid to Africa*; and Richard Jolly, Louis Emmerij, and Thomas Weiss, *On Human Development Strategies*, UN and Human Development Briefing Note 8, July 2009, UN

Intellectual History Project, Ralph Bunche Institute for International Studies, CCNY Graduate Center, available at: www.UNhistory.org.

42 Stephen Viederman, who had been the director of foreign student admissions at Columbia University and deputy chairman of the Inter-University Committee on Travel Grants at Indiana University (which aided exchanges with the Soviet Union), joined the Corporation in 1965 to assist with the international affairs grant-making, especially as it related to national security and comparative studies. After two years, he left to become executive officer of the Behavioral and Social Science Survey Committee in Washington, DC. With his departure, the Corporation's international affairs grant-making at universities and the focus on comparative research soon came to an end.

43 CCNYAR, 1966, 55.

44 CCNYAR, 1965, 48.

45 CCNYAR, 1967, 60–61.

46 Ibid., 40.

47 CCNYAR, 1969, 41. The final book in the project was published in 1978: Sydney Verba, Norman H. Nie, and Jae-On Kim, *Participation and Political Equality: A Seven-Nation Comparison* (New York: Cambridge University Press), 1978.

48 CCNYAR, 1969, 49. Curle's studies on the ways in which conflict could be channeled in productive directions to minimize violence led to several books, including *Mystics and Militants: A Study of Awareness, Identity, and Social Action* (London: Tavistock, 1972). Curle was also a participant in negotiations that led to the successful and fairly sudden end of the Biafra war in Nigeria. His success illustrates that modest funding can have significant impact, such as contributing to the founding of a new field of study.

49 CCNYAR, 1968, 38. This support built on the continued support to Cornell since 1947 for work overseas; the Rockefeller Foundation also supported the Cornell work in anthropology in the same areas.

50 CCNY, Agenda Book of the Board of Trustees, May 21, 1970, "Discretionary Fund, US: Northwestern University, for Research on Intercultural Relations, $15,000" (agenda item), 34; see also CCNY, Minutes of the Board of Trustees, XXIX–XXXI, 48, January 18, 1962; both at CCNY Records, RBML-CUL.

51 See CCNYAR, 1968, 40; CCNY, Agenda Book of the Executive Committee, December 17, 1969, "Columbia University: Grant of $124,000 for a Study of Independence and Accountability in the Contract States" (agenda item), 10–12; CCNYAR, 1970, 51; CCNY, Agenda Book of the Executive Committee, April 21, 1971, "Study of Independence and Accountability in the Contract State: Appropriation of $25,000 for Expenses of an Anglo-American Conference" (agenda item), 20–22; all at CCNY Records, RBML-CUL. The resulting publication from the first grant was Bruce L. R. Smith and Douglas Chalmers Hague, eds., *The Dilemmas of Accountability in Modern Government: Independence versus Control* (New York and London: St. Martin's Press and Macmillan & Co., 1971).

52 CCNYAR, 1972, 52, and 1973, 54; Martin Edmonds, "Government Contracting and Renegotiation: A Comparative Analysis," *Public Administration* 50, no. 1 (March 1972): 45–64.

53 Closely related to the contract study was a modest grant of $6,000 to enable Robert W. Morse, the former president of Case Western Reserve University and the assistant secretary of the navy for research and development, to explore the issue of the relationship between the Department of Defense and universities; CCNY, Agenda Book of the Board of Trustees, May 13, 1971, "Discretionary Fund, US: Exploration of Relations Between the Defense Department and Universities" (agenda item), CCNY Records, RBML-CUL. One small writing project connected this era with earlier ones and particularly highlighted the close relationship of social scientists

with the war effort. In 1972 the Corporation, responding to a suggestion by Frederick Osborn, a former member of the board, along with other colleagues who had been responsible for setting up the original joint army and navy committee on welfare and recreation (which had received some support from the Corporation), recruited social scientists to assist with these studies on race relations and desegregation, troop morale, and other issues related to the war effort. The civilian-organized group was called the Information Education Division of the Army. Lawrence Cremin of Teachers College agreed to conduct the study; CCNY, Agenda Book of the Board of Trustees, October 12, 1972, "Discretionary Fund, US: Teachers College, Columbia University, for a History of the Information and Education Division of the US Army, $15,000" (agenda item), 49–50, CCNY Records, RBML-CUL.

54　A series of Pifer's presidential essays in the Annual Reports addressed these issues. His last essay as acting president and his first essay as full president led the way: Alan Pifer, "The Nongovernmental Organization at Bay," CCNYAR, 1966, 1–15; and "The Quasi Governmental Organization," CCNYAR, 1967, 1–16.

55　CCNY, Agenda Book of the Board of Trustees, January 15, 1970, "Council on Foreign Relations: Grant of $300,000 Toward Support" (agenda item), 19–20, CCNY Records, RBML-CUL.

56　CCNY, Agenda Book of the Executive Committee, September 17, 1969, "Carnegie Endowment for International Peace: Grant of $75,000 for Visiting Scholars" (agenda item), 9, CCNY Records, RBML-CUL.

57　CCNY, Minutes of the Board of Trustees, 56–57, June 11, 1974, CCNY Records, RBML-CUL.

58　CCNY, Agenda Book of the Executive Committee, September 17, 1969, "Discretionary Fund: Association of Junior Colleges, to Plan Community College Programs for Servicemen in Discharge Centers, $10,000" (agenda item), 11–12, CCNY Records, RBML-CUL.

59　CCNYAR, 1976, 57.

60　In 1966, however, the Corporation explored approaches for college collaboration in offering language opportunities for students in small colleges. Capitalizing on the availability of Title VI support for language training, the foundation provided support for expanding an experiment on independent study learning of foreign languages, using tapes and working with native speakers, that had been successfully demonstrated at Kalamazoo College and the State University of New York at Buffalo. The program, which was focused on the "neglected languages" (Arabic, Chinese, Hindi, Japanese, Portuguese, and Swahili), reached undergraduates in thirty to forty small colleges in the State University of New York system. CCNY, Agenda Book of the Board of Trustees, March 17, 1966, "University of the State of New York, Grant of $167,750 for a Program of Independent Study of Neglected Languages" (agenda item), 11–13, CCNY Records, RBML-CUL.

61　For a nuanced, probing analysis of EWA, see Joyce Mary Hertko, "The Internationalization of American Higher Education During the 1960s: The Involvement of the Ford Foundation and the Carnegie Corporation in Education and World Affairs" (PhD diss., Indiana University, 1996). Hertko provides a detailed perspective on the Overseas Educational Service, its relationship to EWA, its funding, and its work; ibid., 126–135.

62　For the problematic relationship with the Ford Foundation, the unwillingness of the Rockefeller Foundation to provide support, and the continued support from Carnegie Corporation, see ibid., 79–136. In this section, Hertko also describes the waxing and waning of government support for international education that compounded EWA's precarious position.

63　Ibid., 157.

64　Scarfo, "The History of Title VI and Fulbright-Hays," 23–25.

65   In conjunction with other foundations, for example, in 1968 the Corporation awarded a major grant of $130,000, through EWA, to the University Service Center in Hong Kong, which facilitated scholarly research on mainland China. This effort complemented foundation activities attempting to improve understanding of developments in mainland China as a basis for building closer ties. In 1970 the grant was renewed, but with the closing of EWA, the institutional base shifted to the American Council for Learned Societies; CCNY, Agenda Book of the Executive Committee, December 20, 1967, "Education and World Affairs: Grant of $130,000 Toward Support of the Universities Service Centre in Hong Kong" (agenda item), 4–5; CCNY, Agenda Book of the Executive Committee, April 21, 1971, "American Council of Learned Societies: Grant of $100,000 Toward Support of the Universities Service Centre in Hong Kong" (agenda item), 2–4; both at CCNY Records, RBML-CUL. The Luce and Ford Foundations joined in supporting the center in 1968 and renewed funding in 1971 of $40,000 and $100,000, respectively (3–4).

66   Hertko, "The Internationalization of American Higher Education During the 1960s," 151–156.

67   CCNY, Agenda Book of the Board of Trustees, February 13, 1975, "Discretionary Fund, US: International Council for Educational Development, Toward Support of a Seminar on Higher Education in Conjunction with the Aspen Institute, $15,000" (agenda item), 30; CCNY, Agenda Book of the Board of Trustees, February 12, 1976, "Discretionary Fund, US: International Council for Educational Development, Toward Support of a Seminar on Higher Education in Conjunction with the Aspen Institute, $15,000" (agenda item), 42–43; both at CCNY Records, RMBL-CUL. The Ford Foundation provided funding for both meetings as well. The International Council also received support for a study of youth, education, and employment; CCNY, Minutes of the Board of Trustees, February 12, 1976, "International Council for Educational Development, $6,000," 71, CCNY Records, RBML-CUL.

68   For the next ten years, support continued for work in Africa, including the organization of meetings related to audiovisual aids in East Africa, with a 1972 award of $300,000, and another award in 1975 of $250,000 to promote Anglo-American cooperation in assisting higher education in Africa, the Caribbean, the South Pacific, and Southeast Asia. A final grant of $140,000 in 1978 enabled the Overseas Liaison Committee to bring together this working group of scholars and university administrators to continue collaborating on higher education. CCNY, Agenda Book of the Board of Trustees, June 8, 1976, "American Council on Education: Three-Year Final Grant of $140,000 (US & C) Toward Support of the Overseas Liaison Committee" (agenda item), 50–52, CCNY Records, RBML-CUL.

69   CCNY, Agenda Book of the Board of Trustees, April 10, 1975, "Teachers College, Columbia University: Grant of $183,000 (Commonwealth) for Fellowships for African Educators" (agenda item), 6–8, CCNY Records, RBML-CUL. As noted in the agenda item, between 1969 and 1975 the Corporation provided $638,000 for these fellowships; with this grant, the final one, the total came to $831,000; see also CCNYAR, 1975, 58–59.

70   CCNYAR, 1982, 53. See also Andrew Taylor, ed., *Insights into African Education: The Karl W. Bigelow Memorial Lectures* (New York: Teachers College Press, 1984).

71   Now known as The Africa-America Institute (www.aaionline.org).

72   Pifer, CCOH, 122–131.

73   See www.aaionline.org for the history timeline of the African-American Institute.

74   This small grant led, however, to a continent-wide program administered by the African-American Institute, the African Scholarship Program of American Universities; see Pifer, CCOH, 137–142; and Murphy, *Creative Philanthropy*, 88–91.

75   Murphy, *Creative Philanthropy*, 37. The slightly different set of questions about the travel grants program that Murphy raised suggested that it was an area that could be revitalized,

especially regarding leaders from African countries. He noted that, as of 1976, "the Corporation has assisted nearly 1,000 men and women to travel to the United States and Canada (occasionally with side trips to the United Kingdom, West Indies, or other areas).... The influence of the Travel Grants program, however, is not accurately reflected by the numbers, though these are impressive. It is in the quality of the people chosen, and in their later career activities, that one sees the long-term importance of the travel grants." Murphy also explained why he recommended the continuation of the concentration in Africa: "As of about 1970 virtually every university principal or vice chancellor from many Commonwealth countries had travelled to North America with Corporation assistance, as had many of the registrars and other senior officials of the same universities. Large percentages of the newspaper editors, scientists, doctors, and educators from such countries as Australia, South Africa, and New Zealand had first become acquainted with North America through Corporation travel grants.... Often travel grantees later became involved in institutional programs supported by the Corporation, which greatly facilitated communication and enabled the Corporation to make grants with more confidence.... Many travel grantees later helped to forge links between their own institutions and others in Canada or the United States that persisted for many years after the grantee had visited America." He added that "everyone acquainted with it—the grantees themselves, Corporation staff, and the people in North America with whom grantees became friends—lauded it." E. J. Murphy, Past Activities of the Commonwealth Program 1953-1973: A Brief Summary, February 1975, 37, CCNY Policy and Program Files, Commonwealth (General) Program: 1969-1974, Folder 8, Box 4, Series I.D, CCNY Records, RBML-CUL.

76 In addition, three grants over the period 1968 to 1975, for a total of $34,475, enabled a Nigerian educator, Elijah Soladoye from Ahmadu Bello University in Nigeria, to complete his PhD on conflicts in secondary schools in Nigeria resulting from the mix of Nigerian and Western cultures. The support continued through 1975 when he was back in Nigeria and became the principal secretary of the Ministry of Planning in the new state of Kwara and needed a small amount of additional funding to complete his dissertation; CCNYAR, 1968, 43; 1970, 58; and 1975, 61. Another grant of $5,500 enabled a lecturer in chemistry at the University of Ibadan, Ike Azogu, to visit the United States and develop skills in technologically based instructional materials. Additional support permitted the African-American Institute to prepare a directory of graduate programs for students from African countries and the Caribbean along with an evaluation of the ASPAU (African Scholarship Program of American Universities); CCNYAR, 1976, 67; 1982, 53; and 1972, 55.

77 CCNYAR, 1969, 49; 1971, 58; 1973, 51; 1974, 50; 1976, 64; 1979, 65; and 1982, 53. For example, in 1972–1973, with Corporation support, the African-American Institute underwrote a model program of African studies for the state of North Carolina, including the development of state tests and the expansion of this model to other states. In 1975 the Institute received some $260,000 to produce college-level teaching materials. The Institute of International Education also received support in 1970 to provide outreach on Africa for American high school teachers; a modest grant of $13,000 enabled Kenyan and American teachers to meet together, in collaboration with the Kenyan Institute of Education; CCNYAR, 1970, 57.

78 The Inter-Parliamentarian Study Group on Africa, also known as the Anglo-American-Canadian Parliamentarian Conferences, was supported by the Corporation and the Ford Foundation from 1965 through 1980. In addition to Pifer's interest, this program had a champion at the Corporation in Mosher, who remained responsible for these grants throughout their duration. This initiative is fully discussed in Chapter 5.

79 CCNY, Agenda Book of the Board of Trustees, February 11, 1982, "African-American Institute, Three-Year Grant of $303,700 (US and IP-International Program) for the Program on Policy Issues in African-American Relations" (agenda item), 50–53, CCNY Records, RBML-

CUL. The parliamentarian conferences are discussed in Chapter 5. Both the African-American Institute congressional seminars and a reformulation of the parliamentarian conferences were continued: for the former, support continued in the 1980s and 1990s; the latter is still funded in 2014 (see Chapters 7 and 8).

80 Fredericks, *A Second Look*, 6. A slightly different rationale for engagement with the African continent, related to business investments, emerged in 2012; see "Forecasts for Management Decision-making," *The Kiplinger Letter* 89, no. 19 (May 11, 2012).

81 CCNYAR, 1972, 51.

82 CCNYAR, 1973, 54.

83 The Corporation and USAID jointly contributed to establishing the program, in 1979; CCNYAR, 1979, 63; 1981, 67; and 1982, 51–52. In 1980 the African-American Institute received a modest grant of $15,000 to enable African women, particularly Eddah Gachukia, to participate in the Second World Conference of the UN Decade for Women held in Copenhagen that year. Gachukia, a member of the Parliament of Kenya, became a significant Corporation grantee in the next decade; CCNYAR, 1980, 58. The 1982 grant enabled the African-American Institute to hold a conference in Zimbabwe, including women from other African nations, to discuss a wide range of issues and roles associated with women's participation in national development.

84 Three key African-American Institute leaders, in addition to Nielsen, deserve special mention for developing its vibrant programs in the 1970s and early 1980s: Donald Easum, African-American Institute president; Gayla Cook, developer of the Women and African development program; and Frank Ferrari, vice president and head of the policy efforts, starting in 1965, who over 30 years built the African-American Institute into the go-to place for African-American cross-continental debate and discussion.

85 CCNYAR, 1967, 63.

86 CCNY, Agenda Book of the Board of Trustees, May 20, 1965, "African Program" (agenda item), 3–5, CCNY Records, RBML-CUL. This focus was approved when Pifer was acting president but would undergird the grant-making in Africa until 1976. During this period, as in others, the Corporation's major partners in international grant-making, both in the United States and overseas, have been the Ford Foundation and the Rockefeller Foundation. All three foundations contributed to developing area studies initiatives in the United States and then individually began working to strengthen institutions of higher education in Africa and other developing countries. In 1958 the Ford Foundation began its work in and on Africa, including the joint support for Education and World Affairs and the policy outreach programs through Johns Hopkins University and the African-American Institute; its grant-making in Africa for higher education included institution-strengthening and planning activities, and Ford also supported more technical areas in health, agriculture, population, and economic and social policy. Starting in the late 1970s, the Ford Foundation and Carnegie Corporation collaborated closely in supporting initiatives in South Africa; Ford Foundation, *Ford Foundation International Programs*, July 1979. The Rockefeller Foundation, the Corporation's longest-term partner (starting internationally at a significant level in 1920 and including some collaborative funding), again was more complementary in this era. Starting in 1963, the Rockefeller Foundation initiated its University Development Program to strengthen universities in Latin America, Africa, and Asia, including Makerere University, the University of Nairobi, the University of Dar es Salaam, and the University of Ibadan in Africa, all places where the Corporation was also active. The Rockefeller Foundation's activities in African education also included strengthening the ministries of education in Kenya and Tanzania and strengthening the capacity for social science research and education in those countries. The Rockefeller Foundation, like the Ford Foundation, also worked on issues of agriculture, population, and health, often in collaboration. Both Rockefeller and Ford also addressed international affairs and security issues, maintaining these programs even as the Corporation

brought its support to a close. For a concise summary, see Sterling Wortman, "The President's Review," in Rockefeller Foundation annual report, 1980, 20–33. By 1980, all three foundations had considerably reduced their investments in higher education in Africa. It was only in the year 2000 that collaborative support for higher education returned to the agenda of the three foundations, as discussed in Chapter 8.

87 At the same time that the Corporation was closing the grants in the field of child psychology and child development in Africa, the US program, which had supported early childhood studies since the early 1960s, showed increasing interest in cross-cultural initiatives. Somewhat unrelated to the work in Africa, these grants provided funds for several years on complementary topics, such as the grant made in 1969 to Northwestern University for a cross-cultural study of ethnocentrism in premodern communities by Donald Campbell and Robert LeVine. Starting even earlier, in 1968, the Corporation supported an international study of early childhood programs in twelve countries (Cuba, France, Hungary, India, Poland, Israel, Sweden, Switzerland, the United Kingdom, the Soviet Union, Yugoslavia, and a country from Latin America [not yet selected as of the 1969 grant]); CCNY, Agenda Book of the Executive Committee, June 19, 1968, "University of North Carolina: Grant of $37,360 to Plan an International Study of Early Childhood Programs" (agenda item); CCNY, Agenda Book of the Board of Trustees, June 18, 1969, "University of Washington: Grant of $80,125 for an International Study of Early Childhood Programs" (agenda item), 26–28; both at CCNY Records, RBML-CUL. In 1971 the Education Development Center received a grant to bring together researchers from the United States and the United Kingdom to discuss ideas about infants and children and the growth of skills and abilities. Jerome Bruner of Harvard's Center for Cognitive Studies was the American co-chairman; the meeting was sponsored in the United Kingdom by the Developmental Science Trust, funded by the UK-based Ciba Foundation; CCNY, Agenda Book of the Board of Trustees, November 16, 1971, "From the Discretionary Fund for 1971–72: Education Development Center, for a Study Group on the Early Development of Competence" (agenda item), 51–52, CCNY Records, RBML-CUL. Michael Cole at Rockefeller University (who had earlier worked in Liberia and would play a significant role in the next era for grants linked to education in the Soviet Union) received support to conduct collaborative research studies on the relationship of children's cultural context to their intellectual development, including fundamental studies bringing together experimental work in neighborhoods in New York City and Yucatán, Mexico; CCNY, Agenda Book of the Board of Trustees, December 9, 1971, "Rockefeller University: Grant of $250,000 for Research on Cultural Factors in the Development of Learning Abilities" (agenda item), 22–24, CCNY Records, RBML-CUL. Other related grants supported studies of the impact of social policies on child care, family planning, and the care of the aged, as well as a cross-cultural study on the importance of father-son relations for a child's readiness for school. Grants to the United Nations and the American Ditchley Foundation supported conferences on youth issues and policies. Brief descriptions of the various grants may be found in the Annual Reports from 1968 to 1982 under the heading "Early Childhood Development."

88 The project in West Africa ran into bad luck with its timing: it started as the Biafra tensions were building up. Moreover, for a variety of reasons both program directors (Roy D'Andrade and Robert LeVine) encountered trouble over the research, staffing, and procedural issues at Ahmadu Bello University, whose Child Development Institute never took off. Although some interesting papers were produced and a couple of people from the university were trained in child development research, there were no lasting results. CCNY, Agenda Book of the Executive Committee, December 18, 1968, "Ahmadu Bello University: Grant of $117,740 (Commonwealth) Toward the Establishment of a Child Development Research Unit" (agenda item), 30–32, CCNY Records, RBML-CUL; Murphy, *Creative Philanthropy*, 205–209.

89 Murphy, *Creative Philanthropy*, 209–214; Rosenfield, "A Noble Use of Wealth," 36. See, for example, CCNY, Agenda Book of the Executive Committee, April 15, 1970, "University College, Nairobi, Grant of $189,000 (Commonwealth) for Research and Training in Human Development in Collaboration with Harvard University" (agenda item), 9–11; and "Harvard University: Grant of $282,000 (US and Commonwealth) for Research and Training in Human Development with University College, Nairobi" (agenda item), 12, both at CCNY Records, RBML-CUL.

90 CCNY, Agenda Book of the Board of Trustees, April 8, 1976, "University of Nairobi: Final Grant of $383,000 (Commonwealth) for Support of the Bureau of Educational Research" (agenda item), 32–35, CCNY Records, RBML-CUL.

91 Ibid., 32–33; Murphy, *Creative Philanthropy*, 211–214; Rosenfield, "A Noble Use of Wealth," 36. As reported originally in the 1976 agenda item, the output from the Child Development Research Unit was remarkable: "Since 1957, a total of 51 separate research projects dealing with the physical, cognitive, moral, and motivational development of Kenyan children have been undertaken. Almost 80 publications—papers, reports, and theses—have resulted." One of the students who later received her doctorate, Violet Kimani, would be a participant and grantee in several of the Corporation's programs in the 1990s.

92 CCNY, Agenda Book of the Board of Trustees, October 14, 1976, "University of Ghana: Final Grant of $150,000 for Support of the Language Centre" (agenda item), 33–35, CCNY Records, RBML-CUL.

93 CCNY, Agenda Book of the Board of Trustees, June 12, 1973, "University of Ghana: Grant of $187,000 (Commonwealth) Toward Support of the Institute of Journalism and Communication" (agenda item), 16–18, CCNY Records, RBML-CUL. Still addressing the concern about brain drain that had been raised earlier in the Gardner era, in 1969 the Corporation provided a modest grant to the University of Ghana of $14,800 to work with the UN Institute for Training and Research to study the migration of professionals. This was the only Commonwealth country involved in a larger study coordinated by Columbia University; the results of the Ghana survey were then assessed together with the results from the other eleven countries.

94 CCNY, Agenda Book of the Executive Committee, June 15, 1971, "Makerere University: Grant of $300,000 (Commonwealth) for Support of a Program of Research, Curriculum Revision, and Staff Development for Primary Teacher Training in Uganda" (agenda item), CCNY Records, RBML-CUL. Senteza Kajubi, the director, sought to use this support to examine the state of primary education in Uganda and refine the institute's work accordingly.

95 CCNY, Agenda Book of the Executive Committee, June 15, 1971, "University of Nigeria, Nsukka: Grant of $230,000 (Commonwealth) for Support of a Curriculum Development and Instructional Materials Resource Centre" (agenda item), 40–41, CCNY Records, RBML-CUL. The University of Nigeria in Nsukka also received modest support to re-create its journal collection and rebuild the library destroyed during the Biafran War. Corporation funds helped pack and ship books for the library. A closely related grant, several years later in 1975, at the University of Ife aimed to improve in-service training by establishing teacher centers for primary school instruction and improving materials and skills development. The aim was to build a cluster of teaching centers that were integrated with the university and would serve as a model for other universities in Nigeria and in Africa; CCNYAR, 1975, 57–58.

96 CCNY, Agenda Book of the Board of Trustees, June 11, 1974, "Association for Teacher Education in Africa: Grant of $290,860 (Commonwealth) Toward Support" (agenda item), 46–48, CCNY Records, RBML-CUL.

97 CCNY, Agenda Book of the Executive Committee, June 15, 1971, "African Social Studies Programme, Grant of $70,000 (Commonwealth) Toward Support of Workshops and Seminars"

(agenda item), 43; CCNY, Agenda Book of the Board of Trustees, February 14, 1974, "African Social Studies Programme: Grant of $119,000 (Commonwealth) Toward Support" (agenda item); CCNY Records, RBML-CUL. This kind of project was important for building citizen participation, empowering a strong civil society, and nurturing emerging political systems. If this project had been continued on a regular basis, even with modest funding by the Corporation and the Ford Foundation, it might have gone to scale in the countries where the teacher training was taking place. With the change in focus of the Corporation's grant-making, support did not continue.

98 CCNY, Agenda Book of the Board of Trustees, May 21, 1970, "Discretionary Fund, Commonwealth: University of Zambia, for a Workshop on the Teaching of Central and East African History" (agenda item), 36, CCNY Records, RBML-CUL. In 1971 the Corporation provided a modest grant to Harvard University to enable Kenneth Dike, the African historian who had participated as one of the three Nigerian members of the Ashby Commission, to complete a major work on African tribal groups. Dike had left Nigeria during the Biafra War and received an appointment at Harvard; CCNY, Agenda Book of the Executive Committee, September 15, 1971, "Discretionary Fund, Commonwealth: Harvard University, for Research on African History" (agenda item), 24, CCNY Records, RBML-CUL.

99 CCNYAR, 1972, 54.

100 CCNY, Agenda Book of the Board of Trustees, June 12, 1973, "University of Ibadan: Grant of $400,000 (Commonwealth) for Support of the International Centre for Educational Evaluation" (agenda item), 3–6; and "Science Education Program for Africa: Grant of $200,000 (Commonwealth) for Support of Research and Training in Evaluation" (agenda item), 6–8, CCNY Records, RBML-CUL. In 1979, Dyasi and Yoloye requested support to conduct a twenty-year review of science education efforts in Commonwealth Africa to assess the role of the African Primary Science Program and the Science Education Program for Africa in those efforts, and to prepare a book on their findings for others in the field in developing countries; CCNY, Agenda Book of the Board of Trustees, February 22, 1979, "Science Education Program for Africa: Twenty-Month Grant of $70,000 (Commonwealth) for a Review of Science Education in Commonwealth Africa" (agenda item), 45–47, CCNY Records, RBML-CUL.

101 See Institute of Education, University of Ibadan, International Centre for Educational Evaluation, available at: ui.edu.ng/education (accessed February 1, 2014).

102 CCNY, Agenda Book of the Board of Trustees, March 20, 1969, "Discretionary Fund, Commonwealth: University of Sierra Leone, for Support of the Commission on Higher Education, $12,000" (agenda item), 34–35, CCNY Records, RBML-CUL.

103 In June 1973, the Corporation provided $100,000 for the educational sector review, covering some of Porter's time, fees for outside consultants, and meeting costs. The university covered local costs and salaries. Collecting data on educational institutions across the country, the commissioners prepared a draft educational strategy outline, held conferences to critique the outline, and organized implementation planning activities with the government. CCNY, Agenda Book of the Board of Trustees, June 12, 1973, "University of Sierra Leone: Grant of $100,000 (Commonwealth) for an Education Sector Review" (agenda item), CCNY Records, RBML-CUL.

104 CCNY, Agenda Book of the Board of Trustees, December 11, 1975, "University of Sierra Leone: Grant of $376,000 (Commonwealth) for Establishment of a University Planning Unit" (agenda item), CCNY Records, RBML-CUL. The concept of partnership between the government and the universities persisted in Sierra Leone. In the 1980s and 1990s, the Corporation would make grants to researchers in the field of maternal mortality prevention who were drawn from both the government and the universities in Sierra Leone (see Chapter 7). In the mid-

1990s, the Corporation and the British Council would provide funds to the University of Sierra Leone for yet another national review in order to build the national science and technology information system linking all the different educational institutions and government agencies around the country. Unfortunately, the civil war in Sierra Leone ended this work, and the Corporation has not renewed grant-making in the country.

105   CCNY, Agenda Book of the Board of Trustees, October 12, 1972, "Discretionary Fund, Commonwealth: Association of African Universities for Support of a Workshop on 'Creating the African University,' $15,000" (agenda item), 51, CCNY Records, RBML-CUL. In 1972 the Corporation asked University of Wisconsin professor Robert Tabatchnik, based at Makerere University, to evaluate the Africa-based university education institutes and the work they had done over a twelve-year period. The aim of this assessment was to provide guidance for both African policymakers and university leaders as well as the Corporation. Murphy, *Creative Philanthropy*, 225.

106   The Association of African Universities started in 1967 with 34 members; today there are 199 members across 45 countries in Africa. See Association of African Universities, www.aau.org.

107   CCNY, Agenda Book of the Executive Committee, April 15, 1970, "The Chinese University of Hong Kong: Grant of $61,000 (Commonwealth) for Research on the Secondary School Curriculum" (agenda item), 15, CCNY Records, RBML-CUL.

108   CCNYAR, 1972, 53–54. In 1976 the Corporation enabled the Association of Caribbean Universities and Research Institutes to survey non-African cultural resources for programs in African and Caribbean Studies; CCNYAR, 1976, 66.

109   CCNY, Agenda Book of the Board of Trustees, May 21, 1970, "University of the South Pacific, Grant of $149,000 (Commonwealth) for Support of Regional Educational Activities" (agenda item), 30–32; CCNY, Agenda Book of the Board of Trustees, February 10, 1972, "For an Experimental Program in Satellite Communication in Cooperation with the University of Hawaii, $15,000" (agenda item), 49; April 2, 1973, "For an Experimental Program in Satellite Communication in Cooperation with the University of Hawaii, $13,500" (agenda item); April 2, 1973, "Grant of $25,000 (Commonwealth) for Support of its Satellite Communication Project" (agenda item); June 9, 1977, "Six-Month Final Grant of $102,000 (Commonwealth) for Support of Regional Educational Activities" (agenda item), 44–46; all at CCNY Records, RBML-CUL. The grant supported the university's efforts to provide extension services, teacher training, adult education, and curriculum development. On the satellite connections, see The University of the South Pacific, "About USP," available at: http://www.usp.ac.fj/index.php?id=about_usp (accessed May 26, 2012). In contrast, the grants to the other two systems involved travel by staff, not satellite connections. See, for example, CCNY, Agenda Book of the Executive Committee, June 21, 1967, "The University of Botswana, Lesotho, and Swaziland; Grant of $50,000 to Establish Posts in Botswana and Swaziland" (agenda item), 5–6, CCNY Records, RBML-CUL.

110   CCNYAR, 1966, 33–34; 1972, 19, 24; and 1973, 35.

111   CCNYAR, 1970, 58; CCNY, Agenda Book of the Executive Committee, September 15, 1971, "Discretionary Fund, Commonwealth: Chinese University of Hong Kong, for Expenses of Heads of Universities in Developing Countries, $15,000" (agenda item), 24–25, CCNY Records, RBML-CUL. The Corporation also provided support to the Commonwealth Foundation for the Andrew Cohen Fellowships, which enabled African civil servants to visit other African countries; CCNYAR, 1970, 58,.

112   The trustees and Pifer began to discuss issues such as efforts under way to establish foundation standards following the Tax Reform Act of 1969 (CCNY, Minutes of the Board of Trustees, November 18, 1969, 47, CCNY Records, RBML-CUL); "the need for younger

members, increased rotation, and diversification," points on which all "trustees agreed"; (CCNY, Minutes of the Board of Trustees, November 18, 1969, 51, CCNY Records, RBML-CUL); and formalizing the appropriation and spending policies for the Corporation (CCNY, Minutes of the Executive Committee, April 15, 1970, 65, CCNY Records, RBML-CUL).

113 In 1974 Stackpole announced that he would retire in two years; Mosher had left in 1973 to take a position at Harvard. Katherine Ford, program assistant for the Commonwealth Program, also had plans to retire in 1975, after twenty-seven years with the program and forty years with the Corporation.

114 CCNYAR, 1973, 3–16.

115 Ibid., 10.

116 Ibid., 4.

117 Pifer, CCOH, 34–38. Pifer also described the close bond that he and Stackpole formed over the years.

118 CCNYAR, 1973, 5.

119 Ibid., 7. For instance, following his trip to South Africa in the fall of 1973, Pifer reported to the board that "he was impressed with the emerging black leadership there and thought there might be ways in which the Corporation could again be active in South Africa"; CCNY, Minutes of the Board of Trustees, October 11, 1973, 33, CCNY Records, RBML-CUL.

120 CCNY, Minutes of the Board of Trustees, October 10, 1974, 3, CCNY Records, RBML-CUL. As early as June 1973, the trustees had discussed evaluation of Corporation programs and grants, including the work in Africa; CCNY, Minutes of the Board of Trustees, June 12, 1973, 26, CCNY Records, RBML-CUL.

121 E. Jefferson Murphy, "Past Activities of the Commonwealth Program, 1953–1973: A Brief Summary," February 1975, CCNY Policy and Program Files, Commonwealth (General) Program: 1969–1974, Folder 8, Box 4, Series I.D, CCNY Records, RBML-CUL.

122 Such activities might include "conferences, planning exercises, leadership development, policy studies, travel grants, pilot or experimental projects, and projects which increase communication within a region or between the United States and other countries within the Program's mandate. The goals of these projects might include planning economic or social development, communication for cooperative effort, strengthening the capacity of leaders or professionals to exercise their responsibilities, improving the process of policy formation, and improving international relations." Murphy added in an aside: "(It was noted that the Commonwealth program has considerable experience in these activities; much of the effort of the 1950s and early 1960s was devoted to them. Thus the recommendation, though marking a departure from present Program work, would not lead the Program into wholly unfamiliar areas.)" E. Jefferson Murphy, "Trustee Review Committee to Discuss the Future of the Corporation's Commonwealth Program: Recommendations" (summary), March 3, 1975, 2, CCNY Policy and Program Files, Commonwealth (General) Program: 1969–1974, Folder 8, Box 4, Series I.D, CCNY Records, RBML-CUL.

123 The board suggested that these "might include education, cultural development, public administration, the role of women, communication among leaders, communication among professions, techniques of communication, and racial or ethnic relations." Ibid.

124 Ibid., 2–3.

125 Ibid., 3.

126 E. Jefferson Murphy, memo to Alan Pifer, March 11, 1975, CCNY Policy and Program Files, Commonwealth (General) Program: 1969–1974, Folder 8, Box 4, Series I.D, CCNY Records, RBML-CUL.

127 Alan Pifer, "Carnegie Corporation of New York, Commonwealth Program: Future

Directions," April 10, 1975, CCNY Policy and Program Files, Commonwealth (General) Program: 1969–1974, Folder 8, Box 4, Series I.D, CCNY Records, RBML-CUL.

128   Ibid., 2.

129   The narrowing of the program can best be tracked by referring to the introductory sections to the program in the Annual Reports by year and page number: CCNYAR, 1975, 57; 1976, 63; 1977, 52; and 1979 (when the program name changed from the Commonwealth Program to the International Program), 60.

130   For the University of the South Pacific, see CCNYAR, 1975, 60, and 1978, 52; for Canada, see 1975, 60–61. See also Robin Sutton Harris, *A History of Higher Education in Canada, 1663–1960* (Toronto: University of Toronto Press, 1976).

131   The grants to the African-American Institute discussed earlier played a major role in meeting this objective.

132   CCNYAR, 1975, 61.

133   Ibid.

134   Pifer, CCOH, 131–135. The Ford Foundation had supported the leadership exchange program from the beginning in 1958, when it was initially incubated by the African-American Institute, and then when it became free-standing; see, for example, "Grant to the United States–South Africa Leadership Development Program, Inc. for General Support for the Continued Operation of Its Two-way Faculty and Leader Interchange Program, August 18, 1961–March 31, 1973," Ford Foundation records, Grant 06100315, Reels 1335 and 1336, Rockefeller Archive Center (RAC). The exchange had earlier only been able to involve white South Africans, attracting the more liberal ones. Considerable discussion took place between Ford, Carnegie, and Rockefeller Brothers Fund staff members on these activities.

135   CCNYAR, 1975, 61 ($13,000); 1976, 65 ($177,000); 1978, 51 ($7,500) and 61 ($150,000); 1981, 65 ($25,000); and 1982, 50 ($15,000).

136   CCNYAR, 1980, 55. A small grant, also in 1980, from the Corporation's Program Development and Evaluation Fund provided support for South African educators Peter Hunter and Ezekiel Mphahlele to help develop the program and meet with their counterparts in the United States; ibid., 61. William Carmichael, vice president of the Ford Foundation, and Derek Bok, president of Harvard University, co-chaired the program.

137   CCNYAR, 1976, 65; 1978, 51; and 1982, 49–50.

138   Frequent meetings with Ford Foundation and Rockefeller Brothers Fund staff (for the latter, mainly William Moody) working on South Africa took place as the Corporation was defining its new scope. David Hood and the new program assistant, Kristin Anderson, met with F. Champion Ward, a senior Ford Foundation staff member, to discuss "how he would go about planning a program given our budget and geographic scope." Noting that "making grants in South Africa is much more difficult than in the Middle East," he said that the Foundation was moving away from large grants for higher education, manpower development, and university development and toward increasing local analytical capacity. Staff members were contemplating a ten-year program in Nigeria, Brazil, and Thailand. In parting advice, he observed that "there was still too much foreign influence in the actual running of African or international programs" and that local governments needed to have "their own capacity to handle future problems." David Hood and Kristin Anderson, record of interview with F. Champion Ward at Ford Foundation, July 20, 1976, CCNY Policy and Program Files, Commonwealth Program, 1976–1978, Folder 7, Box 5, Series I.D, CCNY Records, RBML-CUL.

139   "Grant to the University of Natal for the 1973 Conference on Legal Aid in South Africa, January 1, 1972–January 30, 1973," Ford Foundation records, Grant 07200097, Reel 1310, RAC. As the Corporation was limiting its South African grant-making in the early 1950s, the Ford

Foundation was getting started. In 1953 it made its first grant in the country to the South African Institute of Race Relations, which the Corporation had supported since its founding (see Chapter 3). For a review of the Ford Foundation's early grants to South Africa, see Middle East and Africa Program Director [J.] Wayne Fredericks, "Southern Africa: 1972 Report," Ford Foundation records, Reports 005996, RAC.

140   David Hood, record of interview with Dean Kenneth Pye and Kristin Anderson, October 4, 1976, CCNY Policy and Program Files, Commonwealth Program (Africa), 1976–1980, Folder 7, Box 5, Series I.D, CCNY Records, RBML-CUL.

141   Kristin Anderson, record of interview with Geoff Budlender, Helene Budlender, David Hood, and Kristin Anderson, October 12, 1976, CCNY Policy and Program Files, Commonwealth Program (Africa), 1976–1980, Folder 7, Box 5, Series I.D, CCNY Records, RBML-CUL.

142   John Dugard, *The Reminiscences of John Dugard: Oral History, 1999,* interviewed by Len Morris, Johannesburg, South Africa, August 7, 1999, Carnegie Corporation Project, Part 2: Oral History, 1996–2004, CCOH-CUL, 2–3 (hereafter "Dugard, CCOH").

143   Golden, "Carnegie Corporation in South Africa," 5; Rosenfield, Sprague, and McKay, "Ethical Dimensions of International Grantmaking," 57–59.

144   CCNYAR, 1977, 54–55.

145   Dugard, CCOH, 4.

146   Ibid.

147   CCNY, Minutes of the Board of Trustees, 78–79, June 8, 1978, CCNY Records, RBML-CUL.

148   Robinson was hired as vice president of the Corporation in 1970 from New York University, where he had been vice president for academic affairs. He had advanced degrees in chemistry and physics from Harvard University, with a PhD in chemical physics, and had been actively involved in issues of science and public policy. He also paid close attention to the South Africa program and investment decisions; CCNYAR, 1970, 62. He was promoted to executive vice president in 1980. As the Corporation continued reviewing its internal investment policies and proxy decisions, it also embarked on investment policy–related grant-making. In 1978 it further reviewed developments, in particular the initiative undertaken by Harvard University and other institutional investors to establish a new monitoring program concerning US corporations' policies in South Africa. On June 15, 1979, the Corporation organized a meeting with Leon Sullivan, the author of the "Sullivan principles," established in 1977 for foreign companies investing in South Africa to follow as a way to confront apartheid; see Marshall University, "A Principled Man: Rev. Leon Sullivan," The Civil Rights History Project, Marshall University, Morrow Library, Special Collections, available at: http://www.marshall.edu/revleonsullivan/indexf.htm. With Reverend Sullivan they discussed his perspective on proxies and investment policies concerning South Africa; CCNY, Minutes of the Board of Trustees, 36, June 14, 1979, CCNY Records, RBML-CUL. Pifer described the meeting recommendation that a task force to develop a monitoring mechanism be set up, which the board later supported; CCNY, Minutes of the Board of Trustees, 51, October 11, 1979, CCNY Records, RBML-CUL. In 1982 a grant to the Investor Responsibility Research Center for $28,000 allowed it to continue its monitoring of the domestic pressures being brought to bear on American companies in South Africa, as well as university investment and disinvestment policies; CCNYAR, 1982, 45. A grant to Yale University in 1982, co-funded by the Ford Foundation, supported a conference on US firms in South Africa to discuss their responsibilities, risks, and opportunities; CCNYAR, 1982, 50. The African-American Institute also organized meetings related to South African business issues and investment policies.

149 CCNYAR, 1978, 50, and 1980, 55.

150 See the University of the Witwatersrand Law School website, available at: http://www. wits.ac.za/academic/clm/law/cals/11159/cals_home.html.

151 CCNYAR, 1978, 50; 1979, 61; 1981, 64; and 1982, 49.

152 CCNYAR, 1977, 55.

153 CCNYAR, 1979, 61.

154 CCNY, Minutes of the Board of Trustees, 19, December 14, 1978, CCNY Records, RBML-CUL.

155 CCNYAR, 1980, 56.

156 CCNYAR, 1982, 50. The Black Lawyers Association had coalesced by 1977; see the Association's website at: www.bla.org.za.

157 For a fuller discussion of this point, see the oral history interviews conducted by Len Morris in Johannesburg with Geoffrey Budlender, Arthur Chaskalson, and John Dugard, August 7, 1999, Carnegie Corporation Project, Part 2: Oral History, 1996–2004, CCOH-CUL. See also Arthur Chaskalson, "The Legal Resources Centre: Why It Was Established and What It Hopes to Achieve," available at: http://www.disa.ukzn.ac.za/wlbpgs/DC/resep80.8/resep80.8pdf (accessed June 5, 2012).

158 Francis Wilson, personal communication with the author, March 23, 2010.

159 As discussed in Chapter 3, the Corporation had earlier supported the Poor White Commission in its examination of the conditions facing Afrikaners living in poverty in South Africa. This controversial work, which bolstered the position of apartheid proponents but also contributed to the field of interdisciplinary social surveys, had led Corporation president Frederick Keppel and several South African advisers, notably Charles Loram and Ernest Malherbe, to discuss how and when to conduct a similar survey for the black population. Wilson's suggestion gave the Corporation the unusual opportunity to make amends for its historical record in South Africa; see Wilson, CCOH, 118–119. Many articles have been written about the first study; one article that provides thoughtful commentary about the two studies is Morag Bell, "American Philanthropy, the Carnegie Corporation, and Poverty in South Africa," *Journal of South African Studies* 26, no. 3 (2000): 481–504. See also Francis Wilson and Mamphela Ramphele, *Uprooting Poverty: The South African Challenge* (New York: W. W. Norton & Co., 1989), ix–xiii.

160 CCNYAR, 1980, 61; see also Wilson, CCOH, 119–121.

161 CCNYAR, 1981, 65.

162 University of Cape Town, Faculty of Commerce, School of Economics, "Francis Wilson," available at: http://www.commerce.uct.ac.za/Economics/staff/fwilson/default.asp; South Africa History Online, "Fikile Charles Bam," available at: www.sahistory.org.za/people/fikile-charles-bam.

163 CCNY, Minutes of the Board of Trustees, 62, 64, December 10, 1981, CCNY Records, RBML-CUL.

164 CCNYAR, 1982, 48.

165 Ramphele, a physician and anthropologist, had been banned, put under surveillance, and forced to live in an isolated part of the country. See Mamphela Ramphele, *A Life* (Claremont, South Africa: David Philip Publishers, 1995), 118–152. When the ban was lifted, she was able to participate actively in the conduct of the work. See Mamphela Ramphele, *The Reminiscences of Mamphela Ramphele: Oral History, 1999,* interviewed by Mary Marshall Clark, August 2, 1999, Cape Town, South Africa, Carnegie Corporation Project, Part 2: Oral History, 1996–2004, CCOH-CUL, 13–15 (hereafter "Ramphele, CCOH").

166 Wilson provided further details to this author: "Bill Carmichael [the Ford Foundation officer] was the smartest program officer in South Africa from any foundation. He was totally

brilliant. He had extremely acute political antennae." Carmichael also provided collaborative support for training and for involving black leadership, including the co-investigator Mamphela Ramphele. Wilson added, however, that with Carnegie Corporation support, he learned how to benefit from a variety of Corporation experiences and approaches. Not only did he use the Myrdal study as a guide, he indicated, but "the quarterly reports put me through the hoops. They were extremely important because they forced the process. Moreover, with the organization in New York there was a lot of experience and I drew on all of it." He stressed that "I got much more than money from the Carnegie Corporation. In fact, money was secondary. Alan [Pifer] was always around. We went traveling together to visit Mamphela in the Transvaal and Fikile Bam in Transkei. Here was the president of Carnegie Corporation driving around in the little car. We talked strategy all the time. What foundation president does that today? It's vitally important that they have such knowledge. Alan knew every single thing about South Africa." Francis Wilson, personal communication with the author, March 23, 2010.

167   Wilson and Ramphele, *Uprooting Poverty*.

168   Mamphela Ramphele, for example, in 1996 became the first female black vice chancellor of a South African university, the University of Cape Town.

169   CCNYAR, 1980, 56.

170   CCNYAR, 1981, 63.

171   CCNYAR, 1982, 45.

172   Rockefeller Foundation, *South Africa: Time Running Out: The Report of the Study Commission on US Policy Toward Southern Africa* (Berkeley: University of California Press, 1981). For a follow-up to the Commission, see Tom Lodge et al., *All, Here and Now: Black Politics in South Africa in the 1980s, Update South Africa: Time Running Out* (New York: Ford Foundation and Foreign Policy Association, 1991), ix.

173   Franklin A. Thomas, personal communication with the author, July 10, 2012.

174   CCNYAR, 1980, 11.

175   Ibid., 12.

176   Ibid., 16–17.

177   CCNYAR, 1980, 12–14; see also David Bonbright, "The Ford Foundation in Apartheid South Africa—Soft Solutions to Hard Problems," *Alliance*, September 1, 2003, available at: http://www.alliancemagazine.org/en/content/ford-foundation-apartheid-south-africa-soft-solutions-hard-problems.

178   The Botswana president, Sir Seretse Khama, represented not only his country but also the leaders of other independent countries in Southern Africa—Zambia, Tanzania, Angola, and Mozambique.

179   CCNYAR, 1979, 62, and 1981, 66.

180   For current information, see the SADC website at: www.sadc.int.

181   CCNYAR, 1978, 50.

182   CCNYAR, 1980, 56.

183   CCNYAR, 1981, 66.

184   Ibid.

185   CCNYAR, 1982, 50–51. In the 1980s and 1990s, under the continuing leadership of Kamba and subsequent vice chancellors, the University of Zimbabwe became a major grantee of the Corporation.

186   Deutsch, "Women in Higher Education"; CCNYAR, 1963, 17–21.

187   CCNYAR, 1977, 52.

188   This set of activities included support for an officer's grant, in 1977, to pull together material on income-generating activities for women and a conference in London organized by the International Cooperative Alliance; CCNYAR, 1977, 53 and 54.

189   CCNYAR, 1978, 49–50, and 1979, 65. A later grant enabled the Council to publish a series of pamphlets on successful women's development experiences, called *Seeds*, co-funded by the Ford and Rockefeller Foundations; CCNYAR, 1982, 52.

190   CCNYAR, 1980, 59.

191   CCNYAR, 1979, 64–65.

192   CCNYAR, 1980, 58.

193   CCNYAR, 1979, 63.

194   CCNYAR, 1980, 57, and 1981, 67.

195   CCNYAR, 1977, 53; 1978, 49; 1980, 57, 58–59; and 1982, 51. Related to the WAND grants, in 1982 the Corporation gave a modest grant of $6,000 to the Association of Caribbean Universities and Research Institutes to shine a light more brightly on ways to strengthen women's potential contributions and advance their interests with a range of employers, educators, and policymakers; CCNYAR, 1982, 51.

196   See The University of the West Indies, "About WAND," available at: http://www.open.uwi.edu/wand/about-wand (accessed June 10, 2012).

197   CCNYAR, 1978, 49.

198   CCNYAR, 1982, 52.

199   CCNYAR, 1978, 50, and 1979, 64. Support for women's activities in Zimbabwe continued in the next era, with a focus increasingly on the NGOs in the country.

200   CCNYAR, 1977, 53.

201   CCNYAR, 1981, 68.

202   Ibid.

NOTES FOR CHAPTER 7

1   This chapter and Chapter 8 reflect the considerably improved asset base for the Corporation. In 1982, when Hamburg became president, the assets were about $381 million. By 1985, they had increased to $564 million. By Hamburg's last year in office, 1997, the assets had risen to $1.54 billion. The number of grants also skyrocketed. In 1982, 93 grants and appropriations had been made; in 1985, 166; by 1997, 271. In 1982 there were no US-based international affairs grants, only three Program Development and Evaluation Fund reviews, and only 18 grants for the overseas work. In 1985 there were 37 international affairs grants and 36 in the overseas program. The maximum number of grants made in any one year by the US-based international program was 78, in 1996, and for the overseas program the maximum was 108, in 1992. In this era, the international program made 714 grants and the overseas program 932. Given the greatly increased number of grants, meetings, and consultations, Chapters 7 and 8, while lengthy, cannot be as comprehensive as earlier ones. The narrative portrays the main lines of work, the clusters of grants that informed and implemented program objectives, and the results, when possible. As indicated in the author's note, the Annual Reports, available in the Carnegie Corporation of New York (CCNY) Records, Rare Book and Manuscript Library, Columbia University Libraries (RBML-CUL), provide more detailed information on the grants made in any given year. The Annual Reports from 1998 onward are available online at: www.carnegie.org. For an overview of the international work, see also David Hamburg, "Carnegie Corporation in the 1980s and 1990s," *Carnegie Reporter* 6, no. 1 (Fall 2010): 39–43, available at: www.carnegie.org/publication/carnegie-reporter/single/view/issue/item/348/ (accessed February 8, 2014).

2   Steve Galster, "Volume II: Afghanistan: Lessons from the Last War: Afghanistan: The Making of US Policy, 1973–1990," The National Security Archive, October 9, 2001, 17–28, available at: http://www.gwu.edu/~nsarchiv/NSAEBB/NSAEBB57/essay.html (accessed June 15, 2012).

3 The deaths of the two successors to Leonid Brezhnev, the longtime general secretary of the Communist Party (from 1964 to 1982)—Yuri Andropov (1982–1984) and Konstantin Chernenko (1984–1985)—resulted in Mikhail Gorbachev becoming general secretary in 1985. By early 1986, Gorbachev had introduced *glasnost*, which opened up the Soviet Union, and then *perestroika*, which reformed it. Dumitru Drumea, "The Fall of the Soviet Union and Reunification of Europe," trans. Florent Banfi, *The New Federalist*, May 6, 2008, available at: http://www.thenew-federalist.eu/The-Fall-of-the-Soviet-Union-and-Reunification-of-Europe (accessed August 21, 2012).

4 Raymond L. Garthoff, *The Great Transition: American-Soviet Relations and the End of the Cold War* (Washington, DC: Brookings Institution Press, 1994).

5 Vali Nasr, *The Shia Revival: How Conflicts Within Islam Will Shape the Future* (New York: W. W. Norton and Co., 2006).

6 Thomas L. Hungerford, "Income Inequality, Income Mobility, and Economic Policy: US Trends in the 1980s and 1990s," Cornell University ILR School, March 4, 2008, available at: http://digitalcommons.ilr.cornell.edu/key_workplace/501/ (accessed June 15, 2012).

7 Gustave Ranis, James Raymond Vreeland, and Stephen Kosack, *Globalization and the Nation State: The Impact of the IMF and the World Bank* (Abingdon, UK: Routledge, 2006).

8 T. Akin Aina, "Development Theory and Africa's Lost Decade: Critical Reflections on Africa's Crisis and Current Trends in Development Thinking and Practice," in *Changing Paradigms in Development: South, East, and West: A Meeting of Minds in Africa Workshop Entitled "Paradigms in Development Thinking and Strategies: African, Nordic, and Soviet Experience,"* ed. Margaretha von Troil (Uppsala, Sweden: Nordiska Afrikainstitutet, 1993), 13–20.

9 John Williamson, ed., *IMF Conditionality* (Cambridge, MA: MIT Press, 1983). Structural adjustment was introduced in the 1970s and became the basis for the later, equally problematic, "Washington Consensus," which was centered on macroeconomic policies as the basis for foreign assistance and loans. For a recent review, see Narcis Serra and Joseph E. Stiglitz, eds., *The Washington Consensus Reconsidered: Towards a New Global Governance* (Oxford, UK: Oxford University Press, 2008).

10 See, for example, Adetokunbo O. Lucas, "Health Policies in Developing Countries," and Davidson R. Gwatkin, "Reducing Health Inequalities in Developing Countries," both in Roger Detels et al., eds., *Oxford Textbook of Public Health: The Scope of Public Health*, 4th ed. (Oxford: Oxford University Press, 2002).

11 The South Commission, "The State of the South: The Development Record of the South, 1950–1980," in *The Challenge to the South: The Report of the South Commission* (Oxford: Oxford University Press, 1990), 73–77.

12 Robert A. Pape, *Dying to Win: The Strategic Logic of Suicide Terrorism* (New York: Random House, 2005), appendix 1, 253–263.

13 George H. W. Bush, "Address to the Nation on the Invasion of Iraq (January 16, 1991)," University of Virginia, The Miller Center, available at: http://millercenter.org/president/speeches/detail/3428 (accessed June 24, 2012).

14 David Hamburg, "A Perspective on Carnegie Corporation's Program," Carnegie Corporation of New York (CCNY) Annual Report (CCNYAR), 1996, 9, CCNY Records, Rare Books and Manuscript Library, Columbia University Libraries (RBML-CUL).

15 The Corporation had made a few grants related to atomic energy in the 1940s and nuclear weapons in the 1950s and 1960s, along with a considerable number of grants that defined and extended the fields of national and international security studies, starting in the late 1930s, but the knowledge of those activities had been lost at the Corporation. The election of Hamburg as president saw a full revival of the agenda for securing peace through study and outreach on pre-

venting the proliferation of weapons of mass destruction—first nuclear, then biological, chemical, and conventional—and then through extensive work on preventing deadly conflict.

16 Hamburg had developed interdisciplinary programs in psychiatry and conflict and aggression at Stanford University; selected by President Gerald Ford to be the third president of the Institute of Medicine of the National Academy of Science, he had helped start the program on health policy at Harvard University. A senior consultant to the World Health Organization, a negotiator with the Zairois rebels in Tanzania, and the author of multiple publications, in 1984 he was elected president of the American Association for the Advancement of Science, a significant statement of support and respect from a broad spectrum of the American scientific community. For a full biography, see CRDF Global, "2012 George Brown Award Honoree: David A. Hamburg," available at: http://www.crdfglobal.org/about-us/annual-awards-gala/george-brown-award-archive/lists/2012-george-brown-award/2012-honorees.

17 Similar to the work on nuclear weapons and national security, the knowledge about the extensive involvement of the Corporation in development-related activities had also faded from the Corporation's institutional memory. As mentioned in Chapters 4 and 5, there was little consciousness of prior work such as the decade-long studies teasing apart the complications of technical assistance in developing countries and delving into the fields of economic development and modernization studies, or of the extensive involvement of the Corporation under the Commonwealth Program in the decolonization and independence movement or its history in building networks and strengthening research and education throughout Africa and the Caribbean. Even the 1976 publication by Jefferson Murphy would have surely guided the new staff in the developing-countries work, but they were not aware of the book until many years later. Even taking into account the differences between the eras, the knowledge gained from those earlier activities—especially what was learned about what was and was not effective—might have jump-started some of the later program work by involving some of the experienced former grantees.

18 CCNYAR, 1996, 13.

19 CCNYAR, 1983, 13–14.

20 Ibid., 21.

21 The US-based international program worked in close partnership with the Rockefeller Brothers Fund and the Ford, Rockefeller, and MacArthur Foundations on grants in and on the Soviet Union and on nuclear weapons issues. For the work in Africa and on development issues, the overseas program worked with the Ford, Rockefeller, and MacArthur Foundations, as well as with the Canadian-based International Development Research Centre; in South Africa, it also worked with the Rockefeller Brothers Fund and the W. K. Kellogg and Kaiser Family Foundations. For public outreach and education in the United States, for both programs, the Ford and MacArthur Foundations were significant partners.

22 *Carnegie Reporter* (Spring 2011): 46.

23 John Whitehead, who left in 1985 to become deputy secretary of state under President Ronald Reagan, returned to the board after his term in office ended in early 1989. Warren Christopher, who had been deputy secretary of state under President Carter, served as chairman of the board immediately after Kaplan's tenure, starting in 1990, but had to resign in 1993 when he was appointed secretary of state by President Clinton. Admiral James Watkins, former chief of naval operations under President Reagan, served as chairman of the National Commission on AIDS and, under President George H. W. Bush, as secretary of energy; he stepped down from this position right before he joined the Corporation's board. Sheila Widnall, an aerodynamics scientist, professor, chair of the faculty, and then associate provost at MIT, stepped down from the board to become the first female secretary of the air force under President Clinton.

Ray Marshall, professor of economics and public affairs at the University of Texas and former secretary of labor under President Carter, was engaged in international trade, labor, and educational concerns. Condoleezza Rice, professor of international relations at Stanford University and then provost, was a top specialist in Soviet studies. Thomas H. Kean, former governor of New Jersey, president of Drew University, and committed to international education as well as improving education in the United States, became Corporation board chair in January 1997. Richard Celeste, former head of the Peace Corps and former governor of Ohio, left the board to become ambassador to India under President Clinton. Newton Minow, the first chairman of the Federal Communications Commission and the one who coined the phrase "the vast wasteland," served as honorary counsel for Singapore, worked as a senior lawyer at Sidley Austin in Chicago, and was Corporation board chair from 1993 to 1997. James Johnson, former executive assistant to Vice President Walter Mondale, was chair and CEO of Fannie Mae and active on education and South Africa issues. Robert Rubin of Goldman Sachs, who was especially interested in the South Africa program, left the board to become secretary of the treasury under President Clinton. And Sam Nunn, who was deeply involved in the field of nuclear weapons and their control, was elected to the board almost as soon as he stepped down from the Senate, toward the very end of Hamburg's tenure in late 1996.

24 Jack Clark, a senior executive at Exxon Corporation, played an instrumental role in the work on South Africa. Richard Fisher, chairman of Morgan Stanley, who guided the finance committee, was engaged in a range of international issues as well as early childhood education. Vincent Mai, born in South Africa and a graduate of the University of Cape Town, was actively involved in the country, especially following the end of apartheid, as well as throughout Africa from the perspective of strategic risk investing through AEA Investors. Laurence Tisch, CEO of Loews Corporation, was also involved in international activities through finance and real estate. Richard Beattie, senior partner at Simpson Thatcher and Bartlett, was intensely committed to education at all levels. Bruce Dayton, chairman and CEO of Dayton-Hudson Department Stores (now Target Corporation) was active in philanthropy in Minnesota. Thomas Troyer from the Washington, DC, law firm of Caplin, Drysdale, was one of the leading nonprofit lawyers in Washington. James Renier, elected toward the end of the Hamburg era in 1995, was CEO of Honeywell.

25 Joshua Lederberg, president of Rockefeller University and a Nobel Prize winner, was committed to international scientific exchanges as well as innovations in Internet use. Eugene Cota-Robles, a renowned microbiologist and science educator, was passionate about improving science and technology education for Latino and Mexican American populations. Several members shared the focus of the domestic perspective on early childhood and adolescence as well as education and health. Shirley Malcolm, head of the Directorate for Education and Human Resources Programs of the American Association for the Advancement of Science, was an expert in science and technology in education as well as in the field of women in science and technology. Fred Hechinger, an education reporter and the first education columnist for the *New York Times*, tracked educational innovations around the world and in the United States. James Comer, professor of child psychiatry at Yale University, was a leading expert in early childhood education and creator of the Comer School of Education. Henry Muller, editorial director of *Time* magazine, was committed to educating Americans about international affairs. James Lowell Gibbs Jr., professor of anthropology at Stanford University, was a leader in African studies and a Liberia expert who had done extensive research in the social dimensions of law and community organization. Mary Patterson McPherson was a former president of Bryn Mawr College and vice president of the Mellon Foundation for liberal arts and higher education. Teresa Heinz, born in Mozambique and a graduate of the University of the Witwatersrand, was dedicated to children and environmental issues through her work as president of the Heinz Endowments. And Wilma

Tisch took a special interest in issues of early childhood and adolescence, particularly from the philanthropy and not-for-profit perspective.

26 The review papers from the 1995 retreat complement and extend the discussion in this chapter. They are available at CCNY Records, RBML-CUL.

27 CCNYAR, 1983, 21, 3–22.

28 David A. Hamburg, *The Reminiscences of David A. Hamburg: Oral History, 1996–1998*, interviewed by Mary Marshall Clark, December 10, 1998, Carnegie Corporation Project, Part 2: Oral History, 1996–2004, Columbia Center for Oral History, Columbia Universities Libraries, 321–322 (hereafter "Hamburg, CCOH").

29 CCNYAR, 1983, 3.

30 Ibid., 4–5.

31 Hamburg asked Barbara Finberg, vice president, to chair the Special Projects Committee and to include David Robinson, executive vice president and treasurer; Sara Engelhardt, Corporation secretary; and one representative of the program staff. He asked Avery Russell, director of publications, to serve as program officer and to continue interacting with all programs.

32 David Robinson and Vivien Stewart, both hired by Alan Pifer, were originally Canadian and British, respectively.

33 CCNYAR, 1983, 5; see also Hamburg, "Carnegie Corporation in the 1980s and 1990s," 39. In the 1970s, under the auspices of Pugwash, the association of scientists from the Soviet Union, the United States, and Europe dedicated to avoiding nuclear war, Hamburg had identified a core group of scientists and practitioners from the United States and the Soviet Union to examine different approaches to crisis prevention that would prevent nuclear catastrophe. As this group met in Washington and Moscow and worked with scholars who were also advising their governments, or were even in government themselves, no issues, not even sensitive ones, were off-limits. Thus, when Hamburg became president of the Corporation, he had a group of seasoned advisers—his "key men"—with whom he could consult. This group of colleagues, among whom were Graham Allison from Harvard, Alexander George from Stanford, Senator Sam Nunn, Senator Richard Lugar, and William J. Perry from Harvard and Stanford (who became secretary of defense in 1994), worked with Hamburg and the Corporation trustees and staff members throughout Hamburg's tenure by contributing to program development, implementation, and outreach.

34 The important role of these new "key" advisers, both men and women (unlike Keppel's "key men"), was amplified by program staff such as Frederic "Fritz" Mosher; Deana Arsenian, who, originally from Armenia, had lived in the Soviet Union, was a political scientist, was fluent in Russian, and was hired in 1984 as program assistant for the program; Patricia Moore Nicholas, an administrative assistant hired in 1987; and Deborah Cohen, an administrative assistant hired in 1980.

35 The sections draw on Hamburg's writings (many of which are summarized in his Annual Report essays and his recent *Carnegie Reporter* article, "Carnegie Corporation in the 1980s and 1990s") and on extensive memos prepared by program chairs Fritz Mosher, Jane Wales, and David Speedie, as well as on an article prepared by Adam Stulberg for the *Carnegie Results* series. Adam Stulberg, "Carnegie Corporation and Russia: Grantmaking Amidst Transformation," *Carnegie Results* (Spring 2005), available at: www.carnegie.org/publications/search-publications/pub/128 (accessed February 8, 2014).

36 CCNY, "Avoiding Nuclear War" (program paper), December 1983, CCNY Program Files, Box 11, Series I.D, CCNY Records, RBML-CUL.

37 CCNYAR, 1983, 49 (for one year at $494,100), and 1984, 20–21 (for two years at $1.1 million).

38 CCNYAR, 1983, 50 (for six months at $21,000), and 1984, 21 (for four years at $905,750).

The MIT Defense and Arms Control Studies Program had been funded by the Ford Foundation for fifteen years; CCNYAR, 1984, 21 (for three years at $1.1 million).

39 CCNYAR, 1986 (for $1 million for four years for the RAND/UCLA Center for Soviet Studies); 1985, 56 (for $1.5 million over three years for the W. Averell Harriman Institute for the Study of the Soviet Union); and 1985, 56–57 (for $599,675 over three years for the Berkeley-Stanford Program in Soviet International Behavior).

40 CCNY, "Avoiding Nuclear War," 8.

41 CCNYAR, 1984, 23. A two-year grant of $194,100 covered the first and second volumes.

42 Ibid., 26.

43 CCNYAR, 1985, 56.

44 Avery Russell, "Reducing the Risk of Nuclear War: What Can Scholars Do?" *Carnegie Quarterly* 2 (Spring 1985), available from Carnegie Corporation of New York Office (hereafter "CCNYO").

45 See CCNY, "Avoiding Nuclear War," 62–67, for a discussion of all donors; see also Fritz Mosher for the ANW Program Committee, "Five-Year Review of the Avoiding Nuclear War Program, for the Meeting of the Carnegie Corporation Board of Trustees," January 19, 1989, 13, CCNY Program Files, Box 11, Series I.D, CCNY Records, RBML-CUL. Mosher made the case that many of the institutions chosen for support benefited from a Rockefeller Foundation competition for research awards in the Soviet studies field. Rockefeller had shared its evaluations of the requests, leading to the choices made by the Corporation. One result was a grant to Duke University for the work of Jerry Hough, co-funded by the MacArthur Foundation; CCNYAR, 1989, 73.

46 Russell, "Reducing the Risk of Nuclear War," 2, 4–5, CCNYO. When the MacArthur Foundation sought to build up its grants program in this area, Jerome Wiesner and other MacArthur Foundation board members invited David Hamburg to brief them on the work of the Corporation and his own view of the opportunities for the MacArthur Foundation. To determine the most effective division of responsibility between the two foundations, they asked McGeorge Bundy, former president of the Ford Foundation and former national security adviser under President Lyndon Johnson, and Alexander George, a Corporation grantee and a distinguished scholar on security and Soviet studies, to co-chair a joint committee; David Hamburg, personal communication with the author, June 30, 2011; also discussed in Mosher, "Five-Year Review of the Avoiding Nuclear War Program," 9. Hamburg was well known to the MacArthur Foundation, not only because of his research, writing, and grant-making on these issues but also because he was the first person to be named the John D. MacArthur Professor of Health Policy and Management when he was at Harvard; Michael J. Abramowitz, "Hamburg Assumes MacArthur Chair in Health Policy," *Harvard Crimson*, May 14, 1982.

47 The intent was to review through a social science lens the issues involved in the prevention of war; CCNYAR, 1985, 54. Jacobson pulled together an interdisciplinary group of social scientists and international relations scholars to examine studies on the roots of human conflict and conflict resolution; CCNYAR, 1987, 62.

48 Mosher, "Five-Year Review of the Avoiding Nuclear War Program," 31.

49 Ibid., 32.

50 Ibid., 13.

51 Graham T. Allison, Albert Carnesale, and Joseph S. Nye Jr., eds., *Hawks, Doves, and Owls: An Agenda for Avoiding Nuclear War* (New York, W. W. Norton and Co., 1986), and Joseph S. Nye Jr., Graham T. Allison Jr., and Albert Carnesale, eds., *Fateful Visions: Avoiding Nuclear Catastrophe* (Cambridge, MA: Ballinger, 1988), 299; Mosher, "Five-Year Review of the Avoiding Nuclear War Program," 32.

52 "Address to the Nation on National Security by President Ronald Reagan," March 23, 1983, available at: http://www.fas.org/spp/starwars/offdocs/rrspch.htm. "Reagan had challenged the nation's scientists and engineers to devise an 'impenetrable shield' of defenses that would protect the American population against even the most massive nuclear attack by intercontinental ballistic missiles." David Perlman, "Managing a Delicate Balance: Arms Control and the Strategic Defense Initiative," *Carnegie Quarterly* 32, no. 1 (Winter 1987): 2–3, CCNYO.

53 Mosher, "Five-Year Review of the Avoiding Nuclear War Program," 14-15.

54 All listed in CCNYAR, 1984. In addition to working with the existing institutional grantees, such as Stanford University and MIT, new projects related specifically to the space shield and space weapons. For example, the American Academy of Arts and Sciences (AAAS) conducted an expert review of the state of knowledge in the field; CCNYAR, 1984, 22. The University of California's Institute on Global Conflict and Cooperation, under the leadership of Herbert York, began a longer-term study that focused on the political dimensions (22). The science and technological aspects were analyzed by the American Physical Society in cooperation with the Defense Department (22–23). The AAAS examined the antiballistic missiles weapons treaty; the UN Association of the United States of America conducted studies on developments in space (22). Harold Brown at the Johns Hopkins University School for Advanced International Studies, who had been secretary of defense under President Carter, examined in more depth the political and economic dimensions of the Strategic Defense Initiative and the whole field of militarization of space; CCNYAR, 1985, 51; for a full discussion, see Mosher, "Five-Year Review of the Avoiding Nuclear War Program," 14–21.

55 CCNYAR, 1984, 26.

56 CCNYAR, 1985, 54; see also Mosher, "Five-Year Review of the Avoiding Nuclear War Program," 16.

57 CCYNAR, 1986, 61.

58 "John Adams and Tom Cochran of NRDC swept into the room and made a dramatic announcement: They had just come from the airport on their return from Moscow, where they had negotiated an agreement with the Soviet Academy of Sciences to create a seismic verification system in the USSR (and the United States)." John Tirman, *Making the Money Sing: Private Wealth and Public Power in the Search for Peace* (Oxford: Rowan & Littlefield, 2000), 32. A follow-up grant to the Federation of American Scientists enabled American and Soviet scientists together to explore the verification of arms control agreements, co-funded by the W. Alton Jones Foundation. CCNYAR, 1988, 76.

59 Avery Russell, "Avoiding Nuclear War: Lessons for the Future of US-Soviet Relations," *Carnegie Quarterly* 34, nos. 3-4 (Summer-Fall 1989), CCNYO.

60 As described by Mosher, "Five-Year Review of the Avoiding Nuclear War Program," 17. For example, Alexander George at Stanford and Irving Janis and Richard Ned Lebow at Cornell examined past crises to glean lessons to guide the superpowers in the future; CCNYAR, 1985, 54, 53. John Steinbruner and Bruce Blair at Brookings and Kurt Gottfried and Richard Garwin at Cornell examined the technical aspects of the strategic command and control warning systems; CCNYAR, 1988, 72, 74. The Center for Education on Nuclear War reassessed the different policies of the United States and NATO related to the new US-Soviet INF (Intermediate-Range Nuclear Forces) Treaty; CCNYAR, 1988, 73–74. Herbert Abrams at Stanford studied the potential for accidental nuclear war; Barry Blechman, president of Defense Forecasts, and Janne Nolan of the Council on Foreign Relations and the Brookings Institution reviewed the impact of public pressure and opinion on nuclear doctrine and policy and the information shaping military and political decisions concerning nuclear policy; CCNYAR, 1987, 70, 67. The US Institute of Medicine prepared a book on the medical consequences of nuclear policy, and the International

Council of Scientific Unions' committee on the environment analyzed its environmental and biological effects, including the nuclear winter concept; CCNYAR, 1985, 54, 55.

61 Graham T. Allison, William L. Ury, and Bruce J. Allyn, *Windows of Opportunity: From Cold War to Peaceful Competition in US-Soviet Relations* (Cambridge, MA: Ballinger, 1989)."The 345-page volume reflects a six-year-long collaboration between American and Soviet scholars and policy advisers on the central problems of international security and the risks of inadvertent war in the nuclear age.… It provides perspectives from both sides on 'the most extraordinary achievement' of the postwar period—no nuclear war, no general war, not even a full Soviet-American alert"; Russell, "Avoiding Nuclear War," 2. Allison and his colleagues provided a new political framework presenting guidelines for cooperation, not competition, and "a set of guiding principles for peaceful coexistence now rooted in the US-Soviet relationship"; ibid., 9.

62 CCNYAR, 1984, 23. Two of his publications are, with Jacqueline R. Smith, *Nuclear Ambitions: The Spread of Nuclear Weapons, 1989–1990* (Boulder, CO: Westview Press, 1990) and *The Undeclared Bomb: The Spread of Nuclear Weapons, 1987–1988* (New York: Harper Business, 1990).

63 Paul Leventhal, *Preventing Nuclear Terrorism* (Lanham, MD: Lexington Books, 1987); CCNYAR, 1987, 68.

64 Stansfield Turner, *Terrorism and Democracy* (Boston: Houghton Mifflin, 1991), 274; CCNYAR, 1987, 68–69.

65 CCNYAR, 1987, 65.

66 Ibid., 70; CCNYAR, 1988, 79.

67 Fritz Mosher, "Five-Year Review of the Avoiding Nuclear War Program," 21. Three linked grants in 1988 in particular set the stage: Parliamentarians for Global Action (CCNYAR, 1988, 67); the UN Association of the USA (CCNYAR, 1989, 84), and the Pugwash Conferences on Science and World Affairs, which included representatives from African, Asian, and other non-Western countries (CCNYAR, 1988, 77) .

68 Fritz Mosher, personal communication with the author, June 30, 2011.

69 As Dick Clark mentioned in a 2010 interview, he had been struck by the lack of knowledge about the Soviet Union when he was serving as a senator in Washington. "As Clark was pondering how to resolve the lack of knowledge about Russia in Congress, Carnegie Corporation's then president David Hamburg was thinking along the same lines. Hamburg's particular interest, Clark recalled, was providing scholars with an outlet to policymakers. After Carnegie Corporation provided an initial grant to launch the program, 'I didn't know how long I would do this,' recalled Clark. 'I didn't think of it as a short period or a long period.'" When Clark built the Aspen Institute Congressional Program into an environment for frank, high-quality discussion, the program soon received support from a wide range of foundations on a wide range of themes. Other supporters have included the MacArthur Foundation, the Rockefeller Foundation, the Hewlett Foundation, the Ford Foundation, the Packard Foundation, and the Luce Foundation. In 2011 Clark stepped down after more than one hundred conferences, and former representative Daniel Glickman assumed the gavel. Lee Michael Katz, "Dick Clark: Creating a Lasting Legacy by Educating Congress," *Carnegie Reporter* (Spring 2010): 33–34; CCNYAR, 1984, 27.

70 The grant was originally a three-year grant co-funded by the Rockefeller Foundation and the MITRE Corporation. Joseph Nye of Harvard, Brent Scowcroft, and William Perry served as co-chairs. The Aspen Strategy Group, like the Aspen Congressional Program, was still going strong in 2011. CCNYAR, 1985, 52.

71 Ibid.; Mosher, "Five-Year Review of the Avoiding Nuclear War Program," 23.

72 Mosher, "Five-Year Review of the Avoiding Nuclear War Program," 36–37.

73 Deana Arsenian and David A. Hamburg, "Carnegie Corporation Trip Report: Moscow,

March 7–12, 1988," 7, 25, CCNY Policy and Program Files, Folder 5, Box 14, Series I.D, CCNY Records, RBML-CUL. The timing of this trip was significant. A few months later, Gorbachev announced his policy of democratization, freeing the countries of the Eastern Bloc from their allegiance to the Brezhnev Doctrine. In two years he was no longer general secretary but president of the Soviet Union. By his actions, Gorbachev essentially brought an end to the Cold War. He won the Nobel Peace Prize in 1990.

74   Ibid., 1–2; US embassy in Moscow, press release, March 11, 1988.

75   CCNY, Minutes of the Board of Trustees, April 21, 1988, "Memo from Hamburg to Trustees, dated April 12, 1988," CCNY Records, RBML-CUL. The meetings were clearly glasnost and perestroika in action. The delegation met not only with Gorbachev but with Andre Sakharov, Foreign Minister Eduard Shevardnadze, the foreign policy committees at the Supreme Soviet in the Kremlin, representatives of Soviet Scientists for Peace, Central Committee secretary Anatoly Dobrynin, and then, on the last day, with Gorbachev. Comments read into the *Congressional Record* on March 14, 1988, on behalf of the senators who participated make clear the importance of this remarkable visit. As Senator Simpson concluded his lengthy remarks: "It was a very extraordinary visit where, perhaps, we even had a bit more freedom than would have been the case if we had been part of an official government delegation.… It was an excellent opportunity and hopefully will bear fruit in the form of suitable treaties, ratification, important verification measures, interpretations, linkage, all the things that are so vital to US legislators in the United States." Alan Simpson, "Visit to the Soviet Union," Senate, March 14, 1988, *Congressional Record*, S103–S104.

76   Seweryn Bialer of Columbia University, a Corporation grantee, was the main research adviser. The series was shown in 1988 and received positive reviews. CCNYAR, 1986, 61; Mosher, "Five-Year Review of the Avoiding Nuclear War Program," 24.

77   *Inside Gorbachev's USSR* won the DuPont-Columbia Grand Prize in 1991 for outstanding public affairs production on television. See PBS/Frontline, "Producer Hedrick Smith," available at: www.pbs.org/wgbh/pages/frontline/about-us/producer-hedrick-smith/ (accessed February 8, 2014). See also CCNYAR, 1989, 82.

78   Co-funding by the Rockefeller Family Associates, the Rockefeller Family Fund, and three foundations—MacArthur, General Service, and Winston—enabled the new *Nuclear Times* journal to cover the work of grantees to reach a more activist readership. Two grants in 1989 to the Educational Foundation for Nuclear Science assisted with developing and implementing a marketing plan to bolster readership for the *Bulletin of the Atomic Scientists*; CCNYAR, 1989, 81. Collaborating in 1987, the Public Agenda Foundation and Brown University's Center for Foreign Policy Development conducted public surveys on issues related to international security and the Soviet Union as preparation for a public education campaign, co-funded by the Hewlett and MacArthur Foundations. A narrower set of surveys was funded through the Roosevelt Center in Washington, DC, focusing on nuclear proliferation; CCNYAR, 1987, 71–72. Mosher considered the results of the surveys and their effects on the campaigns inconclusive; Mosher, "Five-Year Review of the Avoiding Nuclear War Program," 36–40, 37.

79   CCNYAR, 1987, 72; 1985, 59; and 1988, 82.

80   From 1986 to 1997, the collaboration was funded to cover a wide variety of educational and exchange activities, focused on computers in elementary education, first under Michael Cole and Alexandra Belyaeva at their institutions (CCNYAR, 1987, 77; 1988, 83–84; 1989, 83; 1990, 89; 1991, 83–84; 1993, 105; and 1994, 77), and then at the International Research and Exchanges Board (IREX), under Daniel C. Matuszewski (CCNYAR, 1994, 73; 1995, 72; 1996, 101; and 1997, 54), for a total of $2,511,500. The grants built on earlier work on cognitive development under Cole, starting in 1984; CCNYAR, 1984, 28.

81 Mosher, "Five-Year Review of the Avoiding Nuclear War Program," 26.

82 Corporation staff members worked closely with another initiative of Velikov's. Established by the Soviets in 1986 and 1987, the International Foundation for the Survival and Development of Humanity aimed to promote similar kinds of collaboration around global problems to explore peaceful solutions to global conflicts and rivalries. One of its great successes was when Andre Sakharov, the Soviet dissident, was allowed to come to the United States to attend a performance at the Metropolitan Opera and also attend the meeting of the Foundation's executive committee at the Corporation. Hamburg, Mosher, and Arsenian provided advice; ibid., 26. The Corporation provided a grant of $500,000 in 1990; CCNYAR, 1990, 85. Nonetheless, the Foundation was not able to find sufficient funding and had to close.

83 This review included discussions by the Avoiding Nuclear War Program with its major advisers: McGeorge Bundy, Marshall Schulman, John Steinbruner, Alexander George, Seweryn Bialer, Ed A. Hewett, and Condoleezza Rice. Patricia Moore Nicholas prepared a report of the discussion for the program; Patricia Moore Nicholas, "Report of the Five-Year Review of the Avoiding Nuclear War Program," January 19, 1989,

84 Ibid., 1.

85 David Hamburg, memo to Board of Trustees, "Five-Year Review of the Avoiding Nuclear War Program," January 6, 1989, 7, CCNY Board Minutes, Box 70, Series I.A.3, CCNY Records, RBML-CUL.

86 Tim Reid, "How Reagan and Gorbachev Made a Real Breakthrough in the Arms Race," *The Times*, February 4, 2009. Mosher, "Five-Year Review of the Avoiding Nuclear War Program," 16.

87 Mosher, Ibid., 11.

88 Ibid., 2. Mosher also noted the active role that David Hamburg played in many of these activities and beyond. Hamburg regularly briefed the White House, including, at times, President Reagan; this connection was vitally important given the backlash experienced by some of the Corporation's domestic activities from Congress (although not in this era; see Phyllis Schlafly, "The Carnegie Blueprint to Nationalize Education," *Human Events* 49, no. 8 [1989], and her *Washington Times* advertisements on the VelHam Project and its deleterious effects on children). Hamburg kept the board fully informed of the risks involved in his activities in this area, both to him and to the Corporation; he made the case that the risks were worth it given the highly positive potential benefits.

89 Nicholas, "Report of the Five-Year Review of the Avoiding Nuclear War Program," 1–5. Board members, such as Joshua Lederberg, emphasized that this was a time when more attention was needed to deal with the US-Soviet relationship and the importance of setting priorities. John Whitehead, having returned to the board from the State Department, and Warren Christopher, not yet back at State, weighed in on the relative merits of continuing to focus on the Soviet Union and nuclear proliferation versus expanding the Corporation's concentration on Eastern Europe. Christopher's comments presciently noted that "the U.S. does not have a policy or approach to react to a possible breakdown of the Soviet Union, which would inevitably affect Eastern Europe." He added, "There is a great need to educate American policymakers on Eastern Europe. Together with nuclear proliferation, this issue is critical"; ibid., 2–5. Helene Kaplan cited the need "to continue and expand support in the areas of nuclear proliferation, terrorism, and accidental and inadvertent nuclear war." Furthermore, "she … called for expanded U.S.-Soviet scholarship in the fields of biological and technical research"; ibid., 5.

90 For a series of articles appearing at the time, see Editors, "From the Archives: 1989," *Foreign Affairs*, available at: http://www.foreign affairs.com/features/collections/from-the-archives-1989 (accessed June 24, 2012).

91 Bush, "Address to the Nation on the Invasion of Iraq (January 16, 1991)."

92   Fritz Mosher, "For Cooperative Security Working Group and Staff, Program on Cooperative Security Review," undated, 10, CCNY Program Files, Box 15, Series I.D; and CCNY Minutes, Box 74, Series I.A.3; both at CCNY Records, RBML-CUL.

93   CCNY, Minutes of the Board of Trustees, October 16, 1990, "Cooperative Security Program, Program Budget Paper, 1990 to 1991" (materials for the board meeting), 10, 11, 26, CCNY Records, RBML-CUL.

94   CCNYAR, 1990, 176. To maintain the focus on nuclear weapons as well as move forward with this new work over the period 1989 to 1990, Hamburg opened up the offices to new temporary appointments: senior specialists, in residence, who would spend time at the Corporation advising him and the staff. Ambassador Herbert S. Okun, on leave from the US State Department from September 1989 to September 1990, consulted on issues of international security and arms control, US-Soviet relations, multinational organizations, and conflict resolution. Graham T. Allison Jr., a Corporation grantee on sabbatical from Harvard University, conducted research, wrote, and advised the Corporation on international security, arms control, US-Soviet relations, strengthening democratic institutions, and conflict resolution. During this period of thematic transition, the program also underwent significant staffing changes. Jane Wales joined the Corporation in 1990 as program officer in Avoiding Nuclear War, and in 1991 she became senior program officer. Wales came from the Secure Society Program at the W. Alton Jones Foundation. She was appointed chair of the Cooperative Security Program in October 1992 when Fritz Mosher, the founding chair of the program, became director of the Project on Philanthropic Strategies. To ensure a full contingent of staff members in the Cooperative Security Program, the Corporation hired David Speedie, who joined on October 1, 1992 as program officer. Previously, he had been at the W. Alton Jones Foundation as co-director of the Secure Society Program, where Wales had been earlier.

95   Among the grantees receiving continued support for work in international security and arms control as well as US-Soviet scientific linkages were: Stanford University (CCNYAR, 1990, 77, and 1991, 85); the Brookings Institution (CCNYAR, 1991, 82–83); the Harriman Institute at Columbia University (CCNYAR, 1991, 88); the University of California at San Diego (CCNYAR, 1991, 83); the Harvard Negotiation Program and Harvard's Avoiding Nuclear War Project (CCNYAR, 1990, 78); the Nuclear Control Institute (CCNYAR, 1991, 89); the work at Princeton led by Frank von Hippel to examine the new Strategic Arms Reduction Treaty and the Treaty on Conventional Armed Forces in Europe (CCNYAR, 1992, 90); the Federation of American Scientists and the Soviet Academy of Sciences (CCNYAR, 1991, 93, 94); projects on regional conflicts supported at Johns Hopkins University and "the Soviet-based Institute of U.S.A. and Canada Studies" under I. William Zartman and Victor Kremanjuk, respectively, (CCNYAR, 1991, 86); and Stanford University, under the leadership of William Perry (CCNYAR, 1992, 87).

96   These grantees often received annual funding: Aspen Institute, both programs (CCNYAR, 1990, 85); AAAS (CCNYAR, 1989, 80); Fund for Peace's National Security Project (CCNYAR, 1987, 72–73); ACLU (CCNYAR, 1991, 101); and SIPI (CCNYAR, 1991, 89).

97   See Fritz Mosher and Jane Wales, "Memo to Corporation Staff, Background for Staff Discussion of the Program on Cooperative Security, Meeting on Dec. 13, 1990," December 11, 1990, Box 15, Series I.D, CCNY Records, RBML-CUL.

98   CCNY, "Program Budget Paper, 1991–1992, Cooperative Security," 28, CCNY Board Minutes, Box 74, Series I.A.3, CCNY Records, RBML-CUL.

99   CCNYAR, 1991, 184; see ibid., 90, for the initial grant.

100   McGeorge Bundy, William J. Crowe, and Sidney David Drell, *Reducing Nuclear Danger: The Road Away from the Brink* (New York: Council on Foreign Relations, 1993).

101 CCNYAR, 1991, 89 and 88. See Janne Nolan, ed., *Global Engagement: Cooperative Security in the Twenty-First Century* (Washington, DC: Brookings Institution, 1994); see also Ashton B. Carter, William J. Perry, and John D. Steinbruner, *A New Concept of Cooperative Security*, Brookings Occasional Papers (Washington, DC: Brookings Institution, 1992), and David Hamburg, "Memo to Warren Christopher, Fritz Mosher, Jane Wales, Subject: Proposed Task Force on Prevention of Proliferation of Weapons of Mass Destruction," November 12, 1990, CCNY Records, RBML-CUL.

102 CCNYAR, 1990, 78, and 1992, 91 (Harvard University); CCNYAR, 1991, 95 (Columbia University); CCNYAR, 1991, 95 (IREX); and CCNYAR, 1991, 96 (Stanford University).

103 CCNYAR, 1992, 98, 100.

104 Other key participants in these efforts included William Perry of Stanford University and Ashton Carter of the Kennedy School of Government at Harvard; see CCNYAR, 1991, 88, 89. In addition, Leonard Spector and Geoffrey Kemp of the Carnegie Endowment for International Peace received a grant of $800,000 in 1992 for the Endowment's activities in association with the project, including its work in the Korean peninsula, the Middle East, and Southwest Asia; CCNYAR, 1992, 88.

105 Senator Nunn indicated that his participation in the Aspen Institute meetings contributed significantly to his thinking; Katz, "Dick Clark," 4. Nunn provided his perspective at the June 11, 1992, meeting of the Carnegie Board of Trustees: "Senator Nunn then discussed his initiative, undertaken together with Senator Lugar, to authorize $400 million to go to the former Soviet Union to reorient its military mission, destroy nuclear and other high technology weapons, and convert its military research and production facilities to civilian uses.... He reviewed the factors that overcame initial skepticism within the House and Senate about the proposal and suggested activities that would contribute to arms reductions, military demobilization and reorientation, and private sector involvement in these issues." Following his presentation, Ashton Carter described the vital importance of the Nunn-Lugar initiative and "outlined the dangers inherent in the post-Soviet nuclear world and the leading role of the Nunn-Lugar initiative in mobilizing a US response to these developments." At the same meeting, Cyrus Vance, who had served as secretary of state under President Carter from 1997 to 1980, discussed issues that later were to feature more significantly in the Corporation's work. He "reported on recent events in Yugoslavia and analyzed the factors that contributed to the outbreak and continuation of hostilities there. He reviewed various proposals for ending the fighting and preventing the escalation of hostilities in other formerly Communist areas of Europe and Asia. He concluded that the challenge before the United Nations and the world community is organizing a multilateral response to crises in an era of local hot wars rather than dealing with an over arching bipolar Cold War." All quotes from CCNY, Minutes of the Board of Trustees, 1–2, June 11, 1992, CCNY Records, RBML-CUL. William J. Perry (then assistant secretary of defense), John B. Steinbruner (director of foreign policy studies at the Brookings Institution), and Senator Richard G. Lugar talked to the trustees about the work in cooperative security and the Nunn-Lugar initiative at a later board meeting; CCNY, Minutes of the Board of Trustees, 69–71, October 14, 1993, CCNY Records, RBML-CUL.

106 Ashton B. Carter, "Origins of the Nunn-Lugar Program," presentation to the presidential conference on "William Jefferson Clinton: The 'New Democrat' from Hope," Hofstra University, November 10–12, 2005, available at: belfercenter.ksg.harvard.edu/files/hofstra_presidential_conference_presentation_november2005.pdf (accessed June 28, 2012).

107 CCNY, "Program Budget Paper, 1993–1994, Cooperative Security," 25, CCNY Board Minutes, Box 74, Series I.A.3, CCNY Records, RBML-CUL. As described in the paper, cooperative security, a reality that had seemed so positive with the changes occurring over the period

1990–1991, had turned brutally elusive. The war in the Balkans, arising out of the situation in Yugoslavia that Cyrus Vance had talked about at the 1992 board meeting, was stubborn and violent. A cluster of grants was related to the situation. Cyrus Vance, along with former UK foreign minister David Owen, tried to mediate the conflict. John Steinbruner of Brookings and John Ruggie, dean of the Columbia School of International and Public Affairs research, each tried to evaluate "collective security options for coping with civil violence in sovereign states." Abram Chayes and Antonia Chayes did work on the role of multilateral institutions in peacekeeping in these disintegrating situations. And Shibley Telhami and his colleagues at Cornell University examined "the interaction between domestic and international politics in ethnic conflicts, in particular the role of external actors from the international community in internal conflict"; ibid., 28–31.

108   CCNYAR, 1992, 94, and 1994, 67 (IREX Project on Ethnic Relations); 1992, 100, and 1994, 68 (Conflict Management Group); 1992, 97, and 1994, 72 (Lawyers Committee for Human Rights); 1992, 46, and 1994, 71 (Helsinki Watch and Human Rights Watch); and 1993, 106 (for quote), and 1994, 71 (Institute for East-West Studies); see also CCNY, "Program Budget Paper, 1993–1994, Cooperative Security," 30.

109   Staff transitions also prompted internal reflection. Jane Wales had been asked to assist the Clinton administration transition team on issues related to national security. Consequently, she took a leave of absence from December 1992 to January 1993. In August 1993, she was appointed associate director for international affairs and national security in the Office of Science and Technology Policy. David Speedie was appointed acting chair of the program; CCNYAR, 1993, 155–156. Continuity in this dynamic program was maintained by program assistant Patricia Moore Nicholas and Patricia Aquino-Macri, Deborah Cohen, and Lynn Di Martino of the administrative staff.

110   CCNYAR, 1993, 11.

111   The Commission was established as an operating project of the Corporation with an office in Washington and support for Commission study reports, meetings, and the preparation of a final report by the end of December 1997 to be widely disseminated, both regionally and internationally. The grants program would fund the more in-depth, larger-scale studies and scholar-policymaker dialogues. Hamburg co-chaired the Commission with former secretary of state Cyrus Vance. The commissioners represented a wide range of countries and organizations and were chosen for the significant roles they had played in conflict prevention, whether nationally, regionally, or internationally: Gro Harlem Bruntland, Norway; Vivendra Dayal, India; Gareth Evans, Australia; Alexander L. George, United States; Flora MacDonald, Canada; Donald F. McHenry, United States; Olara A. Otunnu, Uganda; David Owen, United Kingdom; Shridath Ramphal, Guyana; Roald Z. Sagdeev, Russia; John D. Steinbruner, United States; Brian Urquhart, United Kingdom and United States; John C. Whitehead, United States; and Sahabzada Yaqub-Khan, Pakistan.

112   A number of staffing decisions had to be made before these changes could be implemented. David Speedie, acting chair since October 1993, was named program chair as of October 1, 1994, following trustee approval of the change in the name and theme of the program from Cooperative Security to Preventing Deadly Conflict. Astrid Tuminez, who had been working since September 1992 as a part-time research associate in the program on conflict resolution issues, joined as program officer in July 1994. In November 1994, Suzanne Wood, deputy director of the Salzburg Global Seminars in Austria, joined as program officer. For more details, see CCNY, "Program Budget Paper, 1994–1995, Cooperative Security," 25–28, CCNY Program Files, Box 21, Series I.D, CCNY Records, RBML-CUL.

113   In both the Bush and Clinton administrations, Holl had served on the National Security

Council as director for European political and security affairs. She had extensive service in the US Army and held a PhD in political science from Stanford University and a JD from Georgetown University.

114   CCNYAR, 1997, 47.

115   Carnegie Commission on Preventing Deadly Conflict, *Preventing Deadly Conflict* (New York: CCNY, 1997).

116   The program not only supported the work of the Commission on the Prevention of Deadly Conflict but also continued support for a number of grantees working in depth on global security: the Gorbachev Foundation, for a project to "focus global attention on pressing international issues" (CCYNAR, 1993, 78); Columbia University, American Assembly, for an examination of the role of international nongovernmental organizations in state-building in the former Soviet Union, the redesign of political institutions, the democratization of the rule of law, the evolution of human rights norms, and the management of ethnic and civil conflict (CYNAR 1995, 61); Australian National University, for a study of the UN and its role in conflict resolution and prevention (ibid., 62); the Canadian Centre for Global Security, for the financing of the UN (CCNYAR, 1995, 80); the National Endowment for Democracy's international forum for democratic studies (ibid., 66); the National Research Council, for a project on response mechanisms and strategies by outside interveners in national conflicts (ibid., 76); and a new program, the Center for Preventive Action of the Council on Foreign Relations, which was established in part by the Corporation in 1994 and continued to focus on preventive strategies in various global hotspots (ibid., 60, 80). A joint program with UNITAR, the United Nations Institute for Training and Research, and the International Peace Academy offered joint seminars and training for senior-level UN staff members and diplomats; CCNYAR, 1994, 75, and 1996, 77.

117   For work on strengthening democratic institutions, Corporation staff recognized the challenges in sustaining the previous euphoria in the region. The program continued to focus on Russia—the Russian parliament, the Russian Federation, the Russian military, neighbors of Russia, and the Russian media. Grantees included, for example, Harvard University (with military personnel) (CCNYAR, 1994, 66); Harvard (Russian democratization) (CCNYAR, 1995, 67); Stanford University (defense enterprises) (CCNYAR, 1995, 70); New York University's Russian-American Press Center (CCNYAR, 1995, 71); IREX, for continuing the VelHam Project (CCNYAR, 1995, 72); the Center for Post-Soviet Studies, for work on the former Soviet Union and in Central Asia (CCNYAR, 1995, 70); and the RAND Corporation, to strengthen policy analysis skills among scholars from Russia and the CIS (Commonwealth of Independent States) (CCNYAR, 1997, 52). Others built on the earlier projects about ethnic conflict in the post-Soviet Union era: Columbia University, for work on global stability and the post-Soviet state (CCNYAR, 1994, 69); the Project on Ethnic Relations, for on-the-ground negotiating with the Hungarian minority groups and the governments of Slovakia and Romania (CCNYAR, 1994, 67); Partners for Democratic Change, to explore establishing centers for conflict resolution in the Soviet Union and Eastern and Central Europe (CCNYAR, 1994, 70); Harvard University, for studies of ethnic conflict (CCNYAR, 1994, 69); and the Carnegie Endowment for International Peace, to establish the Moscow Center for Russian and Eurasian Programs (CCNYAR, 1993, 104).

118   Grants continued the work on multiple aspects of proliferation: the Brookings Institution, for cooperative and nuclear security (CCNYAR, 1997, 55); Stanford's Center for International Security and Arms Control (CCNYAR, 1997, 56); Harvard's Center for Science and International Affairs (CCNYAR, 1997, 56); the National Academy of Sciences' Committee on International Security Arms and Control (CCNYAR, 1997, 59); MIT's Defense and Arms

Control Studies Program (CCNYAR, 1997, 57); and the Carnegie Endowment for International Peace, for work on nuclear nonproliferation (CCNYAR, 1994, 61, and 1996, 94).

119 Harvard and the University of Sussex promoted a global agreement on the nonproliferation of chemical and biological weapons; CCNYAR, 1995, 80. The Henry L. Stimson Center focused on ensuring ratification of the chemical weapons convention signed by 150 nations in January 1993; CCNYAR, 1996, 93. The National Academy of Sciences' Committee on International Security and Arms Control worked on an issue that was becoming an increasing concern with regard to nuclear proliferation—contact between US policymakers and military elites in China on arms control issues; CCNYAR, 1996, 94.

120 University of Maryland Foundation, WIIS, co-funded by the Ford Foundation and later Citibank (CCNYAR, 1995, 78); Monterey Institute of International Studies (CCNYAR, 1995, 74); Harvard University, PONARS (CCNYAR, 1996, 101, and 1997, 55); Harvard University, Project Liberty ("connecting a new generation of experts, from new European democracies and Western European and North American counterparts, first grant"), co-funded by the Rockefeller Brothers Fund, Pew Charitable Trusts, and European donors (CCNYAR, 1994, 72).

121 Tirman, *Making the Money Sing*, 134; Sada Aksartova, "In Search of Legitimacy: Peace Grant Making of US Philanthropic Foundations, 1988–1996," *Nonprofit and Voluntary Sector Quarterly* 32, no. 1 (2003): 42.

122 CCNYAR, 1983, 19.

123 Ibid, 19–20.

124 Ibid., 21.

125 Ibid. Hamburg was commenting on work over the course of the 1970s that emphasized the vital role of local communities as participants in, not objects of, development planning and implementation. See Aina, "Development Theory and Africa's Lost Decade," 20–23; Taylor et al., *Empowerment on an Unstable Planet*, 27–29.

126 While David Hood continued to be consulted by the Corporation on Southern Africa after he departed, the Corporation hired David Devlin-Foltz, who had worked with the Ford Foundation on public understanding of development and South Africa, to take over. From 1986 to mid-1990, Dr. Adetokunbo O. Lucas led as program chair. After Lucas's departure to assume the chair in international health at Harvard, Hamburg asked Patricia Rosenfield to serve as program chair. Rosalie Karefa-Smart served as program assistant, including focusing on maternal health. David Robinson and Avery Russell remained engaged with the Southern Africa grant-making. Russell also shaped the focus on increasing media coverage as part of the public understanding of development issues.

127 David Hood, consultant, memo to David Hamburg, president, "Subject: Carnegie Corporation in South Africa," November 1, 1984, CCNY Board Minutes, Box 63, Series I.A.3, CCNY Records, RBML-CUL. Hood also mentions the overall thrust of the program.

128 Attending from the Corporation were President David Hamburg; John Taylor, chairman of the board; Helene Kaplan, vice chairman of the board; Ruth Hamilton, a member of the Carnegie board and a member of the Rockefeller Foundation–funded Study Commission on US Policy Toward Southern Africa; Alan Pifer, president emeritus of the Corporation and a former member of the Rockefeller Study Commission on US Policy Toward Southern Africa; David Robinson, executive vice president; and David Hood, consultant to the Corporation.

129 Wilson and Ramphele, *Uprooting Poverty*, xi–xii.

130 David Hamburg, memo to Carnegie Corporation trustees, "Subject: South Africa in Context," November 28, 1984, CCNY Board Minutes, Box 63, Series I.A.3, CCNY Records, RBML-CUL. A further indication of Hamburg's commitment to ameliorating the South Africa situation was his effort to secure the release of Reverend Allen Boesak from prison. Boesak,

a highly visible leader of the newly formed United Democratic Front, a liberal anti-apartheid movement that brought together activists of varying perspectives, had been arrested for leading protests. On August 27, 1985, the UN Special Committee Against Apartheid called on the international community to help obtain Boesak's release; see South African History Archive, "UDF: 30 Years," available at: http://www.nelsonmandela.org/udf/index.php/theme/category/repression. Hamburg responded and mobilized a team of foundation and university leaders—including Norman Brown, president of the Kellogg Foundation, William Bowen, president of the Mellon Foundation, and Derek Bok, president of Harvard University—to go to South Africa. Along with other members from the international community, they pleaded, successfully, for Boesak's release. David Hamburg, personal communication with the author, June 30, 2011. The Corporation funded distribution by the WGBH Educational Foundation of a film on Boesak; CCNYAR, 1985, 49.

131 Hamburg, memo to Carnegie Corporation trustees, "Subject: South Africa in Context," November 28, 1984, 4. At the same time, the trustees were still determining how best to align investment policy with the abiding concerns about apartheid. A special committee of the board was constituted to review all the issues. In 1986 the committee reported to the board, which unanimously approved its plan: concerning companies in the portfolio, or ones being considered for the portfolio, the Corporation would invest only in those companies with investments in South Africa that followed the Sullivan Principles, the code of conduct arrived at by Reverend Leon Sullivan after consultation and negotiations with American companies investing in South Africa. Ad Hoc Committee, memo to the Board of Trustees, "Subject: South Africa Investment Policy," July 30, 1986, CCNY Board Minutes, Box 65, Series I.A.3, CCNY Records, RBML-CUL.

132 Drawing on the paper prepared by senior adviser to the president Elena Nightingale and staff members Jill Sheffield and David Devlin-Foltz, Hamburg emphasized "building connections to mobilize a strong network of cooperating universities in several African countries and the United States … health for education, particularly education of women and girls"; Hamburg, memo to Carnegie Corporation trustees, "Subject: South Africa in Context," November 28, 1984, 3. Working with two consultants—Dr. Fred Sai, one of the world's leading experts on population and reproductive health, a former director of medical services in Ghana, and a professor of community medicine at the University of Ghana, and Peter Bell, former head of the Inter-American Development Foundation and the Ford Foundation officer in Latin America, with deep knowledge of grassroots developments in Latin America and the Caribbean—the program began to make grants focusing on maternal and child health care, nutrition, education, family planning, and the status of women; ibid., 4; see also CCNYAR, 1984, 42.

133 In 1984 one new and several continuing grantees were supported: the American Medical Research Foundation, a first-time grant for work on African health issues (CCNYAR, 1984, 49); TransAfrica Forum (principally supported by the Ford Foundation), for its outreach publications on conditions in Africa and the Caribbean (CCNYAR, 1984, 51); the African-American Institute for its programs on women in development activities, travel grants for Africans, and the seminar series for congressional staff members (CCNYAR, 1984, 50); the Overseas Development Council, to plan for a publication with the Council on Foreign Relations examining US aid, with a specific focus on Africa, leading to the 1986 publication *Strategies for African Development* (CCNYAR, 1984, 51); and the Institute of International Education for its South African Education Program (CCNYAR, 1984, 50).

134 See CCNYAR, 1983, 52–55, for all the renewals in and on South Africa. In 1985 the African-American Institute received a grant of nearly $700,000 to cover a series of visits of South Africans to the United States and to continue expanding its briefing and conference program related to policy issues in Africa and South Africa. In submitting this grant to the board, staff

members noted that the Institute had received $5 million from the Corporation since 1960 and was considered a valuable resource for reaching out to African Americans as well as American policymakers about African development issues; CCNYAR, 1985, 46.

135 In 1984 and 1985, the work on maternal and child health intensified, with grants to the International Council of Voluntary Agencies (CCNYAR, 1984, 52); the National Academy of Sciences (CCNYAR, 1984, 52); the United States Committee for UNICEF (CCNYAR, 1984, 54); the National Council on International Health (CCNYAR, 1984, 54); the Pathfinder Fund, for the education of pregnant girls in Africa (CCNYAR, 1985, 42–43); the Program for Applied Technology in Health, to apply its Safe Birth Program in Southern Africa; the Population Council, for work on child survival in Mexico and the Caribbean (CCNYAR, 1985, 45); the University of Texas, for a conference on health along the US-Mexico border; and the International Center for Research on Women, for work on infant mortality (CCNYAR, 1985, 47).

136 CCNYAR, 1983, 56 and 55. Later support, in 1986, of about $250,000 for the University of Minnesota together with Columbia University established the International Women's Rights Action Watch to monitor the United Nations Convention on the Elimination of All Forms of Discrimination Against Women and to develop a specific concentration on women's legal rights in the Commonwealth countries of Africa and the Caribbean. Additional support went to the Pan American Development Foundation to examine issues of credit for women. World Priorities was funded over several years to produce a handbook on the status of women and girls around the world; CCNYAR, 1986, 55.

137 Other foundations were also underwriting this activity. Peter Bell was one of the Corporation's main advisers to assess this work. CCNYAR, 1984, 52–53.

138 Over several years, HRDC's Public Understanding of Development (PUD) subprogram, led by Avery Russell, provided support for the interdisciplinary telecourse on Latin America and the Caribbean in association with WGBH, Columbia, Florida International, and Tufts Universities. Ten one-hour prime-time programs and the college-level program *Americas* were also co-funded by the Annenberg/Community Partnership Program project and the MacArthur and Rockefeller Foundations; CCNYAR, 1984, 53. The University of Southern California Center for International Journalism received support for journalists from Mexico and the Commonwealth Caribbean to participate in its master's program; this grant was co-sponsored by the Ford, MacArthur, and Olin Foundations; CCNYAR, 1986, 60.

139 Other early PUD grants went to Global Perspectives on Education, the Overseas Development Network, the National Council of Returned Peace Corps Volunteers, the Joint PVO (Private Voluntary Organization)/University Rural Development Center, and the Africa News Service. CCNYAR, 1986, 50.

140 With the departure of Jill Sheffield in late 1986 and the hiring of Patricia Rosenfield in May 1987, Lucas and Hamburg were building the team; David Devlin-Foltz remained, joined by a new hire in 1986, Rosalie Karefa-Smart, as program assistant. Avery Russell continued to take the lead on the Second Carnegie Inquiry work in South Africa and in the United States, including ensuring completion of the publications and helping to plan the outreach efforts. She also contributed programmatically to the PUD journalism work. Elena Nightingale, with her special interest in Mexico and the US-Mexico border, contributed to the development of programs in that area under the HRDC auspices. David Robinson continued to advise on South Africa in general, and Barbara Finberg, vice president for the program, advised on the overall program strategy. In turn, Finberg asked Rosenfield to serve on the Special Projects Committee to become more familiar with the overall work of the Corporation and its initiatives.

141 Lucas determined that issues affecting women and their health, particularly the

unnecessary and excessive number of maternal deaths in childbirth, were not being addressed sufficiently, whether nationally or internationally or in African or other developing countries; for details on how he arrived at this decision, see his memoir, Adetokunbo O. Lucas, *It Was the Best of Times* (Ibadan, Nigeria: Bookbuilders, 2010), 271–273. Women's health, in contrast to child health, was a backwater area at the time. No one was shining a bright light on maternal mortality. Two key papers reinforced Lucas's decision: Kelsey A. Harrison, "Child-bearing, Health, and Social Priorities: A Survey of 22,774 Consecutive Births in Zaria, Northern Nigeria," *British Journal of Obstetrics and Gynaecology* 92, suppl. 5 (1985): 1–119; and Allan Rosenfield and Deborah Maine, "Maternal Mortality—A Neglected Tragedy: Where Is the M in MCH?" *Lancet* 2, no. 8466 (1985): 83–85.

142   Edward Horesh, "African Alternative Framework to Structural Adjustment Programme for Socio-economic Recovery and Transformation" (New York: United Nations Economic Commission for Africa, November 1, 2006). See also Organization of African Unity, "African Common Position on Africa's External Debt Crisis, Addis Ababa, 1987," available at: http://archive.lib.msu.edu/DMC/African%20Journals/pdfs/Journal%20of%20Political%20Economy/ajpev2n5/ajpe002005007.pdf; United Nations General Assembly, "UN Program of Action for African Economic Recovery and Development, 1986–1990," eighth plenary meeting, June 1, 1986, A/RES/S-13/2, available at: http://www.un.org/documents/ga/res/spec/aress13-2.htm (accessed June 29, 2012).

143   Nobel Prize, "F. W. de Klerk—Biographical," available at: http://nobelprize.org/nobel_prizes/peace/laureates/1993/klerk-bio.html (accessed August 22, 2012).

144   UN Economic Commission for Africa, "Overview of Economic and Social Development in Africa: An Overview of Africa's Development in the First Half of the 1990s," available at: http://www.uneca.org/cfm1996/pages/overview-economic-and-social-development-africa.

145   CCNY, "Strengthening Human Resources in Developing Countries" (program review paper), January 26, 1988, 1, CCNY Program Files, Box 11, Series I.D, CCNY Records, RBML-CUL.

146   Hamburg sought a charter review to explore the possibility of moving beyond Commonwealth countries. Mexico, as the southern neighbor of the United States, was inarguably a country of clear and compelling interest. Elihu Root Jr.'s firm, now called Dewey Ballantine Bushby Palmer and Wood, one of the Corporation's counsels, prepared the review; the senior partner who led the review was Joseph Califano, the former secretary of health, education, and welfare under President Carter. In examining all the charter concerns, as well as Andrew Carnegie's deed of gift, the conclusion was that the Corporation was not limited in its grant-making to the Commonwealth countries (a view that had been upheld by earlier charter reviews) but rather could undertake supportive activities anywhere in the world if those activities had "substantive impact on the peoples of the United States." This decision put the burden of carefully documenting the potential for such impact on both the grant applicant and the Corporation before making the grant, and then to monitor closely whether that impact was being realized. This was easy to do for grants along both sides of the US-Mexico border, but grants in Mexico had to ensure that any books and papers were produced in English as well as in Spanish and circulated widely to the appropriate recipients in the United States. It was also the responsibility of program staff to ensure that this requirement was met. See Joseph Califano, letter to David Hamburg, June 9, 1987, CCNY Records, RBML-CUL.

147   Major partners during this era for the Corporation's work in developing countries included the Rockefeller, Ford, and MacArthur Foundations; the Pew Charitable Trusts; the Kellogg, Mellon, and Kaiser Foundations; and the International Development Research Centre in Canada. With the intention of obtaining more global dissemination from the grants, many

such partnerships also included the World Health Organization, the Pan American Health Organization, and the World Bank.

148 For more details, see CCNY, "Strengthening Human Resources in Developing Countries," 1–5.

149 Ibid., 43.

150 CCNYAR, 1986, 51–52. The Corporation, along with the Ford Foundation, the Rockefeller Brothers Fund, and the Oppenheimer Trust, among others, had created a cadre of legal talent and institutions, prerequisites for establishing and embarking on constitutional democracy in post-apartheid South Africa. Arthur Chaskalson, for example, became president of the Constitutional Court of South Africa in 1994 and a few years later was appointed chief justice of South Africa. Starting in 1992, Corporation support encouraged the development of programs on women's rights. For an excellent discussion of the legal work in South Africa, see Stephen Golub, "Battling Apartheid, Building a New South Africa," in *Many Roads to Justice: The Law-Related Work of Ford Foundation Grantees Around the World*, ed. Mary McClymont and Stephen Golub (New York: Ford Foundation, 2000), 19–54.

151 CCNYAR, 1986, 50 (for $300,000).

152 Omar Badsha, ed., *South Africa: The Cordoned Heart* (Newlands, South Africa, and New York: Gallery Press and W. W. Norton and Co., 1986). This volume contains 136 photographs amplified in twenty essays by the photographers. Bishop Desmond Tutu wrote in his foreword that these photographs, shown first at the 1984 conference, "were used to bring home to people the harsh realities of South Africa revealed by the Second Carnegie Inquiry into Poverty and Development" (xiii). Badsha commented in his preface that the work had demonstrated the importance of documentary photography as a new genre; in this case, the documentary had also amply illustrated the value and bravery of the artists involved: "These events have brought home to us all, artists, photographers, executives, or workers, that we cannot escape the heavy burden of history and that no one can remain neutral" (xvi). In 1987 the Corporation helped the University of Cape Town establish the Center for Documentary Photography, directed by Badsha, and developed a partnership with Duke University for fellowships and a publishing program; CCNYAR, 1987, 59.

153 Mamphela Ramphele and Francis Wilson, *Children on the Front Line: The Impact of Apartheid, Destabilization, and Warfare on Children in Southern and South Africa: A Report for UNICEF* (New York: UNICEF, 1989).

154 Francis Wilson, presentation to CCNY, luncheon for Francis Wilson, December 15, 1995, available from author. Wilson included a list compiled from those who had written the research papers presented in April 1984 and indicated what a sample of those authors had gone on to do in the new South Africa: president of the Land Court, president of the Constitutional Court, director of the General Department of Land Affairs, assistant city administrator with the Cape Town City Council Community Liaison, director general in the Office of the President, secretary to the cabinet, special legal adviser to President Mandela, minister of justice, and vice chancellor at the University of Cape Town (who was both the first woman for that university and the first black South African).

155 CCNYAR, 1988, 67.

156 Grants were made to the Health Development Unit at the University of the Witwatersrand to provide training for health care workers associated with the National Progressive Primary Health Care Network (CCNYAR, 1988, 68–69), and to the Alexandra Health Centre and University Clinic, which also provided community-based training for University of the Witwatersrand medical students (CCNYAR, 1987, 59).

157 Members of Congress met with experts on the issues from the United States, Europe,

and Southern Africa; CCNYAR, 1989, 65. The Corporation funded other efforts to connect black South Africans with Americans: the Phelps Stokes Fund program to help South African refugee students continue their education in the United States (CCNYAR, 1987, 58, 60, and 1989, 69), and the Institute of International Education and the Educational Opportunities Trust, for a career development fellowship program (CCNYAR, 1987, 57). The Corporation also funded the Southern Africa Research Program at Yale University, established by the Ford Foundation and the National Endowment for the Humanities to support South African scholars; CCNYAR, 1986, 51. Internal scholarships for black students were funded through the University of Cape Town scholarship fund; CCNYAR, 1989, 69–70. Also, under the auspices of the Institute of International Education, the Corporation continued to work with longtime consultant J. Wayne Fredericks to increase interest in and understanding of the situation of South Africa in the United States; CCNYAR, 1990, 73.

158   CCNY, "Strengthening Human Resources in Developing Countries (HRDC), 1992–1993," (program budget paper), 36, CCNY Program Files, Box 21, Series I.D, CCNY Records, RBML-CUL. In addition, the HRDC staff working directly on South Africa had changed. In August 1988, Devlin-Foltz, who had been responsible for the work in South Africa and for the PUD subprogram, moved to Harare, Zimbabwe, to become academic director of the School for International Training college semester program; CCNYAR, 1988, 153. He served as a consultant to the Corporation, assisting with the grants in Southern Africa, until 1991–1992. In 1990–1991, a member of the staff of the Corporation's Education, Science and Technology, and the Economy Program, Yolonda Richardson, joined the HRDC program to focus on work related to Southern Africa and women's rights. With Devlin-Foltz's departure, Richardson assumed responsibility for that subprogram. With the changes in 1990, she had the mandate to enlarge the scope of the work.

159   CCNY, "Strengthening Human Resources in Developing Countries," 1992–1993, 36.

160   Ibid., 36–37.

161   CCNYAR, 1992, 75.

162   For Women's Development Foundation and Women's National Coalition, see CCNYAR, 1993, 85; for South African Council of World Affiliated YWCA and Women's Resource Centre, Natal, see CCNYAR, 1993, 87.

163   See Final Constitution of the Republic of South Africa 1996, "Chapter 9: State Institutions Supporting Constitutional Democracy," available at: http://www.nelsonmandela.org/omalley/index.php/site/q/03lv02167/04lv02184/05lv02193/06lv02204.htm. The Corporation supported the work at the University of the Witwatersrand of Barbara Klugman and her team in building the first women's health network in South Africa, comparable to the National Progressive Primary Health Care Network; CCNYAR, 1992, 76. This gave rise to a vibrant NGO community focused on women's health that has had significant successes and highly positive results. "South African reproductive health policies and the laws that underwrite them are among the most aggressive and comprehensive in the world in terms of the recognition that they give to human rights, including sexual and reproductive rights." Diane Cooper et al., "Ten Years of Democracy in South Africa: Documenting Transformation in Reproductive Health Policy and Status," *Reproductive Health Matters* 12, no. 24 (2004): 70.

164   Two publications present the significant details about the maternal and child health part of the program: Lucas, *It Was the Best of Times*, 271–293, and Kenneth Walker, "Preventing Maternal Mortality," *Carnegie Results* (Spring 2011). "Some 500,000 women the world over die each year (approximately one per minute) from problems experienced in pregnancy and childbirth. Most of these deaths occur in developing countries, especially in Africa.… In some communities, complications in pregnancy and childbirth are the most common cause of death among

women of childbearing age." In contrast, for women in developed countries the risk of dying is "on the order of 5 to 40 per hundred thousand; in Africa, maternal death rates are much higher, in some localities as high as 2,000 per hundred thousand." CCNY, "Strengthening Human Resources in Developing Countries," 1988, 18–19.

165 As noted in the program paper, the meeting was "the first high-level discussion of maternal mortality in developing countries by officials of the relevant specialized agencies of the United Nations system—the World Health Organization, United Nations Development Program, United Nations Fund for Population Activities, and the World Bank"; CCNY, "Strengthening Human Resources in Developing Countries," 1988, 20. The Rockefeller and Ford Foundations also participated. See also Susan A. Cohen, "The Safe Motherhood Conference," *International Family Planning Perspectives* 13, no. 2 (1987): 68. As a result, the World Health Organization developed a Safe Motherhood Program with the aim of reducing maternal mortality and morbidity; the Corporation agreed to collaborate. Program staff noted that while the focus would initially be on reducing maternal morbidity and mortality, "the program intends to expand ... to include maternal and child health more broadly defined." Projects being developed in the Caribbean and at the US-Mexico border, where maternal mortality was a less pressing concern, reflected broader issues related to maternal and child health. CCNY, "Strengthening Human Resources in Developing Countries," 1988, 20.

166 Ibid., 26.

167 Ibid., 26–27.

168 With the aim of improving the status of women in part by achieving wider dissemination of grantee results, the Corporation also supported the WHO's Safe Motherhood Initiative (CCNYAR, 1987, 52); Family Care International, for surveys and meetings on women's health in Africa and elsewhere (CCNYAR, 1988, 64); the Society for Obstetricians and Gynecologists in Nigeria, to address the multiple conditions affecting maternal mortality and the Prevention of Maternal Mortality findings through a series of meetings and follow-up activities (CCNYAR, 1990, 65); and the WHO's Global Commission on Women's Health, to disseminate widely best practices on achieving women's health and identify the links between women's health and human rights, population issues, and economic conditions (CCNYAR, 1993, 80).

169 Dr. Allan Rosenfield and Deborah Maine, then at the Center for Population and Family Health at Columbia University's School of Public Health, agreed to take the lead in helping to identify appropriate institutions, assist in the development of the projects, and serve as network coordinators and advisers. In the final configuration, Columbia University, where Rosenfield and Maine served as dean and research associate, respectively, was the focal point for the Prevention of Maternal Mortality Network, the operational research network; the Network comprised eleven teams—seven in Nigeria, two in Sierra Leone, and two in Ghana; see Deborah Maine (guest editor), "The Prevention of Maternal Mortality Network," *International Journal of Gynecology and Obstetrics* 59, supp. 2 (November 1997). For the members of the Network, see CCNYAR, 1987, 51. Following planning grants, the following institutions were supported as part of the Network: Ahmadu Bello University in Nigeria (CCNYAR, 1990, 66–67); the University of Nigeria, Nsukka (CCNYAR, 1990, 66); Usumanu Danfodiyo University (CCNYAR, 1990, 67); the University of Illorin (CCNYAR, 1990, 67); Paramedical School, Bo, Sierra Leone (CCNYAR, 1991, 68); the University of Ghana Accra Medical School (CCNYAR, 1991, 69); the University of Science and Technology, Kumasi (CCNYAR, 1991, 69–70); the University of Benin Teaching Hospital in Nigeria (CCNYAR, 1991, 69); the University of Calabar in Nigeria (CCNYAR, 1992, 69); the University of Lagos (CCNYAR, 1992, 66); and the Paramedical School, Bombali District, Sierra Leone (CCNYAR, 1993, 65).

170 See Maine, "The Prevention of Maternal Mortality Network"; Walker, "Preventing

Maternal Mortality," 205; and Deborah Maine et al., "The Design and Evaluation of Maternal Mortality Programs" (New York: Columbia University, School of Public Health, Center for Population and Family Health, June 1997).

171   Although the Network cannot claim complete credit for the finding announced in 2010 that the maternal mortality rate is being reduced globally and in African countries, its work since the 1990s has clearly contributed in significant ways to these exceedingly hard-to-achieve and positive results. See Kenneth Walker, "Preventing Maternal Mortality," *Carnegie Results* (Spring 2011), available at: www.carnegie.org/file.admin/Media/Publications/carnegie_results_spring_11_prevention_maternal_mortality.pdf. (accessed February 9, 2014).

172   Reactivating the tricountry framework of the Commonwealth Program, the Royal College of Obstetricians and Gynecologists from the United Kingdom, the American College of Obstetricians and Gynecologists, and the Ghanaian universities guided the program; CCNYAR, 1989, 59–60. Also in Ghana, a program in life-skills training for nurse-midwives reinforced the efforts of the Prevention of Maternal Mortality Network and the university-based training; see CCNYAR, 1990, 63–64 (American College of Nurse Midwives), and 1993, 79 (Ghana Registered Nurse-Midwives Association).

173   Between 1960 and the 1989 start of the program, of the thirty specialists who had been trained, only three returned home; by 2002, of the twenty-six trained, all were practicing at home. Cecil A. Klufio et al., "Ghana Postgraduate Obstetrics/Gynecology Collaborative Residency Training Program: Success Story and Model for Africa," *American Journal of Obstetrics and Gynecology* 189, no. 3 (2003): 692–696; Frank Anderson, Yvette Clinton, and E. Yao Kwawukume, "In-country OB/GYN Training Program Contributes to Retention of Doctors," University of Michigan Health System, UMHS Newsroom, September 29, 2010, available at: http://www2.med.umich.edu/prmc/media/newsroom/details.cfm?ID=1735 (accessed June 25, 2012).

174   CCNYAR, 1990, 65 and 67; 1988, 62 and 65.

175   CCNYAR, 1987, 52. Additional grants supported the country-specific work of Africare and the International Women's Health Coalition to strengthen community-based programs and network-related reproductive health; ibid., 53; see also CCNYAR, 1989, 62.

176   CCNYAR, 1988, 63.

177   Stuart Saunders, *Vice Chancellor on a Tightrope: A Personal Account of Climatic Years in South Africa* (Cape Town, South Africa: David Philip, 2000).

178   Ramphele, with Corporation support over the period 1987 to 1995, had conducted her doctoral research in medical anthropology in the New Crossroads Township; CCNYAR, 1987, 59. She spent part of that time writing her results at the Bunting Institute at Radcliffe College, under a Corporation grant; CCNYAR, 1988, 65–66. This experience led her to propose such an institute at the University of Cape Town; CCNYAR, 1995, 98. See also Ramphele, *A Life.*

179   CCNYAR, 1994, 100, and 1996, 122.

180   Following a meeting in Nairobi in 1990 with the League of Women Voters' Overseas Education Fund, the Corporation began to consider how to develop its work outside of South Africa; CCNYAR, 1990, 68. This led to its support for the pan-African network and its work to build the field throughout Africa; CCNYAR, 1993, 86. The WilDAF network remains active today and is based in Ghana. The Corporation funded complementary activities in East and West Africa—the Women and Law in East Africa Network, based at the University of Nairobi and covering Uganda, Tanzania, and Kenya (CCNYAR, 1995), and Women and Law in West Africa, based at the University of Ghana and covering Ghana, Nigeria, and Sierra Leone (CCNYAR, 1996, 119). Additional support went to the Kenya chapter of the Federation of International Women Lawyers; CCNYAR, 1996, 120.

181   CCNYAR, 1993, 77. Following discussions in 1992 with the Rockefeller Foundation and key representatives of a group of women leaders in education, the Corporation provided a

planning grant for them to meet in Nairobi and plan the launch in late 1992. Both foundations provided support for several years, joined by other American and European donors. In addition, starting in 1991, the Corporation supported a research grants program at the African Academy of Sciences on female education. The Rockefeller and MacArthur Foundations also provided support; CCNYAR, 1991, 73. Eddah Gachukia, a longtime Corporation grantee, was the first executive director of the Forum of African Women Educationalists.

182 Support was given to all the Corporation grantees to develop background papers for use by the international conference and the NGO coordinating secretariat. The Corporation also supported the UN Secretariat to reinforce the planning efforts of conference secretary-general Gertrude Mongella from Tanzania and her team; CCNYAR, 1994, 96; see also CCNY, Board of Trustees retreat, June 7–9, 1995, "Strengthening Human Resources in Developing Countries" (program papers), 49, Staff and Retreat Files, Box 1, Series I.E, CCNY Records, RBML-CUL.

183 In July 2010, the UN General Assembly established a new overarching entity, the UN Entity for Gender Equality and the Empowerment of Women, which aims to build on all the work of the past twenty-five years and obtain the policy changes that have been sought for so many decades.

184 CCNY, Board of Trustees retreat, June 7–9, 1995, "Strengthening Human Resources in Developing Countries," 10–17; Organization of African Unity, *Lagos Plan of Action for the Economic Development of Africa, 1980–2000*, 35, available at: http://www.nepadst.org/doclibrary/pdfs/lagos_plan.pdf.

185 CODIST II, "Africa Urged to Invest 1% GDP on Science, Research," May 2, 2011, available at: http://repository.uneca.org/codist/?q=node/117.

186 At the same time, staff members realized that it was of paramount importance to work in partnership with other foundations and donor agencies, both to obtain sufficient support and to contribute to the sustainability of the effort. The Rockefeller Foundation, Pew Charitable Trusts, and the International Development Research Centre (IDRC) in Canada were major partners from the beginning. Over time the MacArthur Foundation, the Ford Foundation, UNESCO, and the Commonwealth Secretariat became significant partners for the work on science and technology for development. For a few specific grants, the World Bank and the World Health Organization also were active partners. The major pan-African institutional partner was the UN Economic Commission for Africa, along with several regional intergovernmental organizations. Bilateral donor agencies often supported the same activities but not in partnerships as close as the ones mentioned here.

187 These priorities resulted from extensive discussions with Gelia Castillo, a globally recognized agricultural anthropologist from the Philippines and member of the IDRC board; Walter A. Rosenblith, a professor and former provost at MIT, an internationally recognized biophysicist; and senior economist Ralph K. Davidson, former dean of the Purdue University graduate school, former deputy director of the university's Social Sciences Division, and former director of the Rockefeller Foundation's University Development Program. With extensive experience promoting the social sciences in Africa, Asia, and Latin America, Rosenfield was also influenced by the debates in the developing countries following the UN Conference on Science and Technology for Development held in Vienna in 1979 and by the writings of Francisco Sagasti, a World Bank adviser, and Geoffrey Oldham, the head of the science and policy research unit at the University of Sussex. These helped sharpen program staff thinking about the needs and opportunities, particularly the weak linkages across researchers and between scientists, scholars, and policymakers. See CCNY, Minutes of the Board of Trustees, 69, February 18, 1988, CCNY Records, RBML-CUL; CCNY, "Strengthening Human Resources in Developing Countries, January 26, 1988," 6–10.

188 As a contribution to in-depth knowledge in the field, and to further the idea that science

and technology capacity and investments create the potential for successful sustainable development, the Corporation supported for several years the research and writing of Francisco Sagasti,
the chief architect of the main position paper shaping the discussion at the first UN Conference
on Science and Technology for Development in 1979. The culminating publication, published in
2004 with support from the Rockefeller Foundation, assessed the state of knowledge in science
and technology for development, technical and international cooperation, and strategic management for development; it provided the rationale and agenda for building science and technology capacities in developing countries to enhance their competitiveness. Francisco Sagasti,
Knowledge and Innovation for Development: The Sisyphus Challenge for the Twenty-First Century
(Cheltenham, UK: Edward Elgar, 2004), xix; see also CCNYAR, 1993, 76.

   189   Fourteen policymaker/researcher teams—five in African countries and nine in Asian
countries (China, Indonesia, India, Pakistan, the Philippines, Thailand, Ghana, Kenya, Nigeria,
Tanzania, and Uganda)—received team grants to initiate, refine, and conduct research over the
ten years of the program. Topics addressed included providing essential drugs in an efficient
and effective manner, the geographic distribution of rural health services and its effect on the
use of services, appropriate fee structures, and a wide range of factors affecting the supply and
utilization of health services. Each year the program brought the teams together to discuss their
work and findings, and it funded a few career development fellows. The Corporation contributed to the core costs of the program and supported the teams in the African institutions. Pew
Charitable Trusts covered the costs of the teams in Asia, along with the core costs. The coordinating team included director Davidson Gwatkin, a development economist; program administrator Tania Zaman, a development expert from Bangladesh; and consultant Ralph Andreano,
a leading health economist who annually reviewed the work. The external international advisory committee was chaired by Canadian John Evans, director of the Health, Population, and
Nutrition Program at the World Bank and chairman of the Rockefeller Foundation Board of
Trustees. CCNYAR, 1988, 59 (grants to the teams at the Uganda Ministry of Health), 59–60
(the University of Dar es Salaam), 60 (the University of Nairobi), 60 (the University of Ibadan),
and 61 (IIE).

   190   Pew Charitable Trusts required formal systematic evaluation midway through the anticipated life cycle of a grants program before it approved major renewals. The evaluation helped to
identify opportunities for change and strengthened the program. The IHPP resulted not only in
the implementation of policy recommendations but also significant publications, including two
funded by the Corporation: Germano Mwabu et al., *Improving Health Policy in Africa* (Nairobi,
Kenya: University of Nairobi Press, 2004), and Ralph Andreano, *The International Health Policy
Program: An Internal Assessment* (Madison: University of Wisconsin Press, 2001). Andreano
documented in great detail the work of all the teams, the successes, and the areas that needed
strengthening.

   191   The program was established in 1983 by then-dean Harvey Fineberg and Professor
Michael R. Reich, who still led it in 2014. Since 1984, 241 fellows from 51 countries have participated; see Harvard University School of Public Health, "Takemi Program in International
Health," available at: www.hsph.harvard.edu/research/takemi. Starting in 1988, the Corporation,
over ten years, contributed to the core costs of the program and covered expenses for fellows
from Africa; CCNYAR, 1988, 58–59. For more details, see Michael R. Reich, "The Concept
and Practice of International Health in the Takemi Program," *Japan Medical Association
Journal* 48, no. 5 (2005): 246–255; and the reports from the Takemi Program 30th Anniversary
Symposium, October 11–12, 2013, available at: http://www.hsph.harvard.edu/takemi/
takemi-program-30th-anniversary-symposium-october-11-12-2013/.

   192   The idea for the Commission was originally conceived by Timothy Rothermel, direc-

tor of UNDP special initiatives programs; Dr. Joseph Cook, director of the Tropical Disease Program at the Edna McConnell Clark Foundation; and Dr. Richard Wilson, director of the IDRC Division of Health Sciences; see CCNYAR, 1988, 60–61.

193 The Commission on Health Research for Development, *Health Research: Essential Link to Equity in Development* (Oxford: Oxford University Press, 1990), 22–23.

194 The Commission's work led to a number of follow-up efforts. The World Bank issued its first major report on health; World Bank, *World Development Report 1993: Investing in Health* (Oxford: Oxford University Press, 1993). The Commission was followed by the Task Force on Health Research for Development, led by Richard Wilson, the IDRC director of health sciences, with the goal of implementing the recommendations on both country-specific and global research approaches; CCNYAR, 1993, 73. The Task Force evolved into a more formal institution, the Council on Health Research for Development, established in 1993 to promote more strenuously the work around essential national health research and supported, in part, by the Corporation; CCNYAR, 1994, 91. The Council, funded now primarily by the bilateral development assistance agencies, has remained an active player in promoting international and national support for health research. The Corporation joined other donors in support of the Task Force and the Council and also supported a few grants linked to the Council's work to promote essential national health research initiatives in Uganda and Kenya, drawing as well on the IHPP teams—such as grants to the Uganda Council on Science and Technology, under the leadership of Dr. Raphael Owor, faculty of medicine, Makerere University, to implement an Africa-wide network in essential national health research; CCNYAR, 1994, 108, and 1996, 111. Adding to the work of the Council and the IHPP, Lucas, now professor of international health at Harvard, worked with his Harvard colleagues Michael Reich and Karin Dumbaugh to establish, with Corporation support, the Health Leadership Forum, with the aim to promote capacity to set priorities in ministries of health on the basis of essential national health research. This activity was co-sponsored by the Kaiser Family Foundation; CCNYAR, 1993, 74.

195 Dr. Arthur Kleinman, a protégé of David Hamburg's who embodied the interdisciplinary nature of the work as both chair of the Department of Social Medicine at Harvard Medical School and a professor of medical anthropology in the Department of Anthropology at the Harvard School of Arts and Sciences, initiated the request; his co-investigators were Leon Eisenberg, an authority in the field of social medicine and psychiatry, also based at Harvard Medical School, Mary-Jo Good and Kris Heggenhougen in the Department of Social Medicine, and Byron Good in the Department of Anthropology; CCNYAR, 1990, 68.

196 The program supported thirty-two fellows over its ten years, resulting in publications and new courses, as well as university-wide task forces to promote closer connections across the health and social sciences in both training and research; Mary-Jo Del Vecchio Good, Laura Tarter, and Martha Fuller, eds., *East Africa Health and Behavior Fellowship Program in Institutional Strengthening in Social and Medical Sciences* (Boston: Harvard Medical School, Department of Social Medicine, 2000). Two scholars from the University of Nairobi, Dr. Violet Kimani and Dr. Julius Meme, had been part of the Child Development Research Unit at the University of Nairobi under the Corporation's grant in the early 1970s. Kimani led in the development of the interdisciplinary task force in health and social sciences at the University of Nairobi and was an active participant in the other activities in this area.

197 Following discussions with Scott Halstead of the Rockefeller Foundation and International Clinical Epidemiology Network participants Nick Higginbotham, Dennis Willms, Peter Kunstadter, and Glenn Albrecht, the issue of how to promote more globally interdisciplinary research linking health and the social sciences emerged as a key area of shared interest. José Barzelatto and Margaret Hempel of the Ford Foundation and Bertha Mo from the IDRC also

participated. All funded the International Health Social Science Forum, with the secretariat finally established at Mahidol University in Thailand under the leadership of Santhat Sermsri, a social demographer; see CCNYAR, 1991, 74; 1992, 83; and 1993, 74. The Corporation supported the network in Africa; the Ford Foundation supported it in Asia, the Pacific, Latin America, the Caribbean, and the Eastern Mediterranean; and the Rockefeller Foundation and IDRC backed all of them. There were also ties to the European medical sociology group and various groups in North America. At least one comparative publication resulted from the work of the network, providing case studies from the different regional networks, assessing the successes and failures, and discussing the challenges in linking across the different disciplines; Nick Higginbotham, Roberto Briceno-Leon, and Nancy Johnson, *Applying Health Social Science: Best Practice in the Developing World* (London: Zed Books, 2001).

198 The principal investigators from these other efforts, Joseph Wang'ombe, Germano Mwabu, and Violet Kimani, took the lead in getting SOMA-Net off the ground. Coordinated by Anne Pertet, SOMA-Net was based in Nairobi, Kenya. The network established eleven national chapters, published a regular newsletter, and brought together university deans and department heads in curriculum development workshops. SOMA-Net, "Proceedings of the First Social Science and Medicine Africa Network International Conference, Nairobi, Kenya, August 10–13, 1992," SOMA-Net, 1993; CCNYAR, 1992, 84.

199 CCNYAR, 1989, 66.

200 A series of grants to the National Council for International Health, managed by consultant Guraraj S. Mutalik and executive director Russell E. Morgan Jr., led to programs around the country, such as the Women's Council of Alabama (in Birmingham), focusing on primary health care, and a program in Watts, Los Angeles, focusing on the vaccine cold chain and the expanded program of immunization; CCNYAR, 1989, 66. As part of the interest in explicating the impact of sound foreign assistance in health on positive developments in the United States, along with giving greater prominence to the role of health and foreign assistance, the Corporation funded a study by the Board on International Health at the Institute of Medicine/National Academy of Sciences, *America's Vital Interest in Global Health: Protecting Our People, Promoting Economic Interests, and Projecting US Influence Abroad* (Washington, DC: National Academies Press, 1997), co-funded by the Rockefeller Foundation and several federal agencies (Rosenfield served on the board then); CCNYAR, 1996, 128.

201 CCNYAR, 1993, 94; 1994, 95; and 1996, 115. One approach that was effective involved work with community-based organizations to increase access for hard-to-reach populations.

202 This research initiative addresses such issues as technological innovation and fish processing by women in Sierra Leone; the impact of international technical assistance on agriculture in Tanzania; farmers' perceptions of technological advancement in rural Swaziland; and appropriate technology for irrigation in Botswana; CCNYAR, 1991, 66. By 2000, the Network was active in 15 countries, had worked with over 700 researchers, and had funded 120 research proposals; CCNYAR, 2000, 50.

203 The Network originally comprised two separate networks: the East Africa Technology Policy Studies Network was led by Hasa Mlawa, a senior technology policy studies researcher based at the Institute for Development Studies at the University of Dar es Salaam, and Akin Adubifa coordinated the West Africa Technology Policy Studies Network, based at the Nigerian Institute of Social and Economic Research in Ibadan; CCNYAR, 1989, 57 and 58. In 1992 and 1993, all the participants agreed that given the commonality of the research questions across East, West, and Southern Africa, the most promising next step for building a vibrant research community across the continent was to merge into one entity, the African Technology Policy Studies Network. The Rockefeller Foundation agreed to join IRDC and the Corporation in

contributing to the Network's costs for administration, research, meetings, and dissemination; the IRDC served as the institutional host for the Network; CCNYAR, 1993, 70.

204   In 1991 board member Ray Marshall suggested that this was an urgent topic and introduced the Corporation to one of the leading researchers in the field at Columbia University, Thierry Noyelle, who developed the network with senior staff members Marcel Namfua and Norbert Lebale at the UN Conference on Trade and Development and then with the UN Department for Development Support and Management Services, supported by the IDRC, the French government, the International Telecommunications Union, and the Corporation. The aim was to build capacity for negotiating effectively by building researcher-policymaker linkages in the field of trade negotiations on the continent, with a particular focus on the cross-border movement of professionals, a concern for both the private and public sectors; CCNYAR, 1992, 85, and 1994, 83. After only four years, the International Telecommunications Union fully supported five countries of the network to work on telecommunications issues; key ministry officials were also positive. For example, at the May 1996 meeting of the UN conference in South Africa—the African Regional Telecommunications Development Conference—the minister of industry and commerce of Zimbabwe said that the Coordinated African Program of Assistance on Services "has gone a long way in assisting Zimbabwe to develop an appropriate legal and regulatory framework conducive to the development of a competitive service sector." Other countries wanted to be included in the network; the "African Regional Telecommunications Development Conference held in May 1996 encouraged all countries to embrace the Coordinated African Program of Assistance on Services project policy findings. The meeting also recommended that this project expand its coverage to other African countries"; CCNY, "Strengthening Human Resources Development Countries, 1996–1997" (program budget paper), 29, CCNY Program Files, Box 22, Series I.D, CCNY Records, RBML-CUL.

205   Despite the positive reactions of ministers, researchers, and UN agencies, a hard-hitting external evaluation supported in 1999 by the IDRC and the Corporation pointed to the need for additional backup with so many countries and so many themes, in addition to the changed policy environment; Dr. Stephen L. Harris and Professor Olu Ajakaiye, "Final Report: CAPAS Program Evaluation," submitted to the IDRC, October 12, 2000, CCNY Records, RBML-CUL. Nonetheless, when funding came to a close, the innovative approach of the intergovernmental working groups and the national roundtables bringing together researchers and policymakers led two interregional networks to fold the CAPAS network into their activities, the Southern African Research Trade Network and the African Economic Research Consortium. Continuation of the CAPAS themes through these two major research networks at least ensured that credible research advice would be given to assist economic and trade planning and action.

206   CCNYAR, 1993, 75.

207   CCNYAR, 1996, 106. Further recognizing the need to build the linkages with key institutions in Africa, Adubifa persuaded UNECA and the Association of African Universities (AAU) to work together to promote university vice chancellors' interest in science and technology. The AAU put together an inventory of such research and then disseminated it widely across the continent. This was one of many activities on which the Corporation embarked with the AAU under the leadership of two secretaries-general, Donald A. Ekong (1987 to 1995) and Narciso Matos (1995 to 1999); Matos would become program chair of the Corporation's Developing Countries Program starting in 2000; CCNYAR, 1992, 81. The work with the AAU resulted in yet another network: the University Science, Humanities, and Engineering Partnerships in Africa Program, developed after a 1996 AAU meeting at the University of Cape Town by Vice Chancellor Stuart Saunders and Deputy Vice Chancellor Martin West: that network remains active today; Nan Warner, "Impact of a Partnership Programme of African Universities: A Study of the Perceptions

of a Group of White South African Academics of Their Learning Experiences," master's thesis in education, University of the Western Cape, submitted October 2004, 13–15, available at: http:// etd.uwc.ac.za/usrfiles/modules/etd/docs/etd_init_9261_1174996337.pdf. Launched with support from the Rockefeller Foundation that was matched by the Corporation, the network's additional donors included the Coca-Cola and Ridgefield Foundations. Partner universities included the University of Botswana, the University of Nairobi, Jomo Kenyatta University of Agriculture and Technology, the University of Dar es Salaam, Makerere University, the University of Cape Town, the University of Zambia, and the University of Zimbabwe; CCNYAR, 1995, 86.

208 Odhiambo, director-general of one of the premier research institutes on the continent, the International Center for Insect Physiology and Ecology, had been the first African scientist to have a major article published in the prestigious journal *Science* in 1967. It was that article, along with his scientific achievements, that propelled him to leadership in the international scientific community. See Thomas R. Odhiambo, "East Africa: Science for Development," *Science* 158, no. 3803 (November 17, 1967): 876–881. Odhiambo was a dynamic, insistent advocate for greater support for African scientists and the use of research results.

209 The program officers responsible for Africa at the Rockefeller Foundation (Vice President Kenneth Prewitt and Associate Vice President Joyce Moock), the Ford Foundation (Africa Program director John Gerhart), the MacArthur Foundation (Vice President Victor Rabinovitch, the former head of BOSTID, the Board on Science and Technology for International Development of the National Academy of Sciences), and the Corporation (Lucas and Rosenfield) met regularly over several years to share ideas and identify opportunities for partnership for joint grant-making in Africa. Odhiambo knew all of them, from their support of initiatives in Kenya and their work in other institutions. Odhiambo not only fully established the Academy, which is still thriving today, but organized a series of Presidential Science Forums to bring attention at the highest levels of government to the importance of science and technology; his colleagues and he developed a network of African science advisers to reinforce the idea that senior governmental leaders would benefit from scientific advice (following the recommendations of the Carnegie Commission on Science and Technology in Government). CCNYAR, 1988, 58 (first grant, co-funded by Third World Academy of Sciences, the World Bank, and the Rockefeller and MacArthur Foundations).

210 With collegial assistance from colleagues at the American Association for the Advancement of Science and the National Academy of Sciences, the Academy published volumes of increasing strength after appointing the distinguished editor Dr. Turner Isoun from Nigeria; see *Discovery and Innovation*, available at: www.ajol.info/index.php/dai/index (accessed February 12, 2014). In an assessment of the journal for the Corporation, Philip Abelson, the longtime, highly respected editor of *Science* magazine, wrote that it was a world-class journal, amply demonstrating that African scientists were globally competitive; CCNY, Agenda Book of the Board of Trustees, October 8, 1992, "African Academy of Sciences: Sixteen-Month Grant of $400,00 Toward Publications, Networking of African Scientific Organizations, and General Support" (agenda item), 92, CCNY Records, RBML-CUL.

211 CCNYAR, 1994, 108.

212 The TWOWS was established in 1989 as a result of the determined efforts of Professor Lydia Makhubu, a respected chemist and vice chancellor of the University of Swaziland. Makhubu was active in the Third World Academy of Sciences and was the only woman member of the Governing Council of the African Academy of Sciences. She launched the TWOWS with the assistance of Sophie Huyer, the coordinator for the Working Group, and others. The Corporation provided limited support to enable African members of TWOWS to participate in the Beijing Conference. CCNYAR, 1994, 108; see also "NASAC-TWOWS Women in Science

Workshop: Proceedings," Nairobi, Kenya, November 30 to December 1, 2009, available at: http://www.interacademies.net/File.aspx?id=10626.

213 CCNYAR, 1994, 106.

214 The AAAS president, Walter Massey, and the team of Amy Gimbel Wilson and Lisbeth Levey organized a series of discussions around the theme of science in Africa held during the annual AAAS meetings, attended by the US scientific community, science journalists and others, and the interested public. From 1991 to 1997, these meetings brought together leading African scientists on themes ranging from achievements and prospects for science in Africa to the opportunities for and constraints on scientific careers for African women; CCNYAR, 1990, 56. As part of an effort to enhance African journalists' capacity to write about science and technology, the African Council on Communication Education received funding for a conference on promoting science and technology through communications in October 1991; CCNYAR, 1991, 81.

215 As a direct linkage to build strength in science and technology in African countries, in 1994 NYAS chief executive officer Rodney Nichols and Susan Raymond, the policy director, suggested to the Corporation's Human Resources in Developing Countries Program staff a series of case studies to examine seven science rich–science poor states in the United States where science and technology policies had helped to promote economic development and to share the findings with African colleagues drawn from a cross-section of government, the private sector, and academia. Over five years, with three grants totaling $500,000, the NYAS produced six case studies and a series of conferences presenting the findings both in the United States and in Africa; CCNYAR, 1994, 84; 1995, 87; and 1997, 63. As the cases showed, "the attainment of such social goals as economic growth and improved health and housing is largely dependent on the ability to benefit from science and technology"; CCNYAR, 1995, 87; see also Susan Ueber Raymond, ed., "Science-Based Economic Development: Case Studies Around the World," *Annals of the New York Academy of Sciences* 798 (December 1996).

216 The continuing outreach of the Council on Foundations' international committee under the leadership of Rob Buchanan led the World Bank partnership office under Joan Martin Brown and President James Wolfensohn to organize a meeting with twelve foundation presidents in 1995. The intent was to build collaboration between the foundations and the World Bank, not just in general but on specific themes of mutual interest. David Hamburg volunteered the Corporation to be responsible for collaboration in the area of science and technology for development with the Bank. Carlos Braga, a Brazilian economist and engineer in the private-sector office at the time, was the liaison; Adubifa and Rosenfield were asked to follow up. Together, the World Bank and Corporation teams organized three interrelated activities: an experimental teleconference reaching over three hundred participants on issues in science and technology for development; with the added help of staff from BOSTID and the National Academy of Sciences, under Michael Greene, a panel of African scholars and scientists held a World Bank meeting on "Knowledge for Development" in Toronto in 1997; and as an outgrowth of these activities, for the first time a foundation-like grants program, InfoDev, was established at the World Bank. CCNYAR, 1997, 62.

217 Under the leadership initially of Thomas Ratchford, then Amy Gimbel Wilson and Lisbeth Levey, and with the strong support of AAAS president Walter Massey, a special focus on partnership with science and technology institutions in Africa was developed, with continuing support from the Corporation for a variety of activities over the ten years. In addition, Wilson and Levy became advisers to Corporation grantees about their work related to access to information as well as on new initiatives related to electronic communications.

218 Grantees were: Davy Koech, director of the Biomedical Sciences Research Centre, and James Muttunga, senior researcher at the Kenya Medical Research Institute, for options

assessment in developing a new information management system for their partners in Kenya and globally, enabling the Institute to purchase computers and software, train staff, and develop electronic indications across its nine centers; Helga Patrikios, medical librarian at the University of Zimbabwe, Faculty of Medicine, for a CD-ROM reader and subscription to enhance the capacity of her faculty and their ability to publish in internationally respected journals; Ogunlade Davidson, professor of mechanical engineering at the University of Sierra Leone, to develop a national science and technology information system; CCNYAR, 1988, 61. A later grantee was medical librarian Regina Shakakata, the University of Zambia, Faculty of Medicine, to develop an information system that could connect the different branches of the faculty scattered around the country; CCNYAR, 1991, 66.

219 Other early grantees in this area were: Gabriel Ogunmola at the University of Ibadan, to assess the feasibility of developing a science and technology database for Nigeria (CCNYAR, 1989, 59); the Faculty of Science at the University of Zimbabwe, to install desktop publishing (CCNYAR, 1990, 61); Lola Dare, executive director of CHESTRAD (Centre for Health Sciences Training, Research, and Development) Nigeria, through the University of Ibadan, to review issues in health and development (CCNYAR, 1992, 83); and Mrs. Adekimpe O. Ike, university librarian at Abubakr Tafawa Balewa University, for science and technology information systems (CCNYAR, 1991, 65). One of the many follow-on grants enabled the overhaul of the University of Dar es Salaam library, and John Newa, director of the library, was able to acquire two CD-ROM workstations, subscriptions to scientific databases, and desktop publishing capacity; CCNYAR, 1994, 88. Two later grants for university-wide local area networks went to the University of Zimbabwe and the University of Cape Coast, Ghana; CCNYAR, 1997, 64. Ogunlade Davidson, a leading technology researcher from the University of Sierra Leone, and Abator Thomas, a librarian with the British Council, with support from the Corporation and the British Council, launched in 1993 the Sierra Leone Science and Technology Information Network, a nationwide information system connecting more than 401 research institutions around the country. Unfortunately, soon after the launch, the system was crashed by the violence that engulfed Sierra Leone soon after the planning period; CCNYAR, 1991, 66.

220 CCNYAR, 1993, 72. African Regional Centre for Technology director B. J. Olufeagba and Michael Nageri, head of the Information and Documentation Division, along with BOSTID executive director Michael Dow and senior program officer Wendy D. White, developed this idea further following conversations with Corporation program staff.

221 UNECA, *The African Information Society Initiative: A Decade* (Addis Ababa, Ethiopia: UNECA, 2008). Consultants such as John Daly, then with USAID, and Michael Jensen, then with the IDRC and based in South Africa, along with PADIS, the major UNECA grantee, guided the program on these activities; CCNYAR, 1994, 86. With considerable leadership from UNECA, especially from Nancy Hafkin, the founder of the PADIS, and Karima Bounema, director of the Division of Information Sciences, and input from other players, including African ministries of information, these activities coalesced in 1996 in the creation of the still-active and vital African Information Society Initiative. In 1997 Hafkin, with input from Adubifa, also helped establish the ongoing Partnership for Information and Communication Technologies in Africa; see United Nations, Economic Commission for Africa, "Essential Readings," available at: http://www.uneca.org/fr/publications/african-information-society-intitative-aisi-decades-perspective (accessed February 12, 2014).

222 The Corporation resumed support for the Association of Commonwealth Universities meetings, whose participants were university leaders from the Caribbean and African countries. CCNYAR, 1987, 54, and 1992, 82.

223 Sir Dr. George A. O. Alleyne, who was appointed assistant director of PAHO in 1990

(and subsequently served as PAHO director from 1995 to 2003), brought many of these ideas to the attention of the HRDC staff. CCNYAR, 1988, 63; 1989, 61; 1992, 84; and 1993, 81.

224   Three additional Caribbean-wide grants focused on economic and women's development in the region: (1) a grant supported Caribbean Resource Development Foundation meetings (CCNYAR, 1988, 67), and following discussions with Sir Alastair McIntyre, vice chancellor of the University of the West Indies, (2) a small grant of $25,000 in 1990 enabled the university to hold a symposium in honor of the distinguished economist Sir W. A. Lewis, who many decades earlier had been a Corporation grantee, and (3) a grant to publish and circulate widely the symposium proceedings, presenting the latest thinking in economic development for the region (CCNYAR, 1990, 72). Support also continued for the Women and Development Network at the University of the West Indies (CCNYAR, 1990, 63).

225   Discussions in 1988 with Dr. Desmond Ali, a senior technology researcher in Trinidad, led the Corporation staff to urge Ali to consult with Odhiambo and the African Academy of Sciences, as well as consider seriously including the social sciences in their purview. As noted in the history provided on the Caribbean Academy of Sciences website (http://www.caswi.org.jm/casprofile.html), "After much (sometimes painful) debate, the social sciences were included." The Corporation provided support for the launch through the University of the West Indies. CCNYAR, 1988, 61.

226   Sir Kenneth Stuart, former dean of medicine at the University of the West Indies in Jamaica and a medical adviser to the Commonwealth Secretariat, and David Picou, a senior nutrition researcher and executive director of the Tropical Metabolism Research Unit at the university, asked for support to prepare a strategic plan. Stuart and Picou consulted with representatives of national health organizations in the United States, Canada, and the United Kingdom to examine ways to promote research and strengthen the Council's finances. Two grants from the Corporation enabled the Council to implement the plan, build a stronger set of institutional relations within and outside the region, and increase capacity for essential national health research in the region following the participation of eight health ministers at a Harvard University seminar as part of the Health Leadership Forum. CCNYAR, 1991, 63, and 1994, 92.

227   In 1997 a name change—to the Caribbean Health Research Council—made it possible for non-Commonwealth individuals and countries to participate. See World Public Health Nutrition Association, "John Waterlow and Michael Latham: Sons of Empire," May 2011, available at: http://www.wphna.org/2011_may_hp2_waterlow_latham.htm.

228   David Hamburg and Mexico's minister of health, Guillermo Soberon, the former rector of Universidad Nacional Autónoma de México, talked in the mid-1980s about the role of American philanthropy in fostering vital research in the United States and the feasibility of establishing a viable philanthropic organization in Mexico dedicated to fostering health research and addressing a range of key issues for Mexico, including the brain drain concerns.

229   Part of the support included opening a chapter in Juarez to link with the US-Mexico border program, described earlier. One innovative program on health economics, under the leadership of Julio Frenk, director of the Foundation's Centre for Health and the Economy, issued a series of publications on the state of the Mexican health system and health care in relation to the economy that generated major discussion, debate, and policy actions in the country. With the innovative funding structure that Soberon developed with his business donors, including a debt swap from the World Bank in the 1990s, along with support from the Rockefeller Foundation and USAID, the Foundation is still going strong in 2012. Over ten years, the Corporation provided $3,825,000. CCNYAR, 1987, 51, through CCNYAR, 1997, 66.

230   David Devlin-Foltz, personal communication with the author, June 30, 2011.

231   As discussed throughout this book, educating Americans about international affairs has

long been an area of the Corporation's attention. Following World War I, the founding trustees of the Corporation, particularly Elihu Root, sought to educate Americans about the world. Following World War II, with extensive support for area studies and international affairs, grants from the Corporation encouraged the development of area studies and international affairs programs to blanket the country, with the aim of educating citizens usually, but not always, at the university level about other nations or regions. In the 1960s, the public outreach attention was increasingly focused on Africa. In the late 1970s, the focus shifted to enhancing international communications. CCNY, "Strengthening Human Resources in Developing Countries," 1988, 41–42.

232　CCNYAR, 1988, 64–66, and 1989, 65. Aspen received support for the Southern Africa Policy Forum from 1989 to1993 for $1,518,000; CCNYAR, 1993, 84. From 1994 to 1996, the meetings, with $700,000 in support, focused on multilateral diplomacy and development assistance; CCNYAR, 1996, 105. The African-American Institute received about $250,000 a year from 1988 to 1996 to cover meetings, a major conference on Africa that alternated between the United States and Africa, special sessions and site visits for US congressional staff, and regular briefings for congressional aides, for a total of $2,397,500, under the leadership of Vivian Lowery Derryck, president, and two vice presidents, Frank Ferrari and Steve McDonald; in 1997, with a new president, Mora McLean, formerly of the Ford Foundation, a grant of $200,000 assisted with a strategic planning process; CCNYAR, 1997, 72. The Overseas Development Council, under the leadership of President John Sewell and two program directors, William Hellert and then Christine Contee, received support of about $200,000 for specific research; as of 1990, the Council had held over 150 conferences for 7,000 participants. To link more closely with Corporation interests, in 1989 the Council organized meetings with Tom Odhiambo and Tim Tihane, vice president of the World Bank. Twenty meetings were held in 1990 on health issues, economic development, and foreign aid; CCNYAR, 1990, 70. From 1988 to 1996, grants totaled $1,075,000. This cluster of grantees—the African-American Institute, the Aspen Institute, and the Overseas Development Council—assiduously organized programs to educate Congress about all the developments in Africa and on development issues in general. Although the Aspen Institute's efforts may have assisted in the sanctions efforts for South Africa, the others were, at their core, continuing education programs for congressional staff members. Evaluations in 1989 and 1994 indicated that they were effective in this regard, but turnover and internal pressures from many competing programs made the impact hard to assess. Without these activities, however, it was certain that information on developments in Africa would not have been easily available to key congressional aides.

233　All reported in CCNYAR, 1988, 68–67, except the Overseas Development Network (CCNYAR, 1989, 66–67) and the National Council of Returned Peace Corps Volunteers (CCNYAR, 1990, 72).

234　CCNYAR, 1988, 66.

235　This information included the film *The Cry of Reason: Beyers Naude—An Afrikaner Speaks Out* (nominated for an Academy Award) by Robert Bilheimer, Worldwide Documentaries (CCNYAR, 1987, 60), and two major meetings of the Association of Western West European Parliamentarians for Action Against Apartheid to discuss assistance in Southern Africa, especially in light of sanctions (CCNYAR, 1988, 67). TransAfrica Forum and its president, Randall Robinson, were deeply immersed in the Free South Africa Project (CCNYAR, 1989, 68), and the Africa Fund, an energetic anti-apartheid group led by Jennifer Davis and Dumisani Kumalo, also helped with outreach for the inquiry (CCNYAR, 1989, 69). A modest grant of $50,000 went to the Southern African Development Coordination Conference, initiated a decade earlier with Corporation support, to hold a conference on decoupling the economies in Southern

Africa from South Africa and disseminating understanding of the Conference's role in the region (CCNYAR, 1989, 68).

236 An additional impetus was the departure for Zimbabwe of David Devlin-Foltz, the staff member responsible for these activities. The consultants Karen Mulhauser and Judith Justice recommended continued support for the policymaker-outreach grantees since their programs were well received by members of Congress and congressional staff. The consultants, however, found it harder to assess the impact of the broader public education activities and suggested streamlining many of those to focus on areas of interest to the Corporation and the Ford Foundation, such as Africa and the other subprogram themes, not on broader development issues.

237 Wolpe, a retired congressman from Michigan, had been responsible for the sanctions legislation against South Africa. He prepared a series of case studies on Southern Africa focusing on the positive developments, including the political and economic reforms; he also organized a series of roundtable discussions for journalists and diplomats, and he co-directed the American Assembly with Ambassador David C. Miller Jr.; CCNYAR, 1995, 110; 1996, 130; and 1997, 74. Reinforcing Wolpe's work, the Corporation also supported the Investor Responsibility Research Center in preparing information about Southern Africa now that investments in the region were acceptable. In addition, a bulletin on African democratization, *Africa Demos*, intended for scholars in the United States as well as Africa, was funded at Emory University's Carter Center and edited by Richard Joseph, who was in charge of the Center's Africa program; CCNYAR, 1994, 105.

238 The meeting held in March 1997 was the first American Assembly to focus on Africa since 1958, when the Corporation had also provided support; CCNYAR, 1997, 72, 74. The meeting and publications were funded by the Corporation and the Ford Foundation with contributions from the Rockefeller Foundation, International Paper, and Maurice Tempelsman. Wolpe helped to write background material and the final report for the Assembly. Ninetieth American Assembly, meeting on "Africa and US National Interests," Arden House, Harriman Institute, Columbia University, March 13–16, 1997, available at: http://americanassembly.org/event/Africa-and-us-national-interests. From the same project, see also David F. Gordon, David C. Miller Jr., and Howard Wolpe, *The United States and Africa: A Post–Cold War Perspective* (New York: American Assembly, 1998), available at: http://americanassembly.org/publication/united-states-and-africa-post-cold-war-perspective (both accessed February 12, 2014).

239 Keeping in mind the recommendations of the consultants, but also recognizing the considerable gap that existed in the field, Richardson and Rosenfield agreed to recommend support of these efforts in 1993 at the level of $200,000 over two years to work toward launching the Constituency as an independent organization. CCNYAR, 1993, 91.

240 This review was conducted by Salih Booker in 1994. In 1993 John Gerhart had been appointed director of the South Africa office, based in Johannesburg, for the Ford Foundation. Conversations with acting director James Trowbridge and then-director Timothy Bork resulted in a series of activities jointly sponsored with the Ford Foundation to respond to the needs identified at the Africare meeting and to enlarge the American and African American Constituency for Africa.

241 Imani Countess, Loretta Hobbs, Doug McAdam, William Minter, and Linda Williams, *Making Connections for Africa: Report from a Constituency Builders' Dialogue* (Washington, DC: Africa Policy Information Center, 1997).

242 The preparatory meetings were held in Atlanta, Chicago, San Francisco, Denver, Baltimore, and Boston. Three policy forums were organized at UCLA, the University of Oklahoma, and Texas Southern University. The summit activities involved all the HRDC staff and many of their Ford Foundation colleagues, including Shepard Forman and Mahnaz

Ispahani, the staff members responsible for work on peace and security in Africa and elsewhere, and Anthony Romero when he assumed responsibility for Africa upon the departure of Timothy Bork. In 1995 the Corporation agreed to support individual participants in the summit activities, while the Ford Foundation provided major support for the summit coordinating committee and outreach activities. The summit was first led by MacArthur DeShayzer, a former member of the National Security Council Africa Policy, and then by Leonard Robinson, the former deputy assistant secretary of state for Africa and president of the US-African Development Foundation. The individual institutions that reinforced summit activities included: TransAfrica Forum, for its continued research and analysis on US policy toward Africa (CCNYAR, 1995, 107); the Africa Fund, to maintain its focus on Southern Africa (CCNYAR, 1995, 108); the Africa Policy Information Center, to contribute briefing papers on constituency-building (CCNYAR, 1995, 109); and the Constituency for Africa, for its national outreach and networking activities (CCNYAR, 1995, 108).

243 The Africa Society on the National Summit on Africa, "History: National Summit on Africa," available at: http://africasummit.org/about-the-society/history/.

244 Melvin P. Foote, "Africa: Under the Baobab Tree—Africa Loses a Giant in the US Congress," allAfrica, April 11, 2012, available at: http://allafrica.com/stories/201204111235.html. One positive sign remains foreign direct investment, which increased from $9 billion in 2000 to over $88 billion in 2008—in contrast to overseas development assistance flows of $44 billion for 2008; see UN Office of the Special Adviser on Africa and NEPAD-OECD Africa Investment Initiative, "FDI in Africa," policy brief 4, October 2010, available at: http://www.un.org/africa/osaa/reports/2010_FDIbrief; and Max Fisher, "How Should the Media Cover Africa? Nick Kristof Debates an African Critic," *The Atlantic*, July 3, 2012.

245 The program's scope benefited from the knowledge gained by other Corporation programs engaged in work on conflict and democracy, namely, the Cooperative Security Program and the work of the Special Projects Committee. Also informing these plans were consultations with African, European, and American advisers and partners, the Regional Commission on Africa of the African Academy of Sciences' work on the regional nature of African conflicts (see Anyang' Nyango', *Regional Integration in Africa: An Unfinished Agenda* [Nairobi: Academy Science Publisher, 1990]), and Francis Deng's analyses of the origins of conflict in Africa, supported by the Corporation's Special Projects program. Hamburg, others at the Corporation, and, among many others, UN secretary-general Boutros Boutros-Ghali expressed the increasing concerns of many leaders and practitioners about the role of peacekeeping in promoting peace and other UN activities. Boutros-Ghali's report prompted considerable debate and discussion about what action should be taken to implement an agenda that focused on preventive diplomacy; Boutros Boutros-Ghali, *An Agenda for Peace: Preventive Diplomacy, Peacemaking, and Peacekeeping*, June 17, 1992, available at: http://www.unrol.org/files/A_47_277.pdf. Along with the work of the Carter Center's International Negotiations Network Council and Francis Deng's research and writings at Brookings, all set in the context of the increasing potential for destructive internal conflict, Corporation staff members became convinced that this aspect of the program on transitions to democracy in Africa should concentrate on grants related to strengthening institutions that were focused on peace and conflict prevention on the continent as the crucial prerequisites for building and sustaining vibrant democracies and economies.

246 Discussed more fully in CCNY, "Strengthening Human Resources in Developing Countries" (program budget papers), 1994–1995, 42–44; 1995–1996, 24–27; 1996–1997, 34–38; CCNY Program Files, Boxes 21, and 22, Series I.D, CCNY Records, RBML-CUL.

247 The Forum received support over the years originally from the UN Development Program. The Corporation supported the Forum annually from 1988 to 1997 (except in 1996) at

approximately $200,000, along with the MacArthur and Rockefeller Foundations, the governments of Finland and Sweden, the Ford Foundation (once Obasanjo had rotated from its board), the Frederic Neumann Foundation, an individual from Zaire, and several Nigerian corporations; for the first significant grant; see CCNYAR, 1989, 56. At the annual Africa Forum meeting held in 1991 in Kampala, Uganda, agreement was reached on a framework for governance and development in Africa that promoted democracy and called for a process that would link security, stability, and development, much like the Helsinki Conference in Europe. Under Obasanjo, the Kampala declaration was promoted widely around the continent. The Organization of African Unity acknowledged these linkages; together, these two groups and other regional and national institutions followed a two-pronged approach: obtain high-level political agreement on these requirements for democracy, and develop the next generation of leaders; CCNYAR, 1992, 66.

248 Hans D'Orville, the president of the African Leadership Foundation, which housed the Forum, managed the activities. While Obasanjo was still in prison, a grant for $50,000 helped promote the activities in the United States. CCNYAR, 1996,129.

249 With this change, it was no longer possible for the Corporation to provide support.

250 Ambassador Garba was a scholar of political institutions, a national military leader, the former foreign minister of Nigeria, and the ambassador to the United Nations, resulting in his presidency of the General Assembly. He had personal experience with connecting conflict resolution and democratic institution-building through his work with leading UN peacekeepers, notably in Cyprus; see, for example, Joseph Garba, *Diplomatic Soldiering: Nigerian Foreign Policy, 1975–1979* (Ibadan, Nigeria: Spectrum Books, 1987). Also contributing to the project design and implementation were Ambassador Jonathan Moore of the Carnegie Endowment for International Peace, a close colleague of Garba's; Jean Herskovits, a consultant to the project; and J. Wayne Fredericks, a consultant to the Corporation on Southern Africa; CCNYAR, 1992, 80. The project was co-funded throughout its duration by the Corporation (for a total of about $752,700 over the six years), the Ford Foundation, and Friedrich Ebert-Stiftung.

251 As Garba wrote, "These days the twin topics of democracy and the future of the military preoccupy the African continent. There is no doubt about it—Africa has too many soldiers with no particular purpose.... Today almost every country on the continent is groaning under ... bloated military budgets." The meetings identified new approaches to building regional and subregional security architecture and touched on issues concerning democratic transitions, how to minimize violence, and how to ensure peace and stability following the transition to democracy. In particular, while national issues were deemed important, participants at the various meetings decided that regional perspectives might be the most productive for moving forward with the interplay of political and military concerns. Joseph Nansen Garba, *The Southern Africa Peacekeeping and Peacemaking Project*, vol. 2 (New York: Institute of International Education, 1994), v.

252 When the positive responses to the recommendations and the increasing violence in West Africa prompted the project to examine issues throughout the continent, the project was renamed the Sub-Saharan African Security Project, and its institutional base was moved to the International Peace Academy. A particularly delicate meeting was held in Nigeria to discuss West African and Nigerian issues. The challenges of peacekeeping in Liberia and Sierra Leone were also fully aired at this meeting. The meeting in Nigeria received support from Shell Nigeria. In the foreword to the final meeting report, Lieutenant General Sophie Nyanja, commander of the South African National Defense Force, summarized the situation in 1997: "When viewed against the backdrop of Africa's instability at the time, the conference assumed the dimension of urgency and currency.... It can only be hoped that the exercise lays the foundation for greater interregional cooperation and exchanges"; Lieutenant General Sophie Nyanja, foreword to Jean

Herskovits, *Africans Solving African Problems: Militaries, Democracies, and Security in West and Southern Africa* (New York: International Peace Academy, 1998), iii (report of a meeting in Abuja, Nigeria, December 1–4, 1997). As a complement to this effort in South Africa, the Corporation examined a different approach to building for peace when it provided modest support in 1992 for Archbishop Desmond Tutu to conduct writing and research on his efforts to build for peace during apartheid; CCNYAR, 1992, 81.

253 CCNYAR, 1993, 92. From 1993 to 1997, the International Peace Academy worked on these issues in Africa and elsewhere with support from both the Strengthening Human Resources in Developing Countries and the Preventing Deadly Conflict Programs, for a total $625,000.

254 Ibid.

255 Margaret Vogt, senior associate in the Africa program, was responsible for the NGO activities, which were jointly funded by the Corporation, the MacArthur Foundation, and the Joyce Mertz Gilmore Foundation, as well as by the governments of Sweden, Australia, Denmark, Finland, and the Netherlands; see International Peace Academy, *Civil Society and Conflict Management in Africa: Report of the IPA/OAU Consultation, May 29–June 2, 1996* (Cape Town and New York: International Peace Academy, 1996), and OAU/IPA, *Report of the Joint OAU/IPA Task Force on Peacemaking and Peacekeeping in Africa* (New York: IPA, March 1998).

256 The last two publications from this project were: Francis M. Deng et al., *Sovereignty as Responsibility: Conflict Management in Africa* (Washington, DC: Brookings Institution, 1996), and Francis M. Deng and Terence Lyons, eds., *African Reckoning: A Quest for Good Governance* (Washington, DC: Brookings Institution, 1998). See CCNYAR, 1998, 49 (for $200,000).

257 The grant to the Council, funded over three years from 1995 to 1998 for slightly over $250,000, was intended to identify a strategic niche in this field so that the Corporation could concentrate its grant-making on the most promising lines of inquiry; CCNYAR, 1995, 110, and 1996, 124; Mamadou Diouf, *Political Liberalisation or Democratic Transition: African Perspectives*, New Path Series 1 (Dakar, Senegal: CODESRIA, 1998). The findings became available when the Corporation was entering a period of transition and was thus unable to use them fully. The US Social Science Research Council helped with dissemination; CCNYAR, 1995, 111.

258 The Association's deputy president, George Nzongola-Ntalaja, was already working with the Organization of African Unity on the OAU/IPA conflict resolution mechanism. The first grant in 1995 of $50,000 over ten months contributed to the Association's efforts to hold meetings on issues in democratization, to build national chapters, to move from Nairobi to Harare, and to issue its multilingual newsletter. After its grant was renewed in 1996 for $150,000 over two years, the Association conducted research on issues related to politics and public policy with a focus on building a democratic culture; it also continued to promote national chapters, with a newly appointed administrative secretary, Kwame Ninsin, a political scientist from Ghana. The Association also received support from the Swedish International Development Agency and the National Endowment for Democracy. By 1996, there were ten active chapters and eight more were in the planning stages. CCNYAR, 1994, 106; 1995, 101; and 1996, 125 (for a total of $225,000, co-funded by the Swedish International Development Agency and the National Endowment for Democracy).

259 See, for example, "The Khartoum Declaration on Africa's Refugee Crisis," OAU Doc. BR/COM/XV/55.90, 1990, University of Minnesota, Human Rights Library, available at: http://www1.umn.edu/humanrts/africa/KHARTO.htm (accessed June 24, 2012).

260 Furthermore, conversations with James H. Michel, newly elected chair of the Paris-based Development Assistance Center of the Organization for Economic Cooperation and Development (OECD), led Corporation staff members to believe that if suitable models were identified, bilateral donors would be interested in learning about them. The OECD was beginning

to address the same issues; see OECD, "DAC in Dates: The History of OECD's Development Assistance Committee," 2006, 26–29, available at: www.oecd.org/dataoecd/3/38/1896808.pdf (accessed July 4, 2012). Staff members were unaware of the earlier concern of their historical counterparts at the Corporation in the late 1940s and early 1950s about this very same set of issues about the effectiveness of development assistance. Had they had access to the reports of Elling Aannestad, for example, the work might have moved in different directions (see Chapter 4).

261 CCNYAR, 1994, 88; 1996, 126; and 1997, 71 (for a total in this era of $822,500). Following a conference in 1992, a smaller roundtable discussion with an advisory group in 1993 led to the Carter Center plan in 1994 "to establish country-level working groups to prepare development plans that could be presented to a consortium of donors." Because of President Carter's interest in working with President Cheddi Jagan of Guyana in addressing issues of development and conflict prevention, Guyana (where the Corporation had been active several decades earlier, supporting the library, university, and other educational initiatives) was selected as a pilot country. With strong support from Minister of Finance Bharrat Jagdeo, planning started. Together a team from Guyana and the Carter Center arrived at the idea of "drafting a national development strategy that would clearly articulate the country's policy framework and could be the basis for setting development priorities and guiding international assistance." Discussions were held with labor unions, women's groups, farmers' cooperatives, indigenous peoples' groups, teachers, students, academics, journalists, and members of Parliament—including the opposition. Indeed, the leader of the opposition, Dennis Hoyt, became a very strong backer of this national initiative. Ambassador Gordon Streeb et al., "Toward a New Model of Development Cooperation: The National Development Strategy Process in Guyana," in *A Report of the Global Development Initiative's Advisory Group Meeting and Review of Lessons Learned in Guyana* (Atlanta: Carter Center, 1997), 6.

262 The team included: Ambassador Gordon Streeb and Jason Calder from the Carter Center; Rayman Mohamed, Brian Lewis, and Fadia Gafoor in Guyana; and Roger Norton and Viodla Villalaz, the consulting team who provided expert advice and assistance. When Minister Jagdeo became president of Guyana in 2006, he took his commitment to implementation of the national development strategy with him into the presidency. As he notes in his official biography: "While Minister of Finance, the President led the production of Guyana's National Development Strategy with the support of former US President Jimmy Carter's Carter Center. This led to the Carter Center and President Jagdeo working with leaders in Africa who drew on Guyana's experience with its National Development Strategy for lessons that could be applied in other countries," www.learn.environment.utoronto.ca/home/seminars_and_workshops/speaker-biographies/bharrat_jagdeo. Other agencies and foundations were also involved, including the Inter-American Development Bank, the World Bank, the W. Alton Jones Foundation, Citibank Corporation, the Ford Foundation, the Charles Stewart Mott Foundation, and the Turner Foundation. See Guyana's National Development Strategy, available at: http://www.guyana.org/NDS/NDS.htm; see also Global Development Initiative, *Toward a New Model of Development Cooperation: The National Development Strategy Process in Guyana* (Atlanta: Carter Center, 1997).

263 Endorsed by Council president John Sewell, the project director, Nicholas van de Walle, a political economist, organized teams of researchers in Botswana, Burkina Faso, Ghana, Kenya, Mali, Senegal, Tanzania, and Zambia, linking African scholars with counterparts in seven aid-giving countries: Canada, Denmark, France, Japan, Sweden, the United Kingdom, and the United States. The program aimed to elucidate the following: "the relationship between donors and recipients to determine its effect on two areas: decisions about aid allocation and coordination, and the sustainability of aid-funded programs." After a 1994 planning grant from the Corporation, the Council received renewed support in 1995 at the level of $182,000 for eighteen

months, and other bilateral donors, including USAID, also supported this work. Additional grants for a total of $85,000 in 1996 supported dissemination in the United States and in Africa. The UN Development Program contributed to the dissemination efforts. CCNYAR, 1995, 104.

264   In testimony before the US Senate Committee on Foreign Relations' Subcommittee on African Affairs, van de Walle presented the results of the studies and recommendations on "The Future of Aid to Africa." He reviewed the results of the studies and suggested ways to improve aid effectiveness, particularly focusing on the role of donors working with the state and the processes they should follow. He continued to emphasize study findings about the role of each country in taking leadership on aid; CCNYAR, 1996, 127. Two activities undertaken by the Aspen Institute reinforced the Council's recommendations and were related to these efforts. Starting in 1992, with support from both the Cooperative Security Program and the HRDC Program, the Institute held a series of discussions on multilateral diplomacy on topics such as the United Nations, the world economy, and the environment and sustainable development; CCNYAR, 1994 and 1996. Drawing on some of the research funded by the Corporation, and co-funded by the Corporation and the Rockefeller Foundation, the Institute then organized roundtables in 1997, bringing together foreign policy experts and decision-makers to consider ways to restructure foreign assistance to be most effective. The Institute's Dick Clark often noted the challenge of this area, since few, if any, members of Congress were elected because of their support for foreign aid; CCNYAR, 1997, 73. In addition, the Corporation contributed to the national planning (later policy) association's discussions on foreign assistance with the business community; CCNYAR, 1995, 109, and 1997, 73.

265   The Corporation grant enabled the founding president of Synergos, Peggy Dulaney, and the executive director, S. Bruce Shearer, to assess, with local partners, the feasibility of a grant-making foundation in either Ghana or Zimbabwe. With the assistance of the W. K. Kellogg and Charles Stewart Mott Foundations, including support for site visits to like-minded institutions in Appalachia and elsewhere in the United States, the Organization of Rural Associations for Progress and Synergos established a steering committee, whose members were leading members of Zimbabwe communities. Andrea Johnson worked closely with the planning committee on behalf of the Corporation. The grants were divided between Synergos and the Organization of Rural Associations for Progress, for a total of $375,000. When the Western Regional Foundation of Zimbabwe was launched in 1997, Invioletta Moyo was named executive director, with the participation of Thandiwe Cornelia Nkoma, executive coordinator of the Organization of Rural Associations for Progress; see CCNYAR, 1992, 67 (Synergos).

266   CCNYAR, 1997, 71 (Organization of Rural Associations for Progress); see also Worldwide Initiatives for Grantmaker Support, "Global Status Report: Zimbabwe," *Community Foundation Global Status Report*, 2010, available at: http://wings-community-foundation-report. com/gsr_2010/assets/images/pdf/ZIMBABWE_final_2010GSR.pdf. Based on the success in Zimbabwe, staff continued to explore alternatives to development assistance. A discretionary grant in 1996 supported the follow-up activities to a meeting held in Uganda by the Dag Hammarskjold Foundation of Sweden in conjunction with the African Association for Public Administration and Management; see Sven Hammrell and Olle Nordberg, eds., "Autonomous Developments Funds," *Development Dialogue* 2 (1995): 1–99. The recommendation from the meetings held in 1995 was to establish autonomous development funds as an alternative to individual foreign aid projects. Like the other activities the Corporation was funding, this was an attempt to reinforce a national strategy for external development assistance. Although this meeting did not result in a national fund, the Corporation felt that it was worth taking at least a modest risk on the endeavor; CCNYAR, 1996, 132 (AAPAM), and 1997, 75 (Dag Hammarskjold Foundation).

267　From 1988 to 1991, Corporation grants, along with support from many other donors, including the Ford Foundation, assisted the World Commission on Environment and Development under the leadership of the prime minister of Sweden, Dr. Gro Harlem Brundtland, in organizing meetings to promote the recommendations in the final report, *Our Common Future*, and to establish an institution for further promulgating the findings after the Commission had dissolved, the Centre for Our Common Future, based in Geneva, Switzerland, under the leadership of William "Chip" Lindner. The Centre's follow-up reached into almost every corner of the world and was instrumental to the successful preparations for the "Earth Summit"—the UN Conference on Environment and Development in Rio de Janeiro, June 3–14, 1992; CCNYAR, 1988, 65; 1989, 56; and 1991, 64 (grants totaled $740,000).

268　In 1990, after three years of deliberations, the South Commission, chaired by Julius Nyerere, president of Tanzania, and led by Mamohan Singh, former head of the planning commission of India, secretary-general of India, and now prime minister of India, issued the report *The Challenge to the South* (Oxford: Oxford University Press, 1990), which argued for greater control of the development and governance agenda in developing countries by the countries themselves. The terms of the South Commission did not permit "Northern" donors to fund its work, but it would accept support for disseminating the report and for the follow-on institute, the South Centre. In 1991 the Corporation supported the follow-up, including organizing round-tables for policymakers, researchers, and funders throughout the United States and Africa, and provided support for the South Centre, including its newsletter, published four times per year. CCNYAR, 1991, 79; 1995, 106; and 1996, 133 (for a total of $235,000).

269　The Commission on Global Governance, launched as a follow-up to the 1991 Stockholm Initiative on Common Security (inspired by German leader Willy Brandt), was co-chaired by Ingvar Karlsson, prime minister of Sweden, and Sir Shridath Ramphal, former secretary-general of the British Commonwealth and former foreign minister of Guyana. The Corporation contributed to the costs of publication and dissemination of the final report, released in January 1995; Commission on Global Governance, *Our Global Neighbourhood* (Oxford: Oxford University Press, 1995). The report came up against the economic boom that was starting in the late 1990s and did not make much of a dent in international deliberations; it is only in the twenty-first century that the issues addressed by the Commission, particularly those that focus on appropriate mechanisms to achieve global governance, are being revived; CCNYAR, 1994, 106; 1995, 106; and 1996, 131 (for a total of $356,000).

270　The program had already supported the international Independent Commission on Health Research, which, given the involvement of Lucas and Rosenfield in the planning and Lucas as a member of the Commission, resembled more closely the Corporation-initiated Commission on the Prevention of Deadly Conflict. These three commissions were organized independently of the Corporation and had completed their discussions or were close to completion when the Corporation became involved.

271　Rohinton Medhora, personal communication with the author, July 18, 2011.

272　The ongoing networks include, for example, the African Technology Policy Studies Network, the Prevention of Maternal Mortality Network, the Forum of African Women Educationalists, the University Science, Humanities, and Engineering Partnerships in Africa, and the African Women's Development and Communication Network.

273　Tirman also mentioned the work of the MacArthur Foundation in the field of civil society initiatives, including mediation support, and the new work of the W. Alton Jones Foundation in fostering the strength of NGOs in India and Russia. He concluded: "It is in these ways that the giants of philanthropy make very profound contributions to the prevention effort, and quiet ones at that. They have as a group moved a long way in the last decade toward a more active, indigenously oriented funding profile emphasizing civil society and integrated concepts of global security." Tirman, *Making the Money Sing*, 134–135.

274 CCNYAR, 1984, 96. Finberg, vice president at the time, had been associated with the foundation since 1959. She had been responsible for moving ahead with the early childhood agenda and identifying talented grantees, such as High Scope. Equally important for the Special Projects Committee was her early training in international relations at Stanford University, the American University in Beirut, and the US State Department. Barbara D. Finberg, *The Reminiscences of Barbara D. Finberg: Oral History, 1997,* interviewed by Brenda Hearing, November 20, 1997, Carnegie Corporation Project Part 2: Oral History, 1996–2004, Columbia Center for Oral History, Columbia University Libraries, 289–291 (hereafter "Finberg, CCOH").

275 In the earliest days of the Special Projects Committee, staff members joining Finberg included David Robinson, the executive vice president at the time, and Sara Engelhardt, the secretary. The Committee would call on staff members to participate in the working group, and for a short time Patricia Rosenfield was the program representative. Other program staff included Bernard Charles, Ellen Nightingale, and Yolonda Richardson. When Geraldine Mannion joined the Corporation, after holding positions at the Rockefeller and Ford Foundations, including in their programs on international security, the Committee began to be more organized by programmatic themes and to take on a few special initiatives. As Finberg noted in a 1995 retreat paper, "Since 1984, special projects averaged 12 to 13 percent of the annual budget, ranging from a low of $3 million to a high of $7.26 million." CCNY, Minutes of the Board of Trustees, 63, June 7–9, 1995, "Program Retreat Papers, Special Projects," Staff and Retreat Files, Box 1, Series I.E, CCNY Records, RBML-CUL.

276 To develop the Corporation's work in this area, nearly six years before establishing the Commission on Preventing Deadly Conflict, Hamburg saw the opportunity to encourage former president Jimmy Carter in his newly established presidential center to undertake a special initiative in this area. In early 1988, Hamburg asked Rosenfield to join him in a meeting with President Carter and his staff assistant James Brasher at the Carter Center in Atlanta to discuss the range of activities at the Carter Center and to identify specific areas for collaboration. These discussions led to concerns about both internal and intra-country conflict. Rosenfield worked on the first grants to follow up those discussions. Later grants funded the meetings and fact-finding work of the network to complement government negotiators and mediators, the International Negotiations Network Council, and separate task forces, a core group of scholars, the council, and a series of working papers. At a second annual meeting in January 1993, representatives of NGOs around the world who had participated in conflict resolution activities, such as women's groups in Liberia, came together to talk about ways to make the work more effective; CCNYAR, 1988, 88; 1989, 90–91; 1990, 67; 1992, 107; 1993, 122; and 1995, 124 (for a total of $2.54 million). This work of the Carter Center was co-funded by the MacArthur Foundation, the Rissho Kosei Kai Foundation of Japan, other international foundations, the Norwegian and Swedish governments, and the Dana M. Greeley and Ford Foundations.

277 In 1995, with the establishment of the Carnegie Commission on the Prevention of Deadly Conflict, the Special Projects Committee made its last grants in the area of conflict prevention and resolution.

278 In 2002, Carter received the Nobel Prize "for his decades of untiring effort to find peaceful solutions to international conflicts, to advance democracy and human rights, and to promote economic and social development." "The Nobel Peace Prize 2002," Nobelprize.org., available at: http://www.nobelprize.org/nobel_prizes/peace/laureates/2002/ (accessed February 12, 2014).

279 The Corporation contributed to covering the costs of the secretariat at Duke University, the meetings and preparation of briefing papers, and then the dissemination of the final report.

The commission was co-chaired by Arthur Levitt, chairman of the American Stock Exchange, and Sonja Picado, executive director of the Inter-American Institute for Human Rights in Costa Rica. The research and coordination staff was headed by William Ascher, a political scientist and co-director of Duke's Center for International Development Research. CCNYAR, 1988, 88, and 1989, 92 (for a total cost of $375,000).

280 CCNY, Minutes of the Board of Trustees, 72, June 7–9, 1995, "Program Papers, Special Projects," CCNY Records, RBML-CUL.

281 Prosser Gifford of the Woodrow Wilson Center and Russell Phillips of the Rockefeller Brothers Fund introduced Deng—an international lawyer, scholar on political developments, and diplomat who had been the Sudanese ambassador to Sweden and the United Nations—to Devlin-Foltz and Rosenfield in 1987. Because the HRDC program was not then working on these issues, the Special Projects Committee agreed to support Deng's research plans. Originally developed through a planning grant to the Woodrow Wilson Center, Deng then moved to the Brookings Institution to work in its foreign studies program, directed by Carnegie grantee John Steinbruner. Deng drew together scholars from Africa, Europe, Japan, and the United States to design the research agenda and identify case studies and appropriate authors from Africa. The support for the next six years enabled several teams of scholars to conduct the case studies, focusing on such issues as institution-building and the use of regional approaches in the role of governance. A special set of studies addressed the challenges arising from conflicts over national identity. The project was co-funded by the Rockefeller Brothers Fund. CCNYAR, 1988, 88; 1989, 91; 1990, 98; 1992, 107, 194; 1996, 122 (for a total from the Special Projects Committee of $1,500,000).

282 The first volume framed the studies; Francis M. Deng and I. William Zartman, *Conflict Resolution in Africa* (Washington, DC: Brookings Institution, 1991). More than seven volumes resulted from these studies on multiple dimensions of the origins of conflict in Africa. Deng also contributed to the work of the Carnegie Commission on Preventing Deadly Conflict, sharing the findings of this project and assisting with specific studies for the Commission.

283 CCNYAR, 1990, 25 (George Mason University), and 1994, 127 (Northern Ireland Inter-Group Relations Project).

284 The Inter-American Dialogue had been incubated by Dick Clark at the Aspen Institute through grants from the HRDC program from 1984 to 1986, for a total of $315,000. When the Inter-American Dialogue became an independent entity, the Special Projects Committee provided support, from 1989 to 1995, for a total of $950,000; CCNYAR, 1989, 91. The Inter-American Dialogue was co-funded by the Ford, Hewlett, MacArthur, and Rockefeller Foundations and by others from the region. Director Peter Hakim focused on regional and national developments in strengthening democratic practice, guaranteeing human rights, and promoting economic cooperation. It remains the main publication on these themes for the region.

285 The Citizens Network for Foreign Affairs, founded in 1985, filled a gap at the time by focusing on rural incomes and agricultural productivity. CCNYAR, 1987, 84.

286 The Pacific Council for International Affairs was launched in 1994 with support from the Corporation of $200,000 and co-funding by the Ford, MacArthur, and James Irvine Foundations as well as from corporations and individual donors. The Pacific Council, based at the University of Southern California, was conceived by Abraham Lowenthal as an effort to enhance American interest in foreign policy on the West Coast. CCNYAR, 1997, 82 (incubated at the University of Southern California, with an earlier grant from the Corporation of $200,000), and 1994, 120.

287 CCNYAR, 1997, 82.

288 David Robinson, former executive vice president and treasurer of the Corporation, and a physicist, had been asked by Hamburg to serve as executive director and launch the twenty-two-member commission, co-chaired by William Golden, chair of the board of the American

Museum of Natural History, national science adviser for President Truman, and one of the originators of the idea, and by Joshua Lederberg, Corporation trustee, Nobel scientist, and president and professor at Rockefeller University; CCNYAR, 1988, 84, 151–152. Geri Mannion was responsible for the officer-assisted grants over the years of the Commission, 1988 to 1993. As noted in the 1996 Annual Report, the Commission produced nineteen reports and over three hundred recommendations, and it covered all branches of government, state governments, and nongovernmental organizations, as well as issues in mathematics education, foreign policy and national security, and development assistance. The Congressional Center was established. Several reports and recommendations had international implications, and HRDC grantees responded. The report on science advisers, for example, persuaded Odhiambo to present these ideas to African heads of state through the African Academy of Sciences. The report on international affairs recommended science attachés in US embassies around the world. The report on international environmental issues related to the Brundtland Commission.

289 The aim of the Task Force, as described in the Corporation's 1993 Annual Report, was "to assess the changing circumstances for international development and aid policy and the organizational implications of these changes for the United States." With a one-month grant of $175,400, the Carter Center held its major conference on global book development cooperation in December 1992. Co-chaired by President Carter and UN Secretary-General Boutros Boutros-Ghali, participants included former heads of USAID, current leaders of development assistance organizations, foundation staff members, representatives from developing countries and the George H. W. Bush administration, and members of Congress and the Clinton transition team. CCNYAR, 1993, 117; see also Carter Center of Emory University, "Conference for Global Development Cooperation," *Conference Report Series* 4, no. 2 (December 1992): 4–5.

290 The issues shaping the program reflected concerns in all three Corporation programs and led Mannion, Speedie, and Rosenfield to identify this as a promising joint activity that was out of program but would reinforce much of the work; CCNYAR, 1994, 26; 1996, 156; and 1997, 85. By 2012, the UN Studies Program was run as a think tank under International Security Studies and led by Professor Paul Kennedy. See Yale Law School, "International Programs at Yale University," available at: http://www.law.yale.edu/academics/internationallawyaleuprograms.htm (accessed February 12, 2014).

291 Although not discussed here, the grants on strengthening US democracy, especially those related to immigrant integration and democratic institutions such as voter participation, became a vibrant grants program under the next administration. In this case, the Special Projects Committee nurtured activities started under Alan Pifer, ensured their viability, and strengthened them sufficiently that they flourished under the leadership of Mannion for many years.

292 The Public Affairs Department's charge to advance the education of the public included support for disseminating the work of scholars funded at major universities and think tanks; widely circulating the results of conferences; promoting exchanges between academics and other experts, practitioners, policymakers, and members of the press; synthesizing knowledge and best practices drawn from experiments, models, and demonstrations to test new ideas as well as evaluation studies; and serving as a clearinghouse of information. CCNY, Minutes of the Board of Trustees, 77–82, June 7–9, 1995, "Diffusion of Knowledge: Carnegie Corporation's Dissemination Program," Staff and Retreat Files: Program Retreat Papers, Public Affairs, Box 1, Series I.E, CCNY Records, RBML-CUL.

293 Russell, like Finberg, came to the Corporation with an abiding interest in international affairs and made special contributions in that area, both by handling officer-assisted grants and by helping to design the subprogram activities in public understanding of development for the HRDC Program. Avery Russell, "The Second Fifty Years: A Personal View," *Carnegie Reporter* 6,

no. 2 (Spring 2011): 27, 28, available at: carnegie.org/publications/carnegie-reporter/single/view/issue/item/387 (accessed February 12, 2014).

294   Under John Gardner and Alan Pifer, the pathbreaking grants and commissions that led to the establishment of the Center for Public Broadcasting initiated the Corporation's continuing support for investing in documentaries and series on public television and public radio—including grants in support of the establishment of the Children's Television Workshop, which led to the peerless television show *Sesame Street*.

295   In addition to work with television and radio, the Corporation continued to promote the results of grantee efforts, both domestic and international, by supporting the *Carnegie Quarterly*, the publication that in 1952 had replaced Robert Lester's *Audits of Experience*. The Corporation also issued Carnegie meeting papers, occasional papers, and special reports. With its interest in dissemination, the Corporation was one of the first foundations to experiment with developing a Web presence. In 1994 it invested in a gopher server (an early alternative to the World Wide Web that is no longer in use) on the Internet. By 1995, commission reports, the issues of *Carnegie Quarterly*, and report essays were available online.

296   CCNYAR, 1995, 157, and 1996, 114.

297   Extending over eight years, the project brought in twelve institutional partners for academic and policy colloquium conferences, seminars, and press briefings in New York, Washington, DC, and Durham, North Carolina. Support also included a traveling photography exhibition based on photographs in the interim report, a two-part public television series, film showings, posters, and educational materials. The grants involved special support for the training of black South Africans in documentary photography. *South Africa: The Cordoned Heart*, the book of photographs and essays, and *Uprooting Poverty* were the main publications disseminated in the United States.

NOTES FOR CHAPTER 8

1   This volume tells the story of Carnegie Corporation's international activities up through the one-hundredth anniversary of the foundation's first board meeting on November 10, 1911. This chapter discusses the Corporation's international work in the era that began with the presidency of Vartan Gregorian, who assumed office in July 1997. Because that era is ongoing, I have occasionally included information relating to grants and events that reach beyond the Corporation's centennial in 2011.

2   Like the previous period, these years reflect a greatly improved asset base for the Corporation. In 1997, when Vartan Gregorian became president, the market value of the assets was nearly $1.54 billion. By 2011, the value had increased to $2.55 billion, despite the adverse effects of the 2008 financial recession. That is, by 2007 the assets had reached the value of $3.07 billion, the high for the era so far, and then dropped by 2009 to $2.43 billion. The number of grants also skyrocketed, but not at a level commensurate with the rise in budget, because grants were larger in budget and longer in time frame. In 1997 and 1998, 164 grants and 7 appropriations in total were made. Over the period 1997 to 2013, the cumulative grants totaled slightly more than $1.4 billion; from 1997 to 2011, the international grants related to international peace and security and based in US institutions totaled slightly more than $215 million, and through 2012 the ones related to Commonwealth Africa were $198 million. Given the greatly increased number of grants, meetings, and consultations, this chapter portrays the main lines of work, the clusters of grants informing and implementing the objectives of the programs, and, when possible, the results; moreover, since the era is open-ended, it is premature to declare that results have been achieved, except as interim and except when initiatives have been closed.

3 For contemporary as well as historical assessments, see United Nations Development Policy and Analysis Division, *World Economic Situation and Prospects 2011*, ST/ESA/334 (New York: UN, 2011), available at: http://www.un.org/esa/analysis/wess/wesp.html; and UN Department of Economic and Social Affairs, *The Global Social Crisis: Report on the World Social Situation 2011*, ST/ESA/334 (New York: UN, 2011), available at: http://undesadspd.org/ReportontheWorldSocialSituation/2011.aspx.

4 See, for example, a range of books by a mix of practitioners and scholars: Dirk Eilinghoff, *Rethinking Philanthropic Effectiveness: Lessons from an International Network of Foundation Experts* (Gutersloh, Germany: Verlag Bertelsmann Stiftung, 2005); William Damon and Susan Verducci, *Taking Philanthropy Seriously: Beyond Noble Intentions to Responsible Giving* (Bloomington: Indiana University Press, 2006); Helmut K. Anheir and Diana Leat, *Creative Philanthropy: Towards a New Philanthropy for the Twenty-First Century* (Abingdon, Oxon, UK: Routledge, 2006); Joel L. Fleishman, *The Foundation: A Great American Secret: How Private Wealth Is Changing the World* (New York: Public Affairs, 2007); Paul Brest and Hal Harvey, *Money Well Spent: A Strategic Plan for Smart Philanthropy* (New York: Bloomberg Press, 2008); Claire Gaudiani, *Generosity Unbound: How American Philanthropy Can Strengthen the Economy and Expand the Middle Class* (New York: Broadway Publications, 2010); Anheir and Hammack, *American Foundations*; Olivier Zunz, *Philanthropy in America: A History* (Princeton, NJ: Princeton University Press, 2011); and David C. Hammack and Helmut K. Anheier, *A Versatile Institution: The Changing Ideals and Realities of Philanthropic Foundations* (Washington, DC: Brookings Institution Press, 2013).

5 Delia K. Cabe, "Nation Building: Shedding Its Isolationist Stance, the United States Begins Reaching Out to Its Global Neighbors," *Kennedy School Bulletin* (Spring 2002). The Corporation also addressed the consequences of intensive national security measures for individual rights in the United States and elsewhere.

6 An excellent overview is given in UN Economic Commission for Africa (UNECA), *Reflections on Africa's Development: Essays in Honour of Abdoulie Janneh* (Addis Ababa, Ethiopia: UNECA, 2012). In that volume, Emmanuel Nnadozie, "Transforming Economic Growth into Sustainable Development in Africa," 151–183. Nnadozie also sketches the fads in development strategies that have deformed development assistance: "commercialization through cash cropping (… up to 1979); community development, integrated rural development and participatory development (1955–1973); regional integration for industry and … food (1970–1979); basic human needs (1970–1979); regional integration … (1973–1989); supply shifters in agriculture (1973–1989); first-generation structural adjustment on demand management (1980–1984); second-generation structural adjustment on equity with growth (1985–1999); and sustainable development (1990–present)" (ibid., 183, 159).

7 See UN Development Policy and Analysis Division, *World Economic Situation and Prospects 2011*; UN Department of Economic and Social Affairs, *The Global Social Crisis: Report on the World Social Situation 2011*.

8 "Ted Turner Donates $1 Billion to 'UN Causes,'" CNN Interactive, September 19, 1997, available at: http://edition.cnn.com/US/9709/18/turner.gift/index.html; and Laurie Dhue, "Sharing the Wealth: Ted Turner's Not the First Big Giver," CNN Interactive, September 19, 1997, available at: http://edition.cnn.com/US/9709/19/donations/index.html (both accessed July 7, 2012). See also Carnegie Corporation of New York (CCNY) Annual Report (CCNYAR), 2000, 23; those issued from 1911 to 1997 can be found in CCNY Records, Rare Books and Manuscripts Library, Columbia University Libraries (RBML-CUL). From 1998 on, the Annual Reports are available at: www.carnegie.org/publications/annual-report/.

9 Lawrence and Mukai, *Foundation Growth and Giving Estimates: Current Outlook 2011*.

When Hamburg's presidency started in 1982, the equivalent was 23,770 foundations with assets of about $59 billion and grant-making of $5 billion.

10 Ibid., 3, 5.

11 For 1997, see Internal Revenue Service, "Table 1. Large Nonoperating Private Foundations Panel Study: Selected Financial Data, 1985–1997, in Constant Dollars," available at: www.irs. gov/pub/irs-soi/97pf01fd.xls (accessed July 7, 2012); the Corporation ranked tenth in 1985, with assets of $970,733,101. For 2012, see Foundation Center, "Top Funders, as of January 25, 2014," available at: http://foundationcenter.org/findfunders/topfunders/top100assets.html (accessed February 15, 2014).

12 Gregorian's published doctoral dissertation on the political history of Afghanistan is still widely used in graduate programs. Vartan Gregorian, *The Emergence of Modern Afghanistan: Politics of Reform and Modernization, 1840–1946* (Palo Alto, CA: Stanford University Press, 1969).

13 CCNYAR, 1997, 9.

14 Ibid., 10.

15 CCNYAR, 2000, 21.

16 One of the striking features of the Gregorian era is the considerable amount of documentation for nearly every activity. Previously, program activities were documented through the presidents' annual essays, staff members' detailed analytical summaries of major grant programs (in the "Audit of Program" and *Carnegie Quarterly*), and the occasional board reviews, such as in 1975 and 1995. Starting around 2000, in addition to publishing the presidential essays and books, the Public Affairs Department expanded its dissemination activities and targeted materials to different audiences and constituencies. Publications such as *Carnegie Results, Carnegie Reporter,* and the *Carnegie Challenge Papers* have enlarged external understanding of the Corporation's programs, as well as the work of others in the sector. All the Annual Reports for this era are publicly available online. With the Corporation's centennial year falling within this time frame, and perhaps also because the president is a historian, explicit attention has been given to the historical continuity of the programmatic areas and even to that of specific grants.

17 The board members (dates of service in parentheses) in 1997 were: Chairman Thomas H. Kean (1991–2002, chair 1997–1998, reelected 2007–2012), president of Drew University and former governor of New Jersey; Helene L. Kaplan (1980–1990, chair 1984–1990, reelected 1993–2006, chair 2002–2006, honorary trustee 2006–present); of counsel Skadden, Arps, Slate, Meagher & Flom LLP, deeply involved in the Corporation's work in South Africa; Richard F. Celeste (1993–1998), appointed ambassador to India in 1997 but participated in selection process; James P. Comer (1990–1998), professor of child psychiatry at Yale University and associate dean of the Yale School of Medicine, making major contributions in the education of disadvantaged minority students; Teresa Heinz (1993–2000) of Heinz Philanthropies, born in Mozambique, graduate of the University of the Witwatersrand; James A. Johnson (1992–2000), CEO of Fannie Mae and former executive assistant and foreign policy adviser to Vice President Walter Mondale; Vincent Mai (1994–2002), born in South Africa, graduate of the University of Cape Town; Shirley M. Malcolm (1992–2000), AAAS program head, active in international science issues promoting the role of women in science; Henry Muller (1992–2000), editorial director of Time Inc. and former *Time* magazine foreign editor, interested in international issues; former US Senator Sam Nunn (1997–2005), responsible for significant foreign policy legislation, including the Nunn-Lugar legislation developed in association with Corporation grantees; James J. Renier (1996–2000), former chairman and chief executive officer of Honeywell, Inc., committed to nonprofit work on K-12 education; Condoleezza Rice (1994–1998), a top Russian expert, Corporation adviser, and grantee through her work at Stanford, and later secretary of state after serving as national security adviser; Marta Tienda (1996–2004), social demographer

at Princeton University, with extensive experience in Latin America; Wilma "Billie" S. Tisch (1994–1998), active in philanthropic and social service organizations, former chair of the WNYC Foundation board and a trustee of UJA-Federation, United Way of New York City, and Hunter College School of Social Work; Admiral James D. Watkins (1993–1998), former secretary of energy under President George H. W. Bush, worked on issues related to overseas security issues, including Law of the Seas; Judy Woodruff (1995–2003), at the time, prime anchor and senior correspondent for CNN and formerly chief correspondent for the *MacNeil/Lehrer NewsHour* (now co-anchor of that show), with a focus on political and international news, and one of the founders of the International Women's Media Foundation; and honorary trustee Caryl P. Haskins, former head of the Carnegie Institution of Washington, who had been involved in international science, including work and writings on the Amazon.

18   The internationally based board members included: Pedro Apse (2004–2012), CEO of Protego, SA, a consulting company in Mexico City, an international lawyer, a former secretary of finance under Carlos Salinas, and undersecretary of planning; Ana Palacio (2005–2013), senior vice president and general counsel of the World Bank, the first woman foreign minister of Spain (with the People's Party government of the early 2000s), and a member of the European Parliament; Kofi Annan (2007–2010, honorary trustee 2010–2012), former secretary-general of the United Nations and recipient of the Nobel Peace Prize, from Ghana, living in Switzerland. The other trustees elected to the board during the Gregorian era were: Martin Liebowitz (1998–2007), member of the Corporation's external investment advisory group since 1995, vice chairman and chief investment officer for TIAA-CREF; Ambassador Olara Otunnu (1998–2007), special representative of the UN secretary-general for children in armed conflict, former president of the International Peace Academy (a Corporation grantee), former minister of foreign affairs of Uganda, and former permanent representative of Uganda to the UN; Raymond Smith (1999–2007), chairman of Rothschild North America and leader in the telecommunications industry, with experience on advisory boards to the Library of Congress focused on science and education issues; Ruth Simmons (1999–2004; pressing obligations as president of Brown University prevented her from accepting a second term), French scholar, president of Smith College, former vice provost at Princeton, and provost at Spelman College; Admiral William Owens (1999–2008), chief executive officer and vice chairman of Teledesic LLC, a global broadband satellite communications company, former vice chairman of the Joint Chiefs of Staff specializing in national security and technological issues; Bruce Alberts (2000–2008), biochemist and molecular biologist, president of the National Academy of Sciences, connecting with academies globally; Governor James Hunt (2001–2008), national leader in education, former governor of North Carolina; Geoffrey Boisi (2001–2008, reelected to new term in 2009), chairman and CEO of Roundtable Investment Partners, former vice chairman of JPMorgan Chase, focused on the global marketplace, education, and philanthropy; William J. McDonough (2002–2003; left early when appointed chairman of the Public Company Accounting Oversight Board), banker, president and CEO of the Federal Reserve Bank, member of the board of directors of the Bank for International Settlements in Basel, Switzerland, and former diplomat with the US State Department and the US Navy; Ambassador Shirin Tahir-Kheli (2002–2003; left early when appointed senior director of the National Security Council), political scientist, born in India (now Pakistan), professor at Johns Hopkins University Foreign Policy Institute and founding director of the South Asia Program, alternate US representative to the UN for Special Political Affairs, former director of Political Military Affairs, former director of Near East and South Asian Affairs for the National Security Council, and former member of the policy planning staff of the US Department of State; Ambassador Thomas Pickering (2003–2011), senior vice president for international relations at the Boeing Company, former undersecretary of

state for political affairs, personnel rank of "career ambassador," the highest in the US Foreign Service, former ambassador to Russia, India, the United Nations, Israel, El Salvador, Nigeria, and Jordan; Fiona Druckenmiller (2004–2008; unexpected obligations prevented her from accepting a second term), philanthropist, also on the board of American Museum of Natural History, Human Rights Watch, and Adopt a Minefield; Richard Riley (2004–2012), lawyer, law firm senior partner, former governor of South Carolina, and former secretary of education under President Clinton; Janet Robinson (2005–2013), publisher, CEO of the New York Times Company, and a former public school teacher; Richard Brodhead (elected in 2005), educator, president of Duke University, and former provost of Yale University; Norman Pearlstine (elected in 2005), editor and reporter, editor-in-chief of *Time* magazine, former senior editorial leader of the *Wall Street Journal* in Europe and Asia; Thomas Kean (former trustee 1991–February 2002; reelected 2005–2012; reelected chair in 2009; honorary trustee 2012–2013; reelected to board and chair 2013), educator and politician, president of THK Consulting, former governor of New Jersey, former chair of the National Commission on Terrorist Attacks upon the United States; Amy Gutmann (2006–2013), political scientist and philosopher, president of the University of Pennsylvania, former provost of Princeton University; Susan Hockfield (elected in 2006), neuroscientist, president of MIT, former provost of Yale University; Kurt Schmoke (elected in 2007, board vice chair), lawyer, dean of Howard University Law School, former mayor of Baltimore, with dedicated work in South Africa; Ralph Cicerone (elected in 2008), electrical engineer and atmospheric scientist, president of National Academy of Sciences, former chancellor of the University of California at Irvine; James Wolfensohn (elected in 2009), Australian investment banker, chairman of Wolfensohn & Company, former president of the World Bank; Richard Beattie (elected in 2009, former board member 1987–1996), lawyer, chairman of Simpson Thatcher and Bartlett LLP, former general counsel of the US Department of Health, Education, and Welfare under President Carter, member of the New York City Board of Education, special adviser to the secretary of state and special emissary for Cyprus under President Clinton; Don Randel (elected in 2010), medieval scholar, president of the Andrew Mellon Foundation, and former president of the University of Chicago; Stephen A. Oxman (elected in 2011), lawyer, senior adviser at Morgan Stanley, former assistant secretary of state for European and Canadian affairs under President Clinton; Ambassador Edward Djerejian (elected in 2011), founding director, James A. Baker III Institute for Public Policy, Rice University, former ambassador to Israel and Syria, assistant secretary of state for Near East affairs, special assistant to President Ronald Reagan, long career in the foreign service; John Hendricks (elected in 2011 for a term starting in March 2012), founder and chairman, Discovery Communications, creator of the Discovery Channel, founder, American Association of University Consultants; and the Honorable Ann Claire Williams (elected 2011 for a term starting in March 2012), US Court of Appeals judge for the Seventh Circuit, former US district judge for the Northern District of Illinois, first chief of the Organized Drug Enforcement Task Force, active internationally in training lawyers and judges, including for international criminal tribunals for Rwanda and Yugoslavia.

19 The trustees were supportive of the changes in the education and democracy work as well, but that work is only touched on in this chapter. Gregorian and the trustees also reviewed the policy on trustee roles and responsibilities as established by an earlier Board of Trustees in 1971. The updated policy, reviewed in 1997 and approved by the trustees on January 8, 1998, emphasized that "a primary responsibility of the board … is to focus its attention on the effectiveness of the Corporation's program as a whole, from a policy standpoint. While retaining final grantmaking authority, the board should play a greater role in setting, reviewing, and revising the broad objectives of the Corporation rather than scrutinize individual proposals for grants.… The board should consider from time to time whether new areas should be entered and work in old areas

discontinued.... The board, furthermore, should advise and support the president and staff in those areas in which the more detached point of view and more diverse experience of trustees can add to the in-depth analysis and specialized expertise of the staff." CCNYAR, 1997, 12; approval reported in CCNYAR, 1998, 85; see also CCNYAR, 1999, 89.

20 CCNYAR, 1999, 89.

21 CCNYAR, 1997, 9–18.

22 Ibid., 11.

23 Among many others, Gregorian's questions include: "What are we doing? Why are we doing it? How well are we doing it, especially in relation to the work of other foundations? How does it serve Carnegie Corporation's overall mission to advance and diffuse knowledge and understanding?" Other questions further illustrate his approach to proposal review during his tenure: "Does the Corporation perceive itself as an incubator of ideas or as a sustainer of institutions that play that role? How do we combat the age-old problem of scatteration in our grant-making, while retaining the flexibility to respond to a tantalizing idea or a target of opportunity? How do we evaluate our programs? Is there merit in recognizing the 'illuminating failure' as well as the obvious success, in order to learn lessons from experience? Would we achieve our objectives more efficiently if we made fewer grants and larger commitments or many more little ones? If we know what our entry strategy is, what will be our exit strategy? How can we intelligently and imaginatively harness technological progress in order to achieve our goals? How effectively, in the electronic age, is the Corporation reaching its various audiences and constituencies?... Finally, what are some important new issues facing our nation and the world that we should deal with? Where is our comparative leadership advantage? Should we 'go it alone' as we often have in the past or increasingly seek partners? How do we achieve the right balance between continuity and change?" Ibid., 11.

24 Ibid.

25 For more details, see ibid., 12.

26 CCNYAR, 1999, 89; for details on program guidelines for 1998–1999, see CCNYAR, 1998, 89–97.

27 Vartan Gregorian, "New Directions for Carnegie Corporation of New York: A Report to the Board," CCNY, February 2, 1999, available at: carnegie.org/fileadmin/Media/Publications/PDF/New_Directions_Gregorian_Board_Report.pdf (accessed February 15, 2014).

28 For the first couple of years, David Speedie continued as chair of the International Peace and Security Program, Patricia Rosenfield stayed on as chair of the International Development Program, and Vivien Stewart remained chair of the Education Program. Geraldine Mannion, the program officer in charge of special projects, which had included the democracy grant-making, was promoted to chair for the Strengthening US Democracy Program and Special Projects Committee. As expected, however, some staff soon departed. Even though he was no longer working on international issues, the departure of Fritz Mosher in 1998 after forty years of service left a significant gap in knowledge of the deep history of the international and national activities in the United States and Africa. In addition, Vivien Stewart, who had been at the foundation for twenty-eight years and had worked on Commonwealth projects at first, particularly those related to population, left in 2000 to work with Ambassador Olara Otunnu to advise on education issues related to children and armed conflict; CCNYAR, 1998, 87, and 2000, 96. In addition, in 1999 the Carnegie Commission on Preventing Deadly Conflict completed its work and the staff left for other positions; CCNYAR, 1998, 87, and 2000, 96.

29 In 1999 Avery Russell, who had been at the Corporation for twenty-nine years and served as director of publications and public affairs and as a program officer, stepped down from those positions but remained a special adviser to the president. Also in 1999, treasurer Jean Grisi, who had been at the Corporation for fourteen years, left for another position. In 2000, Dorothy

Knapp, who had been at the Corporation since 1986 and had worked closely, as corporate secretary, since 1996 with the international programs and was a Russian specialist, stepped down. Idalia Holder, director of human resources, the other member of the administration leadership in 1997, retired in 2006. CCNYAR, 1999, 91; 2000, 96; and 2006, 61.

30   In December 1998, Edward Sermier, former chief financial officer of the New York Philharmonic and a former deputy director of the office of the mayor of New York, joined as vice president and chief administrative officer. In January 1999, Ellen Shuman, a former Yale University investment director for real estate and capital market activities, was hired as vice president and chief investment officer. In June 1999, Neil Grabois, former president of Colgate University and former provost at Williams College, became vice president and director for strategic planning and program coordination (the traditional vice president for program position). And in October 1999, Susan Robinson King, former assistant secretary for public affairs at the US Department of Labor and a longtime broadcasting journalist, became vice president for public affairs. CCNYAR, 1998, 86–87 (Sermier and Shuman), and 1999, 90–91 (Grabois and King).

31   The results of the Corporation's different investment policies over the century are described in Karen Theroux, "Weathering the Financial Storms of a Century," *Carnegie Reporter* 6, no. 1 (Fall 2010): 26–29, available at: http://carnegie.org/publications/carnegie-reporter/single/view/article/item/264/.

32   Gregorian introduced another innovation: academic advisers. Each program was asked to identify several external advisers who would meet periodically with the team, point to new ideas and new breakthroughs, advise on strategy, and serve as a sounding board for the new ideas for the team as well. The advisers worked quite differently in different areas: they had significant strategic input in the International Peace and Security Program and played an essential role for the Carnegie Scholars program.

33   For a history of the Council and its scope of work, see CCNY, "Programs and Accomplishments, 1996–2000, Section 6: Council on Evaluation Purpose and Progress," 1–4. Material on all the evaluation work for this period is available in CCNY Reports, RBML-CUL, and at CCNY Offices (CCNYO).

34   The Council met regularly, nearly every six weeks, between 2001 and the end of 2006, and members discussed levels of evaluation: grant by grant, clusters of grants, and program by program. Both international programs provided excellent guidance because they had engaged evaluation consultants to help develop and review their higher education institution grants in African countries and Russia. One in particular, Johann Mouton, founder and director of the Evaluation Research Agency in South Africa, introduced the Council to the use of formative, midcourse, and summative (final) evaluations.

35   One grant-related innovation, however, was the introduction of "end-of-grant summaries." Program officers would prepare a brief statement on material not in the official record, comparable to mini-oral histories. These summaries were placed in the grant files and made available to trustees, staff members, and, eventually, scholars.

36   Starting in fiscal year 2003 and following guidelines prepared by the Council, the papers described the context and rationale, the goals, the theory of change, the objectives, the implementation strategy and tactics, the indicators, the impact, and the evaluation. If approved by the board, the strategy papers would guide the programs for three to five years; meanwhile, modest updates would be submitted to the board along with the budget requests; for more detail, see CCNYAR, 2002–2003, 82–83. While detailed planning and annual program papers had been prepared in the previous era, these differed in at least two main aspects: they all followed a common structure, and all focused on stating explicit indicators of success and outcomes.

37   CCNY, "Programs and Accomplishments, 1996–2006," circulated November 2006,

CCNYO. In addition to presenting the accomplishments and some of the failures of a program, staff members prepared material on grant-making, the evolution of the programs, the various activities of the Council on Evaluation, the role of technical assistance, the academic advisers, the foundation partners, and the data on numbers of grants and grant publications. For each program, there were several layers of review; the most important was comparing the results with the anticipated outcomes. This document provides one of the key guides to the approaches and results of Corporation grant-making over the first ten years of the Gregorian presidency.

38   Vartan Gregorian, "Meeting the Challenges of the 21st Century," October 1, 2007, 2, available at: carnegie.org/fileadmin/Media/Publications/PDF/meeting_the_challenges.pdf (accessed February 23, 2014).

39   Ibid., 2–3, 20.

40   By the summer of 2008, the new leadership team at the Corporation was in place. Two of the vice presidents, Grabois and Sermier, had left. The position of vice president for program was now divided into two: a vice president for the national program and a vice president for the international program; these positions were filled by Michele Cahill and Deana Arsenian, respectively. The position of vice president for administration, chief administrative officer, and corporate secretary was filled by Ellen Bloom, who joined the Corporation after twenty years with American Express; in her previous position, she had been senior vice president of global talent, responsible for global diversity, learning systems, executive development, and retention, staffing, and leadership effectiveness. To complete the team, Gregorian promoted Jeanne D'Onofrio to chief of staff and operations in the president's office and Susan King to vice president for external affairs and program director for the journalism initiative, special initiatives, and strategy. Ellen Shuman maintained her position as vice president and chief investment officer; CCNYAR, 2007, 70–71. Shuman retired in July 2011 and was replaced by two vice presidents and co-chief investment officers for investments, Kim Y. Lew and Meredith Bradley Jenkins, and Robert J. Seman was promoted to vice president and chief financial officer; CCNYAR, 2011, 64.

41   Working with a consulting firm, the Parthenon Group, the two vice presidents and the program staff developed a coherent evaluation strategy that was presented and approved by the board at its December 2010 meeting. Michele Cahill and Deana Arsenian, "A Proposed Systemic Approach to Program Evaluation," November 22, 2010, 2, CCNYO.

42   Ibid. With trustee approval, implementation of the evaluation strategy began in the Corporation's centennial year, 2011, with the aim of assessing effectiveness, improving programs, and informing policy and procedures. "As we move forward, we will utilize evaluation while also appreciating its limitations." Ibid., 4.

43   In this era, almost every program undertook international activities, even the investment team, whose international activities, primarily in India, China, and selected countries in Africa, were related to grant-making through the enhancement of the Corporation's assets. As vital as the investment team's work is to the success of the grant-making efforts, it is not discussed in this book. As noted in note 1, this chapter reflects work in progress under the leadership of President Gregorian, with the ending date of the one-hundredth anniversary of the Corporation's Board of Trustees' first meeting on November 10, 1911, when the trustees received the deed of gift from the founder and his charge to them. In some instances, as appropriate, later work is included.

44   Gregorian strengthened the Corporation's international US-based grant-making by hiring Deana Arsenian, the staff member who had been working with David Hamburg and Fritz Mosher from the earliest days of the Avoiding Nuclear War Program. Arsenian, who had joined the Corporation in 1984, left in 1989 to become assistant director of the Watson Institute for International Studies at Brown University; she returned in 1997 as program officer in the newly formed International Peace and Security Program under the leadership of David Speedie.

In addition to Speedie, she found the same team in place—Patricia Moore Nicholas, Deborah Cohen, Lynn Di Martino, and Patricia Aquino-Macri. In 1999 Gregorian hired Stephen Del Rosso, program director at the Chicago Council on Foreign Relations, to join the team as senior program officer with responsibility for the New Dimensions of Security Initiative, the part of the program charged with the direct implementation of the recommendations of the Commission on the Prevention of Deadly Conflict. As noted in the 1999 annual report, "Del Rosso is recognized for his deep knowledge of international relations and his work in supporting defining foundation programs in the field"; CCNYAR, 1999, 93. Del Rosso not only had extensive overseas experience as a career US Foreign Service officer for ten years but had been a grant-making partner with the Corporation for five years at Pew Charitable Trusts in Philadelphia, where he had been responsible for the work on conflict resolution. He knew the field and the Corporation's work.

45 There were a few other staffing changes. In 2002 Gregorian asked Speedie to serve as his special adviser and initiate a new program on Islam; he then asked Arsenian and Del Rosso to alternate as chairs of the program. Following the restructuring in 2007, when Arsenian became vice president and the position of chair became that of program director, Del Rosso was appointed to the role and Nicholas was promoted from program associate to project manager for the international program, with increasing special responsibilities for the work on Russia and other powers, as well as on nuclear security. In 2009 Carl Robichaud joined as program officer with responsibility for the nuclear proliferation grant-making. Robichaud most recently had been at the Century Fund working on Afghanistan and nuclear security issues. Hillary Wiesner, who joined the Corporation in early 2007 to direct the Islam Initiative, had deep knowledge of the field. Prior to joining the Corporation, she had served as senior executive officer and secretary of the directorate at the United Nations Educational, Scientific, and Cultural Organization (UNESCO-Paris). Wiesner's research focused on the history, religions, and archaeology of the ancient Mediterranean and Near East, drawing on her BA in religion from Harvard, MA from the University of Chicago on the ancient Mediterranean world, and PhD from Harvard's Committee on the Study of Religion. She had also written on dialogue and ethics across cultures, women and religion, religion and science, and tolerance and human rights.

46 CCNY, "Program Development Papers, October 1998–October 2000, International Peace and Security," 1, Folder 5, Box 22, Series I.D, CCNY Records, RBML-CUL.

47 Ibid., 2.

48 For one approach of the Corporation, see Lee Michael Katz, "The Aspen Institute Congressional Program: A Nonpartisan Success Story," *Carnegie Results* (Summer 2007), available at: http://carnegie.org/fileadmin/Media/Publications/PDF/carnegie_results_summer07.pdf.

49 The individuals who had been trained by the Corporation, a generation of specialists starting in the early 1980s, moved in and out of policymaking positions over time and became the core of informal and formal foreign policy advisers; CCNY, "Program Development Papers, October 1998–October 2000, International Peace and Security," 14. The team also highlighted two challenges. In 1997 and 1998 in the United States, domestic issues preoccupied policymaker interests: "We are operating in a climate in which 60 percent of the U.S. House of Representatives do not possess a passport and claim this as a badge of honor on the campaign trail"; ibid. Moreover, despite the indications of foundation interest, the program team pointed to the shrinking number of foundations in the field, for example, the program changes at the Pew Charitable Trusts and the Rockefeller Brothers Fund.

50 Essentially, the Corporation and its major funding partners, especially the MacArthur Foundation, have invested over the past twenty-five years in creating fields related to national security that are likely to persist in vital importance throughout the twenty-first century, and

certainly throughout the first quarter of the twenty-first century. Working with key partners on a continuing basis is a long-standing practice of the Corporation. As Frederick Keppel, the fifth president, wrote: "In reviewing the activities of the year item by item ... the outstanding element has seemed to the writer to be their essentially cooperative nature. This he believes to be characteristic of the educational foundations as a whole ... but it is an aspect of foundation activities not as fully understood and appreciated as it might be.... Apart from its relations with sister institutions founded by Mr. Carnegie, and with other educational foundations, all of which are steadily growing closer, the Corporation has during the year under review been in direct contact in the consideration of its general program or of specific action within that program with no fewer than 83 national bodies representing different aspects of educational and cultural activity." Keppel then mentioned that working closely with these institutions, as well as with representatives from colleges and universities, would give "some conception of the network of responsible men and women the country over who are working with the Carnegie Corporation for the 'advancement and diffusion of knowledge and understanding' among the people of the United States." CCNYAR, 1925, 25–26.

51 Comparable to the 1980s and 1990s, Corporation grantees have entered government in both Democratic and Republican administrations. Notable examples (with their positions as of 2011) include: William Perry (former) secretary of defense; Ashton Carter, deputy secretary of defense; Rose Gottemoeller, acting undersecretary of state for arms control and international security and chief negotiator of the New Strategic Arms Reduction Treaty; Gary Samore, White House coordinator for arms control and weapons of mass destruction; Susan Rice, US ambassador to the United Nations; and Mitchell Reiss, director of policy planning at the Department of State.

52 In addition, at various stages the team developed three relatively short-lived subprograms that were subsequently either folded into one of the three major subprograms or dropped: US policy options, technology and scientific advances, and "other."

53 As discussed in Chapter 4, in the late 1940s and early 1950s the Corporation was involved in measures to achieve the peaceful uses of atomic energy through the establishment of the Atomic Energy Commission in the United States and the international arrangements at the United Nations. At the request of William Fox, the Corporation also supported the Council on Atomic Age Studies at Columbia University, established by Dwight D. Eisenhower, then the president of Columbia. From the mid-1960s until 1983, as noted in the previous chapter, there was essentially no grant-making directly related to the use of nuclear weapons. A condition of David Hamburg's acceptance of the presidency was establishing the program Avoiding Nuclear War. He also developed a close partnership with the MacArthur Foundation on a variety of complementary issues associated with the use of nuclear weapons as well as in work on Russia, at the time the other major nuclear power. For a more detailed discussion of the grant-making transition between the two periods at the Corporation, see Barry Rosenberg, "Towards Nuclear Nonproliferation: An Evolving Strategy," *Carnegie Results* (Summer 2004), available at: http://carnegie.org/fileadmin/Media/Publications/summer_04nuclear.pdf.

54 CCNYAR, 2007, 14; see also Rosenberg, "Towards Nuclear Nonproliferation."

55 Sharon K. Wiener, *Our Own Worst Enemy? Institutional Interests and the Proliferation of Nuclear Weapons Expertise*, Belfer Center Studies in International Security (Cambridge, MA: MIT Press, 2011), 241–289.

56 Lee Michael Katz, "Opening the Closed Cities of the Soviet Union," *Carnegie Results* (Winter 2010): 2, available at: http://carnegie.org/fileadmin/Media/Publications/PDF/carnegie_results_winter10.pdf; see also CCNYAR, 1999, 43 (via Tides Center); 2000, 60; 2002–2003, 34; and 2004–2005, 30.

57 Katz, "Opening the Closed Cities of the Soviet Union," 4.

58 Ibid., 8–9.

59 Ibid., 9.

60 See Wiener, *Our Own Worst Enemy?* 264–289; and Katz, "Opening the Closed Cities of the Soviet Union," 6–12. Susan Eisenhower, a Corporation academic adviser and grantee, made a comment about the Corporation's role in the area of nonproliferation and the nuclear cities that still has salience: "We all benefited hugely from Carnegie Corporation's commitment to this area.... The Corporation continued to support programs in this area long after other foundations had moved on elsewhere.... Issues of this importance to American national security are just not going to go away because political circumstances have changed." Katz, "Opening the Closed Cities of the Soviet Union," 11.

61 See, for instance, CCNYAR, 2001, 41; 2002–2003, 109; and 2004–2005, 128.

62 CCNY, "Programs and Accomplishments, 1996–2006, International Peace and Security," 4, CCNYO.

63 Ibid., 5; see also CCNYAR, 2006, 15.

64 For the National Academy of Sciences, see CCNYAR, 2000, 59; 2002–2003, 33; and 2004–2005, 30. For the Brookings Institution, see, for instance, CCNYAR, 2000, 53; for the Council on Foreign Relations, see, for instance, CCNYAR, 2000, 62.

65 For the Brookings Institution and the Council on Foreign Relations, see CCNYAR, 2002–2003, 34–35. For other examples, see CCNYAR, 2009, 8, and 2011, 5 (Arms Control Association); 2009, 13 (Hudson Institute); 2002–2003, 33, and 2011, 12 (Princeton University); 2007, 16 (Nonproliferation Policy Education Center through the Institute for International Studies); 2011, 11 (Natural Resources Defense Council); 2011, 12 (Partnership for Global Security); and 2007, 17, and 2011, 9 (Henry L. Stimson Center). Budgetary issues associated with nuclear weapons, for example, formed the core of a grant to the Center for Strategic and Budgetary Assessments; its study results contributed to the 2010 Quadrennial Defense Review; CCNYAR, 2008, 16. The American Academy of Arts and Sciences brought together nuclear experts with industry experts to discuss issues associated with civilian nuclear energy; CCNYAR, 2011, 4. The *Bulletin of Atomic Scientists* (CCNYAR, 2011, 6) and the National Security Archive Fund (CCNYAR, 2004–2005, 34) provided public-oriented outreach on nuclear matters, including the nuclear nonproliferation–related treaties.

66 George Perkovich et al., *Universal Compliance: A Strategy for Nuclear Security* (Washington, DC: Carnegie Endowment for International Peace, 2005). Adding to the Corporation's support was support from the MacArthur Foundation, the Nuclear Threat Initiative, the Compton Foundation, and the New Land Foundation. As the authors state in the preface, preparing this document was a multistage process that took eighteen months of consultations with experts within and outside the United States. It was originally released as a draft at "the Carnegie Endowment's June 2004 International Non-Proliferation Conference attended by 721 participants from over twenty countries. Over 9,000 copies of the draft report were distributed, with the authors inviting readers to critique the work to help improve the final strategy"; ibid., 5. Not only did the authors travel to all current and potential nuclear countries, but they also met with think tanks and UN agencies all over the world. The authors both proposed a strategy for global nuclear nonproliferation and recommended ways to enforce it; furthermore, they suggested applications in different crises, including those in Pakistan, India, China, Iran, the Middle East, North Korea, and Northeast Asia.

67 Beyond contributing to the debate and discussion in Congress, *Universal Compliance* had significant policy impact at the executive-branch level, particularly with the appointment in 2009 of a Carnegie grantee, the former head of the Carnegie Moscow Center (established with Corporation support) and report author Rose Gottemoeller, as assistant secretary of state for arms control, verification, and compliance. In this capacity, as noted in her State Department

biography, she was the chief negotiator of the new 2010 Strategic Arms Reduction Treaty with the Russian Federation. US Department of State, "Biography: Rose Gottemoeller," available at: http://www.state.gov/r/pa/ei/biog/121630.htm.

68   CCNY, "Programs and Accomplishments, 2006, International Peace and Security," 5, CCNYO; CCNYAR, 2002–2003, 109.

69   For more details on the Nuclear Threat Initiative, its origins, and its work, see Lee Michael Katz, "Nuclear Threat Initiative: Working to Reduce Nuclear Dangers with a Goal of Ultimately Ending Nuclear Weapons as a Threat to the World," *Carnegie Results* (Summer 2011), available at: http://carnegie.org/fileadmin/Media/Publications/PDF/nuclear_threat_initiative_results_summer_11.pdf.

70   CCNY, "Programs and Accomplishments, 2006, International Peace and Security," 6, CCNYO.

71   See Nuclear Security Project, Nuclear Tipping Point website at: www.nucleartippingpoint.org. For a review, see Dennis Lim, "It's Time to Start Worrying Again," *New York Times*, July 16, 2010.

72   See NTI: Building a Safer World website at: www.nti.org. Nunn and his colleagues have been writing op-eds and giving interviews toward this aim. See, for example, Bernard Gwertzman, interview with George P. Schultz, former secretary of state, "Confronting a Nuclear Tipping Point," Council on Foreign Relations, March 12, 2010, available at: http://www.cfr.org/arms-control-disarmament-and-nonproliferation/confronting-nuclear-tipping-point/p21633.

73   Gregorian, "New Directions for Carnegie Corporation of New York," 33.

74   See US Chemical Weapons Convention, "CWC Treaty: Preamble," available at: http://www.cwc.gov/cwc_treaty_preamble.html; Tanya Syed, "Ancient Persians 'Gassed Romans,'" *BBC News*, January 19, 2009, available at: http://news.bbc.co.uk/2/hi/science/nature/7837826.stm (accessed October 28, 2012); Jan van Aken and Edward Hammond, "Genetic Engineering and Biological Weapons," *EMBO Reports* 4, supp. 1 (June 2003): S57–S60, available at: http://www.ncbi.nlm.nih.gov/pmc/articles/PMC1326447/.

75   The Stimson Center focused on implementing the Chemical Weapons Convention and strengthening the 1972 Biological and Toxin Weapons Convention. In 1999 the Corporation supported the Center in developing a clearinghouse project that would provide vital information on the subject of proliferation, including a new focus on international proliferation in Russia and China. The Corporation also enabled the Stimson Center to undertake a joint activity with China's Fudan University; CCNYAR, 2000, 60. The Federation of American Scientists supported its scientist constituency in speaking out on these issues; ibid., 58. The grants to the Harvard-Sussex program, linking Harvard University and the University of Sussex in England, aimed to strengthen research and training on the global elimination of biological and chemical weapons; ibid., 59. In addition, the University of Bradford received a grant to develop a website on international biotechnology treaties ("genomics gateway") and then to prepare a review of bioweapons from 1945 to the present; CCNYAR, 2002–2003, 31, 111.

76   Three documents describe and analyze the full complement of Corporation activities on this theme. (Karen Theroux provides the overview of all the grant-making.) Michael J. Zuckerman, "Biosecurity: A Twenty-First Century Challenge," *Carnegie Challenge Paper* (2005); Karen Theroux, "Crafting Strategies to Control the Biological Weapons," *Carnegie Review* (Spring 2009), available at: http://carnegie.org/fileadmin/Media/Publications/PDF/carnegiereview_bioweapons2009.pdf; Joyce Baldwin, "Jefferson Science Fellows: A Vision for Harnessing the Knowledge of Academic Scientists to Help Inform US Policymaking Takes Shape," *Carnegie Results* (Summer 2010), available at: http://carnegie.org/fileadmin/Media/Publications/jefferson_science_fellows_carnegie_results_summer_10_extra.pdf.

77   CCNY, "Programs and Accomplishments, 1996–2006, "International Peace and Security," 7, CCNYO.

78   Zuckerman, "Biosecurity," 11.

79   Patricia Moore Nicholas, the program staff member responsible for the biological weapons grant-making, noted that "the events of that day affected what happened in Geneva [where the treaty negotiations took place] and solidified what we at the Corporation had learned earlier. Subsequently we had a meeting with our grantees, scholars and other funders on 'defining the debate' to determine what should happen next"; Theroux, "Crafting Strategies to Control the Biological Weapons," 9. As Zuckerman added, the "day-long session on biosecurity, bringing together its grantees working on the issue, leading research scientists, medical educators, biologists and policymakers focused on the need for building partnerships of science and policy in biosecurity"; Zuckerman, "Biosecurity," 11. See also CCNY, "Programs and Accomplishments, 2006, International Peace and Security," 7, CCNYO.

80   National Research Council, Committee on Research Standards and Practices to Prevent the Destructive Application of Biotechnology, *Biotechnology Research in an Age of Terrorism* (Washington, DC: National Academies Press, 2004). The five grantees were Harvard, MIT, Princeton, the University of California at San Diego, and the University of California at Berkeley. For more details, see Theroux, "Crafting Strategies to Control the Biological Weapons," 9.

81   Theroux, "Crafting Strategies to Control the Biological Weapons," 9.

82   Baldwin, "Jefferson Science Fellows," 1–2; CCNYAR, 2004–2005, 126. The MacArthur Foundation provided the first grant, and Carnegie Corporation joined in later; the State Department provided additional matching support.

83   As Atkinson described it, there were some conditions for this to work. After convincing eighteen universities to participate, he went to the foundations to see if they would provide support for the stipends. Then he developed the submission and approval process via the National Research Council at the National Academies of Science, the institution that also served as fiscal agent for the foundation resources; Baldwin, "Jefferson Science Fellows," 3. Nicholas, in a speech to the fellows in 2006, emphasized that the mission of the program "lies at the center of our own strategy to build the capacity to manage the biological security challenge by bringing together two quite independent but critical cultures: the policymaking community and the biological science community"; Patricia Moore Nicholas, "Inauguration of the 2006 Class of the Jefferson Fellows to the Department of State," CCNY, June 2006, CCNYO.

84   Baldwin, "Jefferson Science Fellows," 2, 5.

85   For an updated number of fellows, see Ray Gamble, personal communication to Patricia Moore Nicholas, September 12, 2012; see also Jefferson Science Fellows, Fellowships Office, "Jefferson Science Fellow Biographies and Profiles," available at: http://sites.nationalacademies.org/PGA/Jefferson/PGA_046613.

86   Baldwin, "Jefferson Science Fellows," 8.

87   CCNY, "Programs and Accomplishments, 1996–2006, International Peace and Security," 5, CCNYO. The Corporation's grant-making in this area led to the development in 2009 of ongoing consortia, such as the Virtual Biosecurity Center, organized by the Federation of American Scientists in conjunction with the National Academy of Sciences, the American Association for the Advancement of Science, and the Center for Strategic and International Studies. This effort was also dedicated to building and reinforcing connections and communication across policymakers and scientists. It promoted the work of others, as noted by one of the participants, Michael Stebbins from the Federation of American Scientists: "'One of Pat Nicholas's goals was to bring together the work of all the groups that were getting funded by the Corporation,'" says Stebbins. "'We would take a lecture from Princeton, for example, stream it and then archive it.

We would disseminate other groups' reports. I had my doubts, thinking 'it can't be this easy to get an idea, fund it and have the government adopt it.' But that's what's happened"; Theroux, "Crafting Strategies to Control the Biological Weapons,'" 11.

88 The Global Health and Security Initiative is described in "NTI's Global Health and Security Program Receives Major Grant from Google Foundation," NIT, January 27, 2008, available at: www.nti.org/newsroom/news/nti-receives-grant-google-foundation/ (accessed March 29, 2014).

89 CCNY, "Program Papers, October 2001–October 2002, International Peace and Security," 73, Folder 5, Box 22, Series I.D, CCNY Records, RBML-CUL.

90 Wade Boese, "US Withdraws from ABM; Global Response Muted," *Arms Control Today* (July–August 2002), Arms Control Association, available at: http://www.armscontrol.org/act/2002_07-08/abmjul_aug02 (accessed July 25, 2012).

91 CCNY, "Program Strategy and Budget Papers, October 2003, International Peace and Security," 16, Folder 5, Box 22, Series I.D, CCNY Records, RBML-CUL. The advisers were: Susan Eisenhower, chairman of the Dwight D. Eisenhower World Affairs Institute; Shireen Hunter, distinguished scholar at Georgetown University; Jack Matlock, former ambassador to the Soviet Union; Rajan Menon, professor at Lehigh University; John Steinbruner, director of the Center for International and Security Studies, University of Maryland; Jack Snyder, professor at Columbia University; and Thomas Weiss, professor at the City University of New York.

92 Ibid., 13. Program staff defined the Corporation's comparative advantage as "based on our knowledge and experience in the related area of WMD [Weapons of Mass Destruction], extensive contacts in the security and scientific communities, access to relevant corporate representatives and understanding of the international security environment. In short, we are well positioned to fill an important gap in this neglected area of the emerging security agenda." Ibid.

93 CCNYAR, 2002–2003, 31.

94 Ibid., 108.

95 Ibid., 109.

96 Barry Rosenberg, "The Weaponization of Space: Divided Viewpoints, Uncertain Directions," *Carnegie Challenge Paper* (2004): 1.

97 Secure World Foundation, "Space Sustainability 101," available at: http://swfound.org/space-sustainability-101/.

98 CCNY, "Program Budget Papers, October 2004–October 2005, International Peace and Security," 4, CCNYO.

99 Joseph Montville, an active participant in Carnegie Corporation's International Peace and Security Program, originated the idea of Track II. A career Foreign Service officer, social psychologist, and ethicist, Montville coined the term at a 1980 brainstorming session at the Esalen Institute on ways to engage with the Soviet Union: he defined what he was doing as "Track I diplomacy" and what the others were doing as "Track II"—"a concept to characterize unofficial initiatives aimed at fixing a conflict situation." At the 1980 meeting, he realized that those unofficial initiatives could "establish dialogue and communication and … mobilize adversaries on both sides on how to solve a problem…. Formal diplomacy, Track I diplomacy, simply doesn't have those toolkits"; M. J. Zuckerman, "Track II Diplomacy: Can 'Unofficial' Talks Avert Disaster?" *Carnegie Reporter* 3, no. 3 (Fall 2005): 4, available at: http://carnegie.org/publications/carnegie-reporter/single/view/article/item/136/. As a consequence of Montville's writing about Track II, practicing it, and encouraging others to do the same, the concept has now become much more widely accepted, despite remaining skeptics; see Joseph V. Montville, "Track II Diplomacy: The Work of Healing History," *Whitehead Journal of Diplomacy and International Relations* (Summer–Fall 2006): 15–25.

100 Hussein Agha, Shai Feldman, Ahmad Khalidi, and Zeev Schiff, *Track II Diplomacy: Lessons from the Middle East*, BSCIA Studies in International Security (Cambridge, MA: MIT Press, 2003). Drawing on Montville's conceptual breakthrough, these authors differentiate among the variety of Track II talks, Track II settings, Track II participants, and Track II accomplishments. They emphasize the non-official nature of these activities, recognizing that Track I½, a more recent variation on the theme, could involve the officials participating in the Track I talks. They make the point that ongoing official talks are not necessary for Track II meetings, especially in long-standing conflicts (2–3).

101 Ibid., 196.

102 Supported under the New Dimensions of Security Subprogram, discussed later in this chapter. In 2000 the Corporation supported Johns Hopkins University and the Institute of Global Environment and Energy in the 21st Century in "the launching of 'Track-II,' or unofficial diplomatic talks to address the technical aspects of water management in South Asia.... Members of the project, which brought together government officials, scholars, business leaders and other experts, produced a final report that was disseminated to policymakers and ultimately promoted technical solutions to regional problems while fostering cooperative relations among the neighboring countries." Karen Theroux, "Strengthening the Work of the United Nations: A Sustained Strategy for Peace," *Carnegie Results* (Spring 2006): 9, available at: http://carnegie.org/fileadmin/Media/Training_Sandbox/spring_06_results.pdf; see also CCNYAR, 2000, 55.

103 Staff member Stephen Del Rosso has been the main program officer supporting the Track II efforts; previously, David Hamburg and David Speedie were involved. And as President Gregorian has pointed out, a prime practitioner of Track II diplomacy was Andrew Carnegie himself, in his fervent behind-the-scenes attempt to persuade former US president Teddy Roosevelt to take a major role in efforts to prevent the outbreak of World War I. Even before that, Carnegie was involved in issues regarding the Spanish-American War and the Philippines in the late 1890s; see Chapter 1; see also Zuckerman, "Track II Diplomacy," 9–10. Thus, the tradition of Track II diplomacy is firmly embedded in the actions of the founder and as his legacy in two of his institutions—the Carnegie Endowment for International Peace and Carnegie Corporation of New York.

104 CCNYAR, 2002–2003, 34. As noted in the 2004 Annual Report, these grantees' main activities included "unofficial diplomatic efforts to assist decisionmakers in India and Pakistan in designing nuclear risk-reduction and escalation control measures considered useful and credible by both sides." CCNYAR, 2004, 31.

105 CCNYAR, 2004, 31. Pugwash stands for the Pugwash Conference on Science and World Affairs.

106 CCNY, "Programs and Accomplishments, 1996–2006, International Peace and Security," 5, CCNYO.

107 Stephen Del Rosso, personal communication with the author, February 10, 2013.

108 CCNYAR, 2004–2005, 128.

109 CCNYAR, 2006, 30.

110 CCNY, "Program Budget Paper, Fiscal Year 2009–2010, International Peace and Security," 9, CCNYO.

111 See, for example, Laura Rosen, "The Cable: New White House WMD Coordinator Attended Unofficial US-Iran Dialogue in His Private Capacity," *Foreign Policy*, February 3, 2009.

112 Ibid.

113 CCNY, "Program Strategy/Budget Paper, Fiscal Year 2010–2011, International Program," 25, CCNYO.

114 See Kelsey Davenport, "History of Official Proposals on the Iranian Nuclear Issue,"

Arms Control Association, January 2013, available at: http://www.armscontrol.org/factsheets/iran_Nuclear_Proposals (accessed February 15, 2013).

115   As one Corporation grantee reported in confidence to program staff, "If our fingerprints can be found, we have failed." Stephen Del Rosso, personal communication with the author, February 17, 2014.

116   Stephen Del Rosso, personal communication with the author, February 10, 2013.

117   The parties meet, if not regularly, at least with sufficient frequency to give a focus to the Track II discussions and offer a "receptor site" for any suggestions or recommendations that emerge from those discussions. Ibid.; CCNY, "Program Strategy/Budget Paper, Fiscal Year 2010–2011, International Program," 24–25, CCNYO.

118   See, for example, CCNYAR, 2004–2005, 27–28, and 2011, 6 (University of California at San Diego); 2004–2005, 30, 36 (National Committee on American Foreign Policy); 2002–2003, 111, 2011, and 2004–2005, 126–127 (Social Science Research Council); 2001, 41–42, 2002–2003, 111, and 2011, 30 (Institute for Foreign Policy Analysis); 2010, 16 (Stanford University); and 2004–2005, 29, and 2011, 7 (Center for Strategic and International Studies). Each grantee contributed differently; for example, the Institute on Global Conflict and Cooperation at the University of California, under the leadership of Susan Shirk, analyzed and indexed the Track II multilateral dialogues on the denuclearization of the Korean peninsula. The National Committee on American Foreign Policy continued an active dialogue with the North Koreans. The Social Science Research Council, with support from the Corporation, has since 1995 conducted behind-the-scenes work under the leadership of Leon Sigal and provided background information to policy officials and the media. The Institute for Foreign Policy Analysis held workshops and conducted research on confidence-building measures. Stanford's Center for International Security and Cooperation, funded since 1983, addressed issues in Track II diplomacy as part of its broader research and training program. The Center for Strategic and International Studies brought together specialists in Russian and North Korean security issues and produced and disseminated a model threat reduction program for North Korea.

119   Zuckerman, "Track II Diplomacy," 11; see also CCNYAR, 2004–2005, 36.

120   Zuckerman, "Track II Diplomacy," 11; Del Rosso, who has attended most of these sessions, gave his own assessment: "These people all have gravitas and since they are not working for the government, they can stand back and give more candid assessments of what was going on.... Several of the policymakers, including those from Asian countries, noted how useful it was to have these experts there to set the framework for discussions and allow issues to be probed and questions to be raised that policymakers could run with or respond to." Ibid., 6.

121   Stephen Del Rosso, personal communication with the author, February 17, 2014.

122   CCNY, "Program Strategy/Budget Papers, Fiscal Year 2010–2011, International Peace and Security," 24, CCNYO.

123   CCNY, "Program Strategy/Budget Papers, Fiscal Year 2010–2011, International Program," 21, CCNYO. The other foundations are the John D. and Catherine T. MacArthur Foundation, the Hewlett Foundation, the Ploughshares Fund, and other funders in the Peace and Security Funders Group. The Corporation annually spent $6.4 million between 2008 and 2011, making it the largest donor in the field at the time. Ibid.

124   As discussed more fully in Chapters 4, 5, and 6, work on and about Russia, on the margins of Corporation discussions since World War I, directly entered the grants portfolio in the late 1940s through the support of the Russian Research Center at Harvard University until the mid-1960s. From 1983 to 1994, the Soviet Union featured as the geographic center of the Corporation's US-based international grant-making and geopolitical concerns.

125   CCNY, "Program Development Papers, 1998–2000, International Peace and Security," 7, Folder 5, Box 22, Series I.D, CCNY Records, RBML-CUL.

126 Ibid.

127 CCNYAR, 1998, 38, 41.

128 CCNYAR, 2000, 63.

129 Ibid., 63–64.

130 See, for example, discussion of the International Research and Exchanges Board in CCNYAR, 1999, 41.

131 Under the initiative, grants were recommended for a series of study groups. "The study groups will explore such topics as the safety of Russia's weapons of mass destruction, the interplay between economic reform and political democratization, the problems of social cohesion, and the relationship between the central government and the regional authorities. The participants will be Western and Russian experts with diverse intellectual and professional backgrounds, representing the academe, research institutions, business and journalism communities, and nongovernmental organizations." CCNY, "Program Papers, October 1999–October 2000, International Peace and Security," 15, Folder 5, Box 22, Series I.D, CCNY Records, RBML-CUL.

132 CCNY, "Programs and Accomplishments, 1996–2006, International Peace and Security," 3, CCNYO. This initiative led to continuing support for long-term dialogue-promoting grantees, as presented in CCNYAR, 2002–2003, 27 (Aspen Institute Congressional Program and Aspen Strategy Group) and 29 (Conflict Management Group and Harvard's Kennedy School of Government program).

133 Support to PONARS was renewed over many years, including, eventually, support for expansion into other areas of foreign policy interest to both the United States and Russia, such as Eurasia. In addition to the face-to-face and electronic discussions within the network, the group's annual conference in Washington, DC, gives young scholars the opportunity to share their findings with policymakers in Washington. See the discussion of the Center for Strategic and International Studies in CCNYAR, 2002–2003, 104.

134 CCNY, "Program Papers, October 2001–October 2002, International Peace and Security," 77, Folder 5, Box 22, Series I.D, CCNY Records, RBML-CUL.

135 Ibid., 77–79.

136 Andrei Shleifer and Daniel Treisman, "A Normal Country: Russia After Communism," *Journal of Economic Perspectives* 19, no. 1 (2005): 151–174; see also CCNY, "Program Papers, October 2000–October 2001, International Peace and Security," 66–67, Folder 5, Box 22, Series I.D, CCNY Records, RBML-CUL.

137 As presented in CCNYAR, 2001, 35 (American International Health Alliance); 36 (Columbia University); 37 (Council on Foreign Relations and Emory University); 36–37 (Conflict Management Group); 38 (George Washington University East West Institute); and 39 (Richard Nixon Library and Birthplace Foundation).

138 Ibid., 36 (Carnegie Endowment for International Peace, for the Moscow Center) and 38 (Moscow School of Political Studies and International Institute for Strategic Studies).

139 Ibid., 39 (Rutgers University).

140 Ibid., 35–36 (Aspen Institute, for the Aspen Study Group), 36 (Aspen Institute, for the Congressional Program), and 39 (Richard Nixon Library and Birthplace Foundation).

141 CCNY, "Program Papers, October 2002–October 2003," 60–61, CCNYO.

142 Program staff also sought to maintain close connections and complementary activities with other foundation donors, including the MacArthur Foundation, the Ford Foundation, the Eurasia Foundation, and the Open Society Institute. These foundations, recognizing the declining support for Russia from other foundations, were working together and considering working with some of the new foundations in Russia, such as the New Eurasia Foundation.

143 For a review of USAID support in Russia and Eurasia, see USAID, "20 Years of USAID

Economic Growth Assistance in Europe and Eurasia," July 24, 2013, available at: http://www.usaid.gov/where-we-work/europe-and-eurasia/20-years-economic-growth-assistance.

144   CCNY, "Program Strategy and Budget Papers, 2003, International Peace and Security," 25, CCNYO.

145   Ibid.

146   CCNYAR, 2002–2003, 103.

147   Two working groups contributed to building collaboration between US and Russian experts on multilateral relations—a RAND group working on Russian relationships with NATO and an Atlantic Council group working on ways to integrate Russia with the European Union; ibid., 102–103, 106. Participants briefed policymakers, testified before Congress, and published op-ed pieces. The Corporation trustees, president, staff members, and grantees recognized that this was a long-term undertaking, but agreed that it was worth the investment to build strong relations between the United States, Russia, and European countries.

148   The military-to-military program connecting Russia and the United States was initiated in 1991 by Robert D. Blackwill, with Corporation funding. By 2006, with continued support and a parallel program focusing on the Black Sea region, the grant's results included having reached "910 participants in a capacity-building program aimed at senior military officers and foreign policy decisionmakers from 11 Black Sea countries (including Russia) and the United States. Informal tracking of participants has shown career advancement for 60 percent of them." CCNY, "Programs and Accomplishments, 1996–2006, International Peace and Security," 4, CCNYO.

149   See, for instance, CCNYAR, 2002–2003, 103 (Aspen Institute, for the Congressional Program).

150   By fiscal year 2006, the New Eurasia Foundation had fulfilled Corporation stipulations and the foundation was launched with a $1 million onetime Corporation grant. The foundation, based in Russia, was "a collaborative endeavor among American, Russian, and European public and private funders to foster democracy in Russia. [It] has replaced the Eurasia Foundation in Russia." The Foundation is still going strong to this day. See the website for the New Eurasia Foundation at: www.neweurasia.ru/en/.

151   CCNYAR, 2004–2005, 129 (Mercy Corps), and 12 (Moscow School of Political Studies). Support for PONARS continued as Corporation staff members remained convinced of the importance of bringing younger scholars together from Russia, the United States, and, increasingly, Eurasia to meet with senior policymakers and experts from these three areas and develop strong ties for their work. With a new focus on Eurasia, PONARS relocated to the George Washington Elliott School of International Affairs, after having been located at Harvard University (late 1990s), the Council on Foreign Relations (2000 to 2001), the Center for Strategic and International Studies (2001 to 2007), and Georgetown University (2007 to 2009). See the website for PONARS Eurasia at: www.ponarseurasia.org; see also CCNYAR, 2010, 12–13.

152   CCNY, "Strategy and Program Budget Papers, Fiscal Year 2008–2009, International Program," 37, CCNYO (emphasis in original). Eurasia was entering the discussions more regularly. One focus was around energy resources in Eurasian countries. At meetings held at the Corporation from 2007 to 2008, this was a major topic of interest, especially the role of Eurasia as a "geostrategically important region that was unfolding as a battle ground for influence and access to energy resources by the United States, Russia, China and other major powers"; ibid., 38; see also Eugene Rumer, "Eurasia: A World Order," *Carnegie Reporter* 3, no. 4 (Spring 2006): 2–11. In addition, in 2007 the Corporation's internal structure changed to bring together all geographically related programs under the overarching international and national programs. The new International Program now comprised grants related to Russia, weapons of mass destruction, new dimensions of security, African institutions of higher education, women's undergraduate

education in Africa, and revitalization of public libraries in Africa. The National Program comprised grants programs on educational reform, democracy, immigrant integration and migration, special projects, and the Carnegie Scholars Program (the last three areas having extensive international dimensions); Vartan Gregorian, "Carnegie Corporation of New York: Meeting the Challenges of the Twenty-First Century," October 1, 2007, CCNYO.

153 These were the Brookings Institution, the Carnegie Endowment for International Peace, the Center for Strategic and International Studies, the Council on Foreign Relations, the Stimson Center, the Nixon Center, the Aspen Institute, the World Security Institute, and others. Some new institutions were brought into the mix not only for funding but also to participate in the discussions: the New America Foundation, the Center for American Progress, the Center for New American Security, and others. The university-based programs also continued to be supported, particularly those at Harvard University, Stanford University, and MIT, as well as the University of California system including Berkeley and San Diego.

154 CCNY, "Strategy and Program Budget Papers, Fiscal Year 2008–2009, International Program," 38, CCNYO.

155 Ibid., 39.

156 With the reorientation of program goals, longtime grantees such as the Center for Strategic and International Studies shifted to bring Russian and Eurasian emerging experts to the United States to interact with their US counterparts; CCNYAR, 2011, 7. Support also continued to the Carnegie Moscow Center and its programs in Moscow and Russia comparable to those of the Corporation; CCNYAR, 2011, 6. Track II activities related to Russia and US concerns were funded at the National Defense University and Georgetown University (CCNYAR, 2009, 14), the Nixon Center (CCNYAR, 2009, 15), and the International Institute for Sustained Dialogue (Dartmouth conference) (CCNYAR, 2011, 10). Key areas included security issues, foreign policy concerns, and relations with post-Soviet Eurasia. Continued commitment to the next generation and strengthening young scholars in the United States and in Russia led to a joint program at the University of Maryland Center for International Security Studies and the Moscow-based Institute for US and Canada Studies; CCNYAR, 2011, 13. The aim was to undertake "training in research initiatives aimed at producing a cohort of security specialists in both the United States and Russia"; see CCNY, "Program Strategy/Budget Papers, Fiscal Year 2009–2010, International Program," 14, CCNYO.

157 This commitment is reminiscent of the early 1960s, when trustee Frederick Osborn, taking note of the extensive efforts of the Corporation concerning Russia, urged similar attention to China as an increasingly important and not well-understood global power (see Chapters 5 and 6). In this era, as in others, the leadership and trustees tried to work within the charter constraints while developing a focus on China, as evidenced by the grants discussed in this section. A report from China expert Harry Harding was commissioned to advise on the relevant programs in this era. For an early discussion about China, see CCNY, "Strategy and Budget Paper, Fiscal Year 2008–2009, International Program," 38–40, CCNYO.

158 For some of the early grants, see CCNYAR, 2008, 19 (Carnegie Endowment for International Peace and the Financial Services Volunteer Corps); for the National Academy, see CCNY, "Strategy and Budget Paper, Fiscal Year 2008–2009 International Program," 39, CCNYO.

159 CCNY, "Program Budget/Strategy Papers, Fiscal Year 2009–2010, International Program," 15, CCNYO. Among the new grantees receiving support along with the continuing cluster of institutional partners were: the New America Foundation, to strengthen programs on Russia, China, and Iran; the College of William and Mary, for a study on negotiating with terrorists and radicals undertaken by Mitchell B. Reiss; and George Washington University's Elliott

School, for a new project examining non-American perspectives on a wide range of foreign policy and security issues. New approaches for connecting think tanks, academic centers, and the public included: the Tobin Project, for online foreign policy discussions; New York University's Center for Global Affairs; the Choices Program at Brown University's Watson Institute for International Studies; and the New York–based Center for Media and Security. See CCNY, "Strategy/Budget Papers, Fiscal Year 2010–2011, International Program," 30–35, CCNYO.

160 CCNYAR, 1997, 16.

161 Kishkovsky mentioned a pending World Bank loan of $50 million to strengthen social science education at Russian universities, including Tomsk State University, and fund Internet connectivity at thirty-three higher education institutions through the Open Society Institute (established by philanthropist George Soros). As she pointed out, "33 Internet centers have been established at various higher education institutions. One Moscow-based institute, which is pioneering distance learning, has increased its student body from 5,000 to 32,000 and sends out over three tons of course materials monthly"; Sophia Kishkovsky, "A Bright Future for Russian Higher Education," *Carnegie Reporter* 1, no. 1 (Summer 2000): 4, available at: http://carnegie. org/publications/carnegie-reporter/single/view/article/item/3/. A student she interviewed made a point, which the Corporation shared, about the future of Russian higher education grant-making: "This is a period of transition with an old intelligentsia that does not understand the new system and no new intelligentsia that can say how better to do things…. I know that we are capable of changing this situation for the better…. In my opinion, the situation in Russia will be changed by those in my generation who are going from one system to another, through this great change, and didn't become pessimists, those who are not saying that everything is falling apart, but who are doing something. The future is ours"; ibid., 12.

162 CCNYAR, 1999, 41. See also American Council of Learned Societies, "ACLS Humanities Program in Belarus, Russia, and Ukraine," available at: www.acls.org/programs/hp/ (accessed September 14, 2012).

163 Karen Theroux, "Strengthening Scholarship and Research in the Former Soviet Union," *Carnegie Review* (April 2008), 6, available at: http://carnegie.org/fileadmin/Media/Publications/ PDF/carnegiereview_russia2008.pdf. The program team also noted the need for greater coordination among the several donors in support of higher education in the former Soviet Union. The intention was to develop an advisory group in 1998, bringing together representatives from the World Bank, the Ford Foundation, the Open Society Institute, the Spencer Foundation, and the Bertelsmann Foundation in Germany, among others. The Corporation participated in other initiatives as well, including the MacArthur Foundation–funded Russian Science Initiative, a large consortium of foundations and governments engaged in economic research and education, with a focus on Russia and the Ukraine, and the faculty-incentive program in the social sciences and humanities already under way between the Open Society Institute and the US Information Agency. For the full program discussion, see CCNY, "Program Development Papers, October 1999–October 2000, Higher Education in the Former Soviet Union," 1–23, Folder 5, Box 22, Series I.D, CCNY Records, RBML-CUL.

164 Ruble described the process: "Soon … we began the process of conducting hundreds of interviews throughout the FSU [Former Soviet Union], which pointed out the number-one problem: everybody was underpaid. Ultimately, however, we would learn the more serious result of the economic collapse for academia was isolation. With the disintegration of the Soviet Union, the local and regional scholarly networks that sustained indigenous intellectual communities had been weakened, if not totally destroyed. We felt American funders could end some of the isolation by creating horizontal networks among scholars." Theroux, "Strengthening Scholarship and Research in the Former Soviet Union," 4.

165 Arsenian built on the recommendations of the needs assessment team from the Kennan Institute and convinced two colleagues in Moscow—the head of the Open Society Institute's higher education program, Andrey Kortunov, and his deputy director, Irina Laktionova—to join her in site visits across the country. As she noted, "We visited a dozen Russian universities across the country and met with 500 to 600 academics to gauge their perceptions of their needs. In essence, we aimed to test the findings of our needs assessment.... What we learned confirmed the basic recommendations.... And it led us to modify our program through the creation of university-based, autonomous centers that could serve as umbrellas for an array of academic activities ... we approached the Russian Ministry of Education and Science and held a number of meetings with then deputy minister Alexei Borisovich Vinogradov, our proposal to the ministry reflected the needs identified by Russian academics. This was a key factor in getting the Ministry to join us through financial support and endorsement"; Theroux, "Strengthening Scholarship and Research in the Former Soviet Union," 6–7. One of the advantages in Arsenian's leadership of this effort was her early schooling in Moscow, her fluency in Russian, and her deep experience with the Corporation as well as with American higher education. Her background and experiences greatly facilitated the development of a program that otherwise could have been very sensitive for an American-based international philanthropy.

166 "The Challenge: Academic Freedom in the Former Soviet Union," *Carnegie Reporter* (Summer 2000): 13, available at: http://carnegie.org/publications/carnegie-reporter/single/view/article/item/4/. David Speedie, program chair of the International Peace and Security Program since 1993, commented on how this activity reinforced other efforts at the Corporation: "'For the past decade, we've been deeply involved in the Russia question ... bringing leaders in the Russian military, political and scientific fields together with their counterparts in the United States. Together, they've grappled with the security and peace questions faced by these two pivotal world nations and created new and important relationships.... We think this work in the humanities and social sciences is an important investment in the intellectual life of Russia'"; ibid., 14. Gregorian reinforced the commitment by invoking the overarching aim: "If we succeed ... Russian scholars will be integrated into the international intellectual community and that will be a major contribution, not only for Russia and the former states, but for the world"; ibid. The Corporation was making a major commitment to the major goal of supporting the CASEs in all their dimensions, including fellowships for scholars, travel for attendance at conferences and meetings, institutional support, support to hold workshops, conferences, and other institutional outreach and connecting efforts, library publication access, and opportunities to disseminate the research throughout Russia and abroad.

167 The Kennan Institute organized the competitive selection process through a "Request for Proposal" (RFP). The first three institutions supported in 2000 were regional state universities: Tomsk, Voronezh, and Ural State. In 2001, five more were added: Far Eastern, Irkutsk, Kalingrad, Novgorod, and Saratov. In 2003, the final and ninth institution, Rostov State University, was supported, along with an additional four centers, starting in 2003, from outside of Russia in the former Soviet states of Armenia, Azerbaijan, Belarus, and Georgia. Theroux, "Strengthening Scholarship and Research in the Former Soviet Union," 9.

168 Ibid., 17–20. Complementing the work of the American Council of Learned Societies and its fellowships on the humanities, the BRHE program's work on strengthening the sciences, and the nine CASE institutions, the Corporation also supported the Caucasus Research Resource Centers, bringing together the CASEs in Armenia, Azerbaijan, and Georgia, and the National Council for Eurasian and East European Research, to support exchanges and fellowships for the CASEs; ibid. Several other programs were supported either to bolster the work at the individual CASEs or to provide enhanced opportunities for CASE participants: the International Research

and Exchanges Board and its university administration program; Bard College, to strengthen the partnership between St. Petersburg University and Bard in the creation of a liberal arts college, Smolny College; access to American higher education through the University of California at Berkeley; a program at Georgetown University, working with the European University in St. Petersburg; a joint program between the University of Maryland and the Moscow-based School of International Security and World Politics; a program between the University of Michigan and the European University in St. Petersburg; the Civilian Education Project, to enable scholars from the former Soviet Union to return home for teaching appointments; Stanford University, to build on the Internet opportunities for the distance education program in international relations; and Temple University, to help strengthen research methodologies in the social sciences and humanities. Support to the Salzburg Seminar Program focused on strengthening the capacity of university administrators in former Soviet Union institutions. A key program for the CASEs was the journal distribution project at the New School University, which provided subscriptions to scholarly journals and back volumes for the libraries. More details on all of these can be found in the program papers and annual reports from 2000 to 2008.

169   Mark S. Johnson, "Research, Scholarship, and Collaboration: Legacies of Carnegie Corporation of New York's Higher Education in the Former Soviet Union (HEFSU) Initiative, 1998 to 2008," *Carnegie Results* (Spring 2009): 7–8, available at: http://carnegie.org/fileadmin/ Media/Publications/PDF/carnegie_results_spring_09_rev.pdf. For a different perspective on foundation programs based on Princeton University professor Stephen Kotkin's examination of the Ford Foundation support for higher education in Russia, see Scott Jaschik, "Lost Opportunity in Russia," *Inside Higher Education*, January 31, 2007, available at: http://www. insidehighered.com/news/2007/01/31/russia (accessed August 11, 2012).

170   Johnson, "Research, Scholarship, and Collaboration," 10.

171   Ibid., 2.

172   Johnson identified four domains of accomplishments: "publishing high quality academic research in diverse disciplines; linking innovation in the social sciences more directly to university-wide strategies for internationalization; helping to foster external partnerships with private businesses, government agencies and civil society organizations; and working to apply new research to innovative teaching." Ibid., 4–5.

173   Ibid., 6. Johnson also pointed to another sign of the overall success of the HEFSU program: the thousands of scholars who benefited from the grants program and the professional and disciplinary networks. Those networks have also led to the development of a local network in the humanities, a new professional association, and the International Association of Humanities Scholars at Kharkiv National University and Eastern Ukraine, Ibid.,9. Networks, however, often depend on external funding and are frequently not sustained after donor support comes to an end.

174   CCNY, "Strategy/Budget Papers, Fiscal Year 2010–2011, International Program," 51, CCNYO.

175   Ibid. Support in Eurasian CASEs continued with grants to the National Council for Eurasian and East European Research, enabling individual scholars to study at American universities, and with similar programs through the University of California at Berkeley and the University of Michigan; in addition, IREX received continued support for its program with university administrators. Ibid., 52, 64.

176   As staff noted, concerning the Eurasian institutions, "The situation is less positive in other post-Soviet countries … as the economic progress has either not filtered down to academic institutions and communities, or has not been sufficient to reach those societal needs"; CCNY, "Strategy and Budget Papers, Fiscal Year 2011–2012, International Program, Higher Education

in Eurasia," 144, CCNYO. The importance of continuing to connect Russians and Eurasian scholars and university administrators to global networks, as well as providing specialized training, prompted the Corporation to provide another round of funding; ibid., 143–147.

177 Johnson, "Research, Scholarship, and Collaboration," 14–15.

178 Gregorian, "New Directions for Carnegie Corporation of New York," 36.

179 Ibid., 20–21. Staff intended to support activities related to the four areas in order to "understand the relationship between access to vital resources and conflict; explore possible solutions to area-specific problems that have the tension between self-determination and territorial integrity at their core; examine practical applications of multi-tiered assistance strategies and peacebuilding with recommendations tailored to specific conflicts; and assess the efficacy of economic measures as instruments of conflict prevention"; ibid., 21; see also CCNY, "Program Papers, October 1999–October 2000, International Peace and Security," CCNYO.

180 See CCNYAR, 1999, 39, for both Stanford University and the UN Institute. A final grant to the National Endowment for Democracy and Princeton University continued the joint forum on democratic federalism; ibid., 39. The International Peace Academy held a symposium in New York in the fall of 1999 with Corporation funding to mark the one-hundredth anniversary of the first international peace conference at The Hague at the Peace Palace funded by Andrew Carnegie; ibid., 39. The War-Torn Societies Project of the UN Research Institute for Social Development enabled the completion of case studies on Eritrea, Mozambique, Guatemala, and Somalia and wide dissemination of the results to the relevant policymakers; ibid., 40. The Conflict Management Group examined the management of ethnic conflict in the former Soviet Union, prepared materials for policymakers in the former Soviet Union with a particular focus on the Caucasus, and developed a network to monitor ethnic and political conflict in the former Soviet Union; ibid., 40. Significant support of $800,000 for the Project on Ethnic Relations allowed it to continue its on-the-ground peacemaking and peace-building in the midst of conflicts in Eastern and Central Europe, the Balkans, and the former Soviet Union. The Project organized seminars for conflicting groups, distributed widely the results of those meetings, and maintained field offices in the region; ibid. A grant of $600,000 continued support for the program under Graham Allison at Harvard University on strengthening democratic institutions in the former Soviet Union; ibid. With the hiring of Stephen Del Rosso in 1999, the program began to address more systematically ways to build on the Preventing Deadly Conflict Commission's legacy.

181 CCNY, "Program Papers, October 2000–October 2001, International Peace and Security," 72, Folder 5, Box 22, Series I.D, CCNY Records, RBML-CUL. While the other two themes—post-conflict peace-building and sanctions and incentives—would not be directly addressed, nonetheless, because of their close relationship to the topic of self-determination, program staff considered it likely that they would be covered in one or more grants.

182 Ibid., 72–73.

183 Del Rosso, however, as noted earlier, had had deep experience working on issues associated with conflict and conflict prevention from his earlier responsibilities at the State Department, the Pew Charitable Trusts, and the Chicago Council on Foreign Relations. During this period, he also completed a PhD in political science at the University of Pennsylvania focused on self-determination.

184 CCNY, "Program Papers, October 2001–October 2002, International Peace and Security," 85, Folder 5, Box 22, Series I.D, CCNY Records, RBML-CUL.

185 For each of these goals, they maintained the approach of building the research base, sharing lessons across grantees, and identifying policy options. Ibid., 86–87.

186 Ibid., 84. Two relevant initiatives by two other foundations, the Rockefeller Foundation's

global inclusion program and the Rockefeller Brothers Fund's global interdependence initiative, related to issues of globalization but from a slightly different perspective than that of the Corporation, making collaboration more difficult. The focus of the Corporation was specifically on permeable state borders and the relationship of that permeability to conflict. Ibid., 85.

187   Ibid., 84–90.

188   Not only was this a set of issues of historic interest and concern, especially in the American Southwest as well as around the world, but there was increasing recognition internationally of the vital importance of the scarce resource of water and the potential for conflict or competition. The World Bank, the UN Development Program, the Water Science and Technology Board of the National Academy of Sciences, the Global Water Partnership, the Rockefeller Brothers Fund, the Rockefeller Foundation, and the Hewlett Foundation were all working on this issue (Hewlett, for example, was planning a new initiative). Ibid., 88.

189   CCNYAR, 2000, 55. The conceptual and substantive linkages between the two aspects of the program, as noted by Del Rosso, were further underscored by the fact that the headwaters of some of the most important and contentious river systems in the world—such as Kashmir, Kurdish territories, Israel-Palestine, and Tibet—are situated in areas where water scarcity issues overlap with contested borders and self-determination claims.

190   This work was undertaken jointly by the Pacific Institute for Studies in Development, Environment, and Security and Oregon State University. CCNYAR, 2001, 34.

191   CCNY, "Program Papers, October 2001–October 2002, International Peace and Security," 90–92, Folder 5, Box 22, Series I.D, CCNY Records, RBML-CUL.

192   CCNY, "Program Papers, October 2002–October 2003, International Peace and Security," 66, CCNYO.

193   Under the Special Opportunities Fund, with a grant of $250,000, the Corporation joined other foundations in establishing the International Center for Transitional Justice, which tackled the complex human rights violations emanating from the concerns about self-determination, sovereignty, and, now, counterterrorism. CCNYAR, 2001, 54.

194   "As significant as the obstacles are to resolving internal conflicts, they are far greater when the United States and others in the international community do not tap all the knowledge available to them.… In particular, a major disconnect exists between the growing body of scholarship on ethnic conflict, intervention, and nation building—and the policymaking organs of national and international institutions." David Callahan, "The Enduring Challenge: Self-Determination and Ethnic Conflict in the 21st Century," *Carnegie Challenge Paper* (2002): 2, 16–17.

195   The grantees included: the Johns Hopkins University School for Advanced International Studies for a Track II, informal diplomatic effort in South Asia; the Pacific Institute for Studies in Development, Environment, and Security and Oregon State University for research and analysis on particular regions at risk, international workshops involving security and water experts, and the development and expansion of Web-based information resources; and the Environmental Change and Security Project of the Woodrow Wilson International Center for Scholars to facilitate sustained dialogue and collaboration among diverse experts and generate knowledge and policy alternatives on a set of critical water issues. For more details, see CCNYAR, 2000, 55, and 2002–2003, 26–27, 101.

196   See CCNY, "Program Papers, October 2002–October 2003, International Peace and Security," 70–71, CCNYO.

197   CCNY, "Program Strategy and Budget Papers, 2003, International Peace and Security," 21, CCNYO.

198   Office of the President of the United States, "National Security Strategy of the United States, September 2002," 1, available at: http://www.state.gov/documents/organization/63562.pdf.

199 The Rockefeller Brothers Fund, the Rockefeller Foundation, the Ford Foundation, the Open Society Institute, and the German Marshall Fund of the United States were all also working on issues related to globalization, but not through the lens of contested borders and sovereignty leading to failed states; CCNY, "Program Papers, October 2002–October 2003, International Peace and Security," 67–68, CCNYO. Grantees such as the Fund for Peace, the Carr Center for Human Rights at Harvard University, and the Center for International Development and Conflict Management at the University of Maryland had all been addressing a range of issues related to the spread of internal conflict and the potential for failed states; CCNYAR, 2002–2003, 26, 100, 112. The Fund for Peace had attempted to bring together policymakers to arrive at deeper understandings of ways to prevent genocide and mass killings on a regional basis, and the Carr Center had examined the relationship between human rights and military interventions; ibid., 100, 112. The Maryland Center in its Peace and Conflict 2003 report had identified both the limited number of cross-boundary conflicts and a core issue: "In a world of increasing tension, these poor and war-ravaged societies are prone to instability and state failure. This combination of growing tension and vulnerable societies presents crucial challenges to U.S. policymakers"; Barry Rosenberg, "Peace and Conflict 2003: A Surprising Trend Emerges," *Carnegie Results* (Summer 2003): 2, available at: http://carnegie.org/fileadmin/Media/Publications/summer_03peaceandconflict_01.pdf.

200 CCNYAR, 2009, 15.

201 CCNYAR, 2001, 33; 2004–2005, 24, 25, 122; and 2002–2003, 108.

202 CCNYAR, 2004–2005, 102.

203 Theroux, "Strengthening the Work of the United Nations," 11–12.

204 CCNYAR, 2004–2005, 56.

205 The assistant secretary-general for peacebuilding support, Carolyn McAskie, in a Corporation interview, raised the concern: "Development holds the key, she says. 'There's a recognized correlation between neglect and conflict, with the most at-risk places not on anybody's donor list.' Political exclusion, economic frustration, and despair are dangerous because 'where there's little hope, the seeds of conflict will find fertile ground.'... The core rationale behind the Peacebuilding Commission ... is helping the international community bridge the crucial conflict-development gap." Karen Theroux, "Peace in Our Time?" *Carnegie Reporter* 4, no. 4 (Spring 2008): 33, available at: http://carnegie.org/publications/carnegie-reporter/single/view/article/item/202/.

206 CCNY, "Programs and Accomplishments, 1996–2006, International Peace and Security," 6, CCNYO.

207 Ibid.

208 Ibid., 7.

209 CCNY, "International Program, Budget Request for FY 2007–2008," August 2007, 4, CCNYO.

210 Stephen Del Rosso, personal communication with the author, February 10, 2013.

211 CCNYAR, 2000, 54 (University of Denver); 2002–2003, 25 (East-West Center); 2004–2005, 121 (University of California at San Diego); and 2006, 17 (Future Generations). Additional activities with continuing grantees included analyzing ways to reform US post-reconstruction efforts through the CSIS (CCNYAR, 2006, 17), advising the UN on the Peacebuilding Commission through the International Peace Academy (CCNYAR, 2002–2003, 100), and engaging in additional research on national and international decision-making structures, such as work with the Stimson Center on the rule of law in postconflict settings (CCNYAR, 2004–2005, 25).

212 For a full list of grantees, see Theroux, "Peace in Our Time?" 31. The list includes other grantees primarily engaged in research, such as the University of Colorado at Boulder, the Center

for Global Development, the University of Cambridge, Duke University, Emory University, Princeton University (focused on Afghanistan), and the Woodrow Wilson International Center for Scholars (for research and training mainly focused on Burundi). Also funded was research on the crucial state-building initiatives in Bosnia and Herzegovina under the Dayton Peace Accords Project.

213 CCNYAR, 2010, 57.

214 CCNYAR, 2009, 10, 12; 2010, 15.

215 Although not specifically focused on Afghanistan, the RAND Corporation has supported the work of James Dobbins and the City University of New York's Global Center on the responsibility to protect and the role of local actors in humanitarian interventions. Other locally focused work includes the post-earthquake state-building work in Haiti of the RAND Corporation, the Institute of State Effectiveness in the lead role in the 2010 donor conference on assistance to Afghanistan, contributions from the Center for Strategic and International Studies that led to reshaping the US development assistance package to Pakistan, and the Public International Law and Policy Group's pro bono legal assistance in the transition of southern Sudan to the new state of South Sudan and in Uganda. Emory University has assisted with regional West Africa security concerns, particularly in Liberia, Guinea, and Sierra Leone. CCNYAR, 2002–2003, 26; 2004–2005, 121; 2006, 17, 18; and 2010, 12.

216 CCNYAR, 2011, 8.

217 CCNYAR, 2010, 14.

218 CCNY, "Strategy/Budget Papers, Fiscal Year 2010–2011, International Program," 28–30, CCNYO. Similar to other parts of the program, staff recognized the value of building capacity for the next generation of analysts. In this instance, as in Russia, the analysts could not be only American or European but needed to be from the countries themselves so that local policies could be shaped by local scholars and practitioners.

219 This effort should find receptive policymakers at the World Bank; see World Bank, *Conflict, Security, and Development, World Development Report 2011* (Washington, DC: World Bank, 2011). Although no foundation provided support for this report, Corporation grantee Bruce Jones was a senior adviser to the team that prepared it (xiii).

220 CCNYAR, 2011, 13. For the complementary grants on peace-building that were funded in the following year (including those supported through a joint call for proposals with the Canadian International Development Research Centre), see Social Science Research Council, "African Peacebuilding Network," available at: http://www.ssrc.org/programs/apn/; and CCNY, "Eliciting and Applying Local Research Knowledge for Peacebuilding and Statebuilding (Africa)," April 4, 2012, available at: http://carnegie.org/news/press-releases/story/news-action/single/view/eliciting-and-applying-local-research-knowledge-for-peacebuilding-and-statebuilding-africa/ (accessed February 15, 2013).

221 CCNYAR, 1997, 17.

222 Gregorian had written a presidential essay in the summer of 2001 on this theme that was subsequently revised and published as a book; Vartan Gregorian, *Islam: A Mosaic, Not a Monolith* (Washington, DC: Brookings Institution Press, 2003). In 2003 David Speedie, former program chair of International Peace and Security, was asked to serve as special adviser to the president and develop the groundwork for an Islam Initiative project. Wiesner designed the program strategy, based on prior foundation activities as well as consultations with others in the field. In recognition of its global reach, the Islam Initiative became part of the International Program in the fall of 2007, following the restructuring of the Corporation's grants programs.

223 CCNY, "Strategy and Budget Papers, 2008–2009, Islam Initiative," 40–41, CCNYO.

224 Ibid., 40.

225 CCNYAR, 2008, 8.

226 SSRC, "Academia in the Public Sphere Grants Program," available at: http://www.ssrc. org/programs/academia-in-the-public-sphere-grants (accessed July 29, 2012). As noted by program staff in 2011, the program had been favorably reviewed by an external evaluator: "The program was particularly successful in building first-time linkages between Islamic and area studies specialists with communication departments and journalism schools on university campuses. The program has had several layers of impact: Individual impacts on the creators and users of content, which led to broadcasts, podcasts, web sites, editorials, workshops with journalists, and dozens of town meetings; institutional impact on the winning centers, which have increased their public and campus visibility through new outreach and teaching programs in the field of Islamic and area studies; and impact on the Title VI system, as the majority of the nation's 125 Title VI national resource centers applied for grants and both winning and losing centers received advice and coaching from SSRC [Social Science Research Council], improving their chances for further funding from Title VI for outreach programs." CCNY, "Strategy/Budget Papers, Fiscal Year 2010–2011, International Programs," 38, CCNYO.

227 CCNYAR, 2010, 18.

228 CCNYAR, 2008, 8. A small number of other grants supported the follow-up activities of the Carnegie Scholars and policy outreach with the Aspen Institute. Building on Carnegie Scholar initiatives at Northwestern University, the African Studies Program was supported to expand work specifically on African Islamic studies; CCNYAR, 2006, 44. Robert Pape, a Carnegie Scholar, received support to build from his Carnegie Scholarship work on suicide terrorism to develop a center for data collection, publication, and outreach on terrorism and counterterrorism strategies; CCNYAR, 2004–2005, 60; see also Karen Theroux, "The Truth Behind Suicide Terrorism: A Carnegie Scholar's Pioneering Research Project Aims to Dispel Myths and Reshape Policy," *Carnegie Results* (Fall 2009), available at: http://carnegie.org/fileadmin/Media/Publications/PDF/carnegie_results_fall09.pdf. To connect scholars with the policy community, grants backed the Aspen Institute's Congressional Education Forum on Islam, where the Corporation has joined other funders, including the Ford Foundation; CCNYAR, 2009, 19.

229 CCNY, "Strategy and Budget Papers, Fiscal Year 2008–2009, Islam Initiative," 41, CCNYO.

230 See, for example, Caryle Murphy, "The Library of Alexandria: A Treasure House of Knowledge Rises Again," *Carnegie Reporter* 5, no. 4 (Spring 2010): 2–10, available at: http://carnegie.org/publications/carnegie-reporter/single/view/article/item/248/; CCNYAR, 2009, 19 (Bibliotheca Alexandria); 2010, 18 (Institute for Advanced Study); and 2011, 16 (Yale University Press).

231 CCNYAR, 2010, 17, 18.

232 Ibid., 17. Further facilitating the outreach efforts of specialists, the University of Arizona was supported to create an online directory of programs and expertise in the field. CCNYAR, 2009, 19.

233 CCNY, "Program Budget/Strategy Papers, Fiscal Year 2009–2010, International Programs," 20, CCNYO.

234 CCNYAR, 2009, 19.

235 Ibid., 19–20.

236 CCNYAR, 2008, 8, and 2009, 20.

237 See R. J. Smith, "Media Council Dialogue Summary: Media and the Muslim World: Enriching the American Dialogue," September 29–30, 2009, Paley Center for Media, available at: http://assets.paleycenter.org/assets/media-council/Documents/Media-and-the-Muslim-World-Paley-Center-Report.pdf (accessed August 20, 2012).

238 For a fuller discussion, see CCNY, "Strategy/Budget Papers, 2011–2012, International Program," 128–133, CCNYO.

239 Ibid., 130.

240 One approach is to ensure continued resources for the research, networks, and outreach. Since the Corporation remains one of the most significant donors in the field, staff members have been committed to attracting other donors. In 2008 the Corporation and the Rockefeller Brothers Fund brought in other funders to establish a donors group. Staff members have also attended meetings of funders based in the Middle East; ibid., 133. The grant-making related to research and capacity building in the Arab region and some centers of excellence in the United States continues as of this writing.

241 CCNYAR, 1997, 16.

242 For nearly the first two years, from 1997 to 1999, program staff members remained the same: Rosenfield as chair, Richardson and Adubifa as program officers, and Johnson as program associate.

243 For the first time, Jefferson Murphy's book *Creative Philanthropy* was used in planning a new program at the Corporation. Staff found another volume to be of great value as well: James S. Coleman, with David Court, *University Development in the Third World: The Rockefeller Foundation Experience* (Tarrytown, NY: Pergamon Press, 1993). For more information on the Rockefeller Foundation program, see Rockefeller Archive Center, 100 Years: The Rockefeller Foundation, "Education: University Development," available at: Rockefeller100.org/exhibits/show/education/university-development (accessed February 22, 2014).

244 The structural adjustment programs of the World Bank and the International Monetary Fund in the 1970s and 1980s encouraged governments to reduce their investments in higher education; Corporation and Rockefeller and Ford Foundation programs related to higher education institutions also came to a close at that time. For African leadership responses, see UN Economic and Social Council/ Economic Commission for Africa, "Report of the Third/AAU Conference of Vice Chancellors, Presidents, and Rectors of Institutions of Higher Learning in Africa," February 19, 1987. Long-standing grantee Professor Walter Kamba, the first vice chancellor of the University of Zimbabwe, marshaled a scathing response to the initial document of the World Bank's major review of education from his vice chancellor colleagues, who called the World Bank plan "neocolonialist." Kamba himself said, "University cutbacks would keep the continent in 'a state of dependency for all time' by undermining the drive to train African professionals and technicians who can replace expatriate experts"; Steve Askin, "College Crisis Across Africa," September 23, 1988, *Christian Science Monitor*. The final document did not revise the Bank's policy; see World Bank, *Education in Sub-Saharan Africa: Policies for Adjustment, Revitalization, and Expansion* (Washington, DC: World Bank, 1988). For a detailed review, see Joel Samoff and Bidemi Carrol, "Conditions, Coalitions, and Influence: The World Bank and Higher Education in Africa," February 7, 2004, paper presented at the annual conference of the Comparative and International Education Society, Salt Lake City, March 8–12, 2004.

245 The Ford and Rockefeller Foundations and Carnegie Corporation participated in both of these groups. For an example of the Working Group, see Bill Saint and Kees van den Bosch, "Donors to African Education: Working Group on Higher Education," *NORRAG News*, January 11, 1991, available at: http://www.norrag.org/issues/article/180/en/donors-to-african-education (accessed July 31, 2012). A Corporation-funded meeting reviewed these experiences and others in 2003; Burton Bollag, "Improving Tertiary Education in Sub-Saharan Africa: Things That Work," report of a regional training conference held in Accra, Ghana, September 2003, World Bank Africa Region Human Development Working Paper Series, available at: http://siteresources.worldbank.org/INTAFRREGTOPEDUCATION/Resources/444659-1212165766431/ED_

Tertiary_education_SSA.pdf (accessed July 31, 2012). For the Association for the Development of Education in Africa website, see www.adeanet.org.

246 Association of African Universities and the World Bank, *Revitalizing Universities in Africa: Strategy and Guidelines* (Washington, DC: World Bank, 1997). One of the model institutions was the University of Cape Town under the leadership of former vice chancellor Stuart Saunders and then–vice chancellor Mamphela Ramphele, both grantees and longtime associates of the Corporation. Cape Town provided a viable model of institutional transformation in blending equity and excellence.

247 Jennifer F. Klot, "New Directions for Africa: Trends in Economic Development, Governance, and Knowledge Use," report of the meeting convened by Carnegie Corporation of New York, November 9–11, 1997, *Carnegie Meeting Papers* (undated); CCNY, "Program Paper, October 1998–October 2000, International Development," 2, Box 22, Series I.D, CCNY Records, RBML-CUL.

248 CCNY, "Program Development Papers, October 1998–October 2000, International Development," 17. The paper concluded with the guidance provided by Kenneth Prewitt, then serving as president of the Social Science Research Council and also as a consultant to the Corporation on higher education in general; Prewitt was a longtime colleague and co-funder of activities in Africa when he was vice president of the Rockefeller Foundation. He noted that "African countries are confronting a set of trends faced by universities throughout the world." These included "the promotion of privatization, fee-based education, and vocational training." He expressed concern that "the public interest element of higher education is in serious danger of being lost. That is, there will be declining capacity to conduct basic research, to debate and refine national values, to influence policy, and to build continuity across generations"; ibid, 19.

249 Gregorian, "New Directions," 41.

250 Ibid., 45.

251 Ibid.

252 Ibid., 47. In addition, after consulting with UK and US librarians concerned about libraries in Africa, staff members concluded: "In the resource scarce environment of Africa, public libraries are seen by many as the logical information hub. Their role in improving literacy levels, increasing access by students and the general public to books, journals, and eventually information technologies, and providing a quiet haven for study is potentially significant. Public libraries have the mandate to serve as a democratic source of information and knowledge, but the low priority given them by governments and by public, private, and international funders has led to a severe deterioration of stock and services. With the exception of those in South Africa, most are in a parlous state." Ibid.

253 CCNY, "Program Papers, October 1999–October 2000, International Development," 1, Box 22, Series I.D, CCNY Records, RBML-CUL.

254 The discussions included, from the Rockefeller Foundation, Gordon Conway, president, Lincoln Chen, vice president, and Joyce Moock, associate vice president; Gregorian led the Corporation's discussions, with Rosenfield as staff. The idea for a partnership stemmed from the Rockefeller Foundation's commitment to revitalizing Makerere University following the destructive years for Uganda under Idi Amin and from Gregorian's commitment to strengthening universities in Africa. Without both of these prior conditions, it is unlikely that the larger foundation partnership would have developed.

255 CCNY, "Program Papers, October 1999–October 2000, International Development," 5–8.

256 The results of the studies showed that "the University of Dar es Salaam has incorporated targets for increasing the percentage of women in the student body and on the academic staff

into its strategic plan; a university committee has been appointed to design a plan to achieve the objective. The governing bodies of Makerere University have approved a plan to address women's concerns, and a committee has been appointed to determine how best to implement the plan"; CCNY, "Program Papers, October 1999–October 2000, International Development," 11. The first grants reinforced these accomplishments; CCNYAR, 2001, 22.

257 At the University of Dar es Salaam, the energetic and creative vice chancellor, Matthew Luhanga, had been advising the Corporation from the beginning of this effort and made it clear why the focus on working with the vice chancellors and university senate–approved strategic plans was vitally important for sustainability, a point endorsed by Gregorian and the program staff.

258 CCNYAR, 1999, 45.

259 CCNY, "Program Papers, October 1999–October 2000, International Development," 15.

260 Proposed partners included the Ford Foundation, the Rockefeller Foundation, the Open Society Institute, the Mellon Foundation, the Kellogg Foundation, the Aga Khan Foundation, the MacArthur Foundation, and the Gates Library Foundation (the 1997 precursor of the Bill and Melinda Gates Foundation). Recognizing the crucial importance of bilateral and multilateral donors in sustaining development initiatives undertaken by any foundation, staff members also recommended working with the International Development Research Centre, the US Agency for International Development, the Swedish International Development Cooperation Agency, the Norwegian Agency for Development Cooperation, the Danish International Development Agency, and the British Department for International Development, as well as the UN agencies, such as the UN Development Program and UNESCO, the International Telecommunication Union, and continuing the partnership with the World Bank.

261 The search, which also involved then-program chair Rosenfield, drew on advice and guidance from colleagues throughout the African continent, as well as in the World Bank and in European initiatives relating to African education. Matos had been vice chancellor of Eduardo Modlane University in Mozambique and executive director of the Association of African Universities. By mid-2000, the program nearly completely changed staff. Akin Adubifa left in 2000 and became the executive director of the Nigerian Academy of Sciences; Yolonda Richardson had already left by 1999 to assume leadership responsibilities at Africare, a grantee from the 1990s, and soon became senior vice president. Gregorian asked Rosenfield in 2000 to assume the chair of the newly formed Carnegie Scholars Program and to serve as special adviser to the new vice president, Neil Grabois, whose responsibilities included strategic planning and program coordination.

262 As stated in the program paper for 1999–2000, "Evaluation is envisioned as a central mechanism to facilitate accountability and learning within the program.... Each element—the strategy developed by the Corporation, the strategy as interpreted by grantees, and implementation—will contribute to the success of the program, ... clear standards of performance and accomplishment ... will be communicated to grantees and partners.... Succinct, common sense information on program performance will be made available for review by Corporation staff members and the Board. The consultant will also be asked to address the problem of taking best practices and going to scale." CCNY, "Program Papers, October 1999–October 2000, International Development," 17. Even before the Corporation had made a commitment to programmatic evaluation, the International Development Program had hired a consultant, Johann Mouton, a professor from the University of Stellenbosch in South Africa, to establish an evaluation plan for the university-strengthening grants, with milestones to assess grantee progress. He and his team provided ongoing advice to the Corporation and the African universities.

263 "Criteria for selecting universities to receive support through the new initiative include: Being located in a country undergoing systemic public policy reform.... Supporting innovation,

particularly through the use of new technologies, to better position the institutions to meet the specific needs of their countries.... Engaging in a strategic planning process in which a key element is a commitment to helping build national capacity for social and economic development.... Having creative, broad-based institutional leadership." Carnegie Corporation of New York, Rockefeller Foundation, Ford Foundation, and John D. and Catherine T. MacArthur Foundation, "Four Foundations Launch $100 Million Initiative in Support of Higher Education in African Countries" (press release), April 24, 2000, available at: http://carnegie.org/news/press-releases/story/news-action/single/view/four-foundations-launch-100-million-initiative-in-support-of-higher-education-in-african-countries/ (accessed February 22, 2014).

264   A 2003 article in the *Carnegie Reporter* provides the early background on the partnership and a list of the early partnership grants; Ambika Kapur, "The Foundation Partnership to Strengthen African Universities: Four Foundations Share One Vision of the Future," *Carnegie Reporter* 2, no. 2 (Spring 2003): 38, available at: http://carnegie.org/publications/carnegie-reporter/single/view/article/item/80/. By the terms of the 1961 revised charter, the Corporation maintained an explicit commitment to work in and with countries in Africa that were members of the Commonwealth as of 1948; Mozambique became a member of the Commonwealth in 1995. In 2004 the trustees reviewed the Commonwealth policy and then agreed to continue the Commonwealth Program Special Fund policy: "The board ... passed a resolution to allow the Corporation to expend up to 7.4 percent of its income from general funds, including interest, dividends and net realized gains from investments, toward its Commonwealth Program." CCNYAR, 2004–2005, 94.

265   For details on the partnership as a collaborative, see the case study by Susan Parker, "Lessons from a Ten-Year Funder Collaborative: A Case Study of the Partnership for Higher Education in Africa," September 2012, Partnership for Higher Education in Africa, available at: www.foundation-partnership.org. Originally staffed by Lisbeth Levey (a consultant with the Ford and Rockefeller Foundations on partnership tasks and a Corporation grantee in the prior era) as facilitator, a small staff, hired with resources contributed by each of the foundations, assisted with meetings, travel, small grants, and Partnership publications. In 2006 Suzanne Grant Lewis was hired as the Partnership coordinator (16–18, 23–24). The Corporation's longtime partner, the Institute of International Education, served as fiscal agent for joint Partnership activities, working in collaboration with the New York University Partnership office. Parker lists the more than forty staff and advisers across the foundations, including the Partnership office, who contributed to the partnership over the ten years (45–46).

266   Ibid., 19–21, 27–30. See also Suzanne Grant Lewis, Jonathan Friedman, and John Schoneboom, "Accomplishments of the Partnership for Higher Education in Africa, 2000–2010: Report on a Decade of Collaborative Foundation Investment," Partnership for Higher Education in Africa, 7–8, available at: www.foundation-partnership.org. A few collaborative activities are discussed later in this chapter.

267   For details about the rationale and early stages of this work, see Daniel Akst and Mike Jensen, "Africa Goes Online," *Carnegie Reporter* 1, no. 2 (Spring 2001), available at: http://carnegie.org/publications/carnegie-reporter/single/view/article/item/14/.

268   Two Corporation board members, Admiral Owens and Ambassador Pickering, urged increasing attention to and support for upgrading information and communication technologies. With this kind of encouragement from the trustees and the president, staff members began to explore in more detail the complicated issue of reducing the costs of increased access to bandwidth, the seemingly insurmountable barrier identified by the Partnership and the Partnership institutions.

269   CCNY, "Program Budget Papers, October 2005–October 2006," 5, CCNYO. Johnson led the Corporation's effort with backing from program and Corporation leadership.

270   The Corporation then specifically invested in the Nigerian ICT Forum, which took over the work from the African Virtual University for the bandwidth consortium. The Nigerian ICT Forum also allowed considerable access to the Internet through greatly discounted prices; CCNYAR, 2004–2005, 116, 119; see also CCNY, "Strategy/Budget Papers, Fiscal Year 2010–2011, International Program," 45, CCNYO. MIT's I-Labs initiative enabled three of the universities to conduct real-time laboratory experiments and support e-learning and distance education activities in the sciences, all greatly facilitated by the results of the bandwidth consortium. A grant to the Tertiary Education Network of South Africa trained university technicians in the efficient use of bandwidth. See Parker, "Lessons from a Ten-Year Funder Collaborative," 21, 27; and Lewis et al., "Accomplishments of the Partnership for Higher Education in Africa, 2000–2010," 3.

271   CCNY, "Strategy/Budget Papers, Fiscal Year 2010–2011," 46–47, CCNYO. In addition to its success with modern communications and dissemination, the Partnership helped develop a more traditional way of reaching out and communicating the results of research, the *Journal of Higher Education in Africa*. Initiated with a grant made by all four foundations to Boston College, it was later expanded to include a joint activity with the Council for the Development of Social Science Research in Africa (CODESRIA), which is currently responsible for publishing the journal. It is the only journal focused on higher education research activities on the continent. See details in Parker, "Lessons from a Ten-Year Funder Collaborative," 20.

272   All quotes from CCNY, "Program Budget Papers, October 2005–October 2006, International Development Program," 5–6, CCNYO. Building on the Partnership commitment to joint undertakings, the individual foundation-specific activities, the commitment to renewed support, and the recommendations of the evaluators, the Partnership coordinating committee began to develop a strategic plan for joint activities for the period 2004 to 2010. In addition to establishing a forum for the exchange of information on a regular basis, a new plan also included leadership and management training for university leaders, strengthening regional organizations devoted to university-strengthening and the promotion of scientific research; enhancing university access and reducing the cost of access to the Internet and information technologies; building a Partnership website as both a promotional and informational outreach activity; supporting a new journal on higher education in Africa; and supporting specific studies on higher education in Africa. Recognizing the importance of strategic communications, the international development program began to work closely with the Public Affairs staff to develop training workshops on the continent to reach out to university leaders and communications specialists so that they could more effectively present their universities and advocate for support based on their accomplishments. CCNYAR, 2004–2005, 163.

273   Lewis et al., "Accomplishments of the Partnership for Higher Education in Africa, 2000–2010," v.

274   By the end of the Partnership in 2010, the participants had supported an extensive review report, an evaluation of the Partnership itself, and a publication on the perspectives of African participants; for in-depth details of the results of the investments by the foundations, both collectively and individually, see ibid. In addition to Kapur, "The Foundation Partnership to Strengthen African Universities," and Parker, "Lessons from a Ten-Year Funder Collaborative," two other publications analyze the activities and challenges faced at various stages: Karen Theroux, "A Quiet Revolution: Foundation Partners Spur Change in African Higher Education," *Carnegie Reporter* 5, no. 2 (Spring 2009): 38–47, available at: http://carnegie.org/publications/carnegie-reporter/single/view/article/item/216/; and Megan Lindow, *Weaving Success: Voices of Change in African Higher Education* (New York: Institute of International Education, 2011). More details are also found on the website at: www.foundation-partnership.org.

275   Lewis et al., "Accomplishments of the Partnership for Higher Education in Africa, 2000–2010," 1–2.

276 Among these partnerships are, notably, the work in support of the Green Revolution by the Rockefeller Foundation and the Ford Foundation in conjunction with the World Bank, leading to the establishment of the still vital Consultative Group on International Agricultural Research; and the Rockefeller Foundation, Ford Foundation, and Population Council collaboration in support of population and development fellowships; see Joan Spero, *The Global Role of US Foundations* (New York: Foundation Center, 2010), 4. Foundation collaboration during the last phase of apartheid in South Africa, from 1977 to 1994, was more informal but also had a major impact in that country (see Chapters 6 and 7). There are more such partnerships at the national level, such as the Four Freedom Fund, a five-foundation initiative that includes the Corporation; Karen Theroux, "Four Freedoms Fund: A Pioneering Foundation Partnership Advocates for Immigrants," *Carnegie Results* (Winter 2008), available at: http://carnegie.org/fileadmin/Media/Publications/PDF/carnegie_results_winter_08_rev.pdf. Daniel M. Fox has described the multi-foundation consortium on the Americans with Disabilities Act of 1990; personal communication with the author, October 19, 2012, and Daniel M. Fox, *Power and Illness: The Failure and Future of American Health Policy* (Berkeley: University of California Press, 1993).

277 Lewis et al. "Accomplishments of the Partnership for Higher Education in Africa, 2000–2010," v.

278 CCNYAR, 2009, 3, 4; 2010, 9; Parker, "Lessons from a Ten-Year Funder Collaborative," 27.

279 Lewis et al., "Accomplishments of the Partnership for Higher Education in Africa, 2000–2010," 7.

280 Because the volume of work was rapidly expanding in this regard, Matos hired a new program associate, Courtenay Sprague, in 2001. With her background and training in proposal development and preparation of case studies at the Harvard Business School, her skills reinforced Matos's skills in university leadership, management, and strategic planning.

281 Lewis et al., "Accomplishments of the Partnership for Higher Education in Africa, 2000–2010," 13. The Ford Foundation provided $90,424,051, or 21 percent, over ten years (ibid., 29); the Rockefeller Foundation provided $74,360,192, or 17 percent, over ten years (ibid., 83); the MacArthur Foundation provided $58,164,472, or 13 percent, over ten years (ibid., 61); the Mellon Foundation provided $50,351,200, or 11 percent, over five years (ibid., 73); the Hewlett Foundation provided $29,415,894, or 7 percent, over five years (ibid., 41); and the Kresge Foundation provided $11,714,461, or 3 percent, over the ten years, or 7 percent over the three years of its actual participation (ibid., 51).

282 Makerere University received a grant to support strategic planning in 2000; CCNYAR, 2000, 49. The University of Dar es Salaam incorporated gender mainstreaming into its plans; CCNYAR, 2001, 29. Both universities received their first major institution-strengthening grants in 2001; CCNYAR, 2001, 25.

283 CCNYAR, 2001, 25, 26, 28. The Corporation made a few university grants to follow up on discussions among Corporation leadership and staff concerning ways to bring a more interdisciplinary perspective to HIV/AIDS research. Onetime grants were made to the University of Natal and the University of the Witwatersrand; ibid., 26–28. Finally, and also in response to those conversations, a series of onetime grants addressed issues in improving the teaching of mathematics, science, and engineering at the University of Natal, NBI Foundation, Rhodes University, and the University of South Africa; ibid. A final grant to the university partnerships program, USHEPiA (University Science, Humanities, and Engineering Partnerships in Africa) at the University of Cape Town, bringing together the sciences, humanities, and engineering and co-funded by the Mellon and Rockefeller Foundations, linked the University of Cape Town with Dar es Salaam, Makerere, and other universities in East and Southern Africa; ibid., 24–25.

284 CCNYAR, 2002–2003, 20, 22.

285 CCNYAR, 2001, 27.

286 The first two had already been part of the Corporation's portfolio of activities in Nigeria; this was the first time the Corporation had made a grant to the University of Jos. The MacArthur Foundation also supported Ahmadu Bello and Port Harcourt University in Port Harcourt, Nigeria. Thus, five universities in Nigeria were part of the partnership. CCNYAR, 2002–2003, 97 (Ahmadu Bello University), and 98 (Obafemi Awolowo University and University of Jos).

287 Ibid., 20, 97, 98. The University of Ghana at Legon had been a Corporation grantee in the past, starting with library support in the 1930s for its precursor institution, Achimota College.

288 Ibid., 98.

289 CCNY, "Program Papers, October 2002–October 2003, International Development," 50–51, CCNYO.

290 Because of the high degree of flexibility needed with this initiative, staff members made the case to the president and the board that it should be handled as an "officer's assisted grant," that is, as a program with a technical assistance portfolio that could be drawn on as opportunities became available. With responsibility for making the request to the president and reporting regularly on activities and results, staff identified three technical assistance partners that offered workshops on proposal writing, fund-raising, alumni development, and raising the institutional profile: Pamoja, Inc., the Council for Advancement and Support of Education (CASE), and the South African Institute for Advancement (INYATHELO); CCNYAR, 2004–2005, 23, 118; 2006, 13. These three institutions, the first one based in the United States, the second in multiple countries, and the third in South Africa, became regular partners in assisting the universities, whose needs, such as in research or financial management, were identified by the Corporation in conjunction with university leadership or independently by the leadership.

291 Kader Asmal, Minister of Education, "National Plan for Higher Education," February 2001, on behalf of Ministry of Education South Africa, available at: http://sun025.sun.ac.za/portal/page/portal/Administrative_Divisions/INB/Home/Documentation/Documentation_National/National%20Plan%20for%20Higher%20Education%20in%20South%20Africa.pdf.

292 CCNY, "Program Strategy and Budget Papers, October 2003, International Development Program," 9, CCNYO.

293 For considerable detail about the work in South Africa over the first five years and the plans for the new phase, see CCNY, "Program Budget Papers, October 2004–October 2005, International Development Program," appendices 1–4 (1–15), CCNYO.

294 Ibid., 7.

295 CCNYAR, 2004–2005, 115.

296 The grants to the institutions in Tanzania and Uganda, the first ones to receive university-strengthening support, had received positive external reviews; they had been renewed in 2004 for just under $3 million for each institution. The universities in Nigeria and Ghana had not received their first round of grants until 2005 and were not yet up for renewal; ibid., 19; CCNY, "Programs and Accomplishments, 1996–2006, International Development Program," 1–2, CCNYO. The institutions were the University of Dar es Salaam in Tanzania; Makerere University in Uganda; Ahmadu Bello University, the University of Jos, and Obafemi Awolowo University in Nigeria; the University of Ghana and the University of Education, Winnebago, in Ghana; and the University of Cape Town, the University of KwaZulu-Natal, and the University of the Witwatersrand in South Africa. Systemwide grants were also supported in South Africa, Nigeria, and Ghana.

297 CCNY, "Programs and Accomplishments, 1996–2006, Section 4: International Development," 2, CCNYO.

298   Ibid.

299   More are listed in CCNY, "Programs and Accomplishments, 1996–2006, Section 4: International Development," 2, CCYNO.

300   Consequently, the Corporation asked Johann Mouton, the evaluator for the South Africa university partnership grants, to assist in developing formative evaluation plans with the new universities being supported in South Africa and then put monitoring and evaluation activities in place that would lead to summative evaluation. For the five partnership grants in South Africa, the Corporation commissioned the evaluation team to conduct a summative evaluation and identify which partnerships might benefit from continued support. Mouton also worked with the Corporation in the other four countries. Over the course of the partnership, Mouton and his team conducted evaluations of all the university grants.

301   When the Higher Education in the Former Soviet Union Program ended in 2008, after the new program structure was adopted, a separate program, Higher Education in Eurasia, was established. CCNY, "Strategy and Budget Papers, Fiscal Year 2008–2009, International Program," 46-47, CCNYO.

302   CCNYAR, 2007, 13, and 2011, 16. The work continues as of this writing. See also Centre for Higher Education Transformation, available at: http://www.chet.org.za/programmes/herana-i.

303   Aina, as the Ford Foundation representative for East Africa, served as a member of the Partnership coordinating committee from the beginning. A distinguished Nigerian sociologist, he was associated earlier with the Corporation when he was at the Council for the Development of Social Science Research in Africa. Claudia Fritelli, program officer, formerly at the Markle Foundation (where two Corporation staff members, John Russell and Lloyd Morrisett, had been president over the years), was hired in 2005–2006 to replace Courtenay Sprague (who departed to pursue her PhD in South Africa) and assist with the university-strengthening grants and particularly with the work on e-learning, which the universities participating in the bandwidth consortium had selected as the next issue for the Partnership to tackle.

304   Although this idea did not mesh with the earlier guiding principle that only activities directly related to university-approved strategic plans should be funded, the fact that many of the university partners had submitted proposals relating to science and technology indicated that these themes were core areas of interest to African universities and faculty members; CCNYAR, 2008, 43 (International Program). For more details on the initiative, see Alan Anderson, "African Scientists on the Rise: In Africa, Investments in Leadership Transform Lives and Careers," *Carnegie Reporter* 5, no. 4 (Spring 2010): 12–18, available at: http://carnegie.org/publications/carnegie-reporter/single/view/article/item/251/.

305   CCNYAR, 2010, 7. The networks are the African Material Science and Engineering Network, the African Natural Products Network, the Southern African Biochemistry and Informatics Network for Natural Products, the Sub-Saharan Africa Water Resources Network, and the Western Indian Ocean Regional Initiative. Anderson, "African Scientists on the Rise," 13.

306   CCNYAR, 2008, 6. After demonstrating success with the development of postgraduate degrees and projects, the initiative was renewed for an additional three years at the same amount in 2011; by the end of the next round, more than one hundred students will have been supported. CCNYAR, 2011, 17.

307   CCNY, "Budget Request for FY2007–2008, International Program," 8, CCNYO; CCNY, "Strategy and Program Papers, Fiscal Year 2008–2009, International Program," 43, CCNYO. The American Council of Learned Societies drew on its earlier Corporation-supported fellowship program for scholars in Russia and the former Soviet Union in designing this request.

308   Kenneth Walker, "Will Knowledge Survive? Studying the Humanities at African

Universities," *Carnegie Reporter* 5, no. 2 (Spring 2009): 3–11, available at: http://carnegie.org/publications/carnegie-reporter/single/view/article/item/212/.

309   CCNYAR, 2010, 6, 7, 8, 9. The programs range from economics and civil engineering at the University of Cape Town to sociology at the University of Ghana; food, nutrition, and value addition at Makerere University; computational sciences at Ghana; and academic medicine at the University of the Witwatersrand.

310   Ibid., 9.

311   CCNYAR, 2011, 17.

312   CCNYAR, 2009, 3. A grant to the Consortium for Advanced Research Training in Africa was renewed for $2.5 million over three years in 2011 to enable the Consortium to continue connecting with ten universities and providing doctoral fellowships; CCNYAR, 2011, 16. The Ford Foundation also supported the Consortium.

313   For the King's College–African Leadership Centre partnership, see CCNYAR, 2009, 5. For the SSRC doctoral work, see CCNYAR, 2011, 18. For more details generally, see CCNY, "Strategy/Budget Papers, Fiscal Year 2011–2012," 137, CCNYO.

314   CCNY, "Strategy/Program Papers, Fiscal Year 2010–2011," 45, CCNYO.

315   Over the years of the Partnership, the Corporation directly provided $77.1 million for universities and colleges in the Partnership countries. In addition, under the auspices of the Partnership, the Corporation was one of the major supporters of postgraduate training and research networks, at a level of $3.1 million. For a detailed summary of activities up to 2009, see Theroux, "A Quiet Revolution."

316   The understanding of the collateral constraints limiting women's participation drew on work the Corporation had funded earlier through the Forum of African Women Educationalists and other studies showing that there were few women undergraduates in African universities because of the environment they faced there—limited housing and health care facilities, prejudicial taunts and worse from male students and even male faculty members and staff, the need to stay at home to help with siblings, and the lack of career opportunities for women graduates. For a useful historical and current perspective, see N'Dri Assie-Lumumba, "Empowerment of Women in Higher Education in Africa: The Role and Mission of Research," UNESCO Forum Occasional Paper 11, UNESCO Forum Secretariat, June 2006, available at: http://unesdoc.unesco.org/images/0015/001510/151051eo.pdf (accessed August 12, 2012).

317   CCNY, "Program Papers, October 2000–October 2001," 49, Box 22, Series I.D, CCNY Records, RBML-CUL.

318   For example, the University of Dar es Salaam developed a plan under the auspices of the gender dimension program committee and prepared a request for a gender mainstreaming strategy that the Corporation recommended for support; CCNYAR, 2002–2003, 19. Makerere University incorporated such activities directly into its new strategic plan, organizing a gender equity office and initiating a number of activities to enhance support for women scholars. In addition, Makerere hosted a conference on women's issues, under the auspices of an international group called Winds of Change; ibid., 24. To reinforce the universities' commitment to gender equity, the Corporation also tried to include those responsible for the programs in international initiatives. Returning to support the Institute of Education at the University of London, a significant partner of the Corporation's in the 1960s, the gender equity staff members at the Corporation-supported universities were invited to participate in an international network on investigating interventions in support of women and gender equity in the Commonwealth. They were also invited to participate at the Eighth Interdisciplinary Congress on Women.

319   CCNYAR, 2001, 22.

320   CCNY, "Program Papers, October 2001–October 2002, International Development

Program," 58. The Corporation supported a series of studies in South Africa conducted by the Center for Higher Education Transformation, the African Gender Institute at the University of Cape Town, and the South African chapter of the Forum of African Women Educationalists.

321 CCNYAR, 2002–2003, 19.

322 CCNY, "Program Strategy and Budget Papers, October 2003," 19, CCNYO.

323 Ibid., 13. With approval from the board and Corporation leadership to go forward with the strategy, staff members anticipated continuing the fellowship programs at Makerere University and the University of Dar es Salaam for another six years following the initial three years; ibid., 18–20. Each university is designing innovations that will assist with recruitment and, importantly, retention. The scholarship program in South Africa, managed by the South African Department of Education, has been recruiting from all provinces in the country and is committed to maintaining a policy of racial inclusiveness. In the two countries without tuition fees (Nigeria and Ghana), covering other costs, such as room and board and the cost of using libraries, computers, and laboratories, has facilitated women's participation as undergraduates. Again, the intention is that these nine-year programs will be sufficient to inculcate in the universities a culture of gender equity and recognition of the benefits of increasing the number of women students, so much so that the universities will continue at least modified forms of scholarship programs for undergraduate women after Corporation support comes to an end.

324 Ibid., 22.

325 Ibid., 20–21.

326 CCNYAR, 2004–2005, 117.

327 Lewis et al., "Accomplishments of the Partnership for Higher Education in Africa, 2000–2010," 22–24.

328 In 2011, the board approved a $1 million challenge grant to Makerere University for the Female Scholarship Foundation. CCNYAR, 2011, 18.

329 Makerere University, Gender Mainstreaming Directorate, "Female Scholarship Foundation," available at: http://gender.mak.ac.ug/index.php/female-scholarship-foundation-fsf.html. For additional information on women leaders and fellowship holders at Makerere University and the University of Nigeria, see Anderson, "In Africa, Investments in Leadership Transform Lives and Careers," 16–21.

330 For a detailed discussion of the library program, see Karen Theroux, "Bringing New Life to South Africa's Libraries," *Carnegie Review* (Winter 2012), available at: http://carnegie.org/fileadmin/Media/Publications/carnegie_review_winter_2012_libaries.pdf.

331 CCNYAR, 1999, 45; see also CCNY, "Program Papers, October 2000–October 2001," 53–57, Box 22, Series I.D, CCNY Records, RBML-CUL. Recognizing that the field as a whole in Africa needed revitalization, the Corporation decided to continue working with the International Network for the Availability of Scientific Publications as a major partner to assist with identifying ways to build capacity in the management of public libraries and enhance advocacy for them. It was anticipated that the International Network would also assist the Corporation in organizing special sessions at key international meetings and identify donor partners at the level of $1,062,000 over three years; CCNYAR, 2001, 23–24. In addition, the International Network helped the Corporation convene a donor meeting that led to the formation of a small but dedicated funders network for advancing public libraries throughout Africa, including the Ford Foundation, the Rockefeller Foundation, and the Kellogg Foundation, as well as the library staff at the new Bill and Melinda Gates Foundation, who were building on their work in Canada and Chile to support a program in Botswana. The Mellon Foundation, one of the few foundations that had been committed for several years to both library development and information systems in South Africa, was working through the Mortenson Center for International Development

at the University of Illinois at Urbana-Champaign to support leadership in the public and university libraries of South Africa, and the Kresge Foundation was also supporting work with the National Library of South Africa.

332 For the planning grants, see CCNYAR, 2000, 48; for the first proposals, see CCNYAR, 2002–2003, 20.

333 The first individual library grants are reported in CCNYAR, 2001, 22–24.

334 See CCNY, "Program Papers, October 2001–October 2002," 63, Box 22, Series I.D, CCNY Records, RBML-CUL; CCNY, "Program Papers, October 2002–October 2003," 49–50, CCNYO.

335 This was also a time of program staff changes. In February 2002, Primm Brown retired. Hired a few months later was Rookaya Bawa, a South African national who had over seventeen years of experience in managing public libraries in South Africa; for nearly seven years, from 1995 to 2002, she had directed the KwaZulu-Natal Provincial Information and Library Services. Immediately prior to accepting the Corporation's offer, she coordinated the programs of the Colleges Collaboration Fund, a project of the South African National Business Initiative. CCNYAR, 2002–2003, 165.

336 CCNY, "Program Strategy Paper 2003, International Development Program," 23, CCNYO.

337 Ibid., 24–25. Technical assistance activities through the International Network continued, and new partners for training librarians were added, including the Mortenson Center for International Development in Urbana-Champaign, Illinois.

338 CCNYAR, 2004–2005, 18, 115–116, 116.

339 CCNY, "Program Budget Papers, October 2004–October 2005, International Development Program," 5–6, CCNYO.

340 Ibid.; CCNY, "Program Budget Papers, October 2005–October 2006, International Development Program," 8–9, CCNYO.

341 CCNY, "Program Budget Papers, October 2005–October 2006, International Development Program," appendix 1, "Revitalizing Selected African Libraries," 4.

342 See Theroux, "Bringing New Life to South Africa's Libraries," 4–16, for details on the program's grants for training librarians and strengthening the Library Association of South Africa, improving services to schoolchildren, particularly in rural areas, and enhancing both the physical plant and the internal structures of the libraries along with the following model libraries: the Cape Town Library, the Msunduzi Bessie Head Legal Deposit Library in Pietermaritzburg, Johannesburg City Library, Khayelitsha Township Library in Cape Town, the Richards Bay City Library in Richards Bay, and the Ethekwini Municipal Library in Durban, along with the National Library of South Africa.

343 CCNY, "Strategy/Budget Papers, Fiscal Year 2010–2011, International Program," 48 (emphasis in original), CCNYO.

344 Working with the South African government, the Corporation provided continued support for Internet technology, collection-building, and the preservation programs of the National Library of South Africa and the development of a plan to establish additional nodes in branch libraries in the respective provinces. Toward that end, staff members negotiated a funding partnership with provincial and local governments, along with multinational donor agencies, for continued support for the public and university library activities in Africa. Ibid., 47–48.

345 Ibid., 47 (emphasis in original).

346 For the initial grant to the University of Cape Town in this area, see CCNYAR, 2009, 4.

347 CCNYAR, 2010, 7.

348 CCNY, "Strategy/Budget Papers, Fiscal Year 2010–2011," 48, CCNYO.

349 CCNYAR, 2010, 9.

350 CCNY, "Strategy and Budget Papers, Fiscal Year 2011–2012," 142, CCNYO.

351 Ibid., 135.

352 Carnegie also stated in his extended paean to America, *Triumphant Democracy*, that the strength of American democracy was that "there is not one shred of privilege to be met with anywhere in all the laws. One man's right is every man's right…. The Republic … has proved to the world that the freest self-government of the parts produces the strongest government of the whole." Andrew Carnegie, *Triumphant Democracy* (Garden City, NY: Doubleday, Doran & Co., 1885), 15, 17.

353 Vartan Gregorian, "New Directions," 49.

354 Ibid., 56.

355 Sam Afridi, "Muslims in America: Identity, Diversity, and the Challenge of Understanding," *Carnegie Challenge Paper* (2001): i, available at: carnegie.org/fileadmin/Media/Publications/PDF/muslims.pdf (accessed February 23, 2014).

356 CCNY, "Final Draft, Meeting Report, June 28, 2001," 1, CCNYO. The recommendations from this meeting are incorporated into Afridi, "Muslims in America."

357 Ibid., 12.

358 CCNYAR, 2002–2003, 115–116 (Strengthening US Democracy).

359 Ibid.

360 CCNY, "Program Strategy and Budget Papers, October 2003, Strengthening US Democracy," 21, CCNYO.

361 The foundation partners included the Ford Foundation, the Mertz Gilmore Foundation, the John S. and James L. Knight Foundation, and the Open Society Institute. The Four Freedoms Fund, based at the Public Interest Project, provided collaborative support for work on immigrant integration, particularly at the local level. In this case, even should the Corporation close its programmatic work on these issues, the work would be very likely to continue owing to sufficient donor support developed by the fund. Since 2003, the Four Freedoms Fund has made more than $50 million in grants to over 170 grantees across the country. Current funders include the Carnegie Corporation of New York, the Ford Foundation, the Evelyn and Walter Haas Jr. Fund, the Open Society Institute, the Horace Hagedorn Foundation, the J. M. Kaplan Fund, the Gill Foundation, Unbound Philanthropy, the Northwest Area Foundation, the Western Union Foundation, the Arcus Foundation, and the JPB Foundation. See Public Interest Projects, "Partner and Collaborative Funds," available at: http://www.publicinterestprojects.org/funds-projects/partner-and-collaborative-funds; see also CCNYAR, 2002–2003, 120.

362 CCNYAR, 2002–2003, 39.

363 CCNYAR, 2008, 14. The grants with Sutton Trust were primarily on education issues.

364 Gregorian, "Carnegie Corporation of New York: Meeting the Challenges of the 21st Century," 8–9, 11–12.

365 Over time the special projects activities were clustered under different names and different funds. All of them, however, contained protected resources for out-of-program, cross-program, or, in some cases, preprogram grants. The titles included Special Opportunities Fund and Special Initiatives. The 21st Century Fund, another special fund, has served as a reserve fund for major initiatives. The Special Projects/Special Opportunities Fund made many grants with international components; the ones mentioned here, with their focus on Islam and Muslim communities, are representative.

366 Gregorian, "New Directions," 33.

367 CCNYAR, 2002–2003, 141.

368 The Institute of International Education's Council for International Exchange of Scholars was a partner in this effort. Ibid., 127.

369 Ibid., 127.

370   Ibid., 129.

371   Ibid.

372   Ibid., 47 (through Brown University); CCNYAR, 2007, 29 (as Soliya, Inc.).

373   A series of dialogues at the New School University, starting in 2002, brought together scholars and commentators from both Muslim and non-Muslim countries to develop more common understanding of "Islamic political and social movements as well as accompanying grievances against the West and, in particular, the United States"; CCNYAR, 2002, 52; CCNY, "Program Papers, October 2001–October 2002, Special Opportunities Fund," 2, Box 22, Series I.D, CCNY Records, RBML-CUL. Grants included support for University of Maryland professor Shibley Telhami's annual survey of six Arab countries to assess their concerns and their reactions to the West, specifically the United States; CCNYAR, 2004–2005, 146. The Institute for International Economics analyzed economic and global stability issues related to Islam; ibid. The Brookings Institution held dialogues under the auspices of the Sabah Center, often in Doha; ibid., 148. The Interfaith Center of New York also promoted civic engagement with local Muslim communities; ibid., 58. In 2009–2010, together the Corporation and the Open Society Institute provided support for journalist David Rohde, who had been taken captive in Afghanistan by the Taliban, and for his analyses of the situation in that country. The result was David Rohde and Kristen Mulvihill, *A Rope and a Prayer* (New York: Viking, 2010); CCNYAR, 2010, 35. Support for other out-of-program activities included a focus on increasing American understanding of Africa. Working with the Public Affairs team, the Fund supported Public Radio International to enhance its coverage of Africa with a two-year initiative called "Reconsidering Africa"; CCNYAR, 2002–2003, 129. Harking back to support for the Mexican Health Foundation in the 1990s, a onetime grant was made to the US-Mexico Foundation for grant-making in Mexico; CCNYAR, 2009, 48.

374   Human Rights Watch received core support and a special September 11 recovery grant to monitor human rights issues related to antiterrorism campaigns in the United States and elsewhere, including the war in Afghanistan; CCNYAR, 2002–2003, 129. A special fund for recovery in New York City and elsewhere following the September 11 attacks provided almost $10 million worth of support for rebuilding the libraries of the schools that were most affected in lower Manhattan and the tower for New York Public Radio, as well as for the fund for new citizens at the New York Community Trust; ibid., 53, 125. Following the Asian tsunami in January 2005, the Corporation provided a total of $1 million to support recovery efforts, with $100,000 each going to the American Red Cross, the International Federation of Red Cross and Red Crescent Societies, the International Rescue Committee, Mercy Corps, and Save the Children, and $500,000 going to the United States Fund for UNICEF; CCNYAR, 2004–2005, 150. Following the Katrina disaster in New Orleans, a series of grants were made to support education and community action in that city; CCNYAR, 2006, 48. Following the Haiti earthquake in January 2010, under the International Program focusing on states at risk, a grant to RAND Corporation enabled it to undertake a major study on investing more effectively to build stability following the natural disaster; CCNYAR, 2011, 12.

375   Vartan Gregorian, "New Directions," 33–34. As Gregorian wrote in 2005: "One of my priorities, when I became president of Carnegie Corporation of New York in 1997, was to reestablish the Corporation's historic support for individual scholarship … in harmony with the spirit and concerns of Andrew Carnegie, who believed so deeply in the power of the individual to change the world, and in knowledge and scholarship as the tools that humankind uses to bring about that change. And we sought out scholars who were dedicated to the concept of *public* scholarship, meaning that their work was always intended, in effect, to be outward bound: aimed not only for the enlightenment and comment of their peers and the academic community, but also to be accessible and available to the interested public, to become part of the national conver-

sation about critical issues and to add energy and insight to discussion and debate in our country and indeed, around the world." Vartan Gregorian, "Foreword," in CCNY, "Carnegie Scholars Program: A Five-Year Review, 2000–2004" (2005), vii (emphasis in original), CCNYO.

376 Pertinent international themes would include "nuclear nonproliferation, higher education in the former Soviet Union, water as a source of conflict, the resolution of tensions between concepts of national sovereignty and self-determination … intergroup relations (ethnic, racial, and religious) in the United States, higher education, and the status of women in Africa." Gregorian, "New Directions," 60.

377 Composed of a diverse group of academic leaders, practitioners, journalists, and heads of think tanks and NGOs, each new round drew on a slightly modified list depending on changes in positions and emphases. The list was revised each year by Rosenfield and program associate Heather McKay, as well as by other program staff and the academic advisers. Gregorian approved new nominators. A core group of Corporation program staff reviewers from all four programs dedicated considerable time to reviewing the more than one hundred proposal prospectuses that were submitted each year and selecting the finalists to be reviewed by the members of the external selection committee, who then read the final proposals and made their comments and rankings in writing for consideration at the selection committee meeting. Each staff member read proposals both within and outside their program area, as well as cross-program ones. The academic advisers for the other programs reviewed and commented on topic-specific proposals. Neil Grabois, the program vice president, chaired the external and internal review committees. The four academic advisers for the Carnegie Scholars Program, who constituted the external selection committee, made the final recommendations of Scholars for the president's review, final approval, and presentation to the Board of Trustees.

378 CCNYAR, 2001, 56–57; 2002–2003, 61; and 2004–2005, 60. Topics included analyses of the rule of law across South Africa, Russia, and Mexico and counterterrorism; the North American social contract; the Tanzara railroad; new understanding of the role of institutions in economic development; the world of the international civil servant; state power in Russia; the proliferation of weapons of the United States; the Chechnya conflict in Russia; global income gaps; new voices and globalization; Muslim women; scholarship in western North Africa and pre-eighteenth-century scholarship and social activism; arms control and Russia; political and economic determinants of African development; globalization of the Mafia; terrorism and counterterrorism; Afghanistan; ethnic conflict in Europe; fifty years of foreign aid; comparative constitution development; Islam and the Russian Federation; military strategy and threats; multiculturalism and liberal democracies; US foreign policy toward Saudi Arabia from the end of World War II; the Islamization of Chicago's Arab community; Islam and identity in Central Asia and the Caucuses; Islam and identity in Indonesia, Malaysia, and Singapore; Russian legal reform; ethnicity in Africa; violence and torture; the Muslim Brotherhood; the Iran hostage crisis; Iraqi democracy; international law; suicide terrorism; transatlantic relations; and the role of America in the twenty-first century.

379 To shape the new agenda, in early 2004, Rosenfield and McKay held a series of meetings with scholars and directors of Near East and Middle East studies programs in and around New York City. The sixteen Scholars funded earlier on related themes were also consulted. New academic advisers were selected over the first year of the new program, as required for the review of the more specialized requests. Gregorian worked with Rosenfield and McKay to revise the request to nominators so that it clearly reflected the new focus. Gregorian, Grabois, and staff decided to keep the review and selection process the same. All the conditions under which it had earlier received IRS approval were retained for this new phase, including the citizenship or residency requirement; new US Department of Homeland Security procedures were also followed.

380 CCNYAR, 2004–2005, 60; 2006, 29–30; 2007, 31–32; 2008, 19–26; and 2009, 38–39.

381 Susan King, vice president for external affairs, coined the phrase "Scholars of Vision," which soon became the tagline for the Carnegie Scholars Program. The department designed a public outreach strategy starting with announcements of the Carnegie Scholars in the *New York Times*. Press releases prepared by the department circulated with detailed information about the work of the Scholars to the entire Corporation mailing list and to the Scholars' institutions. For the initial phase of the program, King asked a colleague, Michael de Courcy Hinds, to interview four Scholars, one working on domestic issues, one focused on primarily international issues, and two focused on global concerns; see Michael de Courcy Hinds, "Scholarship for Social Change," *Carnegie Reporter* 2, no. 1 (Fall 2002), available at: http://carnegie.org/publications/carnegie-reporter/single/view/article/item/54/. In 2004 the department commissioned the editor of *Daedalus* and Corporation adviser Stephen Graubard to write an essay clarifying for the public, the nominators, and the nominees the concept and approach of public scholarship; see Stephen Graubard, "Public Scholarship: A New Perspective for the 21st Century" (New York: CCNY, 2004). To bring together the scholarship and the learning from both phases of the program, the Public Affairs Department published two in-depth monographs, "Carnegie Scholars Program, 2000–2004" (2005) and "Carnegie Scholars Program: A Five-Year Review of Scholarship on Islam, 2005–2009" (2010). Importantly, the External Affairs Department provided special training for the Scholars in communications skills, including the writing of op-ed pieces.

382 Throughout the first five years, relatively few submissions were received from scholars working on Africa. It was recognized that much of the work on Africa was taking place by African scholars based on the continent, and reviewers, advisers, and program staff were reluctant to fund Americans to go over and "study" African issues. Nonetheless, it was a glaring gap in the program. International Development Program chair Narciso Matos and program staff member Courtenay Sprague worked with the Carnegie Scholars Program to organize a discussion at the African Studies Association meeting in Boston in 2003 with the current head of the Association and all former heads to discuss how best to promote nominations and selection of scholars working on these issues, recognizing the citizenship or residency requirements for eligibility. With the efforts of several of the former presidents of the Association, a few more nominations were made. However, when the focus turned to Islam, a more respectable number of nominations were received, concerning Islam not only in North Africa but in sub-Saharan Africa as well. Still, scholarship on and in Africa remained a gap among the Carnegie Scholars. CCNY, "Program Strategy and Budget Papers, 2003, Carnegie Scholars Program," 10, CCNYO.

383 Reaching out to the Carnegie Scholars Program, the chair of the International Peace and Security (IPS) Program, Deana Arsenian, suggested that when the focus turned to Islam, it might be of interest to hold a special meeting focused on bringing together the American scholars working on Islam in Russia and scholars working on Islam from the former Soviet Union who were part of the Centers for Advanced Study and Education (CASEs), especially those in Rostov, where the issues were of central concern. Following a planning meeting at the Corporation in November 2006 with scholars from the region, Carnegie Scholars, program advisers, representatives from the New York Times Knowledge Network and the Open Society Institute, and Corporation staff members, and working with IPS advisers Andrey Kortunov and Irina Laktionova, president and executive director, respectively, of the International Scholarship Education (ISE) Center in Moscow, staff identified topics for a meeting in Russia, such as identity, social integration, religion, economic and social dimensions, and ethnic conflict. In the summer of 2007, together with the advisers based in Moscow, Corporation staff members, along with the director of the newly formed Islam Initiative, Hillary Wiesner, and three Carnegie Scholars (fluent in Russian, working on salient issues, and able to interact actively with the CASE scholars), met in Moscow with a wide range of Russian scholars on Islam. After three

days of discussions, participants arrived at shared research topics for possible follow-up collaborations, particularly for those scholars engaged in their research in the region.

384 To promote collaboration from different perspectives across Carnegie Scholars, Wiesner and Rosenfield jointly encouraged Carnegie Scholar Bruce Lawrence, then head of the Duke University Center for Islamic Studies, to host a meeting of Carnegie Scholars in the region in an effort to build regional collaboration. Carnegie Scholars based at institutions in North Carolina, Georgia, Virginia, and Washington, DC, participated in a two-day meeting in the fall of 2009. In addition to meeting with Duke students, they shared in-depth papers on their work and discussed issues of intersection, controversy, and collaboration. The Islam Initiative in 2011 continued to support the Duke Center. CCNYAR, 2011, 15.

385 Several meetings were held from 2005 to 2009 with directors of scholars programs and directors of programs that were related, even tangentially, to issues surrounding Islam. When the Islam Initiative was started, Wiesner established, in collaboration with the Rockefeller Brothers Fund, a more formal network of donors. Even with these efforts, attracting other foundations to the field, especially to promote the funding of scholars, proved difficult. Additional efforts to reach other donors were organized with the New York Regional Association of Grantmakers (Philanthropy Now), the Peace and Security Funders Group, the Open Society Institute, and the Corporation, first by the Carnegie Scholars Program and then by Islam Initiative staff and the Rockefeller Brothers Fund. See earlier discussion in the section on the Islam Initiative.

386 CCNYAR, 2006, 28 (under the Special Opportunities Fund).

387 CCNYAR, 2007, 32.

388 Ibid.

389 As with any scholars program, the significance of the work can only be assessed over time to determine whether the research influenced the field and the public and the findings have remained valid. Some scholars have had direct effects on policymakers and have even entered government, at least for short periods. As public scholars, Carnegie Scholars from both phases wrote op-eds for local, national, and international newspapers, including major articles in the *New York Times Magazine* and other Sunday papers; they provided testimony in Congress and participated in consultations with the US State Department; and they gave local talks at Lions Clubs, Rotary meetings, and university alumni association meetings. Program staff tracked for nearly ten years the short-term impact of the program on the individual scholars. The legacies of these individuals could usefully be followed up over the next decade, keeping in mind Pritchett's observation that the impact from the Corporation's work may not be clear until the following generation.

390 With the departure of Wiesner in 2013, the work on Islam has been folded into the International Peace and Security Program and is focusing on the Middle East. (Wiesner left to direct the Programmes Department of the King Abdullah Bin Abdulaziz International Centre for Interreligious and Intercultural Dialogue in Vienna, Austria.)

391 For the 2006 board retreat on Corporation accomplishments, the department prepared a comprehensive compendium of all of the dissemination activities in relationship to each program, the Journalism Initiative, technical assistance, forums and events, and other activities. This was updated yearly in the program strategy and budget papers. The details were given in each of the annual reports under "Dissemination" until 2007, and from then on under "External Affairs." This section only touches on the extensive work of the department to extend the outreach efforts of all the programs and the Corporation as a whole, both in the United States and internationally; for the latter, the department focused especially on the work in Africa and on Russia and Eurasia.

392 The *Carnegie Reporter*, the *Carnegie Review*, *Carnegie Results*, and the *Carnegie Challenge*

Papers may be even more important to future scholars than they are for the contemporary audience, as significant as that might be, because they reflect—especially the *Carnegie Reporter*—not only the Corporation's efforts but also related programs and grant-making at other foundations.

393   CCNYAR, 2007, 46, and 2004–2005, 63; see also CCNYAR, 2006, "Accomplishments: Dissemination" (in "Scholars" section).

394   As an experiment, two scholars of Islam, Jen'nan Read at Duke University and Brian Edwards at Northwestern University, received additional support to work on their skills in writing for the popular media. Read's research addressed the integration of Muslim Americans into their local communities and the issues arising for Muslim Americans; Edwards, through the lens of American studies programs in Cairo, Fez, and Tehran, examined how the Muslim world, including the Muslim scholarly world, viewed Americans. Robert Pape, based on his revealing work on suicide terrorism, received support from the Islam Initiative and the States at Risk Program through the International Program to extend his work at the University of Chicago in other dimensions of terrorism and conflict. See Theroux, "The Truth Behind Suicide Terrorism."

395   The program, even before the Journalism Initiative, supported journalism activities such as the International Women's Media Foundation; CCNYAR, 2004–2005, 66, 163. For publication examples, see the Joan Shorenstein Center, Carnegie Corporation, Knight Foundation, *Report on the Carnegie-Knight Initiative on the Future of Journalism Education* (Cambridge, MA: Shorenstein Center, 2011); CCNY, "Midterm Report of the Carnegie-Knight Initiative on the Future of Journalism Education," 2007, CCNYO.

396   CCNYAR, 2004–2005, 151–154.

397   CCNY, "Program Strategy/Budget Papers, 2010–2011, External Affairs," 3, CCNYO. At the end of the five years, twelve schools were involved and many more wanted to participate.

398   In keeping with the international nature of Andrew Carnegie's commitment to philanthropy, the Medal celebrates not only American philanthropists but also the best representatives of philanthropy from other countries as well; recipients have included Li Ka-Sheng, based in Hong Kong/China (2011); the Koc family, based in Turkey (2009); the Tata family, based in India (2007); His Highness the Aga Khan, based in France (2005); Tom Farmer, based in the United Kingdom (2005); the Cadbury family, based in the United Kingdom (2005); Kazuo Inamori, based in Japan (2003); and the Sainsbury family, based in the United Kingdom (2003). The Medals have been awarded in New York City, Washington, DC, and Pittsburgh, and overseas in the Scottish Parliament. See www.carnegiemedals.org for developments after 2011.

399   For example, in the twenty-first century, through the Corporation's extensive partnership with the Carnegie Endowment and its field offices, the Corporation now has an even more extensive global reach and is still meeting the terms of its charter.

NOTES FOR THE CONCLUSION

1   Carnegie Corporation of New York (CCNY), Minutes of the Board of Trustees, I, 8, November 10, 1911, CCNY Records, Rare Book and Manuscript Library, Columbia University Libraries (RBML-CUL).

2   From November 10, 1911, to November 10, 2011, Carnegie Corporation, under the leadership of 12 presidents joined by 123 trustees and working with close to 300 staff members, supported grant-making of more than $2.5 billion.

3   James Allen Smith, "Private Foundations and Public Policymaking: A Historical Perspective," in *Foundations and Public Policy*, ed. James M. Ferris (New York: Foundation Center, 2009), 41–45; Hammack and Anheier, *A Versatile Institution*, esp. chs. 1 and 2; and Zunz, *Philanthropy in America*, esp. the introduction and ch. 1. See also the Introduction and Chapter 1 of the present volume.

4 He also contributed more than $1 million to build the Peace Palace and Library in The Hague, for over one hundred years the site of significant meetings, research, and court cases related to peace. David Nasaw, "The Continuing Relevance of Andrew Carnegie's Legacy," lecture delivered at the Peace Palace, The Hague, The Netherlands, August 30, 2012, available at: Carnegie.org/fileadmin/Media/Publications/David_nasaw_hague_lecture_aug12_peace.pdf; and Randall Lesaffer, "The Temple of Peace: The Hague Peace Conferences, Andrew Carnegie, and the Building of the Peace Palace (1898–1913)," Tilburg Law School Legal Studies Research Paper Series 024/2013, Social Science Research Network Electronic Paper Collection, available at: http://ssrn.com/abstract=2350189 (both accessed March 1, 2014).

5 From 1925 to 1935, the Corporation's decision in the British colonies in East, Central, and Southern Africa (the main locus at that time for non-Dominion African grant-making) to invest in community development–centered Jeanes education (described more fully in Chapter 3) rather than higher education has never been fully assessed for both the short-term and longer-term impacts. The Jeanes focus on supporting traveling teachers and building the basis for strong communities through education might seem like an appropriate investment, even a cost-effective one in the late twentieth and early twenty-first centuries, but in the 1930s in African colonies the choice was between limiting opportunity for access to higher education or enhancing it. The Corporation chose the more pragmatic approach.

6 Some critics and supporters of foundations have discussed ways to promote greater risk-taking in grant-making, but they do not draw on the extensive biological, psychological, and political science research on the risk-taking behaviors of people and policymakers to illuminate our understanding of the enabling and constraining factors. For an in-depth analysis of risk-taking and political science that draws on work in psychology and game theory, see Rose McDermott, *Risk-taking in International Politics: Prospect Theory in American Foreign Policy* (Ann Arbor: University of Michigan Press, 1998).

7 For discussions on philanthropy see Caroline Hartnell, "High Risk/High Gain? Why Isn't This More Appealing to Foundations?" *Alliance*, June 18, 2012, available at: http://philanthropynews.alliancemagazine.org/high-risk-high-gain-why-isnt-this-more-appealing (accessed February 10, 2013); Pablo Eisenberg, "A Foundation Leader with Innovation and Risk-taking in His DNA," *Chronicle of Philanthropy*, December 19, 2011, available at: http://philanthropy.com/article/A-Foundation-Leader-With/130131/; Patricia Baker, "Taking Risks at a Critical Time," Grantmakers in Health, March 2010, lead essay for 2010 annual meeting, available at: http://www.gih.org/Publications/MeetingReportsDetail.cfm?ItemNumber=4073.

8 Keppel, *The Foundation*, 100. Keppel added: "Provided the general objective is recognized to be of importance and timeliness, measurability of results is regarded as of secondary importance"; ibid. It is important to note that the risk-taking in this discussion refers to grant-making and not the management of assets. Risk-taking in that area, which might hamper a foundation's capacity to maintain payouts for grants, is irresponsible. No one at the Corporation embraced financial risk-taking that would jeopardize the asset base or the tax-exempt status as part of "speculative" grant-making.

9 CCNY Annual Report (CCNYAR), 1964, 12, RBML-CUL.

10 Drawn from a discussion led by Corporation staff member Andrea Johnson on the differences between legitimate and avoidable failures, February 13, 2013.

11 In that instance, the Corporation's consultants had followed up their site visit with a plan that would bring together the provincial colleges and universities into a federation; although a similar approach had worked in Toronto, it was not favored by most of the local communities in the Maritime Provinces. The trustees had reserved $3 million to support the plan; eight years later, with no plan ever submitted, they realized that it would never go forward and put the money back in the funding pool.

12 Another example of risky grant-making with unintended consequences occurred with the support for the study of American blacks funded by the Corporation in the late 1930s and early 1940s. Keppel did not avoid risk in responding to trustee Newton Baker's suggestion in 1935 that the state of Americans blacks be systematically examined. He did seek to reduce the risk by hiring a foreigner, Gunnar Myrdal, instead of an American—for example, W.E.B. Du Bois had been suggested as someone who would be appropriate for the job—but he continued to argue for the work and obtain support from the trustees. The results more than validated the commitment. Most notably, the Myrdal study contributed to dramatic change in American society by providing the evidence used in the 1954 Supreme Court decision *Brown vs. Board of Education*. However, as Myrdal scholar Maribel Morey has noted, neither Keppel nor the trustees had it in mind that funding this study would contribute to improving education. Rather, they wanted to see more of a social and economic perspective introduced into those policies aimed at improving the conditions facing blacks in the United States by removing the structural obstacles to their improved well-being. While Keppel did not live to see the dramatically important unintended consequences of the Myrdal study, he might have been disappointed in the delayed attention to structural change. For a more detailed analysis of this decision and its unintended consequences, see Maribel Morey, "A Reconsideration of *An American Dilemma*," *Reviews in American History* 40 (2012): 686–692; and Lagemann, *The Politics of Knowledge*, 123.

13 Another iterative sequence in risky grant-making is illustrated by the introduction in the 1960s by Alan Pifer and his colleagues of the work in social justice grant-making, including, for the first time, support for litigation. Any failure of this initiative could have affected the future of the foundation. As described in Chapter 6, this grant-making had positive (and intended) consequences, but it also resulted in the Corporation reducing its presence in its traditional areas of comparative advantage, namely, the support of universities and research initiatives. This risky shift fit perfectly, however, with the intentions of Andrew Carnegie as expressed by the Corporation's mission and his charge to the trustees. In both the American South and South Africa, the grants led directly to understanding and ameliorating the root causes of societal injustice, namely, impeded access to the rule of law by the black populations and, in South Africa, by other victims of race-based injustice, the colored and Asian populations. One key factor that mitigated the risk in undertaking these endeavors was partnership, primarily with three foundation partners, the Ford Foundation, the Rockefeller Brothers Fund, and the Rockefeller Foundation, and with local institutions and actors. These collaborative efforts were very risky, but sharing the risk by working in partnership with like-minded institutions in philanthropy and from the region mitigated that risk.

14 Two other significant examples of highly risky programmatic decisions and actions are the work on Russia and nuclear weapons undertaken by President David Hamburg in the 1980s and 1990s and continued by President Vartan Gregorian in the 2000s, and Gregorian's decision in 1997 to become the first foundation president to address the issue of Islam in the modern world and develop a variety of grant-making programs on this theme, including a revival of support for individual scholars in this area and a program initiative dedicated to it, with institutions in North Africa and the Middle East closely involved. In both instances, although the intended consequences have been positive—the Corporation has continued to make significant contributions to institutional and individual expertise with regard to American foreign policy toward Russia, and Corporation involvement has deepened scholarship in the United States around the subject of Islam and Muslim societies—too little time has elapsed to be able to assess outcomes and unintended consequences. These areas provide distinctive opportunities for future scholarship to deepen understanding of the nature of risk-taking in foundation decision-making and its effects.

15 Vartan Gregorian, "Transparency and Accomplishment: A Legacy of Glass Pockets:

Report of the President," 2004, 9, available at: Carnegie.org/fileadmin/Media/Publications/PDF/Transparency_and_Accomplishment.pdf (accessed March 2, 2014).

16 Sara Engelhardt, *The Reminiscences of Sara Engelhardt, 1998*, interviewed by Brenda Hearing, November 5, 1998, Columbia Center for Oral History (CCOH), Carnegie Corporation Project, Part 2: Oral History, 1996–2004, 239, CCNY Records, CUL. Also quoted in Abigail Deutsch, "A Vision of Social Justice: Carnegie Corporation in the 1960s and Beyond," *Carnegie Reporter* (Spring 2011): 2, available at: http://carnegie.org/publications/carnegie-reporter/single/view/article/item/273/.

17 World Economic Forum, "Long-Term Investing," 2012, available at: http://www.weforum.org/issues/long-term-investing (accessed February 10, 2013); Sandy Edwards, "Philantopic: The Benefits of Multiyear Grantmaking: A Funder's Perspective," *Philanthropy News Digest*, Foundation Center, January 29, 2013, available at: http://pndblog.typepad.com/pnd-blog/2013/01/the-benefits-of-multiyear-grantmaking.html (accessed February 10, 2013).

18 CCNYAR, 1922, 19–20.

19 While it is hard to pin down the exact number of institutions and organizations that Andrew Carnegie created in the United States and abroad, as indicated in Chapter 1, twenty-two exist today, either as independent or as merged organizations (the latter including the various Carnegie Hero Funds).

20 The Church Peace Union, after various changes in its name, since 2005 has been titled the Carnegie Council for Ethics in International Affairs. Its work continues today.

21 For example, the Rockefeller Foundation, historically, has supported work to build the fields of physical and information sciences in the broader fields of medicine, public health, and molecular biology; more recently, the Russell Sage Foundation and the Alfred P. Sloan Foundation have supported field-building work in behavioral economics.

22 Other areas have also benefited from the Corporation's commitment to field-building over the past one hundred years: higher education in the United States, Canada, Australia, New Zealand, Africa, and, more recently, Russia and Eurasia; teacher preparation, particularly in African countries and the United States; child development, starting with work on the cognitive science of the brain in the early 1950s, more focused comparative research in the 1960s, outreach through public television in the 1960s and 1970s, work on literacy through the 1990s and early 2000s and previously, in the 1960s and 1970s, in Commonwealth Africa, particularly Nigeria and Kenya; science and technology education, first in the United States and Canada and later in Russia and African countries; social justice, especially related to African Americans, women, immigrants, and disadvantaged people in general, in the United States and South Africa; and journalism and new media, especially for education, through film and radio in the 1920s and 1930s, public broadcasting, training for Commonwealth journalists through the Nieman Foundation, and, in the 2000s, the journalism initiative.

23 For a particularly relevant discussion, see Mark Solovey, *Shaky Foundations: The Politics–Patronage–Social Science Nexus in Cold War America* (New Brunswick, NJ: Rutgers University Press, 2013).

24 See, for example, Robert Albright, "Is This the Decade of Collaborative Philanthropy?" Foundation Strategy Group, Collective Impact Blog, June 12, 2012, available at: http://www.fsg.org/KnowledgeExchange/Blogs/CollectiveImpact/PostID/303.aspx (accessed February 10, 2013).

25 One area that deserves more attention from the internally focused foundation literature is that of internal program staff teamwork across domestic and international programs, whether focused solely on the American setting, the overseas setting, or support for international studies in American institutions. The Corporation is not alone in failing to meet this challenge: nearly

all foundations struggle to increase internal communication among staff members across different programs. In the Corporation's history, the situation became particularly acute as more staff members were hired in the decades following World War II. When President Devereux Josephs and the trustees in 1946 established the separate British Dominions and Colonies Program, the "silo effect" became apparent. Even though all program staff reviewed all proposals from 1945 until 1983, the programmatic dots were rarely connected, even with the internationally oriented staff working on international issues in the United States and those responsible for the overseas grant-making. The example of support for the UN studies program at Yale University in the 1990s provided one of the rare cross-program activities developed jointly and involving staff members from three separate programs: Special Projects, Preventing Deadly Conflict, and Strengthening Human Resources in Developing Countries (see Chapter 7). Not until 2007 did the trustees and President Gregorian make structural changes to link international grant-making initiatives by bringing together, under one vice president, all international activities (with another vice president responsible for domestic activities), with resulting new initiatives in grantmaking.

26 Theroux, "Bringing New Life to South Africa's Libraries."

27 Patricia L. Rosenfield, "Private Philanthropy, Nonprofits, Business, and Government: Shared and Special Features That Facilitate Cross-sectoral Partnerships in the Provision of Public Goods," in *Non-profit och valfarden (Can Nonprofits Save the Swedish Welfare Model?)*, ed. Kurt Almquist, Viveca Ax:son Johnson, and Lars Tragardh (Stockholm: Axel och Margare Ax:son Johnsons stiftelse for allmannyttiga andamal, 2013), 104–105.

28 Rockefeller Foundation/Social Finance, Inc., "A New Tool for Scaling Impact: How Social Impact Bonds Can Mobilize Private Capital to Advance Social Good," Social Finance, Inc. 2012, available at: http://www.socialfinance.org.uk/resources/social-finance/new-tool-scaling-impact-how-social-impact-bonds-can-mobilize-private-capita.

29 Zunz, *Philanthropy in America*; Michael Lipsky and Stephen Rathgeb Smith, "Nonprofit Organizations, Government, and the Welfare State," *Political Science Quarterly* 104, no. 4 (1989–1990): 625–648; Bruce L. Smith, "Changing Public-Private Sector Relations: A Look at the United States," *Annals of the American Academy of Political and Social Science* 466 (March 1983): 149–164; David C. Hammack, "Nonprofit Organizations in American History: Research Opportunities and Sources," *American Behavioral Scientist* 45 (11) 2002, 1638–1674; Hammack and Anheier, *A Versatile Institution*, ch. 4.

30 See, for example, Foundation for Public-Private Partnerships, Nigeria.

31 For a socially constructive way to modify the metrics, see Geoff Mulgan, "Measuring Social Value," *Stanford Social Innovation Review* (Summer 2010), available at: http://www.ssireview.org/articles/entry/measuring_social_value/ (accessed September 15, 2013).

32 CCNYAR, 1922, 13.

33 Ibid.

34 Ibid.

35 See, for example, David Thayne Leibell, "A Second Golden Age of American Philanthropy," Wealth Management.com, June 23, 2010, available at: http://wealthmanagement.com/financial-planning/second-golden-age-american-philanthropy; Betsy Brill, "Stepping Up to the Lifetime Giving Challenge," Forbes.com, August 2, 2010, available at: http://www.forbes.com/2010/08/02/giving-pledge-gates-intelligent-investing-buffett.html; Harry Bruinius, "Can Warren Buffet and Bill Gates Save the World?" Global Policy Forum, *Christian Science Monitor*, November 20, 2010. A Google search on September 19, 2012, on the use of Carnegie's name to promote philanthropy yielded 195,000 entries.

36 Steven Lawrence and Reina Mukai, "International Grantmaking Update: A Snapshot of US Foundation Trends," Foundation Center, December 2010, 7, available at: http://foundation-

center.org/gainknowledge/research/pdf/intl_update (accessed February 27, 2013).

37 Lijun He, "Join Hands with China: An Analysis of the Development of Chinese Philanthropy," Council on Foundations, 2011, 2–3, available at: www.wawomensfoundation.org/sites/default/files/Join Hands with China-COF.pdf (accessed March 2, 2014).

38 This innovation can also be appropriate for a foundation working in its own country; nonetheless, the significantly different cultural values that are likely to prevail when working in another country make this strategy worth serious consideration for foundations that seek to make grants work in other countries. American foundations with overseas offices are likely to have had experiences in peer partnering with local private foundations that could extend to include other foundations seeking to work in those settings.

39 Barry Knight, "The Value of Community Philanthropy: Results of a Consultation," February 2012, The Aga Khan Foundation U.S.A. and the Charles Stewart Mott Foundation, available at: http://www.mott.org/files/publications/thevalueofcommunityphilanthropy.pdf (accessed September 15, 2013); Jenny Hodgson, "Foundations Join Together to Make the Case for Community Philanthropy," *Effect* (Autumn 2013), available at: JennyHodgson_EFFECT_Winter_2013_Web.pdf (accessed March 2, 2013). For more details on practice, see also www.globalfundcommunityfoundations.org.

40 This kind of partnership could also meet the public accountability concerns of US foundations with their public compact for present and future generations resulting in part from their tax-exempt status and in part from the conditions informing their charter. IRS rules, such as foreign institutional qualifying and reporting requirements, have further complicated the overseas grant-making of American foundations, but recent new rules will reduce those burdens. Charity and Security Network, "Proposed IRS Rule Could Make International Grantmaking Easier," October 4, 2012, available at: http://www.charityandsecurity.org/news/Proposed_IRS_Rule_Could_Make_International_Grantmaking_Easier (accessed October 21, 2012).

41 Iriye, *Global Community*, 8.

42 John Krige and Helke Rausch, eds., *American Foundations and the Coproduction of World Order in the Twentieth Century* (Gottingen, Germany, and Bristol, CT: Vandenhoeck & Ruprecht, 2012).

43 Carnegie, *The Autobiography of Andrew Carnegie*, 207.

NOTES FOR THE ACKNOWLEDGMENTS

1. David Nasaw, *Andrew Carnegie* (New York: Penguin Press, 2006), 297.

SELECTED BIBLIOGRAPHY

ARCHIVES

CARNEGIE CORPORATION OF NEW YORK COLLECTION
Carnegie Corporation of New York Records, Rare Book and Manuscript Library, Columbia
University Libraries (CCNY Records, RBML-CUL)

CARNEGIE CORPORATION OF NEW YORK ORAL HISTORY PROJECT: PART I,
1966–1970; PART 2, 1996–2004, COLUMBIA CENTER FOR ORAL HISTORY (CCOH),
COLUMBIA UNIVERSITY LIBRARIES (CUL)
Beeby, Clarence. *The Reminiscences of Clarence Beeby: Oral History, 1968.* Interviewed by Isabel
S. Grossner.
Buck, Paul. *The Reminiscences of Paul Buck: Oral History, 1967.* Interviewed by Isabel S. Grossner.
Budlender, Geoffrey. *The Reminiscences of Geoffrey Budlender: Oral History, 1999.* Interviewed by
Len Morris.
Chaskalson, Arthur. *The Reminiscences of Arthur Chaskalson: Oral History, 1999.* Interviewed by
Len Morris.
Dollard, Charles. *The Reminiscences of Charles Dollard: Oral History, 1966.* Interviewed by Isabel
S. Grossner.
Dugard, John. *The Reminiscences of John Dugard: Oral History, 1999.* Interviewed by Len Morris.
Engelhardt, Sara. *The Reminiscences of Sara Engelhardt: Oral History, 1997–1998.* Interviewed by
Brenda Hearing.
Finberg, Barbara D. *The Reminiscences of Barbara D. Finberg: Oral History, 1997–1998.* Interviewed
by Brenda Hearing.
Fox, William T. R. *The Reminiscences of William T. R. Fox: Oral History, 1968.* Interviewed by
Isabel S. Grossner.
Gardner, John. *The Reminiscences of John Gardner: Oral History, 1971.* Interviewed by Isabel S.
Grossner.
———. *The Reminiscences of John Gardner: Oral History, 2000.* Interviewed by Sharon Zane.
Hamburg, David A. *The Reminiscences of David A. Hamburg: Oral History, 1996–1998.*
Interviewed by Brenda Hearing and Mary Marshall Clark.
Herring, Pendleton. *The Reminiscences of Pendleton Herring: Oral History, 1967.* Interviewed by
Isabel S. Grossner.
Josephs, Devereux. *The Reminiscences of Devereux Colt Josephs: Oral History, 1969.* Interviewed
by Isabel S. Grossner.
Pifer, Alan. *The Reminiscences of Alan Pifer: Oral History, 1967.* Interviewed by Isabel S. Grossner.

———. *The Reminiscences of Alan Pifer: Oral History, 2000.* Interviewed by Brenda Hearing.

Ramphele, Mamphela. *The Reminiscences of Mamphela Ramphele: Oral History, 1999.* Interviewed by Mary Marshall Clark.

Wilson, Francis. *The Reminiscences of Francis Wilson: Oral History, 1999.* Interviewed by Mary Marshall Clark.

CARNEGIE CORPORATION OF NEW YORK UNPUBLISHED REPORTS, DOCUMENTS, AND PAPERS, 1997–2011, CCNY OFFICES (CCNYO)

ROCKEFELLER ARCHIVE CENTER, SLEEPY HOLLOW, NEW YORK

General Education Board Archive, 1901–1967

Rockefeller Foundation Archives, 1910, 1912–2000

Rockefeller Family Archive: Record Group 2: Office of the Messrs. Rockefeller, 1858, 1879–1961

FORD FOUNDATION ARCHIVES

BOOKS

Adelman, Jeremy. 2013. *Worldly Philosopher: The Odyssey of Albert O. Hirschman.* Princeton, NJ: Princeton University Press.

Agha, Hussein, Shai Feldman, Ahmad Khalidi, and Zeev Schiff. 2003. *Track II Diplomacy: Lessons from the Middle East.* BSCIA Studies in International Security. Cambridge, MA: MIT Press.

Ajayi, J. F. Ade, Lameck K. H. Goma, and G. Ampah Johnson. 1996. *The African Experience with Higher Education.* Accra, North London, and Athens, OH: Association of African Universities, James Currey Ltd., and Ohio University Press.

Allison, Graham T., Albert Carnesale, and Joseph S. Nye Jr., eds. 1986. *Hawks, Doves, and Owls: An Agenda for Avoiding Nuclear War.* New York: W. W. Norton.

Allison, Graham T., William L. Ury, and Bruce J. Allyn. 1989. *Windows of Opportunity: From Cold War to Peaceful Competition in US-Soviet Relations.* Cambridge, MA: Ballinger.

Anderson, Florence. 1961. *Carnegie Corporation Library Program: 1911–1961.* New York: Carnegie Corporation.

Andreano, Ralph. 2001. *The International Health Policy Program: An Internal Assessment.* Madison: University of Wisconsin Press.

Anheier, Helmut K., and David C. Hammack, eds. 2010. *American Foundations: Roles and Contributions.* Washington, DC: Brookings Institution.

Anheier, Helmut K., and Diana Leat. 2006. *Creative Philanthropy: Towards a New Philanthropy for the Twenty-First Century.* Abingdon, UK: Routledge.

Association of African Universities and World Bank. 1997. *Revitalizing Universities in Africa: Strategy and Guidelines.* Washington, DC: World Bank.

Barber, Joseph. 1964. *These Are the Committees.* New York: Council on Foreign Relations.

Bennett, Wendell C. 1951. *Area Studies in American Universities.* New York: Social Science Research Council.

Benoit, Emile, and Kenneth E. Boulding, eds. 1963. *Disarmament and the Economy.* New York: Harper & Row.

Berg, Robert J., and Jennifer Seymour Whitaker, eds. 1986. *Strategies for African Development.* Berkeley: University of California Press.

Berman, Edward H. 1983. *The Influence of the Carnegie, Ford, and Rockefeller Foundations on American Foreign Policy: The Ideology of Philanthropy.* Albany: State University of New York Press.

Bieler, Stacey. 2004. *"Patriots" or "Traitors"? A History of American-Educated Chinese Students.* Armonk, NY: M. E. Sharpe.

Bishop, Matthew, and Michael Green. 2008. *Philanthrocapitalism: How the Rich Can Save the World.* New York: Bloomsbury.

Board on International Health. Institute of Medicine. National Academy of Sciences. 1997. *America's Vital Interest in Global Health: Protecting Our People, Promoting Economic Interests, and Projecting US Influence Abroad.* Washington, DC: National Academies Press.

Bremner, Robert H. 1988. *American Philanthropy.* 2nd ed. Chicago: University of Chicago Press.

Brest, Paul, and Hal Harvey. 2008. *Money Well Spent: A Strategic Plan for Smart Philanthropy.* New York: Bloomberg Press.

Brilliant, Eleanor L. 2000. *Private Charity and Public Inquiry: A History of the Filer and Peterson Commissions.* Bloomington: Indiana University Press.

Brown, E. Richard. 1979. *Medicine and Capitalism in America.* Berkeley: University of California Press.

Bundy, McGeorge, William J. Crowe, and Sidney David Drell. 1993. *Reducing Nuclear Danger: The Road Away from the Brink.* New York: Council on Foreign Relations.

Burdick, Eugene, and William J. Lederer. 1958. *The Ugly American.* New York: W. W. Norton.

Burlingame, Dwight. 2004. *Philanthropy in America: A Comprehensive History.* Santa Barbara, CA: ABC-CLIO.

Bush, Barbara. 1999. *Imperialism, Race, and Resistance: Africa and Britain, 1919–1945.* Florence, KY: Routledge.

Butler, L. J. 2002. *Britain and Empire: Adjusting to a Post-Imperial World.* London: I. B. Tauris & Co.

Campbell, Chloe. 2007. *Race and Empire: Eugenics in Colonial Kenya.* Manchester, UK: Manchester University Press.

Carman, Harry J., Ralph Hayes, Lewis Galantière, et al. 1951. *Appreciations of Frederick Paul Keppel.* New York: Columbia University Press.

Carnegie, Andrew. 1885. *Triumphant Democracy.* Garden City, NY: Doubleday, Doran & Co.

———. 1906. *A League of Peace: A Rectorial Address Delivered to the Students in the University of St Andrews, 17th October, 1905.* Boston: Ginn.

———. 1920. *Autobiography.* Boston: Houghton Mifflin.

———. 1962. *The Gospel of Wealth and Other Timely Essays.* Cambridge, MA: Belknap Press of Harvard University Press. (Originally published in 1900.)

Carter, Ashton B., William J. Perry, and John D. Steinbruner. 1992. *A New Concept of Cooperative Security.* Washington, DC: Brookings Institution.

Coleman, James S., with David Court. 1993. *University Development in the Third World: The Rockefeller Foundation Experience.* Oxford: Pergamon.

Collinson, Michael P., ed. 2000. *A History of Farming Systems Research.* Wallingford, UK, and Rome, Italy: CABI Publishing and Food and Agricultural Organization.

Commission on Global Governance. 1995. *Our Global Neighbourhood.* Oxford: Oxford University Press.

Commission on Health Research for Development. 1990. *Health Research: Essential Link to Equity in Development.* Oxford: Oxford University Press.

Connell, W. F. 1980. *The Australian Council for Educational Research, 1930–1980.* Hawthorn, Victoria: Australian Council for Educational Research Ltd.

Curle, Adam. 1972. *Mystics and Militants: A Study of Awareness, Identity, and Social Action.* London: Tavistock.

Curti, Merle. 1963. *American Philanthropy Abroad: A History.* New Brunswick, NJ: Rutgers University Press.

Cutlip, Scott M. 1990. *Fundraising in the United States: Its Role in American Philanthropy.* New Brunswick, NJ: Transaction Publishers. (Originally published in 1965 by Rutgers, The State University.)

Damon, William, and Susan Verducci. 2006. *Taking Philanthropy Seriously: Beyond Noble Intentions to Responsible Giving.* Bloomington: Indiana University Press.

Delgado, James P., Daniel Lenihan, Larry Murphy, Kili/Bikini/Ejit Local Government Council (Marshall Islands), and National Maritime Initiative (US). 1991. *The Archaeology of the Atomic Bomb: A Submerged Cultural Resources Assessment of the Sunken Fleet of Operation Crossroads at Bikini and Kwajalein Atoll Lagoons, Republic of the Marshall Islands.* Santa Fe, NM: US Department of the Interior, National Park Service, Submerged Cultural Resources Unit, National Maritime Initiative.

Delpar, Helen. 2008. *Looking South: The Evolution of Latin Americanist Scholarship in the United States, 1850–1975.* Tuscaloosa: University of Alabama Press.

Deng, Francis M., Sadikiel Kimaro, Terrence Lyons, Donald Rothschild, and I. William Zartman. 1996. *Sovereignty as Responsibility: Conflict Management in Africa.* Washington, DC: Brookings Institution.

Deng, Francis M., and I. William Zartman. 1991. *Conflict Resolution in Africa.* Washington, DC: Brookings Institution.

Deng, Francis M., and Terrence Lyons, eds. 1998. *African Reckoning: A Quest for Good Governance.* Washington, DC: Brookings Institution.

Diamond, Sigmund. 1992. *Compromised Campus: The Collaboration of Universities with the Intelligence Community, 1945–1955.* New York: Oxford University Press.

Diouf, Mamadou. 1998. *Political Liberalisation or Democratic Transition: African Perspectives.* Dakar, Senegal: CODESRIA.

Dubow, Saul. 1989. *Racial Segregation and the Origins of Apartheid in South Africa, 1919–1936.* New York: St. Martin's Press.

———. 1995. *Scientific Racism in Modern South Africa.* Cambridge: Cambridge University Press.

Dumenil, Lynn. 1995. *The Modern Temper.* New York: Hill and Wang.

Eilinghoff, Dirk. 2005. *Rethinking Philanthropic Effectiveness: Lessons from an International Network of Foundation Experts.* Gutersloh, Germany: Verlag Bertelsmann Stiftung.

Ekbladh, David. 2010. *The Great American Mission: Modernization and the Construction of an American World Order.* Princeton, NJ: Princeton University Press.

Engerman, David. 2009. *Know Your Enemy: The Rise and Fall of America's Soviet Experts.* New York: Oxford University Press.

Falk, Richard A., and Saul H. Mendlovitz, eds. 1966. *The Strategy of World Order.* 4 vols. New York: World Law Fund.

Ferguson, Niall. 2004. *Colossus: The Price of America's Empire.* New York: Penguin.

Fleishman, Joel L. 2007. *The Foundation: A Great American Secret: How Private Wealth Is Changing the World.* New York: Public Affairs.

Ford Foundation. 1999. *Crossing Borders: Revitalizing Area Studies.* New York: Ford Foundation.

Fosdick, Raymond B. 1952. *The Story of the Rockefeller Foundation.* New York: Harper & Brothers.

Fox, Daniel M. 1993. *Power and Illness: The Failure and Future of American Health Policy.* Berkeley: University of California Press.

Fredericks, J. Wayne. 1995. *A Second Look: The Role of Africanists in US Policymaking During the Late 1950s and Early 1960s.* New York: Institute of International Education.

———. 1995. *The Anglo-American-Canadian Parliamentary Study Group on Africa 1965–1980: A Preliminary Review.* New York: Institute of International Education.

Gangewere, Robert J. 2011. *Palace of Culture: Andrew Carnegie's Museums and Library in Pittsburgh.* Pittsburgh: University of Pittsburgh Press.

Garba, Joseph Nansen. 1987. *Diplomatic Soldiering: Nigerian Foreign Policy, 1975–1979.* Ibadan, Nigeria: Spectrum Books.

———. 1994. *The Southern Africa Peacekeeping and Peacemaking Project.* Vol. 2. New York: Institute of International Education.

Gardner, John. 1963. *Self-Renewal: The Individual and the Innovative Society.* New York: Harper & Row.

Garthoff, Raymond L. 1994. *The Great Transition: American-Soviet Relations and the End of the Cold War.* Washington, DC: Brookings Institution.

Gaudiani, Claire. 2010. *Generosity Unbound: How American Philanthropy Can Strengthen the Economy and Expand the Middle Class.* New York: Broadway Publications.

Gifford, Prosser, and William Louis Roger. 1988. *Decolonization and African Independence: The Transfers of Power: 1960–1980.* New Haven, CT: Yale University Press.

Gilman, Nils. 2003. *Mandarins of the Future: Modernization in Cold War America.* Baltimore: Johns Hopkins University Press.

Gladwell, Malcolm. 2008. *Outliers: The Story of Success.* New York: Little, Brown.

Global Development Initiative. 1997. *Toward a New Model of Development Cooperation: The National Development Strategy Process in Guyana.* Atlanta: Carter Center.

Gordon, David F., David C. Miller Jr., and Howard Wolpe. 1998. *The United States and Africa: A Post–Cold War Perspective.* New York: Norton.

Gourley, James E., and Robert M. Lester. 1935. *The Diffusion of Knowledge: A List of Books Made Possible Wholly or in Part by Grants from Carnegie Corporation of New York and Published by Various Agencies During the Years 1911–1935.* Philadelphia: Press of W. F. Fell Co.

Gray, George. 1941. *Education on an International Scale.* New York: Harcourt, Brace.

Greaves, Tom, Ralph Bolton, and Florencia Zapata, eds. 2011. *Vicos and Beyond: A Half Century of Applying Anthropology in Peru.* Lanham, MD: AltaMira Press.

Gregorian, Vartan. 1969. *The Emergence of Modern Afghanistan: Politics of Reform and Modernization, 1840–1946.* Stanford, CA: Stanford University Press.

———. 2003. *Islam: A Mosaic, Not a Monolith.* Washington, DC: Brookings Institution.

Griese, Noel L. 2001. *Arthur W. Page: Publisher, Public Relations Pioneer, Patriot.* Tucker, GA: Anvil.

Grose, Peter. 1996. *Continuing the Inquiry: The Council on Foreign Relations from 1921 to 1996.* New York: Council on Foreign Relations Press.

Grosskopf, Johann Friedrich Wilhelm, Raymond William Wilcocks, Ernst Gideon Malherbe, W. A. Murray, J. R. Albertyn, and Mimie E. Rothmann. 1932. *The Poor White Problem in South Africa: Report of the Carnegie Commission.* Stellenbosch, South Africa: Pro Ecclesia.

Hammack, David C., and Helmut K. Anheier. 2013. *A Versatile Institution: The Changing Ideals and Realities of Philanthropic Foundations.* Washington, DC: Brookings Institution.

Harris, Robin Sutton. 1976. *A History of Higher Education in Canada, 1663–1960.* Toronto: University of Toronto Press.

Hendrick, Burton Jesse. 1932. *The Life of Andrew Carnegie.* 2 vols. Garden City, NY: Doubleday, Doran & Co.

Hendrick, Burton Jesse, and Daniel Henderson. 1950. *Louise Whitfield Carnegie: The Life of Mrs. Andrew Carnegie.* New York: Hastings House.

Herskovits, Jean. 1998. *Africans Solving African Problems: Militaries, Democracies, and Security in West and Southern Africa.* New York: International Peace Academy.

Higginbotham, Nick, Roberto Briceno-Leon, and Nancy Johnson. 2011. *Applying Health Social Science: Best Practice in the Developing World*. London: Zed Books.

Hill, Frank Pierce. 1936. *James Bertram: An Appreciation*. New York: Carnegie Corporation.

Hirschman, Albert O. 1995. *Development Projects Observed, with a New Preface by the Author*. Washington, DC: Brookings Institution. (Originally published in 1967.)

Hooper, Paul F., ed. 1995. *Remembering the Institute of Pacific Relations: The Memoirs of William L. Holland*. Tokyo: Ryukei Shysha.

Hoover, Glenn Edwin. 1970. *Twentieth Century Economic Thought*. New York: Philosophical Society. (Originally published in 1950.)

House, Edward Mandell, and Charles Seymour, eds. 1921. *What Really Happened at Paris: The Story of the Peace Conference, 1918–1919*. New York: Charles Scribner's Sons.

International Peace Academy. 1996. *Civil Society and Conflict Management in Africa: Report of the IPA/OAU Consultation, May 29–June 2, 1996, Cape Town, South Africa*. New York: International Peace Academy.

Iriye, Akira. 1997. *Cultural Internationalism and World Order*. Baltimore: Johns Hopkins University Press.

———. 2002. *Global Community: The Role of International Organizations in the Making of the Contemporary World*. Berkeley: University of California Press.

Jackson, Kenneth T. 1992. *The Ku Klux Klan in the City, 1915–1930*. Chicago: Elephant Paperback.

Jensen, Steffen. 2008. *Gangs, Politics, and Dignity in Cape Town*. Chicago: University of Chicago Press.

Joan Shorenstein Center, Carnegie Corporation, and Knight Foundation. 2011. *Report on the Carnegie-Knight Initiative on the Future of Journalism Education*. Cambridge, MA: Shorenstein Center.

Jonas, Gerald. 1989. *Circuit Riders: Rockefeller Money and the Rise of Modern Science*. New York: Norton.

Keith, Arthur Berriedale. 1921. *War Government of the British Dominions*. Oxford: Clarendon Press.

Kenney, Henry. 1980. *Architect of Apartheid: H. F. Verwoerd—An Appraisal*. Johannesburg, South Africa: Jonathan Ball.

Keppel, Frederick. 1936. *Philanthropy and Learning, with Other Papers*. New York: Columbia University.

———. 1989. *The Foundation: Its Place in American Life*. New Brunswick, NJ: Transaction Publishers. (Originally published in 1930 by Macmillan Co.)

King, Kenneth James. 1971. *Pan-Africanism and Education: A Study of Race Philanthropy and Education in the Southern States of America and East Africa*. Oxford: Clarendon Press.

Kohler, Robert E. 1991. *Partners in Science: Foundations and Natural Scientists, 1900–1945*. Chicago: University of Chicago Press.

Krass, Peter. 2002. *Carnegie*. Hoboken, NJ: John Wiley & Sons.

Krige, John, and Helke Rausch, eds. 2012. *American Foundations and the Coproduction of World Order in the Twentieth Century*. Gottingen, Germany, and Bristol, CT: Vandenhoeck & Ruprecht.

Lagemann, Ellen. 1989. *The Politics of Knowledge: The Carnegie Corporation, Philanthropy, and Public Policy*. Middletown, CT: Wesleyan University Press.

Lambert, Richard D. 1973. *Language and Area Studies Review*. Monograph 17. Philadelphia: American Academy of Political and Social Sciences.

Lancaster, Carol. 2007. *Foreign Aid: Diplomacy, Development, Domestic Politics*. Chicago: University of Chicago Press.

Lawrence, Steven, and Reina Mukai. 2009, 2011. *Foundation Growth and Giving Estimates: Current Outlook*. New York: Foundation Center.

———. 2010. *International Grantmaking Update.* New York: Foundation Center.

Lele, Uma J., Carl K. Eicher, Mandivamba Rukuni, et al. 2003, 2004. *The CGIAR at Thirty-One: An Independent Meta-Evaluation of the Consultative Group on International Agricultural Research.* Washington, DC: World Bank.

Lester, Robert M. 1941. *Forty Years of Carnegie Giving, 1901–1941.* New York: Charles Scribner's Sons.

———. 1942. *A Thirty Year Catalog of Grants, 1911–1941.* New York: Carnegie Corporation.

Leventhal, Paul. 1987. *Preventing Nuclear Terrorism.* Lanham, MD: Lexington Books.

Lindow, Megan. 2011. *Weaving Success: Voices of Change in African Higher Education.* New York: Institute of International Education.

Lodge, Tom, Bill Nasson, Steven Mufson, Khela Shubane, and Nokwanda Sithole. 1991. *All, Here and Now: Black Politics in South Africa in the 1980s, Update South Africa: Time Running Out.* New York: Ford Foundation and Foreign Policy Association.

Lucas, Adetokunbo O. 2010. *It Was the Best of Times: From Local to Global Health.* Ibadan, Nigeria: Bookbuilders.

Magat, Richard. 1979. *Ford Foundation at Work: Philanthropic Choices, Methods, and Styles.* New York: Plenum Publishing.

Mansergh, Nicholas. 1968. *Survey of British Commonwealth Affairs: Problems of Wartime Cooperation and Postwar Change, 1939–1952.* London: Cass, 1968. (Originally published in 1952 by Oxford University Press; reprinted in 1958.)

Marx, Christoph. 2008. *Oxwagon Sentinel: Radical Afrikaner Nationalism and the History of the "Ossewabrandwag."* Berlin: Lit Verlag.

Mazower, Mark. 2012. *Governing the World: The History of an Idea.* New York: Penguin Press.

McCallum, David. 1990. *The Social Production of Merit: Education, Psychology, and Politics in Australia, 1900–1950.* New York: Falmer.

McDermott, Rose. 1998. *Risk-Taking in International Politics: Prospect Theory in American Foreign Policy.* Ann Arbor: University of Michigan Press.

Miles, Robert, and Malcolm Brown. 2003. *Racism.* 2nd ed. London: Routledge.

Morawetz, David. 1977. *Twenty-Five Years of Economic Development, 1950–1975.* Washington, DC: World Bank.

Morrell, Robert, ed. 1992. *White but Poor: Essays on the History of Poor Whites in Southern Africa, 1880–1940.* Pretoria: University of South Africa.

Morris, Morris David. 1979. *Measuring the Conditions of the World's Poor: The Physical Quality of Life Index.* New York: Pergamon Press for the Overseas Development Council.

Mulligan, William. 2010. *The Origins of the First World War.* New York: Cambridge University Press.

Murphy, E. Jefferson. 1976. *Creative Philanthropy: Carnegie Corporation and Africa, 1953–1973.* New York: Teachers College Press.

Mwabu, Germano, Joseph Wang'ombe, David Okello, and Gaspar Munishi. 2004. *Improving Health Policy in Africa.* Nairobi, Kenya: University of Nairobi Press.

Myrdal, Gunnar. 1996. *An American Dilemma: The Negro Problem and Modern Democracy.* New Brunswick, NJ: Transaction Press. (Originally published in 1944 by Harper Brothers; reprinted in 1962.)

Nasaw, David. 2006. *Andrew Carnegie.* New York: Penguin.

Nasr, Vali. 2006. *The Shia Revival: How Conflicts Within Islam Will Shape the Future.* New York: W. W. Norton and Co.

Nielsen, Waldemar A. 1996. *Inside American Philanthropy: The Dramas of Donorship.* Norman: University of Oklahoma Press.

Nolan, Janne, ed. 1994. *Global Engagement: Cooperative Security in the Twenty-First Century.* Washington, DC: Brookings Institution.

Nyango, Anyang. 1990. *Regional Integration in Africa: An Unfinished Agenda.* Nairobi, Kenya: Academy Science Publisher.

Nye, Joseph S., Jr., Graham T. Allison Jr., and Albert Carnesale, eds. 1988. *Fateful Visions: Avoiding Nuclear Catastrophe.* Cambridge, MA: Ballinger.

Pape, Robert A. 2005. *Dying to Win: The Strategic Logic of Suicide Terrorism.* New York: Random House.

Parmar, Inderjeet. 2004. *Think Tanks and Power in Foreign Policy: A Comparative Study of the Role and Influence of the Council on Foreign Relations and the Royal Institute of International Affairs, 1939–1945.* Hampshire, UK: Palgrave Macmillan.

———. 2012. *Foundations of the American Century: The Ford, Carnegie, and Rockefeller Foundations in the Rise of American Power.* New York: Columbia University Press.

Patterson, James T. 1996. *Grand Expectations: The United States, 1945–1974.* New York: Oxford University Press.

Perkovich, George, Jessica T. Matthews, Joseph Cirincione, Rose Gottemoeller, and Jon Wolfstahl. 2005. *Universal Compliance: A Strategy for Nuclear Security.* Washington, DC: Carnegie Endowment for International Peace.

Pifer, Alan. 2005. *Speaking Out: Reflections on Thirty Years of Foundation Work.* Rev. ed. Washington, DC: Council on Foundations.

Price, David H. 2008. *Anthropological Intelligence: The Deployment and Neglect of American Anthropology in the Second World War.* Durham, NC: Duke University Press.

Pritchett, Henry Smith. 1931. *The First Twenty Years of Carnegie Corporation* (speech delivered November 19, 1931). New York: Carnegie Corporation.

Ramphele, Mamphela. 1995. *A Life.* Claremont, South Africa: David Philip Publishers.

Ramphele, Mamphela, and Francis Wilson. 1989. *Children on the Front Line: The Impact of Apartheid, Destabilization, and Warfare on Children in Southern and South Africa: A Report for UNICEF.* New York: UNICEF.

Ranis, Gustave, James Raymond Vreeland, and Stephen Kosack. 2006. *Globalization and the Nation State: The Impact of the IMF and the World Bank.* Abingdon, UK: Routledge.

Reed, Alfred Zantzinger. 1921. *Training for the Public Profession of the Law.* New York: Carnegie Foundation for the Advancement of Teaching.

Reeves, Thomas C. 1970. *Foundations Under Fire.* Ithaca, NY: Cornell University Press.

Roberts, Andrew. 1990. *The Colonial Moment in Africa: Essays on the Movement of Minds and Materials, 1900–1940.* New York: Cambridge University Press.

Rockefeller Brothers Fund. 1958. *The Pursuit of Excellence: Education and the Future of America.* New York: Doubleday.

Rockefeller Foundation. 1981. *South Africa: Time Running Out: The Report of the Study Commission on US Policy Toward Southern Africa.* Berkeley: University of California Press.

Rodgers, Daniel T. 1998. *Atlantic Crossings: Social Politics in a Progressive Age.* Cambridge, MA: Belknap Press of Harvard University Press.

Rohde, David, and Kristen Mulvihill. 2010. *A Rope and a Prayer.* New York: Viking.

Rostow, Walt W. 1960. *The Stages of Economic Growth: A Non-Communist Manifesto.* Cambridge: Cambridge University Press.

Sagasti, Francisco. 2004. *Knowledge and Innovation for Development: The Sisyphus Challenge for the Twenty-First Century.* Cheltenham, UK: Edward Elgar.

Saunders, Stuart. 2000. *Vice Chancellor on a Tightrope: A Personal Account of Climactic Years in South Africa.* Cape Town, South Africa: David Philip Publishers.

Schuknecht, Rohland. 2010. *British Colonial Development Policy After the Second World War: The Case of Sukuymaland, Tanganyika.* Berlin: Lit Verlag.

Serra, Narcis, and Joseph E. Stiglitz, eds. 2008. *The Washington Consensus Reconsidered: Towards a New Global Governance.* Oxford: Oxford University Press.

Shaplen, Robert. 1964. *Toward the Well-being of Mankind: Fifty Years of the Rockefeller Foundation.* Garden City, NY: Doubleday.

Smith, Bruce L. R., and Douglas Chalmers Hague, eds. 1971. *The Dilemmas of Accountability in Modern Government: Independence versus Control.* New York and London: St. Martin's Press and Macmillan & Co.

Smith, James Allen. 1991. *The Idea Brokers: Think Tanks and the Rise of the New Policy Elites.* New York: Free Press.

———. 1991. *Brookings at Seventy-Five.* Washington, DC: Brookings Institution.

Solovey, Mark. 2013. *Shaky Foundations: The Politics–Patronage–Social Science Nexus in Cold War America.* New Brunswick, NJ: Rutgers University Press.

Spector, Leonard S., and Jacqueline R. Smith. 1990. *Nuclear Ambitions: The Spread of Nuclear Weapons, 1989–1990.* Boulder, CO: Westview Press.

———. 1990. *The Undeclared Bomb: The Spread of Nuclear Weapons, 1987–1988.* New York: Harper Business.

Spero, Joan. 2010. *The Global Role of US Foundations.* New York: Foundation Center.

Stackpole, Stephen. 1963. *Carnegie Corporation: Commonwealth Program, 1911–1961.* New York: Carnegie Corporation.

Stock, Chester. 1951. *John Campbell Merriam, 1869–1945: A Biographical Memoir.* Washington, DC: National Academy of Sciences Press. Available at: www.nasonline.org/publications/biographical-memoirs/memoir-pdfs/merriam-john.pdf (accessed December 27, 2013).

Stone, Jean, and Irving Stone, eds. 1996. *There Was Light: Autobiography of a University: A Collection of Essays Written by Alumni of the University of California, Berkeley, 1868–1996.* 2nd ed. Berkeley: University of California Press.

Szanton, David L., ed. 2004. *The Politics of Knowledge: Area Studies and the Disciplines.* Berkeley: University of California Press.

Taylor, Andrew, ed. 1984. *Insights into African Education: The Karl W. Bigelow Memorial Lectures.* New York: Teachers College Press.

Taylor, Daniel, Carl Taylor, and Jesse Taylor. 2011. *Empowerment on an Unstable Planet: From Seeds of Human Energy to a Scale of Global Change.* New York: Oxford University Press.

Thompson, Frank V. 1920. *Schooling of the Immigrant.* New York: Harper and Brothers.

Tilley, Helen. 2011. *Africa as a Living Laboratory: Problems of Scientific Knowledge, 1830–1950.* Chicago: University of Chicago Press.

Tirman, John. 2000. *Making the Money Sing: Private Wealth and Public Power in the Search for Peace.* Oxford: Rowan & Littlefield.

Turner, Stansfield. 1991. *Terrorism and Democracy.* Boston: Houghton Mifflin.

United Nations. Department of Economic and Social Affairs. 2011. *The Global Social Crisis: Report on the World Social Situation 2011.* New York: UN. Available at: http://undesadspd.org/ReportontheWorldSocialSituation/2011.aspx (accessed March 4, 2014).

United Nations. Development Policy and Analysis Division. 2011. *World Economic Situation and Prospects 2011.* New York: UN. Available at: http://www.un.org/en/development/desa/policy/wesp/wesp_archive/2011wesp.pdf (accessed March 4, 2014).

United Nations Economic Commission for Africa (UNECA). 2008. *The African Information Society Initiative: A Decade's Perspective.* Addis Ababa, Ethiopia: UNECA.

———. 2012. *Reflections on Africa's Development: Essays in Honour of Abdoulie Janneh.* Addis Ababa, Ethiopia: UNECA.

Van de Walle, Nicolas, and Timothy A. Johnston. 1996. *Improving Aid to Africa.* Washington, DC: Overseas Development Council.

Verba, Sydney, Norman H. Nie, and Jae-On Kim. 1978. *Participation and Political Equality: A Seven-Nation Comparison.* New York: Cambridge University Press.

Wade, Wyn Craige. 1987. *The Fiery Cross: The Ku Klux Klan in America.* Oxford: Oxford University Press.

Wall, Joseph Frazier. 1989. *Andrew Carnegie.* Pittsburgh: University of Pittsburgh Press. (Originally published in 1970 by Oxford University Press.)

———, ed. 1992. *The Andrew Carnegie Reader.* Pittsburgh: University of Pittsburgh Press.

Ward, Barbara. 1962. *The Rich Nations and the Poor Nations.* New York: W. W. Norton.

Warner, Michael. 2002. *The Office of Strategic Services: America's First Intelligence Agency.* Washington, DC: Central Intelligence Agency, Public Affairs. Available at: https://www.cia.gov/library/center-for-the-study-of-intelligence/csi-publications/books-and-monographs/oss/index.htm (posted March 15, 2007).

Weiner, Myron. 1967. *Party Building in a New Nation.* Chicago: University of Chicago Press.

Werth, Barry. 2009. *Banquet at Delmonico's: Great Minds, the Gilded Age, and the Triumph of Evolution in America.* New York: Random House.

Whitehead, Clive. 2003. *Colonial Educators: The British Indian and Colonial Education Service, 1858–1983.* London: I. B. Tauris & Co.

Wiener, Sharon K. 2011. *Our Own Worst Enemy? Institutional Interests and the Proliferation of Nuclear Weapons Expertise.* Belfer Center Studies in International Security. Cambridge, MA: MIT Press.

Wiley, David S., and Robert S. Glew, eds. 2010. *International and Language Education for a Global Future: Fifty Years of US Title VI and Fulbright-Hays Programs.* East Lansing: Michigan State University Press.

Williamson, John, ed. 1983. *IMF Conditionality.* Cambridge, MA: MIT Press.

Wilson, Francis. 2009. *Dinosaurs, Diamonds, and Democracy: A Short, Short History of South Africa.* Roggebai, South Africa: Umuzi.

Wilson, Francis, and Omar Badsha. 1986. *South Africa: The Cordoned Heart.* New York: W. W. Norton and Co.

Wilson, Francis, and Mamphela Ramphele. 1989. *Uprooting Poverty: The South African Challenge.* New York: W. W. Norton & Co.

Woolverton, John Frederick. 2005. *Robert H. Gardiner and the Reunification of Worldwide Christianity in the Progressive Era.* Columbia: University of Missouri Press.

World Bank. 1988. *Education in Sub-Saharan Africa: Policies for Adjustment, Revitalization, and Expansion.* Washington, DC: World Bank.

———. 1993. *World Development Report 1993: Investing in Health.* Oxford: Oxford University Press.

———. 2011. *Conflict, Security, and Development: World Development Report 2011.* Washington, DC: World Bank.

Yale University. 1921. *Inauguration of James Rowland Angell, LL.D., as Fourteenth President of Yale University, on June 22, 1921.* New Haven, CT: Yale University Press.

Ye, Yeili. 2001. *Seeking Modernity in China's Name: Chinese Students in the United States, 1900–1927.* Stanford, CA: Stanford University Press.

Zunz, Olivier. 2012. *Philanthropy in America: A History.* Princeton, NJ: Princeton University Press.

ARTICLES, PAPERS, BOOK CHAPTERS, DISSERTATIONS,
AND ONLINE DOCUMENTS

Abramowitz, Michael J. 1982. "Hamburg Assumes MacArthur Chair in Health Policy." *Harvard Crimson,* May 14.

Africa Society on the National Summit on Africa. N.d. "History: National Summit on Africa." Available at: http://africasummit.org/about-the-society/history/ (accessed March 3, 2014).

Afridi, Sam. 2001. "Muslims in America: Identity, Diversity, and the Challenge of Understanding." *Carnegie Challenge Paper 2001.* Carnegie Corporation of New York. Available at: carnegie. org/fileadmin/Media/Publications/PDF/muslims.pdf (accessed March 11, 2014).

Aina, Tade Akin. 1993. "Development Theory and Africa's Lost Decade: Critical Reflections on Africa's Crisis and Current Trends in Development Thinking and Practice." In *Changing Paradigms in Development: South, East, and West,* ed. Margaretha von Troil, 11–25. Uppsala, Sweden: Nordiska Afrikainstitutet.

———. 2013. "The State, Politics, and Philanthropy in Africa: Framing the Context." In *Giving to Help, Helping to Give: The Context and Politics of African Philanthropy,* ed. Tade Akin Aina and Bhekinkosi Moyo, 19–27. Dakar, Senegal: Amalion Publishing/TrustAfrica.

Aksartova, Sada. 2003. "In Search of Legitimacy: Peace Grant Making of US Philanthropic Foundations, 1988–1996." *Nonprofit and Voluntary Sector Quarterly* 32, no. 1: 25–46.

Akst, Daniel. 2004. "What Are Foundations For?" *Carnegie Reporter* 3, no. 4 (Fall): 2–9. Available at: http://carnegie.org/publications/carnegie-reporter/single/view/article/item/111/.

Akst, Daniel, and Mike Jensen. 2011. "Africa Goes Online." *Carnegie Reporter* 1, no. 2 (Spring). Available at: http://carnegie.org/publications/carnegie-reporter/single/view/article/item/14/.Albright, Robert. 2012. "Is This the Decade of Collaborative Philanthropy?" Foundation Strategy Group, Collective Impact Blog, June 13. Available at: http://www.fsg. org/ KnowledgeExchange/Blogs/CollectiveImpact/PostID/303.aspx.

Amey, Larry. 2001. "When Libraries Made Headlines." *Australian Library Journal* 50, no. 3: 229–234.

Anderson, Alan. 2010. "African Scientists on the Rise." *Carnegie Reporter* 6, no. 2 (Spring): 12–18. Available at: http://carnegie.org/publications/carnegie-reporter/single/view/article/item/251/.

Assie-Lumumba, N'Dri. 2006. "Empowerment of Women in Higher Education in Africa: The Role and Mission of Research." UNESCO Forum Occasional Paper 11, UNESCO Forum Secretariat (June). Available at: http://unesdoc.unesco.org/images/0015/001510/151051eo. pdf.

Baker, Patricia. 2010. "Taking Risks at a Critical Time." Grantmakers in Health, March 8. Available at: http://www.gih.org/Publications/MeetingReportsDetail.cfm?ItemNumber=4073.

Baldwin, Joyce. 2007. "Promoting Social Justice: A Vision of Philanthropic Activism." *Carnegie Results* (Spring). Available at: http://carnegie.org/fileadmin/Media/Publications/jefferson_science_fellows_carnegie_results_summer_10_extra.pdf.

———. 2010. "Jefferson Science Fellows: A Vision for Harnessing the Knowledge of Academic Scientists to Help Inform US Policymaking Takes Shape." *Carnegie Results* (Summer). Available at: http://carnegie.org/fileadmin/Media/Publications/PDF/carnegie_results_summer_10_FINAL_with_adds_rev.pdf.

Bell, Morag. 2000. "American Philanthropy, the Carnegie Corporation, and Poverty in South Africa." *Journal of Southern African Studies* 26, no. 3 (September): 481–504.

Berger, David. 1983. "White Poverty and Government Policy in South Africa, 1894–1934." PhD diss., Temple University.

Bilger, Dennis, and Randy Sowell. 1999. "Point Four Program of Technical Assistance to Developing Nations." Archival materials (prepared February 1999). Harry S. Truman Library and Museum. Available at: http://www.trumanlibrary.org/hstpaper/point4.htm.

Birkner, Michael J. 2010. "'Not Yet Ready': Australian University Libraries and Carnegie Corporation Philanthropy, 1935–1945." In *Collections, Characters, and Communities: The Shape of Libraries in Australia and New Zealand*, ed. B. J. McMullin, 77–93. Melbourne: Australian Scholarly Publishing.

———. 2013. "'The Wisest Help': Frederick Keppel and His Consultants' Impact on Australian and New Zealand Libraries." *Library and Information History* 29, no. 4 (November 2013): 258–271.

Blakeslee, George. 1930. "The Foreign Policy of the United States." In *Interpretations of American Foreign Policy: Lectures on the Harris Foundation*, ed. Quincy Wright, 1–36. Chicago: University of Chicago Press.

Bloom, L. 1967. "The Coloured People of South Africa." *Phylon: The Atlanta University Review of Race and Culture* 28, no. 2: 139–150.

Bollag, Burton. 2004. "Improving Tertiary Education in Sub-Saharan Africa: Things That Work." Report of a regional training conference held in Accra, Ghana, September 22–25, 2003. World Bank Africa Region Human Development Working Paper Series (April). Available at: http://siteresources.worldbank.org/AFRICAEXT/Resources/no_66.pdf.

Bonbright, David. 2003. "The Ford Foundation in Apartheid South Africa—Soft Solutions to Hard Problems." *Alliance*, September 1. Available at: http://www.alliancemagazine.org/en/content/ford-foundation-apartheid-south-africa-soft-solutions-hard-problems.

Bottomley, John. 1990. "Public Policy and White Rural Poverty in South Africa, 1881–1924." PhD diss., Queen's University.

Boutros-Ghali, Boutros. 1992. "An Agenda for Peace: Preventive Diplomacy, Peacemaking, and Peacekeeping: Report of the Secretary-General Pursuant to the Statement Adopted by the Summit Meeting of the Security Council on 31 January 1992." A/47/277-S/24111, June 17. Available at: http://www.unrol.org/files/A_47_277.pdf.

Brass, Paul, and Ashutosh Varshney. 1999. "Remembering Wiener's Legacy." Rediff on the Net (*India Abroad*), September 23. Available at: http://www.rediff.com/news/1999/sep/23us2.htm.

Brill, Betsy. 2010. "Stepping Up to the Lifetime Giving Challenge." *Forbes*, August 3. Available at: http://www.forbes.com/2010/08/02/giving-pledge-gates-intelligent-investing-buffett.html.

Brown, Korey Bowers. N.d. "Carter G. Woodson." Association for the Study of African American Life and History. Available at: http://asalh.org/woodsonbiosketch.html. (accessed December 28, 2013).

Bruinius, Harry. 2010. "Can Warren Buffet and Bill Gates Save the World?" *Christian Science Monitor*, November 20.

Bujra, Abdalla. 2004. "Pan-African Political and Economic Visions of Development from the OAU to the AU: From the Lagos Plan of Action (LPA) to the New Partnership for African Development (NEPAD)." Development Policy Management Forum Occasional Paper 13. Available at: http://www.dpmf.org/images/OccasionalPaper13.pdf (accessed September 14, 2013).

Bulmer, Martin, and Joan Bulmer. 1981. "Philanthropy and Social Science in the 1920s: Beardsley Ruml and the Laura Spelman Rockefeller Memorial, 1922–1929." *Minerva* 19, no. 3 (September): 347–407.

Cabe, Delia K. 2002. "Nation Building: Shedding Its Isolationist Stance, the United States Begins Reaching Out to Its Global Neighbors." *Kennedy School Bulletin* (Spring).

Callahan, David. 2002. "The Enduring Challenge: Self-determination and Ethnic Conflict in the Twenty-First Century." *Carnegie Challenge Paper 2002*. Carnegie Corporation of New York. Available at: carnegie.org/fileadmin/Media/Publications/PDF/ethnic conflict.pdf (accessed March 11, 2014).

Carnegie, Andrew. 1901. "Wealth." In Andrew Carnegie, *The Gospel of Wealth and Other Timely Essays*, 1–44. New York: Century Co. (Originally published in the *North American Review*, June 1889.)

Carnegie Corporation of New York. 2007. "The Carnegie Trusts and Institutions." Carnegie Corporation of New York. Available at: carnegie.org/fileadmin/Media/Publications/ PDF/carnegie_trusts_Inst_small_low.pdf (accessed March 11, 2014).

Carnegie Corporation of New York, Rockefeller Foundation, Ford Foundation, and John D. and Catherine T. MacArthur Foundation. 2000. "Four Foundations Launch $100 Million Initiative in Support of Higher Education in African Countries." Press release, April 24. Available at: http://carnegie.org/news/press-releases/story/news-action/single/view/ four-foundations-launch-100-million-initiative-in-support-of-higher-education-in-afri- can-countries/ (accessed February 22, 2014).

Carnegie Reporter. 2000. "The Challenge: Academic Freedom in the Former Soviet Union." *Carnegie Reporter* 1, no. 1 (Summer). Available at: http://carnegie.org/publications/ carnegie-reporter/single/view/article/item/4/.

Carter, Gwendolen M. 1983. "The Founding of the African Studies Association." *African Studies Review* 26, nos. 3-4 (1983): 5–9.

Charity and Security Network. 2012. "Proposed IRS Rule Could Make International Grantmaking Easier." October 4. Available at: http://www.charityandsecurity.org/news/Proposed_ IRS_Rule_Could_Make_International_Grantmaking_Easier (accessed October 21, 2012).

Chaskalson, Arthur. "The Legal Resources Centre: Why It Was Established and What It Hopes to Achieve." *De Rebus Proc* 145 (1980): 19–22.

Chu, T. K. 2002. Translator's preface to *Chinese Students Encounter America* by Ning Qian, vii– xx. Seattle: University of Washington Press.

Cohen, Susan A. 1987. "The Safe Motherhood Conference." *International Family Planning Perspectives* 13, no. 2.

Cooper, Diane, et al. 2004. "Ten Years of Democracy in South Africa: Documenting Transformation in Reproductive Health Policy and Status." *Reproductive Health Matters* 12, no. 24.

Cotton, James. 2010. "Carnegie, Rockefeller, and the Role of American Soft Power in the Emergence of International Studies in Australia." Paper presented to the Academy of Social Sciences in Australia Workshop "Philanthropy and Public Culture: The Influence and Legacies of the Carnegie Corporation of New York in Australia." University of Melbourne (February 24–25).

CRDF Global. 2012. "Gala Archive 2012 Honorees: 2012 George Brown Award Honoree: Dr. David A. Hamburg." Available at: http://www.crdfglobal.org/about-us/annual-awards- gala/george-brown-award-archive/lists/2012-george-brown-award/2012-honorees.

Darian-Smith, Kate, Julie McLeod, and Glenda Sluga. 2010. "Philanthropy and Public Culture: The Influence and Legacies of the Carnegie Corporation of New York in Australia." *Dialogue* 29, no. 2 (February). Available at: http://www.assa.edu.au/publications/dia- logue/2010_Vol29_No2.pdf.

Davenport, Kelsey. 2014. "History of Official Proposals on the Iranian Nuclear Issue." Arms Control Association (January). Available at: http://www.armscontrol.org/factsheets/ iran_Nuclear_Proposals (updated January 2013).

Del Vecchio Good, Mary-Jo, Laura Tarter, and Martha Fuller, eds. 2000. "East Africa Health and Behavior Fellowship Program in Institutional Strengthening in Social and Medical Sciences." Boston: Harvard Medical School, Department of Social Medicine.

Deutsch, Abigail. 2010. "Investing in America's Cultural Education: The Carnegie Art and Music Sets." *Carnegie Reporter* 6, no. 1 (Fall): 16–25. Available at: http://carnegie.org/publications/carnegie-reporter/single/view/article/item/265/.

———. 2011. "A Vision of Social Justice: Carnegie Corporation in the 1960s and Beyond." *Carnegie Reporter* 6, no. 2 (Spring): 2–10. Available at: http://carnegie.org/publications/carnegie-reporter/single/view/article/item/273/.

———. 2012. "Women in Higher Education." *Carnegie Results* (Winter). Available at: http://carnegie.org/fileadmin/Media/Publications/Reporter/23/women_in_higher_ed_winter_2011.pdf.

Doob, Leonard W. 1953. "Information Services in Central Africa." *Public Opinion Quarterly* 17, no. 1 (Spring): 7–19.

———. 1957–1958. "The Use of Different Test Items in Nonliterate Societies." *Public Opinion Quarterly* 21, no. 4 (Winter): 499–504.

Drake, Paul W., and Lisa Hilbink. 2003/2002. "Latin American Studies Theory and Practice." In *The Politics of Knowledge: Area Studies and the Disciplines*, ed. David L. Szanton, 34–73. Berkeley: University of California Press.

Drumea, Dumitru. 2008. "The Fall of the Soviet Union and Reunification of Europe." Trans. Florent Banfi. *The New Federalist* (May 6). Available at: http://www.thenewfederalist.eu/The-Fall-of-the-Soviet-Union-and-Reunification-of-Europe (accessed August 21, 2012).

Edmonds, Martin. 1972. "Government Contracting and Renegotiation: A Comparative Analysis." *Public Administration* 50, no. 1 (March): 45–64.

Edwards, Sandy. 2013. "Philantopic: The Benefits of Multiyear Grantmaking: A Funder's Perspective." *Philanthropy News Digest* (Foundation Center), January 29. Available at: http://pndblog.typepad.com/pndblog/2013/01/the-benefits-of-multiyear-grantmaking.html (accessed February 10, 2013).

Eisenberg, Pablo. 2011. "A Foundation Leader with Innovation and Risk-taking in His DNA." *Chronicle of Philanthropy*, December 19. Available at: http://philanthropy.com/article/A-Foundation-Leader-With/130131/.

Ekbladh, David. 2011–2012. "Present at the Creation: Edward Mead Earle and the Depression-Era Origins of Security Studies." *International Security* 36, no. 3 (Winter): 107–141.

Everts, R. Alain. 1993. "The Pioneers: Herbert Isaac Ernest Dhlomo and the Development of Library Service to the African in South Africa." *World Libraries* 3, no. 2 (Spring): 1–2.

Fabricant, Solomon. 1984. "Toward a Firmer Basis of Economic Policy: The Founding of the National Bureau of Economic Research." Available at: http://www.nber.org/nberhistory/sfabricantrev.pdf.

Farish, Matthew. 2005. "Archiving Areas: The Ethnogeographic Board and the Second World War." *Annals of the Association of American Geographers* 95, no. 3: 663–679.

Fisher, Max. 2012. "How Should the Media Cover Africa? Nick Kristof Debates an African Critic." *The Atlantic*, July 3.

Fleisch, Brahm. 1993. "American Influences on the Development of Social and Economic Research in South Africa, 1929–1943." Paper presented at the annual meeting of the American Educational Research Association, Atlanta (April). Abstract available at: http://eric.ed.gov/?id=ED370843.

Foote, Melvin P. 2012. "Africa: Under the Baobab Tree—Africa Loses a Giant in the US Congress." Allafrica.com, April 11. Available at: http://allafrica.com/stories/201204111235.html.

Foreign Affairs, The Editors of. 1989. "From the Archives: 1989." *Foreign Affairs*. Available at:

http://www.foreignaffairs.com/features/collections/from-the-archives-1989 (accessed June 24, 2012).

Foundation Center. 2014. "Top Funders: Top 100 US Foundations by Asset Size." January 25. Available at: http://foundationcenter.org/findfunders/topfunders/top100assets.html (accessed February 15, 2014).

Fox, Annette Baker. 2001. "The Institute of War and Peace Studies: The First Thirty-Five Years." Columbia University. Available at: http://saltzman.obiki.org/about.attachment/fox-man-uscript/Fox%20Manuscript%201.pdf.

Franklin D. Roosevelt Library. N.d. "The Papers of Whitney Hart Shepardson, 1910–1966: A Descriptive List." Available at: http://www.fdrlibrary.marist.edu/archives/pdfs/findin-gaids/findingaid_shepardson.pdf (accessed September 12, 2013).

Frumkin, Peter. 1999. "Private Foundations as Public Institutions: Regulation, Professionalization, and Organized Philanthropy." In *Philanthropic Foundations: New Scholarship, New Possibilities*, ed. Ellen Condliffe Lagemann, 69–98. Bloomington: Indiana University Press.

Galster, Steve. 2001. "Volume II: Afghanistan: Lessons from the Last War: Afghanistan: The Making of US Policy, 1973–1990." National Security Archive, October 9. Available at: http://www.gwu.edu/~nsarchiv/NSAEBB/NSAEBB57/essay.html (accessed June 15, 2012).

Garonzik, Elan. 2001. Review of *Private Charity and Public Inquiry: A History of the Filer and Peterson Commissions* by Eleanor L. Brilliant. *Alliance*, September 1. Available at: http://www.alliancemagazine.org/node/3067 (accessed June 3, 2012).

Given, Lisa M., and Liane McTauris. 2010. "What's Old Is New Again: The Reconvergence of Libraries, Archives, and Museums in the Digital Age." *Library Quarterly* 80, no. 1 (January): 7–32.

Glotzer, Richard. 1995. "Sir Fred Clarke: South Africa and Canada Carnegie Corporation Philanthropy and the Transition from Empire to Commonwealth." *Educational Research and Perspectives* (Australia) 22, no. 1: 1–21.

———. 2005. "Mabel Carney and the Hartford Theological Seminary: Rural Development, 'Negro Education,' and Missionary Training." *Historical Studies in Education* 17, no. 1: 55–80.

———. 2006. "Frederick Keppel and Carnegie Corporation's Interwar Overseas Experts." *American Educational History Journal* 33, no. 1: 47–56.

———. 2009. "A Long Shadow: Frederick P. Keppel, the Carnegie Corporation, and the Dominions and Colonies Fund Area Experts, 1923–1943." *History of Education* 38, no. 5 (September): 621–648.

Golden, Marita. 2004. "Carnegie Corporation in South Africa: A Difficult Past Leads to a Commitment to Change." *Carnegie Results* (Winter). Available at: http://carnegie.org/fileadmin/Media/Publications/winter_04southafrica.pdf.

Golub, Stephen. 2000. "Battling Apartheid, Building a New South Africa." In *Many Roads to Justice: The Law-Related Work of Ford Foundation Grantees Around the World*, ed. Mary McClymont and Stephen Golub, 19–54. New York: Ford Foundation.

Government of Guyana. Ministry of Finance. NDS Secretariat. 1997. *National Development Strategy*. May 26. Available at: http://www.guyana.org/NDS/NDS.htm (accessed March 4, 2014).

Graubard, Stephen. 2004. "Public Scholarship: A New Perspective for the Twenty-First Century." Carnegie Corporation of New York. Available at: carnegie.org/fileadmin/Media/Publications/public_scholarship.pdf (accessed March 11, 2014).

Gregorian, Vartan. 1999. "New Directions for Carnegie Corporation of New York: A Report to the Board." Carnegie Corporation of New York, February 2. Available at: carnegie.org/

fileadmin/Media/Publications/new_directions_gregorian_board_report.pdf (accessed March 2, 2014).

———. 2004. "Transparency and Accomplishment: A Legacy of Glass Pockets: Report of the President." Available at: carnegie.org/fileadmin/Media/Publications/PDF/Transparency%20and%20Accomplishment.pdf (accessed March 2, 2014).

———. 2007. "Carnegie Corporation of New York: Meeting the Challenges of the Twenty-First Century." Carnegie Corporation of New York, October 1. Available at: http://carnegie.org/fileadmin/Media/Publications/PDF/meeting_the_challenges.pdf (accessed March 2, 2014).

Groenewald, C. J. 1987. "The Methodology of Poverty Research in South Africa: The Case of the First Carnegie Investigation, 1929–1932." *Social Dynamics* 13, no. 2: 60–74.

Grubel, Herbert. 1968. "The Reduction of the Brain Drain: Problems and Policies." *Minerva* 6, no. 4: 541–558.

Guy-Sheftall, Beverley. 2010. "The American Negro Academy." In *The Encyclopedia of African American Education*, vol. 1, ed. Kofi Lomotey, 48–49. Thousand Oaks, CA: Sage.

Gwatkin, Davidson R. 2002. "Reducing Health Inequalities in Developing Countries." In *Oxford Textbook of Public Health: The Scope of Public Health*, 4th ed., vol. 1, ed. Roger Detels, James McEwen, Robert Beaglehole, and Hezio Tanaka, 281–296. Oxford: Oxford University Press.

Hamburg, David. 2010. "Carnegie Corporation in the 1980s and 1990s." *Carnegie Reporter* 6, no. 1 (Fall): 39–43. Available at: www.carnegie.org/publication/carnegie-reporter/single/view/issue/item/348/.

Hammack, David C. 2002. "Nonprofit Organizations in American History: Research Opportunities and Sources." *American Behavioral Scientist* 45, no. 11: 1638–1674.

Hammrell, Sven, and Olle Nordberg, eds. 1995. "Autonomous Developments Funds." *Development Dialogue* 2: 1–99.

Harrison, Kelsey A. 1985. "Child-bearing, Health, and Social Priorities: A Survey of 22,774 Consecutive Births in Zaria, Northern Nigeria." *British Journal of Obstetrics and Gynaecology* 92, suppl. 5: 1–119.

Hartnell, Caroline. 2012. "High Risk/High Gain? Why Isn't This More Appealing to Foundations?" *Alliance*, June 18. Available at: http://philanthropynews.alliancemagazine.org/high-riskhigh-gain-why-isnt-this-more-appealing-to-foundations/.

He, Lijun. 2011. "Join Hands with China: An Analysis of the Development of Chinese Philanthropy." Council on Foundations. Available at: http://wawomensfoundation.org/sites/default/files/Join%20Hands%20with%20China-COF.pdf (accessed March 4, 2014).

Hertko, Joyce Mary. 1996. "The Internationalization of American Higher Education During the 1960s: The Involvement of the Ford Foundation and the Carnegie Corporation in Education and World Affairs." PhD diss., Indiana University School of Education (August).

Heyman, Richard Davis. 1970. "The Role of Carnegie Corporation in African Education, 1925–1960." EdD diss., Teachers College, Columbia University.

———. 1972. "C. T. Loram: A South African Liberal in Race Relations." *International Journal of African Historical Studies* 5, no. 1: 41–50.

Hinds, Michael de Courcy. 2002. "Scholarship for Social Change." *Carnegie Reporter* 2, no. 1 (Fall): 12–21. Available at: http://carnegie.org/publications/carnegie-reporter/single/view/article/item/54/.

History Matters Blog. "General Jan Christiaan Smuts." South African History Online: Towards a People's History. Available at: http://www.sahistory.org.za/people/general-jan-christiaan-smuts (accessed September 12, 2013).

Hodgson, Godfrey. 2003. "Obituary: Walt Rostow: Cold War Liberal Adviser to President

Kennedy Who Backed the Disastrous US Intervention in Vietnam." *The Guardian*, February 16.

Hodgson, Jenny. 2013. "Foundations Join Together to Make the Case for Community Philanthropy." *Effect* (Autumn). Available at: http://www.efc.be/programmes_services/resources/Documents/JennyHodgson_EFFECT_Winter_2013_Web.pdf (accessed March 2, 2013).

Horesh, Edward. 2006. "African Alternative Framework to Structural Adjustment Programme for Socio-economic Recovery and Transformation." New York: United Nations Economic Commission for Africa (November 1).

Howze, Glenn. 2003. Review of *The Free Speech Movement: Reflections on Berkeley in the 1960s*, ed. Robert Cohen and Reginald E. Zelnik. *Academe* 89, no. 5 (September–October): 98–99.

Hungerford, Thomas L. 2008. "Income Inequality, Income Mobility, and Economic Policy: US Trends in the 1980s and 1990s." Cornell University ILR School, March 4. Available at: http://digitalcommons.ilr.cornell.edu/key_workplace/501 (accessed September 14, 2013).

Hyland, William G. 1992. "Foreign Affairs at Seventy." *Foreign Affairs* 71, no. 4 (Fall): 171–193. Available at: http://cfr.org/world/foreign-affairs-70/p8277.

Iriye, Akira. 2006. "The Role of Philanthropy and Civil Society in US Foreign Relations." In *Philanthropy and Reconciliation: Rebuilding Postwar US-Japan Relations*, ed. Yamamoto Tadashi, Akira Iriye, and Iokibe Mahota, 37–60. Tokyo: Japan Center for International Exchange.

Jackson, Barbara Ward. 1962. "Cutting Aid to Punish Pakistan: Why the United States Should Be Patient with Assistance." *Foreign Affairs* 41, no. 1.

———. 1962. "Foreign Aid: Strategy or Stopgap?" *Foreign Affairs* 41, no. 1 (October): 90–104.

Jacobs, Sylvia M. 1996. "James Emman Kwegyir Aggrey: An African Intellectual in the United States." In *80th Anniversary Year: Vindicating the Race: Contributions to African-American Intellectual History*, ed. V. P. Franklin and Bettye Collier Thomas, special issue of *Journal of Negro History* 81, nos. 1–4: 47–61.

Jaschik, Scott. 2007. "Lost Opportunity in Russia." *Inside Higher Education*, January 31. Available at: http://www.insidehighered.com/news/2007/01/31/russia.

Johnson, Andrea. 2004. "Softening the Painful Path to Goodbye." *Alliance*, June 1. Available at: http://www.alliancemagazine.org/en/content/softening-painful-path-goodbye.

Johnson, Donald. 2000. "W. E. B. Du Bois, Thomas Jesse Jones, and the Struggle for Social Education, 1900–1930." *Journal of Negro History* 85, no. 3: 71–95.

Johnson, Mark S. 2009. "Research, Scholarship, and Collaboration: Legacies of Carnegie Corporation of New York's Higher Education in the Former Soviet Union (HEFSU) Initiative, 1998 to 2008." *Carnegie Results* (Spring). Available at: http://carnegie.org/fileadmin/Media/Publications/PDF/carnegie_results_spring_09_rev.pdf.

Johnson, R. W. 2008. "The Wrecking of a University." Politicsweb, December 5. Available at: http://www.politicsweb.co.za/politicsweb/view/politicsweb/en/page72308?oid=111909&sn=Marketingweb%20detail.

Johnston, Bruce F. N.d. "Creating Stanford's Food Research Institute: Herbert Hoover, Alonzo Taylor, Carl Alsberg, J. S. Davis, and M. K. Bennett." Available at: http://www.stanford.edu/group/FRI/fri/history/bruce.html (accessed September 14, 2013).

Jolly, Richard, Louis Emmerij, and Thomas Weiss. 2009. "The UN and Human Development." UN Intellectual History Project Briefing Note 8 (July). Ralph Bunche Institute for International Studies, CUNY Graduate Center. Available at: http://unhistory.org/briefing/8HumDev.pdf (accessed September 14, 2013).

Jordan, Alma. 1964. "Public Libraries in the British Caribbean: I." *Library Quarterly* 34, no. 2 (April): 143–162.

Kaplan, Robert D. 2001. "Looking the World in the Eye." *Atlantic Monthly* 288, no. 5 (December): 68–82.

Kapur, Ambika. 2003. "The Foundation Partnership to Strengthen African Universities: Four Foundations Share One Vision of the Future." *Carnegie Reporter* 2, no. 2 (Spring): 35–40. Available at: http://carnegie.org/publications/carnegie-reporter/single/view/article/item/80/.

Karl, Barry D., and Stanley N. Katz. 1981. "The American Private Foundation and the Public Sphere, 1890–1930." *Minerva* 19: 236–270.

Katz, Lee Michael. 2007. "The Aspen Institute Congressional Program: A Nonpartisan Success Story." *Carnegie Results* (Summer). Available at: http://carnegie.org/fileadmin/Media/Publications/PDF/carnegie_results_summer07.pdf.

———.2010. "Dick Clark: Creating a Lasting Legacy by Educating Congress." *Carnegie Reporter* (Spring): 33–34. Available at: http://carnegie.org/publications/carnegie-reporter/single/view/article/item/244/.

———. 2010. "Opening the Closed Cities of the Soviet Union." *Carnegie Results* (Winter). Available at: http://carnegie.org/fileadmin/Media/Publications/PDF/carnegie_results_winter10.pdf.

———. 2011. "Nuclear Threat Initiative: Working to Reduce Nuclear Dangers with a Goal of Ultimately Ending Nuclear Weapons as a Threat to the World." *Carnegie Results* (Summer). Available at: http://carnegie.org/fileadmin/Media/Publications/PDF/nuclear_threat_initiative_results_summer_11.pdf.

Katz, Stanley N. 2012. "Beware Big Donors." *Chronicle of Higher Education* (March 25).

Keohane, Robert O., and Joseph S. Nye Jr. 2000. "Globalization: What's New? What's Not? (and So What?)." *Foreign Policy* 118 (Spring): 104–119.

The Kiplinger Letter. 2012. "Forecasts for Management Decision-making." *The Kiplinger Letter* 89, no. 19 (May 11).

Klufio, Cecil A., E. Y. Kwawukume, K. A. Danso, John J. Sciarra, and Timothy Johnson. 2003. "Ghana Postgraduate Obstetrics/Gynecology Collaborative Residency Training Program: Success Story and Model for Africa." *American Journal of Obstetrics and Gynecology* 189, no. 3: 692–696.

Knight, Barry. 2012. "The Value of Community Philanthropy: Results of a Consultation." Aga Khan Foundation USA and Charles Stewart Mott Foundation (February). Available at: http://www.mott.org/files/publications/thevalueofcommunityphilanthropy.pdf (accessed September 15, 2013).

Korobkov, Andrei. 2011. "Dynamics of Russian Language Programs in USA: Recent Trends." Russkiy Mir Foundation (November 15). Available at: http://www.russkiymir.ru/russkiymir/en/publications/articles/article0222.html.

Kushnick, Louis. 1996. "The Political Economy of White Racism in the United States." In *Impacts of Race on White America*, 2nd ed., ed. Benjamin P. Bowers and Raymond G. Hunt, 48–67. Thousand Oaks, CA: Sage.

Lawrence, Steven, and Reina Mukai. 2010. "International Grantmaking Update: A Snapshot of US Foundation Trends." Foundation Center (December). Available at: http://foundationcenter.org/gainknowledge/research/pdf/intl_update_2010.pdf.

Leibell, David Thayne. 2010. "A Second Golden Age of American Philanthropy." Wealth Management.com, June 23. Available at: http://wealthmanagement.com/financial-planning/second-golden-age-american-philanthropy.

Lesaffer, Randall. "The Temple of Peace: The Hague Peace Conferences, Andrew Carnegie, and the Building of the Peace Palace (1898–1913)." Tilburg Law School Legal Studies Research Paper Series 024/2013. Available at Social Science Research Network: http://ssrn.com/abstract=2350189 (accessed March 4, 2013).

Lewis, Suzanne Grant, Jonathan Friedman, and John Schoneboom. N.d. "Accomplishments of the Partnership for Higher Education in Africa, 2000–2010: Report on a Decade of Collaborative Foundation Investment." CCNY, Partnership for Higher Education in Africa. Available at: http://www.foundation-partnership.org/pubs/pdf/accomplishments. pdf (accessed September 11, 2013).

Link, William A. N.d. "Jackson Davis and the Lost World of Jim Crow Education." Jackson Davis Collection of African American Educational Photographs, Albert and Shirley Small Special Collections Library, University of Virginia. Available at: http://www2.lib. virginia.edu/small/collections/jdavis/resources/linkarticle.html (accessed December 7, 2011).

Lipsky, Michael, and Stephen Rathgeb Smith. 1989–1990. "Nonprofit Organizations, Government, and the Welfare State." *Political Science Quarterly* 104, no. 4: 625–648.

Louw, Johann. 1997. "Social Context and Psychological Testing in South Africa, 1918–1939." *Theory and Psychology* 7, no. 2: 235–256.

Louw, Johann, and Kurt Danziger. 2007. "Psychological Practices and Ideology: The South African Case." In *History of Psychology and Social Practice*, special issue 1 of *Social Practice/ Psychological Theorizing*, ed. Adrian C. Brock and Johann Louw, 6–22. Available at: http:// www.kurtdanziger.com/Joahnn&Kurt.pdf (accessed September 15, 2013).

Lucas, Adetokunbo O. 2002. "Health Policies in Developing Countries." In *Oxford Textbook of Public Health: The Scope of Public Health*, 4th ed., vol. 1, ed. Roger Detels, James McEwen, Robert Beaglehole, and Hezio Tanaka, 281–296. Oxford: Oxford University Press.

Macmillan, Hugh. 2011. "The Travels and Researches of W. M. Macmillan in Southern Africa, 1915–32." Paper presented to the Rhodes History Department Centenary Colloquium, Rhodes University (September 16–17). Available at: http://www.ru.ac.za/media/hode-suniversity/content/conferences/documents/historycentenarycolloquium/Macmillan%20 travels%20and%20researches.rtf (accessed September 15, 2013).

Maine, Deborah (guest editor). 1997. "The Prevention of Maternal Mortality Network." Supplement to *International Journal of Gynecology and Obstetrics* 59, no. S2 (November).

Maine, Deborah, Murat Z. Akalin, Victoria M. Ward, and Angela Kamara. 1997. "The Design and Evaluation of Maternal Mortality Programs." New York: Columbia University, School of Public Health, Center for Population and Family Health (June). Available at: http:// www.amddprogram.org/vı/resources/DesignEvalMM-EN.pdf.

Maylam, Paul. 2012. "A Hundred Years of History at Rhodes University: Some Reflections on the Department's Centenary Colloquium, September 2011." *Historia* 57, no. 1 (May).

McAlmont, Cecilia. 2006. "History of the Week: Developments During the Forty Years Before Independence." *Starbroek News*, April 27.

McCartney, David. 2009. "Jessup, Walter Albert." In *The Biographical Dictionary of Iowa*. Iowa City: University of Iowa Press. Available at: http://uipress.lib.uiowa.edu/bdi/DetailsPage. aspx?id=195.

McIlnay, Dennis. 1998. "Philanthropy at Fifty: Four Moments in Time." *Foundation News and Commentary* 39, no. 5 (September–October). Available at: http://www.foundationnews. org/CME/article.cfm?ID=1053 (accessed September 15, 2013).

Merkx, Gilbert. 2010. "Gulliver's Travels: The History and Consequences of Title VI." In *International and Language Education for a Global Future: Fifty Years of US Title VI and Fulbright-Hays Programs*, ed. David Wiley and Robert S. Glew, 17–32. East Lansing: Michigan State University Press.

Merkx, Gilbert W., Ruth Hayoe, Bernard H. K. Luk, Kenneth King, Marcela Gajardo, Elizabeth King, Albert Motivans, Holger Daun, William J. Brustein, Suzanne H. Rudolph, and Lloyd

Rudolph. 2006. "Comparative Education, Area Studies, and the Disciplines." *Comparative Education Review* 501: 125–148.

Miebow, Charles C. 1944. Review of *A Biography of Abraham Flexner* by Henry S. Pritchett. *Popular Astronomy* 52: 107–108.

Milburn, Caroline. 2010. "Taking Research to the Top of Its Class." *The Age*, April 12. Available at: http://www.theage.com.au/national/education/taking-research-to-the-top-of-its-class-20100409-rxja.html.

Miller Center at the University of Virginia. N.d. "American President: A Reference Resource: Herbert Clark Hoover, Life Before the Presidency." Available at: http://millercenter.org/president/hoover/essays/biography/2 (accessed December 27, 2013).

Miller, Roberta Balstad. 1993. "Science and Society in the Early Career of H. F. Verwoerd." *Journal of Southern African Studies* 19, no. 4 (December): 634–661.

Montville, Joseph V. 2006. "Track II Diplomacy: The Work of Healing History." *Whitehead Journal of Diplomacy and International Relations* 7, no. 2 (Summer–Fall): 15–25. Available at: http://blogs.shu.edu/diplomacy/archived-issues/the-changing-nature-of-diplomacy/.

Morey, Maribel. 2012. "A Reconsideration of *An American Dilemma*." *Reviews in American History* 40: 686–692.

Mulgan, Geoff. 2010. "Measuring Social Value." *Stanford Social Innovation Review* (Summer). Available at: http://www.ssireview.org/articles/entry/measuring_social_value/ (accessed September 15, 2013).

Myers, Robert. 1967. "Brain Drains and Brain Gains." *International Development Review* 5, no. 4: 4–9.

Nasar, Sylvia. 1993. "Kenneth Boulding, an Economist, Philosopher, and Poet, Dies at 83." *New York Times*, March 20.

Nasaw, David. 2012. "The Continuing Relevance of Andrew Carnegie's Legacy." Lecture delivered at the Peace Palace, The Hague, The Netherlands, August 30. Available at: http://carnegie.org/fileadmin/Media/Publications/David_nasaw_hague_lecture_aug12_peace.pdf (accessed March 2, 2014).

Network of African Science Academies (NASAC). 2009. Proceedings of the NASAC-TWOWS Women for Science Workshop, Nairobi, Kenya, November 30–December 1, 2009. Available at: http://www.interacademies.net/File.aspx?id=10626 (accessed March 4, 2014).

New York Times. 1942. "Canada Stresses Educational Aims." *New York Times*, April 4.

———. 1943. "Frederick Keppel" (obituary of Frederick Keppel). *New York Times*, September 10.

Nobel Prize.org. N.d. "F. W. de Klerk—Biographical." Available at: http://nobelprize.org/nobel_prizes/peace/laureates/1993/klerk-bio.html (accessed August 22, 2012).

Nyanja, Sophie. 1998. Foreword to *Africans Solving African Problems: Militaries, Democracies, and Security in West and Southern Africa* by Jean Herskovits. New York: International Peace Academy.

Odhiambo, Thomas R. 1967. "East Africa: Science for Development." *Science* 158, no. 3803 (November 17): 876–881.

Organization of African Unity (OAU). 1990. "The Khartoum Declaration on Africa's Refugee Crisis." OAU Doc.BR/COM/XV/55.90. Available at University of Minnesota, Human Rights Library: http://www1.umn.edu/humanrts/africa/KHARTO.htm (accessed June 24, 2012).

Parker, Franklin. 1972. "George Peabody, 1795–1869: His Influence on Educational Philanthropy." *Peabody Journal of Education* 49, no. 2 (January): 138–145.

Parker, Susan. 2012. "Lessons from a Ten-Year Funder Collaborative: A Case Study of the

Partnership for Higher Education in Africa." New York: Carnegie Corporation of New York (September). Available at: http://www.foundation-partnership.org/pubs/pdf/phea_case_study.pdf (accessed March 2, 2011).

Parmar, Inderjeet. 1999. "The Carnegie Corporation and the Mobilization of Opinion in the United States' Rise to Globalism, 1939–1945." *Minerva* 37: 355–378.

Patterson, David S. 1970. "Andrew Carnegie's Quest for World Peace." *Proceedings of the American Philosophical Society* 114, no. 5 (October 20): 371–383.

Posel, Deborah. 1987. "The Meaning of Apartheid Before 1948: Conflicting Interests and Forces Within the Afrikaner Nationalist Alliance." *Journal of South African Studies* 14, no. 1 (October): 123–139.

Rathgeber, Eva. 1990. "WID, WAD, GAD: Trends in Research and Practice." *Journal of Developing Areas* 24, no. 4: 489–502.

Raymond, Susan Ueber, ed. 1996. "Science-Based Economic Development." *Annals of the New York Academy of Sciences* 798 (December): xiii–xv, 1–346.

Reagan, Ronald. 1983. "Address to the Nation on National Security by President Ronald Reagan, March 23, 1983." Available at: http://www.fas.org/spp/starwars/offdocs/rrspch.htm.

Reich, Michael R. 2005. "The Concept and Practice of International Health in the Takemi Program." *Japan Medical Association Journal* 48, no. 5: 246–255.

Reid, John G. 1984. "Health, Education, Economy: Philanthropic Foundations in the Atlantic Region in the 1920s and 1930s." *Acadiensis* 14, no. 1 (Autumn): 64–83.

Rich, Paul B. 1980. "Administrative Ideology, Urban Social Control, and the Origins of Apartheid Theory, 1930–1939." *Journal of African Studies* 7, no. 2 (Summer): 70–82.

Ringland, Arthur. 1954. *The Organization of Voluntary Foreign Aid: 1939–1953*. US State Department Economic Cooperation Series. Washington, DC: US Government Printing Office (March 15).

Roberts, Andrew. 1986. "The Imperial Mind." In *The Cambridge History of Africa*, vol. 7, 1905–1940, ed. J. D. Fage and Roland Oliver, 73–76. Cambridge: Cambridge University Press.

Robinson, Pearl T. 2004. "Area Studies in Search of Africa." In *The Politics of Knowledge: Area Studies and the Disciplines*, ed. David L. Szanton, 82–122. Berkeley: University of California Press.

Rochester, Maxine. 1996. "American Philanthropy Abroad: Library Program Support from Carnegie Corporation of New York British Dominions and Colonies Fund in the 1920s and 1930s." *Libraries and Culture* 31, no. 2: 342–363.

———. 1999. "The Carnegie Corporation and South Africa: Non-European Library Services." *Libraries and Culture* 34, no. 1 (Winter): 27–51.

———. 2002. "Wise Philanthropy: The Carnegie Corporation and Libraries of the British Commonwealth in the 1920s and 1930s." Paper presented at the 68th International Federation of Library Associations and Institutions' (IFLA) Council and General Conference, Glasgow (August 18–24). Available at: http://archive.ifla.org/IV/ifla68/papers/127-117e.pdf (accessed September 15, 2013).

Rockefeller Foundation/Social Finance, Inc. 2012. "A New Tool for Scaling Impact: How Social Impact Bonds Can Mobilize Private Capital to Advance Social Good." Available at: http://www.socialfinance.org.uk/resources/social-finance/new-tool-scaling-impact-how-social-impact-bonds-can-mobilize-private-capita.

Rodwin, Lloyd. 1994. "Rethinking the Development Experience: Aims, Theories, and Theses." In *Rethinking the Development Experience: Essays Provoked by the Work of Albert O. Hirschman*, ed. Lloyd Rodwin and Donald A. Schon, 3–36. Washington, DC, and Cambridge, MA: Brookings Institution and Lincoln Institute of Land Policy.

Rogers, Kate. 2010. Untitled paper presented to the Academy of Social Sciences in Australia Workshop "Philanthropy and Public Culture: The Influence and Legacies of the Carnegie Corporation of New York in Australia," University of Melbourne (February 24–25).

Rose, Amy D. 1990. "Challenging the System: The Adult Education Movement and the Educational Bureaucracy of the 1920s." In *Breaking New Ground: The Development of Adult and Workers' Education in North America: Proceedings from the Syracuse University Kellogg Project's First Visiting Scholar Conference in the History of Adult Education (March 1989)*, ed. Rae Wahol Rohfeld. Syracuse, NY: Syracuse University Kellogg Project. Available at: http://www-distance.syr.edu/breaking.html (accessed September 10, 2013).

Rosenberg, Barry. 2003. "Peace and Conflict 2003: A Surprising Trend Emerges." *Carnegie Results* (Summer). Available at: http://carnegie.org/fileadmin/Media/Publications/summer_03peaceandconflict_01.pdf.

———. 2004. "Towards Nuclear Nonproliferation: An Evolving Strategy." *Carnegie Results* (Summer). Available at: http://carnegie.org/fileadmin/Media/Publications/summer_04nuclear.pdf.

———. 2004. "The Weaponization of Space: Divided Viewpoints, Uncertain Directions." *Carnegie Challenge Paper*. Carnegie Corporation of New York. Available at Carnegie Corporation of New York Offices.

Rosenfield, Allan, and Deborah Maine. 1985. "Maternal Mortality—A Neglected Tragedy: Where Is the M in MCH?" *Lancet* 2, no. 8466: 83–85.

Rosenfield, Patricia. 2011. "A Noble Use of Wealth: Carnegie Corporation's Commitment to African Higher Education." *Carnegie Reporter* 6, no. 2 (Spring): 32–39. Available at: http://carnegie.org/publications/carnegie-reporter/single/view/article/item/278/.

———. 2013. "Perspectives on Philanthropy: The Role of History as a Guide." *Carnegie Reporter* (Summer): 32–41. Available at: http://carnegie.org/publications/carnegie-reporter/single/view/article/item/327/.

———. 2013. "Private Philanthropy, Nonprofits, Business, and Government: Shared and Special Features That Facilitate Cross-sectoral Partnerships in the Provision of Public Goods." In *Non-profit och valfarden (Can Nonprofits Save the Swedish Welfare Model?)*, ed. Kurt Almquist, Viveca Ax:son Johnson, and Lars Tragardh. Stockholm: Axel och Margare Ax:son Johnsons stiftelse for allmannyttiga andamal.

Rosenfield, Patricia L., Courtenay Sprague, and Heather McKay. 2004. "Ethical Dimensions of International Grantmaking: Drawing the Line in a Borderless World." *Journal of Leadership and Organizational Studies* 11, no. 1: 53–56.

Rozen, Laura. 2009. "The Cable: New White House WMD Coordinator Attended Unofficial US-Iran Dialogue in His Private Capacity." *Foreign Policy*, February 3. Available at: http://thecable.foreignpolicy.com/posts/2009/02/02/new_white_house_wmd_coordinator_attended_unofficial_us_iran_dialogue_in_his_private.

Rumer, Eugene. 2006. "Eurasia: A World Order." *Carnegie Reporter* 3, no. 4 (Spring): 2–11. Available at: http://carnegie.org/fileadmin/Media/Publications/Reporter/PDF/carnegiereporter_v3n4.pdf.

Russell, Avery. 1985. "Reducing the Risk of Nuclear War: What Can Scholars Do?" *Carnegie Quarterly* 2 (Spring).

———. 1989. "Avoiding Nuclear War: Lessons for the Future of US-Soviet Relations." *Carnegie Quarterly* 34, nos. 3–4 (Summer–Fall).

———. 2011. "The Second Fifty Years: A Personal View." *Carnegie Reporter* 6, no. 2 (Spring): 28–29. Available at: carnegie.org/publications/carnegie-reporter/single/view/issue/item/387.

Saint, Bill, and Kees van den Bosch. 1991. "Donors to African Education: Working Group on

Higher Education." *NORRAG News* (December): 44–46. Available at: http://www.norrag. org/cn/publications/norrag-news/online-version/higher-education/detail/donors-to-african-education-working-group-on-higher-education.html (accessed March 11, 2014).

Sammon, M. C., and Geoffrey T. Hellman. 1952. "Talk of the Town: Fast Traveller." *The New Yorker*, June 21.

Samoff, Joel, and Bidemi Carrol. 2004. "Conditions, Coalitions, and Influence: The World Bank and Higher Education in Africa, February 7, 2004." Paper presented at the annual conference of the Comparative and International Education Society, Salt Lake City (March 8–12). Available at: http://www.eldis.org/vfile/upload/1/document/0708/doc17679.pdf (accessed March 11, 2014).

Saxon, Wolfgang. 2005. "Alan Pifer Is Dead at 84; Led Carnegie Corporation." *New York Times*, November 5.

Scarfo, Richard D. 1998. "The History of Title VI and Fulbright-Hays." In *International Education in the New Global Era: Proceedings of a National Policy Conference on the Higher Education Act, Title VI, and Fulbright-Hays Programs*, ed. John N. Hawkins, Carlos Manuel Haro, and Miriam A. Kazanjian, et al., 23–25. Los Angeles: International Studies and Overseas Programs. Available at: www.international.ucla.edu/pacrim/title6/Over2-Scarfo.pdf.

Schlafly, Phyllis. 1989. "The Carnegie Blueprint to Nationalize Education." *Human Events* 49, no. 8: 20.

Schlesinger, Arthur, Jr. 2000. "Who Was Henry A. Wallace? The Story of a Perplexing and Indomitably Naive Public Servant." Review of *American Dreamer: The Life and Times of Henry A. Wallace* by John C. Culver and John Hyde. *Los Angeles Times*, March 12.

Schramm, Carl. 2006. "Law Outside the Market: The Social Utility of the Private Foundation." *Harvard Journal of Law and Public Policy* 30, no. 1: 356–415.

Seekings, Jeremy. 2008. "The Carnegie Commission and the Backlash Against Welfare State–Building in South Africa, 1931–1937." *Journal of Southern African Studies* 34, no. 3 (September): 515–537.

Shepherd, Jody. 2005. "Bibliography of Area Studies in Relation to Higher Education: The Past, Present, and Future." Indiana University Libraries. Available at: http://www.libraries.iub. edu/index.php?pageId=1000308 (accessed May 19, 2012).

Shleifer, Andrei, and Daniel Treisman. 2005. "A Normal Country: Russia After Communism." *Journal of Economic Perspectives* 19, no. 1: 151–174.

Shuman, Edwin L. 1931. "Broad Scope of American Philanthropy." *Current History* 33, no. 5: 702.

Simpson, Alan. 1988. "Visit to the Soviet Union." *Congressional Record* (March 14): S103–S104.

Smith, Bruce L. 1983. "Changing Public-Private Sector Relations: A Look at the United States." *Annals of the American Academy of Political and Social Science* 466 (March): 149–164.

Smith, James Allen. 2006. "The Foundation Center: Fifty Years On." In *Philanthropy in the 21st Century*, ed. Mitch Nauffts, 1–12. New York: Foundation Center.

———. 2009. "Private Foundations and Public Policymaking: A Historical Perspective." In *Foundations and Public Policy*, ed. James M. Ferris, 41–78. New York: Foundation Center.

———. 2012. "Congressional Investigations and the Legitimacy and Accountability of Foundations." October 23. Unpublished presentation to the staff of the Rockefeller Foundation.

Smith, Jennie Carney. 2010. "Anna T. Jeanes Foundation." In *The Encyclopedia of African American Education*, vol. 1, ed. Kofi Lomotey, 49–51. Thousand Oaks, CA: Sage.

Smith, Stephen Rathgeb. 1989–1990. "Nonprofit Organizations, Government, and the Welfare State." *Political Science Quarterly* 104, no. 4: 625–648.

Smyth, Rosaleen. 2004. "The Roots of Community Development in Colonial Office Policy and Practice in Africa." *Social Policy and Administration* 38, no. 4 (August): 418–436.

Social Science Research Council (SSRC). "Academia in the Public Sphere Grants Program." available at: http://www.ssrc.org/programs/academia-in-the-public-sphere-grants-program/ (accessed July 29, 2012).

Sondermann, Fred A. 1966. "Colleges, Universities, and World Affairs: A Review." *Journal of Conflict Resolution* 10, no. 2 (June): 227–239.

South African History Archive. "UDF: 30 Years." Available at: http://www.saha.org.za/udf/?-folder=udf (accessed March 4, 2014).

South Commission. 1990. "The State of the South: The Development Record of the South, 1950–1980." In *The Challenge to the South: The Report of the South Commission*, 25–77. Oxford: Oxford University Press.

Stifel, Laurence D., Ralph K. Davidson, and James S. Coleman. 1982. "Agencies of Diffusion: A Case Study of the Rockefeller Foundation." In *Social Sciences and Public Policy in the Developing World*, ed. Laurence D. Stifel, Ralph K. Davidson, and James S. Coleman, 70. Lexington, MA: Lexington Books.

Stoler, Ann Laura. 2006. "Tense and Tender Ties: The Politics of Comparison in North American History and (Post) Colonial Studies." In *Haunted by Empire: Geographies of Intimacy in North American History*, ed. Ann Laura Stoler, 23–70. Durham, NC: Duke University Press.

Streeb, Gordon, et al. 1997. "Toward a New Model of Development Cooperation: The National Development Strategy Process." In *Guyana: A Report of the Global Development Initiative's Advisory Group Meeting and Review of Lessons Learned in Guyana*. Atlanta: Carter Center.

Stulberg, Adam. 2005. "Carnegie Corporation and Russia: Grantmaking Amidst Transformation." *Carnegie Results* (Spring). Available at: http://carnegie.org/fileadmin/Media/Training_Sandbox/spring_05.pdf (accessed February 8, 2014).

Sutton, Francis X. 1960. "The Ford Foundation's Development Program in Africa." *African Studies Bulletin* 3, no. 4 (December): 1–7.

———. 1987. "The Ford Foundation: The Early Years." *Daedalus* 116, no. 1 (Winter): 41–91.

———. 1988. "US Strengths: Non-Western Area Studies to 1956: The FAFP." July 15. Unpublished. Available from the author.

———. 2006. "Nation-Building in the Heyday of the Classic Development Ideology: Ford Foundation Experience in the 1950s and 1960s." In *Nation-Building Beyond Afghanistan and Iraq*, ed. Francis Fukuyama, 42–63. Baltimore: Johns Hopkins University Press.

Tayler, Judith. 1992. "'Our Poor': The Politicisation of the Poor White Problem, 1932–1942." *Kleio* 24, no. 1: 61.

TC Media Center. 2001. "Teachers for East Africa and Teacher Education in East Africa Hold Fortieth Reunion." *TC Today: The Alumni Magazine of Teachers College, Columbia University* 26, no. 2 (January 1). Available at: http://www.tc.columbia.edu/news.htm?articleID=3773&pub=7&issue=72.

Tchan, Francis J. 1926. Review of *War Government of the British Dominions* by Arthur Berriedale Keith. *Catholic Historical Review* 11, no. 4 (January): 713.

Theroux, Karen. 2006. "Strengthening the Work of the United Nations: A Sustained Strategy for Peace." *Carnegie Results* (Spring). Available at: http://carnegie.org/fileadmin/Media/Training_Sandbox/spring_06_results.pdf.

———. 2008. "Four Freedoms Fund: A Pioneering Foundation Partnership Advocates for Immigrants." *Carnegie Results* (Winter). Available at: http://carnegie.org/fileadmin/Media/Publications/PDF/carnegie_results_winter_08_rev.pdf.

———. 2008. "Peace in Our Time?" *Carnegie Reporter* 4, no. 4 (Spring): 26–35. Available at: http://carnegie.org/publications/carnegie-reporter/single/view/article/item/202/.

———. 2008. "Strengthening Scholarship and Research in the Former Soviet Union." *Carnegie*

Review (April): 17–20. Available at: http://carnegie.org/fileadmin/Media/Publications/PDF/carnegiereview_russia2008.pdf.

———. 2009. "A Quiet Revolution: Foundation Partners Spur Changes in African Higher Education." *Carnegie Reporter* 5, no. 2 (Spring): 38–47. Available at: http://carnegie.org/publications/carnegie-reporter/single/view/article/item/216/.

———. 2009. "Crafting Strategies to Control the Biological Weapons." *Carnegie Review* (Spring): 2–19. Available at: http://carnegie.org/fileadmin/Media/Publications/PDF/carnegiereview_bioweapons2009.pdf.

———. 2009. "The Truth Behind Suicide Terrorism: A Carnegie Scholar's Pioneering Research Project Aims to Dispel Myths and Reshape Policy." *Carnegie Results* (Fall). Available at: http://carnegie.org/fileadmin/Media/Publications/PDF/carnegie_results_fall09.pdf.

———. 2010. "100 Years of Big Ideas: The Best Minds Tackle the Toughest Problems." *Carnegie Reporter* 5, no. 4 (Spring): 22–31. Available at: http://carnegie.org/publications/carnegie-reporter/single/view/article/item/245/.

———. 2010. "Weathering the Financial Storms of a Century." *Carnegie Reporter* 6, no. 1 (Fall): 26–29. Available at: http://carnegie.org/publications/carnegie-reporter/single/view/article/item/264/.

———. 2012. "Bringing New Life to South Africa's Libraries." *Carnegie Review* (Winter): 3–20. Available at: http://carnegie.org/fileadmin/Media/Publications/carnegie_review_winter_2012_libaries.pdf.

Thomas, Daniel. 2011. "Aboriginal Art: Who Was Interested?" *Journal of Art Historiography* 4 (June). Available at: http://arthistoriography.files.wordpress.com/2011/05/daniel-thomas-document.pdf.

Time. 1949. "Yale Builder." *Time*, March 14.

Troyer, Thomas A. 2000. "The 1969 Private Foundation Law: Historical Perspective on Its Origins and Underpinnings." *Exempt Organization Tax Review* 27, no. 1 (January): 52–65.

United Nations General Assembly. 1986. "UN Program of Action for African Economic Recovery and Development, 1986–1990." Eighth plenary meeting, June 1. Available at: http://www.un.org/documents/ga/res/spec/aress13-2.htm (accessed June 29, 2012).

United Nations Office of the Special Adviser on Africa and NEPAD-OECD Africa Investment Initiative. 2010. "FDI in Africa." Policy Brief 4 (October). Available at: http://www.un.org/africa/osaa/reports/2010_FDIbrief.

US Department of Education. Office of Postsecondary Education. International Education Programs Service. N.d. "International Education Programs Service: Fulbright-Hays Programs: The World Is Our Classroom: Archived Information." Available at: http://www2.ed.gov/about/offices/list/ope/iegps/fulbright-hays.html.

US Department of State. 2002. "The Role of Think Tanks in US Foreign Policy." *US Foreign Policy Agenda* 7, no. 3 (November).

US Department of State. Bureau of Educational and Cultural Affairs. N.d. "Fulbright: The Early Years: An Informal History of the Fulbright Program." Available at: http://eca.state.gov/fulbright/about-fulbright/history/early-years (accessed September 15, 2013).

USAID. 2013. "20 Years of USAID Economic Growth Assistance in Europe and Eurasia." July 24. Available at: http://www.usaid.gov/sites/default/files/documents/1863/EE_20_Year__Review.pdf (accessed March 4, 2014).

Wagerson, Margarita B. 2010. "In-Country OB/GYN Training Program Contributes to Retention of Doctors." University of Michigan Health System, UMHS Newsroom, September 29. Available at: http://www2.med.umich.edu/prmc/media/newsroom/details.cfm?ID=1735.

Walker, Kenneth. 2009. "Will Knowledge Survive? Studying the Humanities at African

Universities." *Carnegie Reporter* 5, no. 2 (Spring): 3–11. Available at: http://carnegie.org/
publications/carnegie-reporter/single/view/article/item/212/.

———. 2011. "Preventing Maternal Mortality." *Carnegie Results* (Spring). Available at: carnegie.
org/.../carnegie_results_spring_11_prev_maternal_mortality.pdf.

Weiss, Marc A. 1989. "Richard T. Ely and the Contribution of Economic Research to National
Housing Policy, 1920–1940." *Urban Studies* 26: 115–126. Available at: http://www.globalur-
ban.org/Economic_Research_and_I Iousing_Policy.pdf.

White, Michael. 1996. "Carnegie Corporation Travel Grants to Australian Educators in the
1930s." Paper delivered at the joint conference of the Australian Association for Research
in Education and the Singapore Educational Research Association, Singapore (November
24–29). Available at: www.aare.edu.au/data/publications/1996/whitm96274.pdf (accessed
March 30, 2014).

———. 1997. "Carnegie Philanthropy in the Nineteen Thirties: A Reassessment." *History of
Education Review* 26, no. 1: 1–24.

Whitten, Melissa. N.d. "Large Nonoperating Private Foundations Panel Study, 1985–1997."
US Internal Revenue Service. Available at: http://www.irs.gov/pub/irs-soi/97pfpanl.pdf
(accessed March 4, 2014).

Woods, Thomas E., Jr. 2009. "Warren Harding and the Forgotten Depression of 1920." First
Principles: ISI Web Journal, October 14. Available at: http://www.firstprinciplesjournal.
com/print.aspx?article=1319&loc=b...1.

Woodson, C. G. 1950. "Thomas Jesse Jones." *Journal of Negro History* 35, no. 1 (January): 107–109.

World Economic Forum. 2012. "Long-Term Investing." Available at: http://www.weforum.org/
issues/long-term-investing (accessed September 15, 2013).

World Public Health Nutrition Association. 2011. "John Waterlow and Michael Latham: Sons
of Empire." May. Available at: http://www.wphna.org/htdocs/2011_may_hp2_waterlow_
latham.htm.

Worldwide Initiatives for Grantmaker Support. 2010. "Global Status Report: Zimbabwe."
Community Foundation Global Status Report. Available at: http://wings-community-foun-
dation-report.com/gsr_2010/assets/images/pdf/ZIMBABWE_final_2010GSR.pdf
(accessed March 4, 2014).

Zuckerman, Michael J. 2005. "Biosecurity: A Twenty-First Century Challenge." *Carnegie
Challenge Paper.* Carnegie Corporation of New York. Available at Carnegie Corporation
of New York Offices.

———. 2005. "Track II Diplomacy: Can 'Unofficial' Talks Avert Disaster?" *Carnegie Reporter*
3, no. 3 (Fall): 2–11. Available at: http://carnegie.org/fileadmin/Media/Publications/
Reporter/PDF/carnegiereporter_v3n3.pdf.

WEBSITES

100 Years: The Rockefeller Foundation: www.rockefeller100.org

Africa-America Institute (AAI): www.aaionline.org

African Academy of Sciences (AAS) and Academy of Sciences for the Developing World
(TWAS), *Discovery and Innovation* (journal): www.ajol.info/index.php/dai/index

Alfred P. Sloan Foundation: www.sloan.org

American Council of Learned Societies (ACLS): www.acls.org

Association for Teachers Education in Africa: www.afriate.org

Association for the Development of Education in Africa (ADEA): www.adeanet.org

Caribbean Academy of Sciences (CAS): www.caswi.org

Carnegie Corporation of New York: www.carnegie.org.
Carnegie Council for Ethics in International Affairs: www.carnegiecouncil.org
Carnegie Foundation for the Advancement of Teaching: www.carnegiefoundation.org
Carnegie Medal of Philanthropy: www.carnegiemedals.org
Ford Foundation: http://www.fordfoundation.org
Harvard University School of Public Health, Takemi Program in International Health: www.
  hsph.harvard.edu/research/takemi
Human Rights Area Files (HRAF), Yale University: www.yale.edu/hraf
Institute for International Education (IIE): www.iie.org
National Academy of Sciences, National Academy of Engineering, Institute of Medicine, and
  National Research Council: www.nationalacademies.org
National Bureau of Economic Research (NBER): www.nber.org
Nuclear Threat Initiative (NTI): www.nti.org
Partnership for Higher Education in Africa: www.foundation-partnership.org
Rockefeller Archive Center: www.rockarch.org
Rockefeller Foundation: www.rockefellerfoundation.org
Russell Sage Foundation: www.russellsage.org
Teachers Insurance and Annuity Association of America: www.tiaa-cref.org
TrustAfrica: www.trustafrica.org

INDEX

ABOUT THE AUTHOR

AS SENIOR FELLOW AT THE Rockefeller Archives Center, Patricia L. Rosenfield is developing a series of activities to connect practitioners of philanthropy and scholars of philanthropy; a significant initial focus is on the archives of the Ford Foundation. At Carnegie Corporation, she directed its Scholars Program, and earlier had chaired its program on Strengthening Human Resources in Developing Countries and International Development. Prior to joining Carnegie in 1987, she served at the World Health Organization in Geneva, where she was responsible for a program on social and economic research on tropical diseases. She is a member of the Council on Foreign Relations, and currently serves as a director of the Harry Frank Guggenheim Foundation and trustee of Future Generations. Rosenfield holds an A.B. cum laude from Bryn Mawr College, a Ph.D. from Johns Hopkins University, and an Honorary Doctorate from Mahidol University, Thailand. Rosenfield has written extensively on inter-disciplinary research and philanthropy.